Sassy, our "Social Networking Butterfly," increases your productivity by connecting you to thriving real estate-friendly online communities.

What's Unique to This Edition?

Aside from the expected updated real estate forms and revised laws, rules, and regulations, this new 5th Edition of *Property Management* includes new material and information you won't find in other textbooks. Three examples of new concepts introduced in this 5th Edition include:

(1) Craigslist is rapidly replacing the classified section of the newspaper for advertising rentals and leases—saving time and reducing costs.

(2) Mediation (or arbitration) is playing an increasing role in many tenant forms and property management contracts.

(3) Introduction of our icon Sassy, "The Social Networking Butterfly," as a reminder that social networking sites should be an integral part of your business strategy.

Social Networking

Many real estate professionals participate in social networks or blogs for business purposes. Social networking sites are great tools for property managers to stay connected with clients, reach out to prospects, and build relationships within the real estate community. Increasingly, the most successful professionals advertise their services or products through "online communities" such as Facebook, Twitter, LinkedIn, and Youtube.

Facebook is one of the most popular social networking sites being utilized by real estate professionals, including property managers. It's a user-friendly, user-generated site that allows you to create a profile, join or start groups, and add applications to enhance your page. In addition to your personal profile, where you can include photos, interests, status updates, and more, you can also create groups and fan pages to connect with others who share a common cause or interest.

Twitter, another "hot" social networking site, is a micro-blogging site that allows users to post and read short messages (140 characters max) called "tweets." You can customize your profile with a company profile and photo, and Twitter provides some great applications such as "TweetLister" that automatically posts a listing whenever it becomes available. The immediacy, far-reaching exposure, and no-cost factors make social networking sites like this an increasing substitution for traditional forms of marketing, like direct mail and newspaper advertising.

YouTube is one of the essential networking sites now being used by real estate brokerages and property management firms. Virtual tours of properties can be taken by video phone and posted on YouTube in a matter of minutes. It's easy to use, inexpensive, and offers access to available properties to a universal audience, including local and international prospects.

Some business-related sites that can enhance a property manager's presence on the web include LinkedIn, Craigslist, and Yellowpages.com.

LinkedIn is a business-oriented site mainly used for "professionals networking" – with a sort of "resume" posting appeal. When you join, you create a profile that summarizes your professional expertise and accomplishments. You then invite others from your sphere of influence to connect with you through the site. Your network consists of your connections, your connections' connections, and their connections (a "gated-access" approach).

Craigslist is a mostly free site where you can post properties for sale or for lease, or your services as a professional property manager. It is quickly replacing the newspaper as the place to advertise real estate! It's easy to use and, with the exception of brokered apartments in New York City, costs nothing, and gets immediate responses to posts – no downtime!

Yellowpages.com is just what it sounds like – an online version of the yellow pages, but with exposure to millions of viewers unlike the paper version!

PROPERTY MANAGEMENT

5TH EDITION

WALT HUBER
GLENDALE COLLEGE

ARLETTE LYONS, CRS, GRI, SRES
MT. SAN ANTONIO COLLEGE

WILLIAM PIVAR, JD
PROFESSOR EMERITUS

COPYRIGHT© 1991, 1995, 2003, 2005, 2007, 2010 - Fifth Edition

EDUCATIONAL TEXTBOOK COMPANY, INC.
P. O. Box 3597
Covina, California 91722
(626) 339-7733
FAX (626) 332-4744
etctextbooks.com, etcbooks.com, or **appraisal-etcbooks.com**
(Constructive suggestions are welcome)

Call Glendale College Bookstore to order all ETC books:

1-818-240-1000 ext. 3024
1-818-242-1561 (Direct)

Library of Congress Cataloging-in-Publication Data
Real Estate Finance/Huber, Walt; Lyons, Arlette, CRS, GRI, SRES; Pivar, William, JD
5th ed.
Includes index

1. Real Estate Business – United States 2. Real Estate Property – United States

ISBN: 0-916772-82-9 (10-Digit Number)
ISBN: 978-0-916772-82-6 (13-Digit Number)

Preface

Meet Sassy, our Social Networking Butterfly. She's there to remind you that using social networking sites should be an integral part of your business strategy. Like most real estate professionals, property managers are now embracing the use of the Internet, smart phones, and social networking sites.

> *Sassy's world of mobile connectivity today has impacted every aspect of property management – allowing us to improve our performance for both owners and tenants.* **– Walt Huber**

Social networking saves us time. We no longer have to wait 3-5 days for an ad to appear in the classified section of the newspaper and then wait another day before responses start coming in. With a few clicks on your home computer or smart phone, you can get immediate results with virtually no downtime in the placing of the ad or the responses to that ad!

Not only can placing ads on sites like Craigslist and other local rental sites save you time, but also money! For the time being anyway, most social networking sites are free, unlike expensive newspaper ads. My, how the field of property management has changed!

> *I often receive calls from people who are parked outside of my rental and would like to view it <u>immediately</u>. Cell phones have changed how fast customers get a hold of the property manager – most of whom want to schedule a showing <u>instantly</u>, if possible.*
> **– Walt Huber**

Walt Huber is a well-known author of numerous real estate textbooks, serves as Real Estate Coordinator at Glendale College, and has extensive family-owned property management experience.

Arlette Lyons is a well-respected and popular professor of both Real Estate Practice and Property Management at Mt. San Antonio College. She is also a successful broker and owner of Lyons and Associates Realty, Inc. of West Covina, California, and manages a large portfolio of rental properties.

Dr. William Pivar is Professor Emeritus at the College of the Desert, Palm Desert, California, and is not only a prominent real estate attorney, but also served as a property management officer for the General Services Administration, which is the real estate management agency of the federal government.

Special thanks to the people who helped design and produce this book: Philip Dockter, art director, Melinda Winters and Troy Monroe Stacey, cover design, Rick Lee, prepress and layout editor, and Colleen Taber, executive editor.

We appreciate the advice given to us by property manager extraordinaire, Alex Tolocenco.

A special thanks to "our sailboat buddy," William A. McGrath, JD, of Sacramento City College.

Acknowledgments

Derry Knight
American River College

Chris M. Hamilton
Antelope Valley College

E. Denis Roden
Cabrillo College

Jay Mumford
Chabot College

Carol Jensen
City College of San Francisco

Doug Housley
College of the Canyons

Jeff Eddy
College of the Sequoias

Bernie Mnichowicz
Cosumnes River College

Rick Chehab
De Anza College

Ivan G. Eagleson
De Anza College

Olivia Anderson
East Los Angeles College

V.J. Cleva
East Los Angeles College

Elliot Dixon
East Los Angeles College

R.C. Lipscomb
East Los Angeles College

D.E. Rodriguez
East Los Angeles College

Dr. Donna Grogan
El Camino College

Dr. Robert Bowers
Fullerton College

Jack Flynn
Glendale College

Reynan Ledesma
Glendale College

Craig Luna
Glendale College

Walt Zozula
Glendale College

Dr. Chris Hamilton
Golden West College

Jim Cunningham
Long Beach City College

James Scott
Laney College

Ron Maricich
Los Angeles Harbor College

Patricia Moore
Los Medanos College

Ignacio Gonzalez
Mendocino College
Director, Mendocino County Planning and
Building Services

Ed Culbertson
MiraCosta College

Acknowledgments

Robert Palazzo
Moorpark College

Arlette Lyons
Mt. San Antonio College

Mary Ann Zamel
Mt. San Antonio College

Patrick Hogarty
Sacramento City College

William A. McGrath
Sacramento City College

Nick Zoumbos
San Bernardino Valley College

Dr. Nick Sacorafas
San Diego Mesa College

John Wallace
San Diego Mesa College

Nick Faklis
San Joaquin Delta College

Steve Herndon
Santa Rosa Junior College

M. Joel Carlson
Santiago Canyon College

Kim Tyler, JD
Shasta College

Mike Anderson
Ventura College

Chris Grover
Victor Valley College

Jerome Fox
West Los Angeles College

Ruben Ramos
Yuba College

Chris Sorenson, Director
H.E.L.P.

Dionne Falk
Managing Deputy Director
DRE

Anthony Jones
Real Estate Appraiser
San Jose

Ken Combs
Del Mar College, Texas

360 Training.com
Austin, Texas

CELI
Canton, Texas

CETC
Garland, Texas

Key Realty School
Las Vegas, Nevada

Table of Contents

Table of Contents

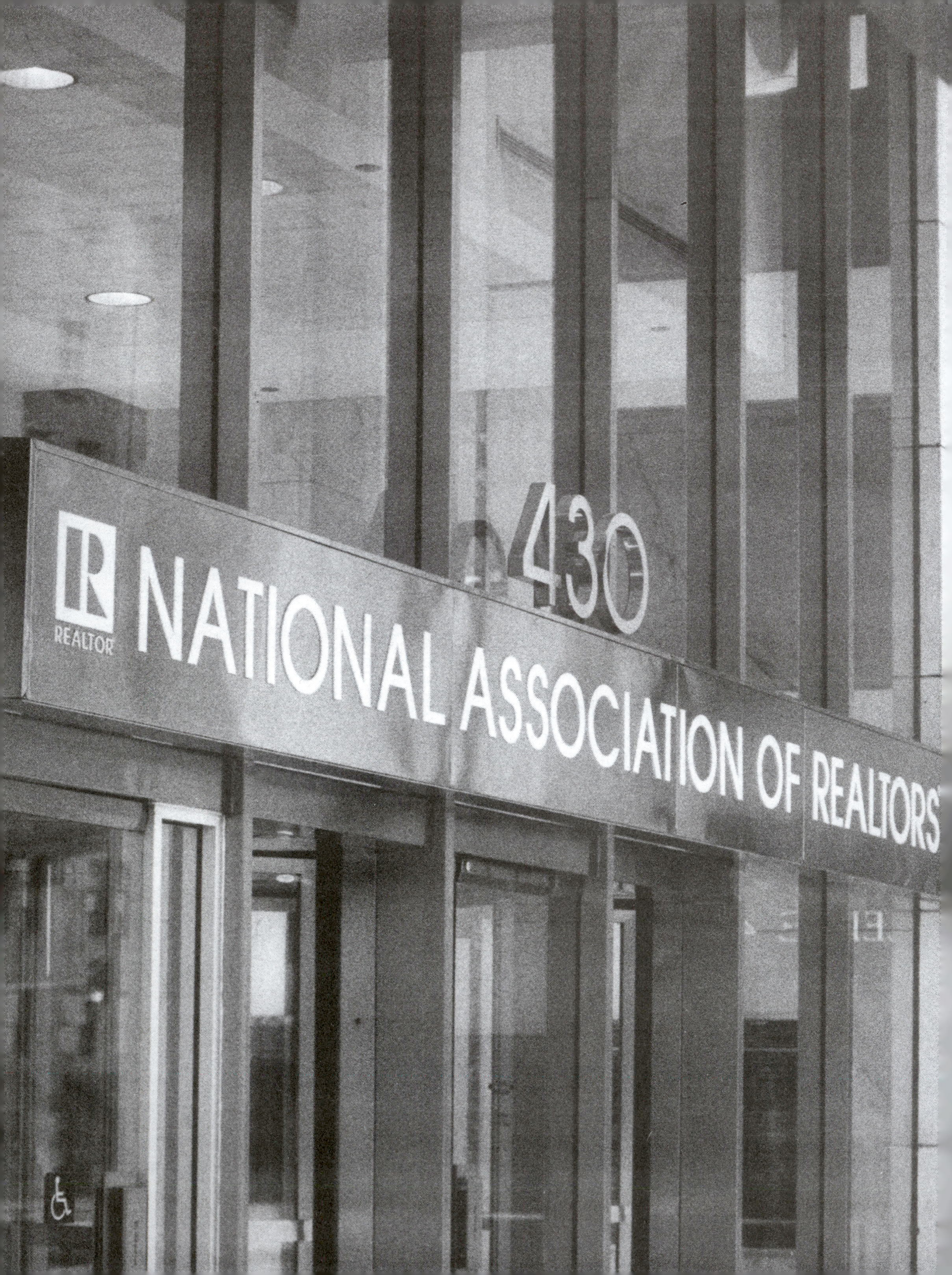
REALTOR
NATIONAL ASSOCIATION OF REALTORS
430

Chapter 1
Property Management – A Profession of Service

KEY WORDS AND TERMS

Accredited Management Goal Oriented
  Organization (AMO)
Accredited Marketing Director (AMD)
Accredited Residential Manager (ARM)
Accredited Shopping Center Manager (ASM)
AIR Commercial Real Estate Association (AIR)
Association Management Specialist (AMS)
Building Owners and Managers Institute (BOMI)
Certified Leasing Specialist (CLS)
Certified Facility Manager (CFM)
Certified Manager of Community Associations (CMCA)
Certified Property Manager (CPM)
Certified Shopping Center Manager (SCSM)
Community Associations Institute
Completed Staff Work
Corporate Property Managers
Economic Life
Electric Elevator
Employee Manager
Facilities Management Administrator (FMA)
Franchises
Independent Property Manager
Industrial Revolution

International Council of Shopping Centers (ICSC)
International Design and Development Award
International Facility Management Association
International Real Estate Institute
MAXI Award
Moldboard Plow
Professional Community Association Manager
  (PCAM)
Property Management Association (PMA)
Real Estate Investment Trust
Real Property Administrator (RPA)
Senior Certified Marketing Director (SCMD)
Senior Certified Shopping Center Manager (SCSM)
Structural Steel
Systems Maintenance Technician (SMT)
System Maintenance Administrator (SMA)
Urban Land Institute (ULI)
Vacancy Factor

CHAPTER 1 OUTLINE

VOICE OF EXPERIENCE:

As a property manager, you need to be aware of the four major money-making reasons owners invest in rental property. They include:

1. Appreciation (buy low, sell high)

2. Cash flow (income after expenses)

3. Income tax advantages (interest and depreciation)

4. Equity buildup (monthly reduction of loan principal)

I. The History of Property Management

A professor once said, "The first property management job was to assign living spaces on Noah's Ark!"

We aren't absolutely certain as to the accuracy of this statement, but we do know that property management has been around for several thousand years. The ancient Egyptians had overseers to manage their estates as did the Greeks and Romans. While they utilized mostly slave labor, their job was to supervise the upkeep of the estates to protect the value and to maximize the income. This isn't much different than the goals of modern day property management.

In the middle ages, property managers in Europe collected rents from the serfs for a lord or vassal. Part of the rent was kept by the lord or vassal and the rest was sent up along the feudal chain to another lord, vassal or king.

Later, in England, estate managers handled the affairs of vast estates including housing for workers, maintenance of improvements as well as agricultural supervision. In

prerevolutionary America, estate managers carried on much of these same duties, often for holders of land grants who were absentee owners.

In modern history, a number of events increased the importance of and changed the scope of property management.

Large cities were an early phenomena of the Mediterranean areas. Because of a warmer climate and long growing seasons, more food was produced per agricultural worker. This freed labor from agricultural pursuits and allowed the growth of major cities. In ancient Rome, there were many buildings six and seven stories high that were rented to citizens. Rome had its rent collectors and property managers. Large cities did not emerge in central Europe until hundreds of years later.

A. THE MOLDBOARD PLOW

Prior to the moldboard plow, the earth was tilled with a stick or iron spike that was dragged by horse, oxen or a human being. These tools made a narrow furrow in the hard earth. The growth of plantings was limited by the compaction of the soil.

The *MOLDBOARD PLOW had a curved plate attached to the spike that could lift and turn over a wide furrow of ground.* The yield from the land increased dramatically. In middle Europe, this freed labor for other pursuits. It allowed for a nonagricultural lifestyle and was a factor in the growth of the cities. The growth of the cities required housing, which was primarily rental housing, and with this housing the need for management.

B. THE INDUSTRIAL REVOLUTION

The industrial revolution in England, with the harnessing of water power and then steam, allowed for factories to mass produce goods that were once produced by hand or otherwise unavailable. The need for workers in the factories brought laborers in from farm communities, leading to a rapid growth of cities and in rental housing. The industrial revolution spread from England to other European countries and the United States. Steam, and later electric power, allowed for horizontal growth of factories that earlier had power conveyed from water wheels by gears, drive shafts, and belts, which necessitated vertical factories.

C. THE ELECTRIC ELEVATOR

The Otis elevator was the first practical elevator and was powered by electricity. This invention allowed for the creation of skyscrapers.

It provided dependable vertical travel, thus allowing tall buildings to be constructed. This increased the value of land in the central cities as it allowed for greater utilization of ground space. Building heights were still limited by the fact that the lower floors required extremely wide walls to support the masonry construction of the upper floors.

D. STRUCTURAL STEEL

The use of structural steel allowed for modern day skyscrapers. The steel frame allowed relatively light exterior sheathing, which made tall buildings possible without the loss of space from massive supporting lower walls. This allowed for additional rental space.

E. THE GREAT DEPRESSION

The Depression that followed the stock market crash of 1929 resulted in thousands of properties being foreclosed and held by lenders who could not find buyers. The Great Depression was actually a boost for professional management.

As proven by the Great Depression, no matter what the economy is, there are always opportunities. Keep your options open for the benefit of your owners.

II. Career Opportunities in Property Management

There is a present need for trained professional property managers in a number of areas. Numerous specialties are available within the property management field to utilize a wide range of talent.

In a slow market, a general brokerage firm that offers property management as a side business may produce the necessary income to keep the company economically afloat.

Property managers fall into different categories:

Employee Manager. This manager is an employee of an owner or corporation and has management duties dealing with one or more properties.

Resident Manager. A manager of an apartment property who "resides on the premises" and does not need a real estate license in most states. Check your state's licensing laws.

Independent Property Manager. These managers handle property individually or with the assistance of their employees. They handle property for more than one owner and have agency duties toward each client they represent.

There are a number of employment opportunities within the property management field.

A. THE GOVERNMENT

Federal, state, county and local governmental units as well as agencies of the government employ property managers. Although titles vary, property managers are responsible for maintenance, repair and protection of real property that is government owned or leased for governmental use. In some cases they actually lease government property to others.

The *GENERAL SERVICES ADMINISTRATION is the real estate management agency for the federal government.* It is the largest single employer of property management personnel in the world.

gsa.gov
General Services Administration

B. REAL ESTATE INVESTMENT TRUSTS (REITs)

We are seeing a rapid growth in **REAL ESTATE INVESTMENT TRUSTS (REITs)**. *These trusts buy and manage income properties for the benefit of their stockholders.*

REITs are publicly traded and, by law, must distribute 90 percent of their gross taxable income from operation to their shareholders.

They have an advantage over corporate structures in that they are not taxed on earnings distributed to shareholders. Therefore, they avoid the double taxation of corporations. Many large developers, limited partnerships and other property owners become REITs in order to have liquidity. REIT shares have a ready market. Many are listed on the stock exchange (New York, American or NASDAQ).

Today, REITs are the primary buyers of large income properties because of their easy access to capital. They can raise capital by selling common stock, preferred stock or bonds. They can also borrow from commercial lenders. Some REITs have open lines of credit approaching the billion dollar mark. While some REITs operate in just a few geographical markets, others operate nationwide.

nareit.com
National Association of Real Estate Investment Trusts (NAREIT)

Some REITs specialize in types of property. As an example, some REITs buy fast food restaurants of particular franchisees and lease them to the operators. There are a half dozen REITs that only own factory outlet shopping centers. Others own only apartments or shopping centers.

Many REITs operate based on opportunity. They may buy or even develop properties that are residential, office, commercial and industrial in nature. Some REITs look for distress properties with serious problems. They then solve the problems. Others only want quality properties.

Because of the significant ownership role of REITs, they are a prominent employer of property managers.

CEOs of REITs tend to have backgrounds in development or finance rather than property management.

A reason for this could be the fact that many REITs were development companies just a few years ago. These companies went public to be able to liquefy assets (stocks) and because of the ability of REITs to both raise equity capital and to borrow funds. Some property managers are now rising to the top as executives retire.

REITs raid other REITs for employees by paying them what they are worth. Many property managers are now making executive salaries from $100,000 to one-half million dollars per year.

REITs have been one of the best things that ever happened for property management as far as increasing the manager's income is concerned.

Because REITs are publicly traded, management is under tremendous pressure from large institutional stockholders to show significant growth in funds from operations. This is the standard measurement for REIT performance.

Because of this pressure, there is a need to show improvements quarter by quarter. This is unfortunate, because in looking at the short term, long-term goals tend to come secondary. Immediate expenses of a property upgrade might be delayed. Maintenance expenses might also be reduced and staff might suffer layoffs. These short-term fixes to increase FFO (Funds From Operation) might in the long term be detrimental to the shareholders even though they offer instant gratification.

Property managers, in some instances, know that growth rates of the past cannot be sustained. When growth rates slow or funds from operations actually show a decline, stocks tend to tumble.

Management often has income related to stock performance, so management suffers as well. It is expected that a number of REITs, currently the darlings of Wall Street, will tumble as to stock prices. The REITS themselves are generally healthy; it's just that they cannot show the growth in earnings quarter after quarter that was expected by stock market analysts.

C. FINANCIAL INSTITUTIONS

Between foreclosure and disposition of property, it must be managed. While many financial institutions use independent property management firms, there are still thousands of property managers employed by financial institutions.

VOICE OF EXPERIENCE:

Independent contractors working as property managers have more control than employees. You may have to work longer hours and be available more days, but you also have the ability to work for as many clients as you choose.

D. CORPORATIONS

Many large corporations have over one-half of their assets in real property.

In recent years, they have begun to realize that property management is an executive function and not necessarily a blue-collar function. Property management has been raised to the vice presidential level in many corporations.

Corporate property management might include leasing space and the supervision of leases. The property manager working in a major corporate environment might have responsibilities for space alterations and maintenance for both corporate owned and leased space. In many cases, maintenance is separated from corporate property managerial duties and is given to plant superintendents or plant engineers.

Corporate property managers are often responsible for the security of excess property until it is needed or disposed of. However, in many cases security is handled by the plant superintendent rather than a property management duty.

Corporate property managers may act as lessors as well as lessees in subleasing or leasing corporate-leased or corporate-owned property.

E. FRANCHISES

Franchises realize the importance of property management concerning leasing and maintenance. Expansion would not be possible without good property management.

F. EMPLOYEES OF PRIVATE OWNERS

Some real estate brokers and nonlicensees work as employees of individual owners rather than as agents. They manage one or a group of properties for the owner with employee responsibilities.

G. PRIVATE MANAGEMENT FIRMS

Many real estate brokerage offices operate property management services. It's a valuable function that should lead to property value appreciation and future sales.

Some just handle a few properties while others are well-staffed divisions handling hundreds of properties for dozens if not hundreds of separate owners.

There are many firms that exclusively handle property management. By not competing with general brokerage offices, they are able to obtain a significant portion of their business from referrals.

Some property management firms specialize in particular types of property while others only perform a single property management function, such as leasing agents.

VOICE OF EXPERIENCE:

Some large real estate firms may have leasing/property management divisions completely separate from their selling and listing functions. This is not necessarily good for agents, as the separation of functions may cause a salesperson to lose potential future sales by turning over his/her client to another department for management duties.

H. ONSITE MANAGEMENT

The greatest number of property managers are onsite managers who live and/or work exclusively at a property where they have management duties.

They are generally employees of either the property owners or of a management firm. Most residential managers are employed to manage residential property but onsite managers are found in other areas, such as mini-warehouse management.

III. Why Owners Choose Management

Most owners choose property management for both economic and personal reasons.

A. ECONOMIC REASONS

Property managers can simply do a better job of management than most owners because of training and experience.

A professional property manager has a better understanding of the rental market. They are more likely to locate tenants and negotiate leases having more favorable terms than are owners who relegate property management to a part-time business.

VOICE OF EXPERIENCE:

Whether an owner or a property manager, becoming emotionally involved with your tenants' personal lives and problems is not a good idea.

Even owners who have the training and ability to do an excellent management job of their own property, nevertheless, will use professional managers. The reason is the value of the owner's time. A surgeon can better use valuable time performing surgery than trying to collect rent from a delinquent tenant or making calls for repairs to a property.

Using a property manager should never cost the owner, but should always be cost effective!

The Main Financial Benefits of Hiring a Property Manager

Increased Rents. The property manager is less eager to give away rent or lower rents when the necessity to do so is not indicated by market conditions.

Reduced Vacancy Factor. By qualifying prospective tenants, the property manager can select tenants who will have a longer tenancy period. This can be aided by lease terms. This results in lower turnover of tenancy which equates to a lower vacancy factor and a higher bottom line.

Reduced Tenant Damage. Through qualifying tenants and requiring reasonable property damage bonds, the probability of damage to the premises is reduced and when damage does occur, the damage bond is usually sufficient to cover the damage.

Reduced Repair Costs. Good property management will include preventative maintenance programs that will reduce the likelihood of costly emergency repairs for operating systems.

Reduced Expenses. Because of purchasing power in managing a great many units, property managers can obtain services and supplies at significant discounts from the prices offered to an individual owner. In addition, a professional manager is less likely to be taken advantage of by a vendor or service provider.

Management Planning. A professional property manager will plan ahead for changes in tenant mix, changes in uses, changes in lease terms, etc. based on the goals of the owner.

Prolonged Economic Life. Property goes through a period of development and lease up. It then goes through what can be a lengthy period of maturity and, finally, it enters a period of decline usually resulting in abandonment or demolition.

Some properties go from the development through the decline phases rapidly and others very slowly. There are apartment structures in Europe that have been desirable for several hundred years. Physically, nonresidential structures can maintain an economic life span far longer than the 39 years that the IRS offers for depreciation. Property management cannot only extend a property's life span, it can reverse the clock through remodeling or restoration.

B. PERSONAL REASONS

Many property owners realize that they don't have the temperament to deal with tenants or problems. Some let problems bother their peace of mind. Others are too nice and end up being taken advantage of by tenants. These property owners hesitate to get tough concerning rule violations, rent collections and evictions. There are thousands of owners who give their tenants below-market rent. They're afraid to raise rents or just don't want to appear to be a bad person. In many cases, owners have run their properties as charitable institutions rather than in a businesslike manner.

Those owners who recognize their shortcomings choose professional management.

IV. Attributes of a Successful Manager

While an estimated two-thirds of our national wealth is in real estate, we have far more stock brokers than property managers.

In recent years, we've come to realize the importance of professional property management. The stock market has played a significant part in this realization. The success of some Real Estate Investment Trusts (REITs) has led to the understanding that all managers are not the same. Professionals who plan their work and work their plan can outperform the pack.

Property managers must be both detail and people oriented. Emotion should not enter into the transaction. This is not easily done.

As a property manager, you must be meticulous as to record keeping, follow through on tenant complaints and problems, and continually strive to do things better.

Property managers must understand the needs and goals of both owners and tenants. While acting as an agent for the owner they must, nevertheless, treat tenants with fairness and understanding.

Specific qualities that a successful manager should possess include the following.

A. MENTAL STAMINA

As the property manager, you must remain focused on a problem and seek a solution. The "hotshot" salesperson who wants to close a transaction and then forget it will not succeed in property management, where the work just begins with the lease.

B. INTEGRITY

As a property manager, your word must be your bond when dealing with owners, tenants and contractors. Those you deal with know that they can rely on you to carry out what it is you said will be done.

VOICE OF EXPERIENCE:

Organization is key! The more properties you manage, the more organized you will need to be. Keep all records separate (especially finances) and keep extensive notes on the status of projects, expected completion dates, checklists, and calendars for each property. Computer programs with mail message capabilities will make communication as easy as the click of a mouse. A very secure safe with a mail slot is indispensable.

C. ORGANIZATIONAL SKILLS

As a property manager, you must be organized so that multiple problems can be addressed and followed up on at the same time.

D. BRAVERY

You may not view it as such, but property management is a field that requires bravery. As a property manager, you cannot hesitate to deliver bad news to an owner or tenant. You cannot be coerced by attorneys in lease negotiations or give in to unreasonable demands by irate tenants. This all requires bravery.

E. PEOPLE SKILLS

We normally view property management as simply a management of fixed assets. It is more than this. As the manager, you will deal with people as much as you do with property. Some writers talk about the property manager who manages people. We don't like this use of the word "managing." Managing denotes using . A good property manager does not use people.

As the property manager, you have to work with people to create a harmonious and mutually beneficial relationship.

Interpersonal relation skills are important for success. However, these skills can be learned. As a property manager, you must be able to correct problem behavior in a tenant or worker without generating resentment or personal animosity.

You must become a listener more than a teller. You must strive to understand other people and what it is that they want. Don't view this as the manipulation of people. It is working with people for mutual advantages.

F. ABILITY TO PRIORITIZE

As the property manager, you cannot allow yourself to become focused on pennies and forget the dollars. You must first focus your efforts and resources on the most important problems.

VOICE OF EXPERIENCE:

Priorities will differ among owners. As the property manager, you cannot forget that you stand in the shoes of the owner (as an agent of the owner), but you must also recognize the tenants' concerns. Also, you may want to consider additional fees for properties being rehabbed, vacant for long periods of time, and income participation in late fees.

G. GOAL ORIENTED

As a property manager, you cannot manage by simply putting out fires or oiling the hinge when it squeaks. You must set goals for a property in coordination with the owner. When the owner knows the goals and has been a part of their development, you will then remain focused on these goals. You must periodically review actions and policies as to reaching/adjusting those goals.

Setting goals doesn't necessarily mean that the goals will be reached. However, your efforts as property manager to reach them will only help the property and the owner.

H. COMMUNICATION SKILLS

As the property manager, you must be able to clearly and succinctly explain an idea, problem or solution in writing as well as verbally.

In learning to outline a letter, you need to organize your thoughts and priority of messages to be conveyed. You will then be able to use this organizational skill verbally by thinking through what has to be communicated before engaging your tongue.

I. TEAM ORIENTED

As a property manager, you must realize that you are not a prima donna but part of a management team. The onsite manager, accountant, and even maintenance personnel are part of the team and must be treated as team members. If one does not do his or her job, everyone will suffer.

J. ABILITY TO DELEGATE

Anyone can say, "Do This!" This is not delegation.

Delegation involves giving a person "authority" as well as "responsibility."

All too often, a person is held accountable without the authority to do something correctly.

Delegation also involves a system to monitor progress without appearing to look over a person's shoulder. Instead of asking, "Is it done yet?" a better way would be to ask, "What is the status of …?"

Some offices have short morning meetings where the status of all actions are reviewed. This helps persons feel that they are team members and also to understand what others are doing and profit from other agents' problematic situations.

K. FLEXIBILITY

As a property manager, you must be flexible. You must be able to think in terms of alternatives, "...if this happens" or, "Who could use this property?"

L. BE PART OF THE SOLUTION

Anyone can spell out a problem. However, no one likes the bearer of bad news. As a good property manager, you need to look at a problem as a challenge. The first thing you must analyze is:

1. What happened? Am I sure of the facts?
2. What will be the result of what happened?
3. What are the alternatives to alleviate the problem?
4. What is the best of these alternatives?
5. Why is it the best alternative?
6. Does this need to be replaced or can it be repaired?

As a property manager, you must then communicate the problem, the alternatives and your recommendations to your owners or supervisors. This is known as **COMPLETED STAFF WORK.** Never present a problem without recommending a solution. Be prepared to defend your solution.

Completed staff work is what management is all about.

If you cannot think or analyze, you become redundant and may very well be replaced by a computer. Once you become involved in completed staff work, you will find that people will be more willing to listen to you and follow your advice.

M. ACCEPT RESPONSIBILITY

Instead of blaming others or using the bland excuse of "It just happened," be willing instead to accept responsibility and correct errors.

N. BENEFIT ORIENTED

Property management is concerned with maximizing the long-term benefits that can be derived from real estate.

O. AGENCY FOCUSED

Instead of being "me" focused, as a property manager, you must think about your principal as being the primary purpose of business. The interest of your client must always come first. If you can adopt this attitude, you will serve your principal well and in turn you will be successful.

VOICE OF EXPERIENCE:

Doing "for" others rather than "to" others will result in referral business, long-term relationships and prosperity. Tenants will most likely become buyers; property owners will most likely want to exchange for larger and more expensive rental properties.

P. A MONEY MANAGER

As a property manager, you can best meet your owners' needs by fully understanding their needs and financial situation. This would include making payments on debt service, and even arranging financing for improvements and renovations. You should periodically review an owner's debt service and consider refinancing if it would be in the best interest of that owner.

Completed staff work would involve knowing the interest rates, locating a lender and preparing a loan application for the owner to sign. A number of property management contracts provide this service for a fee.

V. Licensing Requirements

In most states, renting or leasing real property in an agency capacity for others generally requires a real estate broker's license.

This license requirement extends to offering to rent, soliciting rental listings, and negotiation of leases and/or rental terms. There are exemptions to the licensing requirement. The following are true for California, but you should check with your state's laws concerning who does or does not need a license.

A. OWNERS

An owner need not be licensed to manage his or her own property.

B. WITHOUT COMPENSATION

Depending on the state, doing acts without compensation may exempt a person from licensing requirements.

The *California Attorney General 32 Ops Atty Gen. 210* stated that "for a compensation" is critical to require licensing. According to the Attorney General, unless the buying and selling of promissory notes secured by a deed of trust is done "for a compensation," the person buying and selling such notes is not a real estate broker within the requirements of the real estate law. Based on this reasoning, compensation would also be a critical requirement for licensing of property managers.

C. POWER OF ATTORNEY

Persons holding an executed power of attorney from an owner of real property can sell or lease the property under the power of attorney.

This is based on the legal concept that if a person can deal with their property, then they can transfer that right to another. Courts have not allowed this exception to be used by a nonlicensee to conduct an ongoing property management business.

In some states, employees of licensed property management firms are allowed to show property, accept rental applications and deposits, as well as to provide rental information to others without being licensed.

Case Example

Sheetz v. Edmonds, 201 C.A. 3d 1432 (1988)

Sheetz managed 23 separate properties for compensation. All of the properties were owned by a friend. Sheetz was not licensed, although engaged full time in property management. Sheetz was operating under a power of attorney which he claimed allowed him an exemption from Department of Real Estate licensing.

The Real Estate Commissioner issued a cease and desist order for Sheetz to stop managing these properties. Sheetz was the plaintiff in this action against Edmonds (the Real Estate Commissioner).

The Court of Appeals upheld the action of the real estate commissioner. The court determined that the exemption for a power of attorney applied to particular transactions or very limited periods. The exemption cannot be used as a substitute for obtaining a broker's license.

In this case, it was clear that the power of attorney was given for the purpose of evading licensing requirements.

Check with your state's real estate department to verify whether or not a real estate license is required to be a property manager.

D. HOTEL MANAGER

A manager of a hotel, motel, or auto and trailer park, resident manager of an apartment building, apartment complex, or court or an employee of any such manager, generally need not hold a broker's license. Check with your state's licensing laws to verify this.

E. TRANSIENT OCCUPANCY

In many states, any person or entity (including an employee of a broker) who solicits or arranges and accepts reservations and/or money for transient occupancies is generally exempt from licensing. Check with your state's licensing laws.

F. RESIDENT MANAGERS

In many states, resident managers of apartment buildings generally need not be licensed as real estate brokers, even though they handle rentals as part of their duties. Again, check with your state's licensing laws.

VI. Professionalism in Property Management

As a property manager, you need to realize the need to improve your current skills and to learn new skills to meet the needs created by today's property management requirements. The professionalism of the industry has grown from within the industry itself and has not been mandated by others.

"Trade associations" meet the needs of professional property managers for today and tomorrow. It's important to be up-to-date on industry regulations and standards that are constantly being updated.

A. INSTITUTE OF REAL ESTATE MANAGEMENT (IREM)

The **INSTITUTE OF REAL ESTATE MANAGEMENT (IREM)** *is an institute of the National Association of REALTORS®. IREM offers educational and professional programs in property management.*

IREM was founded in 1933. Guidelines were established that covered protection of clients by using trust funds and employee bonding as well as agreeing not to accept any form of kickbacks from contractors and suppliers without full disclosure to the clients.

irem.org
Institute of Real Estate Management (IREM)

In 1938, IREM set qualification standards for its professional designations.

1. Certified Property Manager (CPM)

The Certified Property Manager (CPM) designation is the most prestigious and widely recognized designation for professional property management.

To become a CPM, candidates must meet criteria set forth by IREM and obtain 260 points, 160 of which are required.

a. Criteria

1. Be a candidate for at least one year.
2. Be currently in the real estate management business.
3. Either hold a real estate license or certify that you are not required to have one.
4. Be a member or affiliated with a local board of REALTORS®.
5. Be approved by your local IREM chapter.
6. Continue to subscribe to the Code of Ethics of the Certified Property Managers.
7. Be current with all national and chapter service fees.
8. Have at least a high school diploma and complete an application.

b. 160 Required Points

These points are received from three areas:

1. IREM courses;
2. Management plan (developed for an actual property);
3. Experience.

c. 100 Elective Points

Elective points are earned by completing elective courses as well as attaining other professional designations.

2. Accredited Residential Manager (ARM)

Specialists in residential property management are designated as Accredited Residential Managers (ARM).

Unlike the CPM designation that covers various types of property, the ARM designation is strictly for residential property. Candidates must:

1. submit letters of recommendation;
2. pass a designated examination;
3. meet experience requirements.

3. Accredited Management Organization (AMO)

The Accredited Management Organization (AMO) designation is given to firms rather than to individuals.

Property Management – A Profession of Service

To attain the AMO designation, the firm must have a person with a CPM designation in charge of the firm's management operations and must have authority and responsibility in a number of designated areas. The executive CPM must also complete an IREM course covering "Managing the Management Company."

4. Educational Courses

IREM offers educational courses in over 85 cities as well as correspondence courses covering a wide range of management and management-related topics. Besides national courses, there are also local chapter network courses. Course offerings include:

MKL402 – Marketing and Leasing Strategies for Multifamily Properties
MKL403 – Marketing and Leasing Strategies for Office Buildings
MKL404 – Marketing and Leasing Strategies for Retail Property
BDM601 – Expanding Your Business
HRS402 – Managing Human Resources for Optimal Results
HRS603 – Enhancing Your Leadership Style
FIN402 – Identifying Financial Alternatives at the Property Level
ASM401 – Transforming Client Expectations into Business Success
ASM402 – Improving Income Property Performance
ASM603 – Financing and Valuation Strategies for Real Estate Assets
ASM604 – Measuring Performance of Real Estate Assets
ASM605 – Applying Investment Criteria to Real Estate Asset Decisions
LRM402 – Risk Management: Protecting People, Property and Profits
LRM603 – Avoiding Surprises: Trends in Regulation and Legislation
MKL201 – Mastering the Essentials of Marketing and Leasing
FIN201 – Mastering Property Budgeting and Accounting
HRS201 – Managing and Motivating a Property Team
LRM201 – Do's and Don'ts of Fair Housing Practice
MNT201 – Managing Maintenance Operations
CLM201 – Managing Small Commercial Properties
MTF201 – Managing Public Housing
MTF202 – Managing Government-Insured Multifamily Housing
MTF203 – Managing Community Associations
MTF204 – Managing Single-Family Homes and Small Residential Properties
ETH800 – Ethics for the Real Estate Manager

IREM also offers a binder of 57 forms for leasing, occupancy, record keeping and reporting, maintenance, personnel management, etc., with the right to print these forms on your photo copiers.

They also offer (for a nominal fee) general management contract forms, condominium association management forms, as well as forms for both office building inspection and office building management. Checkout irem.org for their (IREM) up-to-date offerings and requirements.

B. BUILDING OWNERS AND MANAGERS ASSOCIATION INTERNATIONAL (BOMA)

Founded in 1907, the **BUILDING OWNERS AND MANAGERS ASSOCIATION INTERNATIONAL (BOMA)** *is a federation of 94 local associations with over 16,000 members representing more than six billion square feet of commercial property in North America.*

BOMA has local chapters in all major cities. BOMA holds an annual convention which is a major event as well as an important office building show.

BOMA has an educational institute (BOMI) that promotes the interests of the real estate industry through programs of personal development and by collecting, analyzing and disseminating information.

boma.org

Building Owners and Managers Association International (BOMA)

BOMI offers several important designations.

1. Real Property Administrator (RPA)

To earn the prestigious designation RPA, a candidate must complete the following courses that are offered by the Institute:

1. The Design, Operation and Maintenance of Building Systems, Part I.
2. The Design, Operation and Maintenance of Building Systems, Part II.
3. Property Manager's Guide to Commercial Real Estate Law.
4. Real Estate Investment and Finance.
5. Environmental Health and Safety Issues.
6. Ethics is Good Business - Short Course.

In addition to the above required courses, the RPA also requires two of the following electives:

1. Risk Management and Insurance.
2. Fundamentals of Real Property Administration.
3. Leasing and Marketing for Property Managers.
4. Asset Management

2. Facilities Management Administrator (FMA)

BOMA offers a Facilities Management Administrator (FMA) designation that requires completion of seven mandatory courses and an ethics course.

3. Additional Designations

BOMA also offers a Systems Maintenance Technician (SMT) and Systems Maintenance Administrator (SMA) designation upon completion of required courses.

BOMA courses prepare individuals not only for top management positions, but also for hands-on operating positions working in the trenches.

C. NATIONAL PROPERTY MANAGEMENT ASSOCIATION (NPMA)

Founded in 1952, the **NATIONAL PROPERTY MANAGEMENT ASSOCIATION (NPMA)** *consists primarily of property managers in the Washington, D.C. area.* There are monthly meetings and special seminars. They do have members in other areas of the country.

npma.org
National Property Management Association (NPMA)

NPMA has a number of excellent publications that are guides to specifying and obtaining services by contract. Topics include:

1. *Lighting for Safety and Security*
2. *Roofing: A Guide to Specifying and Obtaining Services by Contract*
3. *Safety and Security: A Guide to Obtaining Services by Contract*
4. *Swimming Pool Management: A Guide to Specifying and Obtaining Services by Contract*
5. *Pest Control: A Guide to Specifying and Obtaining Services by Contract*
6. *Risk Management and Insurance: A Guide to Specifying and Obtaining Services by Contract*
7. *Elevator Maintenance: A Guide to Specifying and Obtaining Services by Contract*
8. *Grounds Care: A Guide to Specifying and Obtaining Services by Contract*
9. *Painting: A Guide to Specifying and Obtaining Services by Contract*

From the above partial list of publications (which are also available to nonmembers), you can see that PMA is a "hands on" type of organization. They also have a monthly bulletin with informative articles about upcoming seminars. "How To Collect Rent" is an example of one of the PMA's more practical seminars.

D. INTERNATIONAL REAL ESTATE INSTITUTE (IREI)

Membership in the **INTERNATIONAL REAL ESTATE INSTITUTE (IREI)** *includes the professional designation RPM (Registered Property Manager).* There are no educational requirements for this designation, but the institute does offer educational programs and numerous publications including the *Global Real Estate News*.

iami.org/IREI/home.cfm
International Real Estate Institue (IREI)

E. URBAN LAND INSTITUTE (ULI)

The *URBAN LAND INSTITUTE (ULI) was founded in 1926 as a nonprofit education and research institute. Its 13,000 members cover the entire spectrum of land use and development.* The ULI sells over 50,000 books annually offering professional information. They also conduct seminars. While primary emphasis is on development, the ULI also researches and publishes excellent material on the leasing and management of both residential and commercial properties.

uli.org
Urban Land Institute (ULI)

F. AIR COMMERCIAL REAL ESTATE ASSOCIATION (AIR)

This association has available excellent lease and contract forms for both industrial and commercial property. We have included a number of their forms in this book.

airea.com/HOME/Home.aspx
AIR Commercial Real Estate Association (AIREA)

Another organization that offers a complete set of property management forms is Professional Publishing. For sample forms you can call this company at 1-800-288-2006.

formulator.com
Professional Publishing - Property Management Forms

G. INTERNATIONAL COUNCIL OF SHOPPING CENTERS (ICSC)

The *INTERNATIONAL COUNCIL OF SHOPPING CENTERS (ICSC) is a specialty organization that offers a number of excellent educational programs as well as professional designations and marketing awards.* They also publish an extensive array of books covering all aspects of shopping center management.

icsc.org
International Council of Shopping Centers (ICSC)

1. Certified Leasing Specialist (CLS)

This designation is obtained by meeting experience and educational requirements as well as passing a written examination.

1. Experience requirements include full-time (85 percent) experience in shopping center leasing for at least four of the prior six years.
2. Completion of ICSC Leasing I and Leasing II certificate courses as well as the ICSC Leasing II Advanced Certificate Program, including 30 hours of college-level continuing education courses in approved areas.
3. Pass the written CLS examination.
4. Continue a mandated program of continuing education after achieving the CLS designation.

2. Certified Shopping Center Manager (CSM)

Over 2,400 professionals from all over the world have achieved this prestigious designation. Requirements include experience, education substitution, and passing a comprehensive examination:

1. A candidate for the CSM designation must have had four years experience as a manager of a shopping center. Experience must include maintenance, leasing, marketing and promotions. An applicant can substitute designated course completions for the fourth year of experience.
2. Pass a six-hour, two-part examination.

3. Accredited Shopping Center Manager (ASM)

The *ACCREDITED SHOPPING CENTER MANAGEMENT (ASM) designation is only available to international members practicing outside the United States.* Requirements for this designation are similar to the CSM designation requirements, and the examination is parallel to the CSM examination.

4. Accredited Marketing Director (AMD)

The *ACCREDITED MARKETING DIRECTOR (AMD) designation is available for candidates who have served as a shopping center marketing director for four years or served as a shopping center manager with duties encompassing those of a shopping center marketing director.*

Educational requirements may be substituted for the fourth year of experience. The AMD examination consists of 100 items and is administered over a period of four and one-half hours.

5. Senior Level Accreditation

Senior level designation is available for Certified Shopping Center Managers (SCSM) and Certified Marketing Directors (SCMD).

Qualifications include achievement of the CSM or CMD designations plus continued educational requirements. CSM or CMD designations must have been held for three years.

6. Awards

ICSC has an award program based on an International Marketing Competition (The MAXI Award) as well as International Design and Development Awards.

The MAXI award is given in a number of categories:

1. Community service
2. Public relations
3. Consumer or trade advertising
4. Sales promotion and merchandising
5. Grand opening, expansion, and renovation
6. Retailer development
7. Center productivity

The International Design and Development Awards Program has two general categories:

1. Innovative design and construction of a project
2. Renovation or expansion of an existing project

H. COMMUNITY ASSOCIATIONS INSTITUTE (CAI)

The **COMMUNITY ASSOCIATIONS INSTITUTE (CAI)** *acts as a clearinghouse for ideas and practices for successful operations and management of all types of residential common-interest housing.* Membership includes "condominium homeowner associations," property management firms, and service providers.

caionline.org
Community Association Institute (CAI)

CAI offers workshops, conferences, educational programs, as well as books, periodicals, and newsletters. They also have a website for subjects relating to common-interest developments. There are currently 59 local chapters including 10 chapters in California.

CAI offers a number of professional designations.

1. Certified Manager of Community Associations (CMCA)

The CMCA designation certifies that a manager has the basic knowledge necessary to manage any type of community association. Some tasks involved may be budgeting and attending monthly homeowner association meetings.

Requirements for the CMCA designation include completion of the M-100 Essentials of Community Association Management course, passing the M-100 examination and passing the National Certification Exam. Recertification is required every two years.

2. Association Management Specialist (AMS)

This designation is available for candidates who have passed the M-100 course and have had at least two years of association management experience in specific functional areas. The certification must be renewed every three years.

3. Professional Community Association Manager (PCAM)

This is the highest professional designation available from CAI.

To achieve this designation, candidates are required to possess at least three years of experience in common-interest development management plus having graduated from an extensive educational program set forth by CAI. The designation must be renewed every three years through work experience, service activities and continuing education.

I. INTERNATIONAL FACILITY MANAGEMENT ASSOCIATION (IFMA)

The *INTERNATIONAL FACILITY MANAGEMENT ASSOCIATION (IFMA) is an international organization of management involved in coordinating the physical workplace with the people and work of the firm.* They primarily deal with managing industrial and commercial facilities. Membership is available to professionals and educators involved in at least two of the following activities:

1. Long-range facility planning;
2. Annual facility planning;
3. Facility financial forecasting and budgeting;
4. Real estate acquisition and/or disposal;
5. Interior space planning;
6. Architectural and engineering planning and design;
7. Environmental health and safety;
8. New construction and/or renovation work;
9. Maintenance and operations management of the physical plant;
10. Facility business functions.

ifma.org
International Facility Management Association (IFMA)

IFMA has programs and conventions around the world and offers specialized councils for specialized management that include health care facilities, academic facilities, museums/cultural institutions, religious facilities, research and development facilities, sports and recreational facilities, etc.

Members can earn the Certified Facility Manager (CFM) designation through education and testing.

VII. CHAPTER SUMMARY

Property managers need to know that owners/investors are looking to make money through:

1. appreciation
2. cash flow
3. tax advantages
4. equity buildup

Property management originally evolved from the needs of the wealthy to have someone care for their estates. The moldboard plow, the electric elevator, structural steel, and the Great Depression all contributed greatly to the need for property management.

Property managers fall into a number of categories:

1. Employee managers
2. Resident managers
3. Independent property managers

There are a variety of employment opportunities for property managers at the present time. They include:

1. Government
2. Real Estate Investment Trusts
3. Financial institutions
4. Corporations
5. Franchises
6. Employees of private owners
7. Private management firms
8. Onsite management

Owners choose professional management for various reasons including:

1. Increasing rents
2. Reducing vacancy factors
3. Reducing repair costs
4. Reducing tenant damage
5. Reducing expenses
6. Management planning
7. Prolonging economic life
8. Freedom from various daily property management tasks.

Attributes of a successful property manager include:

1. Mental stamina
2. Integrity
3. Organizational skills

4. Bravery
5. People skills
6. Ability to prioritize
7. Goal oriented
8. Communication skills
9. Team oriented
10. Ability to delegate
11. Flexibility
12. Be part of the solution
13. Benefit oriented
14. Agency focused
15. A money manager

A number of professional organizations provide important management training, have excellent publications and recognize career development with professional awards and recognition.

The Institute of Real Estate Management (IREM) is affiliated with the National Association of REALTORS®.

They offer many programs and classes. IREM also offers professional designations of Certified Property Manager (CPM), Accredited Residential Manager (ARM) and Accredited Management Organization (AMO).

The Building Owners and Managers Association International (BOMA) has an extensive educational program and offers a number of professional designations including Real Property Administrator (RPA), Facilities Management Administrator (FMA), Systems Maintenance Technician (SMT) and Systems Maintenance Administrator (SMA).

The National Property Management Association (NPMA) has a number of excellent publications available to members and nonmembers.

The International Real Estate Institute (IREI) offers the Registered Property Manager (RPM) designation. They also provide worldwide contacts for members.

The Urban Land Institute (ULI) provides books, studies, and seminars. They sponsor research in many areas concerning property management.

The AIR Commercial Real Estate Association (AIR) has developed lease and contract forms for industrial, office, and commercial property.

The International Council of Shopping Centers (ICSC) offers a variety of educational programs and offers professional designations including Certified Leasing Specialist (CLS), Certified Shopping Center Manager (CSM), Accredited Shopping Center Manager (ASM), Accredited Marketing Director (AMD), Senior Certified Shopping Center Manager (SCSM) and Senior Certified Marketing Director (SCMD).

The Community Associations Institute (CAI) is involved in common ownership residential management. They offer professional designations including Certified Manager of Community Associations (CMCA), Association Management Specialist (AMS) and Professional Community Association Manager (PCAM).

The International Facility Management Association (IFMA) specializes in the evolution of the office.

VIII. CHAPTER QUIZ

1. The high-rise office buildings were made possible because of:
    a. the moldboard plow.
    b. structural steel.
    c. the electric elevator.
    d. both b and c.

2. Which of the following property management areas employ the largest number of people?
    a. Franchise leasing
    b. Government
    c. REIT management
    d. Private management firms

3. Characteristics of REITs include:
    a. publicly traded.
    b. purchasers of large properties.
    c. not taxed on profits passed on as dividends.
    d. all of the above.

4. Benefits offered by professional property management include:
    a. lower vacancy factors.
    b. higher rents.
    c. prolonging economic life.
    d. all of the above.

5. Personal attributes for success in property management include:
    a. people skills.
    b. goal oriented.
    c. flexibility.
    d. all of the above.

6. CPM stands for:

    a. Certificate in Property Management.
    b. Corporate Property Manager.
    c. Certified Property Manager.
    d. Consumer Protection Marketing.

7. ARM stands for:

    a. Association of Retail Managers.
    b. Accredited Residential Manager.
    c. American Restaurant Management.
    d. Alliance of Residential Managers.

8. AMO stands for:

    a. Accredited Management Organization.
    b. American Maintenance Organization.
    c. Association of Management Officers.
    d. Alliance of Management Organizations.

9. BOMA stands for:

    a. Benevolent Order of Managing Agents.
    b. Building Owners and Managers Association.
    c. Builders, Operators, and Managers Alliance.
    d. Building Operators Maintenance Association.

10. RPA stands for:

    a. Real Property Administrator.
    b. Residential Property Administrator.
    c. Real Estate Professional Alliance.
    d. Repair, Protect, and Administer.

ANSWERS: 1. d; 2. b; 3. d; 4. d; 5. d; 6. c; 7. b; 8. a; 9. b; 10. a

Chapter 2
Preparing for Management

KEY WORDS AND TERMS

Agency
Appreciation
Bonding
Capital Gains
Cash Flow
Depreciation
Gross Multiplier
Hedge Against Inflation
Hold-Harmless Clause
Impossibility of Performance
Incapacity
Indemnification
Inventory List
Lease File
Leveraged
Management Plan

Mutual Agreement
Negative Cash Flow
Occupancy Rules and Regulations
Operating Account
Operating Procedures
Psychic Income
Pro-forma Statement
Rent Rolls
Resident Manager
Service Contracts
Slumlord
Stabilization
Takeover Checklist
Waiver of Subrogation
Zero-Based Budgeting

CHAPTER 2 OUTLINE

I. Owner Benefits

You must understand what an owner wants in order to develop a management plan. There are a number of benefits that real property offers to investors. One or more of these benefits will be owner goals.

A. INCOME

CASH FLOW is the cash left over after cash expenses. It is money that an owner can spend. Since cash flow does not deal with non-cash expenses (depreciation), cash flow is affected by the entire amount of a mortgage payment, although only the interest portion is deducted for tax purposes. Cash flow takes into consideration all monies earned and all monies that are spent, i.e., debt payments, operating expenses, and capital expenditures (CFBT = cash flow before taxes).

Some owners are concerned with immediate cash flow while other owners are more concerned with long-term cash flow benefits. An owner who has the greatest concern for immediate cash would be reluctant to make improvements or changes in use or tenancy that could have a short-term negative effect on the cash flow. Owners who take a long-term approach are generally more secure financially. They will make improvements, change use and type of tenant if it makes economic sense as a long-term investment.

If an owner is highly leveraged (a high loan-to-value ratio) it usually doesn't take much to turn a positive cash flow into a negative cash flow or vice versa. Such owners might resist improvements or more than minimum maintenance.

When selling an income property, gross income shown on the books is more important than cash flow to some owners.

The owner wants high scheduled rents to show a low *GROSS RENT MULTIPLIER (sale price divided by gross rent).* Such owners are interested in selling the property at the maximum price or obtaining a maximum loan on the property. Therefore, they want you to get the highest rent possible even if it requires rent concessions. The seller is aware that buyers use the gross rent multiplier to eliminate overpriced properties.

VOICE OF EXPERIENCE:

When making a purchase offer on any property, recommend that the sellers provide a copy of their tax return (probably Schedule E only) where the income and expense information is shown.

B. SECURITY

Historically, real estate has acted as a hedge against inflation.

While prices in particular areas may decline, generally over the long term, real estate values have risen at a greater rate than inflation. Besides values, rents, on the whole, have also risen at a rate above the inflation rate as measured by the Consumer Price Index.

Even though real estate is less risky than most other forms of investment, there nevertheless are risks. Owners differ as to the risks they are willing to accept. As an example, an owner who wants to avoid risks might want a long-term lease at a below-market fixed rent from a financially secure national firm over a lease offering higher rents and rent escalation from a local firm. The degree of risk an owner is willing to accept would be reflected in the management plan for the property.

C. MAINTAINING THE PROPERTY

Most prudent owners want their properties maintained to protect their investment. They realize that proper maintenance directly relates to both vacancy factors and rents.

Managing property for an owner who is the occupant of the property would not involve renting or rent collection. Management would focus around maintaining the property and possibly property improvements.

D. DEPRECIATION AND CAPITAL GAINS

Some owners like the fact that part of their income can be sheltered from taxation by depreciating the building and improvements. The fact that real estate is one of the last tax shelters appeals to them.

Capital gains tax rates have been reduced to 15 percent. This makes a shorter term hold and sale more attractive to some owners. We can expect to see more speculators involved in real estate in the future. Without the capital gains advantage, most real estate investors have been buying with the idea of a relatively long holding period or 1031 exchanges.

E. APPRECIATION

Because real estate has risen in value so dramatically since World War II, many owners expect the values to continue to rise. Some owners are willing to accept negative cash flows now in order to gain future appreciation.

If an owner expects the appreciation of land value and eventually expects to demolish the structure, then this would affect the management plan, as the owner would resist improvements to the property.

F. PSYCHIC INCOME

Some owners don't care what the building looks like, it's the profit and loss statement that matters to them. Other owners are very concerned about the image that their property conveys. They want **PSYCHIC INCOME**, *the prestige that goes with being able to say they own a trophy property*. Some even want their name on the building even though they don't occupy a unit, and despite the fact that the name could be a valuable commodity when negotiating a long-term lease.

VOICE OF EXPERIENCE:

Donald Trump is one perfect example of an owner of trophy buildings. He just loves to have his name on his holdings. It's important to understand your owners' goals, such as pride of ownership.

Owners who seek prestige want their property to shine as to maintenance. Usually these owners are not highly leveraged. Therefore, it doesn't take too much to produce a positive bottom line. While the return on equity for such an owner might be less than for other investment properties, this type of owner will probably be happy if the property has good tenants and is well maintained.

G. COMBINATION OF BENEFITS

The benefits that an owner expects from ownership are likely a combination of benefits listed, with greater emphasis on just one or two of them.

What owners don't want is aggravation. They want a relatively problem-free investment. If there is a problem, they want to know you will solve it for them.

II. The Management Plan

Your **PROPERTY MANAGEMENT PLAN** *is an analysis of the present state of the property's physical condition, nature of tenants, rents, lease provisions, etc., and what you expect to achieve and how you will achieve it.* Your management plan should seek to fulfill the owner's goals.

Your property management plan might be prepared prior to obtaining the business. The prepared plan would be used as a tool to persuade owners that you, as the property manager, understand their property and their goals and will be able to meet those goals.

What owners want must be an integral part of your management plan.

If you regard your management plan as an important document, owners will treat it in a similar manner. Therefore, place your management plan in a finished binder and indicate on

the cover that it was prepared for a particular property and owner. Each client's needs are unique—it's important to remember that.

We recommend that the management plan be formally presented to the owner at a time and place where it can be explained in detail without interruption. Your office is ideal.

A. PROPERTY ANALYSIS

Your analysis of the property should include the following:

1. Location of the Property

The strengths and weaknesses of the location should be considered. Location is one factor that cannot be changed.

2. The Physical Structure

This includes construction type and quality, age, and general conditions of the property, including deferred maintenance.

3. Grounds and Parking

Evaluate the condition of the grounds and adequacy of parking.

4. Current Tenants

Who the current tenants are, rent levels, and current vacancies are important. Consider the strengths and weaknesses of current tenants and the relationship of current rent to market rent.

5. Area Analysis

The analysis includes the demographics and changes in the area, as well as the vacancy factor for similar property in the area. New construction in the area and changes in property use must be covered as to how it will affect the subject property.

Chamber of Commerce information can be valuable. It will probably have supporting data. Major banks have economists who prepare a variety of reports as to regions and particular cities. This information can be invaluable in supporting your management plan.

6. Other Possible Uses

Consider different uses of the property, if applicable.

7. Photos

Include photos to emphasize points being made, such as deferred maintenance, competing properties, etc. Digital cameras are worth their expense.

B. GOALS

The "management plan" might include one-year goals as well as longer term five-year goals.

The goals should be measurable and meaningful. The intermediate steps proposed in the management plan should lead naturally toward those goals.

Goals might include control relating to the growth of expenses or to actually reducing expenses. Goals might be to increase rents, obtain longer-term leases as well as to reduce the vacancy factor.

Showing a desired rent schedule is not enough. Your management plan must show how you will arrive at this goal.

Your plan might actually call for increasing expenses to upgrade the physical plant. This would in turn result in an immediate reduction in cash flow in order to insure later benefits of greater cash flow and property value.

Your management plan might include giving priority to corrective action of the condition of the property. It would include a time table for corrective action. You plan might even include financing arrangements to cover corrective action and/or property improvements.

VOICE OF EXPERIENCE:

Penny pinching now by avoiding needed repairs, will eventually negatively affect the owner's cash flow. Problems do not go away, they just get bigger.

Suggested improvements should include estimated costs for the work. You have to realize that your plan must sell the owner on the benefits of making the improvements and any change in operations.

VOICE OF EXPERIENCE:

Always get three estimates for improvements, informing each bidder that you are shopping for the best estimate. The lowest is not always the best.

You must keep in mind that your management plan involves much more than planning. It is a tool for action. The plan is worthless if not implemented.

C. PRO-FORMA STATEMENT

Your property management plan should include a budget for the first year based on anticipated expenses and anticipated revenue which is your **PRO-FORMA STATEMENT***.* Assumptions made in your pro-forma statement should be clearly explained. The owner must realize that your anticipated income will be directly related to the anticipated expenses, and that a change in net income might not be possible without a change in the budget. In some cases, a pro-forma statement can be based on a change in use.

Your desired rent schedule should be included and your figures should consider current lease restraints on rent adjustments.

Zero-based budgeting can be used effectively to show owners what can be done. **ZERO-BASED BUDGETING** *requires every expense to be justified as well as every staffing position.* It starts from scratch rather than with the prior year's budget. All too often, managers simply add on inflationary adjustments to prior years of expenses to estimate the next year's expenses. This common approach does not consider if the last year's budget was excessive, or too lean and, if so, where is the fat or inadequacies in the budget.

D. STAFFING

Your management plan should include present staffing and any recommended changes in staffing. Any changes should be supported.

E. COST SAVINGS

If savings are possible through your purchasing power, use of contract work, etc., your management plan should spell out just what these savings will be.

F. RESERVE REQUIREMENTS

Your management plan should justify the amount of funds to be held as a reserve against unbudgeted expenses.

G. ECONOMIC CHANGES

Property is not managed in a vacuum. National and local economic conditions will affect your plan. They affect rents, vacancy factors, and costs. A wise property manager stays abreast of local news— companies moving in and out, companies laying off staff, etc.

Any assumption that you make should be clearly stated in your management plan. You must be as realistic as possible. Owners know if the neighborhood where the property is located is declining. They want the truth, not a "Pollyanna" approach.

H. MARKETING PLAN

The management plan should cover how you intend to market the vacant space. This could include:

1. Signs;
2. Press releases;
3. Preparation of property briefs and brochures;
4. Advertising preparation;
5. Advertising budget and media selections;
6. Open houses (residential);
7. Providing information to cooperating brokers;
8. Phone contacts;
9. Personal contacts, and
10. Using present tenants as a source of leads.

I. MANAGEMENT PLAN PRIOR TO CONSTRUCTION

Property management can actually begin prior to construction.

Persons having extensive experience in leasing will have a good feel for which amenities will have little if any effect on rents for the unit being planned and which amenities will have significant economic effects.

As an example, a trash compactor might add just a little to the rent, but it could add additional maintenance costs to a particular rental range and area. A convertible den might be more important than a formal dining area where there is a kitchen dining nook. Tennis courts might not be economical amenities in some areas but in other areas they would be economically very viable additions.

VOICE OF EXPERIENCE:

All improvements are not equal. Always consider options before spending your owner's money.

Besides amenities, at least one developer of high rise office structures has the initial blueprints reviewed for maintenance purposes. Some of the suggestions the developer adopted were wall-hung stools and partitions to reduce cleaning time, washbasins accessible for the handicapped, redesigned janitorial closets to permit cleaning carts and electrical hall outlets for vacuums and floor polishers. Small details of operation and use can be easily provided for in the planning stages but, if not solved, can create problems in operation.

For large projects, the leasing start-up and applicable maintenance contracts and staffing decisions should be made prior to completion.

Some large apartment developments spend almost a year for stabilization (a reasonable occupant level). Shortening the time frame can mean significant savings to the owners.

III. Refusing Management

Just as a sale listing should be refused when the agent feels he or she cannot adequately represent the owner or where the problems associated with listing outweigh the reward, property managers must evaluate whether or not they want to manage a property for an owner.

A. SPECIALIZATION

A property management firm may refuse to manage a property because of its geographical location. A property outside of the area where the firm is operating might require more effort to manage the property than the rewards justify.

A firm that specializes in residential management might turn down the opportunity to manage a small industrial complex knowing that they lack the expertise to handle industrial leases.

> **VOICE OF EXPERIENCE:**
>
> *Acquire expertise in your field. Do not practice on your owners. Taking specialized classes at community colleges or universities is an excellent way to improve your performance and your owner's bottom line.*

B. UNREALISTIC FEES

Abraham Lincoln said, "A lawyer's time is his stock in trade." What Lincoln meant was that a lawyer's advice and experience is what the lawyer is selling and therefore his or her time requires compensation. The same holds true for property management.

As a property manager you can't stay in business if you're not adequately compensated. Compensation has to cover the time and expenses spent on each project.

Don't try to buy a management contract by cutting fee schedules or agreeing to accept what an owner offers if you do not feel the compensation is adequate. Accepting bargain-basement fees will affect your efforts. It will also affect your reputation if you perform at less than maximum effectiveness.

When you allow one owner a significant break on fees, that owner may brag about how he or she beat you down. When other property owners discover your two-tier fee schedule, they're going to be unhappy even though you are doing an excellent job for them. The owners will feel you have taken advantage of them.

In competitive situations where you have shown what you can do, always compete on a professional basis and not because of lower prices.

You may have seen a famous cartoon of two hobos sitting in an open boxcar. The caption reads, "You too! I was always the low bidder!" You must be fair to yourself as well as others and earn your true worth.

If you stick to your fee schedule, you'll find that when an owner asks you to cut your fee they generally have already decided that you will handle their property. They're just trying to see if they can save at your expense and how good a negotiator you are.

C. SLUMLORDING

Don't accept a management position where an owner wants to milk a property for rents without regard to tenant services. It's important to be fair to all parties.

Unfortunately, property owners with large numbers of aliens as tenants often take advantage of them as the owner knows the tenant won't complain about uninhabitable conditions. These owners will want you to act in their place and carry on as they would. By taking the management position you open yourself to liability under the law and lose your own self respect in the process. You're damaging your professional reputation in the community and it will negatively affect your economic status because other owners will be unwilling to entrust their properties to you.

There could be other reasons for the owner to milk a property and not do reasonable repairs and maintenance. An owner may intend to demolish the structure to use the site for a more productive purpose. The owner could be facing foreclosure and simply wants to grab the last few months rent before the property is lost to the lender. The effect is the same for whatever reason. You don't want to be a party to an attempt by the owner to maximize income at the expense of reasonable treatment of tenants.

D. NEGATIVE CASH FLOWS

Management of rental property that can be expected to result in a negative cash flow for an owner should be avoided unless the owner fully understands the financial picture and has the resources and willingness to support the property. *NEGATIVE CASH FLOW exists when cash disbursements exceed cash (rental) income, requiring the owner to continue to put more money in the property.*

Some owners of negative cash flow properties are reluctant to approve necessary repairs, are slow to make payments to the management company and can create a nightmare for the property manager.

E. CODE VIOLATIONS

Avoid getting involved in property that is currently in violation of codes or zoning ordinances unless the owner has shown the ability and willingness to correct any problems.

Some owners offer management so that the manager appears as a buffer between the owner and public authorities. You don't want to be the one who has to answer to a judge regarding any violations of the property. The problems of such properties can far outweigh the benefits of what otherwise appears to be a very lucrative management contract.

We know of a property manager who returned a new management contract where the owner had already accepted the tenant. The manager was to merely consummate the lease and collect the rent. The manager discovered that the tenant, who was to pay an extremely high rent, had a criminal record and planned to use the property for an illegal purpose.

F. PLAYING SCROOGE

Owners who otherwise manage their own property might offer you the management because they don't want to get involved in particularly unpleasant tasks. As an example, several management firms declined an offer to manage an apartment building that had received approval for condominium conversion. The owner wanted the manager to collect rents for one month and give 30-day notices to all the tenants. Management was to cease when the tenants left. A management contract of this sort makes the manager a "bastard" and provides no real benefits.

In this case, had the owners been willing to provide adequate funding to assist the tenants in relocating, and your managerial duties included tenant relocation, then handling this would not reflect negatively on your firm.

G. OWNERS WANT TO CONTROL

Management can be a disaster when owners refuse to give up control. Sometimes it can be a lack of complete trust in you and other times it is just the personalities of the owners. Owners may want you to react more as an employee than as their agent. You're asking for trouble if you accept the management contract with untenable conditions placed on your actions that allow the owner to become a co-manager.

To give back a management contract is better than trying to share management duties.

The Chinese have a proverb, "A pig with two masters shall surely starve." Owners who constantly visit their property and give orders to maintenance personnel and onsite managers tend to interfere with proper management. Orders from owners tend to give priority to what they want rather than what good management would dictate. Confusion sets in and it becomes a situation for the resident manager and staff of "damned if you do and damned if you don't."

Some owners want approval of very minor expenses or want you to deal only with particular service providers. In one case, an owner required a particular service provider who gave exorbitant billings. The owner then received cash rebates from that service provider.

You don't want to get involved in tax fraud.

Even where there is no fraud involved, if forced to use a particular contractor or service provider that you did not choose, you lose control over these people and end up with no say in requiring quality and the timeliness of job completion. Some owners want to do their own repairs or contract for them. This affects the manager's ability to properly deal with tenants.

An atmosphere of trust and respect should exist between the manager and the owner.

You can readily see that changes are required if 10 percent of your management income is derived from property that takes 50 percent of your management time.

IV. The Property Management Contract

The **PROPERTY MANAGEMENT CONTRACT** *is the agency agreement between an owner and a property manager and must clearly set forth the obligations of the parties.*

We have included the Building Owners and Managers Association International (BOMA) Standard Agency Management Agreement as **Figure 2-1**. This management agreement can be adapted for commercial, industrial, or office property. (In Chapter 5, we have included a shorter management agreement form which we feel is better suited for residential property although the BOMA form could be used.)

Pay attention to the notation on the cover page of the BOMA contract. It is intended as a guide in preparing management agreements and should not be used without the assistance of legal counsel. Revisions to the contract may be required to comply with state law or to meet the requirements of specific transactions.

A. ARTICLE I

Article I of the form clearly states that this is an exclusive agency for managing and leasing the described property.

B. ARTICLE II

Article II of the form sets forth the term of this management contract. This particular contract provides for automatic one-year renewals (after the original term) unless a 60-day written notice is given prior to the end of the contract or any renewal period. The contract provides that the owners shall be obligated for contracts for services, supplies and alterations entered into by the property manager while the contract is in effect.

Figure 2-1

MANAGEMENT AGREEMENT

THIS AGREEMENT made as of the _____ day of _____, 19_____,
by and between _____,
(hereinafter referred to as "Owner"), and _____
(hereinafter referred to as "Manager"),

WITNESSETH:

In consideration of the mutual promises and covenants contained herein, Owner and Manager agree as follows:

ARTICLE I

Exclusive Agency. Owner hereby appoints Manager as the sole and exclusive leasing, rental agent and manager of the property described on Schedule 1 attached hereto (hereinafter referred to as the "Building") and Manager hereby accepts such employment.

ARTICLE II

Term of Agreement. The term of this agreement shall commence _____, 19_____, and shall continue for a period of _____ years until _____, 19_____, and is automatically renewed thereafter for successive periods of one year each until terminated by either party upon not less than 60 days' written notice prior to the end of the initial term or any renewal period. Upon termination, Owner shall remain bound by the obligations of all contracts for services, supplies and alterations Manager has entered into in connection with the performance of its obligations hereunder.

ARTICLE III

a. *Rental of Building.* Manager shall use its best efforts to rent all space in the Building which is now vacant or may become vacant during the term of this agreement. When appropriate, Manager shall engage the services of other real estate brokers to lease space in the Building who shall be paid from such commissions as may become due to Manager under the terms of this agreement.

b. *Negotiation of Leases.* Owner shall refer all inquiries concerning the rental of space in the Building to Manager. All negotiations with prospective tenants shall be conducted by Manager or under its direction. Manager shall have the authority to execute on behalf of Owner all leases or rental agreements for periods of less than _____ year(s). Manager shall execute all leases covering a term of _____ year(s) or more with the prior written approval of Owner.

c. *Advertising.* Subject to the approval of Owner and at Owner's expense, Manager shall advertise such space as is available for rent and arrange for such signs, renting plans, brochures and other forms of advertising as may appear advisable. Owner agrees to reimburse Manager for all out-of-pocket expenses, including, but not limited to, long distance telephone calls and, with Owner's prior approval, the cost of out-of-town travel.

d. *Rental Rates.* Rental rates for space in the Building shall be established by Owner. Manager shall, promptly following the execution of this agreement and from time to time thereafter, make recommendations to Owner with respect to rental rates.

e. *Compensation.* As compensation for renting and leasing space in the Building, Owner shall pay Manager as set forth in Schedule 1.

ARTICLE IV

a. *Management of Building.* Manager shall manage the Building in an efficient and businesslike manner having due regard for the age and physical condition of the Building. Manager, through its employees and independent contractors, shall supply complete operational services for the Building.

BOMA International Standard Agency Management Agreement

b. *Repairs.* Manager shall, in the name of and at the expense of Owner, make or cause to be made such ordinary repairs and alterations as Manager may deem advisable or necessary. However, not more than $_____ shall be expended for any one item of repair or alteration without Owner's prior written approval, except emergency repairs if, in the opinion of Manager, such repairs are necessary to protect the Building from damage or to maintain services to tenants as called for in their leases.

c. *Service Contracts.* Manager shall, in the name of and at the expense of Owner, contract for those utilities and other building operation and maintenance services Manager shall deem advisable; provided that, no service contract shall be for a term exceeding one year without the prior written approval of Owner. Manager shall, at Owner's expense, purchase and keep the Building furnished with all necessary supplies. All expenses shall be charged to Owner at net cost and Owner shall be credited with all rebates, refunds, allowances and discounts allowed to Manager.

d. *Reimbursement.* Owner agrees to reimburse Manager for all out-of-pocket expenses, including, but not limited to, long distance telephone calls and, with Owner's prior approval, the cost of out-of-town travel.

e. *Employees.* Except as provided on Schedule 1, all persons employed in the operation of the Building shall be employees of Manager or a legal entity owned or controlled by Manager. Manager shall make disbursements and deposits for all compensation and other amounts payable with respect to persons who are employed in the operation of the Building, including, but not limited to, unemployment insurance, social security, workmen's compensation and other charges imposed by a governmental authority or provided for in a union agreement. Manager shall maintain complete payroll records. All payroll costs, including, but not limited to, those enumerated herein, are operating expenses to be reimbursed to Manager from Owner's funds received by Manager.

f. *Expenditures.* All expenditures authorized by this agreement shall be considered operating expenses to be paid from Owner's funds received by Manager. In the event disbursements shall be in excess of the rents collected, Owner agrees to pay such excess promptly on demand.

g. *Monthly Statements.* Manager shall, by the _____ day of each month, render to Owner a statement of receipts and disbursements for the preceding month. Manager shall, after deducting its compensation and any other sums due it from Owner, hold or expend such sums as Owner may have directed herein or otherwise and remit the balance to Owner.

h. *Collection and Segregation of Funds.* Manager shall collect the rent and other income from tenants of the Building. All funds received by Manager for or on behalf of Owner (less any sums properly deducted by Manager pursuant to any of the provisions of this agreement) shall be deposited in a bank in a special account maintained by Manager for the deposit of funds of Owner and not mingled with the funds of Manager.

i. *Bonding Employees.* All employees of Manager who handle or are responsible for Owner's funds shall be bonded by a fidelity bond in an adequate amount.

j. *Interest and Tax Payments.* Manager shall pay interest or amortization on mortgages, taxes, assessments, premiums on insurance or reserves for such items only as designated on Schedule 1.

k. *Special Services.* At the request of Owner, Manager will perform the following special services for Owner: (i) supervise remodeling, (ii) provide special accounting, and (iii) act as property consultant. If such special services are provided, additional fees shall be payable in an amount agreed upon between the parties.

l. *Legal Proceedings.* Manager shall, at Owner's request and expense, engage counsel and cause such legal proceedings to be instituted as may be necessary to enforce payment of rent or to dispossess tenants. Manager shall have the authority to compromise disputes with tenants involving setoffs or damage claims so long as the amount involved does not exceed one month's rent payable by such tenant.

m. *Compensation.* As compensation for management of the Building, Owner shall pay Manager as set forth in Schedule 1.

ARTICLE V

a. *Indemnification.* Owner agrees: (i) to hold and save Manager free and harmless from any damage or injuries to persons or property by reason of any cause whatsoever either in and about the Building or elsewhere when Manager is carrying out the provisions of this agreement or acting under the express or implied directions of Owner, (ii) to reimburse Manager upon demand for any moneys which Manager is required to pay out for any reason whatsoever, under this agreement or in connection with, or as an expense in defense of any claim, civil or criminal action, proceeding, charge or prosecution made, instituted or maintained against Manager or Owner and Manager, jointly or severally, affecting or due to the conditions or use of the Building or acts or omissions of Manager or employees of Owner or Manager, or arising out of or based upon any law, regulation, requirement, contract or award relating to the hours of employment, working conditions, wages or compensaton of employees or former employees, and (iii) to

BOMA International Standard Agency Management Agreement

defend promptly and diligently, at Owner's sole expense, any claim, action or proceeding brought against Manager or Manager and Owner jointly or severally arising out of or connected with any of the foregoing, and to hold harmless and fully indemnify Manager from any judgment, loss or settlement on account thereof. The foregoing provisions of this Article shall survive the termination of this agreement, but this shall not be construed to mean that Owner's liability does not survive as to other provisions of this agreement. Nothing contained in this Article shall relieve Manager from responsibility to Owner for gross negligence or willful misconduct, unless such gross negligence or willful misconduct is covered by Owner's insurance on behalf of Manager.

b. *Compliance with Laws.* If Owner shall fail or refuse to comply with or abide by any rule, order, determination, ordinance or law of any federal, state or municipal authority, Manager, upon giving twenty-four hours' written notice mailed to Owner at its address as hereinafter set forth, may terminate this agreement.

c. *Insurance.* Owner agrees to carry public liability, elevator liability and contractual liability (specifically insuring the indemnity provisions contained in Article IIIa), steam boiler (if applicable), and such other insurance as the parties agree to be necessary or desirable for the protection of the interests of Owner and Manager. In each such policy of insurance, Owner agrees to designate Manager as a party insured with Owner, the carrier and the amount of coverage in each policy shall be mutually agreed upon by Owner and Manager. A certificate of each policy issued by the carrier shall be delivered promptly to Manager by Owner. All policies shall provide for 10 days' written notice to Manager prior to cancellation.

d. *Waiver of Subrogation.* Owner shall procure an appropriate clause in, or endorsement on, each of its policies for fire or extended coverage insurance and on all other forms of property damage insurance including, but not limited to, coverage such as water damage, property damage, boiler and machinery insurance and sprinkler leakage insurance, covering the Building or personal property, fixture or equipment located thereon whereby the insurer waives subrogation or consents to a waiver of the right of recovery against Manager, and having obtained such clause or endorsement of waiver of subrogation or consent to a waiver of right of recovery, Owner hereby agrees that it will not make any claim against or seek to recover from Manager for any loss or damage to property of the type covered by such insurance.

ARTICLE VI

If the Building is sold prior to termination of this agreement, Manager shall represent Owner in connection with the sale. Owner shall pay Manager a commission for these services in accordance with Schedule 1.

ARTICLE VII

a. *Bankruptcy and Insolvency.* In the event a petition in bankruptcy is filed by or against either Owner or Manager, or in the event that either shall make an assignment for the benefit of creditors or take advantage of any insolvency act, either party hereto may immediately terminate this agreement by written notice. Remedies set forth hereinabove shall be in addition to and shall not exclude any other remedy available under applicable law to the parties hereto.

b. *Independent Contractors.* It is expressly understood and agreed that Manager will act as an independent contractor in performance of this agreement. No provision hereunder shall be intended to create a partnership or a joint venture with respect to the Building or otherwise.

c. *Notice.* Any notice required or permitted under this agreement shall be given when actually delivered or when deposited in the United States mail as certified mail addressed as follows:

To Owner:

To Manager:

or to such other address as may be specified from time to time by either party in writing.

d. *Suit or Action.* If suit or action is instituted in connection with any controversy arising out of this agreement, the prevailing party shall be entitled to recover, in addition to costs, such sum as the court may adjudge reasonable as attorneys' fees in such suit or action and on any appeal from any judgment or decree entered therein.

BOMA International Standard Agency Management Agreement

e. *Assignment and Amendment.* All terms and conditions of this agreement shall be binding upon the parties hereto and their respective successors and assigns. This agreement may not be modified or amended except by written agreement of the parties.

IN WITNESS WHEREOF the parties hereto have executed this agreement in duplicate as of the date first here-inabove written.

_____
Owner

_____
Manager

**BOMA INTERNATIONAL
STANDARD
AGENCY MANAGEMENT
AGREEMENT**

NOTE: *The foregoing form has been distributed by the Agency Management Committee of Building Owners and Managers Association International as a guide to members to assist in preparing management agreements. It is likely that revisions will be needed to comply with the laws of various jurisdictions and to meet the requirements of individual transactions. The foregoing form should not be used without the assistance of legal counsel.*

BOMA International Standard Agency Management Agreement

SCHEDULE 1 TO MANAGEMENT AGREEMENT

DATED _____

1. The property covered by the management agreement is described as follows:

2. Owner shall compensate Manager for renting and leasing space in the Building, including expansion of space occupied by existing tenants, as follows:

For lease renewals, Manager shall be compensated as follows:

Manager shall be entitled to compensation for expansion space and renewals at the rates specified above upon the exercise of options contained in leases negotiated by Manager, even though such options are exercised after the termination or expiration of the agreement. Upon termination of the agreement pursuant to the provisions of Article II, Owner shall recognize Manager as the broker in any pending negotiations for lease of space in the Building. In the event of the consummation of a lease with a person with whom Manager was negotiating at the date of termination of the agreement, Owner shall pay Manager a commission at the rate prescribed above.

3. Manager's compensation for management of the Building shall be as follows:

4. In the event of a sale of the Building, the commission payable to Manager shall be as follows:

5. Manager shall pay, subject to availability of Owner's funds, mortgage payments, BOMA dues, taxes, assessments, premiums on insurance or reserves for such items as follows:

6. The following persons engaged in the operation of the Building shall be employees of Owner:

SCHEDULE 1

BOMA International Standard Agency Management Agreement

A management contract length should be related to the services provided.

As an example, a short-term contract, even one for one year, would not be appropriate if the contract provided only a percentage of the rents received (no rental fees) if there were a significant number of vacancies. In such a contract, the owner could take advantage of you and let you stabilize the property. You would do the hard work and the owner would take over when the property was fully leased.

VOICE OF EXPERIENCE:

Rental fees and property management service fees are different fees for different services. Owners pay either a flat fee or a percentage fee for the property management portion of the contract. Often a leasing fee is charged upon a renewal or rental agreement, although some companies do not do so.

A straight percentage might be appropriate for a one-year contract if the property had a reasonable vacancy factor and was relatively well run. Similarly, if you only received a short-term management contract you would not want to take on trying to get a poorly managed building in shape. This could mean changing the tenant mix and on-site personnel, instituting new rules and regulations, evicting problem tenants, changing rents, etc.

When things are done right and you have policies and procedures in place with relatively stable tenants, then you stand to profit from past efforts. Don't accept an obligation without the rewards.

C. ARTICLE III

1. Rental

The manager agrees to use his or her best efforts to rent all space and keep the space rented during the duration of the management contract. The manager has the authority to use other real estate brokers in leasing the space, however, the property manager shall be responsible for paying their commissions out of the commissions received by the property manager.

2. Lease Negotiation

The owner agrees to refer all rental inquiries to the manager who will have the authority to execute leases on behalf of the owner. The period of leases that can be executed by the manager would be set forth. Leases for longer periods require the prior written approval of the owner.

3. Advertising

The manager has the authority to place signs on the property for rentals and prepare advertising material. This contract calls for owner reimbursement of all of the manager's out-of-pocket expenses, including long distance telephone calls. The owner's prior approval is required for out-of-town travel.

Residential property management contracts generally do not provide for the owner to pay for advertising costs. Some contracts may provide for a separate leasing fee.

4. Rental Rates

This clause clearly provides for rental rates to be established by the owner. The manager can merely make recommendations.

5. Compensation

The managers compensation is set forth in Schedule I.

Lease renewals may or may not be compensated. Whenever a company expects compensation on renewals, it must be noted in the property management agreement.

D. ARTICLE IV

1. Management of Building

The property manager agrees to manage the property in an efficient and businesslike manner, considering the age and physical condition of the property, supplying complete operational services.

2. Repairs

Acting for the owner, the manager can make ordinary repairs and alterations. Owner's prior written approval is required for any one item of repair or alteration that exceeds a specified dollar limit. This limit should be reasonably high enough so that constant owner approval is not necessary. Too low a limit would indicate an owner's lack of trust in the manager.

The dollar limit can be exceeded in emergencies where repairs are required to protect the building or to maintain tenant services.

3. Service Contracts

The manager is authorized to contract for services and utilities. Contracts exceeding one year shall require the prior written approval of the owner.

This clause also authorizes the manager, at the owner's expense, to keep the building furnished with necessary supplies.

The owner is to be charged the net costs and shall be credited with any rebates, refunds, allowances and discounts allowed to the manager (no secret profits).

4. Reimbursement

The owner agrees to reimburse the manager for out-of-pocket expenses.

5. Employees

Schedule I to this contract specifies those employees who shall be employees of the owner. All other employees are employees of the manager. The manager will be responsible for unemployment insurance, worker's compensation, payroll deductions, social security contributions, etc. for the manager's employees. Payroll costs for employees of the manager shall be reimbursed from owner funds. Naturally, each contract has its own provisions and is negotiable.

The property management contract spells out the agreement as to whether the manager or the owner will be the employer.

6. Expenditures

Expenditures provided for in the management contract are operating expenses that may be paid from funds of the owner received by the manager (rents). Any expenses in excess of rents shall be paid on demand by the owner.

7. Monthly Statement

This clause provides the date during the following month for the monthly statement. The amount due the owner after the deduction of management compensation shall be sent to the owner unless agreed otherwise.

8. Collection and Segregation of Funds

The manager has responsibility for rent collections and rents shall be deposited in a bank account and not commingled with the manager's own funds (see Chapter 11).

9. Bonding of Employees

All employees of the manager who handle or are responsible for owner funds shall be bonded by a fidelity bond of an adequate amount.

10. Interest and Tax Payments

The manager shall make mortgage, tax, special assessment and insurance payments or set up reserves for the payments if designated in Schedule I.

11. Special Services

Special services such as supervision of remodeling, special accounting and property consulting shall be performed by the manager at the owner's request. Additional fees shall be agreed upon for special services.

12. Legal Proceedings

At the owner's request and consent, the manager shall hire attorneys and commence legal proceedings to enforce payment of rent or to dispossess tenants. The manager has the power to settle disputes with tenants involving set-offs or damage claims providing the amount does not exceed one month's rent for such tenant.

13. Compensation

The manager's compensation is set forth in Schedule I.

E. ARTICLE V

1. Indemnification

The owner agrees to hold the manager harmless (hold harmless clause) for damages or injuries to persons or property when the manager is carrying out provisions of this contract and to reimburse the manager for defense costs regarding such claims.

The manager is not relieved of liability for gross negligence or willful misconduct unless covered by owner's insurance.

2. Compliance with Laws

Failure of the owner to comply with a rule, order, determination, ordinance or law (federal, state or municipal) allows the manager to terminate the agreement upon 24-hour written notice.

3. Insurance

The owner agrees to carry public liability, elevator liability, contractual liability, steam boiler and other insurance agreed to be necessary to protect the owner and manager's interests. The owner agrees to name the manager as a party insured. The amount of coverage shall be agreed by the parties. Policies of insurance shall provide for 10-day written notice to the manager prior to cancellation.

4. Waiver of Subrogation

The property insurance coverage shall provide that the insurer waives any substitution rights against the manager. Otherwise the insurer, after paying a claim, could go against the manager for reimbursement if the insurer believed that the manager was responsible for the loss.

F. ARTICLE VI

This clause provides that a sale of the property prior to termination of the management contract shall entitle the manager to a commission for services in accordance with Schedule I.

G. ARTICLE VII

1. Bankruptcy and Insolvency

In the event of bankruptcy or an assignment to benefit creditors by one party, the other party may terminate the contract by written notice.

Termination does not exclude any other remedy available under the law. A party could still sue for damages.

2. Independent Contractor

The parties agree that the property manager is an independent contractor in the performance of this contract. The property manager is not a partner or joint venturer.

3. Notice

This provision provides as to where owner and manager notices are to be sent.

4. Suit or Action

If a lawsuit is instituted concerning the performance of this contract, the prevailing party is entitled to costs plus reasonable attorney fees. (This provision will reduce the likelihood of a frivolous lawsuit.)

Note: Some management contracts provide for either consensual or mandatory arbitration of disputes. You need to check with the legal department of your local association of Realtors®.

5. Assignment or Amendment

The terms of this agreement are binding on the successor and assigns of the parties.

Any modification or amendment to the contract must be in writing.

H. SCHEDULE I

Schedule I includes the following.

1. Description of the Property

The description must be clear and unambiguous.

2. Manager Compensation for Leasing

The leasing commission would be set forth. It ordinarily is a percentage of rent received for the entire lease. The fee for lease renewal might be the same as for leasing but it could be less or negotiated down to "0."

The leasing fees apply to expansion space as well as renewal options exercised after the expiration of the management agreement.

If you, as the manager, were negotiating with a prospective tenant when the management contract was terminated and a lease was later consummated, you are entitled to a leasing commission.

3. Management Commission

The management commission is separate from the leasing commission and would ordinarily include a minimum commission against a percentage of gross receipts.

4. Sale Commission

This clause provides a separate commission to be paid to you, the manager, if the property is sold.

As the manager, you need not be a party to the sale to be entitled to a sales commission.

5. Payments by Manager

This clause sets forth what payments you, the manager, makes on behalf of the owner such as insurance, taxes, mortgage payments, etc.

6. Employees of Owner

This paragraph would specify which employees or categories of employees will be employees of the owner.

IV. Agency Termination

Agencies, such as management contracts, can be terminated in a number of ways. These include:

1. Expiration of the term of the agency.
2. Impossibility of performance such as the taking of the property under management contract by eminent domain.
3. Mutual agreement. Parties can agree to end the agency.
4. Bankruptcy of the principal or agent.

5. Incapacity of principal or agent. An example would be a party being declared incompetent.

Either the principal or the agent can cancel a management contract since courts will not force an agency relationship on anyone. However, if either party cancels without just cause, they can be held liable for damages resulting from the wrongful cancellation.

An exception to the right to cancel is an agency coupled with an interest. As an example, if the management company loans an owner money to make renovations as part of a management contract, then the agent would have a financial interest in the property and the agency could not be unilaterally canceled.

Case Example

Pacific Landmark Hotel, Ltd. v. Marriott Hotels, Inc., 19 C.A. 4th 615 (1993)

In order to obtain a 50-year management contract from a hotel, Marriott Hotels, Inc. had a subsidiary corporation make a $23 million loan to the hotel.

The owners of the hotel sued Marriott to cancel the management contract because of breach of contract. Marriott prevailed in Superior Court based on the finding that Marriott had an agency coupled with an interest since they had made a substantial loan to the hotel.

This decision was reversed by the Court of Appeals which held that because a corporation is a separate entity and the loan was made by a separate corporation, Marriott did not have an agency coupled with an interest so the management contract could be cancelled.

VI. Takeout Checklists

Your work begins when you receive a signed management contract. There are many things that must be done quickly for a smooth transition of management from an owner or another manager to you.

A formal checklist of required forms is important or you are almost certain to miss something.

Things you want or information required would include:

1. Names of all owners as well as social security numbers.
2. Owner's home address.
3. Owner's home telephone number.
4. Owner's business address.
5. Owner's business telephone number and e-mail address.
6. Name, address, and telephone number of the person authorized to act as agent of the owner in the event the owner is unavailable or cannot be located.

7. Resident manager's name.

8. Resident manager's telephone number. (Resident manager must be notified of their status and who to contact. They must also be given information about accepting lease deposits, lists of contractors, etc.)

9. Resident manager compensation as well as any contract of employment.

10. Resident manager's social security number.

11. Names, addresses, telephone numbers and social security numbers of other employees as well as their compensation.

12. Payroll records of all employees.

13. Copies of all existing service contracts. (Service providers will have to be notified regarding where to send billings.)

14. Information and/or contracts for any work in progress. (Contractors will have to be notified regarding billings.)

15. Copies of all leases (lease file). (Tenants will have to be notified where to send rents.)

16. Security deposits should be turned over to you and deposited in your trust account. These deposits are then turned over to the owner.

17. Information on vacancies and rent schedules. (You want to review current marketing procedures, rents, and institute a new marketing plan if rent adjustments are called for.)

18. Keys. You want copies of all keys now kept by the resident manager.

19. Inventory lists. (If there is an inventory or owner-owned personal property, including maintenance equipment, you will need a copy. If there is none, one should be prepared.)

20. Occupancy rules and regulations. (You want a copy of present rules and regulations that might need to be modified. If there are none, you should consider what is required.)

21. Copies of insurance policies. (You'll want to review present coverage and make recommendations for change if needed. You'll also want to notify insurance agents that future correspondence should go to you as well as being named as an insured under liability policies.)

22. Copies of last tax statement. (You will want the tax parcel number to have future tax statements sent to you. If taxes appear too high, you should consider an appeal.)

23. Mortgage payment book. (If you are to make mortgage payments you will need the payment book. You should also notify the mortgagee that you are managing the property and that payment receipts or other correspondence should be sent to you.)

24. Leases in progress. (You will want copies of rental applications and information as to their status and verifications and credit checks.)

25. Evictions in progress. (You want to know the status of any three-day or 30-day or 60-day notices, depending on your state, as well as unlawful detainer actions.)

26. Rent rolls and back rent. (You want copies of rent rolls and the amount of back rent or security deposits that are due.)

27. Files. (You want the tenant files, contractor files and other records kept. The records may have to be placed in a compatible format with your record keeping system.)

28. Monies owed by former tenants. (If the debts have not been turned over to collection, you should make a decision as to what should be done. If the owner or prior manager has turned over any collections to a collection agency, they should be notified that checks and correspondence should go to you.)

29. Last utility bills. (Notify utility providers that future billings shall be sent to you.)
30. Washer - Dryer/Vending Machines. You need to know who owns any coin operated machines. If owned by others, you want copies of the contracts (to notify vending companies that checks go to you). If owned by the property owner, you want to know how receipts are presently being handled.
31. Trash removal information. You want to know the name, address and telephone numbers of the trash carrier and if there is a written contract. (You should notify the trash company of any change as to billing.)
32. Unpaid past due or presently due bills and any contested charges. (You want to be able to pay just bills as well as defend against improper charges).
33. Building plans. (If available, building plans could be helpful for renovation or improvements.)
34. Operating account. (You will likely require a check from the owner to set up an immediate operating account so bills can be paid and the reserve amount agree upon can be kept in the account.)
35. Copies of last year's operating statement. (This can be used to analyze progress or discover problems.)

As soon as possible, you, as the property manager, should complete the following:

1. Meet with the resident manager and review all current operating procedures. The manager should be instructed verbally and in writing as to your specific requirements.
2. The resident manager should be given a copy of his or her job description.
3. All vacant units should be inspected by you (the property manager) and any resident manager.
4. Repairs, renovations and present maintenance should be reviewed with the resident manager and maintenance staff.
5. A property inspection, with a written report, should be conducted with the resident manager, maintenance supervisor (if applicable) and you.
6. Review the tentative management plan with the resident manager. If none was prepared, work should commence on the management plan. The tentative plan might require some revisions.
7. Tasks that require immediate attention should be prioritized with the resident manager and the maintenance supervisor.

Additional requirements for property takeover will be dictated by the nature of the property.

VII. CHAPTER SUMMARY

Benefits that owners obtain by the ownership of rental property include:

1. Income.
2. Security.
3. Depreciation.
4. Capital gains taxation.
5. Appreciation.
6. Pride of ownership (Psychic income).

By understanding benefits of ownership and what an individual owner of a particular property is seeking, you can prepare a management plan. A management plan would include an analysis of the plus and minus features of a property as to:

1. Location.
2. Physical structure.
3. Current tenants.
4. Current rents and lease terms.
5. Area analysis.
6. Other possible uses.
7. Photographs.
8. Goals of management.
9. Priority of actions.
10. Pro-forma statement.
11. Proposed staffing.
12. Areas of cost savings.
13. Financial reserve requirements.
14. Economic changes likely to effect management.

There are times when good business practices would dictate that you, as a property manager, should refuse management opportunities.

1. Specialization. Management situations removed from your physical area of activity and/or outside you area of expertise.
2. Unrealistic fees offered by an owner.
3. Slumlord opportunities where expenses are to be severely restrained and the object is to milk the property.
4. Negative cash flow situations where the owner is reluctant to subsidize proper management activities.
5. Property with code violations where the owner is unwilling or unable to correct the situation.
6. Short-term management opportunities to relieve the owner of an unpleasant task.
7. Situations where the owner doesn't have enough faith in you to give up control.

The BOMA property management contract included in this chapter can be used for commercial, industrial and office properties. It is intended as a guide, not to be used without legal counsel review. Elements of this contract, include:

1. Exclusive agency to lease and manage.
2. Term of the contract with an automatic renewal unless notice is given.
3. Managers agreement to use best efforts.
4. Manager to handle leases. The authority as to lease term without owner's approval is set forth.
5. Owner's obligation for advertising costs.
6. Owner sets the rentals, the manager advises.
7. Property manager agrees to manage in an efficient manner.
8. Owner's permission is required for repairs above a set amount.
9. Manager is not to enter into service contracts beyond one year without owner's permission.
10. The owner agrees to reimburse the manager for out-of-pocket expenses.
11. Employees not designated as employees of the owner are employees of the manager who is responsible for insurance and withholding although costs are to be reimbursed by the owner.
12. The manager may use rent money for owner-obligated expenses.
13. The manager will supply owner with a monthly statement and remittance.
14. The manager will not commingle funds of owner with manager's funds.
15. Employees responsible for funds will be bonded.
16. The manager shall make designated payments from rent receipts.
17. Special services provided by the manager will be performed at agreed upon fees.
18. The manager shall commence legal action at owner's direction and expense. Manager has authority to settle disputes without owner's concurrence for up to one month's rent paid by the tenant involved.
19. The owner agrees to hold the manager harmless for property damage and personal injury arising from the management contract.
20. Landlords breach or failure to comply with a law or legal order shall allow the manager to terminate the agreement.
21. The owner agrees to carry designated liability coverage to protect the manager.
22. The owner's insurance carrier shall waive subrogation rights.
23. The sale of the property shall entitle the manager to a stated commission.
24. Bankruptcy or insolvency acts of one party shall allow the other party to terminate the agreement.
25. The property manager is to be an independent contractor.
26. The location where notices are to be sent is set forth.
27. In the event of a lawsuit, the prevailing party is entitled to costs and attorney fees.
28. The contract shall be binding on assigns and successors in interest.

The schedule attached to the contracts describes the property and sets forth lease commissions, lease renewal commissions, management commissions and sales commissions if property is sold. The payments that the manager shall make on behalf of the owner are set forth and who shall be an owner employee is covered.

Agencies such as management contracts can be terminated by:

1. Expiration of term
2. Impossibility of performance
3. Mutual agreement
4. Bankruptcy
5. Incapacity
6. Unilateral action by either party

The one contract that cannot be terminated unilaterally is an agency coupled with an interest.

When taking over management, there should be a checklist because documents and information are needed by the manager for a smooth transition.

VIII. CHAPTER QUIZ

1. Benefits of ownership of investment property include all, except:
    a. risk.
    b. appreciation.
    c. pride of ownership.
    d. capital gains tax on sale profits.

2. A property analysis included in a management plan would cover:
    a. the locational advantages and disadvantages of the property.
    b. the physical structure.
    c. current tenants and rents.
    d. all of the above.

3. What is a Pro-Forma Statement?
    a. The current rent schedule
    b. An audited operating statement
    c. A statement as to anticipated rents and expenses
    d. A chart showing the changes in vacancies

4. Zero-based budgeting is based on:
    a. no expenses for maintenance.
    b. 100 percent occupancy.
    c. starting with zero and justifying every budgeted item.
    d. anticipated revenue equaling anticipated expenses.

5. A property manager should consider refusal of management when:
   a. the manager lacks the expertise to properly handle management.
   b. the owner refuses to allow the manager to take any action without prior approval.
   c. the owner wants the manager to avoid making repairs.
   d. for all of the above situations.

6. A slumlord wants:
   a. maximum rents with minimum tenant services.
   b. minimum rents and minimum tenant services.
   c. maintenance to take precedence over revenue.
   d. the manager to think in terms of long-term benefits of properly maintaining property.

7. Negative cash flow management involves:
   a. tax free income.
   b. continued infusion of cash by the owner.
   c. unreported cash income.
   d. preparing records showing cash expenses that were not actually paid.

8. The length of a management contract should:
   a. never be less than five years.
   b. be under one year.
   c. ideally be on a month-to-month basis.
   d. be related to problems to be corrected and services to be provided.

9. A management contract can be terminated because of:
   a. bankruptcy of either party.
   b. mutual agreement between owner and manager.
   c. impossibility of performance.
   d. any of the above.

10. A management contract cannot be unilaterally canceled by an owner when:
   a. the manager does not wish cancellation.
   b. the manager has an interest coupled with an agency.
   c. the owner owes the manager an outstanding debt.
   d. the contract is for a stated period and it has yet to expire.

ANSWERS: 1. a; 2. d; 3. c; 4. c; 5. d; 6. a; 7. b; 8. d; 9. d; 10. b

SUBLEASE
Keegan & Coppin
ONCOR
INTERNATIONAL
Worldwide Real Estate Services
415-461-1010
www.KeeganCoppin.com
JOSH JONES
THEO BANKS

Chapter 3
Leases and Leasing

KEY WORDS AND TERMS

AIDS (Prior Occupant)
Assignment of Lease
Capacity
Compensation
Consumer Price Index
Contracts of Adhesion
Credit Reports
Death on Property
Estate for Years
Flat Lease
Flood Hazard Area
Gross Lease
Hazardous Substances
Lead-Based Paint Disclosure
Lease
Lease Renewals
Legal Purpose
Lessee

Lessor
Letter of Intent
Master Lease
Military Ordnance
Mutuality
Net Lease
Options to Renew
Percentage Lease
Periodic Tenancy
Proposal to Lease
Qualifying Tenants
Recording
Rent Incentives
Statute of Frauds
Sublease
Sublessee
Sublessor
Win/Win Negotiating

CHAPTER 3 OUTLINE

I. Lease – Definition

A *LEASE is a contract that transfers possession from an owner (lessor) to a tenant (lessee).* While the tenant is entitled to exclusive possession during the term of the lease, the lessor retains title and reversionary rights to take possession at the end of the lease. As a property manager, you may charge a fee for leasing in addition to monthly property management commissions.

Because a lease is a contract, the four basic contractual requirements apply.

Mutuality. This refers to a meeting of the minds. The lease must be clear and unambiguous as to its terms, compensation and property to be leased.

Capacity. The parties must be of legal age and have the mental capacity to contract.

Legal Purpose. To be enforceable, the lease must be for a legal purpose. A lease that specifies an illegal use is void.

Consideration. While courts seldom are concerned with the adequacy of consideration, there must be consideration flowing from the lessee to the lessor and vice versa. It is usually money but it could be anything of value.

A lack of "adequate consideration" could be used to show that the lease was not freely entered into because of undue influence or the presence of fraud, both of which would allow the injured party to void the lease.

II. Statute of Frauds

Every state has a statute of frauds indicating which documents must be in writing.

The statute of frauds requires certain instruments to be in writing. They must be signed by the person who is being held to the instrument. Generally included among the instruments that must be in writing are leases for more than one year. Therefore, oral leases one year or less need not be in writing and are binding, but not recommended.

State *STATUTES OF FRAUDS usually require contracts (leases) to be in writing if, by their terms, they cannot be fully performed within one year.* Therefore, an oral six-month lease, which could ordinarily be enforceable, would be unenforceable if it were not to commence for seven months. By the terms of such a lease, it would take more than one year for full performance (13 months).

Even though a lease might not have to be in writing, it certainly "should" be in writing.

VOICE OF EXPERIENCE:

By setting forth lease terms as a written contract you are protected against a situation where the lessee claims the verbal agreement was different from the agreement you claim it to be. Actually, both parties are protected by writing since people tend to have "convenient" memories and remember agreements in a manner selectively beneficial to them.

III. Types of Leases

A. ESTATE FOR YEARS

*Leases can be for a fixed term. Such leases are known by the legal term **ESTATE FOR YEARS**. A one-month vacation rental would be an estate for years in that it has a definite termination date when possession must be returned to the lessor.*

B. PERIODIC TENANCY

A lease that automatically renews itself, unless notice is given by either party to cancel it, is known as a **PERIODIC TENANCY**. In most states, the notice requirements to cancel a periodic tenancy would be the length of the rent paying period, but no more than 30 days.

Do not confuse 30 days with one month—they are not the same.

A weekly rental would only require seven days notice, which is the length of the rent paying period. A lease for less than one year that automatically renews itself generally requires a 30-day notice of termination. California has a 30-day notice for the tenant and landlord if the tenant has had possession for under a year and 60 days if he/she has had possession for over a year. It may be 30 days if the owner is selling the property.

A 30-day notice is not universal for ending a periodic tenancy. As an example, the notice period is 45 days in Hawaii.

VOICE OF EXPERIENCE:

In California, the notice requirements changed from 30 days to 60 days to 30 days again and then back to 60 days all in the course of a few years. This is an example of why you need to keep abreast of real estate laws and regulations in your state! Property managers are well advised to have a lawyer handle termination of tenancy notices at the owner's expense. It protects you and your owner/client in the long run!

Just as a notice must be given to terminate an estate for years, the same notice requirement must be given by the lessor to change the terms of the lease, such as a rent increase.

Month-to-month tenancies are the most common of the periodic tenancies.

C. RENT-PAYING PROVISIONS

Rent can be a fixed sum or a variable sum according to some formula. Several types of leases are based on rent-paying provisions.

1. Gross Lease

A *GROSS LEASE, also known as a "flat lease," is a lease where the tenant pays a fixed rent.* Generally, residential leases are gross leases, although many commercial and industrial leases also provide for a fixed rental. With a gross lease the lessor pays the taxes and insurance. Maintenance costs can be either the responsibility of lessor or lessee based on the provisions of the lease. A gross lease for a long term, such as five years, might have a provision for rent increases at various times over the period of the lease.

2. Net Lease

A *NET LEASE is a lease where the lessor is given a flat amount of rent each month and the tenant pays taxes, insurance, maintenance and other expenses that would otherwise be the owner's responsibility.* Investors love net leases because they have no operational responsibilities. All they need to do is collect their rent.

Net leases are generally for commercial or industrial property and extremely rare for residential property.

SALE-LEASEBACKS usually provide for net leases where the investor buys the property from the seller and the seller becomes the buyer's tenant. There can be many variations as to net leases where the lessor is responsible for some costs.

Net leases are usually long-term leases and often contain provisions for rent increases. The most common provision ties the rent to the Consumer Price Index (CPI).

The lessor is able to maintain the same purchasing power from the rent money. It would otherwise be reduced because of cheaper dollars due to inflation. Net leases are covered in Chapters 4 and 7.

3. Percentage Lease

A **PERCENTAGE LEASE** *is where the rent is tied to the gross income of a business.* They are generally used for shopping centers. Percentage leases require a minimum rent coupled with the percentage of the gross. Generally, businesses with a higher markup pay higher percentages as rent under percentage leases. Percentage leases and the applicable clauses protecting the lessor are covered in Chapters 4 and 7.

D. CORPORATION LEASE

Where either the lessor or lessee is a corporation, the board of directors must give approval to corporate officers to sign the lease or management contract. You, the property manager, need to know who has the authority to contract.

Should a corporation lease out all of its corporate property, the lease must be approved by a majority of the stockholders, since the corporation could be putting itself out of the business set forth in its corporate charter.

E. GROUND LEASE

A **GROUND LEASE** *is a lease of land only.* Ground leases are used extensively by Indian tribes in leasing their land. They are also used for commercial property.

Ground leases are usually long-term leases.

At the end of the lease, the lessor gets possession of the property and generally the improvements placed on the **property by the tenant.** Many of the free-standing sites in shopping centers, such as those pads for fast food restaurants, are ground leases. The tenant puts up the building and is responsible for all improvements. The owner keeps title to the property and pays no capital gains taxes, although he or she is taxed on the rent.

Ground leases are usually net leases where the tenant pays taxes as well as all other expenses. They may also have a percentage of the rent feature where they include a percentage of the gross in addition to the net amount. This may be in conjunction with a Consumer Price Index feature of the net lease.

The CPI and the additional percentage serve to give the owner protection against inflation.

Many large chains like ground leases since they avoid tying up huge sums of cash in land. Another advantage is that some owners will accept a much lower rent than the cash value of the land would normally dictate because they realize that they are going to own the tenant's improvements at the end of the lease.

As an example, it is hard for an owner of land worth $1,000,000 to turn down a net lease offer of $45,000 a year when the owner will not only get back the property in 25 years, but will own the improvements as well. In addition, the appreciation in value will belong to the owner who did not have any taxes or other carrying costs until that time. After 25 years, the owner knows that he or she can sell the property, lease it to others or lease it to the original lessee from a position of great strength.

From the viewpoint of the tenant, the use of the land is only costing them four and one-half percent a year. The improvements will be fully amortized over the term of the lease. It is a win/win situation.

IV. Assignment and Subleasing

Unless a lease specifically prohibits assignment or subleasing, a lease can be assigned or subleased (landlord's approval may not be unreasonably withheld).

A. ASSIGNMENT

In an *ASSIGNMENT, the lessee becomes an assignor and assigns or transfers all of his or her interest in the property to another party, the assignee.* While the assignee becomes primarily liable to the original lessor for complying with the lease terms and the payment of rent, the assignor remains secondarily liable. Therefore, should the assignee default on the rent, the original lessee can be held liable for the rent (see **Figure 3-1**).

Figure 3-1

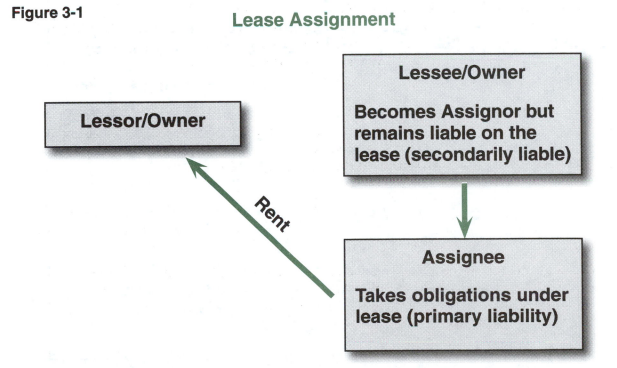

Lease Assignment

B. SUBLEASE

Under a *SUBLEASE, the lessee under a lease becomes a landlord and leases to his or her own tenant.* The sublessee pays the sublessor (original lessee) who then pays rent to the lessor (owner). Unlike an assignment, the lessee remains primarily liable on the lease. The sublessee is not liable under the original lease and has no contractual obligation to the lessor (owner). The sublessee is only liable to the sublessor.

The advantage to a lessee that a sublease offers is that it is possible to make money on the difference between what the sublessee is paying and what is due under the original lease. As an example, assume a tenant has a long-term lease at $1,000 per month, but no longer wants to occupy the property. If the leased value of the premises had increased, the lessee would be economically ahead to sublease rather than assign the lease. If the lessee could sublease for $2,000 per month then he or she could keep $1,000 per month and pay the original lessor the $1,000 rent (see **Figure 3-2**).

Figure 3-2

Advantage to Lessee of a Sublease

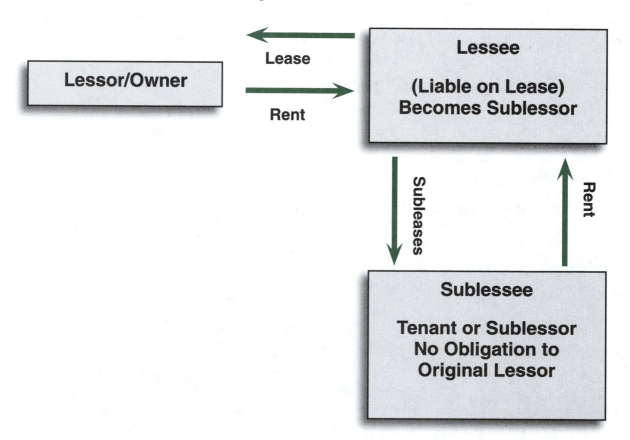

V. Qualifying Tenants

Having a poor or problem tenant is not necessarily better than not having a tenant. A poor tenant can mean rent not collected, damage to the property, lawsuits, general aggravation and the loss of rental opportunities to other tenants. With a tenant in possession you cannot rent to a qualified tenant.

> *Finding out about problems with tenants after they take possession is too late. You want to qualify the tenant before a lease is signed and possession is given.*

Qualifying means that you want to determine not only the tenant's character problems and habits that could make him or her undesirable, but also the tenant's ability and willingness to meet lease obligations.

For residential leases, the prospective tenant should fill out an application to lease. The application should give you a basis for investigating and determining if the application to rent shall be approved or rejected. Qualification of tenants is covered in greater detail in Chapter 5.

A. INCOME DETERMINATION

As part of the application, you should request a pay stub showing the present employer and gross income. You also want to see the applicant's photo identification (driver's license). There have been many cases of potential renters using other person's names in order to qualify for a rental which they would not be able to qualify for had they used their own names.

You should check with the present employer and past employers as indicated on the application. While they might not want to verify present or past income, they will verify period of employment. A significant discrepancy between what the applicant has stated and what the employer states indicates a problem.

The length of employment is important as is the length of past employment. A person who has had relatively short periods of employment with significant gaps between the employment periods, coupled with a present recent employment appears to present significant risks.

You might want to use a ratio of income to rent to determine qualifications of a tenant. A ratio is not very good to use because you might make exceptions. If you made an exception for one person and turned down an applicant with a similar income ratio, you could become involved in a civil rights case if the person turned down was a member of a minority or protected group (see Chapter 13).

Hard and fast rules do not take into account income which might not appear on a pay stub, such as gifts from family.

B. CHARACTER

A person's credit history, how he/she honored prior financial commitments, is a good predictor of how he/she will honor lease obligations. A person who is constantly late in paying other bills will likely be late in paying rent as well.

You can run a credit check with one of the credit agencies if your office is a member. There is a problem with using only one credit reporting agency. Because the three national services are independent of each other, one service might give a prospective tenant a clean bill of health creditwise, while another agency might have information about a judgment entered for unpaid rent due a prior landlord.

There are firms that will supply you with credit information from more than one reporting service.

Advantage Information, LLC provides a tenant screening service for real estate brokers. They will supply credit reports using two of the three services (Experian, TransUnion, and Equifax). Brokers may obtain applications for the services at no charge. They simply need to complete the application, fax it to Advantage Credit Services and wait for the reply (usually within 20 minutes). The broker will be faxed two credit reports with problems highlighted. The fee for this service is currently $18 for each screening (individual owners pay a higher fee than do brokers).

tenantscreeningservice.com
Advantage Information, LLC - Tenant Screening Service

If a credit report service does not have any information about a prospective tenant, you should treat it as a red flag. Check prior landlords and references. A good approach is to contact references and ask them names of other persons who are familiar with the prospective tenant. These people are less likely to have been coached about what to say.

An **Application to Rent/Screening Fee** form (see **Figure 3-3**) can be used to obtain the information you will need for qualifying a tenant, as most state's forms include extensive questions concerning personal and credit information.

Figure 3-3

CALIFORNIA
ASSOCIATION
OF REALTORS®

APPLICATION TO RENT/SCREENING FEE
(C.A.R. Form LRA, Revised 11/09)

I. APPLICATION TO RENT

THIS SECTION TO BE COMPLETED BY APPLICANT. A SEPARATE APPLICATION TO RENT IS REQUIRED FOR EACH OCCUPANT 18 YEARS OF AGE OR OVER, OR AN EMANICIPATED MINOR.

Applicant is completing Application as a (check one) ☐ tenant, ☐ tenant with co-tenant(s) or ☐ guarantor/co-signor.
Total number of applicants _____ .

PREMISES INFORMATION

Application to rent property at _____ 123 Sail Avenue, Marina del Rey CA   90292 _____ ("Premises")
Rent: $ _____ per _____ Proposed move-in date _____

PERSONAL INFORMATION

FULL NAME OF APPLICANT _____
Social security No. _____ Driver's license No. _____ State _____ Expires _____
Phone number: Home _____ Work _____ Other _____
Email _____
Name(s) of all other proposed occupant(s) and relationship to applicant _____
_____
Pet(s) or service animals (number and type) _____
Auto: Make _____ Model _____ Year _____ License No. _____ State _____ Color _____
Other vehicle(s): _____
In case of emergency, person to notify _____ Relationship _____
Address _____ Phone _____
Does applicant or any proposed occupant plan to use liquid filled furniture? ☐ No ☐ Yes   Type _____
Has applicant been a party to an unlawful detainer action or filed bankruptcy within the last seven years? ☐ No ☐ Yes
If yes, explain _____
Has applicant or any proposed occupant ever been convicted of or pleaded no contest to a felony? ☐ No ☐ Yes
If yes, explain _____
Has applicant or any proposed occupant ever been asked to move out of a residence? ☐ No ☐ Yes
If yes, explain _____

RESIDENCE HISTORY

Current address _____ | Previous address _____
City/State/Zip _____ | City/State/Zip _____
From _____ to _____ | From _____
Name of Landlord/Manager _____ | Name of Landlord/Manager _____
Landlord/Manager's phone _____ | Landlord/Manager's phone _____
Do you own this property? ☐ No ☐ Yes | Did you own this property? ☐ No ☐ Yes
Reason for leaving current address _____ | Reason for leaving this address _____
_____ | _____

EMPLOYMENT AND INCOME HISTORY

Current employer _____ | Supervisor _____ From _____ To _____
Employer's address _____ | Supervisor's phone _____
Position or title _____ | Phone number to verify employment _____
Employment gross income $ _____ per _____ | Other $ _____ per _____ Source _____
Previous employer _____ | Supervisor _____ From _____ To _____
Employer's address _____ | Supervisor's phone _____
Position or title _____ | Employment gross income $ _____ per _____

Applicant's Initials (_____) (_____)

Reviewed by _____ Date _____

EQUAL HOUSING OPPORTUNITY

LRA REVISED 11/09 (PAGE 1 OF 2)

APPLICATION TO RENT/SCREENING FEE (LRA PAGE 1 OF 2)

Agent: WALT HUBER	Phone:	Fax:	Prepared using zipForm® software
Broker: WALT HUBER REALTOR			

Property Address: _123 Sail Avenue, Marina del Rey CA 90292_____ Date: _____

CREDIT INFORMATION

Name of creditor	Account number	Monthly payment	Balance due

Name of bank/branch	Account number	Type of account	Account balance

PERSONAL REFERENCES

Name _____ Address _____
Phone _____ Length of acquaintance _____ Occupation _____
Name _____ Address _____
Phone _____ Length of acquaintance _____ Occupation _____

NEAREST RELATIVE(S)

Name _____ Address _____
Phone _____ Relationship _____
Name _____ Address _____
Phone _____ Relationship _____

Applicant understands and agrees (i) this is an application to rent only and does not guarantee that applicant will be offered the Premises; and (ii) Landlord or Manager or Agent may accept more than one application for the Premises and, using their sole discretion, will select the best qualified applicant.

Applicant represents the above information to be true and complete, and hereby authorizes Landlord or Manager or Agent to: (i) verify the information provided; and (ii) obtain credit report on applicant.

If application is not fully completed, or received without the screening fee: (i) the application will not be processed, and (ii) the application and any screening fee will be returned.

Applicant _____ Date _____ Time _____

Return your completed application and any applicable fee not already paid to. _____
Address _____ City _____ State _____ Zip _____

II. SCREENING FEE

THIS SECTION TO BE COMPLETED BY LANDLORD, MANAGER OR AGENT.

Applicant has paid a **nonrefundable** screening fee of $ _____, applied as follows: (The screening fee may not exceed $30.00 adjusted annually from 1-1-98 commensurate with the increase in the Consumer Price Index.) A CPI inflation calculator is available on the Bureau of Labor Statistics website, www.bls.gov. The California Department of Consumer Affairs calculates the applicable screening fee amount to be $37.57 as of 2006.

$ _____ for credit reports prepared by _____ ;

$ _____ for _____ (other out-of-pocket expenses); and

$ _____ for processing.

The undersigned has read the foregoing and acknowledges receipt of a copy.

_____ _____
Applicant Signature   Date

The undersigned has received the screening fee indicated above.

                                                                        DRE Lic. # _____
_____ _____
Landlord or Manager or Agent Signature   Date

Published and Distributed by:
REAL ESTATE BUSINESS SERVICES, INC.
a subsidiary of the California Association of REALTORS®
525 South Virgil Avenue, Los Angeles, California 90020

LRA REVISED 11/09 (PAGE 2 OF 2)

Reviewed by _____ Date _____

APPLICATION TO RENT/SCREENING FEE (LRA PAGE 2 OF 2)   Untitled

VOICE OF EXPERIENCE:

By checking with prior landlords you will find out about problems in paying rent as well as character issues. Landlords prior to the present landlord will likely be more forthcoming with information. If a present landlord has had no problems with a tenant and you indicate that he or she wants to rent from you, it would not be in the landlord's best interests to be honest. On the other hand, former landlords will have no such interests and are more likely to be honest with you. In some cases, they will be eager to tell you about unpleasant relations that they have had with a tenant.

VI. Proposal to Lease

When lessor and lessee are serious about leasing, but many of the terms have not yet been agreed upon, they may exercise a letter of intent that shows the parties' intent to negotiate in good faith to effectuate a lease.

A letter of intent with a major retail tenant will influence lesser retail tenants to commence negotiations for space.

It may also be a factor in obtaining permanent financing for the project. Financing could be arranged contingent upon finalizing a particular lease or leases.

Figure 3-4 is CAR's **Residential Lease or Month-To-Month Rental Agreement**. This proposal includes rent, terms of the lease, good faith deposits, etc. This proposal is not a binding contract on either party until they have both signed a mutually agreeable lease.

VII. Drafting Leases

VOICE OF EXPERIENCE:

Always use the latest forms. If a problem occurs that could have been avoided by using the latest form, then you, the professional property manager, will face potential liability. You should also demand that any other parties to the transaction use the latest forms!

A. USE OF STANDARD FORMS

As a property manager, you should not attempt to modify standard clauses in a lease, prepare new clauses or prepare complex leases by the cut-and-paste method utilizing clauses from other leases. First of all, it exposes you, the property manager, to liability should your draftsmanship create results not contemplated that work to the detriment of the owner.

Figure 3-4

RESIDENTIAL LEASE OR
MONTH-TO-MONTH RENTAL AGREEMENT
(C.A.R. Form LR, Revised 11/08)

Date_____, _____ ("Landlord") and
_____ ("Tenant") agree as follows:

1. PROPERTY:
   A. Landlord rents to Tenant and Tenant rents from Landlord, the real property and improvements described as: *123 Sail Avenue, Marina del Rey CA 90292* ("Premises").
   B. The Premises are for the sole use as a personal residence by the following named person(s) **only**: _____
   C. The following personal property, maintained pursuant to paragraph 11, is included: _____
      _____ or ☐ (if checked) the personal property on the attached addendum.

2. TERM: The term begins on (date) _____ ("Commencement Date"), **(Check A or B):**
   ☐ A. **Month-to-Month:** and continues as a month-to-month tenancy. Tenant may terminate the tenancy by giving written notice at least 30 days prior to the intended termination date. Landlord may terminate the tenancy by giving written notice as provided by law. Such notices may be given on any date.
   ☐ B. **Lease:** and shall terminate on (date) _____ at _____ ☐AM/ ☐PM. Tenant shall vacate the Premises upon termination of the Agreement, unless: **(i)** Landlord and Tenant have extended this agreement in writing or signed a new agreement; **(ii)** mandated by local rent control law; or **(iii)** Landlord accepts Rent from Tenant (other than past due Rent), in which case a month-to-month tenancy shall be created which either party may terminate as specified in paragraph 2A. Rent shall be at a rate agreed to by Landlord and Tenant, or as allowed by law. All other terms and conditions of this Agreement shall remain in full force and effect.

3. RENT: "Rent" shall mean all monetary obligations of Tenant to Landlord under the terms of the Agreement, except security deposit.
   A. Tenant agrees to pay $ _____ per month for the term of the Agreement.
   B. Rent is payable in advance on the 1st (or ☐ _____) **day** of each calendar month, and is delinquent on the next day.
   C. If Commencement Date falls on any day other than the day Rent is payable under paragraph 3B, and Tenant has paid one full month's Rent in advance of Commencement Date, Rent for the second calendar month shall be prorated based on a 30-day period.
   D. PAYMENT: Rent shall be paid by ☐ personal check, ☐ money order, ☐ cashier's check, or ☐ other _____, to (name) _____ (phone) _____ at (address) _____, (or at any other location subsequently specified by Landlord in writing to Tenant) (and ☐ if checked, rent may be paid personally between the hours of _____ and _____ on the following days _____). If any payments is returned for non-sufficient funds ("NSF") or because Tenant stops payment, then, after that: (i) Landlord may, in writing, require Tenant to pay Rent in cash for three months and (ii) all future Rent shall be paid by ☐ money order, or ☐ cashier's check.

4. SECURITY DEPOSIT:
   A. Tenant agrees to pay $ _____ security deposit. Security deposit will be ☐ transferred to and held by the Owner of the Premises, or ☐ held in Owner's Broker's trust account.
   B. All or any portion of the security deposit may be used, as reasonably necessary, to: **(i)** cure Tenant's default in payment of Rent (which includes Late Charges, NSF fees or other sums due); **(ii)** repair damage, excluding ordinary wear and tear, caused by Tenant or by a guest or licensee of Tenant; **(iii)** clean Premises, if necessary, upon termination of the tenancy; and **(iv)** replace or return personal property or appurtenances. **SECURITY DEPOSIT SHALL NOT BE USED BY TENANT IN LIEU OF PAYMENT OF LAST MONTH'S RENT.** If all or any portion of the security deposit is used during the tenancy, Tenant agrees to reinstate the total security deposit within five days after written notice is delivered to Tenant. Within 21 days after Tenant vacates the Premises, Landlord shall: **(1)** furnish Tenant an itemized statement indicating the amount of any security deposit received and the basis for its disposition and supporting documentation as required by California Civil Code § 1950.5(g); and **(2)** return any remaining portion of the security deposit to Tenant.
   C. **Security deposit will not be returned until all Tenants have vacated the Premises and all keys returned. Any security deposit returned by check shall be made out to all Tenants named on this Agreement, or as subsequently modified.**
   D. No interest will be paid on security deposit unless required by local law.
   E. If the security deposit is held by Owner, Tenant agrees not to hold Broker responsible for its return. If the security deposit is held in Owner's Broker's trust account, **and** Broker's authority is terminated before expiration of this Agreement, **and** security deposit is released to someone other than Tenant, **then** Broker shall notify Tenant, in writing, where and to whom security deposit has been released. Once Tenant has been provided such notice, Tenant agrees not to hold Broker responsible for the security deposit.

5. MOVE-IN COSTS RECEIVED/DUE: Move-in funds made payable to _____
   shall be paid by ☐ personal check, ☐ money order, or ☐ cashier's check.

Category	Total Due	Payment Received	Balance Due	Date Due
Rent from _____ to _____ (date)				
*Security Deposit				
Other _____				
Other _____				
Total				

*The maximum amount Landlord may receive as security deposit, however designated, cannot exceed two months' Rent for unfurnished premises, or three months' Rent for furnished premises.

Tenant's Initials (_____)(_____)
Landlord's Initials (_____)(_____)

LR REVISED 11/08 (PAGE 1 OF 6)

RESIDENTIAL LEASE OR MONTH-TO-MONTH RENTAL AGREEMENT (LR PAGE 1 OF 6)

Agent: WALT HUBER   Phone: Fax: Prepared using zipForm® software
Broker: WALT HUBER REALTOR

6. LATE CHARGE; RETURNED CHECKS:

A. Tenant acknowledges either late payment of Rent or issuance of a returned check may cause Landlord to incur costs and expenses, the exact amounts of which are extremely difficult and impractical to determine. These costs may include, but are not limited to, processing, enforcement and accounting expenses, and late charges imposed on Landlord. If any installment of Rent due from Tenant is not received by Landlord within **5 (or ☐ _____) calendar days** after the date due, or if a check is returned, Tenant shall pay to Landlord, respectively, an additional sum of $ _____ or _____ % of the Rent due as a Late Charge and $25.00 as a NSF fee for the first returned check and $35.00 as a NSF fee for each additional returned check, either or both of which shall be deemed additional Rent.

B. Landlord and Tenant agree that these charges represent a fair and reasonable estimate of the costs Landlord may incur by reason of Tenant's late or NSF payment. Any Late Charge or NSF fee due shall be paid with the current installment of Rent. Landlord's acceptance of any Late Charge or NSF fee shall not constitute a waiver as to any default of Tenant. Landlord's right to collect a Late Charge or NSF fee shall not be deemed an extension of the date Rent is due under paragraph 3 or prevent Landlord from exercising any other rights and remedies under this Agreement and as provided by law.

7. PARKING: (Check A or B)

☐ A. Parking is permitted as follows: _____ .

   The right to parking ☐ is ☐ is not included in the Rent charged pursuant to paragraph 3. If not included in the Rent, the parking rental fee shall be an additional $ _____ per month. Parking space(s) are to be used for parking properly licensed and operable motor vehicles, except for trailers, boats, campers, buses or trucks (other than pick-up trucks). Tenant shall park in assigned space(s) only. Parking space(s) are to be kept clean. Vehicles leaking oil, gas or other motor vehicle fluids shall not be parked on the Premises. Mechanical work or storage of inoperable vehicles is not permitted in parking space(s) or elsewhere on the Premises.

OR ☐ B. Parking is not permitted on the Premises.

8. STORAGE: (Check A or B)

☐ A. Storage is permitted as follows: _____
   The right to storage space ☐ is, ☐ is not, included in the Rent charged pursuant to paragraph 3. If not included in the Rent, storage space fee shall be an additional $ _____ per month. Tenant shall store only personal property Tenant owns, and shall not store property claimed by another or in which another has any right, title or interest. Tenant shall not store any improperly packaged food or perishable goods, flammable materials, explosives, hazardous waste or other inherently dangerous material, or illegal substances.

OR ☐ B. Storage is not permitted on the Premises.

9. UTILITIES: Tenant agrees to pay for all utilities and services, and the following charges: _____ except _____ which shall be paid for by Landlord. If any utilities are not separately metered, Tenant shall pay Tenant's proportional share, as reasonably determined and directed by Landlord. If utilities are separately metered, Tenant shall place utilities in Tenant's name as of the Commencement Date. Landlord is only responsible for installing and maintaining one usable telephone jack and one telephone line to the Premises. Tenant shall pay any cost for conversion from existing utilities service provider.

10. CONDITION OF PREMISES: Tenant has examined Premises and, if any, all furniture, furnishings, appliances, landscaping and fixtures, including smoke detector(s).

(Check all that apply:)

☐ A. Tenant acknowledges these items are clean and in operable condition, with the following exceptions: _____

☐ B. Tenant's acknowledgment of the condition of these items is contained in an attached statement of condition (C.A.R. Form MIMO).

☐ C. Tenant will provide Landlord a list of items that are damaged or not in operable condition within 3 (or ☐ _____) days after Commencement Date, not as a contingency of this Agreement but rather as an acknowledgment of the condition of the Premises.

☐ D. Other: _____

11. MAINTENANCE:

A. Tenant shall properly use, operate and safeguard Premises, including if applicable, any landscaping, furniture, furnishings and appliances, and all mechanical, electrical, gas and plumbing fixtures, and keep them and the Premises clean, sanitary and well ventilated. Tenant shall be responsible for checking and maintaining all smoke detectors and any additional phone lines beyond the one line and jack that Landlord shall provide and maintain. Tenant shall immediately notify Landlord, in writing, of any problem, malfunction or damage. Tenant shall be charged for all repairs or replacements caused by Tenant, pets, guests or licensees of Tenant, excluding ordinary wear and tear. Tenant shall be charged for all damage to Premises as a result of failure to report a problem in a timely manner. Tenant shall be charged for repair of drain blockages or stoppages, unless caused by defective plumbing parts or tree roots invading sewer lines.

B. ☐ Landlord ☐ Tenant shall water the garden, landscaping, trees and shrubs, except: _____
   _____

C. ☐ Landlord ☐ Tenant shall maintain the garden, landscaping, trees and shrubs, except: _____
   _____

D. ☐ Landlord ☐ Tenant shall maintain _____ .

E. Tenant's failure to maintain any item for which Tenant is responsible shall give Landlord the right to hire someone to perform such maintenance and charge Tenant to cover the cost of such maintenance.

F. The following items of personal property are included in the Premises without warranty and Landlord will not maintain, repair or replace them: _____

Tenant's Initials (_____)(_____)
Landlord's Initials (_____)(_____)

Reviewed by _____ Date _____

LR REVISED 11/08 (PAGE 2 OF 6)

RESIDENTIAL LEASE OR MONTH-TO-MONTH RENTAL AGREEMENT (LR PAGE 2 OF 6)

Premises: *123 Sail Avenue*
Marina del Rey, CA 90292   Date: _____

12. NEIGHBORHOOD CONDITIONS: Tenant is advised to satisfy him or herself as to neighborhood or area conditions, including schools, proximity and adequacy of law enforcement, crime statistics, proximity of registered felons or offenders, fire protection, other governmental services, availability, adequacy and cost of any wired, wireless internet connections or other telecommunications or other technology services and installations, proximity to commercial, industrial or agricultural activities, existing and proposed transportation, construction and development that may affect noise, view, or traffic, airport noise, noise or odor from any source, wild and domestic animals, other nuisances, hazards, or circumstances, cemeteries, facilities and condition of common areas, conditions and influences of significance to certain cultures and/or religions, and personal needs, requirements and preferences of Tenant.

13. PETS: Unless otherwise provided in California Civil Code § 54.2, no animal or pet shall be kept on or about the Premises without Landlord's prior written consent, except: _____

14. ☐ (If checked) **NO SMOKING:** No smoking is allowed on the Premises. If smoking does occur on the Premises, **(i)** Tenant is responsible for all damage caused by the smoking including, but not limited to, stains, burns, odors and removal of debris; **(ii)** Tenant is in breach of this Agreement; **(iii)** Tenant, Authorized Guests, and all others may be required to leave the Premises; and **(iv)** Tenant acknowledges that in order to remove odor caused by smoking, Landlord may need to replace carpet and drapes and paint entire Premises regardless of when these items were last cleaned or replaced. Such actions and other necessary steps will impact the return of any security deposit.

15. RULES/REGULATIONS:
   A. Tenant agrees to comply with all Landlord rules and regulations that are at any time posted on the Premises or delivered to Tenant. Tenant shall not, and shall ensure that guests and licensees of Tenant shall not, disturb, annoy, endanger or interfere with other tenants of the building or neighbors, or use the Premises for any unlawful purposes, including, but not limited to, using, manufacturing, selling, storing or transporting illicit drugs or other contraband, or violate any law or ordinance, or commit a waste or nuisance on or about the Premises.
   B. **(If applicable, check one)**
      ☐ 1. Landlord shall provide Tenant with a copy of the rules and regulations within _____ days or _____ .
      OR ☐ 2. Tenant has been provided with, and acknowledges receipt of, a copy of the rules and regulations.

16. ☐ (If checked) **CONDOMINIUM; PLANNED UNIT DEVELOPMENT:**
   A. The Premises is a unit in a condominium, planned unit development, common interest subdivision or other development governed by a homeowners' association ("HOA"). The name of the HOA is _____ . Tenant agrees to comply with all HOA covenants, conditions and restrictions, bylaws, rules and regulations and decisions. Landlord shall provide Tenant copies of rules and regulations, if any. Tenant shall reimburse Landlord for any fines or charges imposed by HOA or other authorities, due to any violation by Tenant, or the guests or licensees of Tenant.
   B. **(Check one)**
      ☐ 1. Landlord shall provide Tenant with a copy of the HOA rules and regulations within _____ days or _____ .
      OR ☐ 2. Tenant has been provided with, and acknowledges receipt of, a copy of the HOA rules and regulations.

17. ALTERATIONS; REPAIRS: Unless otherwise specified by law or paragraph 29C, without Landlord's prior written consent, **(i)** Tenant shall not make any repairs, alterations or improvements in or about the Premises including: painting, wallpapering, adding or changing locks, installing antenna or satellite dish(es), placing signs, displays or exhibits, or using screws, fastening devices, large nails or adhesive materials; **(ii)** Landlord shall not be responsible for the costs of alterations or repairs made by Tenant; **(iii)** Tenant shall not deduct from Rent the costs of any repairs, alterations or improvements; and **(iv)** any deduction made by Tenant shall be considered unpaid Rent.

18. KEYS; LOCKS:
   A. Tenant acknowledges receipt of (or Tenant will receive ☐ prior to the Commencement Date, or ☐ _____):
      ☐ _____ key(s) to Premises,   ☐ _____ remote control device(s) or garage door/gate opener(s),
      ☐ _____ key(s) to mailbox,   ☐ _____ ,
      ☐ _____ key(s) to common area(s),   ☐ _____ .
   B. Tenant acknowledges that locks to the Premises ☐ have, ☐ have not, been re-keyed.
   C. If Tenant re-keys existing locks or opening devices, Tenant shall immediately deliver copies of the keys to Landlord. Tenant shall pay all costs and charges related to loss of any keys or opening devices. Tenant may not remove locks, even if installed by Tenant.

19. ENTRY:
   A. Tenant shall make Premises available to Landlord or Landlord's representative for the purpose of entering to make necessary or agreed repairs, decorations, alterations, or improvements, or to supply necessary or agreed services, or to show Premises to prospective or actual purchasers, tenants, mortgagees, lenders, appraisers, or contractors.
   B. Landlord and Tenant agree that 24-hour written notice shall be reasonable and sufficient notice, except as follows: 48-hour written notice is required to conduct an inspection of the Premises prior to the Tenant moving out, unless the Tenant waives the right to such notice. Notice may be given orally to show the Premises to actual or prospective purchasers provided Tenant has been notified in writing within 120 days preceding the oral notice that the Premises are for sale and that oral notice may be given to show the Premises. No notice is required: **(i)** to enter in case of an emergency; **(ii)** if the Tenant is present and consents at the time of entry or **(iii)** if the Tenant has abandoned or surrendered the Premises. No written notice is required if Landlord and Tenant orally agree to an entry for agreed services or repairs if the date and time of entry are within one week of the oral agreement.
   C. ☐ (If checked) Tenant authorizes the use of a keysafe/lockbox to allow entry into the Premises and agrees to sign a keysafe/lockbox addendum (C.A.R. Form KLA).

20. SIGNS: Tenant authorizes Landlord to place FOR SALE/LEASE signs on the Premises.

21. ASSIGNMENT; SUBLETTING: Tenant shall not sublet all or any part of Premises, or assign or transfer this Agreement or any interest in it, without Landlord's prior written consent. Unless such consent is obtained, any assignment, transfer or subletting of Premises or this Agreement or tenancy, by voluntary act of Tenant, operation of law or otherwise, shall, at the option of Landlord,

LR REVISED 11/08 (PAGE 3 OF 6)

Tenant's Initials (_____)(_____)
Landlord's Initials (_____)(_____)

Reviewed by _____ Date _____

RESIDENTIAL LEASE OR MONTH-TO-MONTH RENTAL AGREEMENT (LR PAGE 3 OF 6)

terminate this Agreement. Any proposed assignee, transferee or sublessee shall submit to Landlord an application and credit information for Landlord's approval and, if approved, sign a separate written agreement with Landlord and Tenant. Landlord's consent to any one assignment, transfer or sublease, shall not be construed as consent to any subsequent assignment, transfer or sublease and does not release Tenant of Tenant's obligations under this Agreement.

22. **JOINT AND INDIVIDUAL OBLIGATIONS:** If there is more than one Tenant, each one shall be individually and completely responsible for the performance of all obligations of Tenant under this Agreement, jointly with every other Tenant, and individually, whether or not in possession.

23. ☐ **LEAD-BASED PAINT (If checked):** Premises was constructed prior to 1978. In accordance with federal law, Landlord gives and Tenant acknowledges receipt of the disclosures on the attached form (C.A.R. Form FLD) and a federally approved lead pamphlet.

24. ☐ **MILITARY ORDNANCE DISCLOSURE:** (If applicable and known to Landlord) Premises is located within one mile of an area once used for military training, and may contain potentially explosive munitions.

25. ☐ **PERIODIC PEST CONTROL:** Landlord has entered into a contract for periodic pest control treatment of the Premises and shall give Tenant a copy of the notice originally given to Landlord by the pest control company.

26. ☐ **METHAMPHETAMINE CONTAMINATION:** Prior to signing this Agreement, Landlord has given Tenant a notice that a health official has issued an order prohibiting occupancy of the property because of methamphetamine contamination. A copy of the notice and order are attached.

27. **MEGAN'S LAW DATABASE DISCLOSURE:** Notice: Pursuant to Section 290.46 of the Penal Code, information about specified registered sex offenders is made available to the public via an Internet Web site maintained by the Department of Justice at www.meganslaw.ca.gov. Depending on an offender's criminal history, this information will include either the address at which the offender resides or the community of residence and ZIP Code in which he or she resides. (Neither Landlord nor Brokers, if any, are required to check this website. If Tenant wants further information, Tenant should obtain information directly from this website.)

28. **POSSESSION:**
   A. Tenant is not in possession of the premises. If Landlord is unable to deliver possession of Premises on Commencement Date, such Date shall be extended to the date on which possession is made available to Tenant. If Landlord is unable to deliver possession within **5 (or ☐ _____) calendar days** after agreed Commencement Date, Tenant may terminate this Agreement by giving written notice to Landlord, and shall be refunded all Rent and security deposit paid. Possession is deemed terminated when Tenant has returned all keys to the Premises to Landlord.
   B. ☐ Tenant is already in possession of the Premises.

29. **TENANT'S OBLIGATIONS UPON VACATING PREMISES:**
   A. Upon termination of this Agreement, Tenant shall: **(i)** give Landlord all copies of all keys or opening devices to Premises, including any common areas, **(ii)** vacate and surrender Premises to Landlord, empty of all persons; **(iii)** vacate any/all parking and/or storage space; **(iv)** clean and deliver Premises as specified in paragraph C below, to Landlord in the same condition as referenced in paragraph 10; **(v)** remove all debris; **(vi)** give written notice to Landlord of Tenant's forwarding address; and **(vii)** _____
   B. All alterations/improvements made by or caused to be made by Tenant, with or without Landlord's consent, become the property of Landlord upon termination. Landlord may charge Tenant for restoration of the Premises to the condition it was in prior to any alterations/improvements.
   C. **Right to Pre-Move-Out Inspection and Repairs:** **(i)** After giving or receiving notice of termination of a tenancy (C.A.R. Form NTT), or before the end of a lease, Tenant has the right to request that an inspection of the Premises take place prior to termination of the lease or rental (C.A.R. Form NRI). If Tenant requests such an inspection, Tenant shall be given an opportunity to remedy identified deficiencies prior to termination, consistent with the terms of this Agreement. **(ii)** Any repairs or alterations made to the Premises as a result of this inspection (collectively, "Repairs") shall be made at Tenant's expense. Repairs may be performed by Tenant or through others, who have adequate insurance and licenses and are approved by Landlord. The work shall comply with applicable law, including governmental permit, inspection and approval requirements. Repairs shall be performed in a good, skillful manner with materials of quality and appearance comparable to existing materials. It is understood that exact restoration of appearance or cosmetic items following all Repairs may not be possible. **(iii)** Tenant shall: **(a)** obtain receipts for Repairs performed by others; **(b)** prepare a written statement indicating the Repairs performed by Tenant and the date of such Repairs; and **(c)** provide copies of receipts and statements to Landlord prior to termination. Paragraph 29C does not apply when the tenancy is terminated pursuant to California Code of Civil Procedure § 1161(2), (3) or (4).

30. **BREACH OF CONTRACT; EARLY TERMINATION:** In addition to any obligations established by paragraph 29, in the event of termination by Tenant prior to completion of the original term of the Agreement, Tenant shall also be responsible for lost Rent, rental commissions, advertising expenses and painting costs necessary to ready Premises for re-rental. Landlord may withhold any such amounts from Tenant's security deposit.

31. **TEMPORARY RELOCATION:** Subject to local law, Tenant agrees, upon demand of Landlord, to temporarily vacate Premises for a reasonable period, to allow for fumigation (or other methods) to control wood destroying pests or organisms, or other repairs to Premises. Tenant agrees to comply with all instructions and requirements necessary to prepare Premises to accommodate pest control, fumigation or other work, including bagging or storage of food and medicine, and removal of perishables and valuables. Tenant shall only be entitled to a credit of Rent equal to the per diem Rent for the period of time Tenant is required to vacate Premises.

32. **DAMAGE TO PREMISES:** If, by no fault of Tenant, Premises are totally or partially damaged or destroyed by fire, earthquake, accident or other casualty that render Premises totally or partially uninhabitable, either Landlord or Tenant may terminate this Agreement by giving the other written notice. Rent shall be abated as of the date Premises become totally or partially uninhabitable. The abated amount shall be the current monthly Rent prorated on a 30-day period. If the Agreement is not terminated, Landlord shall promptly repair the damage, and Rent shall be reduced based on the extent to which the damage interferes with Tenant's reasonable use of Premises. If damage occurs as a result of an act of Tenant or Tenant's guests, only Landlord shall have the right of termination, and no reduction in Rent shall be made.

33. **INSURANCE:** Tenant's or guest's personal property and vehicles are not insured by Landlord, manager or, if applicable, HOA, against loss or damage due to fire, theft, vandalism, rain, water, criminal or negligent acts of others, or any other cause. **Tenant is**

Tenant's Initials (_____)(_____)
Landlord's Initials (_____)(_____)

LR REVISED 11/08 (PAGE 4 OF 6)

Reviewed by _____ Date _____

RESIDENTIAL LEASE OR MONTH-TO-MONTH RENTAL AGREEMENT (LR PAGE 4 OF 6)

advised to carry Tenant's own insurance (renter's insurance) to protect Tenant from any such loss or damage. Tenant shall comply with any requirement imposed on Tenant by Landlord's insurer to avoid: (i) an increase in Landlord's insurance premium (or Tenant shall pay for the increase in premium); or (ii) loss of insurance.

34. **WATERBEDS:** Tenant shall not use or have waterbeds on the Premises unless: **(i)** Tenant obtains a valid waterbed insurance policy; **(ii)** Tenant increases the security deposit in an amount equal to one-half of one month's Rent; and **(iii)** the bed conforms to the floor load capacity of Premises.

35. **WAIVER:** The waiver of any breach shall not be construed as a continuing waiver of the same or any subsequent breach.

36. **NOTICE:** Notices may be served at the following address, or at any other location subsequently designated:
Landlord: _____ Tenant: _____
_____ _____
_____ _____

37. **TENANT ESTOPPEL CERTIFICATE:** Tenant shall execute and return a tenant estoppel certificate delivered to Tenant by Landlord or Landlord's agent within 3 days after its receipt. Failure to comply with this requirement shall be deemed Tenant's acknowledgment that the tenant estoppel certificate is true and correct, and may be relied upon by a lender or purchaser.

38. **TENANT REPRESENTATIONS; CREDIT:** Tenant warrants that all statements in Tenant's rental application are accurate. Tenant authorizes Landlord and Broker(s) to obtain Tenant's credit report periodically during the tenancy in connection with the modification or enforcement of this Agreement. Landlord may cancel this Agreement: **(i)** before occupancy begins; **(ii)** upon disapproval of the credit report(s); or **(iii)** at any time, upon discovering that information in Tenant's application is false. A negative credit report reflecting on Tenant's record may be submitted to a credit reporting agency if Tenant fails to fulfill the terms of payment and other obligations under this Agreement.

39. **MEDIATION:**
    A. Consistent with paragraphs B and C below, Landlord and Tenant agree to mediate any dispute or claim arising between them out of this Agreement, or any resulting transaction, before resorting to court action. Mediation fees, if any, shall be divided equally among the parties involved. If, for any dispute or claim to which this paragraph applies, any party commences an action without first attempting to resolve the matter through mediation, or refuses to mediate after a request has been made, then that party shall not be entitled to recover attorney fees, even if they would otherwise be available to that party in any such action.
    B. The following matters are excluded from mediation: **(i)** an unlawful detainer action; **(ii)** the filing or enforcement of a mechanic's lien; and **(iii)** any matter within the jurisdiction of a probate, small claims or bankruptcy court. The filing of a court action to enable the recording of a notice of pending action, for order of attachment, receivership, injunction, or other provisional remedies, shall not constitute a waiver of the mediation provision.
    C. Landlord and Tenant agree to mediate disputes or claims involving Listing Agent, Leasing Agent or property manager ("Broker"), provided Broker shall have agreed to such mediation prior to, or within a reasonable time after, the dispute or claim is presented to such Broker. Any election by Broker to participate in mediation shall not result in Broker being deemed a party to this Agreement.

40. **ATTORNEY FEES:** In any action or proceeding arising out of this Agreement, the prevailing party between Landlord and Tenant shall be entitled to reasonable attorney fees and costs, except as provided in paragraph 39A.

41. **C.A.R. FORM:** C.A.R. Form means the specific form referenced or another comparable form agreed to by the parties.

42. **OTHER TERMS AND CONDITIONS; SUPPLEMENTS:** ☐ Interpreter/Translator Agreement (C.A.R. Form ITA);
☐ Keysafe/Lockbox Addendum (C.A.R. Form KLA); ☐ Lead-Based Paint and Lead-Based Paint Hazards Disclosure (C.A.R. Form FLD)

The following ATTACHED supplements are incorporated in this Agreement: _____
_____
_____
_____

43. **TIME OF ESSENCE; ENTIRE CONTRACT; CHANGES:** Time is of the essence. All understandings between the parties are incorporated in this Agreement. Its terms are intended by the parties as a final, complete and exclusive expression of their Agreement with respect to its subject matter, and may not be contradicted by evidence of any prior agreement or contemporaneous oral agreement. If any provision of this Agreement is held to be ineffective or invalid, the remaining provisions will nevertheless be given full force and effect. Neither this Agreement nor any provision in it may be extended, amended, modified, altered or changed except in writing. This Agreement is subject to California landlord-tenant law and shall incorporate all changes required by amendment or successors to such law. This Agreement and any supplement, addendum or modification, including any copy, may be signed in two or more counterparts, all of which shall constitute one and the same writing.

44. **AGENCY:**
    A. **CONFIRMATION:** The following agency relationship(s) are hereby confirmed for this transaction:
    Listing Agent: (Print firm name) _____
    is the agent of (check one): ☐ the Landlord exclusively; or ☐ both the Landlord and Tenant.
    Leasing Agent: (Print firm name) _____
    (if not same as Listing Agent) is the agent of (check one): ☐ the Tenant exclusively; or ☐ the Landlord exclusively; or ☐ both the Tenant and Landlord.
    B. **DISCLOSURE:** ☐ (If checked): The term of this lease exceeds one year. A disclosure regarding real estate agency relationships (C.A.R. Form AD) has been provided to Landlord and Tenant, who each acknowledge its receipt.

45. ☐ **TENANT COMPENSATION TO BROKER:** Upon execution of this Agreement, Tenant agrees to pay compensation to Broker as specified in a separate written agreement between Tenant and Broker.

Tenant's Initials (_____) (_____)
Landlord's Initials (_____) (_____)

Reviewed by _____ Date _____

EQUAL HOUSING OPPORTUNITY

RESIDENTIAL LEASE OR MONTH-TO-MONTH RENTAL AGREEMENT (LR PAGE 5 OF 6)

46. ☐ **INTERPRETER/TRANSLATOR:** The terms of this Agreement have been interpreted for Tenant into the following language: _____ . Landlord and Tenant acknowledge receipt of the attached interpretor/translator agreement (C.A.R. Form ITA).

47. FOREIGN LANGUAGE NEGOTIATION: If this Agreement has been negotiated by Landlord and Tenant primarily in Spanish, Chinese, Tagalog, Korean or Vietnamese. pursuant to the California Civil Code Tenant shall be provided a translation of this Agreement in the language used for the negotiation.

48. OWNER COMPENSATION TO BROKER: Upon execution of this Agreement, Owner agrees to pay compensation to Broker as specified in a separate written agreement between Owner and Broker (C.A.R. Form LCA).

49. RECEIPT: If specified in paragraph 5, Landlord or Broker, acknowledges receipt of move-in funds.

> Landlord and Tenant acknowledge and agree Brokers: **(a)** do not guarantee the condition of the Premises; **(b)** cannot verify representations made by others; **(c)** cannot provide legal or tax advice; **(d)** will not provide other advice or information that exceeds the knowledge, education or experience required to obtain a real estate license. Furthermore, if Brokers are not also acting as Landlord in this Agreement, Brokers: **(e)** do not decide what rental rate a Tenant should pay or Landlord should accept; and **(f)** do not decide upon the length or other terms of tenancy. Landlord and Tenant agree that they will seek legal, tax, insurance and other desired assistance from appropriate professionals.

Tenant agrees to rent the Premises on the above terms and conditions.

Tenant _____ Date _____
Address _____ City _____ State _____ Zip _____
Telephone _____ Fax _____ E-mail _____

Tenant _____ Date _____
Address _____ City _____ State _____ Zip _____
Telephone _____ Fax _____ E-mail _____

☐ **GUARANTEE:** consideration of the execution of this Agreement by and between Landlord and Tenant and for valuable consideration, receipt of which is hereby acknowledged, the undersigned ("Guarantor") does hereby: **(i)** guarantee unconditionally to Landlord and Landlord's agents, successors and assigns, the prompt payment of Rent or other sums that become due pursuant to this Agreement, including any and all court costs and attorney fees included in enforcing the Agreement; **(ii)** consent to any changes, modifications or alterations of any term in this Agreement agreed to by Landlord and Tenant; and **(iii)** waive any right to require Landlord and/or Landlord's agents to proceed against Tenant for any default occurring under this Agreement before seeking to enforce the Guarantee.

Guarantor (Print Name) _____
Guarantor _____ Date _____
Address _____ City _____ State _____ Zip _____
Telephone _____ Fax _____ E-mail _____

Landlord agrees to rent the Premises on the above terms and conditions.
Landlord _____ Landlord _____

Address _____
Telephone _____ Fax _____ E-mail _____

REAL ESTATE BROKERS:

A. Real estate brokers who are not also Landlord under this Agreement are not parties to the Agreement between Landlord and Tenant.

B. Agency relationships are confirmed in paragraph 44.

C. **COOPERATING BROKER COMPENSATION:** Listing Broker agrees to pay Cooperating Broker (Leasing Firm) and Cooperating Broker agrees to accept: **(i)** the amount specified in the MLS, provided Cooperating Broker is a Participant of the MLS in which the Property is offered for sale or a reciprocal MLS; or **(ii)** ☐ (if checked) the amount specified in a separate written agreement between Listing Broker and Cooperating Broker.

Real Estate Broker (Listing Firm) _____ DRE Lic. # _____
By (Agent) _____ DRE Lic. # _____ Date _____
Address _____ City _____ State _____ Zip _____
Telephone _____ Fax _____ E-mail _____

Real Estate Broker (Leasing Firm) _____ DRE Lic. # _____
By (Agent) _____ DRE Lic. # _____ Date _____
Address _____ City _____ State _____ Zip _____
Telephone _____ Fax _____ E-mail _____

Reviewed by _____ Date _____

LR REVISED 11/08 (PAGE 6 OF 6)

RESIDENTIAL LEASE OR MONTH-TO-MONTH RENTAL AGREEMENT (LR PAGE 6 OF 6)

Untitled

Secondly, preparing a lease using other than what is regarded as a standard industry lease could be construed as the unauthorized practice of law. (You are doing it for another and are compensated in the form of management and/or leasing fees.) Giving legal advice to others in the course of management could also be regarded as the unauthorized practice of law.

Don't attempt to use a standard lease that is not appropriate for the tenancy and don't attempt to alter a legally approved lease.

As an example, you should not use a residential lease form for a property including both residential and commercial areas.

Case Example

People v. Landlords Professional Services, 215 C.A. 3d 1599 (1989)

The Court of Appeals in affirming a judgment against the defendant pointed out that the sale of legal forms and detailed manuals on how to complete the forms was legal. However, in this case the defendant advertised that they accomplished evictions. Clients discussed evictions with counselors who offered specific legal information. This action constituted the unlawful practice of law.

While there are a great many standardized lease forms covering commercial and industrial properties, if any lease form is to be materially altered or a new lease drafted, competent legal counsel should be sought.

A point to remember is that lease ambiguities are generally resolved against the party drafting the lease. Therefore, it behooves you as the property manager to make certain that the lease is clear. If a lease form includes a clause you do not understand, see an attorney; don't take chances with your license and your clients' economic well being.

Care must be taken so that the original lease plus all possible options will not exceed any statutory term limitation.

In most states, statutes provide maximum periods for leasing. In California, and a number of other states, the maximum period for a property situated in a city or town (urban) is 99 years. A one-year lease with unlimited options to renew for one-year periods could exceed 99 years. Such a lease should be avoided since the courts in some states would not enforce the lease.

B. TITLE OF LEASE

Some lessors entitle their lease "Proposal to Lease." It is a proposal by the tenant to lease that includes all the lease terms and conditions. When signed by the lessee, it becomes a binding lease.

The title "Proposal to Lease" is used simply to make the document less menacing to a tenant than "Lease." However, it is clear that this is, in fact, a lease when signed by the lessor.

The authors consider this practice deceptive and unprofessional. In case of a dispute, any ambiguity may backfire against the maker.

C. LEASES PREPARED BY LESSEES

You should be on your guard when a tenant or tenant's attorney has prepared a lease on a form with which you are not familiar. While it may appear clear, you should protect yourself from liability by having the lease reviewed by an attorney. The attorney should also review your customary lease form so that any differences can be noted.

With the advent of laser printers, some landlords (and even tenants) will prepare leases that appear to be "standard form leases." You may demand that only the forms your company endorses be used.

Some will also include a form number. Unfortunately, some people will use this technique to try to take advantage of the other party.

You do not want to be a party to any deception. Even if the lease was prepared by your client, you want to make certain the tenant fully understands the lease provisions, especially any unusual provisions in the lessor's favor. You may wish to suggest to the lessee that he or she also have the lease reviewed by an attorney.

You must be fair to all parties.

D. CONTRACT OF ADHESION

A **CONTRACT OF ADHESION** *is a one-sided contract where one party has superior bargaining ability and will not allow any modification.* It is a take-it-or-leave-it proposition. A contract will be construed strictly against the party creating the contract, so it needs to be free from ambiguity.

A contract of adhesion, such as a lease, that a court determines to be so unfair as to be oppressive, will not be enforced. The courts will consider the agreement unconscionable.

Oil companies and cable companies offer "take-it-or-leave-it leases" to lessees, as do franchisors. There cannot be any negotiations.

E. EXPIRATION DATE

For residential property, you want your leases to expire when rentals are in most demand in your area.

In a college area, you would want one-bedroom rentals to expire before the beginning of the next term when there will be peak demand. This will avoid lengthy vacancy periods. Three-bedroom units are normally sought by families with children of school age. Leases expiring after the end of the school year and prior to the coming school year, such as July 1 and August 1, will likely be at a time of greatest demand.

In cold climates, apartments having pools are most desirable for tenants June 1, July 1 and August 1, when the pool is a positive feature. On December 1, the renter is not likely to be greatly influenced by the presence of a swimming pool.

When you do rent a property during a period of low rental activity, such as December 1, you should consider having the initial lease for a period other than one year so that the lease will expire during a more desirable rental period, such as September 1. Subsequent lease extensions or renewals can be for a one-year or multi-year period.

If a tenant takes occupancy on October 8, you would want the October rent prorated so that November rent comes due on November 1. Having all rents due on the same date allows ease in record keeping and late fee calculations. You are less likely to overlook a delinquency.

F. LENGTH OF THE LEASE

A number of years ago, an attorney/entrepreneur became a multimillionaire by subleasing whole floors of large office buildings, where he provided thousands of young attorneys with private offices, secretarial, telephone answering, and support services, including well-equipped law libraries.

Unfortunately, office space became overbuilt and building developers went bankrupt, leaving lenders with vacancies that drove down rental prices. He lost tenants because the terms of his master lease didn't allow him to match the lower rents being offered.

To protect himself, he could have entered shorter term master leases with multiple extension options. Then, based on higher vacancy factors, he could have renegotiated lower rents, and passed them on to his tenants. Few building owners would refuse to consider concessions at a time when building vacancy rates were over 20 percent.

As a lessor, if you believe that rents will go up significantly and there will be a relatively low vacancy factor, then shorter term leases would be in your best interest.

However, if you believe that vacancy factors will increase, resulting in lower rents, you should lock in tenants with long-term leases. Tenants, on the other hand, would prefer a short-term lease with options to renew. In the following two examples, the right of renewal is discussed.

Remember that the market value of the property is directly affected by the quality of its

Case Example

MTBD v. Handlery Hotel, Inc., 73 Cal.App.4th 517 (1999)

The court discussed the concept of a right to renewal as follows:

"A tenant's right of renewal of a lease refers to a legal right, and this exists only when the lease expressly grants to the tenant the option to renew the lease at the end of its term. A mere expectation, or even, probability, that the lease will be renewed based upon past practice and present good relations between the landlord and tenant, is not a legal right of renewal. It is nothing more than speculation on chance."

Smith v. Huckera, 501 S.E.2d 877 (Ga.App. 1998)

A provision for the renewal of a lease must specify the terms and conditions of the renewal with such definite terms and certainty that the court may determine what has been agreed on, and if it falls short of this requirement, it is not enforceable. It must be certain and definite as to the time the lease is to extend and the rent to be paid.

Lease renewals must be clearly noted and the right for additional broker's compensation, if any, must be explicitly stated.

VIII. Lease Negotiations

There is no lease until the lease has been agreed to.

Parties can change their minds at any time during the negotiation process.

VOICE OF EXPERIENCE:

The 1st of the month is an excellent time to collect all rents. With multiple properties, all rents should come in at the same time, no matter when the tenants take possession. Prorations until the 1st or 15th of the month can easily accomplish this task.

The advantage of using a printed lease form prepared by a form company is that tenants feel it is standard boiler plate and they are less likely to insist on changes.

When you have a great many leases in one building, it is preferable for management to have lease terms as identical as possible. When each lease is negotiated from scratch, it can lead to a management nightmare if each of the many clauses are different.

While residential leases are usually contracts of adhesion because the tenant must accept the lease offered or walk away, leases for commercial and industrial property are likely to be the result of negotiation as to price and/or terms.

A. UNDERSTANDING POSITIONS AND EXPECTATIONS

When negotiating a lease as an agent of the lessor, you want to make the best deal possible for your client. The tenant and/or the tenant's representative wants to make the best deal possible for the tenant.

Remember, although you represent the lessor in negotiations, you must be fair to all the parties.

Each party is likely to have an opening position advantageous to him/her as well as an idea about how low or how high he/she can go. As an example, see **Figure 3-5**.

Figure 3-5

Tenant's Position

Low	High
$800	$1,200

Compromise in the Middle at $1,200

Lessor's Position

Low	High
$1,200	$1,800

As you can see from Figure 3-5, an agreement should be reached. This is not always the case because a tenant who does not know if a lessor will come down to his/her price range might look elsewhere.

A different situation is set forth in **Figure 3-6**.

Figure 3-6

Tenant's Position

Low	High
$800	$1,500

No Middle = No Compromise No Agreement

Lessor's Position

Low	High
$1,700	$2,200

It would appear that in this situation an agreement is impossible. This is not necessarily the case. Negotiations will often convince or influence a person to justify a change in position. One party may reduce expectations or both parties might change positions so that a positive agreement can be reached.

Each party is motivated by factors that are not apparent to the other party. As an example, buyers who have purchased property will often reveal that they would have paid more if they had to and sellers in the same transaction have revealed that they would have accepted less.

The market dictates what options are available.

When you experience many vacancies and/or there is competition in the marketplace from similar properties that have been vacant for some time, the tenants have a great deal of leverage in negotiations. Sometimes tenants don't perceive this power and fail to use it. On other occasions, they assume that they have leverage power when in actuality they do not. If the negotiations are to be successful, this perception of power has to be deflated.

An example of deflating the tenant's perception of power would be in negotiating a lease extension. If the tenant believes you need the tenant more than the tenant needs you, then the tenant might demand a reduction in rent for a lease extension. You might be able to reduce the tenant's expectations by notifying the tenant that you will be showing the premises to a prospective tenant. Always use a real person interested in the rental you will be showing. A tactic like this can change a current tenant's attitude from, "I'll get a reduction in rent" to "I don't want to relocate because it means a loss in business." If you can reduce the tenant's expectations, then the tenant asking for major rent concessions might end up happy with only minor concessions or even a slight rent increase.

Again, care must be taken to avoid appearing too tough or you could end up losing your tenant.

In a market situation where there is a very low vacancy factor for similar properties and you have several prospective tenants, it is a lessor's market that is advantageous to your client. Nevertheless, in preparing for negotiations you should determine:

1. what you want,
2. what you must have, and
3. what is not too important.

You should consider letting the market determine what you want. In Chapter 5 you will find that tenants, not owners, make the ultimate decision about rents. You must consider the supply and demand features of the marketplace. If a particular tenant is important to you, you must consider the fact that too high a rent will mean a marginal or loss operation.

You can expect vacancies if your commercial center tenants are not making a reasonable profit, so a diversity of business types may be preferred.

B. GIVE A LITTLE

In residential leases there are usually many tenants and few, if any, items to be negotiated. Tenants expect to either accept the lease offered or to look elsewhere. Owners know that to negotiate different rents for different tenants will create ill will among tenants who are paying more than others. There is little room, if any, for negotiations. Commercial and industrial leases are far different as various tenants offer various advantages to a lessor. There are usually many areas subject to negotiation, including rent.

Always let the tenant gain something by the negotiation process; you want happy tenants.

This is especially important when an attorney represents the tenant. The tenant and/or attorney leave the negotiations feeling as if they are winners; that you have given them something they otherwise would not have gotten. Even when you are dealing from a position of strength and you know you don't have to give any concessions, you still want the tenant to be a winner. You can do this by asking for terms or clauses which, while favorable for you, you're willing to forgo. In setting forth your position, you will have built-in concessions to be made during the negotiation process.

This is win/win negotiating. If the negotiations result in a lease, your working relationship with the tenant will be better because the tenant will regard you as reasonable.

On the other hand, if you adopt a win/lose philosophy where you convey a take-it-or-leave-it approach, you will lose lease opportunities where you could have gained almost everything you wanted. Even though the owner's position is reasonable, the inability to give any concessions during negotiations will result in tenants looking elsewhere. Assume a dealer wanted $8,000 for a used car. You would be pleased with yourself for saving $1,000 if you could buy the car for $7,000. On the other hand, if the dealer wanted $7,000 for the car and was unwilling to lower the price, you would probably shop elsewhere even though it may not be in your best interest to do so.

If a tenant feels that you're unreasonable but gives in to your position, you will have generated ill will that could come back to haunt you at a later date.

A lease extension might come at a time when the tenant is in a position of strength and may want to humiliate you.

VOICE OF EXPERIENCE:

You never win an argument with a client—you just lose a client and a commission. As a property manager, you should explore all reasonable options and demonstrate the willingness to negotiate and give up at least a little bit, even if it is just to satisfy the client that he/she is not dealing with a rigid winner-take-all mentality.

In negotiating a lease, keep in mind that the overall objective can often be reached by alternative paths. Examples would be items such as basic rents, graduated lease terms, what is included or not included with the rent, the period of the lease, minimum rent on percentage leases, and percentage of the gross.

Assume a prospective tenant indicates that he or she will not pay more than $2,000 per month. The tenant might nevertheless agree to a $1,700 per month lease plus a pro-rata share of parking lot maintenance and security costs, even though the total might be $2,300 per month.

Never get personal or emotional in negotiations—be professional.

While you may feel that the tenant's position is unreasonable and that the attorney representing the tenant is the most obnoxious person you have ever met, don't let them know it. Show respect for the other party as a person but disagree with that person's position.

Although you may be treated rudely during what is otherwise a successful negotiation, you may have to deal with the party in the future. You want the other party to regard you as a fair and reasonable person, so act that way.

C. DO IT QUICKLY

The advantage of face-to-face negotiations is that you can sense agreement or hostility and agreements can be made quickly. You want a quick negotiation.

The longer a period of lease negotiations, the greater the tenant's apprehension and demands.

They are likely to look elsewhere in the event that they are unsuccessful in reaching an agreement. Often a tenant will obligate himself or herself to other space when an agreement with that tenant could have been quickly made. The longer the negotiations process the greater the likelihood the negotiations will fail.

You should continue on other points of the negotiations even though you seem to have reached an impasse on a particular point. Write down the terms with which you agree or check them off indicating agreement. When everything is agreed upon except for the impasse item, you should define the problem. As an example:

"Except for the amount of base rent, the other aspects of the lease are acceptable to you, is that correct?"

Now that the problem has been clearly defined as a single item (or several), you should make the prospective tenant justify his or her position:

"Why do you feel that the base rent of $1,200 per month that I have proposed is excessive?"

You want the tenant to justify his or her objection. This will give you an opportunity to reinforce the advantages that the property offers.

If it is clear that a concession is necessary, you must have the tenant's position if he or she has not given it. As an example:

"Based on what you have expressed, what is the highest figure you would pay as base rent?"

You need a tenant's position from which to negotiate up. Even though it was stated as a maximum, it seldom is and should not be assumed as a maximum. Any stated position should be treated as a position from which to negotiate.

VOICE OF EXPERIENCE:

If a lease is to be prepared by others and is not to be signed at the conclusion of negotiations, prepare a "memo of understanding" that sets forth the provisions agreed to and have the memo signed by the prospective tenant and yourself. Copies go to both parties. This reduces the chance of a tenant claiming that the lease does not reflect what was agreed upon during negotiations.

A memo of understanding reduces the probability that the tenant will go elsewhere or try to renege on any agreement. The memo could be a binding contract if it is complete. The memo should clearly set forth:

1. rent and any escalation;
2. costs to be paid by lessor and/or lessee;
3. services to be provided by lessor;
4. period of the lease and any renewal periods and their terms;
5. deposits;
6. any concessions such as modifications by the owner or free rent;
7. responsibilities of the tenant;
8. each lease clause (reference a standard lease if a standard clause is to be used);
9. late rent;
10. assignment and sublease;
11. use of premises.

D. RENT INCENTIVES

Owners like to show high rents to bankers for refinancing as well as to prospective buyers when they wish to sell and to establish a base rent in the event of subsequent rent control.

The only way to get above-market rents is to offer something special.

Rental concessions should be considered for several other reasons. If you are taking over a new structure, or one that has recently been rehabilitated, you want to stabilize the structure (fill vacancies) as soon as possible. This could eliminate a negative cash flow for the owner. Rental concessions can give you an edge on the competition.

Rental concessions should be considered where there are many vacancies or there has been a vacancy for a long period of time, such as a commercial building vacant over a year.

Rental concessions might be absolutely necessary if the rent being asked is more than market rent for similar available properties. Rental concessions can take several forms.

1. Free Rent

Free rent is the most common concession offered.

While a first month's free rent is more effective than the 12th month's free rent on a one-year lease, it does tend to attract renters who have a greater likelihood of defaulting on lease obligations. However, don't reduce property damage bonds or other deposits. If tenants move in without money, you risk never seeing any money, even when you thought you properly qualified them.

An effective variation on free rent is to offer it to your present tenants. As an example, offer one month's free rent if the new tenant can bring in someone else to lease a unit. Since the tenant does not get a rental incentive, he or she is less likely to move when the lease expires.

VOICE OF EXPERIENCE:

Tenants who receive rental incentives are more likely to leave at the end of their leases than are tenants who do not receive incentives. The likelihood of moving increases directly with the amount of incentives given. Obviously, when incentives are given, it is because a favorable tenant market is in place.

2. A Desirable Premium

One landlord offered a free 31-inch color television set as a rental concession. Her costs were less than half the month's rent. It enabled the landlord to rent out the new building in record time.

A promotion in a golf course community offered a Callaway custom-fitted driver in exchange for leases signed by a particular date.

A different incentive offered by a developer was one year's prepaid cable television with all the premium channels. The developer's costs were less than offering a month's free rent. He reported greater rental success with this promotional incentive.

Instead of giveaways, some lessors advertise a very attractive rent to bring in prospective tenants. In addition to the rent, they charge for parking, trash removal, etc. We consider this practice deceptive and recommend it be avoided.

3. Name That Building

For single-tenant and multi-tenant buildings, offering the building name can be a tremendous incentive for a tenant to sign a lease. A tenant's name on a structure or complex adds prestige to the tenant's firm.

Names such as "The Superior Insurance Building," "Thompson, Inc." or "The Hydraulic, Inc. Industrial Center" will mean a great deal to tenants and it doesn't cost the owner one dime.

Giving away the name should only be done when the tenant is leasing a significant portion of the space under a long-term lease. The name will give you leverage for all of the lease terms.

One successful property management firm uses doctored photographs of buildings to show the name of the prospective tenant on the entrance to the building as well as large letters across the front of the structure.

A picture can be worth a thousand words.

Of course, the owner's approval should be obtained before you give away the name, especially if it currently bears the owner's name.

4. Give Them the Building

Several national corporations have demanded and received equity positions in the buildings they occupy when negotiating a lease for a significant amount of office space located in areas where a high vacancy rate exists.

Typically, they would take around 10 percent in corporate stock or as a limited partnership. Giving away part of the building can make economic sense if it turns a negative cash flow situation into an investment with a significant positive cash flow.

Some lessors have come up with a variation on this idea. When a building has a high debt and is vacant, an owner realizes he has an asset with questionable value. By offering a prospective tenant an equity position up to 50 percent to sign a reasonably long-term lease, the offer becomes nearly impossible to turn down.

The tenant pays a rent that pays the mortgage and more. The tenant gets one-half of the cash flow from the building, and income increases as lease payments escalate.

When the mortgage is paid off, the tenant still has the equity position in the property. The tenant is tied to the property because leaving would mean the equity value would greatly diminish.

E. LEASE RENEWALS

When negotiating renewals or extensions, consider the fact that it costs money to move. Besides the time and expense of moving and the indirect expenses associated with new stationery, decorating items, etc., commercial tenants are likely to suffer a loss in business both during and after their relocation.

Because of the bother and costs associated with moving, a tenant will generally be willing to pay a premium over comparable vacant units to remain at a location.

Residential tenants are more likely to move because of rent increases than are commercial tenants, who value their present patronage.

A rent increase from five percent to ten percent, even though not indicated by market conditions, will generally be accepted by a commercial tenant. However, you could end up with a vacancy if you get too greedy.

You want to make the increase seem reasonable rather than arbitrary when you offer a tenant a new lease at a higher rent. As an example, you can show cost increases such as taxes and insurance as the reason. There is always some rise in costs.

You might be in a situation where you have several vacancies and a commercial tenant needs a downward adjustment in the rent to survive. Rather than lowering the rent, offer to defer a portion of the rent. As an example, instead of paying $1,800 per month rent, a tenant may pay $1,000 per month and sign a note for $9,600 for the balance of the one-year lease. You haven't reduced rents and there is a possibility that the tenant will recover financially and make good on the note. Later, if the tenant is able to pay the full rent, you have the tenant pretty well locked in until the arrearage can be paid off.

Don't offer to defer rent without the owner's written consent. Always get the landlord's approval when his/her income/profit is concerned.

F. DEALING WITH IMPASSE

There are several ways to overcome an apparent impasse. You can go on to other points. However, if the impasse remains, try one of the the following methods.

1. Break Bread

You can defuse a tightening situation over coffee or a meal. Ask questions about the prospective tenant, his or her interests and family. Try to be physically close, but always give the other person space. Coming within three feet of someone's face is considered an intrusion and places that person on the defensive.

At the end of the break, ask the prospective tenant:

"You like the property and I would like to rent it to you. What will it take to reach an agreement?"

G. FOREIGN LANGUAGE NEGOTIATIONS

If you negotiate a lease in any language other than English, make certain the tenant fully understands the lease as written. If not, it's important to have a neutral translator.

You should provide the tenant with a copy of the lease in the language in which it was negotiated, if possible.

In several states, if a residential lease is negotiated primarily in Spanish, or if the lessee requests it, a Spanish translation of the lease must be provided to the lessee. Most form companies have lease forms in Spanish and some have translations in several languages.

VOICE OF EXPERIENCE:

Never translate, even if you know the language. There is too much room for misunderstanding and liability. The best possible solution is to use a printed form in the language of the lessee, particularly if the exact same form is offered in English. That way everyone (including yourself) knows and agrees to the same thing. If not available, then let the lessee select and pay for a translator of his/her choice.

H. RECORDING LEASES

Generally, possession is considered constructive notice that a person has an interest in real estate.

If a lender made a loan on a property where a tenant was in possession, a foreclosure of the loan would leave the lender owning the property subject to the lease rights of the tenant. However, if the lease had been signed but the tenant had not yet taken possession of the property, a lender would not have constructive notice of the tenant's rights. So a later foreclosure of a loan could leave a tenant subject to eviction by the foreclosing lender.

Property managers for franchises and corporations, which lease a great deal of space, generally record their leases as soon as they are signed.

This is especially important if there is going to be a significant time lapse between the time the lease is entered into and the time the lessee will be taking possession. Recording also gives a later lienholder constructive notice so a foreclosure of a trust deed or mortgage entered into after the lease was recorded would result in the foreclosing lienholder taking possession subject to the rights of the tenant.

I. DISCLOSURES

As a property manager, you are generally the agent of the owner, and have a duty to the owner to obtain the most advantageous lease possible. However, you also have duties of fair play and honesty towards prospective tenants.

If, as a property manager, you know that a property is unsuited or cannot be used for the intended purpose of the prospective tenant, then you must disclose this information. As an example, an intended use might be prohibited by zoning or restrictive covenants. Disclosure would be required if you knew of these restrictions. Similarly, you should disclose any negative information you possess that a prospective tenant would want to know.

Other disclosures are mandated by state statutes in addition to those mentioned above. These types of disclosures might include the following.

1. Hazardous Substance

If hazardous substances were known to have been released or present on the property, or if the owner has reasonable cause to believe hazardous substances are on the property, then lessees might have to be notified of this fact.

Failure to notify the prospective tenant about any hazardous substance could be the basis for the tenant voiding the lease and possibly obtaining damages.

2. Lead-Based Paint

When leasing residential property built prior to 1978, the lessor must provide the lessee with a pamphlet warning of the hazards from lead-based paint.

The EPA's **Lead-Based Paint Renovation, Repair, and Painting Program (RRP)** affects property managers, contractors and others who disturb painted surfaces. It applies to anyone who performs renovations for compensation in residential houses, apartments, and child-occupied facilities built before 1978. Not only must a lead pamphlet be distributed before starting renovation work, but firms are required to be certified (8-hour training course) and the EPA can impose steep fines or jail time for noncompliance.

Providing the lead-based paint pamphlet is a federal requirement.

3. Flood Hazard Area

The lessor might be required to disclose to the lessee the fact that the leased premises are within a flood hazard area.

4. Military Ordnance

Leases of residential property might require the lessor to disclose to the lessee any knowledge of a former military ordnance location that might contain explosive materials within a stated distance of the rental.

5. Death

Some states exempt lessors from any liability for failure to disclose to a lessee that a death occurred on the property more than a designated time period prior to entering a lease agreement.

VOICE OF EXPERIENCE:

If you feel that the death or manner of death is information that a prospective tenant would want to know, you should disclose, even if the disclosure is not required by state law. When in doubt, disclose!

6. AIDS

In a number of states, statutes provide that a lessor is under no obligation to disclose to a lessee that a previous occupant was HIV positive or had AIDS.

VOICE OF EXPERIENCE:

The statutes generally do not prohibit disclosure, but indicate that you need not disclose. You should be aware that if you make such a disclosure, you could be held responsible for slander or libel if you are incorrect.

You have a duty to answer honestly, based on knowledge that you possess, if a prospective tenant asks about the death or affliction of a prior tenant. If you don't know, then that should be your answer. If you know, you must answer truthfully.

7. Stigmatized Property

STIGMATIZED PROPERTY is property that has developed an undesirable reputation in the community. As an example, if a property had been written up in a national tabloid as being haunted or this belief was held in the community, then the property would be stigmatized. If the property was the scene of a particularly brutal murder, it could be stigmatized to the point where many people would not want to occupy it, even at a reduced rent.

An apartment would be stigmatized where three separate renters died in violent accidents over a one-year period.

If, over its 10-year life span, nine occupants of a commercial business location had gone bankrupt, the location would be considered unlucky by many. Some people believe strongly in luck and will not want to occupy any structure that they consider unlucky.

You have a duty to an owner to use your best efforts to lease property when you are acting as an agent. You also have a duty to prospective tenants of fair and honest dealing. Placing yourself in the prospective tenant's shoes, if you would want to know particular facts or beliefs about a property prior to leasing it, then you should disclose this information to your tenant. This is nothing more than the application of "The Golden Rule."

VOICE OF EXPERIENCE:

"The Golden Rule" is "Do unto others as you would have them do unto you." In other words, treat others as you would want to be treated—not necessarily as the law strictly mandates.

IX. CHAPTER SUMMARY

A lease is a contract. The four basic requirements of a contract apply:

1. Mutuality - clear meeting of the minds about the essential terms of the lease;
2. Capacity to contract;
3. Legal Purpose;
4. Consideration.

A fifth requirement (writing) applies to leases of over one year and leases which, by their terms, cannot be completed within one year (Statute of Frauds).

Leases for a fixed term are estates for years, while leases that renew themselves unless terminated are periodic tenancies.

A gross (or flat) lease has a fixed-level rental amount. In a net lease, the lessor receives a fixed amount and the lessee pays all property expenses, including taxes and insurance. With a percentage lease, the tenant pays a minimum rent (usually) plus a percentage of the gross income.

Leases that do not specifically prohibit assignment or sublease can be assigned or subleased. An assignment is a transfer of all of a lessee's interest, although the lessee remains secondarily liable on the lease. A sublease is a new lease between the original lessee and a sublessee. The sublessee is the tenant of the original lessee, and the original lessee remains primarily liable on the lease. Tenants should be qualified by checking income, credit history and rental history.

A real estate broker should not prepare a lease other than a standard form as it could be regarded as an unauthorized practice of law.

The court might regard a one-sided, take-it-or-leave-it lease as unconscionable and refuse to enforce it (Contract of Adhesion).

Leases should be written to expire in prime rental periods. With a long-term lease, the lessor risks not being able to take advantage of escalating rents that are not reflected in the lease or its escalations.

In lease negotiations, a win/win attitude results in a greater chance of a favorable conclusion, as well as better tenant relations. As lessor, you should try to have an area for concession.

Rent incentives can be used to rent property quickly, obtain a competitive edge on the market, and even obtain above-market rent. Incentives don't have to be monetary.

Tenants in possession are more likely to accept an increase above the market rental for a lease renewal than a prospective tenant who is considering the rental.

Leases may be recorded. They give constructive notice of the tenant's interest and would thus take priority over later mortgages and trust deeds.

While you, as a property manager, have agency duties to an owner you represent, you have a duty of fair play and disclosure to the prospective tenant. If you know of problems with the property that could affect the tenancy or intended use, then the problems should be revealed to the tenant. The lessor should also reveal hazardous substances that may have been released on the premises and if the property is located in a flood hazard zone.

If it is known that residential property is within a distance specified by statute of a facility where explosive ordnance may be found, then this must be disclosed.

By law, a lead-based paint pamphlet is to be provided to tenants for residential rentals built prior to 1978. The EPA's Lead-Based Paint Renovation, Repair, and Painting Program (RRP) regulates the handling of lead-based painted surfaces, including those made by landlords, carpenters, plumbers, handymen, etc.

A lessor need not reveal death from any cause on the premises if disclosure is not required by state statute. The fact that a prior resident had AIDS or was HIV positive is usually exempt from disclosure.

X. CHAPTER QUIZ

1. Which of the following is NOT a requirement for every lease?

    a. Mutuality
    b. Legal purpose
    c. In writing
    d. Consideration

2. A lease that automatically renews itself, in the absence of notification by either party, is what kind of lease?

    a. A gross lease
    b. A percentage lease
    c. A periodic tenancy
    d. An estate for years

3. A tenant pays taxes, insurance and all maintenance expenses. What kind of lease does she have?

    a. Net lease
    b. Gross lease
    c. Percentage lease
    d. Flat lease

4. Which of the following tenants would be MOST LIKELY to have a percentage lease?

    a. Residential tenant
    b. Manufacturer
    c. Government agency
    d. Jewelry store

5. A transfer by a lessee of all interest in a lease to a third party, who agrees to accept the lease obligations, would be a:

    a. sublease.
    b. assignment.
    c. contract of adhesion.
    d. percentage lease.

6. When the value of the premises has increased significantly above the rent specified in the lease, an economic tenant would be better off to:

    a. assign the lease.
    b. sublease the premises.
    c. void the lease.
    d. renegotiate a higher rent.

7. In qualifying a prospective **tenant, you should be interested in the tenant's:**
   a. income.
   b. credit history.
   c. rental history.
   d. all of the above.

8. If you believe that rents will increase significantly in the near future, the leases you negotiate for owners, should:
   a. prohibit assignment.
   b. be for relatively short terms.
   c. include renewal options.
   d. be estates for years.

9. Rent incentives are most likely to be given when:
   a. there is low unemployment.
   b. the rent is set below-market rent.
   c. there is a high vacancy factor.
   d. the tenant only marginally qualifies.

10. When is a lessor most likely to successfully obtain an above-market rent?
    a. When giving rent incentives
    b. When negotiating a lease renewal
    c. Both a and b
    d. Neither a nor b

ANSWERS: *1. c; 2. c; 3. a; 4. d; 5. b; 6. b; 7. d; 8. b; 9. c; 10. c*

Chapter 4
Lease Clauses

KEY WORDS AND TERMS

Accelerated Payments
Arbitration
Assignment
Attorney Fees
Automatic Renewal
Bad Checks
Bankruptcy
Breach of Lease
COLA
Common Areas
Competition Clause
Complete Agreement
Covenant to Remain in Business
CPI
Destruction of Premises
Eminent Domain
Estoppel Certificate
Escalator Clause
Excuse from Performance

Extension of Lease
Fixtures
Grace Period
Guarantors
Hold Harmless Clause
Holdover Clause
HVAC
Joint and Several Liability
Late Charges
Lead-Based Paint Disclosure
Limitation on Occupants
Merchant Associations
Minimum Rent
Net Sales
Noncompetition Clause
Non-Disturbance Clause
Nonwaiver Clause
Notice of Nonresponsibility
Option to Purchase

Option to Rebuild
Option to Renew
Partial Destruction
Percentage Lease
Possession Clause
Quiet Enjoyment
Radius Clause
Recapture Clause
Renewal of Lease
Rental Interruption Insurance
Rent Control
Right of First Refusal
Security Deposit
Sublease
Surrender
Time is of the Essence
Trade Fixtures
Zero-Tolerance Drug Clause

Chapter 4

> ### CHAPTER 4 OUTLINE
>

I. Administration of Lease Clauses

In order to administer a great many leases, you should attempt to use standard clauses wherever possible.

This is not always possible. A synopsis of each lease can be prepared to indicate the standard clauses for each lease, renewal dates, any options, as well as those clauses that have been rewritten or added with the substance of the changes and additions. For easy access, this data can be in a computer file. The entire lease can also be scanned and saved in the computer file for reference purposes.

VOICE OF EXPERIENCE:

Technology has greatly enhanced the performance of the property manager. Some software programs, such as zipForm®, automatically discard outdated forms, replacing them with the updated ones.

Again, when new clauses are added or changed, legal assistance should be sought. Commercial and industrial leases are more likely to have specially written clauses and alterations to clauses than would residential leases.

II. Lease Clauses

Following are some of the specific clauses utilized in leases. In Chapters 5 and 6, you will find lease forms that include many of the clauses described in this chapter, as well as variations of these clauses.

Some of the clauses and material set forth apply only to residential property, only to commercial or industrial property, to various types of property or for specific types of leases.

The clauses covered are not all-inclusive as new clauses can be formulated to cover any situation. These are simply clauses that are more commonly encountered.

Accelerated Payments. Leases frequently state that a breach of the lease, concerning rent payments, shall accelerate all payments under the lease. What this means is that if there are four years remaining on the lease, the rent for the remaining four years becomes immediately due if the lessee becomes delinquent in rent.

Despite the fact that accelerated payment clauses can be found in many preprinted lease forms, rent acceleration in residential leases is unenforceable in most states.

The fact that a residential tenant agreed to the clause does not make it enforceable. Depending upon state law, the clause may be enforceable for nonresidential leases.

Acknowledgment. Lessee acknowledges that disclosures about the condition of the premises, suitability of the premises for lessee purposes and environmental matters were made to lessee by lessor and/or broker and that no oral representation was made as to the suitability of the premises. The lessee further acknowledges that he or she has investigated the premises and assumes any responsibility for any patent defects. The lessor could still be liable for latent defects that were known but not disclosed.

VOICE OF EXPERIENCE:

Some leases permit tenants three to five days after possession to provide a list of any defects to lessor. It's obvious that a new tenant needs time to check the property after being in the property for a while. Additionally, most leases allow for an inspection prior to termination. This allows the tenant to provide needed repairs in order to get his/her security deposit back.

Advertising. Percentage leases for shopping centers often have advertising requirements for tenants who are to share in joint advertising for the shopping center based on a formula. In some cases, management might also share in such expenses. This obligation would be spelled out in the lease.

Air Conditioning/Heating. This clause sets forth landlords' and tenants' obligations regarding supplying air conditioning, heating, and ventilation. In some cases, air conditioning may be included, in others the tenants might be supplied with chilled water for the tenants' own equipment (commercial leases).

Heating obligations are also set forth in this clause. The term **HVAC** *is frequently used. It stands for Heating, Ventilating, and Air Conditioning.*

Alterations. Some commercial and industrial leases give the lessor the right to elect to be the owner of lessee-installed alterations and utilities or to require their removal at the end of the lease.

This clause prohibits alterations without lessor's consent.

Amendments. The only way the lease can be modified is through a written agreement signed by the parties involved.

Arbitration. An *ARBITRATION CLAUSE may provide for either mandatory or consensual binding arbitration of disputes arising under the lease.* The manner of choosing an arbitrator shall be set forth. One method is to obtain a list of three arbitrators from an arbitration service. Each party eliminates one arbitrator and the remaining arbitrator is chosen for the arbitration.

> *By agreeing to binding arbitration, the parties agree to give up the right to sue in a court of law and the right to appeal.*

However, the advantages are lower litigation costs and a quick resolution of a dispute.

Assignment and Subleasing. When agreeing to long-term leases, most large commercial tenants want the right to assign the lease. Generally, they will agree to an assignment subject to the consent of the owner. They will do so because the lessor (landlord) cannot be unreasonable in his or her refusal to consent to a lease assignment.

> *Generally, this clause prohibits assignment or subletting by the tenant without the consent of the lessor.*

The clause states that acceptance of rent from a third party does not constitute agreement to an assignment and that lessor's acceptance of one assignment or sublease may not be considered acceptance of subsequent assignments or subleases.

VOICE OF EXPERIENCE:

The landlord is permitted to evaluate the new tenant's credit report and background information as he/she did for the previous lessee. A sublease agreement still needs the landlord's approval of all terms and conditions.

The clause may provide for a fee to accompany a request for an approval of assignment or sublease. It may even provide that the lessor has an option to terminate the lease upon receipt of a request for assignment or sublease.

> *Note: There is some disagreement about the enforcement of this termination right.*

The lease might provide that in the event of default the lessor can go against the assignee or guarantor without first going against any other person liable on the lease. Upon default, the clause might provide that sublessee and assignees will be bound by all lease obligations, but that lessor shall not be bound to any deposits made by sublessee or assignee to the original lessee. (The lessor is not responsible for security deposits or other monies sublessees or assignees paid to the original lessee.)

Some commercial and industrial leases provide that the lessor shall have the option to cancel the lease if all or a designated portion of the leased premises is assigned or sublet.

Case Example

John Hogan Enters, Inc. v. Kellogg, 187 C.A. 3d 589 (1987)

A tenant paid a base monthly rent of $2,750 plus an overage based on gross monthly sales. In 1981, the average monthly rent paid was $4,200. In 1982, it was $4,000 and in 1983, it was $3,700. The tenant assigned the remaining nine years of the lease to Phipps for a consideration of $150,000. Phipps wanted the premises for an antique shop which he intended to operate as a hobby. Phipps admitted that the business would not result in rent over the $2,750 base rental because of the nature of the business. The landlord refused to consent to the assignment and Phipps sued for damages.

The Court of Appeals held that the landlord was justified in rejecting the tenant. The landlord does not have to agree to a lease where they will receive less rent.

The court referenced *Kendall v. Ernest Pestana, Inc.* (1985), 40 C. 3d 488 where the California Supreme Court held that a landlord might only refuse to consent to a lease assignment when there is a commercially reasonable objection (which there was in this case).

Trinity Prof. Plaza v. Metrocrest Hosp., 987 S.W.2d 621 (Tex.App. - Eastland 1999)

TEX. PROP. CODE ANN. § 91.005 (Vernon 1995) provides: "During the term of a lease, the tenant may not rent the leasehold without the prior consent of the landlord. This statutory prohibition forbids an assignment as well as a sublease."

The landlord does not have to agree to a lease assignment when this assignment would reduce the expected and agreed upon rents.

Case Example

CARMA Developers v. Marathon Dev. California, Inc., 2 Cal.4th 342, 6 Cal.Rptr.2d 467 (Cal. 1992)

A commercial lease required consent to any assignment or sublease. It also provided that should the tenant request consent to assign or sublet, the lessor could, at its option, terminate the lease and enter into its own lease with the assignee or sublessee.

The tenant requested to sublet a portion of the property and the landlord then exercised the recapture clause which terminated the lease. After the tenant vacated, the tenant sued for breach of contract.

▼

The California Supreme Court stated that even where a lease contains a restriction, the restriction may be declared unlawful as an unreasonable restraint. However, the Court held that a recapture clause in a commercial lease under which lessor might terminate the entire leasehold upon lessee's request for permission to sublet or assign was not an unreasonable restraint on alienation.

718 Associates, Ltd. v. Sunwest N.O.P., 1 S.W.3d 355 (Tex.App - Waco 1999)

As a general rule, if an instrument conveys the entire "term" of the lease without retaining any reversionary interest, the instrument will be construed as an assignment. ... On the other hand, if the conveying party retains any reversionary interest in the estate conveyed, the instrument will be construed as a sublease.

Figure 4-1 is the AIR **Assignment and Assumption of Lessor's Interest in Lease** by the assignee.

Attorney Fees. This provision provides that should there be legal action under the lease, the prevailing party in the lawsuit will be entitled to reasonable attorney fees. This clause reduces the possibility of a frivolous lawsuit.

Authority. Officers of corporations signing the lease acknowledge that they have authority to sign the lease and obligate the corporation based on a resolution of the board of directors.

Bad Checks. The lease should set forth a charge that will be imposed for any check returned because of insufficient funds as well as for a check where the issuer has placed a stop payment. The lease should make it clear that this charge will be in addition to any late payment charge that might be applicable.

A bad check charge should apply to checks written by the tenant as well as third-party checks (checks written by others and endorsed to the property management).

Many property management company offices will not accept third-party checks with the exception of social security and government checks.

If a bad check is replaced by another bad check, your policy should be to immediately start eviction proceedings against the tenant.

Many offices have a policy of evicting tenants who submit two bad checks, while other firms have a modified policy of eviction for two bad checks in one 12-month period. If the tenant is on a lease for one year or more, your lease should provide for termination upon receipt of a bad check. It should also provide that failure to evict does not waive your rights to evict for any later bad check.

Bankruptcy. A clause might provide that tenant bankruptcy or assignment of the lease to creditors shall allow the lessor to, at his/her option, terminate the lease and if so terminated,

Figure 4-1

ASSIGNMENT AND ASSUMPTION OF LESSOR'S INTEREST IN LEASE

1. _____ ("Assignor")
hereby assigns and transfers to _____ ("Assignee") the
interest of Assignor under that certain Lease (the "Lease") dated _____ , by
and between _____ , as Lessor,
and _____ , as Lessee,
concerning the real property commonly known as _____
_____ ("the "Premises").

2.   Assignor also assigns to Assignee the security deposit under said Lease in the sum of $ _____
and the interest of Lessor in any applicable guaranty of said Lease.

3.   This Assignment shall be effective from and after the recordation, in the county where the Premises are located, of the deed passing fee title to the Premises to Assignee.

Dated: _____

ASSIGNOR

By _____
Name Printed: _____
Title: _____

By _____
Name Printed: _____
Title: _____

ACCEPTANCE AND ASSUMPTION

Assignee hereby accepts the above Assignment and assumes all of the rights and obligations of the Lessor accruing from and after the recordation, in the county where the Premises are located, of the deed passing fee title to the Premises to Assignee. Assignee shall defend, indemnify, and hold Assignor harmless with respect to the obligations of Lessor under said Lease accruing from and after said date

Dated: _____

ASSIGNEE

By _____
Name Printed: _____
Title: _____

By _____
Name Printed: _____
Title: _____

NOTICE: These forms are often modified to meet changing requirements of law and industry needs. Always write or call to make sure you are utilizing the most current form: AIR Commercial Real Estate Association, 800 W 6th Street, Suite 800, Los Angeles, CA 90017. Telephone No. (213) 687-8777. Fax No.: (213) 687-8616.

PAGE 1 OF 1

the tenant or assigns will vacate the premises. Generally, the clause would state that the tenant would still be obligated for any losses suffered by the lessor by the default of the lessees. (Guarantors would still be liable.) The lease might also provide that bankruptcy of the lessor would not terminate the lease.

Breach by Lessor. Lessee's rights are set forth for lessor breach. A lessee might have the right to cure a lessor default and deduct costs from the rent up to an amount set forth in the clause.

Broker. In this clause, the tenant either claims that he or she negotiated with a specific broker or without a broker and does not know of any broker who would be entitled to any commission. This statement by a tenant could make it difficult for a leasing agent with an open listing to claim he/she is entitled to a commission from the lessor if not named by the tenant.

The clause might name the brokers involved in the transaction and provide for the amount of compensation they are to receive. The amount of commission might also be provided for exercising any options.

Cleaning. This clause will specify responsibility for cleaning. Some office space is rented with cleaning included in the rent. In large office structures with several hundred tenants, if each tenant hired his/her own cleaner, it could not only result in a logistical nightmare, but could also compromise security. This clause could specify the firm or firms authorized to clean in the building and the tenant agrees not to employ any cleaning firm other than those listed.

Codes. The tenant agrees to comply with all building, safety, health, and fire codes.

Common Areas. This clause sets forth maintenance responsibilities and use of common areas. In many office buildings, there are law libraries available for use by all the tenants. The clause might provide that the use is subject to posted regulations (and charges, if any). The common areas would be defined for the rental.

Competition Clause. This clause would be used in a percentage lease and would prohibit the tenant from opening a competing location within a reasonable radius (expressed in miles) of the location.

A competition clause is sometimes called a "radius clause."

If a tenant did open a competing location, it would siphon off gross income from the other location. One would think that an owner would not wish to compete with his or her own business, but it could make economic sense if the volume was high and the new location had a low fixed rent, rather than a percentage lease.

Complete Agreement. There will usually be a clause indicating that the lease is the complete agreement and there are no verbal understandings or separate agreements affecting the tenancy that are not set forth therein or referenced by the lease.

Condition of the Premises. This provision requires the premises to be free of debris and all systems to be operational at commencement of the lease.

Construction/Contractors.

Commercial leases generally require tenants to use licensed contractors. It's always safer to use licensed contractors who have their own workman's compensation insurance.

There might also be a requirement for preapproval of any contractor by the lessor, or a limitation which a tenant can spend for construction, remodeling, and fixturing.

A commercial lease sets forth the landlord's obligations, or lack thereof, for tenant alterations and construction, although the lessor may agree to take over a portion of alteration and construction costs.

Covenant to Remain in Business. Commercial leases, especially percentage leases, often have this clause printed in the lease. This prevents the tenant from leaving an empty store and paying the minimum rent under the lease. An empty store hurts other tenants and reduces the lessor's income on percentage leases.

While the clause "remain in business" is frequently printed, courts have determined that it is an implied covenant in percentage leases.

Case Example

College Block v. Atlantic Richfield Co., 206 Cal.App.3d 1376 (1988)

A tenant signed a 20-year lease to build and operate a gas station on the plaintiff's land, paying a minimum rent plus a percentage of the gross income. After 17 years, the defendant closed the gas station and paid the minimum rent. The landlord brought action based on an implied covenant in the lease to operate the gas station for the term of the lease. If the gas station were operating, the lessor's income would have exceeded the minimum rent by more than 200 percent.

The Court of Appeals affirmed the trial court which held that a covenant to operate a business is implied in a percentage lease where the minimum rent is not substantial.

McHenry v. Broadfoot, 46 Or.App. 411, 611 P.2d 1174 (Or.App. 1980)

The lessee entered agreement to lease building to be constructed by lessor. Even though lessee notified lessor, before construction began, that he would not fulfill terms of the lease, the Court still found lessor was entitled to damages for "loss of anticipated profit."

 VOICE OF EXPERIENCE:

In the case example of <u>College Block v. Atlantic Richfield Co.</u>, the court found that, when dealing with a percentage lease with a minimum base rent, the landlord is entitled to damages for anticipated loss of income if the tenant is not open for business. The tenant paid a minimal rent thereby increasing his profit for 17 years. The landlord lost money because the tenant breached his contract.

Default by Tenant. This clause provides what constitutes a default and lessor's right to bring suit, re-enter premises, terminate lease, etc. The rights could include rights in any assignment of the lessee or rights in any subleases entered into by the lessee.

Destruction of Premises. This clause sets forth what happens if the premises are destroyed. This could include one of the following:

1. **Termination.** Tenant and/or lessor could have the right to lease termination.

2. **Rent Tolled.** The rent could be *TOLLED, meaning waived, until the premises are available to be used*. The period of the lease could also be tolled (lease would be extended for the period premises were not available). This clause could be based on total and/or partial destruction.

3. **Option to Rebuild.** Lessor might have the option to rebuild or terminate lease. If lessor decides to rebuild, the period to rebuild is set.

4. **Partial Destruction.** The lease could provide for a rent adjustment based on the portion that is useable.

Drugs. A zero-tolerance drug clause might be included in a residential lease. The presence of illegal drugs on the premises shall be treated as proper cause for eviction. This would apply even though the drugs were brought on the premises by a guest.

> *Note: A California court has upheld the right to evict when the tenant's son was found to have drugs in their apartment.*

Earthquake Ordinance. If an earthquake ordinance requires extensive structural work, the lessor shall have the option of performing the required work or terminating the lease and demolishing the structure. If the lessor chooses to make the repairs, the clause could provide for rent abatement while the premises cannot be occupied.

Easements. Lessor shall be permitted to grant easements (such as for utilities) providing such easements do not impair lessee's use of the premises.

Eminent Domain. This provision might provide that the tenant shall have no claim against the landlord if the premises are taken by a public entity by eminent domain. Unless the tenant agrees to waive any claim as to the public agency, the tenant would be entitled to receive compensation under eminent domain for the value of the leasehold, costs of relocation and fixtures. This sum could be considerable.

Entry. Leases should provide for situations when the landlord might enter the premises as well as any notice requirements. In most states, the landlord's right to inspect include:

1. insurance inspection;
2. to inspect for repairs or to make repairs;
3. to check for hazardous material and/or disposal of such material;
4. for appraisal purposes;
5. to show premises to prospective tenants, purchasers and lenders, and
6. in emergency situations.

VOICE OF EXPERIENCE:

Timely and sufficient warning must be given to the tenant (usually 24 hours). Generally speaking, entry should be made during working hours, unless the tenant agrees to be really cooperative. It's not unusual to offer some compensation for this cooperation. The tenant cannot refuse access with proper notice, however.

Escalator Clause. This clause would provide for periodic rent increases. It might be a set increase or an increase determined by the consumer price or other index.

Estoppel Agreement. This clause provides that the lessee will complete an estoppel certificate upon request by the lessor. The certificate sets forth that the lease has not been modified. The tenant has no option to purchase or right of first refusal, the amount of rent, the date the rent has been paid to, the amount of security or lease deposits and that the tenant is not in default.

Estoppel certificates might be required by a buyer if the lessor decides to sell the property. If the lessee fails (or refuses) to exercise an Estoppel Certificate, the lessor can exercise such a certificate.

Eviction. This clause would provide that should the tenant be evicted for the breach of any lease covenant, the tenant agrees to reimburse the landlord for all costs associated with the eviction. Costs would include reasonable attorney fees as well as any rental loss suffered by the landlord through the entire term of the lease.

Excuse From Performance. Lessor's obligations under the lease might be excused by an Act of God (Act of God Clause), labor problems or other problems beyond the control of the lessor, that impair the lessor's ability to meet contractual obligations. Unless provided for in the lease, the lessee's obligations would not be excused for these reasons. The lease might

provide that if the lessor is unable to give the tenant possession on the date indicated, and this delay is for a reason outside the lessor's control, then the rent would be tolled until possession could be given.

Financial Statement. Lessee and any guarantor agree to provide a financial statement to a prospective lender or purchaser if lessor requests same.

Fixtures. *FIXTURES are items of personal property that are attached to, or incoporated into, the land in such a manner as to become real property.* A residential tenant cannot remove fixtures he or she installed unless the lease gave him or her that right. Generally, if there is a question concerning an item being a fixture, the courts will side with the tenant rather than the landlord. Three basic tests are used to determine if an item has become a fixture:

1. **Intent of the Parties.** Did the parties intend the item to stay? This is the most important test. In the lease, parties can agree if items might be removed by the tenant or shall remain as part of the realty.
2. **Adaptability.** If the item is particularly adapted to the property it would likely be a fixture.
3. **Attachment.** Permanent attachment is evidence that the item is a fixture.

A court might determine that a ceiling fan installed by a tenant is not a fixture, but a shower over the bath installed by the tenant is a fixture and must remain.

For commercial and industrial tenants, fixtures are likely be regarded as "trade fixtures" or fixtures that were installed for the purpose of conducting a business or trade and may be removed by the tenant under certain circumstances.

This could include signs, machinery encased in concrete, special cooling systems, etc. The tenant can remove trade fixtures at the end of the tenancy and for a reasonable period thereafter. A tenant would be liable for any property damage that results from the removal of the trade fixtures.

Even though the law on trade fixtures allows removal, leases often specify this right or might take away this right. The parties can agree that particular trade fixtures shall remain with the building.

Grace Period. This clause might provide a grace period for meeting obligations under the lease.

VOICE OF EXPERIENCE:

Naturally, the tenant must leave the property as when he/she rented it. Before and after photographs give a realistic view of the premises.

Guarantors. When a tenant does not appear to have the ability to meet lease obligations or has had serious credit difficulties in the past, landlords would be reluctant to rent to such a tenant unless there is a guarantor. A *GUARANTOR agrees to be liable under a lease if the tenant defaults*. A guarantor could be a supplier or purchaser from the tenant or even a relative of the tenant.

Case Example

Bennett v. Leatherby, 3 C.A. 4th 448 (1992)

LMI leased commercial property for 10 years. The lease contemplated that LMI would sublease the premises to a restaurant franchisee. Leatherby guaranteed the lease for five years after an assignment or subletting. The sublessee defaulted on the lease. The lessor settled with the general partners of the sublessee for $50,000, releasing them from all further claims under the lease. The lessor then brought action against the guarantors (Leatherby) for $228,000 which covered the remainder due under the lease.

The Appeals Court upheld judgment in favor of Leatherby. By releasing the debtor, the guarantors were effectively released. They guaranteed performance by a sublessee and the lessor accepted $50,000 for all amounts due by the sublessee. With nothing further due, the guarantor was released.

The landlord, by releasing the lessee from further obligation, also releases the guarantors. It's important that your legal counsel be well versed on the particular aspects of this case.

State v. French, 945 P.2d 752 (Wash.App.Div.2 1997)

Any material change in a surety's obligation without the surety's consent will discharge the surety's obligation. ... By implication, if a surety consents to an expansion of its obligation, the surety will be liable to the extent of its consent.

If the tenant defaults on the lease, the landlord still has a duty to *MITIGATE DAMAGES*. *This means that the landlord must attempt due diligence to keep damages low.* This would include prompt action upon the default of the tenant, including eviction and a reasonable attempt to again rent the premises.

Failure of the guarantor to execute the guaranty agreement can be considered a default.

Hazardous Substances. The clause might require lessor approval before hazardous substances are used on the premises.

If hazardous substances come onto the premises or are discovered on the premises by the tenant, then the tenant shall immediately notify the lessor.

Any time hazardous material is to be placed on a site you want to make certain that there is an adequate guaranty to cover any loss that may be sustained because the material enters the soil or is not otherwise disposed of properly.

The lease might provide that if hazardous substances are discovered on the property (not due to use or negligence of lessee) and remedial action is required, the lessor shall have the option to terminate the lease if the cost of remedial action exceeds a stated dollar amount. However, the lessee would have the right to pay the excess costs and retain lease rights.

Hold Harmless Clause. In a *HOLD HARMLESS CLAUSE, the tenant agrees that he or she will not hold the lessor responsible for any personal injury or damages.* The clause could provide that the tenant shall indemnify the lessor for any damages suffered by the lessor because of the tenancy. The tenant could also agree to defend the lessor in any lawsuit resulting from the tenancy.

The hold harmless clause can be limited to water damage or it can be all inclusive. For commercial leases, hold harmless clauses are generally held to be valid. Generally, hold harmless clauses are not enforceable for residential leases.

Why do residential lessors continue to insert this clause in a lease? The reason is simple. If a tenant thinks that a landlord is not liable then they are unlikely to seek legal action against the landlord.

> *The hold harmless clause usually will not protect you from damages where the injury resulted from your negligence as the property manager.*

Holdover Clause. Should the tenant remain in possession at the end of the lease or after giving notice to vacate and failing to vacate, the landlord may, at his or her option, evict the tenant or consider the tenant to be on a month-to-month tenancy. The holdover clause generally sets forth a rent for the holdover period that is significantly higher than the rent the tenant was paying. This serves to encourage the tenant to either vacate or negotiate a new lease.

Hours of Operation. The leases of many shopping centers specify hours that the store must be open. Shoppers want all the stores open during similar hours as this is what attracts them to shopping centers.

Improvements (Lessor). If lessor improvements are to be made and the costs will be in excess of the limit set, lessee shall pay the excess prior to the commencement of work.

Insurance. The lease might require that all insurance carriers who provide required insurance be licensed in the state.

> *A net lease specifies who is responsible for property insurance, taxes, and maintenance.*

While the lessee would ordinarily be responsible in such a lease, a modified net lease might provide for lessor responsibility.

If the lessee's use of the premises causes increased insurance rates for the structure or adjacent structures owned by the lessor, the insurance clause could require that the lessee pay these increased costs.

Some commercial net leases require that the lessee carry **RENTAL INTERRUPTION INSURANCE** *so that rent is paid to the lessor if the premises are destroyed or materially damaged.* This provision would customarily protect both lessor and any mortgagor for up to one year's rent.

The insurance clause might require the lessor to carry property insurance up to a percentage of the replacement cost (usually 80 percent).

> *Commercial leases frequently require tenants to carry high-limit liability protection naming both the lessor and lessee as the insured.*

Normally, the lease will require that evidence of the insurance coverage be provided to the property owner.

The lessor might require the tenant to also carry plate glass insurance for the windows and coverage for equipment that is exclusive to the use of the premises.

The tenant might be required to carry a policy of boiler insurance if the boiler is under the tenant's control. **BOILER INSURANCE** *covers damages and liability from a boiler explosion by providing professional inspection to check boiler operations and safety devices to protect against explosion.*

Case Example

Morales v. Fanster, 209 C.A. 3d 1581 (1989)

A lease required that a tenant carry liability insurance covering the premises in a minimum amount of $500,000. In fact, the tenant only carried $300,000 in protection.

A child was injured on the premises and the tenant insurance carrier paid the limit of its policy ($300,000) to the child's parents. The parents then sued the landlord for failing to enforce the lease provision as to the amount of insurance coverage.

The court ruled for the landlord since the landlord had no duty to require a tenant to carry insurance for the benefit of third parties. The fact that the lease required the insurance created no duty on the part of the landlord to enforce the clause.

O'Neill v. Thibodeaux, 709 So.2d 962 (La.App. 3 Cir. 1998)

The contract provided that Liberty agreed to defend, indemnify, and hold Thibodeaux harmless from all claims for damages including the costs of defense. ... Thus, according to the terms of the contract, Liberty was required to defend Thibodeaux against O'Neill's allegation that the building was defective.

 VOICE OF EXPERIENCE:

In the previous case example of <u>Morales v. Fanster</u>, the court determined that the landlord is not responsible for the benefit of third parties. Still, as a property manager, you should enforce all requirements of the lease. Lots of time and money would have been saved if this had been done in the above-mentioned case.

Invalid Provision. This clause provides that if any portion of the lease is held to be invalid, it shall not affect the validity of the remainder of the lease.

Interest. Any amount owed on the lease shall bear interest. The interest rate might be stated or it might be a formula, such as prime rate plus a designated percentage. A common provision is at the maximum legal rate. The clause would make it clear that interest is in addition to any late charges.

Joint and Several Liability. When there is more than one tenant signing the lease, this clause provides that the tenant shall be jointly and severally liable. This means that in the event the lease is breached, the landlord can sue one tenant separately, or all the tenants, and a suit against one tenant will not act to discharge the obligations of the other tenants.

Law Governing Agreement. This clause specifies which state laws govern any contract interpretation or dispute. It likely is the state where the property is located or the law of the state where the landlord is headquartered.

Lead-Based Paint Disclosure. The *FEDERAL REAL ESTATE DISCLOSURE AND NOTIFICATION ACT requires that owners disclose to buyers and renters the presence of lead-based paint and/or lead-based paint hazards for single-family residential dwellings.* These are single-family dwellings or single-family dwelling units (apartments) intended for residential use.

Lead-based paint hasn't been used in residential property since 1978.

The law requires known information or reports of lead-based paint for housing built prior to 1978. It is unlikely you would have knowledge or records of lead-based paint, but generally, most old oil-based paint used prior to the mid-1970s had a lead base.

The lessor or agent must supply prospective tenants of housing built prior to 1978 with a copy of the Environmental Protection Agency's pamphlet entitled, "Protect Your Family From Lead-Based Paint."

The lessee must acknowledge receipt of the pamphlet and the agent must sign and date it. Agents must maintain records of the notice for three years after commencement of the rental. (Also see the EPA's **Lead-Based Paint Renovation, Repair, and Painting Program (RRP)** on page 95.)

Violation of the rule can lead to civil and criminal penalties. For more information about lead-based paint, you can call the **Environmental Protection Agency at 1-800-424-LEAD**. In lieu of the federal disclosure, state disclosure, such as the California pamphlet entitled *Environmental Hazards: A Guide for Homeowners, Buyers, Landlords, and Tenants*, should be supplied to prospective tenants. A lead-based paint disclosure form can be found in Chapter 5.

Liability for Damages. This clause might provide that the landlord shall not be liable for damages to or loss of tenant property caused by acts of third persons (including theft), acts of God, plumbing breaks and leaks, electrical problems, etc. This clause would advise tenants to obtain insurance coverage if they desire to have their property protected against loss.

Limitations on Occupants. A landlord can limit the number of persons that can occupy a property. However, the number of persons must be reasonable.

The general rule of HUD is that limiting occupancy to two persons per bedroom is reasonable.

Occupancy is of importance to a lessor because the greater the number of occupants, the greater the wear and tear on the unit and common areas. In addition, if the landlord supplies any utilities, the usage increases with higher occupancy.

Besides limiting the number of persons allowed, the clause can limit the period for which guests can remain in the unit. This protects the lessor regarding the claim that permanent residents are actually guests. As an example, guest stays could be limited to 30 days.

Locks. This clause sets forth the tenant rights, if any, to make duplicate keys and put in additional locks. If tenants are allowed to change locks, the clause might specify the type of lock and the duty to provide keys to the lessor for emergency entry. This clause also makes tenants liable for damages to any locks.

Merchant Association. This shopping center and mall clause requires tenants to join a merchants association and be subject, as additional rent, to the dues and assessments of the association as well as the maintenance of a marketing and public relations staff.

Noise Levels. Malls and shopping center leases likely prohibit the use of outside speakers. The lease might also include a maximum decibel level for noise emanating from the premises.

Noncompetition. Just as an owner doesn't want tenants to compete in another location (See **Competition Clause**), tenants don't want other tenants to compete with them. Some tenants, like greeting card stores, might want lease provisions that restrict the lessor from leasing to a competitor. A delicatessen may want a clause prohibiting the lessor from opening a delicatessen in the shopping center or leasing another delicatessen.

A tenant with significant economic clout will often negotiate noncompetition clauses.

Nonwaiver. This clause basically says that the lessor's failure to declare a lessee default shall not waive the lessor's right to declare a default for a subsequent breach. The lessor has not waived the obligation of the tenant.

Notice of Nonresponsibility. The landlord shall have the right to post a notice of nonresponsibility on the premises.

> *In some states such as California, the failure of the lessor to post a notice of nonreponsibility within ten days of knowledge that the tenant has authorized construction work makes the property subject to mechanics' liens for which he/she may be responsible.*

Notices. This clause provides that all notices shall be in writing and designates the person(s) to be served. It might provide for service by registered mail.

Operating Costs. A lease might provide that certain operational costs, such as parking lot maintenance, exterior lights, security services, etc., be paid by the tenants. The lease would have to specify which operational costs the tenants would bear and how the costs would be apportioned to the various tenants.

Option to Purchase. It is often necessary for lessors of commercial buildings to give a tenant an option to purchase. If the landlord wants the tenant and the tenant insists on the option, then completion of the lease agreement may hinge on giving the tenant this option.

> *To be enforceable, options to purchase require that consideration be given to the optionor (the owner). Options are assignable.*

Options are often given at prices that are so high that neither the lessor nor leasing agent believe that the option will ever be exercised. Changing situations, as well as market changes, can result in the exercise of the option. Unless the management contract or a separate document provides for commission upon the option being exercised, the broker would have located a buyer for just management and/or rental fees.

A clause similar to the following could be set forth in the lease (if not covered in the property management contract):

> "In the event that the option to purchase is exercised during the period of or during any extension of this lease, then the lessor or agrees to pay [broker] [   ] percent of the option price at close of escrow. The lessor also irrevocably assigns such commission rights to the broker and hereby instructs the escrow holder to disburse such funds to the broker upon close of escrow."

The option to purchase could be set forth as an addendum to the lease such as **Figure 4-2**.

Option to Renew (or Extend). Options can be for lease extensions. They might allow the tenant to extend the lease for one or more periods of time at the same rent or higher rent. Courts have held that options to extend leases at market rent are enforceable because market

Figure 4-2

OPTION AGREEMENT

(To be used with a Purchase Agreement. May also be used with a Lease.)

(C.A.R. Form OA, Revised 4/08)

Date _____ , at _____ , California
_____ ("Optionor"), grants to
_____ , ("Optionee"),
on the following terms and conditions, an option ("Option") to purchase the real property and improvements situated in
(City) _____ *Marina del Rey* _____ , County of _____ ,
California, described as _____ *123 Sail Avenue* _____ ("Property") on the terms and
conditions specified in the attached: ☐ Real Estate Purchase Agreement ☐ Other _____ ,
which is incorporated by reference as a part of this Option.

1. **OPTION CONSIDERATION:**
   A. _____ Dollars ($ _____),
      payable upon acceptance of this Option, or, if checked, ☐ _____ ,
      by ☐ cash, ☐ cashier's check, ☐ personal check, or ☐ _____
      made payable to _____ .
   OR B. ☐ (If checked) Mutual execution of the attached lease specified in paragraph 2A.
   OR C. ☐ (If checked) Both 1A and 1B.

2. ☐ **LEASE (If checked)**
   A. The attached Lease Agreement dated _____ , between Optionee as Tenant and Optionor as Landlord, is
      incorporated by reference as part of this Option.
   B. If the Option is exercised, the lease shall terminate on the earliest of (i) the date scheduled for Close Of Escrow under the
      Purchase Agreement, or as extended in writing, (ii) the Close Of Escrow of the Purchase Agreement, or (iii) mutual cancellation
      of the Purchase Agreement.

3. **OPTION PERIOD:** The Option shall begin (on date) _____ , and shall end at 11:59 p.m.
   (or at ☐ _____), on (date) _____ .

4. **MANNER OF EXERCISE:** Optionee may exercise the Option **only** by delivering a written unconditional notice of exercise, signed
   by Optionee, to Optionor, or _____ , who is authorized to receive it.
   A copy of the unconditional notice of exercise shall be delivered to the Brokers identified in this Agreement.

5. **NON-EXERCISE:** If the Option is not exercised in the manner specified, within the option period or any written extension thereof,
   or if it is terminated under any provision of this Option, then:
   A. The Option and all rights of Optionee to purchase the Property shall immediately terminate without notice; and
   B. All Option Consideration paid, rent paid, services rendered to Optionor, and improvements made to the Property, if any, by
      Optionee, shall be retained by Optionor in consideration of the granting of the Option; and
   C. Optionee shall execute, acknowledge, and deliver to Optionor, within **5 (or ☐ _____) calendar Days** of Optionor's request,
      a release, quitclaim deed, or any other document reasonably required by Optionor or a title insurance company to verify the
      termination of the Option.

6. **EFFECT OF DEFAULT ON OPTION:**
   A. Optionee shall have no right to exercise this Option if Optionee has not performed any obligation imposed by, or is in default of,
      any obligation of this Option, any addenda, or any document incorporated by reference.
   B. In addition, if a lease is incorporated by reference in paragraph 2A, Optionee shall have no right to exercise this Option if
      Optionor, as Landlord, has given to Optionee, as Tenant, two or more notices to cure any default or non-performance under
      that lease.

7. **OPTIONOR DISCLOSURE:**
   A. Unless exempt, if the Property contains one-to-four residential dwelling units, Optionor shall within **7 (or _____) Days After**
      entering into this Option provide to Optionee (i) a Real Estate Transfer Disclosure Statement, a Natural Hazard Disclosure
      Statement, a Notice of Private Transfer Fee and other disclosures required by Civil Code §§1102 and 1103 et seq.,
      (ii) ☐ a preliminary title report, and (iii) ☐ _____
   B. If any disclosure or notice specified in 7A is delivered to Optionee after the Option is Signed, Optionee shall have the right to
      cancel this Option within **3 Days After** delivery in person or **5 Days After** delivery by deposit in the mail by giving written notice
      of cancellation to Optionor or Optionor's agent.

Optionee and Optionor acknowledge receipt of copy of this page, which constitutes Page 1 of _____ Pages.
Optionee's Initials (_____) (_____) Optionor's Initials (_____) (_____)

Reviewed by _____ Date _____

OA REVISED 4/08 (PAGE 1 OF 3)

OPTION AGREEMENT (OA PAGE 1 OF 3)

| Agent: WALT HUBER | Phone: | Fax: | Prepared using zipForm® software |
| Broker: WALT HUBER REALTOR | | | |

Property Address: _____ Date: _____

8. **PURCHASE AGREEMENT:**
   A. All of the time limits contained in the attached Purchase Agreement, which begin on the date of Acceptance of the Purchase Agreement, shall instead begin to run on the date the Option is exercised.
   B. If this Option is exercised and Optionee cancels pursuant to any contingency in the attached purchase agreement, including but not limited to any right of inspection or financing provision, all option consideration paid, rent paid, services rendered to Optionor, and improvements to the Property, if any, by Optionee, shall be retained by Optionor in consideration of the granting of the Option.
   C. If this Option is exercised, upon close of escrow of the attached Purchase Agreement, ☐ all, or ☐ $ _____ , of the Option Consideration, and ☐ (if checked) $ _____ per month of rent actually paid by Optionee, shall be applied toward Optionee's down payment obligations under that Agreement. Optionee is advised that the full amount of the option consideration applied toward any down payment may not be counted by a lender for financing purposes.

9. **DISPUTE RESOLUTION:** Optionee and Optionor agree that any dispute or claim arising between them out of this Agreement shall be decided by the same method agreed to for resolving disputes in the attached Purchase Agreement.

10. **DAMAGE OR DESTRUCTION:** If, prior to exercise of this Option, by no fault of Optionee, the Property is totally or partially damaged or destroyed by fire, earthquake, accident or other casualty, Optionee may cancel this Agreement by giving written notice to Optionor, and is entitled to the return of all Option Consideration paid. However, if, prior to Optionee giving notice of cancellation to Optionor, the Property has been repaired or replaced so that it is in substantially the same condition as of the date of acceptance of this Agreement, Optionee shall not have the right to cancel this Agreement.

11. **OPTIONEE INSPECTION:** Optionee ☐ has, ☐ has not conducted inspections, investigations, tests, surveys and other studies of the Property prior to entering into this Option.

12. **RECORDING:** Optionor or Optionee shall upon request, execute, acknowledge, and deliver to the other a memorandum of this Option for recording purposes. All recording fees and taxes shall be paid by the party requesting recordation.

13. **OTHER TERMS AND CONDITIONS, including attached supplements:** _____
    _____
    _____
    _____
    _____
    _____
    _____
    _____
    _____
    _____
    _____

14. **ATTORNEY FEES:** In any action, proceeding, or arbitration between Optionee and Optionor arising out of this Option, the prevailing Optionee or Optionor shall be entitled to reasonable attorney fees and costs from the non-prevailing Optionee or Optionor.

15. **BROKER COMPENSATION FROM OPTIONEE:** If applicable, Optionee agrees to pay compensation to Broker as specified in a separate written agreement between Optionee and Broker.

16. **TIME OF ESSENCE; ENTIRE CONTRACT; CHANGES:** Time is of the essence. All understandings between the parties are incorporated in this Option. Its terms are intended by the parties as a final, complete, and exclusive expression of their agreement with respect to its subject matter, and may not be contradicted by evidence of any prior agreement or contemporaneous oral agreement. **This Agreement may not be extended, amended, modified, altered, or changed, except in writing signed by Optionee and Optionor.**

17. **TERMS AND CONDITIONS OF OFFER:** This is an offer for an option to purchase Property on the above terms and conditions. This Option and any supplement, addendum, or modification, including any photocopy or facsimile, may be signed in two or more counterparts, all of which shall constitute one and the same writing. Optionee has read and acknowledges receipt of a copy of this offer.

Optionee and Optionor acknowledge receipt of copy of this page, which constitutes Page 2 of _____ Pages.
Optionee's Initials (_____) (_____)   Optionor's Initials (_____) (_____)

OA REVISED 4/08 (PAGE 2 OF 3)

Reviewed by _____ Date _____

EQUAL HOUSING OPPORTUNITY

OPTION AGREEMENT (OA PAGE 2 OF 3)

Untitled

Property Address: _____ Date: _____

18. EXPIRATION OF OFFER: Unless Acceptance of Offer is signed by Optionor, and a signed copy delivered in person, by mail, or facsimile, and personally received by Optionee, or by _____, who is authorized to receive it, by (date) _____ , at _____ ☐ AM ☐ PM , the offer shall be deemed revoked.

OPTIONEE _____

OPTIONEE _____
Address _____
_____

Telephone _____ Fax _____

19. BROKER COMPENSATION FROM OPTIONOR: If applicable, Optionor agrees to pay compensation to Broker as specified in a separate written agreement between Optionor and Broker.

20. ACCEPTANCE OF OPTION: Optionor warrants that Optionor is the owner of the Property or has the authority to execute this Agreement. Optionor accepts and agrees to grant an Option to purchase the Property on the above terms and conditions.

If checked: ☐ SUBJECT TO ATTACHED COUNTER OFFER, DATED _____ .

OPTIONOR _____

OPTIONOR _____
Address _____

Telephone _____ Fax _____

REAL ESTATE BROKERS:
A. Real Estate Brokers are not parties to the Agreement between Optionee and Optionor.
B. **COOPERATING BROKER COMPENSATION:** Listing Broker agrees to pay Cooperating Broker and Cooperating Broker agrees to accept, (i) the amount specified in the MLS, provided Cooperating Broker is a Participant of the MLS in which the Property is offered for Option or a reciprocal MLS; or (ii) ☐ (If checked) the amount specified in a separate written agreement (C.A.R. Form CBC) between Listing Broker and Cooperating Broker.

Broker _____ By _____ Date _____

Address _____

Telephone _____ Fax _____

Broker _____ By _____ Date _____

Address _____

Telephone _____ Fax _____

Published and Distributed by:
REAL ESTATE BUSINESS SERVICES, INC.
a subsidiary of the California Association of REALTORS®
525 South Virgil Avenue, Los Angeles, California 90020

Reviewed by _____ Date _____

OA REVISED 4/08 (PAGE 3 OF 3)

OPTION AGREEMENT (OA PAGE 3 OF 3)

Untitled

rent is ascertainable. Some leases provide that the parties choose a third party to determine what the market rent will be. However, the authors strongly recommend rent be specified or a formula for determining the rent be set forth in the lease.

A notice to renew should be timely or the right will ordinarily be lost. However, there are exceptions where a late notice to renew might be excused.

Case Example

Burroughs v. Ben's Auto Park, Inc., 27 C.2d 449 (1945)

The Court of Appeal held that agreement between lessor and lessee constituted a renewal creating a new and distinct tenancy, and not an extension stretching the former terms of the lease.

Cumberland Center v. Southeast Mgmt., 492 S.E.2d 546 (Ga.App. 1997)

In deciding whether a succeeding lease is substantially a renewal of a preceding lease or altogether a new lease, the determination can be based on whether the succeeding lease employs drastically different terms, not simply somewhat different considerations, i.e., is the lessee occupying substantially the same space under substantially the same terms? If the succeeding lease employs substantially the same terms as the preceding lease, it may be considered a renewal even though technically a "new" lease.

VOICE OF EXPERIENCE:

New lease vs. lease extension—this is the question! In either of the case examples above, when writing the lease, it would have been safer to state "This is a new tenancy and not an extension."

Parking. Leases for both commercial and residential properties might have parking clauses specifying reserved parking areas for tenants and/or customers. If the lease is subject to any parking rules or charges they will be referenced in this clause.

The tenant may be protected in that the lease might prohibit the lessor from reducing parking by placing additional structures in the present parking area. (Often a lessor will place a kiosk, such as for photo services, in the parking area to increase income.)

The parking clause might specify lessor and/or lessee responsibilities for maintenance of the parking areas.

Parking rules and regulations might include:

1. right to issue parking stickers as well as to refuse to reissue stickers for vehicles violating rules;
2. right to have violating vehicles towed away at lessee's expense;
3. limitation on size of vehicles allowed (such as full-size sedans);
4. parking charges and validation procedures;
5. agreement that lessor shall not be liable for damage to or theft from parked vehicles;
6. prohibition against washing or waxing vehicles in parking areas, and
7. rights of lessor to modify parking rules and regulations.

Performance Under Protest. The parties might pay amounts due under the lease without waiving any rights to dispute the amounts by indicating that payment is made under protest. In this way they retain the rights to seek arbitration or legal remedies.

Pets. A pet provision might allow pets, prohibit pets completely, or allow pets subject to certain restrictions.

Even though a landlord has a no-pet prohibition in the lease, the landlord cannot exclude seeing-eye dogs and support animals utilized by handicapped tenants.

Possession. The lease would specify when possession is to be delivered to the tenant. Because a tenant in possession might not vacate, which would require legal action, the lease should provide that neither the owner nor agent will be liable for any damages resulting from the lessor being unable to provide possession when due. While the lease will remain in effect and cannot be voided by the tenant, the clause would provide that rent shall not start until possession is given.

Prohibited Use. This clause prohibits any illegal use of the premises. It might also prohibit any use that increases the lessor's insurance premiums without the lessor's consent or a use that interferes with other tenants' rights to quiet enjoyment of the premises. The clause could also prohibit specific activities such as topless entertainment or adult bookstores.

Quiet Enjoyment. *QUIET ENJOYMENT means that the landlord will not interfere with the tenants rightful use of the premises.* Some leases, nevertheless, set forth the rights of these tenants.

There is an implied covenant of quiet enjoyment in every lease.

A breach of quiet enjoyment could be a landlord's making noisy repairs late at night, landlord's wrongful entry into the tenant's rental unit, a landlord's failure to provide heat when required to do so by the lease, etc.

A tenant can treat a landlord's failure to provide quiet enjoyment of the premises as a breach of the lease (constructive eviction), and can vacate the premises and be excused from further rent obligations. Tenants will often look for some fault to find a basis to claim constructive eviction.

If a court determined that the landlord's actions (or failure to act) were not sufficient to justify the tenant's breaking the lease, then the tenant would still remain liable for rent under the lease even though he or she has vacated the property.

Renewal of Lease. A lease might provide for renewal as well as a time period to exercise the renewal. A tenant's failure to exercise the renewal right by a specified date might be forgiven if the tenant had made significant improvements to the property and the lessor knew that the tenant intended to renew. To allow the lessor to refuse a renewal and demand higher rent in such a case would result in unconscionable damage to the tenant. The late renewal should be excused.

A lease with unlimited renewal options is not necessarily invalid, however, it cannot exceed any statutory limit.

Other Leases. This clause provides that the lessee will not hold the lessor liable for any lease violation of any other tenant.

Outside Displays. This clause might be used to prohibit or require lessor approval to place merchandise or displays outside the premises, such as on walkways.

Recapture Clause. *A RECAPTURE CLAUSE in percentage leases provides the lessor with the opportunity to cancel the lease after a stated period of time unless a particular annual volume of gross sales is reached.* As an example, if a store strives for full markups and avoids clearing-inventory clearance sales, the volume is likely to be less than expected from the type of business and square feet leased.

VOICE OF EXPERIENCE:

If your shopping center has a waiting list of potential tenants with high sales records, then termination of an under-performing tenant's lease might be in order. A recapture clause allows this termination to be done legally.

Receipt of Lease (Rules). By signing the lease, the lessee acknowledges receipt of a copy of the lease. The clause might also cover tenant rules and regulations. The tenant also acknowledges that he or she has read the lease and rules (if applicable).

Recording. The lessor and lessee agree to acknowledge the lease (before a notary) if requested by the other party so that the lease can be recorded. Recording would give constructive notice of the lease interests.

Remedies. The lessor remedies in the event of lessee default are set forth. They include termination of tenant's right to possession and rerenting to mitigate damages, suing for damages, leaving the tenant in possession and suing as the rent becomes due, etc.

Removal of Property. If a tenant abandons the premises leaving behind personal property, this clause authorizes the lessor to remove the property left behind and store it. Generally, the property can be sold if not claimed, and storage fees paid, after a statutory period (90 days in California). The proceeds would first apply to the cost of the sale, then the cost of storage and removal and the balance then applied to any monies owed to the lessor under the lease. Any balance should go to the lessee.

Renewal. A lease might contain a clause that provides for automatic renewal of the lease. This places the burden of nonrenewal upon the tenant. The lease provides that unless the tenant notifies the lessor to the contrary within a stated period prior to the expiration of the lease, it automatically is renewed.

In some states, such as California, the clause is voidable by the party who did not prepare the lease unless the renewal or extension clause appears in at least eight-point boldface type immediately prior to the place where the lessee signs the lease.

In California, the tenant cannot waive the boldface type requirements. Other states have similar limitations on automatic residential lease renewals or extensions. The protection of the requirement for boldface notice for automatic renewal does not generally apply to nonresidential tenants. They are considered more sophisticated so are not afforded this protection.

A "lease renewal" is considered a new lease and it could provide for a change in terms. A "lease extension" is the same lease, but the term is stretched out.

Rent Clause. The lease will specify the amount of rent or provide a formula or means to determine the amount of rent. Generally, the total rent shall be stated for the term of the lease and that it will be paid monthly in advance in a stated amount. For a percentage lease it would list the rent as minimum rent. The lease clause might indicate that the dollars are U.S. dollars. (Note: Other nations may also use the dollar designation.)

The clause might prohibit the tenant from using any set-offs he/she might have against the amount due. (If the tenant claimed the lessor owed him/her money, he/she could not deduct the amount owed from his/her rent payment.)

The clause includes any late charges and the length of any grace period that was provided the tenant before the late charge is assessed.

Most leases do not allow any grace period, although state laws might provide a grace period for residential tenants.

Care should be used in setting late charges. If there is rent control, the late charge could result in rent that exceeds the maximum allowed. Rent control increases may vary from year to year. In Los Angeles, rent control increases have been decreased to 3% annually.

The lease might provide that the last month's rent shall be paid in advance. Because last month's rent is taxed to an owner when it is received, but a security deposit is not taxed unless forfeited, many owners prefer increased security deposits to last month's rent.

Percentage leases generally provide for a minimum rent plus a percentage of the net sales. The lease might define net sales as the gross sales less:

1. returns where credit is given;
2. settlements to customers for defective goods;
3. delivery charges;
4. interest charges (paid by the customer);
5. bad checks;
6. sales taxes;
7. gift certificates sold (until redeemed).

As an encouragement to retail stores to go for a volume business, percentage leases often provide for a decreasing percentage of the gross as volume increases. For instance, a furniture store has 18 percent rent for the first $1,000,000 in sales in a calendar year and 14 percent for the next $1,000,000 and 10 percent for all over $2,000,000. This graduated rent would encourage lower markups and sales. The lower percentages should begin at a figure you would estimate for an annual volume. In this manner, a tenant who achieves lower rent percentages really provides gravy income to the lessor.

Rent adjustment provisions can be set forth in lease addendums.

Rental Inducements. Any inducements, such as free rent given to the lessee to lease the premises, shall be canceled if lessee is in default. Such inducements shall immediately become due, even if cured by the lessee. (This acts as an inducement against lessee default.)

Repairs. This clause might provide that the tenant indicates an inspection of the premises has been performed, and acknowledges that they are in good condition. The tenant also agrees that the premises will not be altered, repaired or changed without the written consent of the lessor.

Case Example

Wu v. Interstate Consol. Indus., 226 C.A. 3d 1511 (1991)

A renewal option in a lease provided that appraisers should set the fair market rental value if the parties could not agree as to the rent for the renewal period. The property, which was leased as a movie theater, was given a fair rental value of $3,000. However, the appraiser pointed out that the fair rental value as shops would be $8,500. The landlord demanded the higher figure.

The Court of Appeals affirmed that the purpose of the option was to allow the business to continue, not to force the tenant to abandon the premises. This was a theater lease and theater rent should apply.

▼

Sage Realty Corporation v. Omnicom Group, inc., 705 N.Y.S.2d 500
(S.Ct. New York County 2000)

Lease provision did not require landlord to compute rent based on union employee's "new hire" rate after new collective bargaining agreement provided for new hire rate at 80% of the minimum regular hourly wage rate.

The clause might also require that repairs be under the control of the lessor, but at the lessee's expense. Some clauses provide that improvements to the premises will remain with the premises at the end of the lease. (See fixture's clause.)

Restoration. Lessee agrees to restore premises to the condition it was in when rented. If lessee has responsibilities for maintenance of systems, they shall be in good and proper operating condition. Damage from removal of fixtures and equipment shall be repaired, unless it has been agreed that they shall remain. This clause could require removal and replacement of contaminated soil.

Right of First Refusal. This means that should the owner wish to accept a bona fide purchase offer from another party, the owner must first allow the tenant to match the offer during a specified time period. If the tenant does not match the offer, then the purchase can proceed. The owner is under no obligation to sell and can refuse any purchase offer.

> *While an owner gives up something when he or she gives a tenant an option, a right of first refusal (or preemptive right) gives absolutely nothing.*

A right of first refusal can be included as to a lease extension. The tenant has the right to match any lease terms offered by another prospective tenant.

There have been cases where an owner has given one tenant a right of first refusal and another an option to purchase. There have been other cases where an owner has given more than one tenant a right of first refusal (see next page for case examples). The reason has been poor lease administration where an owner (or manager) had forgotten or didn't know of a provision buried in a lease given either long ago or by a previous owner or manager. In such cases, the owner and/or manager would be subject to legal expenses and what could be significant damages.

VOICE OF EXPERIENCE:

When the owner gives an "option," he/she gives up the right to sell to other parties, even if they offer more money, but the optionee is not committed. In a "first right of refusal," the seller has the right to accept a better offer if the first buyer refuses to match it.

Rules and Regulations. This clause clearly states that rules and regulations are incorporated into the lease. (To avoid problems, the rules and regulations should be identified and initialed by the parties to the lease and included as an attachment.)

Sale by Lessor. This clause provides that if the lessor sells the premises the lessor shall be relieved of all liability under the lease (no secondary liability if the buyer breaches any provision of the lease).

Case Example

Ellis v. Chevron U.S.A., Inc., 201 C.A. 3d 132 (1988)

A service station lease gave Chevron a right of first refusal as to any new lease when the lease expired. Prior to expiration of the lease, the landlord sought other lease proposals. A proposal received and which was conveyed to Chevron included an offer to construct a new facility on the site and acquire an adjacent site.

Chevron wished to exercise their right of first refusal but would not agree to build a new building or acquire the adjacent site, neither of which they needed.

The court did not agree that the owners had breached an implied covenant of good faith and fair dealing by not restricting the terms as to offers they would entertain. The offer was considered reasonable and if Chevron did not wish to meet it, they could not exercise their right of first refusal.

The court also pointed out that the lease was prepared by Chevron so any ambiguities in the lease should be resolved against Chevron.

> *First rights of refusal must meet more advantageous terms to the lessor. Any ambiguity in the document will be resolved against the maker of the contract.*

Richard Barton Enterprises, Inc. v. Tsern, 928 P.2d 368 (Utah 1996)

Tsern also argues that the trial court erred in ruling that Tsern's obligation to repair the elevator continued after Barton exercised the option to purchase the building because his obligations under the lease were extinguished by Barton's exercise of the option. The general rule is that a lessee's exercise of an option to purchase terminates the lease and all future obligations under the lease.

VOICE OF EXPERIENCE:

First right of refusal usually permits the first offeror to match a subsequent better offer. Whatever the intent is, write it down so no misunderstanding can lead you and your clients to court.

Security. This clause might provide that the lessor is not obligated to employ any security personnel or security services and that the malfunction of any existing security system or the discontinuance of any security service shall not obligate the lessor in any manner.

Security Deposit. The amount of any security deposit will be set forth, as well as the tenant's right to the return of the deposit, and the landlord's right to use the deposit for tenant damage, unauthorized alteration removal, back rent, etc.

Services. Which services will be performed or supplied by the lessor shall be set forth in the lease. As an example, the lease may provide that the lessor will provide a reasonable amount of hot and cold water, heat, air conditioning, janitorial services in common areas, exterior maintenance, etc.

The provision generally provides that the landlord's failure to provide any of the services is not grounds for a tenant's defense of constructive eviction. (This would probably not be enforceable on residential leases.)

The clause might provide that the lessor shall not be liable if failure to provide services results from conditions beyond the control of the lessor.

On net leases, the lessor might require that the lessee shall be obligated to provide service contracts for HVAC, boiler, elevator, pools, landscaping, etc. This would provide the lessor with some assurance that the facilities will be properly maintained.

Signatures. The lease might indicate that it is offered to the tenant, but it shall not be binding on the owner until signed by the owner or an authorized representative of the owner.

Signs. This clause might set forth the right of the tenant to place signs on the premises. These signs may be limited to size, shape, construction, color and lighting. The clause could require that the lessor be responsible for installation of all signs (at lessee's expense).

Smoking. The lease could require the lessee to enforce a no-smoking regulation on the leased premises.

Surrender. Lessee agrees to turn over the premises to the lessor at the termination of the tenancy in the same state as received other than normal wear and tear.

The surrender clause might require a "notice of surrender."

This notice must usually be given at least 30 days prior to the end of the lease stating that the tenant intends to surrender possession to the landlord at the termination of the lease. This notice lets the lessor know that the tenant does not intend to negotiate an extension or a new lease so that the lessor can begin activities to release the premises.

Taxes. Net leases will have a clause that requires the tenant to pay property taxes and insurance. Preferably, this clause will require the tenant to pay one-twelfth of the annual estimated taxes and insurance costs with each monthly payment. This protects a lessor

against a tenant default when taxes are due. The lease might require the lessee to pay personal property taxes on property owned by the lessee prior to delinquency.

Term. This clause spells out the beginning and ending dates of the lease.

Time is of the Essence. This clause indicates dates and times set forth in the lease shall be strictly adhered to. In the absence of this clause a court would likely allow a "reasonable period" beyond a time specified.

Use. The use for which the premises are rented should be set forth. You would likely also want to spell out that the premises may not be used for any other use or purpose without the written consent of the lessor.

Many commercial leases specify what the tenant can sell.

Some even specify items that the tenant cannot sell. In addition, some leases protect tenants in providing that competing stores will not be allowed in the particular shopping center.

Utilities. Tenant obligation for utility costs are set forth in this clause. If the tenants are to pay utilities, and there aren't separate meters, then leases should be clear as to each tenant's share. As an example, it could be based per unit or on the proportion of square feet occupied by each tenant.

Case Example

Pay 'N Pak v. Superior Court, 210 C.A. 3d 1404 (1989)

Tenants, who leased a store in a shopping center, had a lease that restricted the use to the sale of baby-related items. The tenants wished to go out of business and wanted to assign their lease to stores specializing in the sale of ceiling fans and fireplace accessories. The landlord, Pay 'N Pak, operated a home improvement store in the center and refused the assignment since it would bring in stores in competition with them. The tenants sued for compensatory and punitive damages. The trial court sided with the tenants, pointing out that only a minor portion of Pay 'N Pak's business was derived from the sale of fans or fireplace accessories.

The Court of Appeals reversed the trial court, holding that the volume of sales for these items should not have been the sole determinant of whether the refusal to accept an assignment was unreasonably withheld. While a landlord cannot use a clause against assignment for its own economic gain by attempting to charge higher rents, reasonable use restrictions in a shopping center are valid. A landlord may protect itself from competition.

Landlords may refuse lease assignments in order to avoid competition in their own shopping centers. This protects their existing tenants from competitors.

▼

> **Morgan Products v. Park Plaza of Oshkosh,** 598 N.W.2d 626 (Wis.App.1999)
>
> Some of the factors a landlord may reasonably consider when deciding whether or not to sublease are the financial responsibility of the proposed assignee; suitability of the use for the particular property; legality of the proposed use; need for alteration of the premises; and the nature of the occupancy, i.e., office, factory. ... On the other hand, it is not commercially reasonable if the sole basis for a consent denial is so that a landlord can charge a higher rent than the contract rent.

Waiver. A waiver of one term by the lessor shall not be regarded as a waiver of any other term.

Waterbed. While waterbeds are not allowed above the ground floor in some older residential buildings because the weight could cause structural damage, the reason lessors do not want waterbeds is because of potential damage to walls, ceilings and carpeting from leakage.

You can protect yourself by requiring that the tenant carry waterbed insurance to protect your property against damage.

III. CHAPTER SUMMARY

Standard form leases simplify the administration of leases. However, additional clauses and clause alternations might be necessary and may include the following:

Advertising. Sets forth advertising requirements for tenant. (Usually cooperative with other tenant with percentage leases.)

Assignment and Subleasing. This either prohibits or requires lessor approval for assignments or subleases.

Arbitration. It provides for mandatory consensual binding arbitration of lessor/lessee disputes.

Bad Checks. It provides for charges for bad checks.

Bankruptcy. This allows the lessor the option to terminate lease if tenant files bankruptcy or assigns lease to creditors.

Broker. Lessee states that no broker or a named broker helped to negotiate the lease. (Entitlement to commission.)

Codes. Tenant agrees to comply with municipal and state codes.

Common Areas. This covers maintenance and/or use of common areas.

Complete Agreement. The parties acknowledge that there is no agreement other than is set forth in the lease.

Covenant to Remain in Business. This clause requires tenant to remain in business. Otherwise, on a percentage lease, tenant could cease operations and pay the minimum rent.

Default by Tenant. This clause might define default and set forth the lessor's remedies.

Eminent Domain. Tenant rights, if any, if property is taken by eminent domain.

Escalator Clause. Provides for graduated increase in payments for the lease.

Fixtures. It may provide what is (or isn't) a fixture and removal rights, if any.

Guarantors. This indicates that another party agrees to be liable on the lease.

Hold Harmless Clause. Provides that tenant will not hold lessor liable for any injury or property damage caused by the condition of the property.

Hours of Operation. This specifies the hours and days a business must be kept open.

Insurance. This specifies the insurance coverage that the tenant must carry.

Law Governing Agreement. This clause specifies which state law shall apply.

Lead-Based Paint Disclosure. This is a federally mandated disclosure.

Noncompetition. Restrictions are placed on tenants and/or the owner as to competing businesses or products.

Notice of Nonresponsibility. Lessor's right to post the notice for protection against mechanics' liens.

Operating Costs. Sets forth tenant's responsibility for operating costs, such as maintenance of common areas and common area utilities.

Option to Renew. Tenant's option to renew the lease on stated terms.

Possession. The time possession is to be given.

Prohibited Use. Uses that are not allowed.

Quiet Enjoyment. Lessor agrees not to interfere with tenant's proper use of premises.

Receipt of Lease. Tenant acknowledges receipt of lease and applicable occupancy rules.

Renewal. Covers an automatic renewal of the lease unless lessor or lessee gives notice.

Rent. The amount of rent and/or any formulas for determining rent and other charges.

Repairs. Tenant acknowledges the property is in good condition and agrees that alterations and repairs will only be performed with the lessor's approval.

Rules and Regulations. Rules and regulations are incorporated into the lease.

Security Deposit. The amount of any deposit and its purpose.

Services. Specifies what, if any, services shall be supplied by the lessor.

Signatures. The lessor is not obligated until the lessor signs the lease.

Surrender. Lessee agrees to turn over premises to lessor at termination of the lease.

Taxes. Lessee agrees to pay property taxes on a net lease.

Time is of the Essence. Dates stated are considered essential and lateness would breach the agreement.

Use. Sets forth the specified use for which property may be used.

Utilities. Obligations for utility costs are set forth.

IV. CHAPTER QUIZ

1. A purchaser of a commercial building would want the tenant to furnish a(n):

    a. estoppel certificate.
    b. notice of nonresponsibility.
    c. right of first refusal.
    d. lead-based paint disclosure.

2. When a prospective tenant has had credit problems, a lessor is MOST LIKELY to request a(n):

    a. accelerated payment clause.
    b. guarantor.
    c. holdover provision.
    d. recapture clause.

3. A hold harmless clause would likely be unenforceable by a lessor of:

    a. a retail store.
    b. office space.
    c. industrial property.
    d. a residential property.

4. A clause that discourages a tenant from remaining in possession after the lease expires would be a(n):

    a. holdover clause.
    b. right of first refusal.
    c. estoppel certificate.
    d. nonwaiver clause.

5. Tenants A and B sign a lease in which they agree to be jointly and severally liable. If past rent is due, who can the lessor sue?

    a. Tenant A alone
    b. Tenant B alone
    c. Tenants A and B together
    d. Any of the above

6. A tenant hires a contractor to remodel a store. The lessor would be concerned with:

    a. attornment.
    b. the recapture clause.
    c. a notice of nonresponsibility.
    d. a nonwaiver clause.

7. The right to cancel a lease when the tenant's sales are not up to expectations would be set forth in the:

    a. quiet enjoyment clause.
    b. attornment clause.
    c. recapture clause.
    d. accelerated payments clause.

8. In California, boldface eight-point type face would most likely be required in a residential lease that provides for:

    a. lead-based paint removal.
    b. automatic renewal if no notice is given.
    c. a purchase option.
    d. any of the above.

9. A furniture store had a percentage lease specifying rent at 16 percent of net sales for the first $1,000,000 of sales. Sales over $1,000,000 would MOST LIKELY have a percentage of:

    a. 14 percent.
    b. 18 percent.
    c. 24 percent.
    d. 32 percent.

10. A tenant has a right to buy the property from the lessor, but this right only applies should the lessor decide to sell to another. If the lessor is not obligated to sell, this right would be a(n):

    a. option.
    b. right of first refusal.
    c. attornment.
    d. nonwaiver agreement.

ANSWERS: 1. a; 2. b; 3. d; 4. a; 5. d; 6. c; 7. c; 8. b; 9. a; 10. b

DO NOT BLOCK INTERSECTION

THE COW'S END

ADDITIONAL SUMMER WEEKEND BEACH PARKING ←

REAL ESTATE SALES, RENTALS & DEVELOPMENT
SAIL REALTY INC. 821-SAIL
FAMILY OWNED AND OPERATED SINCE 1969

SAIL REALTY INC.

Wa 00

P PARKING ANYONE →

Chapter 5
Residential Property Management

KEY WORDS AND TERMS

Comparative Market Analysis
Confirmation of Lease
Constructive Eviction
Development Fees
Habitability
Lead-Based Paint Disclosure
Moratorium
Population Bulge
Prequalification of Tenants
Qualification of Tenants
Quiet Enjoyment
Quit or Cure

Quit or Pay Rent
Rent Control
Self-Help Eviction
Stratified Housing Market
Supply and Demand
Thirty-Day Notice
Three-Day Notice
Turnover Rate
Uniform Residential Landlords and Tenant Act
Unlawful Detainer Action
Zoning

CHAPTER 5 OUTLINE

I. Residential Defined

Residential property is property where people live, be it single-family residences, condos, apartments, etc.

For the purpose of this text we have included in this chapter the management of homes and apartments. In Chapter 7, we will cover additional residential management property types including mobile home parks, housing for the elderly, single-room occupancy, condominium association housing, etc.

II. Residential Housing Need

A. FAMILY UNITS

The need for residential units is determined more by the number of family units than raw population.

As an example, seven people in one family require but one housing unit, but seven persons who each desire to live alone would mean seven units.

B. ECONOMIC CONDITIONS

While the national economy is important concerning housing needs, the local economy is more important as it can run counter to the national economy. As an example, while housing starts were down during the early 1960s, there were areas where new housing was in great demand, such as areas of government spending for defense programs. In the early 1990s, there was a strong housing market nationally, but most of California's housing market was weak. Layoffs and hiring, plant openings and closings, new public facilities, and military base openings or closures will have a significant effect on the housing need within a local economy.

Economic conditions can influence coupling and uncoupling of family units. In times of high unemployment or high housing costs, families are more willing to share a housing unit than they are when unemployment is low and/or they are able to afford their separate residences.

Where parents live within commuting distance of their jobs, children will often decide that living with their parents is not so bad after all if they find that taxes, rent and car payments leave them nothing left for the good life.

C. SOCIETY CHANGES

At one time, care for seniors was both a moral responsibility and an economic necessity thrust upon children.

Some senior readers may remember three and four generations living within the same household, but we seldom see that today. Because of social security and pension plans, many senior citizens now have the means to live separately from their children. We have also seen the growth of divorce and with it the erosion of duty towards parents. Today, it is more probable that adult offspring sponge off their parents than the other way around.

Differences in lifestyles between parents and children, as well as the desire for privacy, contribute to the demise of extended family households, and the rise in assisted living facilities.

D. INTEREST CYCLES

There is a rental housing need cycle that is closely related to interest rates. When interest rates are low, ownership becomes more affordable and families leave the rental market in favor of ownership. When interest rates rise, the affordability of ownership drops, which keeps many families as renters when they would much prefer ownership.

E. POPULATION BULGES

Bulges in population age groups have effected housing needs. When the baby boomers born after World War II reached marriage age, they created an unprecedented demand for housing, which fueled the inflation of the 1970s. This class of baby boomers created a second-home demand in the 1980s that we can expect to result in an increased demand for retirement housing in the not too distant future.

F. POLITICAL CHANGES

Changes in ordinances, statutes and taxes will affect residential housing needs and costs as well as the likelihood of fulfillment of those needs.

1. Taxes

Low property taxes in a community will encourage people to live and own property within that community.

This encourages renters to then become owners. Low taxes also encourage development of residential rental projects. Lower taxes mean lower costs to owners.

High property taxes have a negative effect on new residential rental developments, which in turn limits new construction.

2. Moratoriums and Limits

Because of problems in supplying services, many communities have placed moratoriums on new housing developments. The effect of moratoriums has been to limit supply of new units to existing housing. This tends to reduce the vacancy factor of existing housing and raise rents.

The same results are achieved by limits on growth. We are witnessing a great deal of the, "I'm aboard, lets raise the drawbridge" mentality. Growth limits are a reality in many communities.

In some areas, growth limits are supported by property owners who realize that growth limits will increase the value of developed property as well as rents. Some supporters just want to keep others out of their areas so that they can continue the lifestyle they currently enjoy. The proponents of no or slow growth often claim to be acting out of a respect for the environment.

Communities experience greater housing pricing when they slow the growth rate below the housing demand for their area.

3. Development Fees

Development fees in many communities have been instituted for schools, police, fire, social services, etc.

These advanced fees must be paid to obtain a residential building permit. In some communities, these permits exceed $10,000 per unit.

Higher development costs result in higher costs for new construction and tend to increase market values of existing residential properties.

New residential rental properties will not be built unless the developers anticipate rents sufficient to cover the higher costs.

Because high development fees tend to limit development, the demand for housing will probably result in higher rents.

4. Rent Control

In some states like California and New York, rent control is legal in specified cities. With rent control, society's burden of providing reasonable or below-market rents is shifted from the community to individual landlords.

Some rent control ordinances are much more lenient than others. As an example, any rent can be charged when a property in Los Angeles becomes vacant because rent control only applies to subsequent increases in rent. In some areas, like San Francisco, the rent control basis remains the same between tenancies.

One of the problems with rent control is that it restricts the new housing supply, rather than meeting the needs of lower income people. It becomes obvious which area a developer will prefer if the choice is developing in a an area with rent control or an area with no rent control.

Developers and investors are motivated by yield and profit. Hence, as land values increase, lot sizes decrease.

Rent control also creates deteriorating structures—landlords will often only provide minimum maintenance to avoid code violations.

In New York, rent control has resulted in a poor utilization of property. Single persons will not give up rent-controlled six- and seven-room apartments to move into one-bedroom units if they have to pay more for the smaller unit.

Renters who can afford to buy have no incentive to purchase homes when housing costs are so reasonable. Many tenants who reside in rent-controlled buildings own vacation homes, while some own homes in the suburbs and only use their rent-controlled units for work-related purposes.

VOICE OF EXPERIENCE:

As a property manager, you should not be concerned about the fairness of rent control, but what the controls allow or don't allow concerning the properties you manage. Also be aware of all rules and regulations.

In some cases, improving the property or renting units furnished will allow a higher rent. There is normally an appeal process to implement the rent increase. You should be aware of this process and understand when an appeal has a reasonable chance of success.

Besides local ordinances, some properties financed under special government loan programs are also limited to rent control. However, you should be aware that many of these programs have escape clauses. Rents may no longer be subject to control if you refinance the property without a government loan. This provides an opportunity to significantly increase income.

Communities with rent control usually establish rent control committees who hear complaints. Unfortunately, some of these committees have gone far beyond the statutes in interpreting what can be allowed.

You should be aware of the statutes in an area so that you will know when to seek legal counsel.

Case Example

City of Santa Monica v. Yarmark, 203 C.A. 3d 153 (1988)

After the California Supreme Court upheld a Santa Monica ordinance that prohibited owners from demolishing residential property, the California Legislature passed the Ellis Act which prohibited local government from requiring a residential landlord to continue to keep residential properties available for leasing. In other words, the state said that a landlord, like any other business, can go out of business.

Santa Monica subsequently passed a measure that a tenant could not be evicted when the purpose was demolition unless the landlord had a demolition permit (a permit would only be granted if the city determined that the building was uninhabitable and beyond any remedy or the landlord agreed to build new rent controlled units).

The court held that the provision against eviction was invalid, as the purpose of the legislation was to evade the Ellis Act. The court pointed out that when local and state law conflict, then the local ordinance is preempted by state law.

State laws will prevail when in conflict with local laws.

Weis v. Lefkowitz, 690, N.Y.S.2d 130 (A.D.2Dept. 1999)

The outcome of this case deals with provisions of a stipulation of settlement and arbitration awards requiring tenant to pay more than the legal rent were unlawful and violative of public policy.

Chapter 5

5. Zoning

ZONING is public control of land use. Value drops when too much land is designated for a particular use. When not enough land is zoned for a particular use, then the value increases based upon the limited supply.

You should be aware that the zoning codes and symbols are not the same between communities. A C-4 zoning in one community might prohibit uses allowed by a C-4 zoning in another community.

By implementing zoning requirements for parking, setback, height, and green space, communities can control density.

Areas requiring more space per unit means that developers will have higher costs per unit because of the need for more land. This discourages new rental housing unless the developer feels that the additional costs will be met by increased rents.

Zoning can be appealed to a zoning appeals board and then to the courts. The courts will only overrule zoning laws if they find that they're too arbitrary or capricious.

Case Example

Berman v. City of West Hollywood Rent Stabilization, 197 C.A. 3d 837 (1988)

A rent control ordinance required landlords to paint all rental units at least once every four years. Berman refused to paint a unit claiming it was rented "as is." The rent control board ordered Berman to reduce rents based on the decrease in maintenance.

The court held that the ordinance was constitutional. The choice of painting or reducing rents was a reasonable means of providing for well-maintained, affordable housing.

Landlords should maintain their properties in good condition in order to avoid vacancies and potential legal liability.

Mayfair York Company v. New York State Divison of Housing and Community Renewal, 658 N.Y.S.2d 270 (A.D.1Dept. 1997)

Defendant did not act irrationally in finding that certain work done to the apartment, claimed by petitioner to constitute "improvements" within the meaning of the Rent Stabilization Code, justifying a rent increase, amounted only to normal maintenance and repair.

> **VOICE OF EXPERIENCE:**
>
> *The courts often side with the tenants where proper maintenance of property is involved. As a property manager, you should always encourage your owner to allow you to keep the property well maintained. It not only improves the value of the property, but may keep you both out of court!*

Zoning that is changed on existing property to disallow a current use generally allows the current use to continue as a nonconforming use. However, the use generally cannot be expanded nor allowed to restart after the use is discontinued.

G. TIME FOR DEVELOPMENT

It takes time for new housing to be developed to fill housing needs. It can take several years to go through the process from land acquisition to renting, because of approval and construction time. The housing market could change in this period of time. Other new projects could become available for rental, thus reducing the need for housing.

Due to costs involved, once land is acquired and approvals and financing obtained, projects must be continued, despite any economic changes.

H. STRATIFIED NEED

The need for housing is stratified by type of housing and rental price. As an example, there may be a tremendous demand for two-bedroom rentals under $500 per month, but a glut of available units at $2,000 per month or more.

New housing might fill one need, but leave another unfulfilled.

III. Residential Management Contracts

There are a number of property management contracts that have been developed by various professional organizations and form companies such as the BOMA form we included in Chapter 2.

The form we have included in this chapter was prepared by Professional Publishing. We like it for its readability and simplicity and we feel it is better suited to residential management situations. The contract describes the property and has a commencement and termination date.

Any management agreement for less than one year is not recommended, as landlords may use you to fill out vacant buildings.

> **VOICE OF EXPERIENCE:**
>
> *If the property has problems, any contract for less than three years is not recommended. This longer term would allow you to recoup some of the benefits from the hard work of solving the property's problems. Otherwise, owners could seek to reduce costs by going to another manager or manage the property themselves. You want to be compensated with higher fees for the work you are to do if you're using a short-term management contract.*

The CAR® **Property Management Agreement** is included as **Figure 5-1**. In this case, the contract applies to a broker acting as a property manager, therefore the terms "broker" and "property manager" are interchangeable.

A. AUTHORITIES AND OBLIGATIONS OF BROKERS/PROPERTY MANAGERS

Advertising, Rental/Leasing, Rent Collection. The broker/property manager might advertise property that is for rent, display signs, screen and select tenants, execute lease signing, and collect rents.

Tenancy Termination. The broker/property manager may terminate tenancies and give notices such as to quit or pay rent.

Repair/Maintenance. The broker/property manager is to provide all reasonably necessary services for proper management (inspection, supervision of maintenance, alterations and repairs, etc.).

Contracts/Services. The broker/property manager may hire, supervise, and discharge required employees and independent contractors. Employee agreements shall be terminable at will. Employees will be owner employees and not the employees of the manager. Broker shall pay employees with appropriate contribution deductions from the gross revenue. The property manager might employ attorneys approved by the owner to enforce the owner's lease rights and to commence legal action.

Note: Commercial management contracts might authorize the employment of attorneys for lease preparation and/or review.

Expense Payments. The broker/property manager shall pay necessary operating expenses as well as expenses authorized by owner. These could include property management compensation, fees and charges, expenses for goods and services, property taxes and other taxes, owner's association dues, assessments, loan payments, and insurance premiums.

Security Deposits. broker/The property manager shall receive deposits from tenants.

Figure 5-1

CALIFORNIA
ASSOCIATION
OF REALTORS®

PROPERTY MANAGEMENT AGREEMENT
(C.A.R. Form PMA, Revised 4/09)

_____ ("Owner"), and
_____ ("Broker"), agree as follows:

1. **APPOINTMENT OF BROKER:** Owner hereby appoints and grants Broker the exclusive right to rent, lease, operate, and manage the property(ies) known as _____ _123 Sail Avenue, Marina del Rey CA 90292_ _____
_____ and any additional property which may later be added to this Agreement ("Property"), upon the terms below, for the period beginning (date) _____ and ending (date) _____ , at 11:59 PM. (If checked:) ☐ Either party may terminate this Property Management Agreement ("Agreement") on at least 30 days written notice _____ months after the original commencement date of this Agreement. After the exclusive term expires, this Agreement shall continue as a non-exclusive agreement that either party may terminate by giving at least 30 days written notice to the other.

2. **BROKER ACCEPTANCE:** Broker accepts the appointment and grant, and agrees to:
   A. Use due diligence in the performance of this Agreement.
   B. Furnish the services of its firm for the rental, leasing, operation and management of the Property.

3. **AUTHORITY AND POWERS:** Owner grants Broker the authority and power, at Owner's expense, to:
   A. **ADVERTISING:** Display FOR RENT/LEASE and similar signs on the Property and advertise the availability of the Property, or any part thereof, for rental or lease.
   B. **RENTAL; LEASING:** Init., sig., renew, modify or cancel rental agreements and leases for the Property, or any part thereof; collect and give receipts for rents, other fees, charges and security deposits. Any lease or rental agreement executed by Broker for Owner shall not exceed _____ year(s) or ☐ shall be month-to-month. Unless Owner authorizes a lower amount, rent shall be: ☐ at market rate; OR ☐ a minimum of _____ per _____ ; OR ☐ see attachment.
   C. **TENANCY TERMINATION:** Sign and serve in Owner's name notices that are required or appropriate; commence and prosecute actions to evict tenants; recover possession of the Property in Owner's name; recover rents and other sums due; and, when expedient, settle, compromise and release claims, actions and suits and/or reinstate tenancies.
   D. **REPAIR; MAINTENANCE:** Make, cause to be made, and/or supervise repairs, improvements, alterations and decorations to the Property; purchase, and pay bills for, services and supplies. Broker shall obtain prior approval of Owner for all expenditures over $ _____ for any one item. Prior approval shall not be required for monthly or recurring operating charges or, if in Broker's opinion, emergency expenditures over the maximum are needed to protect the Property or other property(ies) from damage, prevent injury to persons, avoid suspension of necessary services, avoid penalties or fines, or suspension of services to tenants required by a lease or rental agreement or by law, including, but not limited to, maintaining the Property in a condition fit for human habitation as required by Civil Code §§ 1941 and 1941.1 and Health and Safety Code §§ 17920.3 and 17920.10.
   E. **REPORTS, NOTICES AND SIGNS:** Comply with federal, state or local law requiring delivery of reports or notices and/or posting of signs or notices.
   F. **CONTRACTS; SERVICES:** Contract, hire, supervise and/or discharge firms and persons, including utilities, required for the operation and maintenance of the Property. Broker may perform any of Broker's duties through attorneys, agents, employees, or independent contractors and, except for persons working in Broker's firm, shall not be responsible for their acts, omissions, defaults, negligence and/or costs of same.
   G. **EXPENSE PAYMENTS:** Pay expenses and costs for the Property from Owner's funds held by Broker, unless otherwise directed by Owner. Expenses and costs may include, but are not limited to, property management compensation, fees and charges, expenses for goods and services, property taxes and other taxes, Owner's Association dues, assessments, loan payments and insurance premiums.
   H. **SECURITY DEPOSITS:** Receive security deposits from tenants, which deposits shall be ☐ given to Owner, or ☐ placed in Broker's trust account and, if held in Broker's trust account, pay from Owner's funds all interest on tenants' security deposits if required by local law or ordinance. Owner shall be responsible to tenants for return of security deposits and all interest due on security deposits held by Owner.
   I. **TRUST FUNDS:** Deposit all receipts collected for Owner, less any sums properly deducted or disbursed, in a financial institution whose deposits are insured by an agency of the United States government. The funds shall be held in a trust account separate from Broker's personal accounts. Broker shall not be liable in event of bankruptcy or failure of a financial institution.
   J. **RESERVES:** Maintain a reserve in Broker's trust account of $ _____ .
   K. **DISBURSEMENTS:** Disburse Owner's funds, held in Broker's trust account, in the following order:
      (1) Compensation due Broker under paragraph 6.
      (2) All other operating expenses, costs and disbursements payable from Owner's funds held by Broker.
      (3) Reserves and security deposits held by Broker.
      (4) Balance to Owner.
   L. **OWNER DISTRIBUTION:** Remit funds, if any are available, monthly (or ☐ _____), to Owner.
   M. **OWNER STATEMENTS:** Render monthly, (or ☐ _____), statements of receipts, expenses and charges for each Property.
   N. **BROKER FUNDS:** Broker shall not advance Broker's own funds in connection with the Property or this Agreement.
   O. **KEYSAFE/LOCKBOX:** ☐ (If checked) Owner authorizes the use of a keysafe/lockbox to allow entry into the Property and agrees to sign a keysafe/lockbox addendum (C.A.R. Form KLA).

PMA REVISED 4/09 (PAGE 1 OF 3)

Owner's Initials (_____)(_____)
Broker's Initials (_____)(_____)

Reviewed by _____ Date _____

EQUAL HOUSING OPPORTUNITY

PROPERTY MANAGEMENT AGREEMENT (PMA PAGE 1 OF 3)

Agent: WALT HUBER   Phone: Fax: Prepared using zipForm® software
Broker: WALT HUBER REALTOR

149

4. **OWNER RESPONSIBILITIES:** Owner shall:
   A. Provide all documentation, records and disclosures as required by law or required by Broker to manage and operate the Property, and immediately notify Broker if Owner becomes aware of any change in such documentation, records or disclosures, or any matter affecting the habitability of the Property.
   B. Indemnify, defend and hold harmless Broker, and all persons in Broker's firm, regardless of responsibility, from all costs, expenses, suits, liabilities, damages, attorney fees and claims of every type, including but not limited to those arising out of injury or death of any person, or damage to any real or personal property of any person, including Owner, for: (i) any repairs performed by Owner or by others hired directly by Owner; or (ii) those relating to the management, leasing, rental, security deposits, or operation of the Property by Broker, or any person in Broker's firm, or the performance or exercise of any of the duties, powers or authorities granted to Broker.
   C. Maintain the Property in a condition fit for human habitation as required by Civil Code §§ 1941 and 1941.1 and Health and Safety Code §§ 17920.3 and 17920.10 and other applicable law.
   D. Pay all interest on tenants' security deposits if required by local law or ordinance.
   E. Carry and pay for: (i) public and premises liability insurance in an amount of no less than $1,000,000; and (ii) property damage and worker's compensation insurance adequate to protect the interests of Owner and Broker. Broker shall be, and Owner authorizes Broker to be, named as an additional insured party on Owner's policies.
   F. Pay any late charges, penalties and/or interest imposed by lenders or other parties for failure to make payment to those parties, if the failure is due to insufficient funds in Broker's trust account available for such payment.
   G. Immediately replace any funds required if there are insufficient funds in Broker's trust account to cover Owner's responsibilities.
5. **DISCLOSURE:**
   A. **LEAD-BASED PAINT**
      (1) ☐ The Property was constructed on or after January 1, 1978.
      OR (2) ☐ The Property was constructed prior to 1978.
         (i) Owner has no knowledge of lead-based paint or lead-based paint hazards in the housing except: _____
         _____
         (ii) Owner has no reports or records pertaining to lead-based paint or lead-based hazards in the housing, except the following, which Owner shall provide to Broker: _____
   B. **POOL/SPA DRAIN**
      Any pool or spa on the property does (or ☐ does not) have an approved anti-entrapment drain cover, device or system.
6. **COMPENSATION:**
   A. Owner agrees to pay Broker fees in the amount indicated below for:
      (1) Management: _____
      (2) Renting or Leasing: _____
      (3) Evictions: _____
      (4) Preparing Property for rental or lease: _____
      (5) Managing Property during extended periods of vacancy: _____
      (6) An overhead and service fee added to the cost of all work performed by, or at the direction of, Broker: _____
      (7) Other: _____
   B. This Agreement does not include providing on-site management services, property sale, refinancing, preparing Property for sale or refinancing, modernization, fire or major damage restoration, rehabilitation, obtaining income tax, accounting or legal advice, representation before public agencies, advising on proposed new construction, debt collection, counseling, attending Owner's Association meetings or _____
      _____
      _____
      If Owner requests Broker to perform services not included in this Agreement, a fee shall be agreed upon before these services are performed.
   C. Broker may divide compensation, fees and charges due under this Agreement in any manner acceptable to Broker.
   D. Owner further agrees that:
      (1) Broker may receive and keep fees and charges from tenants for: (i) requesting an assignment, sublease or sublease of the Property; (ii) processing credit applications; (iii) any returned checks and/or ☐ (if checked) late payments; and (iv) any other services that are not in conflict with this Agreement.
      (2) Broker may perform any of Broker's duties, and obtain necessary products and services, through affiliated companies or organizations in which Broker may own an interest. Broker may receive fees, commissions and/or profits from these affiliated companies or organizations. Broker has an ownership interest in the following affiliated companies or organizations: _____
         _____
         Broker shall disclose to Owner any other such relationships as they occur. Broker shall not receive any fees, commissions or profits from unaffiliated companies or organizations in the performance of this Agreement, without prior disclosure to Owner.
      (3) Other: _____
7. **AGENCY RELATIONSHIPS:** Broker shall act, and Owner hereby consents to Broker acting, as dual agent for Owner and tenant(s) in any resulting transaction. If the Property includes residential property with one-to-four dwelling units and this Agreement permits a tenancy in excess of one year, Owner acknowledges receipt of the "Disclosure Regarding Agency Relationships" (C.A.R. Form AD). Owner understands that Broker may have or obtain property management agreements on other property, and that potential tenants may consider, make offers on, or lease through Broker, property the same as or similar to Owner's Property. Owner consents to Broker's representation of other owners' properties before, during and after the expiration of this Agreement.
8. **NOTICES:** Any written notice to Owner or Broker required under this Agreement shall be served by sending such notice by first class mail or other agreed-to delivery method to that party at the address below, or at any different address the parties may later designate for this purpose. Notice shall be deemed received three (3) calendar days after deposit into the United States mail OR ☐ _____.

Owner's Initials (_____)(_____)
Broker's Initials (_____)(_____)

PMA REVISED 4/09 (PAGE 2 OF 3)

Reviewed by _____ Date _____

EQUAL HOUSING OPPORTUNITY
Untitled

PROPERTY MANAGEMENT AGREEMENT (PMA PAGE 2 OF 3)

Owner Name: _____ Date: _____

9. **DISPUTE RESOLUTION**

   A. **MEDIATION:** Owner and Broker agree to mediate any dispute or claim arising between them out of this Agreement, or any resulting transaction before resorting to arbitration or court action, subject to paragraph 9B(2) below. Paragraph 9B(2) below applies whether or not the arbitration provision is initialed. Mediation fees, if any, shall be divided equally among the parties involved. If, for any dispute or claim to which this paragraph applies, any party commences an action based on a dispute or claim to which this paragraph applies, without first attempting to resolve the matter through mediation, or refuses to mediate after a request has been made, then that party shall not be entitled to recover attorney fees, even if they would otherwise be available to that party in any such action. THIS MEDIATION PROVISION APPLIES WHETHER OR NOT THE ARBITRATION PROVISION IS INITIALED.

   B. **ARBITRATION OF DISPUTES: (1) Owner and Broker agree that any dispute or claim in law or equity arising between them regarding the obligation to pay compensation under this agreement, which is not settled through mediation, shall be decided by neutral, binding arbitration, including and subject to paragraph 9B(2) below. The arbitrator shall be a retired judge or justice, or an attorney with at least 5 years of residential real estate law experience, unless the parties mutually agree to a different arbitrator, who shall render an award in accordance with substantive California Law. The parties shall have the right to discovery in accordance with Code of Civil Procedure § 1283.05. In all other respects, the arbitration shall be conducted in accordance with Title 9 of Part III of the California Code of Civil Procedure. Judgment upon the award of the arbitrator(s) may be entered in any court having jurisdiction. Interpretation of this agreement to arbitrate shall be governed by the Federal Arbitration Act.**

   (2) EXCLUSIONS FROM MEDIATION AND ARBITRATION: The following matters are excluded from mediation and arbitration hereunder: (i) a judicial or non-judicial foreclosure or other action or proceeding to enforce a deed of trust, mortgage, or installment land sale contract as defined in Civil Code § 2985; (ii) an unlawful detainer action; (iii) the filing or enforcement of a mechanic's lien; and (iv) any matter that is within the jurisdiction of a probate, small claims, or bankruptcy court. The filing of a court action to enable the recording of a notice of pending action, for order of attachment, receivership, injunction, or other provisional remedies, shall not constitute a waiver of the mediation and arbitration provisions.

   "NOTICE: BY INITIALING IN THE SPACE BELOW YOU ARE AGREEING TO HAVE ANY DISPUTE ARISING OUT OF THE MATTERS INCLUDED IN THE 'ARBITRATION OF DISPUTES' PROVISION DECIDED BY NEUTRAL ARBITRATION AS PROVIDED BY CALIFORNIA LAW AND YOU ARE GIVING UP ANY RIGHTS YOU MIGHT POSSESS TO HAVE THE DISPUTE LITIGATED IN A COURT OR JURY TRIAL. BY INITIALING IN THE SPACE BELOW YOU ARE GIVING UP YOUR JUDICIAL RIGHTS TO DISCOVERY AND APPEAL, UNLESS THOSE RIGHTS ARE SPECIFICALLY INCLUDED IN THE 'ARBITRATION OF DISPUTES' PROVISION. IF YOU REFUSE TO SUBMIT TO ARBITRATION AFTER AGREEING TO THIS PROVISION, YOU MAY BE COMPELLED TO ARBITRATE UNDER THE AUTHORITY OF THE CALIFORNIA CODE OF CIVIL PROCEDURE. YOUR AGREEMENT TO THIS ARBITRATION PROVISION IS VOLUNTARY."

   "WE HAVE READ AND UNDERSTAND THE FOREGOING AND AGREE TO SUBMIT DISPUTES ARISING OUT OF THE MATTERS INCLUDED IN THE 'ARBITRATION OF DISPUTES' PROVISION TO NEUTRAL ARBITRATION."

   | Owner's Initials _____ / _____ | Broker's Initials _____ / _____ |

10. **EQUAL HOUSING OPPORTUNITY:** The Property is offered in compliance with federal, state and local anti-discrimination laws.

11. **ATTORNEY FEES:** In any action, proceeding or arbitration between Owner and Broker regarding the obligation to pay compensation under this Agreement, the prevailing Owner or Broker shall be entitled to reasonable attorney fees and costs from the non-prevailing Owner or Broker, except as provided in paragraph 9A.

12. **ADDITIONAL TERMS:** ☐ Keysafe/Lockbox Addendum (C.A.R. Form KLA); ☐ Lead-Based Paint and Lead-Based Paint Hazards Disclosure (C.A.R. Form FLD)

13. **TIME OF ESSENCE; ENTIRE CONTRACT; CHANGES:** Time is of the essence. All understandings between the parties are incorporated in this Agreement. Its terms are intended by the parties as a final, complete and exclusive expression of their Agreement with respect to its subject matter, and may not be contradicted by evidence of any prior agreement or contemporaneous oral agreement. If any provision of this Agreement is held to be ineffective or invalid, the remaining provisions will nevertheless be given full force and effect. Neither this Agreement nor any provision in it may be extended, amended, modified, altered or changed except in writing. This Agreement and any supplement, addendum or modification, including any copy, may be signed in two or more counterparts, all of which shall constitute one and the same writing.

Owner warrants that Owner is the owner of the Property or has the authority to execute this contract and acknowledges Owner has read, understands, accepts and has received a copy of the Agreement.

Owner _____ Date _____
Owner _____
       Print Name   Social Security/Tax ID # (for tax reporting purposes)
Address _____ City _____ State _____ Zip _____
Telephone _____ Fax _____ E-mail _____

Owner _____ Date _____
Owner _____
       Print Name   Social Security/Tax ID # (for tax reporting purposes)
Address _____ City _____ State _____ Zip _____
Telephone _____ Fax _____ E-mail _____

Real Estate Broker (Firm) _____ Date _____
By (Agent) _____ DRE Lic. #: _____
Address _____ City _____ State _____ Zip _____
Telephone _____ Fax _____ E-mail _____

| Reviewed by _____ Date _____ |

Trust Funds. The broker/property manager shall deposit all receipts collected for owner, less any sums properly deducted or disbursed, in a financial institution whose deposits are insured by an agency of the United States government.

Reserves. The broker/property manager shall maintain a reserve in broker's trust account.

Disbursements. The broker/property manager shall disburse owner's funds held in the broker's trust account in the order shown in the management agreement.

Owner Distribution. The broker/property manager shall remit funds, if any are available, monthly to owner.

Owner Statements. The broker/property manager shall submit monthly statements to the owner.

B. OWNER'S RESPONSIBILITIES

Provide Ducumentation. The owner shall provide all documentation, records, and disclosures as required by broker to manage and operate the property.

Lead-Based Paint Disclosure. The owner shall disclose to the broker the date of construction and any knowledge of the presence of lead-based paint.

Compensation for Management Services. There could be a flat monthly fee for a property or a fee could be a percentage of gross monthly income and may be coupled with a minimum. The flat fee and percentage could be included in the management contract.

Compensation for Leasing and Evictions.

Leasing compensation is usually a percentage of the total lease rent paid in the year received for the term of the lease.

Some contracts provide for higher percentages in the early years. Fees for renegotiated leases could be lower than for new leases. The leasing fee may be lowered or eliminated if a contract has a higher percentage of the gross.

Compensation for Preparing Property for Rental or Lease.

Compensation for Managing Property During Extended Periods of Vacancy.

Overhead and Service Fee.

Compensation for Other Services. The owner might agree to pay advertising costs or additional costs and/or fees.

C. ADDITIONAL OWNER OBLIGATIONS

Agency Relationships. Broker shall act as a dual agent for owner and tenant(s) in any resulting transaction (sale).

D. NOTICE

This provision requires all notices to be in writing and specifies manner of delivery and place of delivery.

E. DISPUTE RESOLUTION

Owner and broker agree to **mediate** any dispute or claim arising between them out of this agreement, or any resulting transaction before resorting to arbitration or court action, subject to certain conditions.

Owner and broker agree that any dispute or claim in law or equity arising between them regarding the obligation to pay compensation under this agreement, which is not settled through mediation, shall be decided by neutral, binding arbitration.

F. EQUAL HOUSING OPPORTUNITY

The property is offered in compliance with federal, state, and local anti-discrimination laws.

G. ATTORNEY FEES

In any legal dispute between owner and broker, the prevailing party shall be entitled to reasonable attorney fees. This provision reduces the likelihood of frivolous lawsuits.

H. TIME

TIME IS OF THE ESSENCE, which means that the time set forth in this agreement means the time stated and not within a reasonable period thereafter.

IV. Policies

Existing "policies" should be reviewed when a firm takes over management of a property.

As the new property manager, you may wish to make changes to the policies based on the owner's needs, demands of the marketplace, vacancy factor, etc.

A. SECURITY DEPOSITS

You will have to make decisions about the types of and amounts of security deposits for new leases. You might consider asking for the first and last month's rent in advance plus a security deposit.

Chapter 5

VOICE OF EXPERIENCE:

If tenants tell you that they intend to use their security deposit for the last month's rent, you might point out to them that the rental records will show that they did not pay the last month's rent as agreed and that you were forced to take the rent out of their security deposit. You might also mention that these facts could be detrimental to their credit report.

Don't threaten to report this information, however it's enough to indicate that an investigation may bring this information to light.

In most states, the amount of a residential security deposits is limited by law.

The **UNIFORM RESIDENTIAL LANDLORD AND TENANT ACT**, *adopted by many states, limits security deposits to one month's rent*. A number of states have greater limits. In California, a security deposit cannot exceed two month's rent for an unfurnished unit and three month's rent for a furnished unit. The California Code of Civil Procedure allows landlords to take three weeks to account for the security deposit. (It was formerly two weeks). Failure to do so within the allotted time could subject the landlord to $600 in damages.

Security deposits may be applied to damages as well as unpaid rent. However, they cannot apply to normal wear and tear.

In many states, nonrefundable deposits, such as a general cleaning charge or move-in fee, are not allowed. In most states, interest is not paid on security deposits unless agreed to by the parties.

Besides the security deposit, you should require a deposit for keys and garage door openers. Of course, this security deposit information is stated in both property management and leasing contracts.

Case Example

Korens v. R.W. Zukin Corp., 212 C.A. 3d 1054 (1989)

Tenants brought a class action against a landlord for failure to pay interest on their security deposits. In ruling for the landlord, the court pointed out that neither the lease nor California statute requires interest on security deposits. If the tenants had expected interest, they should have negotiated this fact in their leases.

To avoid litigation, have all legal agreements spelled out in the lease.

B. PETS

Allowing pets will reduce the vacancy factor for many apartments, as well as increase the average tenancy period.

An increased tenancy period reduces the costs associated with preparing a property for rental and related rental costs. In addition, property that accepts pets may rent at a premium compared to similar property where pets are not allowed. It also helps avoid down times while negotiating another lease.

While an owner can decide not to allow pets, this refusal cannot apply to seeing eye dogs or support animals. In fact, a greater property damage bond cannot be charged than is required of tenants who do not own pets.

Handicapped persons are protected by the Americans With Disabilities Act.

VOICE OF EXPERIENCE:

If you allow pets, you might want to increase property damage bond requirements as pets can ruin carpeting and damage hardwood floors. Most pet owners are so attached to their animals that they're more than willing to pay for this additional coverage if it means they can keep "Fluffy" and still live in the building of their choice.

Case Example

People v. Parkmerced Co., 198 C.A. 3d 683 (1988)

The owners of a 3,400 unit apartment complex charged tenants a first month's rent which was $65 higher than the rent for the remaining 11 months on the one-year leases. In addition, tenants wishing to change apartments were charged a $50 transfer fee.

This action was brought by the District Attorney based on California law requiring the refunding of all security deposits. (California prohibits nonrefundable security deposits). The trial court ruled that Parkmerced should pay $222,000 in civil penalties, $40,000 in attorneys' fees and notify tenants of their right to have these fees refunded.

The Court of Appeals affirmed the award by the trial court. The court pointed out that the charges were not rent but were intended to cover front-end costs associated with moving a tenant in. The court indicated that the penalty charged was not excessive, in fact it was very lenient.

▼

Your state may not nonrefundable security deposits, or any fees that similarly reflect the cost of moving in new tenants.

Radwan v. Dist. of Col. Rental Housing, 683 A.2d 478 (D.C.App. 1996)

Hearing examiner found that Radwan charged Smith rent that exceeded the rent ceiling. Landlord was not entitled to have judgment set aside where landlord failed to proffer any substantive defense to overcharge claim.

C. LEASE PERIOD

Market demand determines the length of leases.

While longer leases tend to reduce the vacancy factor, in an inflationary period the owner must wait until the lease has expired to raise rents.

In residential rentals, leases protect the tenants against rent increases and termination of tenancy during the stated period of time.

You might want leases to expire in the months when it is easiest to rent. As an example, you would want a beach area unit to have a lease expiring on May 1, June 1, or July 1.

D. FURNISHED UNITS

Furnished units can demand significantly higher rents than unfurnished units.

Generally, bachelor and one-bedroom furnished units have the highest demand since such units appeal strongly to singles.

Management fees for furnished units are normally higher than for unfurnished units because of the shorter occupancy periods and greater maintenance, cleaning and inventory expenses.

Kitchen appliances are usually included in a residential lease, even those for unfurnished units. Don't let tenants use their own appliances unless the benefits exceed the problems involved in moving out the owner's appliances and storing them until they will be required again.

VOICE OF EXPERIENCE:

One problem with furnished units is that the turnover is normally greater than for unfurnished units. This is probably due to the fact that moving for the tenants only involves a few trips to their vehicles with personal effects.

Also, be careful not to allow the installation of a T.V. dish directly on the roof. This can cause serious damage to the roof.

E. OCCUPANCY

You cannot discriminate as to family status when renting. However, you can limit the number of occupants, providing you are reasonable in that request. (See Chapter 13 .)

F. QUALIFICATION REQUIREMENTS

You can set qualification standards for your tenants, but the standards must be reasonable and applied uniformly to all applicants for rental.

G. WHO NOT TO RENT TO

As a property manager, you should not rent to a relative or close friend.

Besides giving the appearance of a conflict of interest, a personal relationship with a tenant can cause significant problems. For instance, a tenant may think that he or she is an exception to the rules. You might hesitate to evict or take legal action because of your personal relationship with the tenant. On the other hand, if you treat this tenant the same as any other tenant, you could ruin an otherwise good relationship or cause family-related problems.

In New York, many lessors refuse to rent to attorneys because of their litigious nature. While the authors don't approve of any type of discrimination, attorneys are not one of the protected groups under civil rights laws.

Studies show that attorneys are far more likely to sue landlords than any other occupational group.

Case Example

Harris v. Capital Growth Investors XIV, 52 C.3d 1142 (1991)

This case involved a landlord who had a minimum income policy. The landlord required that a tenant's gross income be at least three times greater than the rent for the unit.

The plaintiff claimed that the income was arbitrary and not based on the actual ability to pay. The plaintiff also alleged that the policy was discriminatory as to sex because women generally have lower incomes than men.

▼

In ruling for the defendant, the California Supreme Court recognized that businesses can justifiably place limitations on their businesses to insure full and timely payment for goods and services. The court held that a minimum income standard was a reasonable means to achieve this goal. The landlord's policy is only economic and did not make distinctions as to any protected category.

> *The landlord has the right to refuse to rent to tenants who cannot prove adequate income, just as a lender may refuse to make a loan to a buyer for the same reason.*

Harris v. Itzhaki, 183 F.23 1043 (9th Cir. 1999)

A plaintiff can establish a FHA discrimination claim under a theory of disparate treatment or disparate impact if the plaintiff can establish that: (1) plaintiff's rights are protected under the FHA; and (2) as a result of the defendant's discriminatory conduct, plaintiff has suffered a distinct and palpable injury.

V. Setting Rents

A. USING COMPARABLES

Setting rents is part art and part science. You should consider comparables when setting rents for any property. For what price are similar size units of similar desirability currently renting? Be concerned with developments having vacancy rates that are not overly low or overly high. As an example, if apartment rentals experience a seven-percent vacancy factor within a community, you would not use comparables of units only having a two-percent vacancy factor. Such a vacancy factor would indicate rents charged are too low since the vacancy factor would be practically nil. Similarly, if you used comparable units having a 20-percent vacancy factor, you could be setting rents too high. You would not then meet the area average for vacancies. Actually, meeting the average should not be a goal.

No property manager's performance should be average. You should be better because you are a professional.

Just as market values for sales prices can be estimated using a comparative market analysis, the same analysis can be performed for setting rental rates. Use the rental of each comparable and add or subtract from the comparable rental for any difference in location and amenities present or lacking in your rental.

In some cases, it is difficult to find comparables. As an example, units with a view generally command a significant rental premium over units without a desirable view. The premium might be as much as 100 percent. You'll find such premiums on some water-view properties. Check on data to determine what you feel is a fair premium for the view. When renting apartment units, if you discover that the view property is renting faster than nonview property, it would indicate your rents are too low for property with a view or too high for nonview property.

As a general rule, you should reevaluate your rents if your rentals in a new structure are going much slower or faster than anticipated.

VOICE OF EXPERIENCE:

In determining a rent schedule or any change in that schedule, you should not be concerned about the rental price current tenants are paying for similar units. You are not competing with occupied units, but with unoccupied units. The only comparison should be with units currently available for rent.

When setting rents, what is not available for lease does not compete with what is available for lease.

B. SUPPLY AND DEMAND (Set By Local Market)

What determines rents? Supply and demand.

If demand for a particular type of property exceeds supply, then rents rise. If demand is less than supply in that neighborhood, rents drop. It is the basic capitalistic market system in action and it works. More products (rentals) will be added to the marketplace as demand increases and rents increase.

The real estate marketplace is different from economic models set forth in textbooks because it is a stratified marketplace. What this means is that there can be a high vacancy factor for high-rent units and a very low vacancy factor for middle-income and low-income units.

Another economic factor to consider is that real estate is immobile, but people are mobile. When rents get too high in one area, people will be willing to commute greater distances to residences in other areas. Rents and housing costs are extremely high in Orange County California. This has led to the growth in housing and tens of thousands of Orange County workers commuting from areas in Riverside County, where costs are significantly less.

C. THE IDEAL RENT

As a rule of thumb, if the "vacancy factor" in an area for a type of property is less than five percent, then the rents are considered too low and can be raised.

As a property manager, what you should be concerned with is that combination of rents and vacancy factor that will result in the highest net. As an example, assume a property has 100 units, each rented at $1,000 per month for a total of $100,000 gross per month.

Assume the rents are raised 10 percent and the property goes from full occupancy to a 10-percent vacancy factor. On the face of these facts, raising the rent 10 percent is not a smart economic decision. Now there are 90 units each rented at $1,100 per month or a gross income of $99,000 per month. The gross income declined one percent with the rise in rent.

Using the same situation, assume the rents were raised five percent and resulted in a three percent vacancy factor. You now have 97 units rented at $1,050 with a total gross income of $101,850. The gross has increased by $1,850 per month, so it would seem to be a good economic decision.

There are other factors to consider in setting rents. If higher rents result in a shorter average tenancy, then savings could erode by necessary costs incurred between tenants, such as professionally cleaning carpets, repainting, etc. Such costs, above the normal wear and tear covered by the property damage bond, can easily average $500 per move, depending on the area and size of the rental. There can also be costs to rerent, such as advertising and even commissions.

As a property manager, you should be more interested in long-term net income than in gross income.

D. WHAT NOT TO USE IN SETTING RENTS

You should establish a rent pricing schedule that is competitive within the neighborhood.

1. Owner Costs

What an owner paid only affects his or her price, not what the local marketplace will allow him or her to receive as rent.

Just because an owner desires a particular rate of return on an investment does not mean that rental should be set to yield that rate. The owner's desired rate of return is only a wish. In renting, you should be concerned with the realities of the marketplace. The owner's desired return might be more or even less than what the market will allow.

2. Appraisals

Appraisals are simply one person's opinion (based on education and experience) of value.

Because a person uses a rental figure in the appraisal does not mean that such a rent is the proper rental for the property.

Appraisers too often use rentals based on what other properties are renting for, which, as previously stated, are not the competition. The competition is other vacant units.

Appraisers also may lack the grasp of a particular stratified marketplace in a particular community. Appraisers also use figures that are fixed as to a point in time. They often don't consider any changes that might influence rents after that date.

A desirable school district will favorably affect rental prices.

E. RAISING RENT

The rental marketplace is not a perfect economic model.

People will not move simply because an equally desirable unit can be rented for a few dollars less than they are currently paying. As an example, assume that rents in an apartment complex were to rise from $500 per month to $520 per month, a four-percent rent increase. It is unlikely that tenants would leave simply because they could rent a similarly desirable unit elsewhere for $500. It costs money to move, so moving would not be an economic decision for such a small difference. Of course, there is a point where rent increases will result in lower total revenue because of tenants moving.

VOICE OF EXPERIENCE:

Small rent increases on a regular basis are more favorably accepted than larger increases spread out over time. In rent controlled areas, the amount of rent increase is dictated by law. Even if property you manage is not located in a rent control area, you can use the percentage allowed by law in those areas as a generally accepted amount of rent increase.

It is possible to raise rents above what is being asked for similar units, but too much difference will make it extremely difficult to rent vacant units unless a rental incentive is provided. Another alternative is to make your units appear more desirable by properly preparing vacant units for rent.

F. WHEN RENTS ARE TOO HIGH

Setting rents too high can be economically unsound for the property owner.

Assume you are asking $500 in rent for a property which should rent for $375. You might find uninformed tenants who will agree to the rent or you might have to give rental incentives (i.e., one month's free rent). Chances are, the time period to find tenants will be longer than it would normally take. This would mean vacant units until they are rented. Your costs to fill those vacancies, such as ads, commissions and incentives, will also be considerably higher than for market-rate rentals.

Tenants will eventually realize that they are paying too much in rent. Unhappy tenants are more likely to abandon the premises before the lease expires than are tenants who recognize that the rent is fair.

> **VOICE OF EXPERIENCE:**
>
> *Charging too much for rents is far more likely to reduce a lessor's net income than would charging lower rents. You need to protect your owner's bottom line by not overcharging (and losing) tenants.*

G. INFLATION AND RENT

Rents can generally be raised to cover inflation. If they can be raised, then the purchasing value of the rent received is not diminished.

Rents usually increase with inflation and provide the landlord with an increase in the net income in excess of the inflationary increase. The reason is that debt service is normally a fixed expense. Look at the following situation before and after a 10-percent inflationary increase. The assumption is that expenses and rent will increase by 10 percent:

	Before Inflation	After Inflation
Gross Rents	$1,000,000.00	$1,100,000.00
Debt Service	-650,000.00	-650,000.00
Operational Expenses	-300,000.00*	-330,000.00*
Positive Cash Flow	$50,000.00	$120,000.00

*These costs, such as property taxes and maintenance, may also increase.

You can see that in the above example a 10 percent increase in the rent coupled with a 10 percent increase in operational expenses (including taxes and insurance) would result in a 140 percent increase in net spendable income (cash flow) for the owner.

However, inflation can increase expenses and not result in a rent increase since rent is determined by forces of supply and demand.

Keep in mind: inflationary rent increases are not a certainty.

Supply and demand of the marketplace indicates what you can get. Historically, rent increases have been able to exceed inflation in most parts of the country.

VI. The Rental Process

A. PREPARING TO LEASE

Any delay in preparing a vacant unit for a rental is costly because every day delayed is a day's rent that can never be recovered.

Waiting two weeks for a crew to remove junk left in an apartment, touch up the painting, and clean the carpet could exceed the cost of preparing the unit for rental. It might be better to pay a premium to people who will get in immediately when a unit becomes vacant and finish the work in a few days.

As a property manager, you should have a roster of reliable trade people to do necessary cleanup and repairs.

You want the unit sparkling to rent it. That means a shine on tile, clean carpets, walls that look freshly painted, clean light fixtures and spotless windows, as well as appliances that gleam. Some property managers use car wax on appliances and fixtures.

All light fixtures should have enough wattage to flood the apartment with light. Window shades, blinds and curtains should be pulled back to have natural light. You want the unit to appear bright and cheerful. Keep in mind that people are not entirely economic when renting. Emotion can trigger desire and you want your properties to evoke positive emotions.

VOICE OF EXPERIENCE:

When there are a number of identical vacant units, you can prepare one as a sample unit. It might even be decorator furnished. This is an excellent rental tool when units have recently been completed. You must be certain that all units will be prepared for rental in an identical manner or you will end up with some unhappy short-term tenants.

B. PREQUALIFYING YOUR PROSPECTIVE TENANTS

Before you take prospects into a unit, you should determine if the unit is within their budget and if the size of the unit meets their needs. You should have also gone over with them all deposit requirements and the policy about pets.

If they can't afford the unit or it is too small, you are just wasting your time and theirs. In the end, you could lose a tenant for a unit which better suits their needs.

Be certain that you obtain names and telephone numbers before showing prospective tenants units.

C. SHOWING TO PROSPECTIVE TENANTS

Turn on all the lights when showing a property and make sure there are no unpleasant odors in the unit.

You should be showing property to prospective renters who are satisfied with the location and size of the property and who can meet the financial requirements.

A straightforward approach is best, even if you're not receiving any feedback from the prospective renters. You (or your leasing agent) should present a closing similar to the following:

> "This apartment is available (now/on July 1) for ($6100 per month [which includes one garage space and one parking space]. It requires a property damage bond of ($500 plus a $15 key deposit). If you like this apartment, I can take your application for rent with a (refundable) deposit of ($500. I will be able to notify you within (24 hours) if your rental application is accepted. Is this satisfactory with you?"

Their answer will be either yes or no. If the answer is yes, begin filling out the rental application that the prospects will then sign. They will also give you their check.

Ask to see a photo ID. You want to be certain that your renters are who they say they are.

D. THE QUALIFICATION PROCESS

As covered in Chapter 3, you should check the applicant's credit as well as check the accuracy of the current employment data. You also want to check with past landlords.

Some states may charge $30 or more for a credit check and other reference screening.

Don't take short cuts or assume because a person drives a fancy car and dresses well that he/she will be a good tenant.

VOICE OF EXPERIENCE:

Be leery of tenants who need immediate occupancy. Always ask permission to check with previous landlords and the reason for moving. The qualification process should be regarded as a priority. Process your inquiries quickly.

E. THE LEASE SIGNING

Notify the applicants as soon as they have been approved. Set up an appointment for them to pay the balance of the first month's rent and any deposits due. The applicants should understand the total financial obligation at the time they sign any lease.

Carefully go over every provision of the lease with the tenant as well as any applicable occupancy rules. Tenants need to understand that the rules are important. The better the tenants understand the rules, the fewer problems you will encounter. The tenants then sign the lease and accompanying rules. They should know where they will obtain the key to the unit. **Figure 5-2** is a sample of the **Residential Lease or Month-To-Month Rental Agreement** prepared by the California Association of REALTORS®.

Figure 5-2

RESIDENTIAL LEASE OR
MONTH-TO-MONTH RENTAL AGREEMENT
(C.A.R. Form LR, Revised 11/08)

Date _____ . _____ ("Landlord") and
_____ ("Tenant") agree as follows:

1. PROPERTY:
   A. Landlord rents to Tenant and Tenant rents from Landlord, the real property and improvements described as: *123 Sail Avenue, Marina*
      del Rey CA 90292 _____ ("Premises").
   B. The Premises are for the sole use as a personal residence by the following named person(s) **only**: _____
      _____ .
   C. The following personal property, maintained pursuant to paragraph 11, is included: _____
      _____ or ☐ (if checked) the personal property on the attached addendum.

2. TERM: The term begins on (date) _____ ("Commencement Date"), **(Check A or B):**
   ☐ **A. Month-to-Month:** and continues as a month-to-month tenancy. Tenant may terminate the tenancy by giving written notice at least 30 days
      prior to the intended termination date. Landlord may terminate the tenancy by giving written notice as provided by law. Such notices may be
      given on any date.
   ☐ **B. Lease:** and shall terminate on (date) _____ at _____ ☐ AM/ ☐ PM.
      Tenant shall vacate the Premises upon termination of the Agreement, unless: **(i)** Landlord and Tenant have extended this agreement in
      writing or signed a new agreement; **(ii)** mandated by local rent control law; or **(iii)** Landlord accepts Rent from Tenant (other than past due
      Rent), in which case a month-to-month tenancy shall be created which either party may terminate as specified in paragraph 2A. Rent shall be
      at a rate agreed to by Landlord and Tenant, or as allowed by law. All other terms and conditions of this Agreement shall remain in full force
      and effect.

3. RENT: "Rent" shall mean all monetary obligations of Tenant to Landlord under the terms of the Agreement, except security deposit.
   A. Tenant agrees to pay $ _____ per month for the term of the Agreement.
   B. Rent is payable in advance on the **1st** or ☐ _____) **day** of each calendar month, and is delinquent on the next day.
   C. If Commencement Date falls on any day other than the day Rent is payable under paragraph 3B, and Tenant has paid one full month's Rent in
      advance of Commencement Date, Rent for the second calendar month shall be prorated based on a 30-day period.
   D. PAYMENT: Rent shall be paid by ☐ personal check, ☐ money order, ☐ cashier's check, or ☐ other _____ , to
      (name) _____ (phone) _____ at
      (address) _____ , (or
      at any other location subsequently specified by Landlord in writing to Tenant) (and ☐ if checked, rent may be paid personally between the hours
      of _____ and _____ on the following days _____). If any payments
      is returned for non-sufficient funds ("NSF") or because Tenant stops payment, then, after that: (i) Landlord may, in writing, require Tenant to pay
      Rent in cash for three months and (ii) all future Rent shall be paid by ☐ money order, or ☐ cashier's check.

4. SECURITY DEPOSIT:
   A. Tenant agrees to pay $ _____ as a security deposit. Security deposit will be ☐ transferred to and held by the Owner
      of the Premises, or ☐ held in Owner's Broker's trust account.
   B. All or any portion of the security deposit may be used, as reasonably necessary, to: (i) cure Tenant's default in payment of Rent (which includes
      Late Charges, NSF fees or other sums due); (ii) repair damage, excluding ordinary wear and tear, caused by Tenant or by a guest or licensee of
      Tenant; (iii) clean Premises, if necessary, upon termination of the tenancy; and (iv) replace or return personal property or appurtenances.
      SECURITY DEPOSIT SHALL NOT BE USED BY TENANT IN LIEU OF PAYMENT OF LAST MONTH'S RENT. If all or any portion of the
      security deposit is used during the tenancy, Tenant agrees to reinstate the total security deposit within five days after written notice is delivered to
      Tenant. Within 21 days after Tenant vacates the Premises, Landlord shall: **(1)** furnish Tenant an itemized statement indicating the amount of any
      security deposit received and the basis for its disposition and supporting documentation as required by California Civil Code § 1950.5(g); and **(2)**
      return any remaining portion of the security deposit to Tenant.
   C. **Security deposit will not be returned until all Tenants have vacated the Premises and all keys returned. Any security deposit returned**
      by check shall be made out to all Tenants named on this Agreement, or as subsequently modified.
   D. No interest will be paid on security deposit unless required by local law.
   E. If the security deposit is held by Owner, Tenant agrees not to hold Broker responsible for its return. If the security deposit is held in Owner's
      Broker's trust account, **and** Broker's authority is terminated before expiration of this Agreement, **and** security deposit is released to someone
      other than Tenant, **then** Broker shall notify Tenant, in writing, where and to whom security deposit has been released. Once Tenant has been
      provided such notice, Tenant agrees not to hold Broker responsible for the security deposit.

5. MOVE-IN COSTS RECEIVED/DUE: Move-in funds made payable to _____
   shall be paid by ☐ personal check, ☐ money order, or ☐ cashier's check.

Category	Total Due	Payment Received	Balance Due	Date Due
Rent from _____ to _____ (date)				
*Security Deposit				
Other _____				
Other _____				
Total				

*The maximum amount Landlord may receive as security deposit, however designated, cannot exceed two months' Rent for unfurnished premises, or
   three months' Rent for furnished premises.

Tenant's Initials (_____)(_____)
Landlord's Initials (_____)(_____)

Reviewed by _____ Date _____

LR REVISED 11/08 (PAGE 1 OF 6)

RESIDENTIAL LEASE OR MONTH-TO-MONTH RENTAL AGREEMENT (LR PAGE 1 OF 6)

Agent: WALT HUBER	Phone:	Fax:	Prepared using zipForm® software
Broker: WALT HUBER REALTOR			

Premises: *123 Sail Avenue*
Marina del Rey, CA 90292   Date: _____

6. LATE CHARGE; RETURNED CHECKS:

    A. Tenant acknowledges either late payment of Rent or issuance of a returned check may cause Landlord to incur costs and expenses, the exact amounts of which are extremely difficult and impractical to determine. These costs may include, but are not limited to, processing, enforcement and accounting expenses, and late charges imposed on Landlord. If any installment of Rent due from Tenant is not received by Landlord within **5 (or ☐ _____) calendar days** after the date due, or if a check is returned, Tenant shall pay to Landlord, respectively, an additional sum of $ _____ or _____ % of the Rent due as a Late Charge and $25.00 as a NSF fee for the first returned check and $35.00 as a NSF fee for each additional returned check, either or both of which shall be deemed additional Rent.

    B. Landlord and Tenant agree that these charges represent a fair and reasonable estimate of the costs Landlord may incur by reason of Tenant's late or NSF payment. Any Late Charge or NSF fee due shall be paid with the current installment of Rent. Landlord's acceptance of any Late Charge or NSF fee shall not constitute a waiver as to any default of Tenant. Landlord's right to collect a Late Charge or NSF fee shall not be deemed an extension of the date Rent is due under paragraph 3 or prevent Landlord from exercising any other rights and remedies under this Agreement and as provided by law.

7. PARKING: (Check A or B)

    ☐ A. Parking is permitted as follows: _____
.

        The right to parking ☐ is ☐ is not included in the Rent charged pursuant to paragraph 3. If not included in the Rent, the parking rental fee shall be an additional $ _____ per month. Parking space(s) are to be used for parking properly licensed and operable motor vehicles, except for trailers, boats, campers, buses or trucks (other than pick-up trucks). Tenant shall park in assigned space(s) only. Parking space(s) are to be kept clean. Vehicles leaking oil, gas or other motor vehicle fluids shall not be parked on the Premises. Mechanical work or storage of inoperable vehicles is not permitted in parking space(s) or elsewhere on the Premises.

  OR ☐ B. Parking is not permitted on the Premises.

8. STORAGE: (Check A or B)

    ☐ A. Storage is permitted as follows: _____

        The right to storage space ☐ is, ☐ is not, included in the Rent charged pursuant to paragraph 3. If not included in the Rent, storage space fee shall be an additional $ _____ per month. Tenant shall store only personal property Tenant owns, and shall not store property claimed by another or in which another has any right, title or interest. Tenant shall not store any improperly packaged food or perishable goods, flammable materials, explosives, hazardous waste or other inherently dangerous material, or illegal substances.

  OR ☐ B. Storage is not permitted on the Premises.

9. UTILITIES: Tenant agrees to pay for all utilities and services, and the following charges: _____ except _____ which shall be paid for by Landlord. If any utilities are not separately metered, Tenant shall pay Tenant's proportional share, as reasonably determined and directed by Landlord. If utilities are separately metered, Tenant shall place utilities in Tenant's name as of the Commencement Date. Landlord is only responsible for installing and maintaining one usable telephone jack and one telephone line to the Premises. Tenant shall pay any cost for conversion from existing utilities service provider.

10. CONDITION OF PREMISES: Tenant has examined Premises and, if any, all furniture, furnishings, appliances, landscaping and fixtures, including smoke detector(s).

    (Check all that apply:)

    ☐ A. Tenant acknowledges these items are clean and in operable condition, with the following exceptions: _____
_____

    ☐ B. Tenant's acknowledgment of the condition of these items is contained in an attached statement of condition (C.A.R. Form MIMO).

    ☐ C. Tenant will provide Landlord a list of items that are damaged or not in operable condition within **3 (or ☐ _____) days** after Commencement Date, not as a contingency of this Agreement but rather as an acknowledgment of the condition of the Premises.

    ☐ D. Other: _____

11. MAINTENANCE:

    A. Tenant shall properly use, operate and safeguard Premises, including if applicable, any landscaping, furniture, furnishings and appliances, and all mechanical, electrical, gas and plumbing fixtures, and keep them and the Premises clean, sanitary and well ventilated. Tenant shall be responsible for checking and maintaining all smoke detectors and any additional phone lines beyond the one line and jack that Landlord shall provide and maintain. Tenant shall immediately notify Landlord, in writing, of any problem, malfunction or damage. Tenant shall be charged for all repairs or replacements caused by Tenant, pets, guests or licensees of Tenant, excluding ordinary wear and tear. Tenant shall be charged for all damage to Premises as a result of failure to report a problem in a timely manner. Tenant shall be charged for repair of drain blockages or stoppages, unless caused by defective plumbing parts or tree roots invading sewer lines.

    B. ☐ Landlord ☐ Tenant shall water the garden, landscaping, trees and shrubs, except: _____
_____

    C. ☐ Landlord ☐ Tenant shall maintain the garden, landscaping, trees and shrubs, except: _____
_____

    D. ☐ Landlord ☐ Tenant shall maintain _____

    E. Tenant's failure to maintain any item for which Tenant is responsible shall give Landlord the right to hire someone to perform such maintenance and charge Tenant to cover the cost of such maintenance.

    F. The following items of personal property are included in the Premises without warranty and Landlord will not maintain, repair or replace them: _____

Tenant's Initials (_____) (_____)
Landlord's Initials (_____) (_____)

LR REVISED 11/08 (PAGE 2 OF 6)

Reviewed by _____ Date _____

RESIDENTIAL LEASE OR MONTH-TO-MONTH RENTAL AGREEMENT (LR PAGE 2 OF 6)

Premises: *123 Sail Avenue* *Marina del Rey, CA 90292*   Date: _____

12. **NEIGHBORHOOD CONDITIONS:** Tenant is advised to satisfy him or herself as to neighborhood or area conditions, including schools, proximity and adequacy of law enforcement, crime statistics, proximity of registered felons or offenders, fire protection, other governmental services, availability, adequacy and cost of any wired, wireless internet connections or other telecommunications or other technology services and installations, proximity to commercial, industrial or agricultural activities, existing and proposed transportation, construction and development that may affect noise, view, or traffic, airport noise, noise or odor from any source, wild and domestic animals, other nuisances, hazards, or circumstances, cemeteries, facilities and condition of common areas, conditions and influences of significance to certain cultures and/or religions, and personal needs, requirements and preferences of Tenant.

13. **PETS:** Unless otherwise provided in California Civil Code § 54.2, no animal or pet shall be kept on or about the Premises without Landlord's prior written consent, except: _____

14. ☐ (If checked) **NO SMOKING:** No smoking is allowed on the Premises. If smoking does occur on the Premises, **(i)** Tenant is responsible for all damage caused by the smoking including, but not limited to, stains, burns, odors and removal of debris; **(ii)** Tenant is in breach of this Agreement; **(iii)** Tenant, Authorized Guests, and all others may be required to leave the Premises; and **(iv)** Tenant acknowledges that in order to remove odor caused by smoking, Landlord may need to replace carpet and drapes and paint entire Premises regardless of when these items were last cleaned or replaced. Such actions and other necessary steps will impact the return of any security deposit.

15. **RULES/REGULATIONS:**
   A. Tenant agrees to comply with all Landlord rules and regulations that are at any time posted on the Premises or delivered to Tenant. Tenant shall not, and shall ensure that guests and licensees of Tenant shall not, disturb, annoy, endanger or interfere with other tenants of the building or neighbors, or use the Premises for any unlawful purposes, including, but not limited to, using, manufacturing, selling, storing or transporting illicit drugs or other contraband, or violate any law or ordinance, or commit a waste or nuisance on or about the Premises.
   B. **(If applicable, check one)**
       ☐ 1. Landlord shall provide Tenant with a copy of the rules and regulations within _____ days or _____.
   OR ☐ 2. Tenant has been provided with, and acknowledges receipt of, a copy of the rules and regulations.

16. ☐ (If checked) **CONDOMINIUM; PLANNED UNIT DEVELOPMENT:**
   A. The Premises is a unit in a condominium, planned unit development, common interest subdivision or other development governed by a homeowners' association ("HOA"). The name of the HOA is _____. Tenant agrees to comply with all HOA covenants, conditions and restrictions, bylaws, rules and regulations and decisions. Landlord shall provide Tenant copies of rules and regulations, if any. Tenant shall reimburse Landlord for any fines or charges imposed by HOA or other authorities, due to any violation by Tenant, or the guests or licensees of Tenant.
   B. **(Check one)**
       ☐ 1. Landlord shall provide Tenant with a copy of the HOA rules and regulations within _____ days or _____.
   OR ☐ 2. Tenant has been provided with, and acknowledges receipt of, a copy of the HOA rules and regulations.

17. **ALTERATIONS; REPAIRS:** Unless otherwise specified by law or paragraph 29C, without Landlord's prior written consent, **(i)** Tenant shall not make any repairs, alterations or improvements in or about the Premises including: painting, wallpapering, adding or changing locks, installing antenna or satellite dish(es), placing signs, displays or exhibits, or using screws, fastening devices, large nails or adhesive materials; **(ii)** Landlord shall not be responsible for the costs of alterations or repairs made by Tenant; **(iii)** Tenant shall not deduct from Rent the costs of any repairs, alterations or improvements; and **(iv)** any deduction made by Tenant shall be considered unpaid Rent.

18. **KEYS; LOCKS:**
   A. Tenant acknowledges receipt of (or Tenant will receive ☐ prior to the Commencement Date, or ☐ _____):
       ☐ _____ key(s) to Premises,   ☐ _____ remote control device(s) for garage door/gate opener(s),
       ☐ _____ key(s) to mailbox,   ☐ _____
       ☐ _____ key(s) to common area(s),   ☐ _____
   B. Tenant acknowledges that locks to the Premises ☐ have, ☐ have not, been re-keyed.
   C. If Tenant re-keys existing locks or opening devices, Tenant shall immediately deliver copies of all keys to Landlord. Tenant shall pay all costs and charges related to loss of any keys or opening devices. Tenant may not remove locks, even if installed by Tenant.

19. **ENTRY:**
   A. Tenant shall make Premises available to Landlord or Landlord's representative for the purpose of entering to make necessary or agreed repairs, decorations, alterations, or improvements, or to supply necessary or agreed services, or to show Premises to prospective or actual purchasers, tenants, mortgagees, lenders, appraisers, or contractors.
   B. Landlord and Tenant agree that 24-hour written notice shall be reasonable and sufficient notice, except as follows: 48-hour written notice is required to conduct an inspection of the Premises prior to the Tenant moving out, unless the Tenant waives the right to such notice. Notice may be given orally to show the Premises to actual or prospective purchasers provided Tenant has been notified in writing within 120 days preceding the oral notice that the Premises are for sale and that oral notice may be given to show the Premises. No notice is required: **(i)** to enter in case of an emergency; **(ii)** if the Tenant is present and consents at the time of entry or **(iii)** if the Tenant has abandoned or surrendered the Premises. No written notice is required if Landlord and Tenant orally agree to an entry for agreed services or repairs if the date and time of entry are within one week of the oral agreement.
   C. ☐ (If checked) Tenant authorizes the use of a keysafe/lockbox to allow entry into the Premises and agrees to sign a keysafe/lockbox addendum (C.A.R. Form KLA).

20. **SIGNS:** Tenant authorizes Landlord to place FOR SALE/LEASE signs on the Premises.

21. **ASSIGNMENT; SUBLETTING:** Tenant shall not sublet all or any part of Premises, or assign or transfer this Agreement or any interest in it, without Landlord's prior written consent. Unless such consent is obtained, any assignment, transfer or subletting of Premises or this Agreement or tenancy, by voluntary act of Tenant, operation of law or otherwise, shall, at the option of Landlord,

Tenant's Initials (_____) (_____)
Landlord's Initials (_____) (_____)

| Reviewed by _____ Date _____ |

LR REVISED 11/08 (PAGE 3 OF 6)

RESIDENTIAL LEASE OR MONTH-TO-MONTH RENTAL AGREEMENT (LR PAGE 3 OF 6)

EQUAL HOUSING OPPORTUNITY

terminate this Agreement. Any proposed assignee, transferee or sublessee shall submit to Landlord an application and credit information for Landlord's approval and, if approved, sign a separate written agreement with Landlord and Tenant. Landlord's consent to any one assignment, transfer or sublease, shall not be construed as consent to any subsequent assignment, transfer or sublease and does not release Tenant of Tenant's obligations under this Agreement.

22. **JOINT AND INDIVIDUAL OBLIGATIONS:** If there is more than one Tenant, each one shall be individually and completely responsible for the performance of all obligations of Tenant under this Agreement, jointly with every other Tenant, and individually, whether or not in possession.

23. ☐ **LEAD-BASED PAINT (If checked):** Premises was constructed prior to 1978. In accordance with federal law, Landlord gives and Tenant acknowledges receipt of the disclosures on the attached form (C.A.R. Form FLD) and a federally approved lead pamphlet.

24. ☐ **MILITARY ORDNANCE DISCLOSURE:** (If applicable and known to Landlord) Premises is located within one mile of an area once used for military training, and may contain potentially explosive munitions.

25. ☐ **PERIODIC PEST CONTROL:** Landlord has entered into a contract for periodic pest control treatment of the Premises and shall give Tenant a copy of the notice originally given to Landlord by the pest control company.

26. ☐ **METHAMPHETAMINE CONTAMINATION:** Prior to signing this Agreement, Landlord has given Tenant a notice that a health official has issued an order prohibiting occupancy of the property because of methamphetamine contamination. A copy of the notice and order are attached.

27. **MEGAN'S LAW DATABASE DISCLOSURE:** Notice: Pursuant to Section 290.46 of the Penal Code, information about specified registered sex offenders is made available to the public via an Internet Web site maintained by the Department of Justice at www.meganslaw.ca.gov. Depending on an offender's criminal history, this information will include either the address at which the offender resides or the community of residence and ZIP Code in which he or she resides. (Neither Landlord nor Brokers, if any, are required to check this website. If Tenant wants further information, Tenant should obtain information directly from this website.)

28. **POSSESSION:**
   A. Tenant is not in possession of the premises. If Landlord is unable to deliver possession of Premises on Commencement Date, such Date shall be extended to the date on which possession is made available to Tenant. If Landlord is unable to deliver possession within **5 (or** ☐ **_____) calendar days** after agreed Commencement Date, Tenant may terminate this Agreement by giving written notice to Landlord, and shall be refunded all Rent and security deposit paid. Possession is deemed terminated when Tenant has returned all keys to the Premises to Landlord.
   B. ☐ Tenant is already in possession of the Premises.

29. **TENANT'S OBLIGATIONS UPON VACATING PREMISES:**
   A. Upon termination of this Agreement, Tenant shall: **(i)** give Landlord all copies of all keys or opening devices to Premises, including any common areas, **(ii)** vacate and surrender Premises to Landlord, empty of all persons; **(iii)** vacate any/all parking and/or storage space; **(iv)** clean and deliver Premises as specified in paragraph C below, to Landlord in the same condition as referenced in paragraph 10; **(v)** remove all debris; **(vi)** give written notice to Landlord of Tenant's forwarding address; and **(vii)** _____
   B. All alterations/improvements made by or caused to be made by Tenant, with or without Landlord's consent, become the property of Landlord upon termination. Landlord may charge Tenant for restoration of the Premises to the condition it was in prior to any alterations/improvements.
   C. Right to Pre-Move-Out Inspection and Repairs. **(i)** After giving or receiving notice of termination of a tenancy (C.A.R. Form NTT), or before the end of a lease, Tenant has the right to request that an inspection of the Premises take place prior to termination of the lease or rental (C.A.R. Form NRI). If Tenant requests such an inspection, Tenant shall be given an opportunity to remedy identified deficiencies prior to termination, consistent with the terms of this Agreement. **(ii)** Any repairs or alterations made to the Premises as a result of this inspection (collectively, "Repairs") shall be made at Tenant's expense. Repairs may be performed by Tenant or through others, who have adequate insurance and licenses and are approved by Landlord. The work shall comply with applicable law, including governmental permit, inspection and approval requirements. Repairs shall be performed in a good, skillful manner with materials of quality and appearance comparable to existing materials. It is understood that exact restoration of appearance or cosmetic items following all Repairs may not be possible. **(iii)** Tenant shall: **(a)** obtain receipts for Repairs performed by others; **(b)** prepare a written statement indicating the Repairs performed by Tenant and the date of such Repairs; and **(c)** provide copies of receipts and statements to Landlord prior to termination. Paragraph 29C does not apply when the tenancy is terminated pursuant to California Code of Civil Procedure § 1161(2), (3) or (4).

30. **BREACH OF CONTRACT; EARLY TERMINATION:** In addition to any obligations established by paragraph 29, in the event of termination by Tenant prior to completion of the original term of the Agreement, Tenant shall also be responsible for lost Rent, rental commissions, advertising expenses and painting costs necessary to ready Premises for re-rental. Landlord may withhold any such amounts from Tenant's security deposit.

31. **TEMPORARY RELOCATION:** Subject to local law, Tenant agrees, upon demand of Landlord, to temporarily vacate Premises for a reasonable period, to allow for fumigation (or other methods) to control wood destroying pests or organisms, or other repairs to Premises. Tenant agrees to comply with all instructions and requirements necessary to prepare Premises to accommodate pest control, fumigation or other work, including bagging or storage of food and medicine, and removal of perishables and valuables. Tenant shall only be entitled to a credit of Rent equal to the per diem Rent for the period of time Tenant is required to vacate Premises.

32. **DAMAGE TO PREMISES:** If, by no fault of Tenant, Premises are totally or partially damaged or destroyed by fire, earthquake, accident or other casualty that render Premises totally or partially uninhabitable, either Landlord or Tenant may terminate this Agreement by giving the other written notice. Rent shall be abated as of the date Premises become totally or partially uninhabitable. The abated amount shall be the current monthly Rent prorated on a 30-day period. If the Agreement is not terminated, Landlord shall promptly repair the damage, and Rent shall be reduced based on the extent to which the damage interferes with Tenant's reasonable use of Premises. If damage occurs as a result of an act of Tenant or Tenant's guests, only Landlord shall have the right of termination, and no reduction in Rent shall be made.

33. **INSURANCE:** Tenant's or guest's personal property and vehicles are not insured by Landlord, manager or, if applicable, HOA, against loss or damage due to fire, theft, vandalism, rain, water, criminal or negligent acts of others, or any other cause. **Tenant is**

Tenant's Initials (_____) (_____)
Landlord's Initials (_____) (_____)

Reviewed by _____ Date _____

RESIDENTIAL LEASE OR MONTH-TO-MONTH RENTAL AGREEMENT (LR PAGE 4 OF 6)

advised to carry Tenant's own insurance (renter's insurance) to protect Tenant from any such loss or damage. Tenant shall comply with any requirement imposed on Tenant by Landlord's insurer to avoid: (i) an increase in Landlord's insurance premium (or Tenant shall pay for the increase in premium); or (ii) loss of insurance.

34. **WATERBEDS:** Tenant shall not use or have waterbeds on the Premises unless: **(i)** Tenant obtains a valid waterbed insurance policy; **(ii)** Tenant increases the security deposit in an amount equal to one-half of one month's Rent; and **(iii)** the bed conforms to the floor load capacity of Premises.

35. **WAIVER:** The waiver of any breach shall not be construed as a continuing waiver of the same or any subsequent breach.

36. **NOTICE:** Notices may be served at the following address, or at any other location subsequently designated:
Landlord: _____ Tenant: _____

37. **TENANT ESTOPPEL CERTIFICATE:** Tenant shall execute and return a tenant estoppel certificate delivered to Tenant by Landlord or Landlord's agent within 3 days after its receipt. Failure to comply with this requirement shall be deemed Tenant's acknowledgment that the tenant estoppel certificate is true and correct, and may be relied upon by a lender or purchaser.

38. **TENANT REPRESENTATIONS; CREDIT:** Tenant warrants that all statements in Tenant's rental application are accurate. Tenant authorizes Landlord and Broker(s) to obtain Tenant's credit report periodically during the tenancy in connection with the modification or enforcement of this Agreement. Landlord may cancel this Agreement: **(i)** before occupancy begins; **(ii)** upon disapproval of the credit report(s); or **(iii)** at any time, upon discovering that information in Tenant's application is false. A negative credit report reflecting on Tenant's record may be submitted to a credit reporting agency if Tenant fails to fulfill the terms of payment and other obligations under this Agreement.

39. **MEDIATION:**
   A. Consistent with paragraphs B and C below, Landlord and Tenant agree to mediate any dispute or claim arising between them out of this Agreement, or any resulting transaction, before resorting to court action. Mediation fees, if any, shall be divided equally among the parties involved. If, for any dispute or claim to which this paragraph applies, any party commences an action without first attempting to resolve the matter through mediation, or refuses to mediate after a request has been made, then that party shall not be entitled to recover attorney fees even if they would otherwise be available to that party in any such action.
   B. The following matters are excluded from mediation: **(i)** an unlawful detainer action; **(ii)** the filing or enforcement of a mechanic's lien; and **(iii)** any matter within the jurisdiction of a probate, small claims or bankruptcy court. The filing of a court action to enable the recording of a notice of pending action, for order of attachment, receivership, injunction, or other provisional remedies, shall not constitute a waiver of the mediation provision.
   C. Landlord and Tenant agree to mediate disputes or claims involving Listing Agent, Leasing Agent or property manager ("Broker"), provided Broker shall have agreed to such mediation prior to, or within a reasonable time after, the dispute or claim is presented to such Broker. Any election by Broker to participate in mediation shall not result in Broker being deemed a party to this Agreement.

40. **ATTORNEY FEES:** In any action or proceeding arising out of this Agreement, the prevailing party between Landlord and Tenant shall be entitled to reasonable attorney fees and costs, except as provided in paragraph 39A.

41. **C.A.R. FORM:** C.A.R. Form means the specific form referenced or another comparable form agreed to by the parties.

42. **OTHER TERMS AND CONDITIONS; SUPPLEMENTS:** ☐ Interpreter/Translator Agreement (C.A.R. Form ITA);
☐ Keysafe/Lockbox Addendum (C.A.R. Form KLA); ☐ Lead-Based Paint and Lead-Based Paint Hazards Disclosure (C.A.R. Form FLD)

The following ATTACHED supplements are incorporated in this Agreement: _____

43. **TIME OF ESSENCE; ENTIRE CONTRACT; CHANGES:** Time is of the essence. All understandings between the parties are incorporated in this Agreement. Its terms are intended by the parties as a final, complete and exclusive expression of their Agreement with respect to its subject matter, and may not be contradicted by evidence of any prior agreement or contemporaneous oral agreement. If any provision of this Agreement is held to be ineffective or invalid, the remaining provisions will nevertheless be given full force and effect. Neither this Agreement nor any provision in it may be extended, amended, modified, altered or changed except in writing. This Agreement is subject to California landlord-tenant law and shall incorporate all changes required by amendment or successors to such law. This Agreement and any supplement, addendum or modification, including any copy, may be signed in two or more counterparts, all of which shall constitute one and the same writing.

44. **AGENCY:**
   A. **CONFIRMATION:** The following agency relationship(s) are hereby confirmed for this transaction:
   Listing Agent: (Print firm name) _____
   is the agent of (check one): ☐ the Landlord exclusively; or ☐ both the Landlord and Tenant.
   Leasing Agent: (Print firm name) _____
   (if not same as Listing Agent) is the agent of (check one): ☐ the Tenant exclusively; or ☐ the Landlord exclusively; or ☐ both the Tenant and Landlord.
   B. **DISCLOSURE:** ☐ (If checked): The term of this lease exceeds one year. A disclosure regarding real estate agency relationships (C.A.R. Form AD) has been provided to Landlord and Tenant, who each acknowledge its receipt.

45. ☐ **TENANT COMPENSATION TO BROKER:** Upon execution of this Agreement, Tenant agrees to pay compensation to Broker as specified in a separate written agreement between Tenant and Broker.

Tenant's Initials (_____)(_____)
Landlord's Initials (_____)(_____)

Reviewed by _____ Date _____

LR REVISED 11/08 (PAGE 5 OF 6)

RESIDENTIAL LEASE OR MONTH-TO-MONTH RENTAL AGREEMENT (LR PAGE 5 OF 6)

Premises: *123 Sail Avenue*
Marina del Rey, CA 90292 _____ Date: _____

46. ☐ **INTERPRETER/TRANSLATOR:** The terms of this Agreement have been interpreted for Tenant into the following language: _____ . Landlord and Tenant acknowledge receipt of the attached interpretor/translator agreement (C.A.R. Form ITA).

47. **FOREIGN LANGUAGE NEGOTIATION:** If this Agreement has been negotiated by Landlord and Tenant primarily in Spanish, Chinese, Tagalog, Korean or Vietnamese. pursuant to the California Civil Code Tenant shall be provided a translation of this Agreement in the language used for the negotiation.

48. **OWNER COMPENSATION TO BROKER:** Upon execution of this Agreement, Owner agrees to pay compensation to Broker as specified in a separate written agreement between Owner and Broker (C.A.R. Form LCA).

49. **RECEIPT:** If specified in paragraph 5, Landlord or Broker, acknowledges receipt of move-in funds.

> Landlord and Tenant acknowledge and agree Brokers: **(a)** do not guarantee the condition of the Premises; **(b)** cannot verify representations made by others; **(c)** cannot provide legal or tax advice; **(d)** will not provide other advice or information that exceeds the knowledge, education or experience required to obtain a real estate license. Furthermore, if Brokers are not also acting as Landlord in this Agreement, Brokers: **(e)** do not decide what rental rate a Tenant should pay or Landlord should accept; and **(f)** do not decide upon the length or other terms of tenancy. Landlord and Tenant agree that they will seek legal, tax, insurance and other desired assistance from appropriate professionals.

Tenant agrees to rent the Premises on the above terms and conditions.

Tenant _____ Date _____
Address _____ City _____ State _____ Zip _____
Telephone _____ Fax _____ E-mail _____

Tenant _____ Date _____
Address _____ City _____ State _____ Zip _____
Telephone _____ Fax _____ E-mail _____

☐ **GUARANTEE:** In consideration of the execution of this Agreement by and between Landlord and Tenant and for valuable consideration, receipt of which is hereby acknowledged, the undersigned ("Guarantor") does hereby: **(i)** guarantee unconditionally to Landlord and Landlord's agents, successors and assigns, the prompt payment of Rent or other sums that become due pursuant to this Agreement, including any and all court costs and attorney fees included in enforcing the Agreement; **(ii)** consent to any changes, modifications or alterations of any term in this Agreement agreed to by Landlord and Tenant; and **(iii)** waive any right to require Landlord and/or Landlord's agents to proceed against Tenant for any default occurring under this Agreement before seeking to enforce this Guarantee.

Guarantor (Print Name) _____
Guarantor _____ Date _____
Address _____ City _____ State _____ Zip _____
Telephone _____ Fax _____ E-mail _____

Landlord agrees to rent the Premises on the above terms and conditions.
Landlord _____ Landlord _____

Address _____
Telephone _____ Fax _____ E-mail _____

REAL ESTATE BROKERS:
A. Real estate brokers who are not also Landlord under this Agreement are not parties to the Agreement between Landlord and Tenant.
B. Agency relationships are confirmed in paragraph 44.
C. **COOPERATING BROKER COMPENSATION:** Listing Broker agrees to pay Cooperating Broker (Leasing Firm) and Cooperating Broker agrees to accept: **(i)** the amount specified in the MLS, provided Cooperating Broker is a Participant of the MLS in which the Property is offered for sale or a reciprocal MLS; or **(ii)** ☐ (if checked) the amount specified in a separate written agreement between Listing Broker and Cooperating Broker.

Real Estate Broker (Listing Firm) _____ DRE Lic. #_____
By (Agent) _____ DRE Lic. #_____ Date _____
Address _____ City _____ State _____ Zip _____
Telephone _____ Fax _____ E-mail _____

Real Estate Broker (Leasing Firm) _____ DRE Lic. #_____
By (Agent) _____ DRE Lic. #_____ Date _____
Address _____ City _____ State _____ Zip _____
Telephone _____ Fax _____ E-mail _____

Reviewed by _____ Date _____

LR REVISED 11/08 (PAGE 6 OF 6)

RESIDENTIAL LEASE OR MONTH-TO-MONTH RENTAL AGREEMENT (LR PAGE 6 OF 6)   Untitled

You should consider giving your tenants a check list with telephone numbers for utilities, post office, school registration, etc.

You might want to sign the lease on the premises where furnished rentals are involved. The tenants should also sign an inventory list of items furnished in the units. We recommend taking polaroid photos of the furnished units prior to renting and have the tenants sign and date each photo. This will help you should there be a dispute later as to damage to the units.

VOICE OF EXPERIENCE:

Polaroid photos are preferred over digital photos, as the latter can easily be modified with a Photoshop® type of software. You don't want your tenant to alter a digital photo when moving out to show that there were no curtains in the unit when he/she moved in, for example, by "photoshopping" them out of the picture. Also, once you take polaroid photos, have the tenant initial and date them in indelible ink.

F. LESSOR DISCLOSURES

A number of lessor disclosures are required. These include the following:

Name and Address on Notices. Tenants of multi-unit dwellings generally must be provided with the name and address of persons who have management responsibility and on whom notices and demands may be served. This provision should be provided in writing if it is not provided in the lease.

Lead-Based Paint Disclosure. For property that was built prior to 1978, tenants must be provide with a disclosure on lead-based paint.

Some states require water heater strapping, smoke detectors, and sex offender disclosures.

VII. Uniform Residential Landlord and Tenant Act

In addition to obligations set forth in the lease, there are legally mandated rights and obligations.

The Uniform Residential Landlord and Tenant Act has been adopted in whole or in part in most states.

In adopting the act, many states have made some modifications to this act.

A. GENERAL PROVISIONS

Unconscionable Leases. Leases that are considered unconscionable will not be enforced. (A lease where a tenant waives his or her legal rights would be considered unconscionable.)

Failure of Lessor to Sign. If a rental agreement is signed by the tenant and delivered to the landlord who fails to sign but accepts rent without reservation, the lease has the same effect as if it were signed and delivered.

If the term of the lease is longer than one year, the unsigned lease would only be valid for one year.

Confession of Judgment. A lease provision where a tenant confesses judgment, if in default, is prohibited.

A confession of judgment gives up the tenant's right to defend actions in court.

Attorney Fees. A provision where the tenant agrees to pay a landlord's attorney fees, regardless of a court decision, is prohibited.

Note: Attorney fees to the prevailing party are proper. Landlords are usually responsible for attorney fees for eviction.

Hold Harmless. A provision where the tenant agrees to hold the landlord harmless for any personal injury or property loss, regardless of landlord fault, would be prohibited.

Knowingly Including Prohibited Provisions. If a landlord knows a provision is prohibited but knowingly includes it in a lease, the tenant is entitled to actual damages plus up to three month's rent and attorney's fees.

Beware, as damage expenses may trickle down to you, the manager.

Security Deposit Limits. While there is no limit on prepaid rent, residential security deposits are limited to one month's rent. (In California, it is two month's rent for unfurnished units and three month's rent for furnished units.)

Accounting for Deposits. Failure to return a deposit can result in return of the deposit plus twice the amount wrongfully held, as well as attorney's fees. (In California, the lessor has 21 days to account for and return funds owed and damages are limited to actual damages plus $600 in exemplary damages.) Time limits and damage amounts may vary from state to state.

A California landlord must account for funds within 21 days of termination of tenancy.

Name of Manager. The landlord must give the tenant the name and address of the manager or person authorized to receive notices and legal service.

Possession. The landlord must deliver possession of the premises at commencement of the lease.

B. LESSOR'S DUTIES

Codes. The landlord must comply with applicable health and safety codes.

Repairs. The landlord must make repairs necessary to keep the premises in a fit and habitable condition. The landlord is not responsible to make repairs for damage caused by the tenant's carelessness, such as a child's toy clogging a toilet.

If the tenant's improper conduct caused a problem that made the premises uninhabitable, the tenant cannot require the landlord to repair. If the tenant interferes with the landlord's ability to make repairs, the tenant cannot require the landlord to make repairs.

Common Areas. The landlord must keep common areas in a clean and safe condition.

Maintenance. The landlord must maintain electrical, plumbing, sanitary, heating, ventilating, air conditioning and other facilities (including elevators) in good and safe working order.

Garbage Receptacles. The landlord shall provide and maintain garbage receptacles and arrange for garbage removal.

Water and Heat. The landlord shall provide water and a reasonable amount of hot water as well as heat, the latter generally between October 1 and May 1. Exceptions to this period of time would be situations where the facilities are under the exclusive control of the tenant.

Working Toilet. There must be a working toilet, washbasin, and bathtub or shower. The toilet, bathtub or shower must be in a ventilated room and the room must provide privacy.

Kitchen Sink. The kitchen must have a sink that cannot be made of absorbent material such as wood.

Natural Lighting. There must be natural lighting in every room (window or skylight). If the windows do not open, there must be ventilation.

Emergency Exits. There must be fire or emergency exits leading to a street or hallway.

Smoke Detectors. There must be smoke detectors in common stairwells and within the dwelling unit when there is more than one unit.

Agreements. Agreements otherwise as to garbage disposal repair, etc., are proper as long as such agreements are made in good faith.

Quiet Enjoyment.

The lessor shall not interfere with a tenant's quiet enjoyment of the premises.

Violation of a lessor's covenant of quiet enjoyment could include:

1. wrongful entry into tenant's space;
2. barring tenant access to his or her space;
3. numerous and/or needless repairs that disturbs the tenant's peace;
4. leasing the property to a third party and giving possession while the tenant has a right of possession.

The breach of the covenant of quiet possession could allow a tenant to terminate the lease without further obligation.

In California, landlords are required to provide written **Notices of Entry** to tenants any time the landlord enters the property, except in the case of emergency, abandonment, or when showing potential purchasers the property.

A 24-hour notice must be given in California and showings must be during normal working hours (9:00-5:00 during the week). Many managers will give incentives to existing tenants to allow better showing conditions.

C. TENANT'S DUTIES

Code Compliance. The tenant must comply with tenant obligations under building and health codes.

Cleanliness. The tenant must keep the premises clean and safe as conditions permit.

Garbage. The tenant must dispose of garbage and waste in a clean and safe manner.

Use of Fixtures and Appliances. The tenant must use electrical, plumbing and gas fixtures and appliances in a proper manner and maintain them in a clean manner.

Protection of Premises. The tenant shall not deliberately or negligently damage, deface, destroy or remove parts of the premises or permit others to do so.

Use of Premises. Tenant shall use the premises only as a dwelling unless agree otherwise.

Conduct. The tenants shall conduct themselves in a manner that will not disturb the peaceful enjoyment of other tenants.

Rules. The tenant shall abide by rules and regulations that promote the safety and welfare of tenants if they apply equally and fairly to all tenants.

End of Tenancy. The tenant shall surrender the premises to the landlord at the termination of the tenancy in a clean and proper manner.

VIII. After Occupancy

A. RENT COLLECTIONS

As a matter of security, rent should only be accepted in the form of a check or money order (see Chapter 9). Cash creates a security problem and places property management personnel at risk.

Rent should be either paid at the resident manager's office or at the central office of the management firm. A procedure needs to be in place for rental collection problems.

Late Payment. Fees charged for late payments set forth in the lease must be strictly and uniformly enforced.

Tenant Promises. One promise by a tenant to pay by a specific date might be allowed, but no further promises should be allowed to deter taking eviction action.

Three-Day Notice. When rent is 15 days late (some firms allow longer periods), the tenant should be served with a notice, generally a three-day notice to quit or pay rent (see **Figure 5-3**).

Unlawful Detainer Action. A three-day notice normally results in tenant compliance. In the event the tenant does not comply, an *UNLAWFUL DETAINER ACTION follows the three-day notice. It is the legal action to evict a tenant who is in default.*

No rent should be accepted (unless payment is in full) after the three-day notice is given or acceptance may defeat the unlawful detainer action. The specific rent due must be set forth.

Asking for more than the amount due could also defeat the action, therefore no late charge should be included.

A tenant has a limited period to respond to an unlawful detainer action. In California, the tenant has five days to file an answer. If the tenant fails to answer the complaint, a judgment will be entered against the tenant. This will authorize the sheriff to remove the tenant and his or her possessions from the property.

Tenant Defenses. The tenant can defend against an unlawful detainer action for the following:

1. That the action is invalid (three-day notice not served, only two days passed before unlawful detainer was served on tenant, etc.).
2. The property was not inhabitable. If a lessor breaches the covenant of habitability, an unlawful detainer will generally not be enforced against a tenant. The landlord has failed to provide a habitable dwelling.

Figure 5-3

CALIFORNIA
ASSOCIATION
OF REALTORS®

NOTICE TO PAY RENT OR QUIT
(C.A.R. Form PRQ, Revised 4/03)

To: _____ ("Tenant")

_____ ("Tenant")

_____ (Street Address)

_____ (Street Address), (Unit/Apartment #)

_____ , _____ _____ (City), (State) (Zip Code) ("Premises").

Other notice address if different from Premises above: _____

_____ .

Notice to the above-named person(s) and any other occupants of the above-referenced Premises:

WITHIN 3 (OR ☐ _____ (BUT NOT LESS THAN 3)) DAYS from service of this Notice you are required to either:

1. Pay rent for the Premises in the following amount, which is past due, to _____

_____ (Name) _____ (Phone)

at _____

_____ (Address)

between the hours of _____ on the following days: _____ .

Past Due Rent $ _____ for the period _____ to _____

$ _____ for the period _____ to _____

$ _____ for the period _____ to _____

Total Due: $ _____ .

OR 2. Vacate the Premises and surrender possession.

If you do not pay the past due amount or give up possession in the required time, a legal action will be filed seeking not only damages and possession, but also a statutory damage penalty of up to $600.00 (California Code of Civil Procedure § 1174). Landlord declares a forfeiture of the lease if past due rent is not paid and you continue to occupy the Premises. As required by law, you are hereby notified that a negative credit report reflecting on your credit record may be submitted to a credit reporting agency if you fail to pay your rent.

Landlord _____ Date _____
(Owner or Agent)
Address _____ City _____ State _____ Zip _____
Telephone _____ Fax _____ E-mail _____

(Keep a copy for your records.)

This Notice was served by:

1. ☐ **Personal service.** A copy of the Notice was personally delivered to the above named Tenant.

2. ☐ **Substituted service.** A copy of the Notice was left with a person of suitable age and discretion at the Tenant's residence or usual place of business and a copy was mailed to the Tenant at Tenant's residence.

3. ☐ **Post and mail.** A copy of the Notice was affixed to a conspicuous place on the Premises and a copy was mailed to the Tenant at the Premises.

Published and Distributed by:
REAL ESTATE BUSINESS SERVICES, INC.
a subsidiary of the California Association of REALTORS®
525 South Virgil Avenue, Los Angeles, California 90020

Reviewed by _____ Date _____

EQUAL HOUSING OPPORTUNITY

PRQ REVISED 4/03 (PAGE 1 OF 1)

NOTICE TO PAY RENT OR QUIT (PRQ PAGE 1 OF 1)

Agent: WALT HUBER	Phone:	Fax:	Prepared using zipForm® software
Broker: WALT HUBER REALTOR			

3. The court will not allow the enforcement of an eviction when it is retaliatory. If a lessor evicts a tenant (for other than failure to pay rent) within a designated period of a tenant complaining to a public authority about violations by the landlord or for tenant organizing activities, the court would view such action as retaliatory eviction and refuse to enforce the action. (California statutes provide a 180-day period.)

4. If the tenant can show that the eviction was based on the fact that the tenant was a member of a protected group, then the eviction could be a civil rights violation. (See Chapter 13.) The action would not be enforced.

Self-Help Evictions. A lessor cannot generally force a tenant to move by removing the door, cutting off utilities, threatening force, changing locks or by physically removing the tenant's possessions. All such actions would expose the lessor to compensatory and likely punitive damages. California Civil Code Section 789.3 provides for damages of $100 per day for cutting off utilities as well as other self-help eviction action.

B. ENFORCEMENT OF CONTRACT PROVISIONS OR RULES AND REGULATIONS

If a tenant fails to meet the lease requirements or rules as agreed to by the tenant, he or she may be served with a Notice to Quit or Cure.

This notice sets forth the tenant's breach and provides that failure to cure the breach within a period of time (generally three days) will result in an action to recover possession (Unlawful Detainer Action). **Figure 5-4** is a sample form of one such notice.

C. 30/60-DAY NOTICE

If a month-to-month tenant has lived in the dwelling for less than a year, a 30-day notice to terminate the tenancy must be given. However, if the month-to-month periodic tenant has lived in the dwelling for one year or more, a 60-day notice to terminate must be given by the landlord (this time frame may change periodically). A tenant may terminate a month-to-month periodic tenancy by giving a 30-day notice.

D. CHANGE IN RENT/COVENANTS

A lessor can change the rent or covenants of the lease, when it is a periodic tenancy, by giving the tenant a notice of the new rent and/or lease terms (generally 30 days).

E. CONFIRMATION OF LEASE

The lease may provide that the tenant will complete a lease confirmation (an estoppel certificate) setting forth the tenant's lease rights. This would be for the purchaser or lender. If a tenant had an option to purchase it could effect the rights of the lender or purchaser if such a right was not disclosed.

Figure 5-4

CALIFORNIA
ASSOCIATION
OF REALTORS®

NOTICE TO
PERFORM COVENANT (CURE) OR QUIT
(C.A.R. Form PCQ, 4/03)

To: _____ ("Tenant")
_____ (Street Address)
_____ (Street Address), (Unit/Apartment #)
_____ , _____ _____ (City), (State) (Zip Code) ("Premises").

Other notice address if different from Premises above: _____
_____ .

Notice to the above-named person(s) and any other occupants of the above-referenced Premises:
WITHIN 3 (OR ☐ _____ (BUT NOT LESS THAN 3)) DAYS from service of this Notice you are required to either:
1.   Perform the following covenant or cure the following breach of your rental agreement: _____
_____
_____
_____
_____

OR 2.   **Vacate the Premises and surrender possession.**
If you do not perform, cure the breach, or give up possession by the required time, a legal action will be filed seeking not only damages and possession, but also a statutory damage penalty of up to $600.00 (California Code of Civil Procedure § 1174). NOTICE: Pursuant to California Civil Code, § 1785.26, you are hereby notified that a negative credit report reflecting on your credit record may be submitted in the future to a credit reporting agency if you fail to fulfill the terms of your rental/credit obligations. Landlord declares a forfeiture of the lease if: **(i)** you do not perform as specified in paragraph 1; or **(ii)** the breach of your rental agreement is not cured and you continue to occupy the Premises.

Landlord _____ Date _____
(Owner or Agent)
Address _____ City _____ State _____ Zip _____
Telephone _____ Fax _____ E-mail _____
(Keep a copy for your records.)

This Notice was served by:

1.   ☐ **Personal service.** A copy of the Notice was personally delivered to the above named Tenant.

2.   ☐ **Substituted service.** A copy of the Notice was left with a person of suitable age and discretion at the Tenant's residence or usual place of business and a copy was mailed to the Tenant at Tenant's residence.

3.   ☐ **Post and mail.** A copy of the Notice was affixed to a conspicuous place on the Premises and a copy was mailed to the Tenant at the Premises.

REBS   Published and Distributed by:
REAL ESTATE BUSINESS SERVICES, INC.
a subsidiary of the California Association of REALTORS®
525 South Virgil Avenue, Los Angeles, California 90020

Reviewed by _____ Date _____   EQUAL HOUSING OPPORTUNITY

PCQ REVISED 4/03 (PAGE 1 OF 1)

NOTICE TO PERFORM COVENANT (CURE) OR QUIT (PCQ PAGE 1 OF 1)

Agent: WALT HUBER	Phone:	Fax:	Prepared using zipForm® software
Broker: WALT HUBER REALTOR			

IX. CHAPTER SUMMARY

The need for housing is affected by a number of factors:

1. The number of family units is more important than the raw population figures.

2. Economic conditions cause coupling and uncoupling of families.

3. Society changes with the decline of extended family residences resulting from social security and pension plans.

4. Interest rates affect rental housing needs in that lower interest rates make ownership possible for more renters.

5. Population bulges result in need for starter housing as well as family and then elderly housing as bulges move through various age brackets.

6. Political changes such as taxes, growth limitations, development fees, rent control and zoning affect the number of new units that will be built to replace deteriorating housing stock.

7. The fact that development from land acquisition to renting can take as much as several years means that there can be a significant lag period between housing need developing and the meeting of that need.

8. Since the housing market is stratified by type of housing and amount of rent, there can be a need for one type of housing at one rental price and a housing surplus at another price.

Property management contracts are the owner/agent contracts. They should be for several years because of the time and effort required to turn around poorly managed property. The word "broker" is interchangeable with "property manager" in the management contract. These contracts include:

1. The authority and obligations of the broker.
2. The broker's rights regarding advertising and tenant selection.
3. The broker's power to negotiate and execute leases.
4. Rent collection authority.
5. The authority to terminate tenancies and give notices.
6. The authority to employ attorneys to enforce owners' rights.
7. The power to provide all management services.
8. The authority to hire and discharge employees.
9. The authority to contract for repairs and to enter service contracts (there may be dollar and time limits).
10. The authority to pay operational expenses, mortgage payments, taxes, insurance, etc.
11. The requirement for proper record keeping.
12. The requirement to submit monthly statements.
13. Special requirements would be added for specific owner or property needs.

Owner obligations would also be set forth in the property management contract. These obligations include:

1. Compensation to property manager for a percentage of gross revenue, minimum fee or a flat fee.
2. Leasing compensation.
3. Compensation for supervision of improvements.
4. Compensation for obtaining refinancing.
5. Compensation for other services.

Other provisions of the property management contract would include an agreement to hold the property manager harmless from expenses and damages arising from the contract, as well as the owner's duty to carry designated insurance coverage. In the event of any dispute, the parties would agree that the prevailing party would be entitled to attorney's fees.

When a property management firm takes over management of a property they should review property policies and make changes where necessary. Areas of change to consider could include rent schedules, security deposits, allowing pets, periods of leases and expiration dates, furnishings of units, occupancy and qualification requirements, etc.

Rents should be competitive with other vacant units on the market, not units already rented. Rents should be set so that the rental rate and vacancy factor combine to produce the maximum net return to the owner. Too high a rent results in too high a vacancy factor and rents too low result in less than a maximization of income, which is a disservice to an owner.

Property should sparkle when placed on the rental market. Prospective tenants should be prequalified before being shown a vacant unit. A rental application should be the result of a successful showing.

The applicant's credit, work, and rental history should be checked during the qualification process. If the applicant is qualified, the lease should be explained in detail as well as rules of the property. All deposits should be received at the time the applicant signs the lease.

By law, the lessor is responsible for:

1. A weather-tight unit.
2. Proper plumbing and gas.
3. Hot and cold water supply.
4. Heating facilities.
5. Proper wiring.
6. Clean and sanitary buildings and grounds.
7. Sufficiently clean garbage receptacles.
8. Stairs, floors and railings in good repair.

9. A working toilet.
10. A kitchen sink of nonabsorbent material.
11. Natural lighting in each room.
12. Emergency exits.
13. Smoke detectors.

The landlord must also not interfere with a tenant's quiet enjoyment of the premises.

The tenant's legal responsibilities include:

1. Cleanliness.
2. Proper garbage disposal.
3. Proper utilization of fixtures and appliances.
4. Not permitting damage to the property.
5. Use as residence only.
6. Surrendering the premises at the end of the lease.

Property management duties, in addition to leasing and maintenance, include setting forth procedures for rent collection and following those procedures, enforcement of contract provisions as well as property rules, adjustments to rents and eviction notices.

The quality of the interpersonal relationships between tenants and with tenants are one determinant of successful management. Tenant problems must be handled promptly.

X. CHAPTER QUIZ

1. Which of the following would be a factor of rental housing needs in an area?

    a. The growth in the number of family units

    b. Changes in the local economy

    c. A lowering of interest rates

    d. All of the above

2. A moratorium on new construction could be expected to:

    a. reduce the vacancy factor.

    b. result in rent increases.

    c. both a and b.

    d. neither a nor b.

3. Rent control can be expected to result in:

    a. reducing new construction.

    b. minimum maintenance of rent controlled units.

    c. uneconomic utilization of property.

    d. all of the above.

4. A property management contract is likely to provide for compensation based on all of the following, except:

    a. a percentage of an owner's net income.

    b. a percentage of an owner's gross income.

    c. a fee for leasing.

    d. a fee for supervision of improvements.

5. A residential lease may properly:

    a. provide for the tenants to waive legal rights.

    b. provide for a confession of judgment should the tenant default.

    c. provide that the tenant pay the lessor's legal fees in any dispute, regardless of fault.

    d. none of the above.

6. Reasons why an owner would allow pets include:

    a. to reduce the vacancy factor.

    b. to increase rents.

    c. to increase the average tenancy period.

    d. all of the above.

7. Which of the following is TRUE when comparing furnished and unfurnished residential units?

    a. Unfurnished units command higher rents.

    b. People stay for longer periods of time in furnished units.

    c. Maintenance costs are greater for furnished units.

    d. Management fees are lower for furnished units.

8. The best way to set rents would be to consider:
   a. the cost of the property.
   b. the return that is desired by the property owner.
   c. operational costs.
   d. rents asked for comparable properties having reasonable vacancy factors.

9. If the vacancy rate remains the same when rents and operational expenses both increase by 10 percent, the owner, whose debt service is a fixed expense cash flow, should see his/her cash flow:
   a. remain the same.
   b. increase less than 10 percent.
   c. increase 10 percent.
   d. increase more than 10 percent.

10. Lessors of residential units have certain legal duties. They include all, except:
   a. the duty to supply heating facilities.
   b. the duty to provide air conditioning facilities.
   c. the duty to provide a working toilet.
   d. the duty to provide for natural lighting in every room.

ANSWERS: 1. d; 2. c; 3. d; 4. b; 5. d; 6. d; 7. c; 8. d; 9. d; 10. b

Chapter 6
Commercial, Office, & Industrial Property Management

KEY WORDS AND TERMS

Absorption Rate
Anchor Tenants
Class A Buildings
Class B Buildings
Class C Buildings
Class D Buildings
Clear Span
Combination Building
Commercial Property
Community Shopping Center
Demographics
Discretionary Purchasing Power
Economic Life
Excess Parking
Factory Outlet
Fire Suppression Systems
Fixturing Allowance

Footloose Industries
Freestanding Retailers
Garden Office Buildings
High-Rise Office Buildings
Industrial Parks
Intelligent Building
Labor-Oriented Location
Loading Docks
Low-Rise Office Buildings
Market-Oriented Location
Mega-Mall
Mid-Rise Office Building
Mini-Mall
Neighborhood Shopping Center
Overbuilding
Pedestrian Shopping Streets
Quality of Life

R&D Facilities
Regional Shopping Center
Sick Buildings
Special Use Structures
Square Footage
Stores
Supply-Oriented Location
Symbiotic Relationship
Tenant Mix
Tenant Quality
Theme Buildings
Transportation-Oriented Location
Trophy Building
Urban Pedestrian Mall
Utility Oriented Location

Chapter 6

CHAPTER 6 OUTLINE

Commercial, Office, & Industrial Property Management

I. Commercial Property Management

COMMERCIAL PROPERTY *involves the buying and selling of commodities or goods.* Primarily, commercial property would be involved in retail sales. A lesser amount of space would be devoted to wholesale operations, restaurants, and service providers, such as lenders who deal with the general public.

A. HOW MUCH COMMERCIAL SPACE?

The requirements for commercial space are not based on raw population figures alone. Other community factors include the following:

Number of Households. The number of households affects the demand for furniture and appliances as well as many other household purchases.

Discretionary Purchasing Power. After fixed expenses, such as mortgage or rent payments, car payments, insurance, basic food purchases, etc., what is left is discretionary income.

The greater the discretionary income, the better the business is for the sale of nonessential goods and services.

Demographics. The age of the residents of an area affects saving and spending. For a large percentage of people in the 45 to 55 age group, a significant portion of their discretionary income is put into savings. On the other hand, the 25 to 35 age group spends a higher percentage of its discretionary income.

Exceptions would be affluent retirement communities. Older populations require less commercial square footage, while a younger population would need more commercial square footage.

As a general rule, the need for commercial space within a community is inverse to the average age of its residents.

Drawing Power of Area. The commercial areas in many communities have drawing power far greater than would ordinarily be expected. As an example, tourists from around the world who come to Los Angeles often want to shop on Rodeo Drive.

Many individual retailers and shopping centers draw customers from a wide geographical area.

In the 1960s, there was a chain of discount department stores in Southern California known as White Front. The chain went through an expansion stage and not only did the volume of the new stores fail to meet expectations, but a number of existing stores also suffered a significant decline in volume. It has been suggested that the failure of White Front was partially based on the fact that the management did not understand fully that the stores were drawing customers from a wide area. While new stores made it more convenient for customers, a loyal customer base was now spread over more stores.

B. TYPES OF RETAIL PROPERTIES

RETAIL refers to the sale of goods or commodities in small quantities directly to consumers.

1. Pedestrian Shopping Streets

PEDESTRIAN SHOPPING STREETS tend to be lined with buildings having no side-yard setbacks, just stores side-by-side.

VOICE OF EXPERIENCE:

Corner locations command the highest rent in pedestrian shopping streets because of greater window display area as well as signage. Visability is always important for retailers. The corner locations are also more visible from vehicular traffic, especially if there is a traffic stop sign or traffic signal.

As a general rule, the closer a location is to the corner on a pedestrian shopping street, the higher the rent. The lowest rent would be in the center of the block. An exception would be a store next to another extremely successful store. Being close to a desired shopping location could bolster sales and allow for greater rent.

In The Sunbelt, the south and west sides of streets tend to have greater sales volume than do north and east sides of the street if other factors are equal. The reason for this is that the greatest volume of sales tend to be after 12 PM when the south and west sides of the street are shaded from the hot sun.

The volume of foot traffic on pedestrian shopping streets affects sales volume and rents. Often a few businesses mixed with other uses will cause pedestrians to cross a street and return on the other side of the street. Banks, savings institutions, brokerage offices, churches, etc., are of little interest to shoppers. A block with few, if any, retail stores is dead space for shoppers and will affect pedestrian traffic.

2. Urban Pedestrian Mall

An *URBAN PEDESTRIAN MALL is a mall open only to foot traffic.* By eliminating vehicular traffic on a street, an urban pedestrian mall can revitalize an urban shopping area. This has been successful in Santa Monica and in Santa Barbara. However, the Fulton Mall in Fresno was not a success. Problems with the Fulton Mall were attributed to a great deal of crime in the area, the opening of an enclosed mall that captured many of the upscale shops plus the fact that there was only one anchor tenant on the street.

3. Strip Centers

A *STRIP CENTER is a line of shops that attract vehicular traffic rather than foot traffic.* Stores in many strip centers fail to support each other. Shopping at one store does not bring the shopper into neighboring stores. Customers tend to park close to the store in which they are interested.

VOICE OF EXPERIENCE:

Easy access is very important in a strip center. If it's too hard to get in and out of, drivers will keep driving. If there's no left turn at a light leading into the mall, people will not always make the effort to go a block or two past the mall and make a u-turn. Adequate parking is also a concern.

Volume increases if strip center stores offer similar appeal to shoppers so that each store "feeds" the other with customers, such as a four-store building selling women's shoes, dresses, women's sportswear and a beauty parlor. This is a *SYMBIOTIC RELATIONSHIP, where each store helps the other,* which means success for the merchants and for the owner of the building.

4. Mini-Malls (Convenience Center)

MINI-MALLS are small centers with an anchor tenant that is a fast food store or convenience store, such as a 7-11® store. A mini-mall generally has less than 10,000 square feet and other shops could include a dry cleaner, donut shop, delicatessen, etc. The center provides for quick ingress and egress (in and out).

5. Neighborhood Shopping Center

Neighborhood shopping centers have a supermarket as a primary anchor tenant. *ANCHOR TENANTS are the primary draw for a shopping center.* Stores between the anchor tenants benefit from the foot traffic.

Additional anchor tenants for neighborhood shopping centers could be a chain drug store or variety store. Customers frequent this type of anchor tenant at least once per week. A supermarket may have the same foot traffic at least three times per week. A neighborhood shopping center usually consists of 10 to approximately 30 stores.

6. Community Shopping Center

A *COMMUNITY SHOPPING CENTER might have as the primary anchor tenant a department store or a discount store such as Target® or Wal-Mart®.* A major food store might be the other anchor, with all types of shops between the anchor stores. There may be 30 to 75 stores in a community shopping center, including some freestanding pads for fast food outlets, quick lube operations, banks, etc.

A community shopping center, with a large home improvement center as an anchor, may attract other tenants, such as carpet, tile, and drapery stores, all of whom are willing to pay premium rates.

7. Regional Shopping Center

A *REGIONAL SHOPPING CENTER, which could be in excess of one-half million square feet and house several department stores, is likely to be a mall.* The anchor tenants are usually placed at the end of wings in the mall. Shoppers must pass stores between the anchor tenants. The smaller stores pay a premium rent for this foot traffic generated by the anchor tenants.

The greater the draw by anchor tenants, the higher the rent other tenants are able to pay.

Because of the size of the center and distance shoppers have to park from stores, regional shopping centers seldom include major food stores. This eliminates shopping carts and makes store traffic flow smoothly.

When a developer or manager wants to entice a particular high-profile anchor tenant to a shopping center, they may offer a "sweetheart" deal of below-market rent. In some cases, the offer is free rent for one year followed by a percentage lease beginning at below-market level and only reaching market rental in five to seven years. This, of course, would be an extreme inducement.

When anchor tenants line up to lease space, far better lease terms are possible from a management standpoint.

Assume a center has been planned for three major anchors and you have obtained Nordstrom and Macy's by offering rental incentives. Due to the strong draw of these two anchor tenants, chances are you can lease the third location for a premium rate.

Shopping centers have become more than just places to sell merchandise. They have become community gathering areas that have replaced the village green.

Courts have held that shopping centers cannot exclude persons who wish to obtain signatures for petitions or to hand out religious material, as long as the activity doesn't impede commercial use.

Case Example

Union of Needletrades v. Superior Court, 56 C.A. 4th 996 (1997)

A union was involved in a labor dispute with Guess. The union wanted to place pickets at the Guess stores located in numerous malls. Taubman Company refused access because the union would not follow application procedures, nor accept the picket locations specified by mall management. The union sued, claiming that they were denied free speech. The Superior Court refused to issue an injunction allowing the union to picket the stores and the Court of Appeals affirmed.

The court held that the malls were reasonable as to rules, time and place for picketing. The court pointed out that free speech does not mean that the union can impede commerce.

Note: This decision is not in conflict with the landmark case of *Robins v. Pruneyard Shopping Center*, 23 C. 3d 899 (1979). In the Pruneyard case, Robins wanted to put a card table in a corner of a courtyard to obtain petition signatures. The court held that free speech must be protected, even at privately owned shopping centers. The court pointed out that the petitioning in this case was reasonably exercised.

Terry v. Reno, 101 F.3d 1412 (D.C.Cir. 1996)

Protesters have no First Amendment right to "cordon off a street, or [the] entrance to a public or private building, and allow no one to pass who did not agree to listen to their exhortations."

8. Mega-Malls

The four Ghermezian brothers built a mall in Edmonton, Canada, a city of 600,000 people. At the time, the mall, with 5.5 million square feet, was the largest in the world. The mall includes a 360-room hotel, 836 retail stores, a church, dozens of restaurants and an amusement park; all protected from the harsh Canadian winters. Besides strolling bands, tumblers, musicians and singers there is a hockey rink used by the Edmonton Oilers for practice, a full-sized Spanish Galleon floating in its own sea, a Disney-type aquarium with four 28-passenger submarines, a 142-foot high roller coaster with a triple loop, a waterpark with a 120-foot waterfall, indoor wave machine for surfing, powered waterskiing and a lot more.

Edmonton's population could never have supported such a mall but it has been fantastically successful. Per-square foot sales figures are believed to be the highest for any North American mall. With parking for more than 30,000 cars and 250,000 visitors per day, the mall has been credited with a 70 percent increase in Edmonton tourism.

On the negative side, the Edmonton mall has also been blamed for disastrous results to the Edmonton central shopping areas. The Ghermezian brothers believe that if a mall is built right, it will dominate the market. In the case of Edmonton, they were correct.

Malls with amusement features tend to detain people for many hours. A visit to the Edmonton mall can take an entire day, including live theatrical attractions in the evening.

The Ghermezian brothers, along with U.S. associates, built the huge Mall of America near the Minneapolis airport and only minutes away from an existing regional mall. The Mall of America has captured the market and is a vacation destination for hundreds of thousands of people. The mall includes a roller coaster, four-acre water park, over 800 stores, 100 restaurants and more. Like the Edmonton Mall, the U.S. mall is an international tourist destination. The drawing power extends to Europe and Asia.

Mega-malls do not compete with small neighborhood shopping centers, mini-malls, or even factory outlet malls because of different customer appeal.

9. Factory Outlet Centers

FACTORY OUTLET CENTERS are malls featuring stores owned by manufacturers, distributors, or others selling off-price merchandise. Successful outlet malls carry name brand merchandise.

Examples of such outlets are the huge Ontario Mills store and the Cabazon Outlet stores (over 100) located within 50 miles of each other along Interstate 10 in Southern California.

The factory outlets that have failed have been primarily small outlets having 50 stores or less. The larger the number of stores, and the better quality of the stores, the greater the volume per square foot.

Most of the large factory outlet centers are owned by a handful of Real Estate Investment Trusts (REITs) that employ their own management staffs.

10. Large Freestanding Retailers

Some retailers feel that their large retail stores don't need to be in close proximity to other retailers. As an example, a Home Depot® or Wal-Mart® might locate on the outskirts of a shopping area to utilize a large but lower cost site. Their major criteria would be excellent ingress and egress from a major street and being in close proximity to a significant population center. The building is built to the retailer's specifications and leased to them under a long-term net lease (not a percentage lease).

With a "percentage lease," tenants pay a percentage of their gross, sometimes with a flat fee added on.

Even though such retailers can stand alone, they are still draws, and shopping centers and other freestanding stores will be attracted to the outlet, which would then very shortly become the center of another shopping district.

11. Wholesale Operations

While **WHOLESALERS** *might consist of showrooms and some retail businesses, most wholesale locations contain office space, with the majority of the space warehouse related.*

Warehouses with large office areas are ideal for wholesalers.

Wholesale operators often have offices with windows overlooking warehouse operations. The ratio of office space to total wholesale area probably would be one to six. This could vary greatly depending upon the business.

Wholesale operations like to be in close proximity to other wholesalers of similar goods. As an example, the presence of one plumbing wholesaler would make another plumbing wholesaler consider a vacancy in the area. Similarly, car dealerships are often located in close proximity to each other.

Wholesale operators don't need prime locations. They need ingress and egress for trucks and proximity to major streets and highways. Security and a good fire suppression system are also needed. High ceilings allow for expansion where steel storage and second-floor walkways are desirable.

C. TENANT SELECTION

1. Tenant Mix

The tenant mix becomes very important whenever a property has more than one tenant.

As previously stated, you want each tenant to help the other so that they can all be successful. You want your tenants to succeed, even if they are not on percentage leases.

Successful tenants pay rent on time, meet all lease terms, abide by property rules, and are unlikely to move out—a win/win situation.

The worst case of tenant selection we know of was a small eight-store complex with a center court running off a major foot-traffic area in a resort community. Two stores were on the main street with the other stores having access off the courtyard. A religious bookstore rented one of the corner stores. The other corner store was a "head shop," selling legal drug-related paraphernalia such as books on how to grow marijuana, tee shirts and posters. A gourmet coffee shop, an African antiquities store, a bicycle repair shop, a beauty salon, a clock repair store, and an art gallery made up the remaining stores. The eclectic grouping provided minimal, if any, mutual support. After a few years, the only remaining occupant was the religious store. A high turnover rate among the other shops occurred despite bargain rents.

This small center could have rented to eight women's wear stores. This would have made the center a must check location for pedestrian and vehicular shopping. Instead, the owner's leasing philosophy was to rent to whomever came up with the rent first.

VOICE OF EXPERIENCE:

"First come, first served" should not be used for tenant selections. Advise your owner to look at the bigger picture and be more selective in choosing tenants. The long-term success of the businesses directly affects the profitability of his/her investment.

2. Tenant Quality

When a person just starts in business the chance of failure is far greater than for relocating an existing business. The longer a business can exist, the greater its chances of staying in business. If you have two similar prospective tenants, one new to the business and the other with an established clientele, the smart economic decision would be to select the existing business that wants to relocate.

Some types of new businesses have extremely high turnover rates. As an example, less than one-half of the newly opened restaurants will still be in business in the same location 18 months later. An exception would be franchise operations. Certain franchisors study areas to select locations and therefore have a very low failure rate. As an example, it would be unusual for a McDonald's location to close for lack of business. Some franchisors are more interested in initial fees rather than in any long-term franchisee success, often resulting in high failure rates.

In the 1970s, candle shops were in vogue. Candle shops kept opening even though few ever made money.

As a lessor/property manager, you should evaluate the economic viability of various businesses and anticipate their profitability.

A number of major banks have made studies of various businesses and can provide you with figures reflecting the success of a business.

Renting a vacant location in a mall to a temporary tenant for a few months before Christmas might be a good economic decision when you have several vacancies. This type of tenant should otherwise be avoided. A three-month lease could result in a lost opportunity to rent to what could be a long-term tenant.

The depth of a tenant's or lease guarantor's pockets is important in tenant selection.

If a commercial tenant does not have enough financial reserves, the tenant may not be able to last long enough to reach a break-even point, even though, with time, the business idea and operation should have been successful.

We know of one case where the business owners were starting a bakery. They were evicted before they even opened because all their money was spent on equipment and fixtures and nothing was left to pay for the last supplies needed or the rent.

The two major reasons why businesses fail are under-capitalization and lack of knowledge about the business.

D. RENT SETTING

1. Determining Rents

There is no simple rule for determining how much rent a commercial location is worth.

Certainly, a successful merchant who wants to expand would pay more for an adjacent store than would other tenants. Similarly, competitors of a successful business would pay more than others to locate close to their competitor.

Location based on other stores is not the sole factor in determining rents. Parking, ease of ingress and egress, signage, etc. will all affect the desirability of a location.

Generally, smaller stores, such as 2,000 square feet, can command a higher per-square-foot rental than larger stores, such as 100,000 square feet.

In setting commercial rents you should consider what is available from other lessors with similar desirable property. If a property bearing a high degree of similarity as to desirability has been vacant for 10 months, you can assume that the rent being asked is too high.

If there are no similarly desirable locations that are vacant, you should look at the rental rates tenants are paying for similar properties. You can assume that the average rental rate for similar property that is rented is too low or there would be some kind of vacancy factor.

When renewing leases, the prosperity of your tenant has a direct bearing on any rental increase.

If a tenant has a marginal operation, you should consider the effect of a vacancy before rents are raised. You might decide that in the long run you would be better off having the opportunity to seek a stronger tenant at a higher rent. Of course, your current vacancy factor, area vacancies and economic climate should all be considered.

2. Don't Be Unreasonable

As a commercial property manager, you must realize that your success, and that of your owner, depends upon the success of any tenant. You don't succeed if your tenants don't succeed.

As far as the tenant is concerned, an onerous lease can be a burden on the both lessor and the lessee. Failing businesses mean vacancies, additional expenses and revenue which most likely will never be recouped.

In renegotiating leases, lessors and their agents will often try to "put the screws" to commercial tenants because they realize any change in location will have a negative effect on the tenants' businesses. Lessors and agents try for a win/lose negotiation where the landlord wins and tenants lose. This reasoning has validity for some highly profitable businesses. However, it can often lead to lose/lose results if the business fails and the lessor ends up with a vacancy.

VOICE OF EXPERIENCE:

Vacancies can be very expensive. As long as the property is empty, your owner is losing money. Maintenance costs, mortgages, and security costs are ongoing, but there is no income coming in. Not only is the owner's income stream affected, but should the owner decide to sell, the value of the property will be diminished by the vacancy factors.

Some locations, including small shopping centers, have developed a negative reputation in an attempt to maximize rents. A high turnover in tenants, with few lasting more than a year, can lead to difficulties in renting and the need to reduce rents to what would be regarded as below-market rents. In desperation, the lessor may accept marginal tenants not normally considered to fill the vacancies.

3. Bargain Rents

A vacancy can often mean a negative cash flow for an owner. Some owners don't have the resources to withstand an extended vacancy or vacancies. This can result in granting a bargain rent to solve immediate cash flow problems. Bargain rents can create problems, such as:

1. The owner takes an opportunity risk by tying up a property with a below-market rent, and loses the chance to rent the location at market rent to a future prospective tenant.

2. Other tenants will soon learn of the bargain rent and demand lower rents when their leases expire. They feel that the owner is worried that they'll vacate and will agree to the lower rent. They're probably right.

Tenants share a lot of information.

E. PARKING

Parking is an important item for commercial, office, and industrial rentals. There are a number of problems to address with respect to parking, including:

Employees Taking Customer Spaces. In commercial and office leases, employees should have designated parking areas, usually in less desirable areas. The most desirable spaces should be for customers or clients. As the property manager, you should notify tenants if an employee does not comply. Towing a vehicle away might solve the problem of a flagrant violator when contacting the offender fails.

Parking in Someone Else's Spot. When spaces are designated, such as for offices and some retail operations, a person is less likely to park in another's spot if that parking area is designated with a person's name rather than just a number or "reserved" sign.

An employee's feeling of self-worth is another advantage of assigning a parking space by name rather than number.

We all like to see our names in print. This helps employee morale and in turn keeps your tenants happy. This same idea can apply to residential parking.

Tenant Monopolization of Parking. Some tenants use more parking spaces than others. As an example, a real estate office may have 20 salespersons operating out of a 1,200 square foot office. At times, the parking lot can be overflowing with salespersons' vehicles, creating a problem for real estate clients and customers of other businesses utilizing the same parking lot.

One solution would be to locate offsite parking for employees even if you have to pay for that parking. If just one tenant is the cause and you can't arrive at a solution, you could lose tenants and/or bargaining strength when other tenants come up for lease renewal.

You might have to consider not renewing the offending tenant's lease.

Excess Parking. Some properties have more parking or garage space than is required by the tenants. Excess parking can be rented out to others and offers a worthwhile addition to property income. If parking spaces are rented, consider either assigning spaces with names or special numbered stickers to determine if any unauthorized parking is taking place.

VOICE OF EXPERIENCE:

Allowing able-bodied people to use handicapped designated parking spots is not only socially irresponsible, but can lead to disastrous results. For example, unable to find parking on several occasions, a frustrated person with physical disabilities could very well file a complaint accusing you, your owner, and/or your tenant of violating civil rights laws. In addition to the possibility of facing state and federal prosecution for denying access to the handicapped, the complainant may also file a lawsuit in civil court. The financial repercussions could be devastating if the court awards a large damage amount to the offended party.

F. OVERBUILDING

Construction of commercial and office projects tends to be directly related to the availability of mortgage money for the projects.

When money is available, developers scramble for their own projects with a number of them being planned at the same time.

A project can take several years to move through the various stages from land acquisition, the approval process, and construction until the doors are ready to open. Frequently, a great deal of similar space might become available for leasing within the same time frame. In such a situation, the law of supply and demand takes over and prospective tenants have great bargaining power for lower rents and lease concessions. Lower rents, in turn, will attract more prospective tenants to the area and eventually an equilibrium will be reached with the excess space being absorbed.

When the vacancy factor is reduced to a controllable point, rents will start to rise.

G. COMMERCIAL LEASES

Commercial leases could be flat or gross leases, net leases, modified net leases or percentage leases.

Figure 6-1 is the CAR® standard **Commercial Lease Agreement**. You should be familiar with the lease types and clauses from the material in Chapters 3 and 4.

II. Office Property Management

With the growth of service and technical industries, the need for office space has increased dramatically over the past two decades.

Rents vary significantly based on location and the desirability of the space. Rents are usually expressed as a rent per square foot.

Office space is often rented with full janitorial services. Otherwise, there could be a logistical nightmare with maintenance firms numbering in the hundreds working in one building. This could also present a security problem.

A. CATEGORIES OF OFFICE BUILDINGS

Office buildings are categorized by quality as well as by height.

1. Class A Office Buildings

CLASS A BUILDINGS refer to newer, more desirable buildings. Many glass towers fall into this Class A category. They tend to be architecturally distinctive. If you were to be asked to name the three most prestigious or desirable office buildings in your city, chances are that all three would fall into the Class A category.

Because of their desirability, Class A buildings command high rents for office space.

Many image-conscious tenants would not consider locating in anything other than a Class A building.

2. Class B Office Buildings

CLASS B OFFICE BUILDINGS are older, well-maintained structures that have been out done by newer, more extravagant buildings. Class B office buildings still provide desirable space. However, they cannot command the same rents as a Class A office space.

3. Class C Office Buildings

CLASS C OFFICE BUILDINGS are usually older office buildings that are less desirable. Class C office buildings are adequate but they tend to compete on price. When the General Services Administration asks for bids on government office space, Class C buildings usually bring out the low bidders.

Normally not in a prime location, Class C buildings do meet office use requirements.

Figure 6-1

COMMERCIAL LEASE AGREEMENT
(C.A.R. Form CL, Revised 10/01)

Date (For reference only): _____

_____ ("Landlord") and
_____ ("Tenant") agree as follows:

1. **PROPERTY:** Landlord rents to Tenant and Tenant rents from Landlord, the real property and improvements described as: _____
_____ ("Premises"), which
comprise approximately _____ % of the total square footage of rentable space in the entire property. See exhibit _____ for a further
description of the Premises.

2. **TERM:** The term begins on (date) _____ ("Commencement Date"),
(Check A or B):
- ☐ **A. Lease:** and shall terminate on (date) _____ at _____ ☐ AM ☐ PM. Any holding over after the
term of this agreement expires, with Landlord's consent, shall create a month-to-month tenancy that either party may terminate as specified in
paragraph 2B. Rent shall be at a rate equal to the rent for the immediately preceding month, payable in advance. All other terms and
conditions of this agreement shall remain in full force and effect.
- ☐ **B. Month-to-month:** and continues as a month-to-month tenancy. Either party may terminate the tenancy by giving written notice to the other at
least 30 days prior to the intended termination date, subject to any applicable laws. Such notice may be given on any date.
- ☐ **C. RENEWAL OR EXTENSION TERMS:** See attached addendum _____

3. **BASE RENT:**
- A. Tenant agrees to pay Base Rent at the rate of (CHECK ONE ONLY:)
  - ☐ **(1)** $ _____ per month, for the term of the agreement.
  - ☐ **(2)** $ _____ per month, for the first 12 months of the agreement. Commencing with the 13th month, and upon expiration of
  each 12 months thereafter, rent shall be adjusted according to any increase in the U.S. Consumer Price Index of the Bureau of Labor
  Statistics of the Department of Labor for All Urban Consumers ("CPI") for
  _____ (the city nearest the location of the Premises), based on the following formula: Base Rent will be multiplied by the most current CPI
  preceding the first calendar month during which the adjustment is to take effect, and divided by the most recent CPI preceding the
  Commencement date. In no event shall any adjusted Base Rent be less than the Base Rent for the month immediately preceding the
  adjustment. If the CPI is no longer published, then the adjustment to Base Rent shall be based on an alternate index that most closely
  reflects the CPI.
  - ☐ **(3)** $ _____ per month for the period commencing _____ and ending _____ and
  $ _____ per month for the period commencing _____ and ending _____ and
  $ _____ per month for the period commencing _____ and ending _____.
  - ☐ **(4)** In accordance with the attached rent schedule.
  - ☐ **(5)** Other: _____
- B. Base Rent is payable in advance on the **1st (or** ☐ _____ **)** day of each calendar month, and is delinquent on the next day.
- C. If the Commencement Date falls on any day other than the first day of the month, Base Rent for the first calendar month shall be prorated based
on a 30-day period. If Tenant has paid one full month's Base Rent in advance of Commencement Date, Base Rent for the second calendar month
shall be prorated based on a 30-day period.

4. **RENT:**
- A. Definition: ("Rent") shall mean all monetary obligations of Tenant to Landlord under the terms of this agreement, except security deposit.
- B. Payment: Rent shall be paid to (Name) _____ _____ at (address)
_____ , or at any other
location specified by Landlord in writing to Tenant.
- C. Timing: Base Rent shall be paid as specified in paragraph 3. All other Rent shall be paid within 30 days after Tenant is billed by Landlord.

5. **EARLY POSSESSION:** Tenant is entitled to possession of the Premises on _____
If Tenant is in possession prior to the Commencement Date, during this time **(i)** Tenant is not obligated to pay Base Rent, and **(ii)** Tenant ☐ is
☐ is not obligated to pay Rent other than Base Rent. Whether or not Tenant is obligated to pay Rent prior to Commencement Date, Tenant is
obligated to comply with all other terms of this agreement.

6. **SECURITY DEPOSIT:**
- A. Tenant agrees to pay Landlord $ _____ as a security deposit. Tenant agrees not to hold broker responsible for its return.
(IF CHECKED:) ☐ If Base Rent increases during the term of this agreement, Tenant agrees to increase security deposit by the same proportion
as the increase in Base Rent.
- B. All or any portion of the security deposit may be used, as reasonably necessary, to: **(i)** cure Tenant's default in payment of Rent, late charges,
non-sufficient funds ("NSF") fees, or other sums due; **(ii)** repair damage, excluding ordinary wear and tear, caused by Tenant or by a guest or
licensee of Tenant; **(iii)** broom clean the Premises, if necessary, upon termination of tenancy; and **(iv)** cover any other unfulfilled obligation of
Tenant. **SECURITY DEPOSIT SHALL NOT BE USED BY TENANT IN LIEU OF PAYMENT OF LAST MONTH'S RENT.** If all or any portion of the
security deposit is used during tenancy, Tenant agrees to reinstate the total security deposit within 5 days after written notice is delivered to
Tenant. Within 30 days after Landlord receives possession of the Premises, Landlord shall: **(i)** furnish Tenant an itemized statement indicating the
amount of any security deposit received and the basis for its disposition, and **(ii)** return any remaining portion of security deposit to Tenant.
However, if the Landlord's only claim upon the security deposit is for unpaid Rent, then the remaining portion of the security deposit, after
deduction of unpaid Rent, shall be returned within 14 days after the Landlord receives possession.
- C. No interest will be paid on security deposit, unless required by local ordinance.

Landlord's Initials (_____) (_____)
Tenant's Initials (_____) (_____)

Reviewed by _____ Date _____

CL REVISED 10/01 (PAGE 1 of 6)

COMMERCIAL LEASE AGREEMENT (CL PAGE 1 OF 6)

Agent: WALT HUBER	Phone:	Fax:	Prepared using zipForm® software
Broker: WALT HUBER REALTOR			

Premises: _____ Date _____

7. PAYMENTS:

	TOTAL DUE	PAYMENT RECEIVED	BALANCE DUE	DUE DATE
A. Rent: From _____ To _____ Date Date	$ _____	$ _____	$ _____	_____
B. Security Deposit	$ _____	$ _____	$ _____	_____
C. Other: _____ Category	$ _____	$ _____	$ _____	_____
D. Other: _____ Category	$ _____	$ _____	$ _____	_____
E. Total:	$ _____	$ _____	$ _____	

8. PARKING: Tenant is entitled to _____ unreserved and _____ reserved vehicle parking spaces. The right to parking ☐ is ☐ is not included in the Base Rent charged pursuant to paragraph 3. If not included in the Base Rent, the parking rental fee shall be an additional $ _____ per month. Parking space(s) are to be used for parking operable motor vehicles, except for trailers, boats, campers, buses or trucks (other than pick-up trucks). Tenant shall park in assigned space(s) only. Parking space(s) are to be kept clean. Vehicles leaking oil, gas or other motor vehicle fluids shall not be parked in parking spaces or on the Premises. Mechanical work or storage of inoperable vehicles is not allowed in parking space(s) or elsewhere on the Premises. No overnight parking is permitted.

9. ADDITIONAL STORAGE: Storage is permitted as follows: _____ .
The right to additional storage space ☐ is ☐ is not included in the Base Rent charged pursuant to paragraph 3. If not included in Base Rent, storage space shall be an additional $ _____ per month. Tenant shall store only personal property that Tenant owns, and shall not store property that is claimed by another, or in which another has any right, title, or interest. Tenant shall not store any improperly packaged food or perishable goods, flammable materials, explosives, or other dangerous or hazardous material. Tenant shall pay for, and be responsible for, the clean-up of any contamination caused by Tenant's use of the storage area.

10. LATE CHARGE; INTEREST; NSF CHECKS: Tenant acknowledges that either late payment of Rent or issuance of a NSF check may cause Landlord to incur costs and expenses, the exact amount of which are extremely difficult and impractical to determine. These costs may include, but are not limited to, processing, enforcement and accounting expenses, and late charges imposed on Landlord. If any installment of Rent due from Tenant is not received by Landlord within **5 calendar days** after date due, or if a check is returned NSF, Tenant shall pay to Landlord, respectively, $ _____ as late charge, plus ___% interest per annum on the delinquent amount and $25.00 as a NSF fee, any of which shall be deemed additional Rent. Landlord and Tenant agree that these charges represent a fair and reasonable estimate of the costs Landlord may incur by reason of Tenant's late or NSF payment. Any late charge, delinquent interest, or NSF fee due shall be paid with the current installment of Rent. Landlord's acceptance of any late charge or NSF fee shall not constitute a waiver as to any default of Tenant. Landlord's right to collect a Late Charge or NSF fee shall not be deemed an extension of the date Rent is due under paragraph 4, or prevent Landlord from exercising any other rights and remedies under this agreement, and as provided by law.

11. CONDITION OF PREMISES: Tenant has examined the Premises and acknowledges that Premise is clean and in operative condition, with the following exceptions: _____
Items listed as exceptions shall be dealt with in the following manner: _____
_____

12. ZONING AND LAND USE: Tenant accepts the Premises subject to all local, state and federal laws, regulations and ordinances ("Laws"). Landlord makes no representation or warranty that Premises are now or in the future will be suitable for Tenant's use. Tenant has made its own investigation regarding all applicable Laws.

13. TENANT OPERATING EXPENSES: Tenant agrees to pay for all utilities and services directly used to Tenant _____

14. PROPERTY OPERATING EXPENSES:

    A. Tenant agrees to pay its proportionate share of Landlord's estimated monthly property operating expenses, including, but not limited to, common area maintenance, consolidated utility and service bills, insurance, and real estate taxes, based on the ratio of the square footage of the Premises to the total square footage of the rentable space in the entire property. _____

OR B. ☐ **(If checked)** Paragraph 14 does not apply.

15. USE: The Premises are for the sole use as _____
No other use is permitted without Landlord's prior written consent. If any use by Tenant causes an increase in the premium on Landlord's existing property insurance, Tenant shall pay for the increased cost. Tenant will comply with all Laws affecting its use of the Premises.

16. RULES/REGULATIONS: Tenant agrees to comply with all rules and regulations of Landlord (and, if applicable, Owner's Association) that are at any time posted on the Premises or delivered to Tenant. Tenant shall not, and shall ensure that guests and licensees of Tenant do not, disturb, annoy, endanger, or interfere with other tenants of the building or neighbors, or use the Premises for any unlawful purposes, including, but not limited to, using, manufacturing, selling, storing, or transporting illicit drugs or other contraband, or violate any law or ordinance, or committing a waste or nuisance on or about the Premises.

17. MAINTENANCE:

    A. Tenant OR ☐ **(If checked, Landlord)** shall professionally maintain the Premises including heating, air conditioning, electrical, plumbing and water systems, if any, and keep glass, windows and doors in operable and safe condition. Unless Landlord is checked, if Tenant fails to maintain the Premises, Landlord may contract for or perform such maintenance, and charge Tenant for Landlord's cost.

    B. Landlord OR ☐ **(If checked, Tenant)** shall maintain the roof, foundation, exterior walls, common areas and _____
_____
_____

Landlord's Initials (_____) (_____)
Tenant's Initials (_____) (_____)

| Reviewed by _____ Date _____ |

CL REVISED 10/01 (PAGE 2 of 6)

EQUAL HOUSING OPPORTUNITY

COMMERCIAL LEASE AGREEMENT (CL PAGE 2 OF 6)

Untitled

18. **ALTERATIONS:** Tenant shall not make any alterations in or about the Premises, including installation of trade fixtures and signs, without Landlord's prior written consent, which shall not be unreasonably withheld. Any alterations to the Premises shall be done according to Law and with required permits. Tenant shall give Landlord advance notice of the commencement date of any planned alteration, so that Landlord, at its option, may post a Notice of Non-Responsibility to prevent potential liens against Landlord's interest in the Premises. Landlord may also require Tenant to provide Landlord with lien releases from any contractor performing work on the Premises.

19. **GOVERNMENT IMPOSED ALTERATIONS:** Any alterations required by Law as a result of Tenant's use shall be Tenant's responsibility. Landlord shall be responsible for any other alterations required by Law.

20. **ENTRY:** Tenant shall make Premises available to Landlord or Landlord's agent for the purpose of entering to make inspections, necessary or agreed repairs, alterations, or improvements, or to supply necessary or agreed services, or to show Premises to prospective or actual purchasers, tenants, mortgagees, lenders, appraisers, or contractors. Landlord and Tenant agree that 24 hours notice (oral or written) shall be reasonable and sufficient notice. In an emergency, Landlord or Landlord's representative may enter Premises at any time without prior notice.

21. **SIGNS:** Tenant authorizes Landlord to place a FOR SALE sign on the Premises at any time, and a FOR LEASE sign on the Premises within the 90 (or ☐ _____) day period preceding the termination of the agreement.

22. **SUBLETTING/ASSIGNMENT:** Tenant shall not sublet or encumber all or any part of Premises, or assign or transfer this agreement or any interest in it, without the prior written consent of Landlord, which shall not be unreasonably withheld. Unless such consent is obtained, any subletting, assignment, transfer, or encumbrance of the Premises, agreement, or tenancy, by voluntary act of Tenant, operation of law, or otherwise, shall be null and void, and, at the option of Landlord, terminate this agreement. Any proposed sublessee, assignee, or transferee shall submit to Landlord an application and credit information for Landlord's approval, and, if approved, sign a separate written agreement with Landlord and Tenant. Landlord's consent to any one sublease, assignment, or transfer, shall not be construed as consent to any subsequent sublease, assignment, or transfer, and does not release Tenant of Tenant's obligation under this agreement.

23. **POSSESSION:** If Landlord is unable to deliver possession of Premises on Commencement Date, such date shall be extended to the date on which possession is made available to Tenant. However, the expiration date shall remain the same as specified in paragraph 2. If Landlord is unable to deliver possession with 60 (or _____) **calendar days** after the agreed Commencement Date, Tenant may terminate this agreement by giving written notice to Landlord, and shall be refunded all Rent and security deposit paid.

24. **TENANT'S OBLIGATIONS UPON VACATING PREMISES:** Upon termination of agreement, Tenant shall: **(i)** give Landlord all copies of all keys or opening devices to Premises including any common areas; **(ii)** vacate Premises and surrender it to Landlord empty of all persons and personal property; **(iii)** vacate all parking and storage spaces; **(iv)** deliver Premises to Landlord in the same condition as referenced in paragraph 11; **(v)** clean Premises; **(vi)** give written notice to Landlord of Tenant's forwarding address; and **(vii)** _____

_____
All improvements installed by Tenant, with or without Landlord's consent, become the property of Landlord upon termination. Landlord may nevertheless require Tenant to remove any such improvement that did not exist at the time possession was made available to Tenant.

25. **BREACH OF CONTRACT/EARLY TERMINATION:** In event Tenant, prior to expiration of this agreement, breaches any obligation in this agreement, abandons the premises, or gives notice of tenant's intent to terminate this tenancy prior to its expiration, in addition to any obligations established by paragraph 24, Tenant shall also be responsible for lost rent, rental commissions, advertising expenses, and painting costs necessary to ready Premises for re-rental. Landlord may also recover from Tenant: (i) the worth, at the time of award, of the unpaid Rent that had been earned at the time of termination; **(ii)** the worth, at the time of award, of the amount by which the unpaid Rent that would have been earned after expiration until the time of award exceeds the amount of such rental loss the Tenant proves could have been reasonably avoided; and **(iii)** the worth, at the time of award, of the amount by which the unpaid Rent for the balance of the term after the time of award exceeds the amount of such rental loss that Tenant proves could be reasonably avoided. Landlord may elect to continue the tenancy in effect for so long as Landlord does not terminate Tenant's right to possession, by either written notice of termination of possession or by re-renting the Premises to another who takes possession, and Landlord may enforce all Landlord's rights and remedies under this agreement, including the right to recover the Rent as it becomes due.

26. **DAMAGE TO PREMISES:** If, by no fault of Tenant, Premises are totally or partially damaged or destroyed by fire, earthquake, accident or other casualty, Landlord shall have the right to restore the Premises by repair or rebuilding. If Landlord elects to repair or rebuild, and is able to complete such restoration within 90 days from the date of damage, subject to the terms of this paragraph, this agreement shall remain in full force and effect. If Landlord is unable to restore the Premises within this time, or if Landlord elects not to restore, then either Landlord or Tenant may terminate this agreement by giving the other written notice. Rent shall be abated as of the date of damage. The abated amount shall be the current monthly Base Rent prorated on a 30-day basis. If this agreement is not terminated, and the damage is not repaired, then Rent shall be reduced based on the extent to which the damage interferes with Tenant's reasonable use of Premises. If damage occurs as a result of an act of Tenant or Tenant's guests, only Landlord shall have the right of termination, and no reduction in Rent shall be made.

27. **HAZARDOUS MATERIALS:** Tenant shall not use, store, generate, release or dispose of any hazardous material on the Premises or the property of which the Premises are part. However, Tenant is permitted to make use of such materials that are required to be used in the normal course of Tenant's business provided that Tenant complies with all applicable Laws related to the hazardous materials. Tenant is responsible for the cost of removal and remediation, or any clean-up of any contamination caused by Tenant.

28. **CONDEMNATION:** If all or part of the Premises is condemned for public use, either party may terminate this agreement as of the date possession is given to the condemner. All condemnation proceeds, exclusive of those allocated by the condemner to Tenant's relocation costs and trade fixtures, belong to Landlord.

29. **INSURANCE:** Tenant's personal property, fixtures, equipment, inventory and vehicles are not insured by Landlord against loss or damage due to fire, theft, vandalism, rain, water, criminal or negligent acts of others, or any other cause. Tenant is to carry Tenant's own property insurance to protect Tenant from any such loss. In addition, Tenant shall carry liability insurance in an amount of not less than $ _____ . Tenant's liability insurance shall name Landlord and Landlord's agent as additional insured. Tenant, upon Landlord's request, shall provide Landlord with a certificate of insurance establishing Tenant's compliance. Landlord shall maintain liability insurance insuring Landlord, but not Tenant, in an amount of at least $ _____ , plus property insurance in an amount sufficient to cover the replacement cost of the property. Tenant is advised to carry business interruption insurance in an amount at least sufficient to cover Tenant's complete rental obligation to Landlord. Landlord is advised to obtain a policy of rental loss insurance. Both Landlord and Tenant release each other, and waive their respective rights to subrogation against each other, for loss or damage covered by insurance.

Landlord's Initials (_____) (_____)
Tenant's Initials (_____) (_____)

Reviewed by _____ Date _____

Premises: _____ Date _____

30. TENANCY STATEMENT (ESTOPPEL CERTIFICATE): Tenant shall execute and return a tenancy statement (estoppel certificate), delivered to Tenant by Landlord or Landlord's agent, within 3 days after its receipt. The tenancy statement shall acknowledge that this agreement is unmodified and in full force, or in full force as modified, and state the modifications. Failure to comply with this requirement: **(i)** shall be deemed Tenant's acknowledgment that the tenancy statement is true and correct, and may be relied upon by a prospective lender or purchaser; and **(ii)** may be treated by Landlord as a material breach of this agreement. Tenant shall also prepare, execute, and deliver to Landlord any financial statement (which will be held in confidence) reasonably requested by a prospective lender or buyer.

31. LANDLORD'S TRANSFER: Tenant agrees that the transferee of Landlord's interest shall be substituted as Landlord under this agreement. Landlord will be released of any further obligation to Tenant regarding the security deposit, only if the security deposit is returned to Tenant upon such transfer, or if the security deposit is actually transferred to the transferee. For all other obligations under this agreement, Landlord is released of any further liability to Tenant, upon Landlord's transfer.

32. SUBORDINATION: This agreement shall be subordinate to all existing liens and, at Landlord's option, the lien of any first deed of trust or first mortgage subsequently placed upon the real property of which the Premises are a part, and to any advances made on the security of the Premises, and to all renewals, modifications, consolidations, replacements, and extensions. However, as to the lien of any deed of trust or mortgage entered into after execution of this agreement, Tenant's right to quiet possession of the Premises shall not be disturbed if Tenant is not in default and so long as Tenant pays the Rent and observes and performs all of the provisions of this agreement, unless this agreement is otherwise terminated pursuant to its terms. If any mortgagee, trustee, or ground lessor elects to have this agreement placed in a security position prior to the lien of a mortgage, deed of trust, or ground lease, and gives written notice to Tenant, this agreement shall be deemed prior to that mortgage, deed of trust, or ground lease, or the date of recording

33. TENANT REPRESENTATIONS; CREDIT: Tenant warrants that all statements in Tenant's financial documents and rental application are accurate. Tenant authorizes Landlord and Broker(s) to obtain Tenant's credit report at time of application and periodically during tenancy in connection with approval, modification, or enforcement of this agreement. Landlord may cancel this agreement: **(i)** before occupancy begins, upon disapproval of the credit report(s); or **(ii)** at any time, upon discovering that information in Tenant's application is false. A negative credit report reflecting on Tenant's record may be submitted to a credit reporting agency, if Tenant fails to pay Rent or comply with any other obligation under this agreement.

34. DISPUTE RESOLUTION

A. MEDIATION: Tenant and Landlord agree to mediate any dispute or claim arising between them out of this agreement, or any resulting transaction, before resorting to arbitration or court action, subject to paragraph 34B(2) below. Paragraphs 34B(2) and (3) apply whether or not the arbitration provision is initialed. Mediation fees, if any, shall be divided equally among the parties involved. If for any dispute or claim to which this paragraph applies, any party commences an action without first attempting to resolve the matter through mediation, or refuses to mediate after a request has been made, then that party shall not be entitled to recover attorney fees, even if they would otherwise be available to that party in any such action. THIS MEDIATION PROVISION APPLIES WHETHER OR NOT THE ARBITRATION PROVISION IS INITIALED.

B. ARBITRATION OF DISPUTES: (1) Tenant and Landlord agree that any dispute or claim in Law or equity arising between them out of this agreement or any resulting transaction, which is not settled through mediation, shall be decided by neutral, binding arbitration, including and subject to paragraphs 34B(2) and (3) below. The arbitrator shall be a retired judge or justice, or an attorney with at least 5 years of real estate transactional law experience, unless the parties mutually agree to a different arbitrator, who shall render an award in accordance with substantive California Law. In all other respects, the arbitration shall be conducted in accordance with Part III, Title 9 of the California Code of Civil Procedure. Judgment upon the award of the arbitrator(s) may be entered in any court having jurisdiction. The parties shall have the right to discovery in accordance with Code of Civil Procedure §1283.05.

(2) EXCLUSIONS FROM MEDIATION AND ARBITRATION: The following matters are excluded from Mediation and Arbitration hereunder: **(i)** a judicial or non-judicial foreclosure or other action or proceeding to enforce a deed of trust, mortgage, or installment land sale contract as defined in Civil Code §2985; **(ii)** an unlawful detainer action; **(iii)** the filing or enforcement of a mechanic's lien; **(iv)** any matter that is within the jurisdiction of a probate, small claims, or bankruptcy court; and **(v)** an action for bodily injury or wrongful death, or for latent or patent defects to which Code of Civil Procedure §337.1 or §337.15 applies. The filing of a court action to enable the recording of a notice of pending action, for order of attachment, receivership, injunction, or other provisional remedies, shall not constitute a violation of the mediation and arbitration provisions.

(3) BROKERS: Tenant and Landlord agree to mediate and arbitrate disputes or claims involving either or both Brokers, provided either or both Brokers shall have agreed to such mediation or arbitration, prior to, or within a reasonable time after the dispute or claim is presented to Brokers. Any election by either or both Brokers to participate in mediation or arbitration shall not result in Brokers being deemed parties to the agreement.

"NOTICE: BY INITIALING IN THE SPACE BELOW YOU ARE AGREEING TO HAVE ANY DISPUTE ARISING OUT OF THE MATTERS INCLUDED IN THE 'ARBITRATION OF DISPUTES' PROVISION DECIDED BY NEUTRAL ARBITRATION AS PROVIDED BY CALIFORNIA LAW AND YOU ARE GIVING UP ANY RIGHTS YOU MIGHT POSSESS TO HAVE THE DISPUTE LITIGATED IN A COURT OR JURY TRIAL. BY INITIALING IN THE SPACE BELOW YOU ARE GIVING UP YOUR JUDICIAL RIGHTS TO DISCOVERY AND APPEAL, UNLESS THOSE RIGHTS ARE SPECIFICALLY INCLUDED IN THE 'ARBITRATION OF DISPUTES' PROVISION. IF YOU REFUSE TO SUBMIT TO ARBITRATION AFTER AGREEING TO THIS PROVISION, YOU MAY BE COMPELLED TO ARBITRATE UNDER THE AUTHORITY OF THE CALIFORNIA CODE OF CIVIL PROCEDURE. YOUR AGREEMENT TO THIS ARBITRATION PROVISION IS VOLUNTARY."

"WE HAVE READ AND UNDERSTAND THE FOREGOING AND AGREE TO SUBMIT DISPUTES ARISING OUT OF THE MATTERS INCLUDED IN THE 'ARBITRATION OF DISPUTES' PROVISION TO NEUTRAL ARBITRATION."

Landlord's Initials _____ / _____   Tenant's Initials _____ / _____

Landlord's Initials (_____) (_____)
Tenant's Initials (_____) (_____)
Reviewed by _____ Date _____

EQUAL HOUSING OPPORTUNITY

COMMERCIAL LEASE AGREEMENT (CL PAGE 4 OF 6)   Untitled

Premises: _____ Date _____

35. JOINT AND INDIVIDUAL OBLIGATIONS: If there is more than one Tenant, each one shall be individually and completely responsible for the performance of all obligations of Tenant under this agreement, jointly with every other Tenant, and individually, whether or not in possession.

36. NOTICE: Notices may be served by mail, facsimile, or courier at the following address or location, or at any other location subsequently designated:
Landlord: _____ Tenant: _____

_____ _____

_____ _____

_____ _____

Notice is deemed effective upon the earliest of the following: **(i)** personal receipt by either party or their **agent**; **(ii)** written acknowledgement of notice; or **(iii)** 5 days after mailing notice to such location by first class mail, postage pre-paid.

37. WAIVER: The waiver of any breach shall not be construed as a continuing waiver of the same breach or a waiver of any subsequent breach.

38. INDEMNIFICATION: Tenant shall indemnify, defend and hold Landlord harmless from all claims, disputes, litigation, judgments and attorney fees arising out of Tenant's use of the Premises.

39. OTHER TERMS AND CONDITIONS/SUPPLEMENTS: _____

_____

_____

_____

_____

_____

_____

_____

_____

_____

_____

_____

_____

The following ATTACHED supplements/exhibits are incorporated in this agreement: ☐ Option Agreement (C.A.R. Form OA)

_____

_____

40. ATTORNEY FEES: In any action or proceeding arising out of this agreement, the prevailing party between Landlord and Tenant shall be entitled to reasonable attorney fees and costs from the non-prevailing Landlord or Tenant, except as provided in paragraph 34A.

41. ENTIRE CONTRACT: Time is of the essence. All prior agreements between Landlord and Tenant are incorporated in this agreement, which constitutes the entire contract. It is intended as a final expression of the parties' agreement, and may not be contradicted by evidence of any prior agreement or contemporaneous oral agreement. The parties further intend that this agreement constitutes the complete and exclusive statement of its terms, and that no extrinsic evidence whatsoever may be introduced in any judicial or other proceeding, if any, involving this agreement. Any provision of this agreement that is held to be invalid shall not affect the validity or enforceability of any other provision in this agreement. This agreement shall be binding upon, and inure to the benefit of, the heirs, assignees and successors to the parties.

42. BROKERAGE: Landlord and Tenant shall each pay to Broker(s) the fee agreed to, if any, in a separate written agreement. Neither Tenant nor Landlord has utilized the services of, or for any other reason owes compensation to, a licensed real estate broker (individual or corporate), agent, finder, or other entity, other than as named in this agreement, in connection with any act relating to the Premises, including, but not limited to, inquiries, introductions, consultations, and negotiations leading to this agreement. Tenant and Landlord each agree to indemnify, defend and hold harmless the other, and the Brokers specified herein, and their agents, from and against any costs, expenses, or liability for compensation claimed inconsistent with the warranty and representation in this paragraph 42.

43. AGENCY CONFIRMATION: The following agency relationships are hereby confirmed for this transaction:
Listing Agent: _____ (Print Firm Name) is the agent of
(check one):
☐ the Landlord exclusively; or ☐ both the Tenant and Landlord.
Selling Agent: _____ (Print Firm Name) (if not same as Listing Agent) is the agent of
(check one): ☐ the Tenant exclusively; or ☐ the Landlord exclusively; or ☐ both the Tenant and Landlord.
Real Estate Brokers are not parties to the agreement between Tenant and Landlord.

Landlord's Initials (_____) (_____)
Tenant's Initials (_____) (_____)

Reviewed by _____ Date _____

CL REVISED 10/01 (PAGE 5 of 6)

EQUAL HOUSING OPPORTUNITY

COMMERCIAL LEASE AGREEMENT (CL PAGE 5 OF 6) Untitled

Premises: _____ Date _____

> Landlord and Tenant acknowledge and agree that Brokers: (i) do not guarantee the condition of the Premises; (ii) cannot verify representations made by others; (iii) will not verify zoning and land use restrictions; (iv) cannot provide legal or tax advice; (v) will not provide other advice or information that exceeds the knowledge, education or experience required to obtain a real estate license. Furthermore, if Brokers are not also acting as Landlord in this agreement, Brokers: (vi) do not decide what rental rate a Tenant should pay or Landlord should accept; and (vii) do not decide upon the length or other terms of tenancy. Landlord and Tenant agree that they will seek legal, tax, insurance, and other desired assistance from appropriate professionals.

Tenant _____ Date _____
_____
(Print Name)
Address _____ City _____ State _____ Zip _____

Tenant _____ Date _____
_____
(Print Name)
Address _____ City _____ State _____ Zip _____

Landlord _____ Date _____
(owner or agent with authority to enter into this agreement)
Address _____ City _____ State _____ Zip _____

Landlord _____ Date _____
(owner or agent with authority to enter into this agreement)
Address _____ City _____ State _____ Zip _____

Agency relationships are confirmed as above. Real estate brokers who are not also Landlord in this agreement are not a party to the agreement between Landlord and Tenant.

Real Estate Broker (Leasing Firm) _____ DRE Lic. # _____
By (Agent) _____ DRE Lic. _____ Date _____
Address _____ City _____ State _____ Zip _____
Telephone _____ Fax _____ E-mail _____

Real Estate Broker (Listing Firm) _____ DRE Lic. # _____
By (Agent) _____ DRE Lic. # _____ Date _____
Address _____ City _____ State _____ Zip _____
Telephone _____ Fax _____ E-mail _____

Published and Distributed by:
REAL ESTATE BUSINESS SERVICES, INC.
a subsidiary of the California Association of REALTORS®
525 South Virgil Avenue, Los Angeles, California 90020

Reviewed by _____ Date _____

EQUAL HOUSING OPPORTUNITY

CL REVISED 10/01 (PAGE 6 OF 6)   COMMERCIAL LEASE AGREEMENT (CL PAGE 6 OF 6)   Untitled

4. Class D Office Buildings

If you have watched old detective movies on television, the location of the detective's office always seems to be in a *CLASS D BUILDING, which are the least desirable, seedy type buildings.*

Because Class D buildings offer the lowest rent, maintenance is often minimal. Lessors of nonresidential property have no statutory duties to maintain the property. The responsibilities for and level of maintenance would be specified in the lease. Tenants in Class D buildings are there because they can't pay for Class A space and don't expect Class A maintenance. Class D buildings will probably be razed when the vacancy factor rises and income is not sufficient to maintain operational expenses.

5. Garden Office Buildings

A *GARDEN BUILDING is a one-story building, usually located in a suburban area.*

6. Low-Rise Office Buildings

A *LOW-RISE BUILDING would usually be from three to six stories high.* It can have an elevator or be a walk-up. Some low-rise offices are located on the top floor of an older commercial building.

7. Mid-Rise Office Buildings

While the definition varies, we classify a *MID-RISE BUILDING as from four to twelve stories high.* These buildings are usually located in small communities or at the periphery of high-rise structures.

8. High-Rise Office Buildings

While we classify a *HIGH-RISE BUILDING as six to twelve stories, there isn't any real standard as to height.*

B. REPOSITIONING OFFICE BUILDINGS

What were once lower rent, less desirable structures have become highly desirable office locations because of features of the buildings or because of other tenants.

In the 1950s and 1960s, some older buildings with open-laced iron elevator housings, rotundas and an abundance of marble were "modernized" by coverings of formica material. Frescos were painted over and these "ancient" buildings were turned into nondescript structures.

Attitudes are changing from "new is better" to "old is more desirable."

Sound, older buildings that have retained their architectural distinction or have been restored to their former elegance are now highly desirable structures. They are sought by firms that wish to convey an image of conservatism and solid trust. Law firms, accountants, investment consultants, insurance agencies and stockbrokers all have flocked to these structures. These tenants have driven up rents to match or exceed those of a new, Class A office structures.

Quite often, tenants refurbish their offices with antique furniture, light fixtures and solid wood paneling to convey what they consider to be a desirable and prestigious image.

An old office structure in Milwaukee, Wisconsin, called the Mackie Building, once housed the Grain Exchange. The floor space was later used as a private athletic club before being closed off to gather dust for several decades. Turning back the clock over 100 years, the building was restored by the owners. This former exchange is now a focal point for society charity affairs and civic functions. It went from one swing ahead of a wrecking ball to a highly desirable location. The owners heeded the advice of management to the benefit of their profits.

Class C and D office buildings can command Class B rent if the demand for the particular space is there.

Tenants will pay more to be in particular buildings because of other tenants. Therefore, a theme building can take itself out of competition with similar office space.

An example of such a building would be one which housed several wholesale jewelers, yet had a great deal of vacant space. The management changed the name of the building to The Jewelry Exchange and actively sought tenants who were in various aspects of the jewelry business, such as jewelry settings, jewelry repair, antique jewelry, etc. The owners had an excellent security system installed and contracted for a guard service. They began renting space by offering free rent and very attractive lease terms. As the vacancy rate went down they were able to significantly increase rents and raise rents on lease renewals.

Tenants are happy because they are able to "feed off" each other due to their related businesses. In addition, buyers come to the building because of the concentration of wholesale jewelers. This is a win/win situation for both landlord and tenants.

Other theme buildings can be design centers as well as wholesale marts for shoes, women's wear, furnishings, etc.

C. TROPHY BUILDINGS

TROPHY BUILDINGS *are image structures*. They were built with pride of ownership in mind. Trump Tower and the Pan Am Building are examples of trophy buildings.

Although usually not economically sound when built, as the return seldom justifies the expenses of construction, inflation has provided attractive returns to these structures over a period of time.

Trophy buildings incur high costs per-square foot of rentable space because of features like central atriums, as well as elaborate public and plaza areas. They are built to impress and provide a platform for company names.

Trophy buildings tend to bring a premium price when sold. During the 1970s and 1980s, Japanese investors were principal buyers of U. S. trophy properties. They had bid up the price among themselves and purchased buildings based on the low cost the Japanese investors had to pay for borrowing in Japan. The investors often used Japanese stocks and Japanese real estate as collateral on their loans.

The collapse of the Japanese stock market coupled with a collapse in Japanese real estate prices led to a situation where Japanese owners suddenly had little, if any, equity in their Hawaiian and other U.S. buildings. To make matters worse, a U.S. recession and our savings and loan debacle led to a glut of empty office space.

Japanese lenders ended up owning these buildings and a need for cash led to the sale in a buyer's market. Many U.S. REITs bought up premier properties for prices in the 50 percent of reproduction cost range.

As the property manager of a trophy building, you have to play the hand you are dealt. You have to provide a high level of maintenance expected by the owners, attract and keep quality tenants at relatively high rents. If the owners purchased the building at a bargain price from a lender, then you could provide a respectable or even outstanding return for the owners.

The nation is once again experiencing a strengthening of the marketplace. The vacancy factor is materially decreasing. New office buildings are being built, including several in the "trophy" category.

VOICE OF EXPERIENCE:

Las Vegas is a hot spot for new trophy buildings. High-rise upscale condo buildings with prestigious pedigrees, like the Trump name, are selling like hotcakes.

D. THE INTELLIGENT BUILDING

Over the past few years we have been hearing a lot about *INTELLIGENT BUILDINGS that offer shared electronics for the tenants*. Some of these services, such as video conferencing capabilities, are attractive features that could influence tenants. However, some of the electronic features offered have become unnecessary because of lower cost technology available. Use of e-mail and low-cost, high-powered computers have obviated the need for some of the shared facilities offered. As technology advances, intelligent buildings will still have a strong selling point in marketing space.

Buildings prewired with high-speed, fiber optic T-1 Internet lines, for example, are highly desirable.

E. COMBINATION BUILDINGS

In central cities, office buildings often have commercial tenants on the first floor. Commercial tenants can pay much more per-square foot than office tenants can pay for desirable space.

In high-rise office structures, the lower floors are the least desirable because they are noisier and lack views.

Also, any lower floor windows that can be opened allow exposure to more polluted air than do the upper floors. Rents tend to increase with height.

*Besides stores on the first level, **COMBINATION BUILDINGS** might have restaurants and bars on the second level or at basement level, accessible by escalators and stairs.*

Some well-known office towers have apartments. San Francisco has a number of office towers where several floors house executive-type apartments. Trump Towers in New York and the infamous Watergate complex in Washington, D.C. fall into this category of combination buildings.

F. R&D FACILITIES MANAGEMENT

A ***RESEARCH AND DEVELOPMENT (R&D) FACILITY*** *may have offices for engineers, draftsmen, and computers, as well as a general administration function.* In addition, there might be laboratories and/or a fabrication area for production of models and prototypes. There might also be test facilities on site. The makeup of an R&D facility varies, based upon the area of research and development involved.

R&D facilities are frequently in industrial-type parks or freestanding buildings. They are often prestigious buildings with extensive grounds. On a per-square foot basis, not as many people work in an R&D facility as would work in a general office environment.

R&D differs from industrial and most office management in that R&D facilities frequently require an extremely high level of cleaning.

G. SICK BUILDINGS

Tenants have complained of illnesses working in some office buildings. Quite often, in order to save energy, these buildings have sealed windows and air circulates through a ventilation system. Legionnaires Disease is a worst case scenario. It is believed to be caused by bacteria in the cooling towers and/or ventilation system.

Far more common are chemical reactions. Many people are sensitive to chemicals used in building products and furniture. Fumes are emitted from synthetic carpets, woodchip

partitions, and even paints. Some people have become seriously ill from working in a "sick building."

At the first indication of a problem, you should contact an HVAC (Heating, Ventilating and Air Conditioning) engineer who has had experience with sick buildings.

Remedies might include:

1. Cleaning of all duct work and water towers.
2. Modification of the ventilation system to provide fresh air rather than recirculation.
3. Windows changed so that they can be opened.
4. Removal and replacement of carpets, fabrics or chipboard products in the building that are believed to cause health problems. (Chemicals are used as binders in chipboard products.)

If a property develops a reputation as a sick building, you will have rental difficulties as well as possibly an effect on tenant retention. Competitors will be sure to let prospective tenants know of the problems with your building.

H. DEMOLITION OF SERVICEABLE OFFICE BUILDINGS

A number of profitable office structures in a good state of repair have been demolished. The reason for tearing down a sound structure is pure economics. Rising values have resulted in some buildings no longer bringing in an acceptable rate of return on the value of the property.

As an example, assume an office building was built on a site for a total cost of $3,000,000. Let us assume that the building could produce a net income of $300,000 for the owners. This 10 percent rate of return would make this building economically sound. However, assume greater demand caused the site value to increase to $30,000,000. If the owners wanted a seven percent return then the owner should expect a return of $2,100,000 just on land value plus a return on the value of the structure. But if all they were receiving was $300,000 it would mean the building exceeded its economic life. Even if almost new, such a building would be demolished to build a structure capable of providing the required return based on land value and building costs. Low-rise structures replaced by high-rise office buildings are perfect examples of what happens when land becomes too valuable for the structure. Property managers often recommend that owners replace their buildings.

I. VACANCY FACTOR

1. By Category

The office vacancy factor for an area is not uniform where the category of office buildings is concerned.

As an example, an area might have a 20 percent vacancy factor in a depressed market. However, the vacancy factor for a Class A office building could be 26 percent, while the vacancy factor could be 12 percent for a Class C building.

The highest vacancy factors seem to be in Class A buildings during business recessionary periods. Office tenants will move upward in quality as they perceive their prosperity in periods of great economic growth.

J. NEW CONSTRUCTION

An ongoing problem is new competition for existing vacant space as new space becomes available in the marketplace. The absorption rate for new space is tied to the local economy. New space will mean an increased vacancy factor during a stagnant economic period, unless marginal Class D office space is taken off the rental market.

As a property manager, you try to anticipate the future demand for space.

This is difficult to do. Not only will changes in the national and local economy affect the market but we are also affected by the plans of others. The marketplace is affected by the development of new space. Your perception of the marketplace will affect your strategy in negotiating the length of leases and other lease terms.

Even the experts can be wrong about the demand for space. Just a few years ago, Houston, Texas was loaded with "see-through" office towers (there weren't any tenants or partitions in the new glass towers). Experts predicted that it would take more than 20 years to absorb all this vacant space. The experts were wrong. An economic turnaround resulted in a demand for office space and the vacancies were filled in just a few years. No good economic models exist to anticipate the absorption rate of vacant space. Although you'd like to incorporate every known fact into your planning, it's still as much an art as a science.

K. COMPUTING SQUARE FOOTAGE

Office rents are quoted per square foot. For renting less than a full floor of office space, the price quoted would be for space actually rented. For an entire floor, the quoted square footage rate includes halls, etc. Rents for square footage may be expressed as a monthly or annual figure.

A number of methods are used in measuring square footage. When a prospective tenant provides a quote from another property, you want to make certain that the same method of measuring is being used. It's like one person using a ruler showing 11 inches to the foot while another person has a ruler with 13 inches to the foot.

The authors prefer to use what we regard as a realistic method of measuring. We use the **usable square footage method** developed by the Building Owners and Managers Association. We measure the square footage by diagramming the perimeter of the space. In arriving at the perimeter we measure:

1. The interior of the structure's exterior walls.
2. The exterior of interior corridor walls.
3. The center of partitions used in common with other tenants.

From the total square footage derived by simple geometry of length times width, we deduct areas for venting, elevators and stairwells located within our perimeter measurements.

To find the square footage of entire floors, measure the interior of all exterior walls and exclude ducts, stairwells and elevators.

Because you are figuring in what will be interior hallways, you will have more rentable square footage than for a multi-tenant floor. However, the rent per square foot would be less per square foot when the tenant is to occupy an entire floor rather than just one office suite.

L. FIXTURING ALLOWANCE

Lessors often provide a **fixturing allowance** for the tenant. This allowance is expressed in dollars. Any special requirements that exceed these authorized dollars would be the tenant's responsibility.

As the property manager, you would probably want to specify the contractors to be used to prepare the space. A time period for work will be set and the lease will not begin until work has been completed. By limiting the work to contractors who will meet deadlines, you avoid costly delays that are common with some contractors. As the party authorizing the work, you have control over the work. If prospective tenants want changes, they should be made by change order and the cost agreed to in writing by the prospective tenants.

Some tenants want large, open spaces to hold cubbyhole work stations while other tenants prefer more traditional separate offices. Interior offices go to employees of lesser rank. Window offices go to managerial employees. High-ranking executives would warrant corner offices. Although some office partitions may rise to the ceiling, they are not load-bearing walls and can easily be removed.

VOICE OF EXPERIENCE:

Some fixturing expenses may go to noise reduction. Acoustical tile, partitions faced with sound absorbing materials, carpeting and sound baffles can all be used to reduce office noise in large areas.

M. KEEPING TENANTS HAPPY

Services that a tenant requires within a building can be a strong positive feature for office towers. Examples are restaurants, health clubs, quick-printing service, etc.

The health clubs are often used as a rental perk by offering a tenant several memberships as a part of the rental. While an executive might never consider accepting money, memberships for several executives might be acceptable. The health club benefits from the memberships while helping the landlord rent space.

One Los Angeles office building offers every employee a perk. The building owners have arranged with a health club in the area to provide half-price memberships to all the employees of their tenants. The club was happy to increase gross revenues and the employees who accepted the memberships feel that they received a bargain.

Similarly, offering some free parking space with the lease is a perk. Employers who make the lease decisions tend to get free parking, while their employees pay to park.

A few large office complexes operate elegant executive restaurants at a loss. They provide gourmet-quality cuisine at reasonable prices for designated executives of tenants and their guests. The rent is actually paying for the perk. An executive of a firm who receives such a perk may be more reluctant to relocate.

Some buildings use their roofs as helicopter pads. Others have turned the roof areas into gardens where workers who brown-bag their lunch can relax.

VOICE OF EXPERIENCE:

It helps to visit your tenants and talk to employees. You can plan your approach to emphasize what advantages your property offers, and explore possible further incentives to keep your tenants happy.

N. OFFICE LEASES

Although net leases can be used for office property, tenants generally prefer gross leases that detail their exact rental costs. Most office leases are gross leases.

In multi-tenant buildings, office leases should include a floor plan and specify space leased so that there are no disputes about what space the tenant shall be entitled.

As an attachment to the lease, a copy of the Rules and Regulations for Tenants should be included.

If the lease involves improvements to the property, an attachment will indicate the lessor's responsibility for the improvements and stipulate that the tenant will pay for costs exceeding the lessor's allowance.

Figure 6-3 is the first two pages of a gross office lease for a full-service office space. Most of the provisions of the lease were covered in Chapter 4. The lease form included here was developed by The AIR Commercial Real Estate Association (AIR).

Figure 6-3

STANDARD MULTI-TENANT OFFICE LEASE - GROSS
AIR COMMERCIAL REAL ESTATE ASSOCIATION

1.   **Basic Provisions ("Basic Provisions")**.
        1.1   **Parties**: This Lease (**"Lease"**), dated for reference purposes only _____ .
is made by and between _____
_____
_____ (**"Lessor"**)
and _____
_____
_____ (**"Lessee"**),
(collectively the **"Parties"**, or individually a **"Party"**).
        1.2(a)   **Premises**: That certain portion of the Project (as defined below), known as Suite Numbers(s) _____ ,
_____ floor(s), consisting of approximately _____ rentable square feet and approximately _____
useable square feet(**"Premises"**). The Premises are located at: _____ ,
in the City of _____ , County of _____
State of _____ , with zip code _____ . In addition to Lessee's rights to use and occupy the
Premises as hereinafter specified, Lessee shall have non-exclusive rights to the Common Areas (as defined in Paragraph 2.7 below) as hereinafter
specified, but shall not have any rights to the roof, the exterior walls, the area above the dropped ceilings, or the utility raceways of the building
containing the Premises (**"Building"**) or to any other buildings in the Project. The Premises, the Building, the Common Areas, the land upon which
they are located, along with all other buildings and improvements thereon, are herein collectively referred to as the **"Project."** The Project consists of
approximately _____ rentable/square feet. (See also Paragraph 2)
        1.2(b)   **Parking**: _____ unreserved and _____ reserved vehicle parking spaces at a monthly cost of
$_____ per unreserved space and $_____ per reserved space. (See Paragraph 2.6)
        1.3   **Term**: _____ years and _____ months (**"Original Term"**)
commencing _____ (**"Commencement Date"**) and ending _____
(**"Expiration Date"**). (See also Paragraph 3)
        1.4   **Early Possession**: If the Premises are available Lessee may have non-exclusive possession of the Premises commencing
_____ (**"Early Possession Date"**). (See also Paragraphs 3.2 and 3.3)
        1.5   **Base Rent**: $_____ per month (**"Base Rent"**), payable on the _____ day of each month
commencing _____ . (See also Paragraph 4)
☐ If this box is checked, there are provisions in this Lease for the Base Rent to be adjusted. See Paragraph _____
        1.6   **Lessee's Share of Operating Expense Increase**: _____ percent (____%) (**"Lessee's
Share"**). In the event that that size of the Premises and/or the Project are modified during the term of this Lease, Lessor shall recalculate Lessee's
Share to reflect such modification.
        1.7   **Base Rent and Other Monies Paid Upon Execution**:
                (a)   **Base Rent**: $_____ for the period _____
                (b)   **Security Deposit**: $_____ (**"Security Deposit"**). (See also Paragraph 5)
                (c)   **Parking**: $_____ for the period _____
                (d)   **Other**: $_____ for _____
                (e)   **Total Due Upon Execution of this Lease**: $_____ _____
        1.8   **Agreed Use**: _____
_____
_____ . (See also Paragraph 6)
        1.9   **Base Year; Insuring Party**. The Base Year is _____ . Lessor is the **"Insuring Party"**. (See also Paragraphs 4.2 and 8)
        1.10   **Real Estate Brokers**: (See also Paragraph 15)
                (a) **Representation**: The following real estate brokers (the **"Brokers"**) and brokerage relationships exist in this transaction (check
applicable boxes):
☐ _____ represents Lessor exclusively (**"Lessor's Broker"**);
☐ _____ represents Lessee exclusively (**"Lessee's Broker"**); or
☐ _____ represents both Lessor and Lessee (**"Dual Agency"**).
                (b) **Payment to Brokers**: Upon execution and delivery of this Lease by both Parties, Lessor shall pay to the Brokers for the brokerage
services rendered by the Brokers the fee agreed to in the attached separate written agreement or if no such agreement is attached, the sum of
_____ or _____ % of the total Base Rent payable for the Original Term, the sum of _____ or _____ of the total Base
Rent payable during any period of time that the Lessee occupies the Premises subsequent to the Original Term, and/or the sum of _____
or _____ % of the purchase price in the event that the Lessee or anyone affiliated with Lessee acquires from Lessor any rights to the Premises.
        1.11   **Guarantor**. The obligations of the Lessee under this Lease shall be guaranteed by _____
_____ (**"Guarantor"**) (See also Paragraph 37)
        1.12   **Business Hours for the Building**: _____ a.m. to _____ p.m., Mondays through Fridays (except Building Holidays) and
_____ a.m. to _____ p.m. on Saturdays (except Building Holidays). **"Building Holidays"** shall mean the dates of observation of New
Year's Day, President's Day, Memorial Day, Independence Day, Labor Day, Thanksgiving Day, Christmas Day, and _____

_____   _____
INITIALS   INITIALS

1.13 **Lessor Supplied Services.** Notwithstanding the provisions of Paragraph 11.1, Lessor is NOT obligated to provide the following within the Premises:

☐ Janitorial services
☐ Electricity
☐ Other (specify): _____

1.14 **Attachments.** Attached hereto are the following, all of which constitute a part of this Lease:

☐ an Addendum consisting of Paragraphs _____ through _____;
☐ a plot plan depicting the Premises;
☐ a current set of the Rules and Regulations;
☐ a Work Letter;
☐ a janitorial schedule;
☐ other (specify): _____

2. **Premises.**

2.1 **Letting.** Lessor hereby leases to Lessee, and Lessee hereby leases from Lessor, the Premises, for the term, at the rental, and upon all of the terms, covenants and conditions set forth in this Lease. While the approximate square footage of the Premises may have been used in the marketing of the Premises for purposes of comparison, the Base Rent stated herein is NOT tied to square footage and is not subject to adjustment should the actual size be determined to be different. **Note: Lessee is advised to verify the actual size prior to executing this Lease.**

2.2 **Condition.** Lessor shall deliver the Premises to Lessee in a clean condition on the Commencement Date or the Early Possession Date, whichever first occurs ("**Start Date**"), and warrants that the existing electrical, plumbing, fire sprinkler, lighting, heating, ventilating and air conditioning systems ("**HVAC**"), and all other items which the Lessor is obligated to construct pursuant to the Work Letter attached hereto, if any, other than those constructed by Lessee, shall be in good operating condition on said date, that the structural elements of the roof, bearing walls and foundation of the Unit shall be free of material defects, and that the Premises do not contain hazardous levels of any mold or fungi defined as toxic under applicable state or federal law.

2.3 **Compliance.** Lessor warrants to the best of its knowledge that the improvements comprising the Premises and the Common Areas comply with the building codes that were in effect at the time each such improvement, or portion thereof, was constructed, and also with all applicable laws, covenants or restrictions of record, regulations, and ordinances ("**Applicable Requirements**") in effect on the Start Date. Said warranty does not apply to the use to which Lessee will put the Premises, modifications which may be required by the Americans with Disabilities Act or any similar laws as a result of Lessee's use (see Paragraph 49), or to any Alterations or Utility Installations (as defined in Paragraph 7.3(a)) made or to be made by Lessee. **NOTE: Lessee is responsible for determining whether or not the zoning and other Applicable Requirements are appropriate for Lessee's intended use, and acknowledges that past uses of the Premises may no longer be allowed.** If the Premises do not comply with said warranty, Lessor shall, except as otherwise provided, promptly after receipt of written notice from Lessee setting forth with specificity the nature and extent of such non-compliance, rectify the same. If the Applicable Requirements are hereafter changed so as to require during the term of this Lease the construction of an addition to or an alteration of the Premises, the remediation of any Hazardous Substance, or the reinforcement or other physical modification of the Premises ("**Capital Expenditure**"), Lessor and Lessee shall allocate the cost of such work as follows:

(a) Subject to Paragraph 2.3(c) below, if such Capital Expenditures are required as a result of the specific and unique use of the Premises by Lessee as compared with uses by tenants in general, Lessee shall be fully responsible for the cost thereof, provided, however that if such Capital Expenditure is required during the last 2 years of this Lease and the cost thereof exceeds 6 months' Base Rent, Lessee may instead terminate this Lease unless Lessor notifies Lessee, in writing, within 10 days after receipt of Lessee's termination notice that Lessor has elected to pay the difference between the actual cost thereof and the amount equal to 6 months' Base Rent. If Lessee elects termination, Lessee shall immediately cease the use of the Premises which requires such Capital Expenditure and deliver to Lessor written notice specifying a termination date at least 90 days thereafter. Such termination date shall, however, in no event be earlier than the last day that Lessee could legally utilize the Premises without commencing such Capital Expenditure.

(b) If such Capital Expenditure is not the result of the specific and unique use of the Premises by Lessee (such as, governmentally mandated seismic modifications), then Lessor shall pay for such Capital Expenditure and Lessee shall only be obligated to pay, each month during the remainder of the term of this Lease or any extension thereof, on the date on which the Base Rent is due, an amount equal to 1/144th of the portion of such costs reasonably attributable to the Premises. Lessee shall pay Interest on the balance but may prepay its obligation at any time. If, however, such Capital Expenditure is required during the last 2 years of this Lease or if Lessor reasonably determines that it is not economically feasible to pay its share thereof, Lessor shall have the option to terminate this Lease upon 90 days prior written notice to Lessee unless Lessee notifies Lessor, in writing, within 10 days after receipt of Lessor's termination notice that Lessee will pay for such Capital Expenditure. If Lessor does not elect to terminate, and fails to tender its share of any such Capital Expenditure, Lessee may advance such funds and deduct same, with Interest, from Rent until Lessor's share of such costs have been fully paid. If Lessee is unable to finance Lessor's share, or if the balance of the Rent due and payable for the remainder of this Lease is not sufficient to fully reimburse Lessee on an offset basis, Lessee shall have the right to terminate this Lease upon 30 days written notice to Lessor.

(c) Notwithstanding the above, the provisions concerning Capital Expenditures are intended to apply only to nonvoluntary, unexpected, and new Applicable Requirements. If the Capital Expenditures are instead triggered by Lessee as a result of an actual or proposed change in use, change in intensity of use, or modification to the Premises then, and in that event, Lessee shall either: (i) immediately cease such changed use or intensity of use and/or take such other steps as may be necessary to eliminate the requirement for such Capital Expenditure, or (ii) complete such Capital Expenditure at its own expense. Lessee shall not have any right to terminate this Lease.

2.4 **Acknowledgements.** Lessee acknowledges that: (a) it has been given an opportunity to inspect and measure the Premises, (b) Lessee has been advised by Lessor and/or Brokers to satisfy itself with respect to the size and condition of the Premises (including but not limited to the electrical, HVAC and fire sprinkler systems, security, environmental aspects, and compliance with Applicable Requirements), and their suitability for Lessee's intended use, (c) Lessee has made such investigation as it deems necessary with reference to such matters and assumes all responsibility therefor as the same relate to its occupancy of the Premises, (d) it is not relying on any representation as to the size of the Premises made by Brokers or Lessor, (e) the square footage of the Premises was not material to Lessee's decision to lease the Premises and pay the Rent stated herein, and (f) neither Lessor, Lessor's agents, nor Brokers have made any oral or written representations or warranties with respect to said matters other than as set forth in this Lease. In addition, Lessor acknowledges that: (i) Brokers have made no representations, promises or warranties concerning Lessee's ability to honor the Lease or suitability to occupy the Premises, and (ii) it is Lessor's sole responsibility to investigate the financial capability and/or suitability of all proposed tenants.

2.5 **Lessee as Prior Owner/Occupant.** The warranties made by Lessor in Paragraph 2 shall be of no force or effect if immediately prior to the Start Date, Lessee was the owner or occupant of the Premises. In such event, Lessee shall be responsible for any necessary corrective work.

2.6 **Vehicle Parking.** So long as Lessee is not in default, and subject to the Rules and Regulations attached hereto, and as established by Lessor from time to time, Lessee shall be entitled to rent and use the number of parking spaces specified in Paragraph 1.2(b) at the rental rate applicable from time to time for monthly parking as set by Lessor and/or its licensee.

(a) If Lessee commits, permits or allows any of the prohibited activities described in the Lease or the rules then in effect, then Lessor shall have the right, without notice, in addition to such other rights and remedies that it may have, to remove or tow away the vehicle involved and charge the cost to Lessee, which cost shall be immediately payable upon demand by Lessor.

(b) The monthly rent per parking space specified in Paragraph 1.2(b) is subject to change upon 30 days prior written notice to Lessee. The rent for the parking is payable one month in advance prior to the first day of each calendar month.

2.7 **Common Areas - Definition.** The term "**Common Areas**" is defined as all areas and facilities outside the Premises and within the exterior boundary line of the Project and interior utility raceways and installations within the Premises that are provided and designated by the Lessor from time to time for the general nonexclusive use of Lessor, Lessee and other tenants of the Project and their respective employees, suppliers, shippers, customers, contractors and invitees, including, but not limited to, common entrances, lobbies, corridors, stairwells, public restrooms, elevators, parking areas, loading and unloading areas, trash areas, roadways, walkways, driveways and landscaped areas.

2.8 **Common Areas - Lessee's Rights.** Lessor grants to Lessee, for the benefit of Lessee and its employees, suppliers, shippers, contractors, customers and invitees, during the term of this Lease, the nonexclusive right to use, in common with others entitled to such use, the Common Areas as they exist from time to time, subject to any rights, powers, and privileges reserved by Lessor under the terms hereof or under the terms of any rules and regulations or restrictions governing the use of the Project. Under no circumstances shall the right herein granted to use the Common Areas be deemed to include the right to store any property, temporarily or permanently, in the Common Areas. Any such storage shall be

_____
INITIALS

_____
INITIALS

III. Industrial Property Management

Industrial property includes manufacturing, fabrication, and warehousing facilities.

Some industrial property is designed for specialized purposes, while other space is modified for tenant needs similar to office space modification.

A. LOCATIONAL NEEDS

Locational needs for industrial property are different than commercial property. Most commercial property users want high-traffic locations, while industrial property locations may be oriented as follows:

Supply Oriented. Locations close to the source of raw materials or close to component manufacturers would best suit supply-oriented firms.

Market Oriented. A supplier located close to a prime user of the product would prefer a market-oriented location. A machine shop that produces prototypes may want to locate close to a major customer in order to consult at various stages of preparation.

Transportation Oriented. A company fabricating large steel drums may want to locate close to a railroad line if they use rail transport, or be close to a major highway if they ship by truck. A fabricator of small costly items would probably want to locate close to an airport.

Labor Oriented. A company that wants to manufacture computer-related equipment and hire engineers and skilled fabricators would seek a Silicon Valley location. Where unskilled labor is needed, the supply and cost of such labor is an important location factor.

Utility Oriented. Having low-cost electricity might be an important locational factor to a firm requiring high power needs. A food processing firm might be interested in the quantity and quality of the water.

Quality of Life. Footloose industries do not have excessive problems with transportation or tapping into a particular labor pool. Location would be influenced by the quality of life offered to management. Quality of life factors would be:

1. **Climate.** The sunbelt might be a particular plus.
2. **Hobbies and Special Interests.** If a CEO is an avid skier, then Colorado, Idaho or Utah might be a desirable location for the firm.
3. **Schools.** The quality of education would be important for many executives who have children.
4. **Colleges and Universities.** A location close to a major college or university would appeal to many firms. College and university programs for families and executives themselves are important. Many firms work closely with colleges and universities

by getting involved in doctoral programs and/or consulting with professors on research.

5. **Housing.** Quality and the cost of housing is an important life style consideration.

6. **The Arts.** Areas in which theaters, music and the arts are located attract many firms because of the contribution to quality of life.

7. **Crime.** A low crime rate is important in making a locational decision.

8. **Religion.** Executives in footloose industries will be influenced by religion. They want to be located near other people of similar beliefs. As an example, many Mormons have moved their facilities to Utah from other areas of the country.

9. **Locational Incentives.** Footloose industries would be interested in incentives offered by a community. Incentives include low-cost loans, low or no rent, a moratorium on property taxes, locally sponsored training programs for employees, etc.

Many communities vie for industrial facilities that will employ local residents. These are usually communities having a high rate of unemployment. Often, they will build a facility for the special needs of a user.

VOICE OF EXPERIENCE:

In leasing space to a footloose industry, you might be competing against a community desperate to obtain the same tenant. In this case, you would have to stress locational advantages rather than rental costs.

B. STRUCTURAL NEEDS

1. Historic Structures

When water was used to power factories, it was transferred from waterwheels to machines by belts, chains and shafts more readily done vertically than horizontally. Factories were multi-story facilities during the industrial revolution. These structures were not efficient operations because of the cost of moving goods from one floor to another.

2. One-Story Factories

Manufacturers sought large sites for one-story factories to run modern assembly line businesses. They moved toward suburban areas to obtain the necessary space. Today, factory requirements include:

1. Water quantity for fire suppression systems and water quality for processing application may be necessary. Location to hydrants, quantity of water and water pressure are important for insurance purposes.

2. Adequate power and three-phase wiring is required for some applications.

3. Adequate ceiling height needed for movement of equipment, forklifts, truck operations, etc.

4. Overhead traveling cranes are important for moving heavy equipment or material.

5. Clear-span structures are desirable for ease in changing production lines and moving equipment.

6. Overhead doors provide easy ingress and egress of vehicles, equipment and material.

7. Loading docks are important for receiving and shipping. Some factories want two sets of doors so that the arrival of material does not conflict with shipments.

8. Employee parking is an important consideration in maintaining a work force.

9. Industrial zoning is important, as many communities have various zoning categories for particular uses.

10. Depending upon climate and the type of facility, heating and air conditioning as well as insulation could be significant factors.

11. While leakage may be a problem, underground tanks are nevertheless desirable for many industrial users.

12. Covered, secured, and open storage areas are necessary for different industrial users. Besides the arrival of components and material, there may be a need to store goods prior to shipping.

13. Secure perimeter fencing could be important for many industrial users. Park security could be a leasing consideration if the factory is located within an industrial park.

C. SPECIAL USE STRUCTURES

SPECIAL USE STRUCTURES have a very limited use. Although in one case a grain elevator complex was converted to apartments, generally such a complex has limited use.

Some special use structures, such as a cold storage or freeze storage facility, could easily be converted to another use such as general storage. However, such use would not take advantage of the structure's special features and should only be considered if a tenant cannot be found to use the structure "as is" or with the addition of any special features.

VOICE OF EXPERIENCE:

In recent years, the conversion of special structures for other purposes has been increasing in popularity. A boarded-up old hospital near downtown Los Angeles, for example, is being considered for conversion to low-income housing to address the problems of a growing homeless population. Additionally, the skyrocketing prices of cookie-cutter suburban residential developments and excessive commuting time have contributed to the redevelopment of ignored, rundown, or even blighted, downtown areas.

▼

Across the country, once shabby warehouse districts are experiencing a revitalization. Architecturally interesting or unique buildings are being converted into upscale loft-style condominiums, art galleries, coffee houses, night clubs, and alternative entertainment spaces.

A word of caution, however! A softening of the market, unrealistic expectations by investors, and overdevelopment may lead to a glut of vacancies in these areas. Slower turnover may force short-term investors interested in quick profits, to "cut and run," resulting in a reduction of maintenance, bigger incentives to renters and buyers, and ultimately, price slashing of the units.

D. INDUSTRIAL PARKS

INDUSTRIAL PARKS are subdivisions containing a number of freestanding buildings made up of single-tenant or multi-tenant structures. Large green areas encompass modern industrial parks that present an excellent image. Fountains, waterfalls or colorful plantings can be found at many industrial park entrances. There may be a security gate, although most parks are open with tenants responsible for their own security. Large lots are set aside for parking in the rear of the structures.

Some industrial parks are wholly owned by one individual or entity. Others are developed by investors who purchased one or more sites. Buildings within the park must conform with restrictive covenants dictating setbacks, landscaping, height and possibly even architectural style.

E. WAREHOUSE SPACE

WAREHOUSES are industrial related buildings even though no manufacturing or fabrication takes place on the property.

Historically, warehouses were built near interconnecting transportation routes such as rail lines or sea ports. While major warehouse locations exist, the greater reliance on truck transportation allows warehouses to locate near any major highway.

A great many warehouses are located in Nevada because there isn't any inventory tax.

Warehouse space is marketed by the square foot. Height, size of doors, loading docks, fire suppression system, security system, and insurance rates where the warehouse is located are important factors to lessees.

F. EVALUATING A SITE

Evaluate the location and structure when you have an industrial property for lease. You should target specific types of users as well as particular users. You want to consider the favorable and negative features of your site and how to present them before making a general approach to a specific firm or through an industrial publication.

G. PREPARING TO LEASE

The space should be clean and, where possible, well lighted before it is shown for marketing.

Any delay in preparation should be regarded as costly since waiting for a crew to remove debris from a vacated space would mean lost rent that could far exceed the cleanup cost.

H. INDUSTRIAL LEASES

Industrial leases vary significantly based on the type of property and services included, as well as the length of the lease. Disclosures are often provided for industrial leases to protect the lessor from future lessee claims.

I. CHANGING USES

When vacancies are at a high level, as a property manager, you will seek tenants who are attracted by location and reasonable rent. As the vacancy factor is reduced, you will seek those tenants who are willing to pay much more for the space.

Managers of industrial property in Burbank and Santa Monica, California have been notifying tenants that their leases will not be renewed. They are repositioning their properties to pursue "clean" firms. They are targeting post production entertainment companies and high-tech industries that can pay almost double for the square footage that small industrial shops could pay. (Property managers in other areas are actively seeking these tenants.) Former auto repair shops and machine shops are now renting for $1 and more per square foot. The art-oriented new tenants like the open trusses and skylights of industrial property.

VOICE OF EXPERIENCE:

There is a risk in chasing out small industrial users, as they tend to be located in more volatile areas that may discourage new tenants. In evaluating the potential benefits and drawbacks to pursuing more "upscale" tenants, you should take into consideration the appeal of the building versus the condition of the neighborhood. Some tenants will appreciate the unexploited "rawness" of the property, while others will be turned off by the inconvenience created by a lack of grocery stores, theaters, and cafes.

IV. CHAPTER SUMMARY

Commercial property is property involved in the buying and selling of goods. The commercial space requirements for a community are based upon population, number of households, discretionary purchasing power, demographics of the community and the drawing power of area businesses. Commercial property might be located on pedestrian shopping streets, urban pedestrian malls, strip centers, mini-malls, neighborhood shopping centers, community shopping centers, regional shopping centers, mega-malls, factory outlet centers, freestanding stores and also include wholesale operations.

Tenant selection is very important in multi-tenant facilities. Tenants can contribute to each other's success if properly selected. Quality tenants will help reduce tenant turnover.

Rent setting for an area is not based on comparables alone. Special needs of tenants, locational differences, etc., can affect rents.

A tenant's survivability can be affected if a landlord wants too high a rent. This can mean problems with rent collection, vacancies and additional costs related to renting. Too low rents could mean losing later opportunities to obtain market rent. It could also result in other tenants wanting to negotiate rent reductions.

Parking needs create many problems in nonresidential leasing that must be addressed by management.

Since building nonresidential structures is related to the availability of loans, building and overbuilding tends to run in cycles.

Office buildings are categorized from Class A to Class D, depending on quality and desirability. Office buildings may be one-story garden structures, low-rise, mid-rise or high-rise. Some older office structures can be repositioned as to class by restoration or remodeling. Buildings can be more desirable to occupants because of the theme of the structure.

Intelligent buildings use shared state-of-the-art communication facilities. Some buildings combine commercial, office and residential uses. R & D (Research and Development) facilities include offices, laboratories and might also include fabrication facilities.

Sick buildings have problems such as bacteria (air conditioning ducts, etc.) and/or fume emissions from chemicals used in construction and/or decorating. When a building has exceeded its economic life due to increase in the value of the site, demolition and replacement should be considered.

The vacancy factor of an area will likely differ by class of office structure. When new space becomes available it must be absorbed by increased demand or other space will have to be taken off the market. Otherwise, the vacancy rate will increase. Square footage can be computed in various ways for rental purposes.

Property managers should make clear what methods were used to arrive at any square footage figures. Many office leases provide for a fixturing allowance for new tenants. Expenses beyond the allowance would be the tenant's responsibility.

Perks to management and employees make for happy tenants. Happy tenants are more likely to become long-term tenants.

Most office leases are gross leases. Leases often include a floor plan so that all parties fully understand what is being leased.

Locational needs for manufacturing properties is not based on traffic counts. Important factors include location in relation to supplies, market, transportation, labor supply, utility supply, and the quality of life offered by the community.

Most industrial firms prefer a one-story plant for ease of movement of supplies and the finished product. Of concern to facilities are the water quality, quantity and pressure for products and/or fire suppression, adequacy of electrical service for the tenant's needs, height of structure, overhead cranes, clear span, overhead doors, loading docks, parking, HVAC facilities, storage, underground tanks, as well as the security of the structure and its perimeter.

Special use structures may be very limited in their use, although there is a growing trend towards conversion. Industrial parks have a number of freestanding structures and often attractive green areas.

Warehouse space is industrial related. The best warehouse locations are accessible to transportation. Personal property tax is also a consideration.

A property manager should evaluate a property to be leased, taking into consideration who can use it and the specific strengths of the property for the user. A property manager could target specific industries and firms in marketing the property.

Industrial leases vary significantly based on the type of property, services included and length of the lease.

Commercial, Office, & Industrial Property Management

V. CHAPTER QUIZ

1. Which of the following would be of importance in determining the amount of commercial space required by a community?
    a. The number of households
    b. Discretionary purchasing power of residents
    c. The age breakdown of residents
    d. All of the above

2. An established shopping street that is restricted to foot traffic only would BEST describe a(n):
    a. urban pedestrian mall.
    b. strip center.
    c. neighborhood shopping center.
    d. mini-mall.

3. A shopping center with a single, large department or discount store as an anchor tenant, best describes a:
    a. neighborhood shopping center.
    b. mega-mall.
    c. community shopping center.
    d. mini-mall.

4. A symbiotic relationship would apply to:
    a. industrial sites.
    b. selecting tenants who will benefit by each other.
    c. freestanding single-tenant structures.
    d. the quality of life offered by a community.

5. The best office quality of a building in a community would be:
    a. Class A.
    b. Class B.
    c. Class C.
    d. Class D.

6. A two- or three-story office building would be a:
    a. garden building.
    b. low-rise building.
    c. mid-rise building.
    d. high-rise building.

7. A sick building would MOST LIKELY be the result of:

    a. a tenant going bankrupt.
    b. having elderly tenants.
    c. chemical fumes from construction products and/or furnishings.
    d. desirability of the building.

8. Demolition could be an economic decision for a sound building when:

    a. interest rates rise.
    b. land values rise dramatically but rents do not.
    c. the vacancy factor reaches five percent.
    d. never.

9. Office tenants generally have what kind of lease?

    a. Gross
    b. Net
    c. Percentage
    d. Percentage plus minimum

10. An industrial plant that locates next to its largest customer would be:

    a. supply oriented.
    b. labor oriented.
    c. utility oriented.
    d. market oriented.

ANSWERS: 1. d; 2. a; 3. c; 4. b; 5. a; 6. b; 7. c; 8. b; 9. a; 10. d

 **WESTWOOD MEDICAL**

Chapter 7
Special Management Situations

KEY WORDS AND TERMS

Board of Directors
Clothing Optional
Condominium Association
Corporate-Owned Farms
Docking Facilities
Elderly Housing
Farm/Ranch Management
Gentlemen Farms
Homeowner's Association (HOA)
Hotel/Motel Management
Independent Living
Institutional Management
Inventory Control
Lender-Owned Farms
Life Care
Mediation

Medical Office Management
Mini Storage
Mobile Home Park Management
Nursing Facilities
Public Rooms
Recreational Vehicle Park Management
Residential Hotels
Resort Management
Section 8 Housing
Semi-Independent Living
Short-Term Residential
SROs
Storage Yard
Subsidized Housing
Time Share Management
Undivided Interest Developments

CHAPTER 7 OUTLINE

I. Single-Room Occupancy (SROs)

SROs refer to single-room occupancy. They are usually former transient hotels and motels that, because of a variety of factors, are either marginal or loss operations when rented on a daily basis.

Renting units by the month offers significant operational savings in housekeeping services as well as eliminating the need for full-time desk clerks. By changing from daily occupancy, the operation changes from a hotel/motel management plan and philosophy to a simple multi-unit rental unit.

> *SROs differ from residential hotels in that they do not offer the services a hotel does such as housekeeping, room service, 24-hour desk service, valet service, message service, etc.*

In many population centers there is a tremendous need for SRO units that consist of a single room and bath. They can be rented for significantly less than the normal bachelor (efficiency) or one-bedroom unit. The lower rent makes the units desirable for retirees, single working persons as well as persons receiving some sort of government assistance.

In large metropolitan areas you might find managers who specialize in SROs. They would likely present a management proposal to the owner of a large hotel or motel-type property covering conversion to an SRO.

Property managers may team up with entrepreneurs who either buy or lease property for conversion to SROs with the property manager handling the conversion and operation. Because of the low prices that loss operations can be purchased or leased for, some property managers have elected to operate SROs as principals rather than as agents of others.

A. TENANT QUALIFYING

Because you are renting a single room does not mean that you should be less careful in tenant selection. Problem tenants can result in the exodus of desirable tenants. It can also result in damage to the property and long-term damage to the building's reputation.

If you choose to become a single-room occupancy manager, you should be aware that these units often appear attractive to prostitutes, drug dealers, addicts and other criminal elements. Background credit and rental history is important and must be checked. A prospective tenant who wants immediate occupancy and offers several month's rent in advance is not necessarily superior to having a vacant unit.

A copy of the tenant's driver's license should be kept in the file.

B. SECURITY

Consideration must be given to security in changing a daily rental facility to an SRO. While the room locks and door chains might be adequate, exterior doors should, if possible, be locked with an electronic lock that can be released by individual tenants through a call system. In this way, persons intent on mischief have two locks to go through.

In addition, a 24-hour security camera can be aimed at the entrance as well as any elevators. Service doors would likely already be set up for exit only with panic hardware. See Chapter 9 for a further discussion regarding security.

C. OCCUPANCY

Because of the 1988 Amendment to the Civil Rights Act of 1968, it may not be possible to restrict occupancy to one person.

This could discriminate against married couples, which would be familial status discrimination (see Chapter 13). However, because of the small size of the units, limiting occupancy to two persons would likely be upheld should it be challenged in the courts.

While hotels charge more for a double than a single, you should not charge more for two persons as it could be discriminatory based on familial status. You can, of course, charge more for large size rooms or different amenities, such as a king-size bed.

D. RENTAL PERIOD

Weekly rentals should generally be avoided, as it will result in a greater turnover of tenants and higher vacancy and maintenance factors, which will likely result in lowering the net. In addition, weekly rentals will attract transients and other undesirable tenants.

In property management, having to deal with more individuals increases the likelihood of encountering tenants who become serious problems.

E. LEASE

Renters in SROs should sign a lease, even if it is only a month-to-month tenancy, and pay some sort of property damage bond, even if it is only $50. Renters should also be asked to sign a copy of house rules and be given a copy. The rules may cover cooking in rooms, use of electric heaters, pets, noise, parking, etc.

F. UTILITIES

SROs are generally rented with all utilities. In most instances, the cost of rewiring would make separate utilities an uneconomic conversion.

They usually include heat and air conditioning, light, water and cable television. While telephones will likely be installed in the lobby, laundry room and perhaps other public areas, private telephones would be the tenants' responsibility. The existing telephone system utilizing a hotel or motel switchboard would not be used.

G. FURNISHINGS

SROs are generally rented fully furnished, although some operations will allow a tenant to use his or her own furniture. This would likely lead to a longer term tenancy. A small refrigerator is usually added to the hotel/motel type furnishings.

While SROs generally prohibit hot plate use, some allow the tenants to use their own microwave ovens, if the electrical service will handle such use. Allowing microwaves will increase tenancy periods and avoids clandestine cooking in the rooms.

Some managers include the original televisions but will not replace or repair them. The set becomes the responsibility of the tenant and therefore reduces management's problems.

Most units include basic bedding, linens and towels with additional supplies being the responsibility of the tenant. However, units that do not supply bedding, linens, and towels do not necessarily lose prospective tenants because of this practice.

H. HOUSEKEEPING

SROs should avoid housekeeping other than the lobby, elevators, hallways, and public areas. The individual units should be the responsibility of the tenants. The only time units should be cleaned would be between tenancies. The units should always be rented in a clean and sanitary condition with fresh linens.

I. LAUNDRY ROOM

Usually, space is available for a coin-operated laundry room. The laundry room should be locked with entry only with tenant's keys or by a combination electric lock. Vending machines can be placed in the laundry room and/or in the lobby area.

Income from coin-operated machines can be substantial in an SRO setting.

Therefore, proper maintenance of the equipment is important. Machines should either be on a maintenance contract or should be contracted for with an operator on a split-revenue basis.

VOICE OF EXPERIENCE:

Although a laundry room is a perk for SROs, you need to determine that the operating costs (including the utilities) do not exceed their benefits.

J. RESTAURANTS/BARS

As a property manager, you should avoid managing existing restaurants and/or bars.

The management problems and specialized nature of such operations usually result in disaster.

If feasible, the restaurant/bar operation should be leased out to an operator. Some motels that have converted to SROs have leased restaurant facilities at a very reasonable rent to moderately-priced chain restaurant operators. The SRO owners find that the presence of a food service has aided in renting rooms.

K. PUBLIC ROOMS

In some cases, meeting and banquet rooms can be leased to the onsite restaurant operator. If this is not economically feasible, consideration should be given to convert the space to additional rental units. However, this is not always realistic due to the size of the meeting or banquet room and large windows. Some SROs use old banquet facilities as day rooms for their residents and even provide donuts and coffee on Sunday mornings.

There is a reason for promoting tenant socialization. Tenants who know each other, especially retired persons, are more likely to become permanent tenants.

Space that does not have any rental value and is otherwise not needed for operations should be converted to a storage facility. Air and heat ducts in this space should be closed.

L. 55 AND OLDER

It is possible to restrict occupancy to persons 55 years of age and older (see Chapter 13). This will reduce crime and property damage as well as increase the average occupancy period for your tenants. You should analyze your market to determine if the area supports this restriction before you make a change.

VOICE OF EXPERIENCE:

A 100-unit, older motel or hotel that is occupied entirely by pensioners could provide relatively easy management, and provide an excellent monthly gross income, depending on the marketplace.

M. RESIDENT MANAGER

Most hotel and motel operations include either a large apartment unit for a resident manager or offices that can be converted to such use.

The **RESIDENT MANAGER** *would be responsible for enforcing house rules, taking rental applications, lease signing, supervision of housekeeping and maintenance, handling complaints, and recommending or initiating eviction procedures.* In some cases the resident manager would actually collect the rents.

A resident manager who does the job well will usually insure a smooth operation. A careless resident manager who fails to meet his or her obligations can spell disaster for an SRO operation.

II. Common Interest Developments (CIDs) Management

The **DAVIS-STIRLING ACT** *is a comprehensive body of law which was passed in California to regulate* **Common Interest Developments (CIDs)**. It defines CIDs to include the following:

1. The condominium
2. The stock cooperative
3. The community apartment project
4. The planned development

Because most CIDs are condominiums, we will focus on condominiums.

Management of a condominium means representing the Board of Directors of the Homeowner's Association (HOA) rather than an individual owner.

A. THE BOARD OF DIRECTORS (HOA)

WELL, GOOD LUCK WITH YOUR NEW CONDOMINIUM, MR TRASK... AND REMEMBER- IF ANYTHING AT ALL GOES WRONG WITH YOUR UNIT- ANYTHING- DON'T CALL ME!

The **BOARD OF DIRECTORS** *of a Homeowner's Association (HOA) is elected by the homeowners as their representatives.* The Board of Directors hires the property manager. Rather than dealing with an owner who is economically oriented, members of the association might have separate agendas, which may include the following:

Keep Fees Down. Such a director can drive a manager practically insane with constant questions about individual minor expenses. Often the director is a retired individual who has nothing else to do but be a self-appointed watchdog over expenses.

Self-serving motives can derail good property management.

Keep It Beautiful. This director is very interested in the grounds and possesses a passion for gardening. They often insist on selecting the flowers, plants and colors to be used on the premises.

Be a Chief. Some directors strive to be important and are very impressed with themselves. Such a director can end up going over the head of the property manager in directing maintenance and grounds personnel.

An Obsession. Some people run for office on the Board of Directors because of specific personal agendas. The desires of one individual should not take priority over the whole picture.

Throw Them Out. Some directors run for office because they didn't like the decisions made by previous board members. In their clean-slate approach, they also may want to change the current property management, which they cannot do if the firm has a solid contract. Such a director is politically motivated and may work hard to find a breach of the management contract. Management will be under great scrutiny.

The Time Waster. This type of director loves meetings at every opportunity. They enjoy lengthy meetings with a lot of talking where not much is really said nor accomplished.

The Nit-Picker. This director has a lot of time to worry about little things that the average person would ignore. The nit-picker demands that meetings be run "by the book," requiring management to bone up on association procedures.

The Reasonable Director. Actually, there are few directors who are reasonable in every area and few who are unreasonable all of the time. Directors tend to have a combination of the traits listed and, like all of us, fall into varying shades of grey.

B. HOMEOWNER'S ASSOCIATION (HOA) MANAGEMENT DUTIES

To be a certified condominium manager, you must pass a skills competency test or complete 30 hours of courses.

The California DRE has added a course in Common Interest Developments (CIDs) to satisfy one of the broker statutory requirements. Check your state's department of real estate for similar courses.

Educational Textbook Company has published a textbook for this course entitled *Homeowner's Association Management*, by Walt Huber and Kim Tyler, JD.

Management duties may include the following.

Supervision of Elections. As a property manager, you would see that the election of the Board of Directors is held in accordance with the bylaws of the association.

Enforcement of CC&Rs. The enforcement of covenants, conditions, and restrictions, as well as rules and regulations, must be uniform. Before enforcing a previously unenforced regulation, you should consult with the Board of Directors.

VOICE OF EXPERIENCE:

As the property manager, it will be your duty to enforce the CC&Rs and rules and regulations of the HOA. Before implementing policies that have been inconsistently applied or ignored in the past, you should consult with the Board of Directors. If the Board agrees that it's reasonable to begin enforcing the rule, a bulletin should be issued notifying the association members/homeowners that stricter application of the rule is imminent.

If a court determines a rule is unreasonable, the court will refuse to enforce it.

Recommendation for Rule Changes. As the property manager, you should notify the Board of Directors of any new rule or modification. The recommendation should be specific as to the language of the rule. If the board agrees, copies of the rule should be given to members for a vote. Some associations require only a simple majority to change rules and others require a two-thirds vote.

If you feel a rule is unreasonable, you should consult with the Board of Directors and recommend calling for a vote to eliminate or alter it.

Chapter 7

VOICE OF EXPERIENCE:

If immediate implementation of a previously unenforced rule or a new rule change is not paramount, you can avoid dealing with outraged homeowner association members by allowing for a one month "grace period" before imposing the most severe penalties.

For example, if an existing but ignored or new rule is about to take effect requiring visitors to display a 24-hour parking pass, you might consider "easing" the transition by gradually increasing the consequences. You could instruct parking enforcement personnel to place a one-time warning notice on a noncompliant vehicle during the first week after notification, with a ticket and fine imposed the second week, followed by ticketing, towing, and impound fees the third week. And finally, 30 days after initial notification, if a homeowner is consistently found to be the offending party, he/she may be accused of breaching the HOA CC&Rs and be subject to the consequences of that violation.

Preparation of the Annual Budget. In the preparation of the budget, as the manager you should consider past costs, inflation, necessary modifications to maintenance and any changes in improvements, taxes, insurance, etc. The budget should be submitted for Board approval.

Management of Insurance. As the property manager, you would make certain that the insurance coverage is adequate but not excessive. Coverage would include replacement value for physical improvements from theft, vandalism, and damage from fire, smoke, and water, etc. It may also include earthquake and/or flood damage. Coverage should include high-limit liability insurance for members and a directors' liability policy. Worker's Compensation coverage would be required for any employees.

Supervision of Maintenance. As the property manager, you would be responsible for supervising all maintenance work and repairs.

Case Example

***Portola Hills Community Association v. James*, 4 C.A. 4th 289 (1992)**

CC&Rs banned satellite dishes completely from the community. Jones installed a satellite dish that was not visible to other residents or to the public. The trial court found that the restriction was not reasonable so could not be enforced.

The Court of Appeals affirmed pointing out that under California Civil Code Section 1354, restrictions are enforceable unless unreasonable. Prohibiting a satellite dish that could not be observed by others does not serve any legitimate purpose of the association and was therefore unreasonable. ▼

Jarrett v. Valley Park, Inc., 922 P.2d 485 (Mont. 1996)

Condominium owners sought to enjoin enforcement of a covenant that prohibited installation of television satellite dishes within the village except by developer or its designate. It was held that a plain and unambiguous covenant will be upheld if it is possible to harmonize it with the general plan for the property.

Case Example

Bernardo Villas Mgt. Corp. v. Black, 190 C.A. 3d 153 (1987)

A property manager sued the owner of a condominium unit to enjoin the owner from parking a new pickup truck in his carport and also to recover fines levied against the owner for violations of the CC&Rs. The CC&Rs prohibited the parking of trucks, campers, boats and recreational vehicles in the carports.

Both the trial court and the Court of Appeals ruled in favor of the owner. The court pointed out that California Civil Code Section 1354 holds that CC&Rs are enforceable unless they are unreasonable. Therefore, unreasonable restrictions would be unenforceable. The court pointed out that the presence of the truck in the carport was in no way offensive to a reasonable person. The truck was not used for commercial purposes. The court pointed out that the pickup trucks today are the equivalent of station wagons and convertibles. "One person's Bronco II is another person's Rolls Royce."

Note: This case points out the necessity of condo associations having reasonable covenants, conditions and restrictions. With the appeal, the association expended thousand of dollars to enforce a covenant which they should have realized was unreasonable.

Case Example

Randol v. Atkinson, 965 S.W.2d 338 (Mo.App.W.D. 1998)

Condominium bylaws constitute the rules and regulations that govern the internal administration of the condominium complex. ... We find nothing in the bylaws or the Declaration that, by itself, imposed a duty on the Association and Wind River to ban the use of charcoal grills.

Contracting for Services. Even if a condominium association has its own employees, there are still services that are best contracted for, such as swimming pool maintenance and exterior pest control.

Mediation. Personal problems between homeowners can develop into an ugly situation unless handled in a prompt and judicious manner. As the property manager, you should not try to direct a solution but instead act with the help of both parties to reach an understanding. You can also ask a board member to mediate the dispute.

Mediation and arbitration can aid you as the property manager in your relations with the HOA Board of Directors.

Attending Board Meetings. As the property manager, you may help in preparing a meeting agenda and should attend all meetings to answer any questions and present plans for future work on the premises. In some cases, you might take notes at the meeting and distribute copies to the members.

Many associations have committees for various aspects of the association. As an example, there could be committees for recreation, security, landscaping, etc.

Whenever possible, you should be available to attend committee meetings.

Security and Safety. As the property manager, you should supervise and review security operations and safety procedures and make recommendations to the board for any changes needed.

Collection of Assessments. While the assessments are set by the Board of Directors, you are responsible for collecting assessments from the members.

Legal Action. Legal action to protect or enforce the interests of the association or to collect delinquent assessments should only be commenced after receiving Board of Director approval.

Accounting and Record-Keeping. As the property manager, you need to keep up-to-date accounts of all income and expenses as well as employee records, insurance files, maintenance schedules, etc. These records should be available to the Board of Directors and members. You should never appear to be hiding anything from a member of the association.

Rentals and Sales. The rental or sale of units may not be your responsibility as a property manager. However, some associations prefer that a property manager handle these areas rather than have a number of brokers showing properties within the complex.

VOICE OF EXPERIENCE:

As the property manager, you have an advantage over other agents when engaging in such brokerage activities because you will have built up a relationship with the owners of the complex.

C. PERSONAL RELATIONSHIPS

As a condominium association property manager, you are more likely to lose your client because of personal reasons rather than because of management errors. The following are some points to remember:

Treat Them As Owners. Treat every member of the condominium association as if he or she were a sole owner. Listen to their complaints and let them know what you will do about it and do it.

Avoid Taking Sides. Cliques often form within the Board of Directors and/or association members. Remain neutral. Listen to everyone but say nothing negative about anyone.

Avoid Favoritism. Treat every member the same concerning rules and regulations. Don't give preference because a person is a member of the Board of Directors. Don't allow a member to think that you owe your position to that person.

Don't Lie or Exagerate to Members. Never tell a member you will do something when you don't intend to do it.

VOICE OF EXPERIENCE:

As a professional, you are only as good as your word. Your effectiveness as a property manager depends on the confidence you inspire in others. You must prove your level of competence and ability to follow through before others will trust your advice and decision-making capabilities.

Don't Hide Bad News. If there is an anticipated cost overrun, let the board know as soon as you have made that determination.

Always Complete Staff Work. Never present a problem to the Board of Directors without also presenting possible courses of action, your recommendations and why you think the recommended course of action is best.

People don't want to hear about problems without solutions.

Meet Deadlines. Don't give deadlines you can't meet just to please someone. Be realistic and then try to beat the deadline you have set.

Don't Underestimate Costs. People become angry when work exceeds an estimate. However, coming in under budget is like found money.

Ask for Advice. Although you should be the advisor and not the advisee regarding most management matters, you can use the expertise of members and Board members in many areas. People like being asked for advice about their areas of expertise.

As an example, while preparing specifications for a bid on a new pool heater, you might ask a member who is a heating contractor to review your specifications. You can also ask a person with gardening interests about changing plants for the common areas.

Know Their Names. Some condominium association property managers can address several hundred residents by name. Memory identification tricks can help you remember names, such as repeating the name to yourself three times during introductions and associating the name with someone or something. Most people don't go to this much trouble, but a little effort can make a big difference in personal relations.

Studies have shown that using a person's name frequently in conversation favorably influences that person's opinion of you. If those you deal with feel that you are personally interested in them, they will no doubt be easier to interact with.

Return All Calls Promptly. People get angry when you don't return calls or appear to be hiding from them.

Stop Board Abuses Fast. If Board members begin directing employees or contractors this can lead to confusion and problems. You must inform the Board that you will do whatever they want as long as it is legal, but any directions to the staff must come from you.

Inform all employees and contractors that as the property manager you are to approve all labor.

Watch Out for Employees Working for Homeowners. Your employees must understand that they cannot do work inside owners' units on association-paid time. They must also understand that they are not to accept tips for performing their jobs because some owners will feel others were treated better.

Be Positive. Any problems associated with a planned action of the Board of Directors should be pointed out before they are approved by the Board of Directors. After they are passed is not the time to resist. Ask for clarification if you are uncertain as to what is actually desired. Carry out the Board's wishes with enthusiasm.

Know the Bylaws and CC&Rs. Understand the Board of Director's authority as well as your own.

Never exceed your authority without attempting to first notify the board, except in emergencies.

Understand the CC&Rs. You don't want members to know more than you do about the governing of the association or your authority. Also understand the limitations imposed by the various statutes covering condominium associations.

D. COMPENSATION

Compensation for your management services will usually be a set monthly fee per unit plus actual costs incurred. The association will also probably provide you with an office within the complex. Associations of 1,000 members or more may have a monthly management fee of $8.00 per unit, while a smaller association may charge a monthly fee of $15.00 per unit. One person might be able to handle several smaller associations located in a close proximity, while a large association may require a full-time manager plus someone to handle secretarial and bookkeeping tasks.

III. Resort Area Management

Many property managers in resort areas will rent homes and condominium units by the month or by the *SEASON, which is usually dictated by weather conditions and could be as long as six or seven months.*

The shorter the rental period, the higher the rent and management fee.

Some management companies charge fees from 25 percent to 33 1/3 percent of gross rent receipts plus cleaning expenses. These fees are justified by marketing expenses and the rents collected for the owners.

Property management companies in the Palm Springs area advertise using 800 numbers in Los Angeles and San Francisco, as well as Washington, Oregon, and Canadian newspapers. Inquiries are answered by sending photographs and information on available units and rentals are concluded by telephone using a credit card for the rental deposit.

These firms also obtain business from the referrals of other brokers, who don't handle rentals, by paying referral fees.

Rental firms located in resort areas are often specialty firms that handle these rentals only. However, some brokers have one or more agents designated to handle resort area rentals. Condominium association managers also compete for this business. In some condominium complexes, rental commissions are a significant portion of the property manager's income.

IV. Clothing Optional

There are a number of clothing-optional apartment units located primarily in sun belt areas. Clothing-optional units are not intended to appeal to perversion or voyeurism. These units are rented to nudists who are allowed to wear or not wear clothes in the common areas. Residents are often middle-aged and believe strongly in the healthful aspects of sunshine and physical fitness.

Nudists are willing to pay a premium for these clothing-optional units. Through friendships with other nudists, these units often have long waiting lists.

VOICE OF EXPERIENCE:

Clothing-optional communities may present you with unique tenant-screening challenges. For example, it would seem prudent to conduct a thorough criminal history search of potential tenants to protect current residents from sexual predators. Fair housing laws, however, may prevent you from discriminating against registered sex offenders. If you rent to a known offender and a tenant is victimized by that person, could you be held liable for exposing that person to a known danger? Could a registered sex offender sue you for notifying the community of his/her past criminal record? Those questions are best addressed by a qualified attorney in your state.

A clothing-optional unit should have privacy, such as an interior courtyard with a pool and other recreational facilities which can be reached by entering a solidly-locked, gated area. Resident managers of such units are generally also dedicated nudists. Besides the normal management duties, they might also serve as recreational director.

VOICE OF EXPERIENCE:

From a legal standpoint, it's advisable to rely on accepted rental criteria like credit checks and employment history, although in this unique environment you may want to place a strong emphasis on referrals (especially those of current tenants). Your criteria should abide by state and federal fair housing laws and be applied consistently to all applicants.

V. Single-Family Dwellings

Management of a single-family dwelling is a specialized residential management area.

A large percentage of property management firms and real estate brokers handle some single-family dwellings as a natural progression of their residential sales.

A. OWNERS' GOALS

Owners often hold some single-family dwellings as long-term investments. They expect both income and appreciation in value. As a property manager, you can affect just one of these goals and that is income.

Single-family homes are often placed under property management because the owner is unable to sell the property at what he or she regards as a reasonable price. This owner wants or needs income from the property, usually to meet mortgage payments, until the property can be sold. Additionally, owners may not be sure they want to sell at this time.

Some single-family homes are placed under management because the owners expect to re-occupy the homes at some later date. It may be due to a work transfer out of the area or plans for future retirement. While the owner wants the income, he or she also wants the property maintained. Such an owner is usually more willing to agree to major expenditures. As an example, an owner who wants to sell a property would prefer to patch a leaky roof while an owner who hopes to retire in the house would agree to replace the roof.

Because single-family dwellings generally represent the highest per-unit value of all residential housing, great care must be taken in tenant qualifications. Be sure to check previous landlords' references.

B. MAINTENANCE

In the case of property of lower value, the tenant is responsible for lawn maintenance and even minor repairs. However, the rent might include gardening services and sprinkler maintenance in some higher priced properties.

A pool should be maintained by a service company and the cost included in the rent. Pool maintenance by a tenant could result in black algae growth, which is extremely difficult to control once it has gained a foothold. Improper chemical use can also result in pool stains.

Drive-by inspections on a regular basis are important if there is no resident manager. Also, interior inspections twice a year are very important.

C. UTILITIES

All utilities, except water, should be paid by the tenant. You don't want a tenant to skimp on taking care of landscaping.

D. RENT PROBLEMS

When a tenant's rent is delinquent, or if an eviction notice has been sent out, you should drive by the property daily. You want to know when the property becomes vacant. A single-family property can be vandalized at the cost of tens of thousands of dollars in just a few days.

Furnished homes are particularly vulnerable to vandalism.

E. RENTERS

Who rents single-family homes? People who prefer to be homeowners rather than apartment dwellers. They might lack the down payment to buy, they might be new to the area and wish to rent before they buy, they might be waiting to have a house built or they may not know how long they will be in the area. In some case, hobbies and/or pets preclude apartment living for them.

Because of the high unit value, tenant qualification must be thorough.

F. MANAGEMENT FEES

Generally, management fees for single-family dwellings are much higher than for other types of residential property considering per unit and gross rents. This is necessary because of the problems involved in managing scattered single units. A 6% to 10% monthly fee is customary.

VI. Short-Term Residential Properties

Some efficiency and one-bedroom apartment developments are rented furnished for short-term use to business people who expect an extended stay in a community. Rentals are by the week or by the month. However, some corporations arrange to rent units on an annual basis.

These units are much larger than motel or hotel rooms and provide a far better quality of living for the tenants. The cost per night is less than a decent hotel room. In an area where decent hotel rooms might be $90 per night, an extended-stay unit might rent for $400 per week.

A number of lodging chains have joined this lucrative market by building new facilities specifically to fulfill short-term residential needs.

These rentals customarily include a small kitchen, bedroom, or bed area and a living area with a couch, chairs, work or dining table, etc. Daily housekeeping is usually included. Units might also include telephone answering machines. The management office should offer a copy machine, fax and computer modem.

Management problems and duties are similar to hotel and motel operations except that they do not include any food service. Some premises might include a leased restaurant.

VOICE OF EXPERIENCE:

Marketing of such property would include tourist guides such as AAA, providing information to a Chamber of Commerce and contact with personnel, sales and engineering departments of major area employers.

VII. Hotel/Motel Management

Hotels differ from motels by the services offered.

Hotels offer food service and usually include banquet and meeting facilities, as well as luggage service to the rooms and room service.

Because of housekeeping, accounting, and rental policies, hotel and motel operations require specialized knowledge and experience that few general property managers possess.

A number of colleges and universities offer hotel/motel management programs. Generally these courses include supervision of food service, supervision of housekeeping, promotion of conventions, group sales, etc.

A. ELDERLY HOUSING PROJECTS

As post World War II baby boomers age, they will pass from the ranks of middle-age, to retirees, and then to the category known as elderly.

The three basic categories of elderly housing are independent living, semi-independent living, and skilled nursing facilities. Many independent and semi-independent facilities encourage guests to bring their own furnishings.

B. INDEPENDENT LIVING FACILITIES

A number of independent living facilities include the following features:

Individual Units. Many elderly independent living facilities feature luxurious apartments.

Common Areas. An activity director is usually on the premises to supervise activity programs that might include using common areas for music recitals, bingo, shopping trips, morning coffee hour, religious services, bridge tournaments, craft classes, group exercise sessions, etc.

There may be a number of common areas so that residents have a choice of various activities.

Restaurant. Many facilities include food services for residents. To maintain reasonable costs, some developments include, with the rent, a number of meals per month, such as 20 meals, with additional meals costing more.

While it can be contracted out, many elderly facilities prefer to provide their own food service to insure nutritional quality and desirability of the meals served and to better meet the individual dietary needs of the residents.

C. SEMI-INDEPENDENT LIVING FACILITIES

These facilities might be intermingled with independent living facilities. Semi-independent living facilities might include the following:

Full-Meal Program. Individuals eat all meals on the premises.

Aide Service. An aide stops by one or more times a day to check if the resident is taking his or her medication and assist with bathing, if required. All residents are provided with emergency call buttons in their units.

Housekeeping. Semi-independent living would likely include some level of housekeeping service.

D. NURSING FACILITIES

Skilled nursing facilities are monitored by a 24-hour nursing staff and could include ambulatory and nonambulatory patients.

Generally, they have activity and food service centers separate from the independent and semi-independent care residents. Nursing facilities do not have locks on the doors. Some units use television monitors and personnel to check on residents. Some nursing facilities consist of one room while others may include a full apartment.

E. LIFE CARE FACILITIES

LIFE CARE FACILITIES *include independent living, semi-independent living, and nursing facilities.* A number of major corporations have entered, or are considering entering, the life care market.

Life care provides complete medical facilities, often using Medicare payments.

Some life care facilities require residents to pay a large sum of money down, such as $150,000 per person, plus agree to pay a set fee per month, which would not change. Because of competition, most life care facilities now offer to return all or most of the initial fee upon death or leaving the facility.

VOICE OF EXPERIENCE:

Unfortunately, many life care facilities that cater to uninsured or state-reliant patients have earned terrible reputations. They are often accused of "warehousing" patients, cramming several in a room and providing insufficient and inhuman treatment. "Bottom line" economics is an ever-growing priority, as large corporations take over these facilities. Someone who can balance a strong cost-cutting ability with real human compassion is best suited to manage such a facility.

F. THE PROPERTY MANAGER FOR ELDERLY HOUSING

Property management for elderly housing requires a property management, recreation, social service, food service, and nursing background.

One manager of an elderly housing unit mentioned that the closest she could equate her position to was the director of a summer camp, with bookkeeping responsibilities. Actually, no one person will have all the skills needed. It requires a team effort.

G. SECURITY FOR THE ELDERLY

Security is a prime concern in elderly housing. Most projects have front desks manned 24 hours. Some have two electric entrance doors which can only be opened by front-desk personnel.

H. ALTERNATIVE ELDERLY HOUSING

Some apartments and condos offer special services for the elderly. However, they differ primarily in that occupancy is limited to residents 55 and older. The general quiet atmosphere is attractive to many senior citizens. These units consist of total independent living.

There are hotels that have become retirement hotels and rent month-to-month to senior citizens. They generally have food service and include meals as part of the rental fee. The restaurant can operate efficiently at a profit by offering these prepaid meals. Some retirement hotels offer very little as to activities, while others offer a great deal. Quality can vary significantly. Some are former middle- and low-line commercial hotels, while others were once luxury hotels.

Some hotels with low occupancy have turned a number of lower floors into senior housing and use the more desirable upper floors for hotel rentals.

VOICE OF EXPERIENCE:

As huge numbers of baby boomers (born 1946-1964) reach retirement age and join the ranks of the "elderly," traditional housing options will have to undergo big changes. Institutional-style cafeteria food, bingo games, and group TV rooms will be replaced with gourmet cooking, yoga instruction, and computer classes to cater to a more physically and intellectually active clientele.

VIII. Institutional Management

The armed forces, other federal, state, and local governmental agencies, as well as charities, colleges, and corporations own and operate housing facilities. Managers are generally employees of the appropriate entity. Management includes assigning units, inventory control (furniture where applicable) and maintenance functions. In some cases it also involves collecting rent or fees. Management might include food service or the responsibility to contract for food service.

> *As an institutional property manager, marketing of the housing would not be one of your general functions.*

Some institutional property management involves relatively short-term tenancies. In these cases, there are much greater maintenance requirements. In most cases, for example, housekeeping responsibilities would be involved.

Institutional management is more likely to involve a staff of employees rather than contract services. Bottom-line profits are not likely a consideration. However, a prime consideration would be the avoidance of problems reaching up beyond your position as the property manager.

IX. Subsidized Housing

SUBSIDIZED HOUSING offers below-market rent based on either government ownership or government benefits to the developer. Access to subsidized housing is limited to low-income individuals and families.

Some religious and nonprofit organizations also provide subsidized housing. The quantity of such housing is minimal compared to government-involved housing.

Subsidized rent payments are different than subsidized housing. Under various programs, including HUD's Section 8 Assistance program, the tenant's payment is augmented by the government. While the housing is not subsidized, the payment is. Yearly inspections by the program are conducted.

The basis of subsidized housing is often the loan. A below-market rate loan allows an investor to obtain a fair return on his or her investment with a below-market rate rent. The loan is tied to a developer's agreement concerning the rent.

A. PROBLEMS OF SUBSIDIZED HOUSING

Subsidized housing creates problems for management, including the following:

Gangs and Crime. Subsidized housing often consist of one-parent households depending on the financial assistance of the government. In an environment where poverty and violence breed hopelessness, many young people join gangs for protection and self esteem. Gangs often dominate subsidized housing projects and crime can be rampant. Residents often live in fear. In Chicago and St. Louis, public housing high-rise apartments have been demolished because people were afraid to live in them.

Drug Addiction and Alcoholism. Public housing residents include a high percentage of drug addicts and alcoholics that result from a feeling of hopelessness. People feel trapped in a ghetto and seek the wrong type of relief. This exacerbates the crime problem.

Vandalism and Graffiti. Vandalism and graffiti tend to be the norm, rather than the exception, in some subsidized housing projects managed by governmental agencies. As units become vacant, they are often stripped of plumbing fixtures and appliances.

Inadequate Budget. Property managers who work for government agencies have limited budgets and frequently play a losing "catch-up" game in trying to restore vandalized units, meet legitimate maintenance needs and provide some measure of security.

Impossible Policies. In some public housing projects, social agencies, and not property managers, determine eligibility to reside in the units. Families with histories of domestic abuse, alcoholism, criminal activities and children who have gang ties are admitted into the projects.

As the property manager of a housing project, you may lack the power to evict problem tenants without bureaucratic approval.

Management Negativism. After battling public housing problems, managers who are public employees often take a "go with the flow" attitude. They give up in much the same way as many of their tenants. Managers see no benefit in agonizing over change without government support.

VOICE OF EXPERIENCE:

The most successful public housing managers are often motivated by a strong social conscience. Many have a desire to "give back" to the community in which they grew up or a real conviction to improve the oppressive "human condition" to which the project tenants have become accustomed.

B. SOLUTIONS TO PROBLEMS IN PUBLIC HOUSING

VOICE OF EXPERIENCE:

Rather than allow hopelessness and disappointment to deter you from embracing the challenges of public housing management, consider altering your approach by becoming politically and socially active. As a professional property manager, you can offer valuable insight and realistic options to those authorities and politicians who can enact change within the system.

The following suggestions may potentially improve the way in which public housing is administered:

Greater Management Authority. Many of the public housing problems would be solved if property managers had the authority to screen tenants, set rules and regulations and evict tenants who failed to follow these rules and regulations.

Where private owners receive low-interest loans to build low-income housing, the problems associated with publicly owned housing are far less evident. Managers in such situations are empowered and use it to protect the property and the residents. We are beginning to see some public housing projects adopting a tough line on a no-drugs policy and holding parents liable for the actions of their children.

Welfare Reform. Welfare reform measures across the country are reducing the number of persons on welfare. Even people who are forced to work eventually develop a feeling of self-worth where previously there was only despair.

A positive change in attitude can lead to a desire to be part of the solution rather than part of the problem.

Tenant Organizations. Some public housing projects have developed strong tenant organizations that watch out for the safety of the residents and meet regularly with property management personnel. They report criminal activities and even recommend eviction of problem tenants. Vandalism, graffiti and crime have decreased appreciably in some of these projects.

Privatization. Privatization of public housing projects has been proposed as a solution to many of the problems associated with this type of housing. Privatization with requirements as to rent limits would result in management incentives to protect the property and solve the problems that have plagued public housing. Decisions would be made by trained managers rather than social workers or bureaucrats.

Sell to Residents. In a few trial cases, public housing units have been sold to the residents with positive results. However, it has taken the units out of the inventory for future low-income people.

Elimination of Public Housing. This proposal sounds harsh, but actually has great merit. Under the Voucher and Section 8 systems, persons on public aid can rent anywhere. They are not restricted to what have become racial ghettos in many cities. If there is a housing need and sufficient public assistance in the form of vouchers, private developers will fulfill that need in a far more economical manner than could government. (See *Real Estate Economics*, by Huber, Messick, and Pivar from Educational Textbook Company. There is an order form at the back of the book).

etctextbooks.com
Educational Textbook Company

X. Time Shares

A *TIME SHARE is a divided interest in a unit where a participating owner has exclusive use to the unit during a designated period of time.* The ownership could be in fee simple or it might be a leasehold interest for a designated number of years. Time shares are "fractional ownership," and there are still time shares in some states that are not ownership units, but rather, "right to use" units with ownership vested in the developer/owner.

Time shares tend to be vacation-type units in vacation-type locations. This results in very intensive use of the unit as well as the common areas.

Typically, time shares are sold for 50 weeks a year allowing a two-week period in the "off season" for refurbishing the units.

A. MANAGEMENT DUTIES

As the property manager of a time share property, your duties may differ from other property obligations.

Housekeeping. As the property manager, you must supervise cleaning and preparation of a unit between occupants of that unit. Unlike hotel and motel housekeeping, the work is all scheduled for the same turnover day. Therefore, housekeeping requires a large crew of part-time workers or a cleaning contract to have these housekeeping duties completed.

Units are typically much larger than hotel or motel rooms and contain kitchens and sometimes multiple baths, so cleaning each unit is time consuming. Appliances need to be cleaned so that the unit is in pristine condition for the next occupant.

Inventory Control. Kitchen and decorator items tend to disappear when the unit is vacated. This happens because many units are rented or exchanged or owners have guests and sometimes items are broken and thrown out. At times, decorator items may be exchanged for those of lesser value. Owners sometimes forget that they are only owners for one or two weeks of the year and exercise full ownership prerogatives.

With time shares, inventory checks are necessary, as whatever is not nailed down tends to disappear.

If an item on the inventory list is missing, the previous occupant should be notified immediately and asked to return the item or pay for the value. Never accuse the person of theft. It might have been "inadvertently" packed with their belongings when they left.

New Occupants. Occupants should pick up keys at your management office. A key deposit should be obtained to insure their return. Security is compromised when keys are not returned.

A copy of the rules and any schedule of recreational or other activities should be given along with the keys to the unit. Because many time shares belong to time share trade organizations, rules should be available in German, Spanish, French and Japanese.

Maintenance of Buildings and Grounds. As the time share manager, you are responsible for maintenance of the buildings and grounds by either employees or contracted staff. Pride of ownership is important to time share owners, so units must look like a luxury resort. This can be difficult because common areas are subject to intense use.

Recreation Director. As the property manager, you or your personnel are responsible for recreational activities at many time shares. They might schedule tours, golf tournaments, tennis tournaments, talent shows, theme parties, barbecues, etc.

The purpose is to have "happy campers." Owners will want to come back and not resent paying their monthly fees. In addition, when residents get to know each other, they develop friendships that help to make their stay enjoyable.

Collection of Fees. Time share owners pay a homeowner association fee to cover housekeeping, maintenance, taxes, insurance, and refurbishing of the units. This fee may be collected monthly or quarterly.

HOA fees are a problem, with 100 units sold in 50 separate weekly increments, since it means 5,000 owner statements and collections.

Rentals. As a time share manager, you may also provide a rental service for owners. Rental fees can be 25 percent to 33 1/3 percent of gross rent. A property damage bond is collected at the time of rental. This fee would be returned to the renter after the unit is vacated and inventory is taken. Some management offices will send out notices of other units available during "their week" to owners along with their statements or receipts. Friends often rent during the same week or weeks as the owners.

Another rental method is to notify owners of the same unit that the week prior or after their week is vacant. Owners can then double their vacation stay.

When there are many rentals available, advertising in newspaper classifieds using an 800 number can be effective in areas where many of the owners have permanent residences.

Other Duties. Budgeting and record keeping are similar to those duties of a condominium association manager.

Resales. Some property management offices list resales of units that they manage. Owners may be shocked to find that they must take a significant discount to sell their time shares. Resales of times shares regularly sell for 50 percent or even less than the original sale price.

Techniques used for renting a time share can be effectively used to sell units.

B. MANAGEMENT PROBLEM AREAS

Time share problem areas are similar to those associated with condominium management. Some of the problems become more intensified with time shares.

Rules and Regulations. Times shares are vacation units and while some occupants do not go to extremes, others do. Noise, drunkenness, the use of foul language,

monopolizing recreational facilities, etc., are part of the everyday management problems. Calling the police is an option. However, you should try to solve problems tactfully and without making the offender "lose face."

Collections. Time share owners who have not finished paying for their units are often delinquent in making payments, even though the association bylaws probably provide for late penalties. The lender, if there is one, will be reluctant to pay the fees or foreclose because of the questionable value of the unit. In some cases, lack of collections results in time shares not having sufficient funds to properly service the units. One desert time share development that has had many vacancies in the past few years is scheduled to have all the units sold at a tax sale.

You don't want to be a part of management if the development does not have sufficient funds to cover maintenance, insurance, or taxes.

The rewards would be almost nothing and the aggravation and liability could be excessive.

XI. Mobile Home Parks

MOBILE HOME PARK MANAGEMENT consists of leasing spaces for a tenant's mobile home, or manufactured home, which is a term the mobile home industry prefers. Larger parks should have a resident manager.

In California, parks with 50 or more spaces must have a resident manager.

Besides renting space and collecting rents, management may sell utilities to the tenants, and in some large parks, cable television. As a manager, you may also be responsible for maintenance of common areas, including recreational facilities and a clubhouse, as well as the enforcement of park rules.

A. MOBILE HOME RESIDENCY LAW

State statutes are important to managers of mobile home parks. The purpose of the statutes is to protect the rights of mobile home park owners, as well as owners of mobile homes.

The protection offered mobile home owners under the Mobile Home Residency Laws is necessary because of the fact that mobile homes are really not mobile.

Moving a mobile home will generally result in substantial damage to the unit as well as significant moving and relocation costs. The majority of mobile homes removed from parks are never again used as residences.

The following are requirements of the California Mobile Home Residency Law. A number of other states have similar requirements.

Lease Requirements. Every rental agreement must include:

1. The term of the tenancy and the rent.
2. The rules and regulations of the park.
3. A copy of the Mobile Home Residency Law (it may be an attachment).
4. A requirement that management maintain the improvements of common areas in good working condition.

VOICE OF EXPERIENCE:

If there is an unforeseen breakdown, you as the manager, have a reasonable period to repair. A reasonable period shall be as soon as possible in situations affecting health and safety but not to exceed 30 days, except where demanding circumstances justify a delay.

5. A description of the physical improvements.
6. A listing of services to be provided and will continue to be offered for the term of the tenancy as well as any fees.
7. A provision allowing management to charge a reasonable fee for maintenance of the site where the mobile home is situated if the owner fails to maintain the site and unit in accordance with park rules. Before management can perform the maintenance, the owner must be given 14 days notice for compliance and the notice must state specific conditions to be corrected.
8. All other provisions of the space rental must be set forth.

Cancellation Rights. At the time the rental agreement is first offered to the owner, you, the manager, must give the owner notice that the owner has 30 days to inspect the rental agreement and can void the agreement in writing within 72 hours of signing. If you fail to provide this cancellation information, the homeowner can void the agreement at his/her option upon discovery of this cancellation right.

Automatic Extensions. A lease cannot authorize automatic extensions or renewals at the sole option of either management or of the homeowner.

Exempt From Local Rent Control. The original rental agreement is exempt from local ordinances that establish maximum rents. If the rental agreement is not extended and no agreement over 12 months in duration is entered into, then the last month's rent shall be the base rent for application of local rent control.

Note: The original lease is exempt from rent control, but if the tenant does not extend or enter into a new lease, the last rent under the lease is the base rent for rent control.

Twelve-Month Lease Entitlement. The tenant can request up to a 12-month lease. The tenant is entitled to the same rent as offered by the lessor for a longer term lease or being offered for a month-to-month lease.

Note: Tenants need not accept long-term leases offered by management.

Liability Insurance. Homeowners shall not be required to obtain liability insurance in order to use common areas.

Amendments to Park Rules. Amendments to rules require:

1. A written notice be provided to homeowners at least 10 days prior to a meeting setting forth changes.
2. A meeting with park homeowners for consultation between management and homeowners.
3. That rules may be changed with the consent or without the consent of homeowners upon written notice to the homeowners of not less than six months.

For regulations applicable to recreational facilities, the notice must be at least 60 days.

4. Rules enacted without consultation with homeowners are void and unenforceable.

Right of Entry. Mobile home park management has no right of entry to a mobile home without prior written consent of the owner. If such consent is given, it can be revoked in writing at any time. However, the park does have the right of entry upon the land for maintenance of utilities and park maintenance or if the homeowner fails to maintain the grounds. In the event of an emergency or when the resident has abandoned the mobile home, the park management may enter the mobile home.

Owner Disclosure. Upon the request of a resident, you, as the park manager, must disclose the name, business address and business telephone number of the park owner.

Rent Increase Notice. Notices addressing rent increases must be given at least 90 days prior to the increase.

Unauthorized Fees. Mobile home owners shall not be charged fees other than for rent, utilities and incidental charges for services actually rendered.

Homeowners should not be charged a fee for services rendered that are not listed in the rental agreement unless given a 60-day notice before such fee is imposed.

Pets. No fee may be charged because the homeowner has a pet unless the park provides special facilities or services for pets. The fee charged must be related to the cost of maintenance of the facilities or services and the number of pets kept in the park.

If new rules prohibit pets, the rule generally cannot be applied retroactively. However, a lost or deceased pet cannot be replaced with another pet by an owner.

Guests. A homeowner cannot be charged a fee for a guest who does not stay more than 20 consecutive days or more than 30 days in a calendar year.

No fee shall be charged if a senior homeowner shares a unit with a person giving live-in health or supportive service in accordance with a treatment plan prepared by a physician.

Family Size. Homeowner shall not be charged a fee based on the number of residents in the homeowner's immediate family. Immediate family means homeowner, spouse, parents, children, and grandchildren under the age of 18.

Utility Meter. When management provides submeter utility services, the billing must include meter readings. Management must also post the prevailing residential utility rate schedule of the serving utility. Utility fees must be stated separately on billings.

Security Deposits. Security deposits may be demanded only upon initial occupancy. (No additional security deposits can be demanded.)

For security deposits collected after January 1, 1989, the homeowner can request their return providing the homeowner has paid park rent and other charges within 5 days of due date over the 12 consecutive months prior to the request.

Termination of Tenancy. As the manager, you cannot terminate a tenancy or refuse to renew a tenancy except for the following reasons:

1. Failure of resident to comply with local ordinance or state law regarding mobile homes within a reasonable time after notification of violation.
2. Conduct which constitutes a substantial annoyance to other homeowners or residents.
3. Conviction for prostitution or a felony controlled substance offense anywhere within the park. However, the tenancy cannot be terminated if the person convicted of the offense has permanently vacated and does not subsequently reoccupy the mobile home.
4. Failure to comply with reasonable park rules within seven days after written notice of violation. No notice is required if the party has been given notice of the violation of the same rule on three or more occasions within a 12-month period.
5. Nonpayment of rent, utility or reasonable incidental charges. The park must give a three-day notice (after a five-day grace period). Payment during the three-day period will cure the deficiency. If the homeowner fails to cure the deficiency, a 60-day notice is required to terminate the tenancy.

The legal owner of the mobile home is entitled to notice of the default and can cure the deficiency within 30 days of mailing of the notice.

6. Condemnation of the park.
7. Change of use for the park. However, management must give 15 day's written notice of any appearance before a government body requesting permits or use change.

After all permits have been received, homeowners must be given six month's notice of termination.

Note: A lease cannot be terminated because management wants the site for a person who has purchased a mobile home from the park owner.

Abandoned Mobile Homes. A park may post a notice of belief of abandonment on a mobile home that is unoccupied, rent has not been paid for 60 days and a reasonable person would believe it to be abandoned.

After 30 days from posting the belief of abandonment notice, the park may petition the court for a declaration of abandonment.

If the park management shows, by a preponderance of evidence, that the home is abandoned and no party shows an interest in the mobile home, the court will enter a judgment of abandonment.

As the park manager, you must enter and inventory the mobile home within 10 days of judgment of abandonment and post and mail a notice of intent to sell the abandoned mobile home and its contents. At any time prior to the sale, any person having a right to possession may remove the mobile home from the premises after paying rents and other charges (including court charges).

Within 10 days of notice of sale, you may conduct a public sale of the mobile home and its contents. Management has the right to bid at the sale.

Any amount received over the amount that management is entitled to shall be paid to the county treasurer.

Advertising - For Sale. A homeowner has the right to post a for sale sign on the side of a mobile home facing the street (not to exceed 24 inches wide and 36 inches high).

Showing - For Sale. Agents have a right to show units that are for sale.

Transfer Fees. No transfer fees may be charged to heirs, joint tenants or personal representatives of a deceased owner or his/her agent.

As the manager, the only charge you can impose on a purchase would be for a credit check.

Removal Upon Sale. Upon sale of a mobile home, you cannot require that the mobile home be removed from the park unless it is more than 25 years old or in a significantly rundown condition or disrepair.

Prior Approval of Purchaser. As manager, you may require prior approval of a mobile home purchaser when the mobile home is to remain in the park. Approval cannot be denied if the purchaser is financially able to pay park rent and charges unless, based on prior tenancies, you reasonably determine that the purchaser will not comply with park rules and regulations.

Within 15 days of receipt of information requested by the park from the prospective purchaser, the park shall notify the prospective purchaser in writing of acceptance or rejection.

VOICE OF EXPERIENCE:

Any fees collected for a credit report must be credited to the purchaser's first month's rent. If the prospective purchaser is rejected, the credit fee must be refunded. This differs from the nonrefundable credit fees allowed for apartment rentals.

New Rental Agreement. A purchaser must execute a rental agreement with the park. Failure to do so subjects the purchaser to an unlawful detainer action.

Age Requirement of Purchaser. Purchasers must meet the age requirement, if residency is limited to seniors, in accordance with the Fair Housing Amendment Act of 1988.

Nonwaiver of Rights. Lease agreements cannot require a purchaser or homeowner to waive any rights under the Mobile Home Residency Law.

Rights of Heirs to Sell. If the heirs or personal representatives of a deceased owner have paid rents and fees as they have accrued, they can sell the mobile home. Otherwise the park can insist on its removal. The heirs or representatives may also replace the mobile home with another mobile home prior to sale.

Lienholders' Right to Sell. Lienholders who foreclose can sell the mobile home if all of the rents and fees were paid as they accrued.

Sale of Park - Offer to Homeowners. The park owner shall notify the resident tenant organization, if they have formed an entity for the purpose of buying the park, at least 30 days but not more than one year prior to listing a park for sale or offering it for sale.

Management's Failure to Maintain. After 30-day prior notice, an action for failure to maintain physical improvements or reduction in service may be commenced by a homeowner. The prevailing party would be entitled to attorney fees.

Failure to provide and maintain physical improvements would be considered a public nuisance.

Restraining Order. As manager, you may obtain an injunction against a tenant for a violation of a reasonable rule or regulation.

Tenant Organization. Management cannot prohibit the organization of homeowner groups. Homeowner groups must be allowed to hold meetings in public areas within the park, such as a recreation hall.

B. COURT DETERMINATIONS

Courts have tended to side with the owners of mobile homes rather than park owners, where fairness has been an issue.

Case Example

Rancho Santa Paula Mobile Home Park Ltd v. Evans, 26 C.A. 4th 1139 (1994)

A mobile home park issued new rules requiring occupancy by a registered owner of the mobile home. This clause effectively prohibited subleasing. The Court of Appeals, in reversing the trial court, determined that the total ban on subleasing was unreasonable and therefore unenforceable.

Lake County Trust Company v. Wine, 704 N.E.2d 1035 (Ind.App. 1998)

Plaintiffs, who were class action tenants in a mobile home park, argued that the language of the preamble to the rules imposed a duty of good faith into the rental agreement. The Court held that general contract law does not impose such a duty.

C. CONDO - MOBILE HOME PARK

Some mobile home parks are owned by the homeowners. Each homeowner owns his or her site and the common areas are owned as tenants in common with the other owners.

In such a situation, you assume a different management role. In effect, you are a condominium association manager (covered earlier in this chapter), but the condo units just happen to be mobile homes.

Some of these parks resulted from developer plans when the lots were sold as condominiums. Others were mobile home parks converted to condominiums by owners or purchased by mobile home owners who converted the park to condominiums.

XII. Recreational Vehicle Parks

RECREATIONAL VEHICLES are motor homes, travel trailers, truck campers, camping trailers and other wheeled vehicles intended for recreational or camping use.

The following example applies to California, however, a number of states have laws for recreational vehicles similar to mobile home park legislation. The California Recreational Vehicle Park Occupancy Law covers elements of recreational park management.

A. CALIFORNIA RECREATIONAL VEHICLE PARK OCCUPANCY LAW

The law provides for the following:

Removal of Units. A defaulting owner's unit may be removed from the park after a 72-hour notice is served upon the unit owner. The owner can cure any violations during the 72-hour period.

If an occupant cannot move the vehicle because of physical incapacity or the vehicle is not motorized, the occupant shall have no less than seven days to move it from the park.

The park owner can have the unit taken by the police or sheriff to the nearest secured storage yard.

Reasonable care must be taken for the removal and the appropriate law enforcement agency must be notified of the removal.

Termination of Tenancy. The owner shall not terminate a tenancy or refuse to renew a tenancy unless written notice is given. With respect to this notice:

1. It need not state the cause for termination if the tenant has resided in the park for less than nine months and a 30-day notice is given.
2. The cause of termination must be stated for tenants who have resided on the property for nine months or more. The causes that apply to termination of mobile home leases also apply to recreational vehicles.
3. The notice can be given by the tenant in accordance with park rules.

Recreational vehicle parks place a lien on the recreational vehicle and its contents for unpaid charges of a defaulting owner.

XIII. Farm/Ranch Management

Agricultural management is highly specialized.

While it involves maintenance and improvements to buildings and fences and may involve leasing as a lessor or lessee, your duties as a manager tend to focus on the agricultural aspects. These duties include soil management, economic decisions regarding crops, labor management, equipment purchases or lease, and maintenance and other farming activities.

A. CORPORATE-OWNED FARMS/RANCHES

Corporate management deals with large farming or ranching activities. It is likely to involve leased land as well as corporate-owned land. Decisions as to management are primarily based on economics. The corporate owners are interested in the bottom line—profits. Corporate farm managers customarily have education and training in both agriculture and accounting.

B. LENDER-OWNED FARMS

These are farms owned by lenders due to foreclosures. Generally, the lenders are interested in holding the farms only until they can be sold. However, they may wish to hold them until the market improves, so they can recover their money.

While there are far fewer farm foreclosures than in the past, problems still arise because of debt, weather, etc., that result in foreclosures.

Lenders who take back farms want you, as the manager, to protect the physical improvements and hopefully obtain some income. Since the lenders seldom want to take farming risks, they will generally lease the land one season at a time. Structures will either be boarded up or rented. Your job would be handling leases and seeing that the status quo is maintained.

C. GENTLEMEN FARMS

The owners of so-called GENTLEMEN FARMS reside in a home on a farm, seeking a rural lifestyle and pride of ownership, but they do not wish to actually labor in the fields.

The gentlemen farmer gains satisfaction by riding around his or her property and gazing at the land. Therefore, appearance is rated at least as high, and often higher, than economics. Gentlemen farms can be orchards, ranches, or just general farming. Formerly, the great interest in California was in avocado groves, but the current interest is in vineyards and wineries. In Kentucky, gentlemen farms are likely to be horse ranches.

While profit may be secondary to many gentlemen farmers, they usually seek to make a profit, or the IRS will not allow the tax deductions given to farmers.

As a manager of foreclosed farms and gentlemen farms, you might handle the farms of a number of owners, while as a corporate property manager, you customarily handle farms of just one owner.

XIV. Docking Facilities

Property management does not have to involve real property. Managing a marina requires the same management skills as managing commercial and residential properties.

If the marina includes a launch ramp, repair facilities, fuel services, shops and/or restaurants, they should generally be separately leased. The person who leases the repair facilities would normally also lease the fuel service and launch ramp. Generally, you would want a minimum rent plus a percentage on launching fees, fuel sold and repairs. If there is dry storage, the responsibility should logically fall to the onsite manager who would lease the boat slips.

Marina rent is usually based on size of the slip.

Utilities to slips can and should be metered, especially if live-aboards are allowed or prevalent. Live-aboard slips can rent for significantly higher rents than slips that don't allow occupancy. Local zoning affects your right to allow live-aboards.

You will encounter some live-aboard activity even though you may not allow it. Normally, it is not worthwhile to make an issue of it unless there are complaints.

The biggest problem you will encounter in managing dock space is interpersonal (between the parties).

Some owners will use their boats for constant parties. Loud music and raucous behavior can make life miserable for other boat owners. Therefore, restrictions on noise and behavior must be strictly enforced. Owners cannot be allowed to throw bottles, cans and garbage into the water nor empty their sewage into the harbor.

XV. Medical Offices (MDs)

Managing medical offices differs from other office management in both tenant selection and cleaning requirements.

Medical office rentals usually include cleaning services. The standard of cleaning required is normally much higher than for other office space.

Many MDs only want other MDs in the complex because much of their clientele is through referrals from other MDs. Leases frequently require that a stated percentage of the rental space (which is often 100 percent) will be rented to other MDs.

The most desirable medical buildings are those that are in close proximity to other medical buildings and hospitals.

XVI. Mini-Storage Facilities

Mini-storage facilities are usually the size of a garage or smaller and rent primarily by the month. The facility is often equipped with a light and possibly an interior electrical outlet with a water faucet on the outside of the structure. The units usually come equipped with a roll-up lockable door. A single restroom might be located in the office building on the premises.

Mini-storage facilities are used by individuals who just have too many possessions as well as businesses. Better facilities are usually fenced and have exterior lighting. These facilities are only open for use during designated hours. Normally, a fee is charged for after-hour use.

As a property manager, you may sell unclaimed property providing that you have complied with statutory notice requirements.

VOICE OF EXPERIENCE:

A word of caution to storage unit managers. Extremely negative media attention was recently focused on the management policies of a storage facility when they adhered to the strict "letter of the law" and sold the belongings of a delinquent unit renter. The renter was serving active military duty and had paid his rental fees in advance for the length of time he expected to be out of the country. Unfortunately, his term of duty was extended and war-time complications prevented him from being notified of the impending sale of his belongings. Upon return home, he discovered all his worldly goods had been sold by the storage facility, including irreplaceable family photos and mementos.

Although no laws were broken, sympathy for the renter serving his country will no doubt result in substantial damage to the reputation of the business.

XVII. Storage Yards

STORAGE YARDS are fenced and secured exterior storage areas. Some grounds may have gravel, while others may be paved. Space is rented for storing recreational vehicles, cars, trucks, boats and heavy equipment.

Your management duties will be identical to the management of mini-storage space. In fact, many mini-storage facilities offer contiguous storage yards.

XVIII. CHAPTER SUMMARY

A number of property management situations present different problems and sometimes require special skills.

SROs are single-room occupancy units. Very often they were former hotels and motels that have been converted for long-term residential use. SROs are really mini-apartments without kitchens and present the same management problems and considerations as apartment dwellings.

Condominium association management differs from other property management in that renting is not the primary purpose of management, and the manager deals with a Homeowner's Association (HOA) Board of Directors, rather than an individual owner. A problem in management is that different members of the Board have different agendas. However, management must strive to carry out the wishes of the Board.

Resort-area management involves renting and managing homes and condominiums for monthly or seasonal tenants.

Clothing-optional apartments appeal to nudists. They command premium rents and units must offer privacy from outside viewing.

Single-family dwellings are often managed. They must be carefully watched as there is no resident manager.

Short-term residential properties are a cross between furnished apartments and motels/ hotels. They are rented by the week or month, often for business purposes.

Elderly housing management is growing as our population is graying. The three types of elderly housing are:

1. Independent living.
2. Semi-independent living.
3. Nursing facilities.

Life care facilities are those where the resident is guaranteed that he or she will be taken care of even if skilled nursing care is required.

Institutional management involves handling property management for governmental agencies, the military, colleges, charities and corporations. Managers are usually employees of the owning institution.

Subsidized housing is low-income housing that is either government-owned or housing where owners receive benefits such as below-market interest rates. Public housing projects have been plagued by problems of crime, gangs, drug addiction, alcoholism, vandalism and graffiti. Management has been hindered by inadequate budgets and responsibility without the authority to effectuate change.

Time shares are a divided interest in a unit where the time share owner owns a block of time (usually one week) in a specified unit. These projects are recreationally oriented and are subject to intensive use. The management is concerned with a number of unusual problems associated with a constant change of tenants. These include disappearance of personal property from units, violation of rules by tenants, necessity for weekly housekeeping for all units over a short span of time, recreational leader responsibilities, collection of fees from what could be thousands of owners, etc.

Mobile home park management involves leasing spaces. The manager must understand and comply with any applicable Mobile Home Residency Law which can govern just about every aspect of management.

Recreational vehicle park management is similar to mobile home park management, except the stays are relatively short because the units can readily be relocated. Management is subject to the state Recreational Vehicle Park Occupancy Law.

Farm/ranch management is very specialized, in that it requires expertise in agriculture, as well as property management knowledge. Properties likely to be managed are:

1. Corporate-owned farms and ranches.
2. Lender-owned property.
3. Gentlemen farms/ranches.

The goals of the different types of owners vary from lenders who are primarily interested in protecting the property, corporations that are interested primarily in profit, and gentlemen farmers who want nice looking facilities as a prime objective.

Managers of docking facilities, such as marinas and yacht clubs, are involved in the rental of water space. Many of the skills required for managing other types of property, such as condominiums, are applicable to this type of management.

Medical office management differs from other office management in the degree of cleaning expected, as well as tenant selection.

XIX. CHAPTER QUIZ

1. SRO stands for:

    a. selective residential opportunities.

    b. single-room occupancy.

    c. subsidized residential occupancy.

    d. semi-resort operation.

2. A property manager who was hired by a Board of Directors would most likely be involved in:

    a. the management of a single-family dwelling.

    b. clothing-optional management.

    c. condominium association management.

    d. medical office management.

3. Hotel management differs from condominium management in:

    a. housekeeping supervisory duties.

    b. food service supervision.

    c. both a and b.

    d. neither a nor b.

4. Elderly housing where a resident has his or her own apartment without nursing, health services, or food services would best be described as a(n):

    a. independent living facility.

    b. semi-independent living facility.

    c. nursing facility.

    d. life care facility.

5. A facility for the elderly that provides all levels of care and charges a high entry fee is most likely to be a(n):

    a. nursing home.

    b. SRO.

    c. independent living facility.

    d. life care facility.

6. Problems confronting publicly owned, low-income housing include:

    a. vandalism and graffiti.

    b. crime.

    c. drug and alcohol abuse.

    d. all of the above.

7. Managers of government-owned projects are hampered in their operation because:

    a. they often lack the ability to choose tenants and evict tenants.
    b. of budgetary restraints.
    c. of gang activity.
    d. of all of the above.

8. A fractionalized interest in a specific dwelling unit would BEST describe a:

    a. cooperative.
    b. time share.
    c. condominium.
    d. manufactured home lease.

9. What type of owner would want his or her farm manager to place a greater emphasis on appearance than on financial return?

    a. Corporate owner
    b. Gentleman farmer
    c. Family farmer
    d. Lender-owner

10. Which of the following would be a duty of a condominium association manager?

    a. Management of insurance
    b. Supervision of maintenance
    c. Contracting for services
    d. All of the above

ANSWERS: 1. b; 2. c; 3. c; 4. a; 5. d; 6. d; 7. d; 8. b; 9. b; 10. d

TM

Chapter 8
Liability and Risk Management

KEY WORDS AND TERMS

Binder
Boiler Insurance
Burglary and Theft Insurance
Business Interruption Insurance
Coinsurance Primary Policy
Comprehensive General Liability
Deductibles
Dram Shop Liability
Earthquake Insurance
Employee
Errors and Omissions Insurance
Extended Coverage Policy (Fire Insurance)
Fidelity Bonds
Flood Insurance
Government Seizure
Hazardous Waste
Homeowner Policy
Independent Contractor
Inland Marine Insurance
Innkeeper's Liability
Insurable Interest
Key Man Insurance

Leasehold Insurance
Liability Insurance
Libel
Medical Pay Coverage
Owners, Landlords, and Tenants Liability
Partnership Insurance
Proximate Cause
Record Insurance
Rental Interruption Insurance
Replacement Cost
Respondeat Superior
Risk Management
Robbery Policies
Secondary Policy
Self-Insured
Slander
Standard Policy (Fire Insurance)
Strict Liability
Surety Bonds
Three D Policy
Umbrella Policy
Worker's Compensation Insurance

CHAPTER 8 OUTLINE

I. Liability

Property owners are liable for their own wrongful and negligent actions.

They can also be held liable for the actions of others. Besides actual wrongful acts, they can even be liable for failure to take action.

A. STRICT LIABILITY

STRICT LIABILITY of an owner is liability for an injury to a person or damages to a property without being at fault. The concept of strict liability would make an owner liable for an injury even though the owner was not negligent or acted in good faith.

The case of *Becker v. IRM Corp.*, 38 C. 3d 454 (1985) held that a residential landlord had strict liability for latent property defects. In this case, a recent purchaser of a rental property was held liable when a tenant fell against a shower door that was not made of tempered glass. The California Supreme Court held the landlord to be strictly liable and the fact that the landlord was not aware of the defect did not excuse his liability.

In a rare reversal, the California Supreme Court reversed the IRM decision in *Peterson v. Superior Court*, 10 C. 4th 1185 (1995). The court held that the application of the doctrine of strict products liability to residential property landlords for a defective product in the IRM case was a mistake.

California law now holds that proof of a landlord's negligence is required for a landlord to be liable for damages or injury. Other states generally follow similar reasoning.

B. INJURY AND PROPERTY DAMAGE

A person can be negligent without having any liability. To be held liable, an owner not only has to be negligent but the negligence must be the cause (proximate cause) of an injury or property damage.

Owners are not liable for their negligence unless the negligence caused injury. Without an injury there can be no recovery.

C. LIABILITY FOR EMPLOYEES AND AGENTS

Owners of property can be held liable for actions of their employees and agents within the scope of the employment or agency. The English *DOCTRINE OF RESPONDEAT SUPERIOR is that a master is liable for the actions of his servants while carrying on duties for his or her master.*

1. Within the Scope of Employment

If an agent or employee had an accident during his or her off hours, the principal or employer would not be liable even if there was negligence. The negligence was not within the scope of the agency or employment. However, if the agent or employee put too much chlorine in the swimming pool causing several tenants to suffer eye injuries, the property owner would be liable. The negligence of the agent or employee occurred within the scope of employment or agency.

2. Libel and Slander

"Sticks and stones may break my bones but names will never hurt me" is not a true statement. Words, either written or oral, can result in monetary damages as well as damages to a person's reputation.

A published (written) false statement is **LIBEL**, and could result in damages being awarded to an injured party. If the statement was merely careless or made based on a false belief, then damages would be limited to compensation for the resulting injury. If the false statement was intentionally made by one who knows it to be false, then punitive damages could be awarded that far exceed actual damages. *PUNITIVE DAMAGES are awarded to punish a wrongdoer for outrageous action.*

SLANDER is verbal. Assume, for example, in providing information to a prospective employer, the resident property manager told that employer that a former tenant was "a hopeless alcoholic, her garbage was always overflowing with empty vodka bottles. She's also a tramp. She would bring a different boyfriend or customer home every night."

Assume the property manager had merely confused the person inquired about with another former tenant. It would nevertheless be slander. The property owner and manager would be liable for the damages that resulted from the careless false statements. If the resident manager had a personal vendetta against the former tenant and made those statements with the knowledge that they were false, then the damages awarded could be punitive as well as compensatory.

Because of the danger of slanderous or libelous statements, some property management firms inform resident managers that they are never to discuss tenants and former tenants with anyone other than their supervisors. This is a prudent clause for all property management employment contracts.

Some property management offices take the position that their records are privileged and will only be available to others upon a court order.

D. LIABILITY FOR ACTS OF INDEPENDENT CONTRACTORS

As a general rule, persons are not liable for injuries or damages that result from the negligence of independent contractors. Independent contractors are hired to accomplish a task and are not under the direct supervision of the person who hired them. **In property management, most service providers are independent contractors rather than employees.**

E. LIABILITY FOR ACTIONS OF TENANTS

As expressed in the *Portillo v. Aiossa* case, an owner can be held liable for acts of a tenant, a tenant's pet, or a tenant's child if the property owner knew of the dangerous propensities of the tenant, pet or child and failed to take reasonable measures to protect others from the danger. The problem must have been foreseeable.

F. LIABILITY OFF THE PREMISES

An owner generally does not have any liability outside the perimeter of his or her property.

In some states, the owner may be cited and fined if the tenant does not put away trash containers the same day they are picked up.

G. CRIMINAL ACTIVITY

If you believe that criminal activity is being conducted at a property you manage, it is imperative that you make your suspicions known to the applicable law enforcement authorities. Be completely factual as to the reasons for your beliefs. However, do not share these beliefs with any other person, since, should you be wrong, you may have slandered your tenant, which could lead to civil penalties.

If you knowingly allow criminal activity to take place at a property you manage, as the owner's representative, you could subject an owner to forfeiture of his or her property and possible monetary damages.

Case Example

Portillo v. Aiossa, **27 C.A. 4th 1128 (1994)**

An owner leased a property to a tenant who operated a liquor store. The tenant kept a German Shepherd (guard dog) on the premises and posted a sign warning customers of the dog's mean disposition. A person delivering liquor to the property was seriously injured when the dog attacked him. He sued the landlord.

The trial court found that while the landlord did not have actual knowledge of the dog's disposition (the dog had previously bitten someone), he could have learned about it by a reasonable inspection of the premises. The trial court awarded the plaintiff $300,000. The landlord's defense that he had no actual knowledge was not enough. The landlord was held to a duty to reasonably inspect the premises. The landlord allowed a dangerous situation with the dog kept in an establishment open to the public.

▼

Chapter 8

Note: This case imposes a duty upon a landlord to make a reasonable inspection of the property. If the dog was not present during inspections by the owner then the owner would appear to have a defense against liability.

Owners and/or property managers should inspect the premises at least twice a year and document the inspection.

People sue in the direction of money. This is why landlords are often sued. Tenants may not have the resources or the insurance to satisfy a claim by an injured party.

Miller v. Fickett, 724 N.E.2d 354 (Mass.App.Ct. 2000)

The defendant real estate brokers were obliged to warn the plaintiff of the dangerous condition of the property because of the presence of vicious dogs. The plaintiffs, after being warned, chose to enter the house, thereby assuming the attendant risks to themselves and their four-year-old daughter, Rachel.

Case Example

Davis v. Gomez, 207 C.A. 3rd 1401 (1989)

A tenant began acting strangely. She talked to herself and seemed to be casting spells on others. Other tenants knew she had a gun in her apartment and complaints were made to the manager about her bizarre behavior. The tenant later shot and killed another tenant whose parents then sued the landlord for the wrongful death.

In ruling for the landlord the trial court pointed out that a landlord has no duty to check out the background of a prospective tenant. They also pointed out that a landlord was not in a position to evaluate her as a psychotic. While the landlord could have evicted the tenant, a wrongful eviction would subject the landlord to damages. In this case there was nothing foreseeable as to the murder because she had never before been violent. The landlord was held not to be liable.

Note: The Americans With Disabilities Act now applies to mental problems. If, in a similar situation today, a landlord evicted a tenant with this type of behavior, the landlord would probably be subject to significant penalties.

Although you should carefully screen all tenants, perceived discrimination is always a valid concern of property management.

New York City Housing v. Housing Authority Risk, 203 F.2d 145 (2nd Cir. 2000)

Under New York common law, to hold a landlord liable for torts committed by third parties, a plaintiff must demonstrate that the third parties were intruders with no right or privilege to be on the premises, and that they gained entry because of the landlord's negligence.

Case Example

Rosenbaum v. Security Pacific Corp., 43 C.A. 4th 1084 (1996)

A tenant was afraid to park her car in her assigned garage space because of what she considered inadequate lighting. Because of the fear for her safety, she parked it on the street. One night, after parking her car on the street adjoining her apartment, she was robbed and shot in the head.

The Court of Appeals affirmed the trial court in determining that a landlord was not liable for criminal activity off the premises.

Note: The landlord could have been liable if the assault had taken place in the garage area and inadequate lighting was a contributing factor to the crime.

You should always provide lighting and security in the facility you manage.

Case Example

Alcaraz v. Vece, 14 C. 4th 1149 (1997)

An apartment owner maintained an adjoining city property (10 foot strip off the road). A tenant was injured when he tripped over a depressed meter box in the lawn and fell.

The California Supreme Court held that since the landlord exercised control over the strip of land, the landlord had a duty of care as to the hazard which would be to warn tenants of the dangers.

When you take over maintenance of adjoining properties, you also inherit certain liabilities concerning proper maintenance.

Fithian v. Reed, 204 C.3d 309 (1st Cir. 2000*)*

As homeowners and hosts, the defendants had a duty to take into account the extant circumstances (including those known to them and those of which they should have known) and to maintain their property in reasonably safe condition. ... The standard does not, however, hold homeowners to anticipate and guard against "what is unusual and unlikely to happen," or what, as is sometimes said, "is only remotely or slightly probable."

Case Example

Southland Corp. v. Superior Court, 203 C.A. 3rd 656 (1988)

A customer was assaulted in a vacant lot adjacent to a 7-11 store. The lot was not controlled by the store but customers often parked there. The store's lease provided for nonexclusive use of the lot for extra parking. The 7-11 store did not discourage customers from parking on the lot.

The lot had become a hangout for youths. Store employees had called the police on several occasions to remove loiterers.

The court held that while a property owner or tenant is generally not liable for the condition of property it does not own, possess or control, the tenant in this case exercised sufficient control to charge them with a duty of care. If that duty was breached then the tenant could be liable for resulting damages.

Case Example

McDaniel v. Sunset Manor Co., 220 C.A. 3rd 1 (1990)

A landlord constructed over 1,200 feet of fencing around a large government subsidized housing project. One of the landlord's purposes in constructing the fence was apparently to protect the children since there was a creek adjacent to the property. There were over 300 children living in the project.

A two-year-old child crawled through a hole in the fence and was found in the creek. While her life was saved, she suffered brain damage and became a quadriplegic.

The court held that by building the fence the landlord had a duty to maintain it. Negligence in construction or maintenance would result in liability for the landlord.

Note: The landlord had no duty to build the fence. Without a fence the landlord would not be liable for injuries on adjacent property. In this case, tenants would be lulled into complacency believing that their children were safe playing in a secured area.

With 300 children in the complex, it is reasonable to assume that there was a resident manager onsite (a requirement for 16 units or more). Therefore, maintenance of the premises should have been strictly adhered to.

▼

Plesha v. Edmonds Ex Rel. Edmonds, 717 N.E.2d 981 (Ind.App. 1999)

Dog owners who failed to restrain or contain their dog were liable for injuries sustained by child when dog chased and repeatedly bit him, even though boy and his friend were crossing over dog owner's property.

Case Example

Lew v. Superior Court, 20 C.A. 4th 866 (1993)

Lew was a landlord of an apartment building housing Section 8 tenants (subsidized low income). Neighbors sued, asking for damages for emotional and mental distress caused by the illegal drug activity which occurred on the premises.

The Court of Appeals affirmed the decision by the Superior Court to award a total of $218,325 in damages after determining that the owners knew, or should have known, of the illegal activity and taken reasonable means to alleviate the activity.

> *Knowledge of illegal drug use can result in expensive lawsuit damages and even confiscation of property.*

Hammond v. City of Warner Robins, S.E.2d 422 (Ga.App. 1997)

Evidence showed the ability of methane and other gases to migrate from the landfill, despite abatement efforts, across Holt property and the street, to physically invade appellant's property. ... If a nuisance is found to exist, although there has been only *de minimis* damages to the property interest, appellant may seek damages for "annoyance and discomfort" caused by such nuisance as a result of the maintenance of the nuisance.

Case Example

U.S. v. 141st Street Corp., 911 F. 2d 870 (1990)

A 41-unit apartment managed by the uncle of the owner was the center of a great deal of illegal drug activity. In fact, tenants in 24 of the apartments had been arrested for drug sales. Rents of $2,000 or more per month were charged for substandard apartments.

The police left messages with the President of the Corporation that held title to the property but calls were not returned. The President of the Corporation admitted visiting the property at least once a week but claimed to have no knowledge of any illegal activity.

The court in this case held that government seizure was proper since it was clear the landlord knew of the illegal activity.

Note: In this case, the amount of rent charged and collected would alert any landlord, even if they never visited the property, that it was being used for illegal activity.

Unrealistic rents are a red flag for all parties. If you are aware of any illegal activities, you must inform the owner.

U.S. v. James Good, 114 S.Ct. 492 (1993)

This subsequent case held that prior to government seizure the owner must have prior notice or a hearing. Seizure without a chance to present a defense was held to violate the due process clause of the U.S. Constitution.

H. DRAM (LIQUOR) SHOP LIABILITY

Some states hold the property owner liable for injuries caused by premises serving liquor to minors or to other persons to the point of their intoxication or leading to intoxication. This **DEEP POCKET LEGISLATION** *allows for recovery against the owner (who generally has greater assets—deeper pockets—than the tenants) of real property.* For premises selling liquor, as a lease provision, the tenant should be required to carry DRAM shop liability coverage protecting the lessor up to a stated limit.

I. HAZARDOUS WASTE

Hazardous waste is a term dreaded by owners and property managers. The presence of hazardous waste could leave an owner in a maze of federal, state, county and city laws and ordinances.

Without going into the details of various state and federal laws, the result is that an owner of property can be held liable for hazardous substances on the property that were caused by a tenant, former tenant, or former owner of the property.

HAZARDOUS SUBSTANCES, as defined by the Environmental Protection Agency, include many hundreds of chemical compounds, and just about anything that is toxic and/or flammable.

Cost of hazardous substance cleanup can be substantial. In many cases, the cost can exceed the value of the property.

As a property manager, you can protect your property owner against future liability by requiring the tenant to carry liability insurance that will indemnify the property owner for the cost of removal of hazardous substances. To substantiate the amount of damage to a property, a qualified testing firm dealing in hazardous waste can test the soil and property prior to leasing and at the termination of tenancy. If this is not done, the tenant and/or the insurance carrier will likely claim that the problems were largely pre-existing.

Case Example

Los Angeles Chem. Co. v. Superior Court, 226 C.A. 3rd 703 (1991)

This case made it clear that a regulatory agency cannot enter private property without a search warrant to gather evidence that hazardous wastes are being improperly stored there.

II. Risk Management

There are many different insurance policies. As a property manager, you must be carefully selective to protect your owner's interests, and still not be insurance poor.

There are many more risks than just owner liability and agent liability. There are also risks to property and to income.

The term "risk management" does not mean living with risk, it means reducing risk to an acceptable level.

Insurance allows us to trade now a certainty (premium cost) for a future uncertainty (a loss). In other words, we put the burden of specified losses on an insurance carrier. Most people seek security in their lives, and insurance is able to provide both mental and financial security to the insured.

Insurance will not protect an owner against all risks, such as government seizure of the property, however, it can protect owners against most common risks.

As a property manager, you have a duty to your principal to advise protection against losses that can be insured against. Of course, you have a parallel duty to use your best efforts to

make certain losses do not occur. While preventative measures reduce the likelihood of some types of losses, they cannot eliminate the chance of loss.

As a property manager, you can be helpful in pointing out areas of exposure and will often be able to suggest ways to save money for property owners. You can also file a claim against an insurance agent who misrepresents a policy.

> *As a professional, you will be held to a higher standard of knowledge. It pays to read the fine print.*

Case Example

Eddy v. Sharp, 199 C.A. 3d 858 (1988)

The plaintiff asked Sharp to provide insurance coverage similar to his present coverage. A cover letter with the policy said the policy covered all risks over eight of their listed exclusions, but did not mention that it did not cover damages for water backing up in drains. After a loss, the plaintiff discovered that the policy would not cover the loss.

The Court of Appeals held that an independent insurance agent is the agent of the insured and has both a fiduciary duty as well as a duty of due care. Sharp failed to accurately inform the plaintiff of the policy terms so a duty was breached.

Note: This case applies to independent agents only and not agents for a single insurer.

State Farm Fire & Casualty Company v. Slade, 747 So.2d 293 (Ala. 1999)

With respect to claim for fraudulent suppression of exclusions in insurance policy, the Court stated: [W]e conclude that the trial court correctly held that Carr did not have a duty to disclose the existence of exclusions in the Slade's policy ... as Mr. Slade was a knowledgeable businessman. ... Furthermore, although the value of the fact at issue, i.e., the fact that the policy had exclusions, was important, Mr. Slade could have ascertained the existence of that fact.

Insurance companies set conditions for payment of claims. One is that the carrier must be notified of a loss in a prompt manner. Another condition is that the insured will cooperate with the insurance company and truthfully answer questions concerning a loss. Attempting to defraud the insurance company with inflated loss figures could absolve the carrier from paying the loss even though there was a real loss.

It is possible to obtain more than one insurance policy covering the same risk. When more than one insurance policy exists, the carriers pay the loss equally up to the limits of the lowest policy. The higher limit carrier(s) then pay up to their limits. An exception to the above are policies that state if they are primary or secondary. A secondary carrier has far less risk than a primary carrier since the secondary carrier only pays after the primary carrier has paid up to their insurable limit.

An umbrella policy is a secondary policy that requires minimum primary coverage, but pays losses in excess of that coverage up to the umbrella policy limit.

A. SELF-INSURED

Some of our nation's largest corporations do not insure their property.

These corporations elect to be self-insurers because they realize no single loss or even group of losses would have a significant negative effect on their financial well-being. Rather than pay insurance to a company that has high costs of selling and servicing policies, they can handle their claims at significant savings. Corporate property managers working for multi-billion dollar firms may be in a self-insured situation where risk management would consist of safety procedures to reduce the possibility of loss. However, this is not the situation in which most property managers find themselves.

B. IDENTIFYING AND ADMINISTERING RISKS

Risk management is a function of management.

As a manager, you must identify risks associated with a property, measure the risks, and then decide how to treat the risks. As an example, a meteorite destroying a property is one in a billion chance. Therefore, you might decide that protecting the property from such a calamity would not be in the best interest of your client. The risk of other disasters could be much greater. As a general rule, if you have any doubt, you should either insure or obtain a written directive from the owner not to insure against the risk. *RISK ADMINISTRATION involves making decisions concerning insurance coverage, obtaining the coverage, and reviewing the coverage that may be affected by changes in the economy.*

Some owners will want to keep insurance with their current agent with whom they may have a family or social relationship.

You will need copies of all policies. You should evaluate each policy's adequacy and appropriateness. The basic policies include the following:

1. Fire and extended coverage (including vandalism).
2. Liability (including liability for sprinkler systems).
3. Plate glass coverage.
4. Worker's compensation (if employees will be employees of the owners).
5. Flood and/or earthquake coverage.
6. Rental interruption insurance.
7. Bonding of employees.

In analyzing an owner's insurance coverage, you might discover there is an immediate need for additional protection.

C. BINDERS

BINDERS provide temporary insurance coverage until a policy can be issued. Binders are generally for property and liability protection. You must have agreed with the agent of the insurer regarding the coverage desired in order to obtain a binder.

While the binder can be a separate memorandum or, in some cases, a verbal statement, it is often provided in the application for an insurance policy. The binder is conditional coverage since the insurance company need not issue the policy. The insurance company instead could notify the applicant that a policy will not be issued and temporary coverage shall cease as of a specified date. Fire insurance binders are often issued prior to the payment of any premium.

If you find that you do not have required coverage, you should seek a binder protecting the property and property owner until a policy can be issued.

D. TYPES OF OWNER INSURANCE POLICIES

You can insure against just about any type of loss. The likelihood of loss will, of course, affect the premium.

To insure, you must have an "insurable interest."

Otherwise, a person could insure your property for fire and, in the event of fire, he/she could collect. If this were possible, it is likely that the risk of your property burning down would be materially increased.

Properties that are not profitable for owners tend to be destroyed by fire more often than properties that show a profit. Arson is believed to be the cause of almost 50 percent of business fires. In addition, false and exaggerated claims for damages are often made. This has resulted in significantly higher insurance rates. These higher rates must be paid if you are not in a position to be a self-insurer.

Some of the insurance coverage you should consider for your clients, includes the following.

1. Fire Insurance

Standard Policy. The *STANDARD POLICY of fire insurance is specified peril coverage.* It covers loss from:

1. fire,
2. lightning, and
3. loss from removal of property from the above perils.

HOMEOWNER POLICIES add liability coverage, as well as theft and vandalism, and contents to extended coverage policies. However, they are only available for homeowners residing on the premises.

You want to make certain that casualty policies cover "replacement costs," not just "cash value."

Cash value considers depreciation and, unless you were able to buy used, it would not be enough to replace an asset that was destroyed.

Burglary and theft protection is offered in many extended coverage owner policies. The coverage might also cover mysterious disappearance of property even though there is not evidence of a robbery or burglary. Policies that cover burglary might also cover damage to a property in the course of the burglary. Robbery policies have a limit on reimbursement for cash stolen.

2. Earthquake and Flood Coverage

Normal casualty insurance policies exclude earthquake and flood damage.

There are separate coverage policies that can be added to other casualty loss coverage. They have high deductibles. As an example, earthquake coverage generally has at least a $10,000 deductible, so an $11,000 loss would only pay $1,000 in compensation.

Just because there has been no flood in recent years doesn't mean you should not consider flood insurance. At the very least, you should check a topographic map and study elevations and drain-off. Better yet, some hazard disclosure providers can inform you regarding seismic activity, flood maps, etc.

If you want protection from mud slides, you might need additional coverage. Some flood policies cover mud pouring into a property but do not cover the property itself sliding away. This additional coverage is available.

3. Boiler Insurance

BOILER INSURANCE protects an owner against losses associated with a boiler explosion. Boiler explosions can destroy an entire structure with loss of life. Boilers seldom explode today. The reason can be largely attributed to boiler insurance. The insurers are experts in boiler maintenance and safety and make certain the boiler is properly maintained and is equipped with the proper operating safety valves.

4. Elevator Insurance

ELEVATOR INSURANCE covers liability losses due to failure of elevator equipment.

5. Liability Insurance

LIABILITY INSURANCE covers a property owner's liability to other parties because of the condition or operation of a property.

Liability insurance does not automatically pay a person who was injured or whose property was damaged.

The insurance carrier will only pay if the insured is legally liable for the loss. An insurance carrier may deny a claim of a third party, but if that third party brings a lawsuit against the insured, the insurance carrier has a duty to defend the insured.

In some instances, an insurance carrier could be liable for an amount greater than the insurance coverage. As an example, assume an injured party agreed to settle his or her claim for the limits of the policy. Assume also the insurance company refused to settle and decided to let the court determine liability. Assume an award was in excess of the insurance coverage and the carrier paid up to the insurance limit, leaving the insured liable for the remainder. The insured could sue his or her carrier for this overage. If a court determined that the carrier was unreasonable in failing to settle within the limits of the policy, the court could hold them liable for the amount of the judgment in excess of the insurance coverage.

Libel and slander are not ordinarily included in liability insurance coverage, although they can be added. Generally, libel and slander coverage has a high deductible, such as $10,000.

There are a number of types of liability policies. The *OWNERS, LANDLORDS, AND TENANTS LIABILITY (OLT) INSURANCE coverage pays for damage to property and/or persons caused by ownership, maintenance, or use of the premises.* There are also Comprehensive General Liability (CGL) policies.

6. Medical Pay Coverage

MEDICAL PAY COVERAGE covers actual medical expenses for persons injured on the premises without regard to who was at fault. It is a "no fault" type of policy. If a person trips over his/her own feet while on the property of the insured, medical expenses will be paid up to the limit set forth for medical pay. It is generally included as coverage in a liability or extended coverage policy of the owner.

7. Inland Marine Insurance

INLAND MARINE INSURANCE is not insurance to cover your boat. Generally, it is a transportation-related policy for personal property that can protect bailees of personal property in transit or in storage. Inland insurance also provides "floater policies" for items of personal property and for loss of records, such as accounts receivable. The coverage offered can be for named risks or cover all risks. Management of warehouse facilities should consider inland marine coverage that protects the bailee for loss of the property.

The owner of the property is not the party protected. However, if the insured is held liable for a loss the insurance carrier would indemnify the bailor.

Many buildings have works of art in their lobbies and public areas. They can be insured with an inland marine floater. Other items that are applicable to property management and can be covered by floater policies are signs, stained glass windows and computer systems.

Ranch managers can even insure livestock with an inland marine policy.

8. Rental Interruption Insurance

When a property is made unusable because of an insured loss, the insurance coverage will probably pay for the property loss. However, the owner has other losses. While mortgage payments must be made, the income stream from the property is interrupted by the casualty loss. *RENT INSURANCE gives the owner a cash flow to make up for the lost rent.* Mortgage payments are not excused simply because the property was damaged or destroyed.

9. Fidelity Bonds

BONDING is a process where an insurer agrees to pay for losses resulting from the dishonesty of an employee up to the amount of the bond.

Insurers will check on the person to be bonded. If they refuse to bond the person, then you should consider if you want to allow that employee to have access to client funds.

When a bonding company discovers employee dishonesty, the employer must discharge the employee unless the bonding company agrees to the continued employment. In some cases, payback arrangements are reached.

Fidelity bonds can be written for each individual employee or for a group of named individuals.

You should consider bonding persons with access to funds or property of others. Management contracts often require bonding.

10. Worker's Compensation Insurance

WORKER'S COMPENSATION INSURANCE pays for injuries to employees when the injuries are work related and is required where any employees are involved. It applies both to owners, who have employees, and property managers who employ others. We are now seeing claims that go beyond what we formerly considered injuries. Persons who have had heart attacks have successfully claimed that their attacks were the result of stress on the job.

11. Additional Insurance Coverage

If there are vehicles used at the property for the property, they should have liability coverage. Comprehensive insurance and collision coverage should also be considered.

For hotel and motel management, innkeeper liability coverage should be obtained. *INNKEEPER LIABILITY COVERAGE indemnifies an innkeepker who is held liable for property loss of a guest.* The guest is not insured, just the innkeeper.

There are various packaged crime policies which cover burglary and robbery. A separate policy should be considered if the coverage is not provided in another policy. Some packaged policies also cover fidelity of staff. The *3D POLICY is a comprehensive policy that covers Dishonesty, Disappearance and Destruction.* It applies to personal property, and also covers forgery.

E. TYPES OF TENANT INSURANCE POLICIES

As a property manager, you may be an agent or employee of a tenant. You may also work for a large corporation or franchisor. As such, you would have a different perspective on risk management. Coverage that you would be interested in includes the following.

1. Fire and Extended Coverage

This coverage would apply to tenant property improvements and personal property. Earthquake and/or flood coverage could be added to the fire coverage or it could be a separate policy.

2. Liability Coverage

The more money the insured has, the greater the liability coverage should be because more is at risk. After $1 million in coverage, additional millions are relatively inexpensive protection because the risk decreases to the insurance company. The tenant may wish to obtain additional liability protection with a high-limit umbrella liability policy. The cost of liability protection would depend on tenant use and operations on the leased premises.

3. Medical Pay Coverage

As a matter of goodwill, most tenants want medical pay coverage for persons injured on the premises.

4. Inland Marine Coverage

Personal property of high value, such as decorative items and accounts receivable records, can be covered by these policies. To determine the necessity of such policies, evaluate the coverage provided by other policies. With computer records and disks at various locations, the risk of loss of records has been materially reduced.

5. Fidelity Bonds

Bonds for a tenant would more likely be a function of financial operations rather than property management. The same is true for worker's compensation coverage. On the other hand, innkeeper liability coverage would more likely be of concern to property management.

6. Business Interruption Insurance

This insurance indemnifies the owner of a business for lost earnings while the business is unable to operate. This coverage would significantly reduce the likelihood of a tenant defaulting on the lease after a casualty loss. Therefore, owners prefer that tenants have this coverage.

7. Extra Expense Coverage

Extra expenses deal with the unusual expenses resulting from a casualty loss. It might include the preparation of a temporary location, moving expense, equipment rentals, etc. These expenses would not be covered by business interruption insurance.

Owners must be prepared to pay for interim relocation of tenants while termite eradication work (including tenting) is being performed.

8. Leasehold Insurance

Because many leases provide for lessor cancellation rights when a property is destroyed, this policy protects the tenant's lease value. Increased rents could give an advantageous long-term lease a significant value that would be lost if the lease were canceled.

9. Residential Tenant Coverage

Residents of apartments and rental homes can obtain the equivalent of a homeowner's policy, except that there is no coverage for the structure.

VOICE OF EXPERIENCE:

As a property manager, you might want to consider obtaining an insurance license. Selling tenant's insurance can be a significant profit center for your business.

Because a tenant would have additional living expenses if a casualty loss made their rental uninhabitable, coverage for residential living expenses is available. This insurance covers the excess expenses caused by relocation. Rental value insurance is a little different in that it provides the rental required to lease similar property to that which was destroyed.

F. PROPERTY MANAGEMENT INSURANCE

As a property manager, you must be concerned with risk management for yourself as well as your clients.

Risk management includes fidelity bonding for employees, coverage for personal property including records, liability protection, etc. In addition to coverage set forth for owners and tenants, you might consider additional coverage, including the following.

1. Errors and Omissions

This policy protects you against your "goofs" and defends you in resulting lawsuits. As an example, if your firm allowed an insurance policy to lapse and there was an uninsured casualty loss, you would likely be liable for the loss. An errors and omissions policy would protect you. Errors and omissions policies frequently have high deductibles, such as $10,000. These policies are expensive, but are a necessary part of doing business.

Remember, there is no insurance that covers fraud.

2. Records Insurance

If not covered by other policies, the loss of client files, accounts receivable and payable as well as contracts could be devastating. While insurance is available, many firms use a scanner to copy paper records for their computer and download the material at another location.

3. Automobile Coverage

Any company vehicles should have high-limit liability coverage. Collision and comprehensive policies should also be considered.

Since an employer can be liable for torts (a civil wrong or injury) of employees, a property management office would want copies of employees' automobile coverage showing high-limit liability protection. This is customary in most real estate offices.

4. Key Man Insurance

A property management office may have one or more employees whose loss would have significant effect on the business. As an example, one person's family connections might be responsible for obtaining 40 percent of a firm's business. That person's death could have a significant effect on the business in that major clients could be lost. *KEY MAN INSURANCE allows you to have a term life or accidental death policy on that person's life with your firm as the beneficiary.* You have a beneficial interest in that person's life.

5. Partnership Insurance

If your property management business is a partnership, the death of one partner could be catastrophic to the business.

While heirs of the deceased partner would have no right to conduct the business, they would be entitled to the value of the deceased partner's share of the business. A partner's death often requires the sale of a business to pay off his/herheirs.

PARTNERSHIP INSURANCE would involve policies of insurance on the life of each of the partners, payable to surviving partners. This would be coupled with an agreement that the proceeds of the policy are accepted for the interest of the deceased partner.

6. Surety Bonds

When contracting for major renovations or improvements, you should consider a surety bond from the contractor. A **SURETY BOND** *guarantees the completion of the contract.* All too often, horror cases involve a contractor going bankrupt when only half the job has been completed. The usual results are that the job takes many more months, and in some cases years, to complete with the cost greatly exceeding the original contracted amount. Bonding companies generally require audited financial statements from the contractor before they will issue a bond. Generally, only large contractors can meet the requirements for surety bonding.

G. HOW MUCH INSURANCE?

Be selective in what you insure. You don't want to be insurance poor!

A risk manager must decide on how much insurance to carry. The land is not going to be lost because of a fire so coverage that would include the land would be wasted insurance. You want your owners to be able to obtain protection at a reasonable cost. Additional protection must be weighed against the additional cost.

1. Deductibles

Deductible amounts for losses are really examples of risk sharing. The insured decides he or she is able to bear the risk up to a stated dollar amount.

Insurance companies like deductibles because the majority of casualty losses are small losses. Not having the paperwork of administering minor claims takes a significant burden off of the insurance companies and reduces costs. They offer lower rates as deductibles increase. As an example, an owner might wish to take a $5,000 risk that lowers a premium by a significant amount.

Deductibles simply make risk more affordable and should be considered in applicable situations.

2. Lender Requirements

If a property is encumbered by a mortgage or trust deed, the encumbrance would likely provide that the lienholder be provided with a copy of the insurance coverage. It would also provide that failure to do so would entitle the lienholder to obtain necessary insurance coverage at the owner's expense. When the lender does this, the policy price is usually far more than the coverage would normally cost.

> ### VOICE OF EXPERIENCE:
>
> *As a property manager, it is your duty to not only protect an owner's investment, but to increase its productivity and value. Therefore, you are obligated to monitor all insurance policies. Over-insuring a property diminishes an owner's profits and under-insuring exposes the owner to financial loss or ruin.*
>
> *An owner depends on your skills as a professional to recommend the appropriate insurance coverage based on a realistic evaluation of the risk factors balanced against the cost-effectiveness of the various coverage options.*

Lenders typically require insurance policies to either cover an entire purchase price or their loan. Insurance in these amounts could be excessive or inadequate based on the property. As an example, replacement costs of an office building that was purchased at a time when rents were low and vacancies were high could be several times the purchase price. On the other hand, property where a great percent of value is in the land could have a loan far in excess of the cost to replace the structure. Therefore, a lender wanting insurance coverage for the loan amount would be asking you to throw away dollars buying excess coverage, yet lenders usually require this amount.

In many cases, however, you may convince a lender to adopt a more reasonable approach by obtaining a separate land and structure appraisal. If your loan requires replacement value insurance, you have legal basis for lower coverage and your attorney should be able to convince the lender without the commencement of a lawsuit. However, if the loan requires insurance to a set dollar amount or to the amount of the loan, then your only hope is to use reason to obtain an agreement for lower coverage.

3. 80-Percent Coinsurance

Insurance referred to as 80-percent coinsurance is available for commercial property. Insurance is based on a cost per $1,000 of coverage. Because buildings are seldom totally destroyed, many owners wanted to carry only partial insurance and be self-insured for the balance. This was not in the best interests of insurance companies who wanted premium dollars for the likely portion of any casualty loss as well as for losses that were far less likely to occur. Therefore, insurance companies came up with 80-percent coinsurance requirements for commercial buildings.

Under **80-PERCENT COINSURANCE**, *an owner must carry insurance that covers 80 percent of the replacement cost to be fully reimbursed for any loss*. Even then, the insurance would only pay up to the insured amount, even if there was a 100 percent loss.

Assume an insured only purchased insurance covering 40 percent of the loss and the policy included an 80-percent coinsurance clause. The insured would only be reimbursed for 50 percent of any loss incurred, even if the loss was less than the amount of the policy. The reason for only 50 percent reimbursement is that the insured was only carrying 50 percent of the insurance that should have been carried (40 percent rather than 80 percent).

Proper risk management requires you, as a property manager, to review the adequacy of all insurance coverage. Special attention must be paid to 80-percent coinsurance situations.

If you are handling insurance coverage for a building and you believe your coverage is less than 100 percent of replacement costs, you should have an owner's concurrence as to the coverage. While 80 percent may be an economical decision for commercial property, it is a decision as to risk that should involve the wishes of the owner.

VOICE OF EXPERIENCE:

Because people have selective memories, you should keep a paper trail of your communications with the owner concerning all important decisions, including those involving insurance coverage.

III. CHAPTER SUMMARY

Owners of property are liable for their own wrongful and negligent actions as well as for the actions of their agents and employees. For employee and agent liability, the wrongful or negligent act must have been within the scope of employment. The act also must have been the proximate cause of the injury suffered to persons or property.

An owner is also liable for slander (verbal false statement) and libel (published false statement) that injures another. Owners are not liable for injuries caused by their independent contractors unless the contractor was employed for a dangerous activity.

An owner could be held liable for an injury caused by a tenant, the tenant's child or tenant's pet if the landlord knew, or should have known, about the dangers presented and failed to warn or protect others in a reasonable manner.

Generally, an owner is not liable for injuries that occur off the premises. An exception would be if the owner exercised control over the property where the injury occurred. Another exception would be where the owner attempted to secure a property with a fence but where the fence was faulty, allowing a child to leave the premises and be injured elsewhere.

Owners who knowingly allow criminal activity on their property could be subject to damages and government seizure of their property.

An owner can be liable for hazardous waste released or stored on the property even though the owner was not involved in bringing the hazardous waste onto his or her property.

Risk management involves bringing risk to an acceptable level. By trading a certainty for an uncertainty, insurance makes most risks manageable. However, not every risk is insurable.

Insurance agents who misrepresent a policy can be held liable for that misrepresentation. To collect on an insurance policy, the insurance carrier must be promptly notified of a loss and the insured must cooperate with the insurance company.

Multiple policies of insurance can be issued for the same property and the carriers would equally bear the loss up to their policy limits. An exception would be secondary coverage that would only pay after the primary insurer had reached its policy limit.

Some large firms are self-insured because they have enough financial strength to settle claims themselves and don't see the necessity to pay expensive insurance premiums.

By a verbal or written binder, it is possible to obtain insurance protection prior to a policy being issued.

To obtain insurance, the insured must have an interest in property. This is known as an insurable interest.

Owner insurance policies include:

1. Fire insurance
2. Standard policy
3. Extended coverage policy
4. Earthquake insurance
5. Flood insurance
6. Boiler insurance
7. Liability insurance
8. Medical pay coverage
9. Inland marine insurance
10. Rental interruption insurance
11. Fidelity bonds
12. Worker compensation insurance
13. Innkeeper liability coverage

Tenant insurance protection includes:

1. Fire insurance
2. Liability coverage
3. Medical pay coverage
4. Inland marine coverage
5. Business interruption insurance
6. Extra expense coverage
7. Leasehold insurance
8. Residential tenant policy

Property management companies may want to limit their exposure with:

1. Errors and omissions insurance
2. Records insurance
3. Automobile coverage
4. Key man insurance
5. Partnership insurance
6. Surety and fidelity bonds

Lower insurance rates can be obtained by deductibles. With a deductible, the insured pays the first part of the loss. The higher the deductible, the lower the premium.

Lenders generally want the loan covered by insurance.

The 80-percent coinsurance requires the insured to insure at least 80 percent of the replacement cost in order to be fully covered (up to policy limits).

IV. CHAPTER QUIZ

1. Ownership of rental property makes an owner strictly liable for injury to a tenant:
    a. when there is no injury.
    b. when the negligence was not perceived.
    c. when the owner had no knowledge.
    d. when reasonable inspections would have revealed the problem.

2. Slander that damages a person would be described as a(n):
    a. intentionally false written statement.
    b. unintentionally false written statement.
    c. true statement that damages a person's reputation.
    d. false verbal statement.

3. An owner's liability for acts of a tenant would be based on:
    a. foreseeability.
    b. agency law.
    c. strict liability.
    d. an insurable interest.

4. Obtaining insurance protection before the issuance of a policy is known as a(n):
    a. option.
    b. binder.
    c. bond.
    d. right of first refusal.

5. The standard policy of fire insurance protects an owner for all of the following, except:
    a. fire loss.
    b. lightning damage.
    c. hail damage.
    d. loss suffered in removal of fire-damaged property.

6. Inland marine coverage would be applicable for:
    a. a bailee's stored property.
    b. insuring an expensive painting.
    c. both a and b.
    d. neither a nor b.

7. Fidelity bonds provide protection against:
    a. employees leaving for other employment.
    b. employee theft.
    c. inflation because of rising interest rates.
    d. mysterious disappearance.

8. Who is required to provide worker's compensation insurance?

    a. Firms having in excess of 10 employees
    b. Firms having in excess of five employees
    c. Firms having in excess of one employee
    d. Firms having any employees

9. A property manager accidently rented the same property to two separate tenants. The manager's protection, in this case, would be provided by:

    a. homeowner's insurance.
    b. errors and omissions coverage.
    c. leasehold insurance.
    d. innkeeper liability.

10. A property manager is considering awarding a $300,000 contract for renovation of a commercial building. The protection the property manager would be interested in would be:

    a. a fidelity bond.
    b. a surety bond.
    c. worker's compensation coverage.
    d. errors and omissions coverage.

ANSWERS: 1. d; 2. d; 3. a; 4. b; 5. c; 6. c; 7. b; 8. d; 9. b; 10. b

Chapter 9
Security and Safety

KEY WORDS AND TERMS

Armed Guards
Carbon Monoxide Detectors
Closed-Circuit Alarms
Covert Cameras
Deadbolt
Dual Units
Electronic Gates
Electronic Security Alarm
Emergency Lighting
Emergency Oxygen
Emergency Telephones
Employee Name Tags
Employment Checks
Fire Extinguishers
Fire Doors
Foreseeability of Harm
Guard Gates
Guard Dogs
Guard Patrols
Hasps
Infrared Beams
Inherently Dangerous Areas

Latch Bolt
Microwave Fields
Mortised Lock
Motion Sensor Lighting
Occupancy Rules
Open-Circuit Alarms
Overt Cameras
Proactive Guard Patrol
Reactive Guard Patrol
Security Committees
Smoke Detectors
Solid-Core Doors
Sound Sensors
Speed Bumps
Spot Detectors
Sprinkler Systems
Strike Plate
Tailgating
Television Cameras
Ultrasonic Alarms
Vibration Detectors

CHAPTER 9 OUTLINE

I. Security: An Overview

A. SECURITY DEFINED

Security is more than just feeling secure. It is the knowledge that persons and property have a right to that feeling.

B. SECURITY OBLIGATIONS

As a property manager, you have moral, and in some cases, legal obligations to take reasonable measures to protect your tenants, their guests and the personal property of your tenants and their guests.

1. Foreseeable Harm

A previous history of criminal activity increases the foreseeability of loss or injury and a landlord's duty to take appropriate precautions.

Case Example

Ann M. v. Pacific Shopping Center, 6 C.A. 4th 666 (1993)

An employee of a tenant in a shopping center was raped inside the store during business hours. She claimed that the shopping center had not provided adequate security. The Court of Appeals, as well as the California Supreme Court, upheld the trial court's verdict in favor of the landlord.

The court pointed out that "a high degree of foreseeability is required to order or find that a landlord's duty of care includes hiring security guards." In the absence of similar incidents of violent crime, there was no degree of foreseeability.

Note: If there had been prior violent crimes on the premises, the court seems to conclude that they could have found for the plaintiff.

Don't wait until courts may establish a precedent. Give your tenants security if there is a forseeability of a crime problem.

Case Example

Mata v. Mata, 105 Cal.App.4th 1121 (2003)

An injured bar patron brought a negligence action against the proprietor of the bar and landowner. One of the issues was the scope of the duty of the landowner to patrons. The Court of Appeals stated:

"Because a landlord has relinquished possessory interest in the land, his or her duty of care to third persons injured on the land is attenuated as compared with the tenant who enjoys possession and control. Thus, before liability may be thrust on a landlord for a third party's injury due to a dangerous condition on the land, the plaintiff must show that the landlord had actual knowledge of the dangerous condition in question, plus the right and ability to cure the condition. For example, a landlord with actual knowledge of the presence of a vicious dog kept by the tenant on the leased premises owes a duty of care to the tenant's guests to prevent injury from attack by the dog where the landlord has the right to take possession and remove the animal."

Harm may be foreseeable when the condition of the building does not provide reasonable security. Examples of problems that could result in lessor liability include:

1. unlighted or poorly lighted entry ways and paths;
2. the presence of shrubbery around an entryway that provides a convenient hiding place;
3. broken locks on apartment entrances or locks that can be easily opened with a credit card, and
4. security doors that are left unlocked.

Some areas within a building or types of buildings present a greater foreseeability of loss to property and persons.

2. Advertising Security

Never advertise a property as being safe or secure. It could be considered a warranty of security. An owner could be held liable for a tenant's loss of property and/or physical and emotional injuries if the property was represented to the tenant as being safe in order to rent the premises.

3. Security Disclosure

A lessor who is aware of more than the ordinary security problems in the property, complex, or neighborhood should disclose the risk in writing to the prospective tenant.

Although you, the property manager, probably would not have to tell a prospective tenant that one of the tenants had a car broken into and lost a car radio several months before, a series of crimes may subject you to full disclosure.

When in doubt as to what to disclose, disclose (always in writing).

II. Security and Safety

Security and safety are interrelated. Many methods of obtaining security also help to ensure safety of residents and employees.

Security has become a matter of prime concern for property managers. Managers of large properties frequently use security consultants to identify areas of concern and suggest methods to deal with these matters.

Case Example

Madhani v. Cooper, 106 Cal.App.4th 412

Through their agents, the building managers, the landlords, knew or should have known Moore had engaged in repeated acts of assault and battery against Madhani as well as her mother. If injury to another "is likely enough in the setting of modern life that a reasonably thoughtful [person] would take account of it in guiding practical conduct," it is "reasonably foreseeable." In contrast to the trial court's view, we believe ... it was foreseeable Moore's violent outbursts and physical assaults would eventually result in serious injury to Madhani.

Don't ignore a problem tenant, as the courts may perceive your knowledge of prior behavior as a foreseeable conclusion in the future.

VOICE OF EXPERIENCE:

Without getting personally involved in a couple's problems, you should, nevertheless, keep a journal of domestic disturbances, noise complaints, etc. and never hesitate to call the police to report any violent behavior.

Case Example

Waters v. Housing Authority, 505 NE 2d 922 (1987)

This New York case involved a rape victim who was dragged into a building by her assailant. Neither the victim nor the assailant were residents of the building. The victim alleged that there were no locks on the exterior doors to the building and that the vestibule areas were poorly lighted.

The court held that while a landlord has a duty to offer reasonable protection for the safety of residents and guests, the owner has no duty to general members of the public. The court pointed out that extending the duty of property owners would not result in safer streets.

Note: If the plaintiff had been a tenant in the building, a different decision would have been likely.

Proper lighting is important, regardless of the liability issues.

As a property manager, you should seek help from local police departments. Many police departments will perform a security survey at no cost and make security recommendations. Fire departments will conduct a fire safety inspection. A safety engineer can check a property for dangerous conditions and recommend safety procedures, equipment and changes. Injuries to personnel will increase your worker's compensation contribution, while injuries to tenants will increase insurance costs and possible liability issues.

The best risk management is really risk prevention. It's taking care of eradicating problems before they become legal and financial liabilities. In either case, the problem will still exists and will still have to be handled.

Perfect security is impossible to obtain because whatever we design or work to protect, someone else can find a way to defeat it if they're willing to put in the effort and take the risk. However, thieves, vandals, and those intent on harming others, when given a choice between an easy target and a difficult target, will choose the easy one. Therefore, you want any property that you manage to present as many challenges as possible to those intent on wrongdoing and pose less risk for owners and occupants of those properties.

You will see that there are numerous ways to increase security for both persons and property. You can provide greater security through a combination of many methods.

If there is a breach of security, evidenced by loss or damage to property or injury to persons, you should make every effort to remedy the situation that caused the problem. Keep in mind that courts could determine that a future problem was foreseeable based on past experiences on the property.

A. LIGHTING

Good lighting is always a deterrent to crime.

Persons intent on wrongdoing tend to be extremely surreptitious. They don't want to advertise their presence or intent.

Exterior Lighting. Forget about saving pennies with 15-watt bulbs. You want entryways, parking and garage areas and walkways well lighted. Ornamental 12-volt systems look great for knee-high path lighting and keep costs down, but they don't do much for security. The same holds true for some multi-colored lighting. The tinted lights materially reduce the candlepower for any lighted area. For parking and outside storage areas, consider high-intensity mercury or sodium vapor lamps that are set high enough to give daylight conditions to a wide area. Enough lighting should be used to avoid areas of dark shadows. Exterior lights can be on clock systems that should be reset on a monthly basis to adjust for changes in sunrise-sunset times. Many properties use photoelectric cells that automatically turn lighting systems on at dusk and off again at sunrise.

Motion Sensor Lighting. Flood lights that are on a motion sensor tuned to a high degree of sensitivity and set for at least four minutes can be a deterrent to criminal activity in parking areas as well as along walls and fences. While small animals might cause the lights to come on, it is better to risk scaring a raccoon if you also scare off a thief.

In addition to saving electricity, motion sensor lighting will increase your tenants' sense of well-being and safety.

Motion sensor lights should be set to go on in darkness when a person is within a certain number of feet or yards from the light. Therefore, you should consider having detectors installed that are not a part of the sensor lights.

Entryways and Halls. Entryways and hallways in apartments and office structures should be well lighted. Fixtures should be of a type that it would be difficult to remove or loosen a bulb. Light switches should not be placed in public areas so that criminals cannot easily control the environment.

At times, dangerous conditions are the direct cause of tenants. They find it easier to replace a light bulb in their apartment with one from the hallway or entryway rather than going out and purchasing one. You can solve this problem, cut costs, and make the property safer by using fluorescent lighting in the public areas of the building. Fluorescent tubes don't fit most household fixtures so the problem of theft will be almost nil.

Emergency Lighting. Emergency lights are battery operated and are kept charged by being hard-wired to the building's electrical service. When the electricity goes off, the emergency lights go on. Such lights are a safety feature for vestibules, public hallways, public restrooms, storage areas, laundry rooms, indoor parking areas and enclosed malls. These lights also serve as a security measure where thieves may turn off the electricity.

Locked Circuit Breakers. Circuit breakers that are located in locked rooms or cabinets act as a deterrent to criminals who look for well-labeled breaker systems to cut off exterior or hall lighting.

B. LANDSCAPING

Proper landscaping along pathways and entryways can reduce crime by reducing a criminal's ability to hide.

Avoid large bushes close to entryways and walkways. A pair of six-foot Arbor Vita flanking an entryway may look impressive, but it can be deadly for your tenants and/or their guests. As a rule of thumb, allow at least 20 feet of grass, flowers or very low ground cover along both sides of walkways and entryways.

Large trees and shrubs that allow hiding places should be removed along with low tree branches within 30 feet of entryways, pathways, and parking areas. Areas around the perimeter walls and fences of the property should be relatively clear so that persons walking in the areas can have unobstructed vision for quite a distance. Any object, such as a tree that could be used to scale a fence, climb on top of a structure, or enter the property, should be removed.

C. FENCES AND WALLS

> **VOICE OF EXPERIENCE:**
>
> *Fences do more than make good neighbors. They discourage intrusions. Criminals are opportunistic people who will take the path of least resistance.*

While a healthy young person can scale a six-foot wall, he or she prefers not to. In today's world where most people get in their car to travel one block, criminals will do the same. They want to get as close to the area of planned criminal activity as possible and get away just as easily. Fences and walls make entry and exit activities more difficult.

Lawn furniture that is left too close to walls aids in the exit of the wrongdoer. Heavy or anchored tables can't be used as ladders.

Always be alert to potentially dangerous situations. Look for "red flags" and conduct regular inspections to check for new maintenance and potential security problems.

Chain-link fencing topped with barbed wire is an excellent deterrent for exterior storage areas, as well as perimeter fencing for warehouse or industrial areas. The gate should also have barbed wire topping to deter entry. Gates on chain-link fences should be secured in at least two places or the gate can be twisted to allow a person to squirm through. Chain-link security fencing should be combined with a lighting system flooding an unobstructed grounds area. Having to scale a fence with barbed wire to cross a well-lighted open area is not an inviting environment for criminals.

D. DOORS

Composition. Exterior and apartment doors should be either solid-core wood or metal-clad doors. *HOLLOW-CORE DOORS simply have a light wood framework covered with thin plywood or masonite sheeting.* Hollow-core doors can be easily smashed in, while solid-core doors will resist forced entry much longer.

Metal-clad or solid-core doors provide the greatest resistance to forced entry.

Peepholes. Apartment doors should be equipped with a peephole viewer. The small, wide-angle lens allows tenants to view visitors before opening the door.

Security Chain. Apartment doors should also be equipped with a quality security chain. The chain should be anchored into the wood or metal door frame with at least one-inch screws or longer, depending upon the thickness of the door.

Even the best security chain is limited by the thickness of the door. Short screws won't resist determined kicks to the door.

Sliding glass doors should be equipped with an inside pin through the metal frame and the door so if the lock is forced, the doors cannot be opened. Holes for the pin can be placed so the glass door can be pin-locked while open only an inch or so for ventilation.

Hinges. Hinges should be installed on the inside of doors. As basic as this may seem, there are constant cases where entry was gained by removing the pins and lifting the door off its hinges.

E. LOCKS

Skeleton Key Entry. Although difficult to believe, many burglars gain entry by using a common skeleton key. Many interior locks, especially those in older buildings, and some exterior locks can be opened with this key. Skeleton keys can be purchased at most hardware centers, variety stores, and lock shops.

VOICE OF EXPERIENCE:

Locks that can be opened with skeleton keys only keep honest people out. They're more decorative than deterrent to criminals, allowing easy entry with very little effort. The cost of replacing these ineffective locks is minimal compared to the potential price to be paid if a tenant is victimized.

Burglar Pry Bars. Simple pry bars are available at any hardware store. They are the tool of choice for most burglars. The burglar can rip the wood from around the door lock with a pry bar and gain entry. One lock placed at the top and one at the bottom of a door can make the job of a thief more difficult because the door itself can't be used as leverage to break or loosen the lock.

While quality locks can be picked by professionals if given enough time, most burglars are not professionals and operate with a smash-and-grab technique so they are in and out and away in just a few minutes.

The quicker the burglary, the less the chance of being caught. Therefore, use as many crime deterrents as possible.

Key-in-the-Knob Locks. Most residential locks, and some used for commercial property, are of the key-in-the-knob variety. These knobs are not recommended because the locks can be quickly pried off, leaving the latch bolt exposed for easy removal. Some combination locks have a dead bolt immediately above the key/knob type of lock. Again, ripping off the knob may allow access to the latch bolt as well as the dead bolt above it. One solution is to add an auxiliary dead bolt about six inches above the existing lock.

Mortised Locks. Until recently, most locks were mortised into the center edge of the door leaving very little wood around the lock. This placement created a weakening of the door that left the strongest lock worthless when forced with a bar. Mortise locks also commonly used a cylinder held in place by a single-set screw. A well-equipped burglar could quickly twist the cylinder out of the lock to gain entry.

Beveled Bolts. Thirty years ago, locks had a bolt where the function was more to keep the door closed than to keep intruders out. The latch bolt with a curved or beveled surface could easily be pushed open with a credit card by first running a screwdriver to pull the jamb strip loose. A metal plate driven into the jamb will deter this type of entry. Sophisticated burglars use a curved tool to work around this metal plate.

Strike Plate. The strike plate may also be a weak point on a door. The strike plate should be held in place by screws at least four inches long that go through the jamb into the studs around the door jamb. Some strike plates are heavier and extra long, which require additional screws. Staggered holes can reduce the chances of the jamb splitting when the door is kicked.

Jamb and Casing. One-piece steel jambs and casings will prevent pry bars from entering the edge of a door. The door will still be vulnerable to severe kicking and very few locks and/or doors can hold against a half-dozen vigorous kicks from an athletic 200-pound individual.

Better Locks. As previously stated, more tumblers and sophisticated spacing and depth can make locks more difficult to pick.

Some latch bolts have little bevels as an anti-shimming measure. However, there are ways to get around such deterrents. Burglars can use a bar to push a door over toward the hinges so that the bolt clears the strike plate to open the door. This can be accomplished with most doors, and if the door opening is just a quarter inch too wide for the door, the latch bolt may barely catch the strike plate. Forced entry is quite easy.

Today, better locks are now equipped with longer bolt throws with straight shafts that cannot be pushed open by a credit card or other tools. However, for most locks the latch bolt throw is seldom over five-eighths of an inch so that the bolt isn't much more than one-quarter inch into the strike plate.

Some new locks use a magnetic key. A series of magnets imbedded in the key interface with the lock. These locks are excellent because they are very difficult to pick.

Similar to magnetic key locks are card locks. Push-button coded locks don't require a key and can deter most criminals.

Dead Bolts. *DEAD BOLTS consist of a square face and long throw and cannot be pried open with a credit card or thin metal screwdriver.* The beveled-faced bolt is a latch bolt. Although usually installed on the interior, dead bolts can also be keyed for exterior entry. A reinforced cylinder guard should be used with a keyed dead bolt. The guard is a heavy steel plate that surrounds the cylinder so it can't be twisted out or otherwise tampered with. The guard plate is held in place by screws from the inside of the door that go through an inside plate and into, but not through, the exterior guard plate. The door is "sandwiched" between these two steel plates that hold the locking mechanism and resists prying.

These dead bolts are excellent security locks. Using a lock mechanism with numerous tumblers can make picking the lock difficult.

While it may seem easy in the movies, the use of a tension tool in one hand and a pick in the other against a multi-tumbler lock is, fortunately, a talent few burglars possess.

A double-cylinder dead bolt that requires a key to open both sides is available on the market. This dead bolt is for use in a door with a small window. A burglar who breaks the window still can't reach in and turn the dead bolt. We strongly recommend that you do not use a double-cylinder dead bolt. A person who can't locate the door key or is too nervous to use it may end up trapped in an emergency situation. You may also expose yourself to a liability situation.

VOICE OF EXPERIENCE:

Double-cylinder dead bolts violate fire ordinances in some areas of the country. You should always check with the appropriate local authority in the state and city where the property is located.

Cylinder upgrading should be considered if locks are being picked. Cylinders can be changed without replacing the entire dead bolt assembly. Your local locksmith can assist you in any upgrade decisions.

Dead bolts mounted on the surface of interior doors are easy to install. These dead bolts are quite effective if the screws are long enough to penetrate solid wood. Pine is a relatively soft wood. Hardwoods are the preferred surface for holding dead bolt screws.

Garage-Type Doors. Garage and warehouse doors should be secured by side bolts and bottom bolts.

Padlocks. The quick blow of a hammer or a good bolt cutter will make short work of all but the best padlocks. A thin metal strip can be inserted along the shank in many padlocks to release the lock mechanism.

Padlocks with very short shanks are more difficult to open with a hammer. They also prevent any large bar from being inserted to pry the lock open. In some better padlocks, the key is really a flat piece of metal with magnets inserted that are keyed to a portion of the lock casing.

Hasps. Padlocks, although often used, are easily bypassed by burglars who twist off cheap hasps with a bar. The weakest link is often the hasp. Quality hasps securely fastened should be used in combination with a quality padlock.

F. WINDOWS

Protection Against Breakage. Breaking a window is an easy way to gain entry if a burglar is not concerned about making noise. The only protection against this is metal window grills or bars, metal security curtains, or an unbreakable window. Lexan, a plexiglass-like plastic, is clear and can't be broken with an ordinary hammer. This type of window should be considered for lower windows.

Another solution for lower level windows is the use of glass block windows. The lower windows of some commercial buildings have often simply been bricked over. Windows with wire reinforcement can be broken, but will still resist forcible entry.

There is a safety problem with blocked off windows or the installation of bars or grills. An emergency exit has been blocked. Check with your local building and fire departments before blocking off windows or installing bars. Your actions could be a code violation and you could be held liable for injuries that relate to your action.

Many states now require "break-away" bars on bedroom windows in case of fire or other emergency exit situations. These security bars can be opened from the inside, but not the outside.

Latches. Normal window latches won't protect a double-hung or glide-by window unit from a pry bar. Drilling a hole through the sash and the window casing overlap and inserting a 3/8th inch bolt through the hole provides better security. There are also metal clamps available in hardware stores for light-weight aluminum window casings. For sliding glass doors, burglars will use a bar to either break the locking mechanism or to lift the door out of its track. Here again, you can drill holes through the metal track and window casing to place a pin or heavy nail.

Glass Cutting. If time is not a factor, but noise is, the thief will cut the glass if it is accessible. This gives easy access to reach the latch to open the door or window.

VOICE OF EXPERIENCE:

There is no dishonor in fooling criminals, but it's dangerous to lull a tenant into a false sense of security. Signs and/or labels indicating the property is protected by electronic security even though no such security exists will deter an unsophisticated criminal and are definitely worthwhile. You should, however, make your tenant aware that no security system is in effect.

Metal tape around the edges of windows on some buildings appears to be wired for electronic security even though they are not actually wired. Dummy security systems are intended to deter criminals, not to misrepresent the property to the tenant.

Never let a tenant think you have a security system when you don't. This would be the same as warranting the security and could expose you to legal liability.

G. ELECTRONIC GATES

Some industrial parks as well as condominium and apartment projects can limit access by use of walls, fences and gates.

ELECTRONIC GATES are unmanned gates that swing back or glide open on a track. To enter, a resident or employee will use an opener in his or her car, an electronic card, or punch in a combination at the gate. An electronic eye usually opens an exit gate. Some exits are left open and instead use a one-way barrier that would destroy tires of any vehicle that used the exit for entry purposes. (**Note:** This exit allows entry by pedestrians.)

Radio channels, cards, and code keys can be changed to increase security. As mentioned, you must keep track of openers and cards and change codes when either is reported lost or stolen.

VOICE OF EXPERIENCE:

Unfortunately, when codes are changed some users fail to get the information and become frustrated trying to open the gate. Avoid this headache by making notification or new key dispersal a priority. Keep a list of tenants who are out of town or otherwise unreachable and revisit them often to make sure they aren't inconvenienced by being locked out.

The wooden bar electronic gate is not recommended. All too frequently, a frustrated user will get out of his or her car and will take the end of the wooden bar, and using it like a lever, pull it open causing the board or mechanism to break. Additionally, the wooden bar can come down on the car when the vehicle stops underneath it.

Police, fire, and ambulance services must be given openers or codes in advance for emergency use.

Service personnel can create a problem in that they must be given access. The system becomes less secure as more persons have the codes or openers. Service contractors and employees of service contractors are believed to be the cause of the majority of break-ins within a number of gated residential communities. If true, it can be understandable considering the wealth of many persons living in some of the gated communities and the fact that some service providers, such as gardeners, are paid minimum wages.

Electronic gates must provide for guests and visitors. Some use a telephone so that a tenant can be contacted and remotely open the gate.

A problem with some electronic gates is that an unauthorized car may be able to "tailgate" another vehicle and thus gain entry. A gate that is opened for vehicles can also be opened for foot traffic. A video camera installation coupled with the electronic gate is a better crime deterrent.

VOICE OF EXPERIENCE:

Real estate agents are often advised to wait by the gate and follow a car inside a complex in order to show prospective buyers/tenants a property. If this happens on a regular basis, it's quite likely that a thief would be aware of this easy access.

Speed bumps within gated communities slow traffic. Besides being a safety feature, it is also a security feature in that slow-moving vehicles are more likely to be noticed and stopped if suspect. Speed bumps should be painted with yellow reflective paint as well as warning signs posted to avoid liability for a speed bump-induced accident.

H. GUARD GATE SERVICES

Considering vacations, it takes five full-time employees to man a 24-hour guard gate with just one person. If there is also a roving patrol, such as that used at many retirement communities and large condominium projects, then five additional employees would be required. This is with a one-person patrol. If more than one gate is to be manned, add five more employees for each gate. When you add salaries, social security contributions, worker's compensation, unemployment insurance, time-and-a-half work requirements, and any benefit's package, you can see that security is not a small expense when guard gates are to be manned. In addition to labor costs, there are also equipment and maintenance costs.

Some large developments want special uniforms for their guards. Distinctive looks are meant to make the residents feel important. The problem with the image is it can be costly. One 26-home enclave in the Palm Springs area has a 24-hour manned gate that costs over $2,000 per month in homeowner fees that don't cover clubhouse, golf course, or gardening expenses.

Some multiple-gated communities only operate one gate from 10 P.M. until 6 A.M. and leave other gates locked. This offers significant savings in manning gates. Other developments have resorted to electronic sliding gates.

I. GUARD SERVICES

Founded in 1855, the first paid private security service was Pinkerton, which was formed with the realization that public police forces could not meet all security needs.

Guard services control access as well as prevent or detect unauthorized activities and break-ins.

Some security services will use undercover operators. As an example, one condominium management company had an undercover agent join the gardening staff and shortly thereafter determined who was breaking into condominiums in the gate-guarded community.

Security companies conduct background checks on employees that property managers are considering hiring. Although the fact that a person might previously have been guilty of a theft does not mean that person will steal again, the recidivism rate of criminal activity usually indicates that a person is likely to do so again.

With a few exceptions, most property management firms do not possess the expertise needed to hire, train and supervise an employee guard service.

Therefore, most management firms will contract for professional guard services. After specifications are developed, property management firms go out for competitive bids. Security consultants can help develop guard service specifications and can provide contract supervisory services.

Some guard services simply consist of a drive-through. Others check doors and conduct more drive-by checks. Basically, the service providers will give you what you are willing to pay for.

VOICE OF EXPERIENCE:

Armed guards may pose a risk to tenants and others. They can also create a liability nightmare. Most guard employees or guard services that are contracted for by property management firms are unarmed. Weapons are generally not required, although armed response would be appropriate when responding to an alarm.

Guards can summon authorities with radios and cellular telephones when needed. Your security guards should contact local police to report any suspicion of possible criminal activity on the premises.

At apartment complexes, your security personnel should notify the proper authority when there is evidence of spousal abuse, child abuse or abuse of the elderly. Report only the facts. If information was received by others, report it as such and give names of witnesses.

Security personnel should keep logs of all suspicious behavior, anything out of the ordinary, as well as any action reported to other authorities.

J. GUARD PATROLS

Guard patrols are proactive or reactive. A **PROACTIVE PATROL** *protects or discourages criminal activity by following slow-moving vehicles, checking persons who appear "out of place," and residents who may be acting in a suspicious manner.* **REACTIVE PATROLS** *answer alarms and calls by neighbors and generally act in the capacity of an after-the-fact patrol.* They try to identify and/or catch a perpetrator.

Good proactive patrolling uses random routes and random times, which makes it difficult for criminals to plan avoiding detection by the patrols.

Some guard patrols are equipped with the latest high-tech devices, such as infrared scopes for night vision, allowing intruders to be easily spotted.

K. GUARD DOGS

Fenced facilities such as mini-warehouses, storage yards, and some industrial complexes might wish to consider guard dogs. They do deter criminals. When the fur rises on the dog's back or neck and teeth are bared, even the most fearless criminal will make a hasty retreat.

Guard dogs must be secured when gates are open to tenants and guests. You should also post signs warning the public and intruders about the dogs. A person should be on duty to respond to agitated dogs.

You will have a liability problem if the dogs get loose or children gain access to the guard-dog area and are injured. The doctrine of attractive nuisance would probably apply in this case since dogs do attract small children. It makes no difference that the children are trespassing and that they could read the warning signs.

Concrete should be poured deep enough along fence lines so that the dogs can't dig under the chain link fence.

A number of guard dog companies can supply you with trained dogs. Some owners simply purchase the meanest looking dogs at the pound without regard to their training. This could be dangerous in that a dog could kill rather than only hold at bay an intruder, or worse, attack one of your tenants or employees.

L. ELECTRONIC SECURITY ALARMS

Alarms are not a recent innovation. The first burglar alarm company was founded in 1858.

1. Entry Alarms

Motion detectors, pressure sensitive plates, and wired windows and doors so that opening them breaks or closes a circuit are just some of the electronic means of detecting an entry into a property.

When a circuit is opened or broken, there may be a time delay that allows a person to punch in a code or use a device to cancel an alarm. Often, people forget the code or get flustered and an alarm is set off accidently.

There are open-circuit and closed-circuit alarms. An open-circuit alarm goes off when a circuit closes. A circuit is completed and the alarm goes off when a window is opened.

An open-circuit alarm will not function if a wire is cut.

A *CLOSED-CIRCUIT ALARM has continuous low-voltage current running through the circuit and the alarm goes off when that circuit is broken.* Cutting a wire will set off the alarm. A closed-circuit alarm goes off if the current of electricity is accidentally interrupted or turned off and creates a false alarm. Operating the system by battery and wiring the storage battery to a charger will solve this problem.

A closed-circuit alarm system is the preferred security alarm system.

Vibration alarms are also available that will detect sawing or breaking through a wall.

Electronic intrusion devices are used by individual homeowners and condominium owners. Other users are miniwarehouses, office buildings, and industrial parks.

Alarm Specifications. You should use an independent security consultant to determine if you need a system and, if so, what kind. The consultant will develop required specifications before you put the installation and maintenance of the system out for bids.

Any bid should include multi-year service or have options for service renewal. Otherwise, the installer will have a "lock-in" with respect to future maintenance

services because it is their system. The firm that sold the system could otherwise bargain from a position of strength and significantly increase maintenance fees.

Sounding the Alarm. Formerly, many systems were wired to sound alarms at local police stations. Police were devoting too much time to false alarms. Now, most alarms are wired by telephone directly to central alarm services.

When an alarm goes off, the service will telephone the installation site. A password must be given when the telephone is answered at the site. If not, the service will respond, often with armed guards. The service will coordinate their response with local police.

Unsophisticated burglars will probably be frightened off when a loud piercing alarm goes off. Based on the location, more sophisticated burglars will probably be aware that they have several minutes to work safely.

Alarms can consist of sounds and lights suddenly flooding the premises or flashing on and off. It is very disturbing to intruders.

Alarms that blare continuously disturb the neighborhood. Many alarms are equipped with an automatic shut-off after five or ten minutes. In big cities, false alarms may be so frequent that people regard them as a nuisance and tend to ignore them. In smaller communities, neighbors are more apt to check on an activated alarm going off.

You may incur penalties by the city if your alarm system is set off accidently numerous times.

2. Interior Alarms

Pressure Plates. Besides alarms connected to windows and doors, alarms can be connected to pressure plates placed under carpeting or mats.

Sound Sensors. *SOUND SENSORS really consist of a microphone and an amplifier.* The alarm goes off when any irregular noise exceeds the alarm's setting. Some systems have a silent alarm that goes off at a central listening station. Some systems allow the central station to tune in to the property and listen.

Ultrasonic Alarms. *ULTRASONIC ALARMS use a low-frequency sound wave that reverberates in all directions.* Inanimate objects send back a signal. A moving intruder would set off a change in a signal and set off the alarm. Unfortunately, air disturbances, noise and electrical interference can set off false alarms. Temperature and humidity will affect the range of these detectors.

Microwave Fields. Microwave fields are used by other motion detectors. A disturbance in the field will set off the alarm. Microwaves penetrate material other than metal so motion in another room or unit might set off an alarm. False alarms can occur from "cross-talk" when microwave fields overlap, so more isn't always better. Another problem is that fluorescent lighting is sometimes picked up by microwave detectors and read as a motion due to radiated ionization. Water moving through plastic drains may also be read as motion.

Infrared Beams. As seen in many movies, *INFRARED BEAMS are invisible to the naked eye, but become visable with infrared glasses*. If a beam is interfered with, an alarm goes off. The advantage of these units is that they can cover long distances and can be used outdoors. When used outdoors, they should be set up high enough so that small animals don't set them off.

Spot Detectors. A spot detector is a single-location detector that is set off by touching a particular metal object.

Vibration Detectors. Vibration detectors can be fine-tuned to sense a glass cutter or a person tiptoeing across a floor. They are subject to false alarms from truck traffic, sonic booms and sometimes just the sound of an air conditioner kicking in.

Dual Units. *DUAL UNITS combine two sensor technologies that require both sensors to indicate the presence of an intruder before the alarm goes off*. This unit can be an advantage because it practically eliminates false alarms. However, if one part of the alarm is inoperative the unit is useless. Some new units are now equipped to send an alarm even though one sensor is not working.

VOICE OF EXPERIENCE:

Any alarm is worthless it if isn't turned on. It can be turned on automatically by a clock or manually. If the alarm system is manually operated, a person must be delegated that responsibility and supervised.

3. Alarm Box

The alarm itself should have no external wires that can be cut. The alarm box should be incapable of being disabled with ordinary tools.

M. TELEVISION CAMERAS

Security cameras placed in lobbies, hallways, elevators, storage areas, laundry rooms, etc. can act as a deterrent to crime. Don't hide the fact that security cameras are on the premises. You should consider placing signs to point out this fact. Some vandalism of the cameras may occur, but you may also end up with photos of the vandals themselves.

Mock Cameras. Some stores use mock cameras to discourage shoplifting. Although a good deterrent, you should not use mock cameras because they could give tenants a false sense of security. If you use both real and mock cameras, then advise the tenants and guests that the premises are not totally covered by cameras to record their movements.

Monitoring. While security cameras in large apartment complexes and office buildings may be monitored by guard response, most cameras simply provide 24-hour taped coverage that can later be viewed should a crime occur. Cameras can act as a deterrent, but all you can hope for are photographs of any criminal activity. Tapes should be stored for at least 48 hours before being reused.

Real and mock cameras can reduce the probability of crime and vandalism inside and outside the premises. Use these wisely, disclosing to the tenants that all areas are not always monitored.

Covert Cameras. Most cameras are overt installations in order to deter crime. A covert or hidden camera can be installed if you find it necessary to try to catch the perpetrator or perpetrators where a series of thefts have occurred. Installing hidden cameras is especially important if you suspect that the problem may involve a management employee or employees. Covert equipment, which can be rented, is usually compact in size so that it can be easily concealed, using just a small camera lens opening.

A covert camera can be a good choice if you suspect a crime is an "inside job."

Indoor and Outdoor Cameras. Camera units are available for use either indoors or outdoors. However, keep in mind that any camera is useless unless the viewing areas are well lighted.

Maintenance. Solid-state cameras perform the best with minimum maintenance, although maintenance contracts can be arranged. Guard service employees or management employees can learn to reload the cameras. The cameras can be stationary or set to sweep a viewing area. Cameras are available to record in black and white, but most use color tapes.

Use of Tapes. Tapes can be viewed at high or slow speed as well as viewing per frame. Most tapes record dates and times so the time of an incident can be checked quickly.

Sensors activate some cameras so that they only turn on due to motion. This makes tapes easy to monitor.

Like other elements of security, cameras are only part of a total program.

N. BOMB SEARCH

VOICE OF EXPERIENCE:

If you receive a telephone call about a bomb, immediately notify the authorities and evacuate the premises. It's best to err on the side of caution.

You want the occupants to be moved at least 100 yards from the property because flying debris can injure over a wide area. Leave any search to professionals. Similar action would be prudent if you had reason to suspect that a package on the premises contained a bomb.

Some tenants may generate a degree of hate that could result in a bomb scare. This type of tenant can include birth control centers, governmental offices and some political and religious groups. Strange packages at any location involving these types of tenants should be treated seriously.

VOICE OF EXPERIENCE:

Ask your tenants to notify you if they receive any threats, even if they don't take them seriously. Unlike the police or other law enforcement agencies, you are on the premises on a regular basis and may notice suspicious activity outside the building. You or your security staff are familiar with ordinary comings and goings and are in a good position to notice unusual things or out-of-place people.

O. RENT COLLECTION SECURITY

Not too many years ago, rent collectors used to come to each door to collect the month's rent. These rent collectors carried a lot of money to cash social security and welfare checks. Many lower income tenants without checking accounts would have to buy money orders to send their rent in the mail. So, since tenants didn't have to pay a fee to cash a check with the rent collector, many of them waited for that knock on the door.

Security was a problem in the inner city where most of these rent collectors worked. Carrying a lot of cash, even when accompanied by a guard, is an invitation for disaster. Solutions would include the following.

1. Resident Manager

As a resident manager, you can insist that rents be paid by money orders or checks. In other words, no cash! This method can also protect you from any questions regarding your honesty should there be some missing cash.

Mail Only (Checks and Money Orders). Any problems can be spotted quickly when tenants are required to mail their rent to a central office. However, if this data is not relayed to you as the resident manager, you can be delayed in working to correct problems with late payments and bad checks.

Cash At Office Only. Some property management offices accept cash put into a slot in a safe placed next to an employee who hands out rent receipts, but has no access to the safe. However, this practice could endanger the employee.

VOICE OF EXPERIENCE:

Regardless of what type of property you manage, you should insist that all tenants pay by check or money order. The rent payment schedule should be on the 1st or 15th of the month, no matter when the tenant takes possession.

We suggest that checks and money order be mailed to one address. Upon receipt, all checks should be stamped "For Deposit Only" immediately. After mail delivery or pickups, rents should always be deposited as soon as possible and not left on the premises. A metered self-addressed envelope can be enclosed with rent statements to ease the mailing process for tenants.

P. SHOWING UNITS

A number of reported cases involve assaults on female resident managers and leasing agents while showing vacant units.

As a security measure, you should know the person's name and ask for identification prior to a showing. This is just using common sense. All you have to say is, "Our owner's office policy requires that we see a driver's license or other photo identification of a prospective renter before we show a unit." A serious prospect will not object.

VOICE OF EXPERIENCE:

Always meet potential tenants at the office, not at the property. It's too dangerous to meet complete strangers alone in a vacant property. Many agents have found this out the hard way. Don't allow your desire not to offend someone to overcome your need for self preservation.

Q. EMERGENCY TELEPHONES

The installation of emergency telephones should be considered for large developments. Some large retirement communities have installed emergency telephones that connect to a gate house so that a guard may be notified in case of trouble.

R. EMERGENCY OXYGEN UNITS

Some elderly housing communities have placed emergency oxygen units in public areas such as recreation buildings and pool areas.

S. EMPLOYEE BACKGROUND CHECKS

A number of firms will check the backgrounds of prospective employees. Background checks are particularly important where security personnel are involved. Thefts are often traced to employees who were charged with safeguarding the very items taken. You don't want to be the person who hires the fox to guard the hen house.

T. STAFF SUPERVISION

Condominium associations that hire their own employees are able to more closely supervise the maintenance and grounds staff. Additionally, employees know each other and know the homeowners or tenants. Also, employment may be long term compared to employees of contractors. Intruders are more likely to be caught in a condominium environment than in individual homes where services are separately contracted for by each owner.

U. EMPLOYEE NAME TAGS

Employee name tags, including gardening staff, help the tenants identify individuals and think of them by name rather than just an employee. Claims have been made that name tags reduce employee theft. For instance, tenants would probably remember by name which employees were in an area where a theft occurred.

VOICE OF EXPERIENCE:

Again, use caution! Name tags can be reproduced/copied with relative ease. Still, if you use several of our suggested crime deterrents, you, the property manager, have a better opportunity to provide safety to the tenants and profitability to the owner.

V. OCCUPANCY RULES

Residential units should have occupational safety rules. They might include:

1. Prohibit storing flammable liquids in garages and storage areas.
2. Prohibit small children from using the pool or pool area without supervision.
3. Prohibit children from using any hot spa or sauna.
4. Prohibit the use of bicycles and roller skates on pathways or in halls.
5. No glass containers in pool area.
6. No alcohol in the sauna or hot spa.
7. Hours of pool use.
8. Closing and locking of garage doors.

W. SECURITY COMMITTEES

As the property manager, you might encourage tenants to form security groups. The tenants voice recommendations to you and to each other regarding security matters. Where residential developments are involved, tenants should be encouraged to be aware of strangers and inquire why they are in the area and to write down license numbers of suspicious vehicles.

Tenant meetings help them to know their neighbors by name and, as a result, they are more likely to show concern about the security of their neighbors' property and/or personal well-being.

VOICE OF EXPERIENCE:

Encourage tenants to attend meetings and take an interest in the complex. You too should attend the meetings, as many residents will complain to each other about issues they may not report to you. You can't address problems unless you are aware that they exist.

X. VACANT UNITS

Vacant apartment units and vacant homes are often vandalized. In some instances, the cost of repairs due to vandalism can exceed the value of the property. In some cold-climate areas, if the electricity is cut off the plumbing can freeze, resulting in water damage as well as extensive plumbing and fixture repairs.

If the property will be vacant for some time, have the valves turned off at each plumbing fixture or the water shut off to the property (unless it is needed for landscaping). Also, heat must be maintained in the building, or plumbing must be drained and antifreeze placed in all drains so the traps don't break. The preferred method to drain the plumbing is to use an air compressor to be certain that all water is blown from the lines.

Boarding up the premises might be a wise choice if the property is going to be vacant for some time and other neighboring properties have been vandalized. Alternatives to boarding up property are:

1. Employing a house sitter who would have use of the property until it is rented or used.
2. Paying a neighbor to check the property daily.
3. Installing of alarm systems.

An owner can be subject to liability if a vacant property can be accessed even if it involves a case of trespassing, and more so if a crime is committed on the property.

VOICE OF EXPERIENCE:

Accessibility by intruders must be properly curtailed. Newspapers and mail must be stopped, a light can be left on, and all flyers or advertising should be removed often.

The *ATTRACTIVE NUISANCE DOCTRINE is that an owner can be found liable if his or her property has a condition likely to attract small children and the property poses dangers for children.* As an example, a vacant house could be expected to attract children. If a child were able to enter the house, the owner could be liable for dangerous conditions in the house should they result in injury to the child. If a child fell through a hole in the floor, then the owner could be liable. Cases have held property owners liable for the suffocation of children crawling inside old refrigerators abandoned on the property.

> **VOICE OF EXPERIENCE:**
>
> *Secure all vacant units. Contact neighbors and ask them to contact you if there is any suspicious activity. This is also a benefit to them and may not be as intimidating as contacting the police department.*

Vacant units can become homes to vagrants, drug addicts, and youth gangs. Their presence will increase crime at neighboring properties. You need to keep out such occupants and want to know about any forced entries of properties so you can contact authorities as soon as possible.

Y. FIRE EXTINGUISHERS

Fire extinguishers should be placed in public areas of commercial, office, and residential structures.

Extinguishers enclosed in "break glass" containers reduce theft of the extinguishers, but do not eliminate it entirely.

Fire extinguishers will often disappear within days of replacement in some government subsidized housing projects. Drug addicts and alcoholics look at the extinguishers as found money because they can be sold on the street for a few dollars. Fire codes may require replacement. If a locked "break glass" container is damaged or stolen, the glass and extinguisher will need to be replaced.

You should have a service contract for any fire extinguishers used at your properties. The contractor ensures that all fire extinguishers are fully charged and operable.

Z. FIRE DOORS

Fire doors should be self-closing and are never to be locked, chained closed, or blocked. Fire requires oxygen to burn. Fire doors limit the spread of fire, slow its advance and/or allow the fire to burn itself out due to lack of oxygen. These doors should have a large "Exit" sign posted above them.

Fire exit doors should be equipped with panic hardware for easy opening. Fire doors can be secured from outside entry by simply not having an exterior lock or hardware.

One-way fire exits should have alarms and the door should clearly indicate that opening the door will set off an alarm.

The alarm isn't really for fire alert as much as it is for security and prompt evacuation.

Without the alarm, entrances that you don't want used will be opened by tenants and even propped open allowing others to enter the premises.

AA. FIRE SUPPRESSION

Sprinklers are fire suppression systems.

Most residential properties lack sufficient water supply and pressure for an effective sprinkler system.

The two types of sprinkler heads are a metal plug that melts at relatively low temperature allowing the sprinklers to turn on, and a glass bulb filled with liquid that expands to break the glass setting off the sprinklers when subjected to heat.

Sprinklers should be connected to an alarm water flow in the system that sets off an alarm at the fire station or private security firm.

BB. SMOKE DETECTORS

Smoke detectors should be hardwired rather than battery operated.

VOICE OF EXPERIENCE:

If smoke detectors are battery operated, inspect them regularly to make sure the batteries are working. It's important to demonstrate that you have an honest concern for the tenants' safety. In the not too distant future, in addition to smoke detectors, expect carbon monoxide detectors to be required.

Regular inspection can reduce the likelihood of inoperative units and also their disappearance. Batteries can become disconnected or simply wear out.

Smoke alarms can easily be tested by lighting a length of cotton rope and holding the smoking rope under the detector.

CC. CARBON MONOXIDE DETECTORS

Where garages are built within the same structure as residential units, you should consider carbon monoxide detectors. Actually, it would be a good idea to have detectors in every unit since a heating unit that is not working properly can result in dangerous carbon monoxide levels. These detectors are now quite economically priced at about $25. Tenants should sign for detectors that are provided for them. This small dollar expenditure shows tenants that you are concerned about their safety and protects the owner's investment, as well as limiting liability resulting from defective units.

DD. INJURIES ON PREMISES

You should immediately call for medical assistance if persons are injured on the premises or take them for medical help if they are ambulatory.

Direct pressure should be applied to control any bleeding. Where breathing has stopped, CPR should be administered if you have someone trained in CPR. Don't move injured parties if they cannot move by themselves. Get names and handwritten statements from any witnesses after taking care of the injured parties.

VOICE OF EXPERIENCE:

As a responsible property manager, you should know CPR. Implementing an employee policy requiring CPR certification is also a good idea, especially where numerous children or elderly tenants are in residence. Many local organizations like YMCAs or fire departments offer CPR classes for little or no charge. If you have a large number of personnel, consider paying a professional to come to your office or clubhouse and train everyone at once. Tenant or HOA meetings are also good places to offer classes. You'll be doing both your tenants and the community at large a valuable service. Who knows how many lives will be saved in the long run?

EE. SAFETY RULES

You should establish and enforce applicable safety rules for employees. They might include requiring the use of leather gloves while pruning, use of goggles and a face filter while operating edgers and blowers, as well as precautions regarding the use and storage of flammable material.

Make sure all employees use proper preventative measures.

FF. OCCUPATIONAL SAFETY AND HEALTH ACT (OSHA)

While originally targeted at hazardous waste, OSHA has been expanded to be a matter of some concern to property managers. OSHA applies to interstate commerce, however, very loose interpretations as to what interstate commerce really is has included property management as part of this definition.

One category covered by the act is personal protection, and OSHA has developed standards of safety and health for personal protection. In some cases the standards seem ludicrous, such as the written requirements concerning the placement of toilet paper in bathroom stalls and about 20 pages on ladder safety.

An employer who hires seven or more employees must keep records and file reports with OSHA.

Records must also be kept at the work site. These records include work-related injuries and illnesses.

OSHA covers the maintenance of structures that includes personal protective devices. As an example, goggles must be worn while using certain lawn maintenance equipment.

An OSHA inspection revealing a broken hammer handle that has been taped could result in a significant fine.

Many firms do a self-audit of safety procedures and equipment to avoid any problems. Other firms have independent consultants audit operations for safety violations. OSHA inspectors are like any other people; some act with reason and do not make an issue of minor infractions, while other inspectors tend to go by the book.

OSHA has a number of free documents covering various types of activities.

 osha.gov
Occupational Safety and Health Act (OSHA)

OSHA requires a posting of a log on illnesses and injuries (see **Figure 9-1**).

GG. STATE OSHA

A number of states, such as California, have also passed Occupational Safety Hazards Acts (CAL OSHA in California).

California provides free onsite technical assistance to help identify and correct safety and/ or health hazards. This service is confidential and information will not be made available to OSHA enforcement offices.

VOICE OF EXPERIENCE:

Using the advice in this chapter may cost a little bit more, but will usually increase rents because the income property has a better appearance and provides more security. You and your owner will feel better about providing a safer environment and reducing the risk of lawsuits. Use this book to create a partial checklist.

Figure 9-1

OSHA's Form 300 (Rev. 01/2004)

Log of Work-Related Injuries and Illnesses

Attention: This form contains information relating to employee health and must be used in a manner that protects the confidentiality of employees to the extent possible while the information is being used for occupational safety and health purposes.

U.S. Department of Labor
Occupational Safety and Health Administration

Form approved OMB no. 1218-0176

Year 20____

You must record information about every work-related death and about every work-related injury or illness that involves loss of consciousness, restricted work activity or job transfer, days away from work, or medical treatment beyond first aid. You must also record significant work-related injuries and illnesses that are diagnosed by a physician or licensed health care professional. You must also record work-related injuries and illnesses that meet any of the specific recording criteria listed in 29 CFR Part 1904.8 through 1904.12. Feel free to use two lines for a single case if you need to. You must complete an Injury and Illness Incident Report (OSHA Form 301) or equivalent form for each injury or illness recorded on this form. If you're not sure whether a case is recordable, call your local OSHA office for help.

Establishment name _____

City _____ State _____

Identify the person

(A) Case no.	(B) Employee's name	(C) Job title (e.g., Welder)

Describe the case

(D) Date of injury or onset of illness	(E) Where the event occurred (e.g., Loading dock north end)	(F) Describe injury or illness, parts of body affected, and object/substance that directly injured or made person ill (e.g., Second degree burns on right forearm from acetylene torch)

Classify the case

CHECK ONLY ONE box for each case based on the most serious outcome for that case:

Death (G)	Days away from work (H)	Remained at Work — Job transfer or restriction (I)	Remained at Work — Other recordable cases (J)

Enter the number of days the injured or ill worker was:

Away from work (K)	On job transfer or restriction (L)

Check the "injury" column or choose one type of illness:

(M) Injury (1)	Skin disorder (2)	Respiratory condition (3)	Poisoning (4)	Hearing loss (5)	All other illnesses (6)

Page totals ▶

Be sure to transfer these totals to the Summary page (Form 300A) before you post it.

| Injury (1) | Skin disorder (2) | Respiratory condition (3) | Poisoning (4) | Hearing loss (5) | All other illnesses (6) |

Page _____ of _____

Public reporting burden for this collection of information is estimated to average 14 minutes per response, including time to review the instructions, search and gather the data needed, and complete and review the collection of information. Persons are not required to respond to the collection of information unless it displays a currently valid OMB control number. If you have any comments about these estimates or any other aspects of this data collection, contact: US Department of Labor, OSHA Office of Statistical Analysis, Room N-3644, 200 Constitution Avenue, NW, Washington, DC 20210. Do not send the completed forms to this office.

327

III. CHAPTER SUMMARY

Security is a prime concern of property management. Security involves taking reasonable measures to protect tenants and their property and guests.

Although owners and managers have moral obligations, legal duties are either set forth in statutes or by the courts. Courts are concerned with the foreseeability of loss or injury in determining if a landlord or manager has a duty to maintain and enforce safety precautions.

The many ways in which owners and managers can fulfill their security duties include:

1. Lighting. Wrongdoers prefer darkness to cloak their activities. Lighting in entryways, parking areas, hallways, and other common areas may consist of various types of lights based on need. Emergency lighting should be storage-battery operated.
2. Landscaping allowing a clear view, limiting places to hide and climbing access into units increases safety.
3. Fences and Walls. They restrict entry and criminals prefer to get in and out of property quickly and with ease.
4. Doors. Solid-core doors or metal-clad doors resist forced entry.
5. Peepholes. Having a view of a person at the door makes it more difficult to gain entry to an occupied unit.
6. Security Chain. A quality security chain that is anchored into the door and jamb will resist forced entry.
7. Locks. Quality locks resist picking and forced entry. Key-in-the-knob locks and mortised locks are not much of a deterrent to forced entry. Dead bolts provide better securiy. They should be used with a good strike plate and a solid jamb.
8. Windows. Break-resistant windows resist forced entry. Pins between sliding window units are far better than normal window locks. Pins can also be used for sliding glass doors.
9. Electronic Gates. Electronic gates limit access, but don't protect against access at other points of the premises or crimes by persons who have been given access.
10. Guard Gates. Guard gates are expensive to maintain because of personnel costs.
11. Guard Services. Guard providers will give you whatever services you wish to pay for. You should consider a security consultant to determine specifications for guard services.
12. Guard Dogs. Dogs should only be used in a secured vacated area. They must be secured when tenants are in the area.
13. Electronic Security Alarms. Alarms can be interior or exterior and be connected to intrusion detection devices attached to windows or doors, pressure plates, motion detectors, sounds, heat sensors, etc. They may be connected directly to a police department location, but are most likely connected to a central alarm company office.

14. Television Cameras. Cameras can be a deterrent to criminal activities. For proper use, the area must be well lighted. Tapes can be viewed to determine the identities of any wrongdoers.
15. Bombs. Bomb threats must be taken seriously. Certain tenants such as birth control centers and government offices are more likely to be the subject of threats and/or actual bombs.
16. Rent Collection. By accepting only checks and money orders the danger to property management personnel is greatly reduced.
17. Security in Showing Units. As a safety measure, an employee showing a unit should first request photo identification from a prospective tenant and meet tenants at the office rather than at the property.
18. Emergency Telephones. Emergency telephones connected to guard gates can help to promptly report any emergencies.
19. Emergency Oxygen. Elderly housing developments might have oxygen available in public areas for emergency use.
20. Employment Screening. You reduce the probability of future crimes by checking the backgrounds of job applicants.
21. Staff Supervision. Tight supervision reduces staff crimes.
22. Employee Name Tags. Employees who are known by name among tenants and other staff are more likely to be identified for wrongful activity, if any. This works as a crime deterrent.
23. Occupancy Rules. Rules can reduce both accidents and crime.
24. Security Committees. Involving tenants in security matters results in proactive tenant actions as well as the increased likelihood of catching any wrongdoer after the fact.
25. Vacant Units. Vacant units must be protected against vandalism, illegal occupancy, and the elements.
26. Fire Extinguishers. Fire extinguishers should not only be available on the premises, but also be operable. A maintenance contract should be considered to keep them in working order.
27. Fire Doors. Fire doors should never be locked. The doors should also be self-closing. Panic hardware and alarms should be installed on exterior doors.
28. Fire Suppression Systems. Sprinklers should have an alarm attached to the water supply (flow alarm) that is connected to a central system or fire department.
29. Smoke and Carbon Monoxide Detectors. These detectors are for safety of the tenants.

IV. CHAPTER QUIZ

1. A landlord's duty to provide for security may be determined by:
    a. cost of the property.
    b. foreseeability of harm.
    c. prior criminal activity on the premises.
    d. both b and c.

2. You could be liable to a tenant who was the victim of a crime if you advertised an apartment as being:
    a. behind security gates.
    b. managed by a security conscious firm.
    c. safe.
    d. patrolled by security guards.

3. Which of the following helps in providing for security of the tenants?
    a. A well-lighted parking area
    b. The absence of high bushes and trees around entryways
    c. Emergency lighting in halls and entrances
    d. All of the above

4. The best break-in resistant doors are:
    a. hollow core.
    b. solid core.
    c. those having peepholes.
    d. interior doors.

5. The most secure type of door lock is:
    a. one with the fewest tumblers.
    b. mortised into the door.
    c. one with a knob key.
    d. a dead bolt.

6. The more difficult padlocks to force open have:
    a. long shanks.
    b. hasps.
    c. short shanks.
    d. tumblers.

7. Ways to prevent lower windows from being entered include:
    a. replacing glass with glass block.
    b. replacing glass with Lexan.
    c. window bars.
    d. all of the above.

8. The LEAST desirable electronic gate employs:

    a. a radio controlled opener.

    b. a sliding gate.

    c. a gate that swings open from the center.

    d. a wooden bar that drops.

9. A proactive guard patrol would:

    a. question persons who appear out of place.

    b. respond quickly to alarms.

    c. investigate crimes.

    d. all of the above.

10. Alarms can be activated by:

    a. breaking or opening a circuit.

    b. movement.

    c. vibration.

    d. any of the above.

ANSWERS: 1. d; 2. c; 3. d; 4. b; 5. d; 6. c; 7. d; 8. d; 9. a; 10. d

Chapter 10
Maintenance and Energy Conservation

KEY WORDS AND TERMS

Aluminum Wiring
Automatic Damper Control
Blanket Wrap
Blown Insulation
Built-Up Roofs
Caulking
Contract Specifications
Double-Glazed Windows
Duct Work
E-Value
Energy Conservation
Exterminator
Florescent Lights
Foam Roofs
Force Account
Graffiti
Heating and Air Conditioning Engineers
Improvements
Insulation
Insulation Paint

Maintenance
Maintenance Records
Name Tags
Patch-and-Hope Repairs
Pigeons
Pressure Washing
Preventative Maintenance
Priority of Repairs
R-Value
Rebond Pad
Roof Pitch
Solar Heat
Solar Lights
Standardization
Temporary Help Services
Ten-Day Week
Tile Roofs
Venting
Water Conservation
Weatherstripping

CHAPTER 10 OUTLINE

I. Your Maintenance Program

MAINTENANCE is the upkeep of property. It involves cleaning, repairing and servicing of a property to obtain the use benefits needed at the present time and in the future.

Ideally, the best form of maintenance would be preventative maintenance. You must also know when "deferring maintenance" is appropriate.

Changing filters and belts, oiling bearings, painting, etc., can reduce breakdowns or more costly maintenance or repair.

Problems will occur no matter how good your preventative maintenance program is. Things that can break will break at some time. Repair or replacement then becomes necessary.

You need to be aware of and address replacement issues.

Some maintenance programs deteriorate to the point of "putting out fires" or repairing what has broken resulting in preventative maintenance taking a back seat. If this is the case, long-term economic benefits could be realized by increasing the staff so that part of the work schedules can be spent on preventative maintenance duties.

Keeping records, such as ledgers, stickers, or tags, are methods for checking the preventative maintenance schedule on vehicles and equipment. Tags could be attached to serviced indoor equipment, including a date and signature of the employee performing the task.

Preventative maintenance schedules could be documented in a computer as a reminder of both work performed and checking on work completed.

A. EMPLOYEE VERSUS CONTRACT SERVICES

For many years, battles raged within the General Services Administration of the Federal Government regarding the use of force accounts or contracts for maintenance services. *FORCE ACCOUNT refers to the use of employees versus contract services.*

On the side of force account were government personnel services whose basic existence and size directly related to the number of employees. Property managers preferred the use of contract services because their budgets couldn't be met by using employees. Weighing the use of employees on a federal government pay scale with full health benefits, sick days, vacations and retirement plans made the use of contract labor significantly less expensive in the long run.

A similar situation exists with large unionized corporations. The pay scales and benefits of employees results in their use being more costly than those of contractors. Contractors either provide no health services, or minimum health services, minimum vacation time, and no retirements. When there is a health plan, the employee often must contribute a portion (often one-half) of the health benefit costs. Wage scales usually begin at minimum wage level and don't graduate much beyond this point. By using contract labor, the federal government saved in the neighborhood of 30 percent to 45 percent, which still left a profit for contractors.

Large nonunion building management firms can match the savings possible for cleaning and servicing large office buildings. Work done by employees can mean greater control, but can also mean a heavy supervisory burden.

The authors have had extensive experience with both contract and employee services and strongly recommend contract cleaning services.

Advantages include locking in costs and avoiding little problems so that management can focus on the big issues. There are paperwork advantages that contract labor has over employees. The Social Security contributions, worker's compensation, unemployment coverage, liability protection, and tax withholding are taken care of by the contractor. While you still pay these costs, they are included in the contract price.

We realize that our view is not universal within the property management field. Some property management companies have their own cleaning firms that are actually profit centers for the companies.

The authors prefer that services such as cleaning and landscaping be contracted for and minor repairs be handled by the owner's qualified employees. Being able to direct minor jobs is important for tenant satisfaction.

B. YOUR OWN MAINTENANCE COMPANY

Some management companies totally own maintenance companies that deal in minor repairs and maintenance work. Reasons for controlling a maintenance firm used at a number of properties are:

1. You can achieve better utilization of resources. As an example, a development may only need a handyperson 25 percent of the time for a few months, but 100 percent of the time the rest of the year. The units, however, may be paying a full-time person for

a 40-hour week even though the only work done might be "busy" work. Work done by a contractor could mean big savings to an owner in such cases.

2. By controlling maintenance, you are the one who determines what is to be handled first, making decisions regarding priority or emergency.

3. Saving Costs. Using handypersons to change washers, install new valves in toilets, repair sprinkler systems, replace electrical outlets, etc., can mean significant savings to the owners rather than contracting for work to be done.

4. Your own maintenance company can be a separate profit center because you can save an owner money while still making a reasonable return for the company.

Controlling your own company that is performing the majority of maintenance and cleaning work should not be a problem as long as the owners understand that the firm is yours, what and how the work is priced and that the owner has given written permission to use your firm.

Use of your firm's maintenance organization should not be a requirement of management, but if used, there should be a disclosure regarding ownership.

You have a duty to recommend to owners that employees be used rather than your company if the properties can support a full-time staff and owner-employees offer advantages over your contracting services.

Where feasible, you should obtain competitive bids for significant repairs before deciding to use your maintenance company so as to avoid the appearance of a conflict of interest. Failing to do so would be a disservice to the owners.

Full disclosure is extremely important and avoids any conflict of interest.

Bids will not be competitive unless there is a meeting of the minds between you and the contractors about the work to be performed and materials to be used. As an example, a new commode can be purchased for under $50 to $300. There are many types of commodes that affect operation, maintenance, and initial cost.

Various management associations have developed sample specifications to aid in contracting.

C. PRIORITY OF REPAIRS

While some resident managers might prioritize repairs by who is making the most demands, repairs should be prioritized by importance if several tasks are to be assigned to one employee or an independent contractor.

Special circumstances sometimes affect the order in which tasks are performed.

D. STANDARDIZATION

Your managed properties were probably built by different contractors during different periods. Brands and quality of appliances, fixtures and hardware will vary. Repairs are not always possible because parts are no longer available. At times, replacement of an item makes more sense than trying to repair it.

For replacement, many property management firms use standardized items such as faucets and locks, using good quality items that will require less repair.

VOICE OF EXPERIENCE:

The use of standardized fixtures can be very cost effective. Not only are replacement parts readily available, but no special training or expertise will be required when repairs are needed. Employee maintenance personnel will become familiar with the installation and repair of these items, reducing the time and labor costs.

E. DEVELOPING CONTRACTOR RELATIONS

You want to develop a core of dependable contractors who will do good work at the time they say they will perform the job and whose work is competitively priced.

As a property manager, you should not regard price alone in determining maintenance and repair contracts. Good quality and reliability is every bit as important.

You can build an excellent relationship by giving most of your work to just a few contractors. You can and should expect preferential treatment by contractors in terms of work timeliness, priority emergency responses, and callbacks due to the volume of work you provide.

F. PATCH-AND-HOPE REPAIRS

Advise tenants of any delay in repairs.

You won't be able to always properly repair or replace an item or a system. There could be a delay in obtaining replacement items or parts. This may result in a "patch- and-hope that it will hold" operation. Patch-and-hope work can actually end up more expensive than if the job had been done right the first time. The owners should be notified of when and why a patch-and-hold job is done. The owners could otherwise become agitated when they find out they are paying twice for the same repair. Explain that it is a "stop-gap effort" to avoid losing tenants.

Of course, any repairs that are not critical should be delayed until they can be performed properly. You should explain to the tenants the reason for any delay in repairs.

G. THE 10-DAY WEEK

Maintenance schedules tend to get in a rut when tied to calendar dates.

As an example, mowing the lawn once a week might be scheduled and performed regardless of the need. While lawns might require cutting regularly because of greater growth during the summer months, other times of the year this task could be performed every 8 days, 10 days, or even 12 days, depending upon the need. This can free valuable manpower for other maintenance duties and could even lower staff requirements.

In using an extended week, when lawn care becomes due on a weekend or holiday, move the whole calendar forward to the next work day.

The same can be done for office cleaning tasks that could vary based on need. For instance, floor maintenance should be more frequent during rainy periods than during dry periods.

Pool maintenance may need to be performed daily during warm periods and intensive use. The maintenance could be reduced to two or three times a week during colder periods and reduced usage.

VOICE OF EXPERIENCE:

As a manager, you should be flexible and reschedule work around need rather than becoming a slave to the calendar. However, this method may not be practical for contract services.

H. MAINTENANCE RECORDS

Property managers, including onsite managers, must keep records of all maintenance requests and complaints.

The problem should be logged in detailing when work is requested, what has or is being done to alleviate the problem, when the work was completed and by whom. If a purchase order was written up, then an order number must be assigned so it can be tracked.

The person who reported a problem or made a complaint should be notified as soon as possible detailing how and when the problem will be resolved. In some cases, nothing can be done. As an example, resident managers often receive complaints from tenants that furnaces or air conditioners are too loud, but checks reveal that the units are well maintained and operate properly with no excess noise, loose bearings, or slipping belts. You want to be concerned about problems, however, some people imagine problems or try to find fault with things. It's unfortunate, but all you can do in such situations is to reassure the tenants that what they view as a problem is really normal.

Chapter 10

I. IDENTIFY YOUR MAINTENANCE PERSONNEL

Employee maintenance personnel should be uniformly dressed to make their presence evident to tenants.

They should wear a prominent name tag so tenants know who did what. When tenants identify maintenance personnel by name, the personnel become individuals and tenant/maintenance personnel relations tend to improve. When tenants know personnel by name, they tend to become more understanding and tolerant of problems.

Some personnel of management firms are given personal cards to hand out to tenants when needed. They can tell tenants, "Call me if you have a problem again." Tenants are more likely to be satisfied if they feel that they have a good relationship with your personnel.

J. STAFFING

Professional organizations and the General Service Administration have developed staffing requirements for cleaning services based on the types of properties and the level and frequency of cleaning desired. These staffing requirements are only guides. Special circumstances, as well as climactic conditions, can alter the staffing requirements.

Other maintenance staffing requirements are affected by the age of the property, quality of construction, size of common areas, etc.

II. Specific Maintenance Tasks

A. ROOFS (New)

Know your roofers and determine if they are competent.

If you are replacing an asphalt shingle roof, the labor to install the shingles will exceed the cost of the shingles. It is false economy to buy low-cost shingles. Overlapping heavyweight roofing paper should be used under the roof. Asphalt shingles, wood shingles, and tile can be used on a pitched roof with a 4-inch or greater pitch. This means that for each 12 inches horizontally, the drop vertically should be at least 4 inches.

Roofers will recommend that the first roof be removed when replacing an asphalt shingle roof. However, a second asphalt shingle roof can be installed directly over the original shingles by using at least 1 1/2 inch galvanized nails.

Foam roofs, built-up roofs and rubber roofs can be used on flat or slightly pitched roofs. Rubber roofing is quite expensive, but it provides an excellent roof.

The most widely used built-up roofs may come with a 15-year or 20-year guarantee.

These roofs consist of three sandwiched layers of roofing paper between applied hot-mopped tar. A gravel surface is then applied to reduce running tar and to provide a surface upon which to walk.

Foam roofs normally require an application of reflective and protective paint every two years or they will show deterioration. It can be an excellent roof if applied properly.

Tile roofs seldom have to be replaced.

The only damage tile roofs might sustain are from objects falling on the roof, improperly walking on the roof or tile being blown away by strong winds.

Tile roofs are usually expensive. The cost might be 200 percent greater than the cost of a built-up roof. Tile roofs are also heavy. Replacing singles with tiles will require engineering work to determine what, if any, additional roof supports will be required to support the weight of the tile roof.

A building permit is required to install a new tile roof.

Tile roofs can be of clay or concrete tile. Concrete tile is less expensive. Some concrete tiles are significantly lighter than other tiles, but still heavier than shingles.

Be sure to deal with a reliable roofer who will be around should you encounter problems later.

Tile roofs require at least a 4/12 pitch. They might be used in remodeling a structure that is being repositioned in the marketplace to obtain higher rents.

Flat roof buildings are frequently remodeled with a fake mansard-style roof facade. The edge of the building might have 10 to 12 feet of tile roof at a 6/12 to 10/12 pitch. It is a relatively low-cost remodeling effort and can change the appearance of the building.

B. ROOFS (Repairs)

A roof leak is often not related to where the leak appears to be. Water will follow a rafter or joist and drip through the ceiling, sometimes as far as 20 feet from where the roof leaks.

You can often determine likely spots for future leaks by visually checking a roof to find where the current leak starts.

On built-up roofs there may be cracks in the roofing around vents, the ridge line, or internal valleys in the roof. Long, straight cracks parallel to the eaves where sheets of roof paper overlap usually are the site of many leaks. Repairs are relatively simple by using plastic roofing repair material that is applied with a four-inch scraper. (There are mastics that can be applied when the roof is wet). Simply brush the loose gravel off a strip on both sides of the crack and trowel on about a six-inch wide swath of mastic. This also works for cracks around vents and chimneys.

A licensed roofer should be able to locate the source of the leak. If there are areas where a portion of the pitched roof meets a flat portion, then apply mastic along the juncture. This will probably solve the problem. The same can be done around chimneys and where the roof meets any vertical wall. Apply roof cement when in doubt. It is better to patch 10 areas and find three leaks than it is to patch five areas and only locate two of three leaks.

Asphalt shingle roof leaks can be repaired by using a caulking gun and tubes of roofing cement. Use the best mastic you can buy. Get under the edges of the shingles, around vents and chimneys with the caulking gun. The source of leaks on shingled roofs are normally less obvious than on built-up roofs. New shingles can be inserted using plenty of mastic where there are damaged or missing shingles.

While you will probably not be making roof repairs yourself, if you understand problems with leaks and roof repairs then you can supervise the work and train your employees in this area.

If roof repairs become a regular event, you should probably consider a new roof to preserve the structure.

C. PLUMBING

Your continued patronage has value—negotiate advantageous contracts with your better providers.

Because of the sheer volume of business that you, as a property manager, can offer a plumbing firm, significant savings in costs can be realized by entering into a negotiated contract. The contract might specify a price per call including one-half hour of service and an hourly rate thereafter. Fixed prices might be negotiated for replacement of various sizes of water heaters (both gas and electric).

Contracts can also be negotiated for any drain cleaning services, septic system services, etc. Each owner benefits from the quantity provided by negotiating for many properties.

Minor plumbing work can be performed by general maintenance personnel.

D. FURNACES AND AIR CONDITIONERS

Consider a contract provider for annual services for checking oil and grease, gas levels, belts, bearings, etc. Your contracted cost per unit should be reasonable when it involves a large number of similar units. Servicing can significantly reduce expensive repairs and emergency service calls.

You should also consider negotiating for a price per call contract similar to the plumbing contract previously discussed.

Figure 10-1 is an AIR Commerical Real Estate Association (AIR) service agreement for maintenance of heating, ventilating, and air conditioning. Where HVAC is a tenant responsibility, such a contract would likely be required as a lease provision.

E. PAINT

As a property manager, you may consider using similar carpeting as well as interior and exterior paint in all your units.

When one of the authors was actively engaged in property management, he required the same brand of coffee-colored paint be used for all residential units. By using quality paint, a maintenance worker could touch up a unit between tenants in less than one hour. A little spackle was applied to picture holes and allowed to dry before painting.

For exterior trim, six basic colors of paint were used. Touch up was easy and repainting never required more than one coat.

Consider if the entire building needs repainting or just the trim before going ahead with exterior painting. It is often just the eaves that need to be painted. By using matching paint, the trim can be repainted without doing the entire exterior.

Often, just one or two sides of a building require repainting. With matching colors, you don't have to repaint the whole building.

Owners are thrilled when you save them money. This is the type of savings they'll tell their friends about, which makes your property management fees more than worthwhile.

To match existing paint, you can cut a chip from the wood trim and take it to any major paint store. A machine will compute the color formula to match your chip close enough to the original color. If you use the new paint, paint an entire wall or trim on one side. Don't paint just one small area or the matched paint might be obvious to the naked eye and appear to be a sloppy patch job.

Do not use latex paint to paint decks. Latex paint peels on decking within a year from exposure to the elements. You can match latex colors with a semi-transparent or solid color oil base paint made for decks.

Spray painting is fast, but it can create liability problems. Contractors should be able to verify that they carry high-limit liability protection. Dark colored cars parked half a block away during a spray painting job may develop a speckled appearance from just a gentle breeze.

F. CARPETING

Good quality carpeting is well worth its cost.

Figure 10-1

AIR COMMERCIAL REAL ESTATE ASSOCIATION
STANDARD FORM SERVICE AGREEMENT
[THE USE OF THIS FORM IS DEEMED TO BE IN COMPLIANCE WITH THE HVAC REQUIREMENTS OF LEASE PARAGRAPH 7.1(b)]
HEATING, VENTILATING, AND AIR CONDITIONING

_____ ("Contractor")

agrees to maintain and service certain heating, ventilating, and air conditioning equipment located at _____

_____

for _____ ("Lessee").

This Agreement shall include the maintenance and service of the following equipment:

Description of Equipment	Make	Model	Serial No.
_____	_____	_____	_____
_____	_____	_____	_____
_____	_____	_____	_____
_____	_____	_____	_____
_____	_____	_____	_____
_____	_____	_____	_____

Said service and maintenance shall include the following:

☐ A. **Fans and Blowers**
    1. Lubricate all moving parts as required.
    2. Adjust tension on all belt drives and align when necessary.

☐ B. **Filters**
    1. Clean or replace every _____ days with _____.

☐ C. **Motors and Motor Controls**
    1. Clean, oil, and/or grease.
    2. Check for overload under full operation.
    3. Check contacts and clean as necessary.
    4. Check time clock for proper setting.
    5. Check and adjust operation of all electric or pneumatic controls.

☐ D. **Gas Furnaces**
    1. Check combustion.
    2. Check and clean pilot.
    3. Check fan limit control.
    4. Check pilot safety device.
    5. Check automatic gas valve.

☐ E. **Boilers**
    1. Check combustion.
    2. Check and clean pilot.
    3. Check fan limit control.
    4. Check pilot safety device.
    5. Check low water cut off.
    6. Check automatic water feeder.
    7. Check water strainer.
    8. Check pressure regulator.
    9. Check relief valve.
    10. Drain and recharge expansion tank.
    11. Blow down boiler and controls.
    12. Check automatic gas valve.
    13. Check boiler control settings.
    14. Check steam valves and traps.
    15. Adjust controls as required.

☐ F. **Dampers (Automatic or Manual)**
    1. Check and adjust for correct operation.
    2. Check all linkage and adjust where necessary.
    3. Check fire damper for fusible links.

☐ G. **Compressors**
    1. Lubricate all bearings as required.
    2. Check oil level and pressure.
    3. Check head pressure. (Adjust if required)
    4. Check suction pressure. (Adjust if required)
    5. Check head bolts and anchor bolts. (Adjust if required)
    6. Check refrigerant charge.
    7. Test for leaks.

☐ H. **Evaporate Condenser, Cooling Tower and Air Washers**
    1. Lubricate all motors and pumps and fan bearings.
    2. Check pump packing. (Adjust or replace when required)
    3. Check coil. (Scale or dirt)
    4. Check spray nozzles. (Clean and adjust when required)
    5. Check water strainer. (Clean when required)
    6. Check pump strainer. (Clean when required)
    7. Check float control. (Adjust when required)
    8. Check drip pan and rain connections.
    9. Check drive belts. (Align and adjust when required)
    10. Check rotation of fan.
    11. Check bleeder line. (Adjust when required)
    12. Check water valve setting.
    13. Adjust automatic controls.
    14. Drain and flush sump pan.

☐ I. **Air Cooled Condensers**
    1. Lubricate all motors and fan bearings as required.
    2. Check pump packing.
    3. Check coils. (Scale and dirt)
    4. Check air intake screen. (Clean when required)
    5. Check drip pan and drain connections.
    6. Check drive belts. (Align and adjust when required)
    7. Check rotation of fan.
    8. Adjust automatic controls.

☐ J. **Controls-Electric and/or Pneumatic**
    1. Check thermostat contacts.
    2. Check starter contacts.
    3. Check damper motors.
    4. Air controls-drain water.
    5. Clean air compressor intake.
    6. Check air compressor oil.
    7. Check air compressor motor.
    8. Lubricate air compressor motor.
    9. Spot check stats for calibration.

☐ K. **Fin Coils (Water, Steam or Refrigerant)**
    1. Check for leaks.
    2. Check strainers.
    3. Check coil face for dirt.

☐ L. **Pad Type Evaporative Coolers**
    1. Oil and adjust all motors, bearings and drives as required.
    2. Adjust water distribution over pads.
    3. Check pads for dirt, looseness, sagging or disintegration.
    4. Flush sump and check for leaks.
    5. Adjust float.
    6. Oil and check pump and motor.

8. Check rotation.

9. Align and tighten belts.

10. Check amperage and voltage.

☐ **M. 1. Check Water Treatment Control**

☐ **N. Boiler Water Treatment**

    1. Take water analysis and make recommendations.

Maintenance, and service inspection will occur no less than quarterly and Contractor agrees to provide quarterly maintenance inspection reports, in writing, to both Lessee at the building address shown below and also to Lessee's Lessor _____

located at _____ .

ADDITIONAL TERMS AND CONDITIONS

1. Lessee to receive 10% discount on repair parts.

2. Lessee to receive _____ % discount on labor.

3. Any alterations, additions, adjustments or repairs made by others, unless authorized or agreed upon by Contractor, will be cause to terminate this Agreement.

4. Repairs necessitated by fire, floods, acts of God, abuse or the improper use of equipment listed will be the sole responsibility of Lessee and are not covered by this Agreement.

5. This Agreement does not cover any work or changes which might at some future date be required by government regulations, or insurance company requirements.

6. While this Agreement covers all functional components of the air conditioning system, it does not cover ductwork, structural supports or other sheet metal components which may deteriorate due to corrosion or rust.

7. NEITHER PARTY to this Agreement shall hold the other responsible for any indirect or consequential damage of a commercial nature such as, but not limited to, loss of revenue or loss of use of any equipment or facilities.

8. Contractor's maximum liability based upon any claim or cause of action shall not exceed the yearly contract price of this Agreement.

9. Payment for this Agreement will be net upon receipt of invoice. Contractor reserves the right to discontinue service any time payments have not been made as agreed so long as Contractor first gives at least 15 days prior written notice to Lessor

10. This Agreement may be terminated by either party upon 30 days written notice to the other and to Lessor. A refund for the remaining contract period will be made on a prorata basis, with deduction for work already completed.

11. Lessee shall receive Priority Service.

BILLING ADDRESS

The address for the billing of Lessee shall be: _____

_____ .

CONTRACT PRICE

The price for this service contract shall be $ _____ per year, payable _____ .

TERM

The initial term of this contract shall be from _____ to _____ .

CANCELLATION

In the event that this agreement is canceled or terminated, Contractor agrees to provide written notice of said cancellation or termination to Lessor at the address listed above.

Dated: _____   _____

                                                                      CONTRACTOR

Dated: _____   _____

NOTICE: These forms are often modified to meet changing requirements of law and industry needs. Always write or call to make sure you are utilizing the most current form: AIR Commercial Real Estate Association, 800 W 6th Street, Suite 800, Los Angeles, CA 90017. Telephone No. (213) 687-8777. Fax No.: (213) 687-8616.

DRAFT

The way to save on carpeting is not by using an inexpensive pad. Even good carpeting will wear out fast from a cheap pad. The pad should be at least 9/16th of an inch in thickness and made up of recycled foam chunks (rebond) rather than a pad uniform in color and texture. Rebond pads hold up well and don't mat down like cheaper pads.

You can save on carpeting by obtaining a competitive price on installed, per-square yard carpeting based on quality and pad and by using the same carpeting in several units.

The contract would indicate yardage you used in the prior year and while you're not obligated, if you do buy carpeting, you agree to purchase it from the contractor at the agreed installed price per-square yard.

Your contract could include both residential and commercial carpeting prices and will probably be negotiated rather than given to a low bidder. You want to negotiate with a firm you have worked with before and were satisfied with the promptness and quality of work.

If you use 5,000 yards of carpeting per year at an average price of $18 per yard installed, that amounts to $90,000 worth of business. For that much business you can expect a firm to sharpen their pencils. At $90,000, cutting the cost by $3 per yard would mean a savings of $15,000 and, in the above situation, this price cut may be conservative.

While you may enter such a contract for just one owner's property, you'd be wise do so for multiple owners. The more business you can provide, the better the price break.

Pass on the savings to your owners.

If you can guarantee a minimum number of yards of carpeting, then even greater savings are possible.

We suggest that colors be limited and carpet scraps be stored for future repair purposes. A light neutral Berber carpet with a tight pattern wears well. It doesn't matt down and show traffic patterns and it cleans well. The disadvantage of Berber carpeting is that if a loop is pulled, it can unravel like a run in a nylon stocking. This requires extensive repair work. There are dozens of brands of carpeting with each firm producing a number of grades. The minimum FHA specifications are of a low-quality carpeting that you will not want to use in a rental property. The carpet just would not hold up.

When evaluating carpeting, experts will look at the backing. Padding is also very important.

When the lines of threads are tight and close together on the jute backing, this means it is a denser, better quality carpet. By checking the underside of a very cheap carpeting and expensive carpeting you'll soon realize the difference in carpet quality.

Your carpet dealer will be your best instructor. Because the dealer will want your continued business, he or she will instruct and guide you as to carpet types and quality for your properties.

G. AIR FILTERS

Dirty air filters reduce the flow of air, increase cooling and heating costs, and place unnecessary strain on air conditioning and heating systems.

Tenants have been known to remove filters when air flow decreases. This results in dirt, otherwise trapped in the filter, to flow into the rental space. Dirty streaks form across ceilings and around heating and cooling vents. This results in the need to repaint between tenants. Because removal of a filter is difficult to substantiate, the property damage bond may not cover the cost. The tenant will claim normal wear and tear.

VOICE OF EXPERIENCE:

Because air filters are relatively inexpensive and easy to install, you should install new filters at the beginning of your tenancies and replace the filters on a regular basis.

New metal filters are available that can be washed, however, the washing time of the metal filters may be more costly than simple replacement with fiber glass filters.

In some properties, such as laboratories, cleanliness is of extreme importance. You may use electronic filters to electrically charge particles in the air and trap them. These filters require a regular maintenance schedule.

H. PRESSURE WASHING

Walkways in malls and shopping centers can get filthy over a short period of time with stains, wads of gum, etc.

Pressure washing and/or steam cleaning can be used on walkways, patios, garage floors, concrete driveways, and parking areas. It is a quick way to remove dirt. Most stains can also be removed or be significantly reduced with available detergents on the market that can be used with the pressure washer.

Pressure washing can also be used to clean exterior walls and remove algae-type growth from walls in areas with high moisture and humidity.

Professional pressure washers charge by the job or a per-hour rate. Some management firms own their own pressure washers or purchase them for owners of large properties.

I. GRAFFITI

Some communities will paint over graffiti at no cost.

Gang slogans, messages, and obscenities spray-painted on walls will affect an area economically. Many people are intimidated by areas of heavy graffiti.

One large department store has one of its service personnel go around the exterior of the building at 7 A.M. every morning and roller-paint over any art displays from the night before. After many months, the graffiti has almost ceased because the perpetrators have realized what is happening.

Painted buildings are best touched up with latex-based paint. However, for brick and stone structures, pressure washing, solvents, and even sandblasting may be necessary to obliterate graffiti. Once gone from brick or stone, there are a number of treatments that can be applied to act as a sealer and/or make paint difficult to adhere, allowing pressure washing to quickly remove the graffiti.

J. EXTERMINATORS

Although some tenants will bring roaches, earwigs, ants, etc., into your building because of poor housekeeping, even the most immaculate tenant can't eliminate this problem.

For apartment units, we recommend negotiating a price per unit for monthly extermination service.

When you're negotiating for 1,000 units, you will find that exterminators will develop very sharp pencils. Don't use employees to do extermination work because of liability problems.

K. PIGEONS

As a manager of commercial and office properties, you will often encounter serious problems involving pigeons. They create a mess and are believed to be responsible for the spread of disease. Many properties have more than one person employed on a full-time basis just to clean sidewalks and benches in plaza areas.

The most effective way to eliminate the pigeons is to cut off their source of food.

Pigeons disappear when people stop feeding them. While you have no control over offsite feeding, you can stop tenants, employees, and guests from doing so on your property.

Some commercial firms claim that they can rid your property of pigeons. The schemes include:

1. **Cutouts or Plastic Owls and Snakes.** These scare the pigeons for a short time, however, they soon realize they're no threat.

2. **Ultra-high Frequency Sounds.** The effect does not seem to be permanent.

3. **Recordings of Distress.** Recordings of pigeons in distress or pain are a short-term remedy.

4. **Gooey Substances.** Sticky substances spread on ledges works for awhile, but soon collects dirt that cakes the substances and the pigeons return.

5. **Bed of Nails.** Plastic strips with protruding plastic nails (about 3" x 4" in length) can be attached to ledges to take away the roosting site. While they are effective, they must be applied to every possible roosting area. Even then, you may only find that the pigeons have moved to the next building and still mess your walkways, etc.

Many of these remedies are a double-edged sword: not a perfect solution.

6. **Raptors.** Hawks moving into an area will cause the pigeons to decrease significantly. Check with your Department of Natural Resources or Fish and Game Commission. Making your property more inviting to raptors could have a negative effect. One property manager who managed to attract raptors to his office building received many complaints from horrified tenants witnessing hawks tearing apart pigeons on the ledges of their office windows.

7. **Traps.** State and local officials might approve the use of traps to catch the pigeons. If you release the pigeons rather than destroy them, they will likely migrate back to your property.

8. **Poison. Never use poison.** Dead pigeons cause public relations problems. Also, you could pass the poison on to a protected species such as raptors. In addition, you can expose yourself to great liability even if you received approvals to use poison.

We are not aware of any magic bullet for pigeon control. Your state Department of Fish and Game might have some suggestions based on your situation.

L. GULLS, DUCKS, AND GEESE

Like pigeons, these birds cause problems to property owners. A beautiful landscaped garden and pond can become an eyesore that no one will come near.

Some golf courses have resorted to controlled shooting to try to keep the numbers in check. *ROCKET NETS can catch whole flocks for relocation purposes and have been effective with geese.* You must check with your Department of Fish and Game before dealing with migratory waterfowl. Local ordinances may prohibit shooting them or the use of poison. In Las Vegas, one golf course is using a specially trained sheep dog to chase ducks and geese away from the greens.

M. CLEANING

Depending upon the size and type of cleaning, you can use contract services or employees. You want to set up specifications of the jobs to be done so that personnel and supervisory personnel know what is expected of them.

By attending trade shows, you will discover equipment and products that can make cleaning jobs more efficient as well as provide labor savings.

N. TEMPORARY CLEAN-UP WORK

A relatively low-cost clean-up method is to use a temporary service when you need unskilled labor to do simple jobs around your property. These services cover worker's compensation, unemployment insurance, and carry liability coverage. Hiring temporary service is often quicker than trying to bring in a contractor.

Your local services most likely have people with their own tools who are qualified to perform some trade tasks.

Never hire the jobless who congregate in the early morning hours at the local 7-11® or paint store or other locations because you could create a worker's compensation problem should any hired worker be injured.

In addition, you might find that you're hiring someone with physical or emotional problems or drug or alcohol dependency.

O. ALUMINUM WIRING

Aluminum wiring was used from the 1960s into the early 1970s because it was cheaper than copper.

The price of copper was relatively high because of the Vietnam War. Aluminum wiring tends to oxidize where it meets copper wire or a brass electrical fixture connection. A gap develops and electricity can jump the gap and result in a serious fire hazard.

By removing electrical wall plates, you can usually determine if you have aluminum wiring (a silver-gray wire). An electrical contractor or engineer should be contacted if any corrective measures are needed. It could be just cleaning connections or it could mean rewiring.

III. Improvements

A. DEFINITION

IMPROVEMENTS are additions to property. Improvements are more than just repairs because you are giving the property something that was not there before.

An improvement could be an air conditioner that the building did not have. However, replacing an air conditioning compressor unit and cooling fan assembly are only repairs.

A property owner will prefer that your monthly statement show work performed as a repair rather than as an improvement.

Repairs can be totally written off as an operating expense in the year the work was performed. An improvement must be added to the owner's cost base and only a small portion written off on the improvement each year (depreciation), depending on its lifespan. There are gray areas distinguishing between what are repairs and what are improvements. Don't be dishonest. In such situations, your billings should reflect whether you regard the work performed as maintaining a status or giving the property something it never had.

B. ECONOMIC AND UNECONOMIC IMPROVEMENTS

Overimprovements are not good economic choices.

In determining the economics of an improvement, consider the effect the improvement has on the net income. As an example, assume you want to add a tennis court at a 12-unit apartment building site. Assume the construction costs will be $60,000 and the estimated annual maintenance will be $2,400. Assume that the tennis court can allow you to raise rents $20 per unit per month.

The mathematics of this improvement are:

12 x $20   = $240.00 per month additional income
12 x $240 = $2,880.00 increase in annual gross income

$2,880.00
- 2,400.00 annual maintenance
  $480.00 annual net income

$480 ÷ $60,000 = .008

The investment would provide 8-tenths of one percent return on income. No investor would consider this acceptable. Nevertheless, the investment might be made by an owner who wanted pride of ownership and/or use of the courts.

However, assume a hot spa and sauna could be added for $8,000 that would allow rents to be raised by $20 per month for each unit. Assume estimated maintenance costs at $1,800 per year.

Using these figures:

$20 x 12   = $240 per month rent increase
$240 x 12 = $2,880 per year rent increase

$2,880.00
-1,800.00 maintenance
$1,080.00 net revenue gain

$1,080 ÷ $8,000 = 13.5

A 13.5% return on investment would make this improvement appear economically viable. The numbers speak for themselves.

An uneconomic investment based on present mathematics might nevertheless be economically sound if it keeps vacancies down in a marketplace where an oversupply of units is anticipated. Another factor is if tenants are less likely to move, additional maintenance and vacancy periods are reduced.

The owner of a 15-unit, garden-style office complex recently spent $25,000 on improved landscaping that included a fountain, bird feeders, picnic tables, etc. in an interior courtyard. Although the tenants were on multi-year leases with no chance of rent increases, the owner's sole purpose for the improvements was tenant retention when the leases expired. The owner of this office complex wanted a unique feature that would keep the tenants and their employees happy.

When an area is undergoing a positive change, such as a gentrification of a rundown neighborhood, improvements to bring a property up to par with neighboring properties is normally an economic decision based on potential increases to income and/or value. When the neighborhood is declining, improvements are unlikely to be economically sound.

Curb-appeal improvements, such as new facades or landscaping, don't affect the rental space, but they will affect the rental. Improvements such as these increase interest in the property by prospective renters, and give the tenants a sense of pride that can reduce tenant turnover.

IV. Mechanic's Liens

Unpaid contractors, subcontractors, and material providers can place a lien against property for which they supplied goods or services if they have not been paid. This is called a **MECHANIC'S LIEN. In many states, unlicensed contractors cannot file a mechanic's lien.**

If a tenant has authorized work on the premises, you want to make certain that the contractor cannot go against the property. You would record and post a ***NOTICE OF NONRESPONSIBILITY*** *on the premises to protect against this type of problem. The notice would state that the owner is not responsible for any work on the premises.* This notice must be both recorded and posted within a statutory period of having knowledge of any work that has begun. Failure to do so could subject the owner to liabilities for the work, even though the owner was not the person who authorized it.

As the property manager, your failure to protect the owner could subject you to liability.

The contractor could foreclose on the property to satisfy the judgment if it were not paid.

In shopping centers where stores are being fixtured and/or remodeled by tenants, you will often see notices of nonresponsibility posted on the plywood covering the storefront.

Where ground leases or other leases require the tenants to construct improvements, the owner will generally not be protected by a notice of nonresponsibility.

In many states, prior to filing a lien, a contractor must serve a preliminary notice on the prime contractor, the lender, and the owner.

In representing the owner, if you receive such a notice from a subcontractor then you will want to make certain that the subcontractor is paid. You could pay direct, or as part payment for the work give the prime contractor a check payable to the subcontractor who had filed a preliminary notice.

The filing period of a lien differs by state. Filing a notice of completion may shorten the lien period.

A bill does not have to be paid just because the contractor threatens to file a lien. If the lien is filed, you can get it removed by posting a bond. You can then have the court decide as to the rights involved.

Mechanic's liens seldom become a problem on small repair jobs. They do become problems on large dollar repairs or improvements where subcontractors are involved.

Even though contractors may fail to file a lien, it does not mean that they aren't entitled to be paid. The debt remains even though the lien rights are lost. To enforce the debt, the contractor would have to sue on the debt, obtain a judgment and then go against the debtor's property.

VOICE OF EXPERIENCE:

The longer you're in the business of property management, the longer your list of competent contractors and subcontractors will become. Share information with other professionals. Networking with brokers, builders, and other related fields will help you develop good contacts and give work to those who deserve repeat business.

V. Energy Conservation

From a strictly economic sense, the reduction of energy costs to property owners is a benefit as it increases the bottom-line return on an investment.

An additional benefit and ethical consideration is that the use of less energy produces cleaner air and the saving of nonrenewable resources for the future. Savings in energy and water consumption are earth-friendly activities that all of us should embrace.

Saving on water is becoming more important as our clean water sources are depleted and our need for water increases.

Conservation of our natural resources should concern all.

A. HEATING AND AIR CONDITIONING ENGINEERS

A heating and air conditioning engineer can evaluate your building and make energy-saving recommendations.

Older air conditioning and heating units are less efficient than newer units today. An engineer can evaluate usage and tell you how long it should take to recover the initial costs of installing a new unit so that an economic decision can be made.

The engineer can also recommend economic modifications to existing systems and energy conservation methods for your particular property. Your local gas and electric companies may provide this evaluation as a free service.

B. GOING TO INDIVIDUAL UNITS

Landlords who pay for central air and heat provide no incentive for tenants to conserve energy. Tenants who pay for these services become cost conscious.

Heating and air conditioning engineers can evaluate the possible cost benefit of changing a central system to individual systems for each unit. You will have to figure in any rent adjustments where needed if the tenants are to bear these costs. You can also determine how long it will take to recapture your investment in the individual systems. Sometimes conversion is too costly to make economic sense.

C. AUTOMATIC DAMPER CONTROL

An automatic damper control on a furnace keeps the flue open while the burners are on and closes it when the burners go off. Furnace generated heat, which would otherwise escape the building through the flue, is instead trapped within the building to provide additional heat.

D. ELECTRIC USE CONTROLS

Lower electric rates are possible in many areas. This is possible if you agree to have the electric company install a unit that allows the provider to turn off the air conditioning unit for up to 15 minutes if an overload is threatened within the service. The savings makes sense because this service only affects the air conditioner for relatively short periods of time. Check your local electric utility provider about the availability of this type of plan.

E. WATER HEATERS

You will want to install an energy-efficient water heater, if it is to be replaced, rather than just shopping for the lowest priced unit. Savings can quickly add up for a slightly higher priced unit. If you're using a gas water heater, you will want one with an electronic ignition rather than one where the pilot light is constantly burning up gas.

All water heaters should be wrapped with an insulation blanket and in earthquake-prone states, it is required that they be strapped.

F. LIGHTS

Have you ever seen yard lights turned on in the middle of the day? By operating lights on a single photoelectric cell or a timer you can avoid this problem. A timer should be checked every few weeks to adjust for the change in times of sunrise and sunset and readjusted after any power outage.

More light for less energy is possible by using exterior mercury or sodium vapor lighting.

In common areas, fluorescent lights use considerably less power for the desired level of lighting. The fluorescent tubes produce less light as they get older. Therefore, some managers change them once a year. They claim that following this procedure also avoids flickering tubes and costly trips replacing one tube at a time. This is a time consuming problem in office buildings with thousands of fluorescent lights.

G. FIREPLACES

Fireplaces work because the air traveling over the chimney draws air out of the building. However, what makes for a cheery blaze can be an expensive waste of energy. Unless the flue is closed, cool or hot air will be drawn from the building. In most modern buildings fireplaces are equipped with a metal lever to close off the chimney opening. Fireplaces in older buildings lack this feature.

Many old Victorian homes with multiple fireplaces have been converted to highly desirable office units. As a manager of such property, you want to be certain that the fireplaces are inoperable by blocking off the flues or that glass doors are installed so the air vents can be closed when the fireplaces are not in use.

H. SOLAR HEAT

Solar heaters act as heat collectors drawing heat from the sun and transferring it to a water source. Solar heaters are not likely to be cost effective for heating a structure. However, in some areas of the country they have become quite cost effective in heating water, particularly swimming pools.

Early solar collectors made of plastic soon deteriorated in the sunlight that caused leaks in the system. Products have improved today and prices have also come down. Past installations of solar units were often done at exorbitant prices.

You should evaluate the cost effectiveness of using solar heating for swimming pools because using this system alone is not adequate. You will need a back-up gas heater when the weather cools and the sun does not shine for several days. You will also need a gas heater to back up any solar heating system to reach desired temperatures for use with a spa.

Talk to owners and managers who use particular solar systems about any savings and/or problems.

I. SOLAR LIGHTS

Solar powered lights use a solar battery to receive power from the sun. The lights can then be set to go on at dusk using a photoelectric cell. Lighting is limited to the size of the solar collector. Although not sufficient for security purposes, they can be used to light driveways and for landscaping effects. Solar powered lighting is normally used for limited illumination in noncritical areas where the cost would be excessive for electrical wiring.

J. WATER CONSERVATION

If the owners supply water to the units, as manager, you should be interested in water conservation methods. Low-volume adapters placed on kitchen faucets and showers reduce water usage. These are especially important if owners supply hot water.

Water tanks on older commodes can be fitted with one or two bricks to reduce the use of water. You would then want to check that the commode works properly. Of course, if this method now requires two flushes, it defeats the purpose.

In summer, more water may be used on greenery than is used inside homes. This is a significant area where water savings are possible.

You may want to introduce native plants into the landscaping.

If you don't have an onsite maintenance service, you should sign on with a sprinkler service who will check regularly and adjust and repair the system as needed.

Clocks on automatic sprinkler systems should be adjusted according to the time of year. In warm weather, sprinklers should be on every day and in severe heat, during the evening or early morning hours. Watering can be cut to every second or third day during cold periods. Use also depends upon if you're watering lawns or flower beds, which may require different sprinkler heads and more or less time.

Resident managers or maintenance personnel may find in winter that the sprinklers need only be on 20 to 25 percent of the time that they need to be on during the summer months. Setting sprinkling time is not a real science; the best method is to cut back in the water until the grass begins to look dry and then increase the watering time.

New lawns or rehabilitating neglected lawns requires setting the sprinkler system to several times per day for short periods to keep the ground moist but not washing away the seeding. Evening hours are the best when water pressure is high, such as 11 P.M. to 3 A.M. You would want your resident manager or maintenance personnel to make a visual inspection daily for trouble spots and broken sprinkler heads or lines. They should inspect each clock station approximately every two weeks.

Repairing sprinkler systems is very low-tech work and it only takes PVC cement, a stock of PVC fittings, a few extra pieces of tubing and sprinkler heads to handle most repairs. Should training be required, most home improvement companies regularly conduct classes in the installation and repair of sprinkler systems.

Resident managers should be on the alert to shut off sprinkler systems when the grounds are saturated by rain.

K. VENTING

Dead air space above the ceiling becomes super heated from the sun on the roof. Even with relatively good insulation and passive venting, this hot, dead air space adds to cooling costs.

Wind-powered, rotating turbine-style vents are a low cost way to solve the problem.

The wind-powered vent expels hot air and forces outside air in through other roof or eave vents. Wind-powered vents help but they don't let in much air compared to power vents.

POWER VENTS are large power fans that push air out of the building and can be mounted on the roof or gable end. They can be purchased for approximately $100.

Included with the power vent is a thermostat that allows the fan to turn on when attic space reaches the setting on the thermostat (such as 80 degrees) and turn off when the temperature falls below the setting. One problem with power vents is that in desert communities the fans tend to run 24 hours per day for months on end because of the desert heat. Burned out bearings after two years of constant operation are not uncommon. However, replacement is a half-hour job which is well worth the savings. Most of these fans mounted on sloped or gabled surfaces can be installed within one to two hours. They use no more current than a 16-inch or 20-inch house fan, so the benefits are significant compared to the cost.

L. INSULATION

Sometimes more is better, depending on temperatures in your state.

Insulation is measured by R-VALUE (RESISTANCE VALUE). The higher the R Value, the better the insulation. You should use R Value to evaluate insulation material.

1. Ceiling

If the building has a roof with a pitch and the rooms have flat ceilings then there is dead air space between the ceiling and roof. There should be an access panel to this dead air or attic space. The panel might be in a closet or in an attached garage. To check ceiling insulation is simple with access to this space.

Today, if you have less than 8 inches of insulation, consider adding to make it between 12 inches and 18 inches in the ceiling area. Insulation is light so it will not cause a weight problem for the ceiling drywall unless there is a significant roof leak.

The additional insulation will probably be cost-effective in energy savings within three years.

It is relatively inexpensive in material and labor costs to blow in loose insulation. We feel that this method is the better way to go for flat surfaces rather than using batts of insulation. Batt insulation tacked into place works best for sloped surfaces such as between rafters inside a building.

Any insulation improvements will save the owner money as well as the tenants if they are paying their own heating and cooling bills. Besides justifying a rent increase, lower costs will make the tenant less likely to move.

Insulation can also be placed in a hanging or dropped ceiling. However, the dead air space created between the dropped ceiling and the roof should be vented.

Where you have a flat or pitched roof with a vaulted ceiling and high heating and cooling costs, you might want to consider installing a foam roof. Foam roofs contribute to insulation. Foam roofs should be regularly treated with a special paint that helps to reflect light and prevent the foam from deteriorating.

Another option for a flat roof building is to install two-inch styrofoam planks to the ceiling and apply a plaster-like coating for a finished appearance.

2. Walls

Place your hand on the inside of an exterior wall and on an interior wall. If you feel little difference in the temperature then the insulation is probably adequate.

If the exterior wall feels hot when temperatures soar or cold when the thermometer drops, the insulation may be inadequate or might be nonexistent.

One solution is to apply styrofoam sheets with mastic to the interior of the exterior walls and then finish the surface with a troweled or sprayed treatment. If new aluminum or vinyl siding is planned, styrofoam sheathing can be added.

Insulation was not used in the exterior walls of many old frame structures. You can easily determine if this is the case by removing an electrical plate and checking around the box. To blow in insulation or insert foam insulation, you can cut access holes through either the interior or exterior walls.

The blown insulation often settles so that the upper few inches of the wall ends up with little if any insulation, which can be a problem.

In the past, foam insulation forced into exterior wall cavities caused toxic fumes, creating an allergic reaction in many people.

Before you decide to insulate, consult with a heating and cooling engineer about cost effectiveness based on cost recovery through energy savings, as well as the most effective method and materials to use.

3. Caulking and Weatherstripping

Savings in heating and cooling costs can be achieved by using tubes of caulking that cost about a dollar each.

Check the caulking around windows and doors and where the exterior wall and foundation meet. Another area to check is where the top of the wall meets the soffit. Caulking should be done in areas where it has deteriorated or is missing.

Any exterior painting contracts should include caulking.

Drafts around windows and doors normally indicates a need for better weatherstripping. Your maintenance personnel should be familiar with the best type to use of the various brands on the market.

A snugly fitting threshold with a raised vinyl insert is one of the easiest solutions to a draft coming in from under a door.

4. Windows

Consider double- or triple-glazed window units that provide extra insulation when windows are to be replaced during remodeling.

Storm window units are available that are really add-on exterior glazed units. They are usually double-hung or sliding units installed easily on the exterior of existing windows. They are relatively inexpensive. Some are aluminum frames with built-in plastic moldings for a tight fit over an exterior wall.

In the sunbelt, many people believe that single-glazed windows are adequate, but heat can go both ways. Old, single-glazed windows allow a lot of heat to enter, which raises air conditioning costs in many warm parts of the country.

Reflective tinted windows can also reduce the heat of the sun but also reduce the light entering the building. Again, check with a heating and cooling engineer before attempting to change any windows.

5. Basement Walls

Frost lines in cold climates can be four feet or more into the ground. Concrete block or poured concrete walls do not provide much insulation.

The easiest way to insulate the interior walls of a basement is to apply two-inch thick styrofoam which is available in 4-foot by 8-foot panels. Mastic can be used to apply the styrofoam directly to the basement walls. Plaster can be troweled onto the styrofoam surface for a finished appearance.

6. Basement Windows

While regular windows are often double glazed, basement windows are usually single glazed. This can create heat loss in cold areas. Two solutions are storm window kits, or clear plastic exterior shields which leave dead air space outside the basement windows. These weather shields are readily available.

7. Insulation Paint

RADIANCE PAINT is available in the United States. It has a low E-Value, which means it reflects heat. This paint is applied to interior surfaces. Developers claim that it radiates 40 percent of the heat back into the room in winter and blocks heat from entering in the summer. Energy savings of up to 30 percent have been reported with this paint.

Consider a special reflective paint for flat roofs. Dark colored roofing can be hot because dark colors, such as black, absorb heat, whereas the reflective roof paint is relatively cool and could be cost effective.

This principal of dark colors absorbing heat and light colors reflecting heat can be applied when you decide to reroof with asphalt shingles. In cold areas of the country, where heating costs are greater than cooling costs, a dark colored roofing would be beneficial. If cooling costs are your primary concern, then you would probably be interested in reroofing with white shingles.

8. Duct Work

Dirty ducts slow the passage of air through a structure. For efficient heating and cooling, air ducts should be cleaned with frequency that would vary according to location.

Ducts that carry hot or cold air as well as hot and chilled water pipes should be wrapped with insulation to minimize loss or gain in temperature through heat transfer.

M. COMPUTERIZED BUILDINGS

Over 30 years ago, Honeywell developed a program where computers determined how heating and air conditioning should be operated inside a building. For instance, assume an office building is vacant from 7 P.M. until 7 A.M. the following morning and that at 7 P.M. the temperature outside is 80 degrees with an expected low of 79 degrees. At what temperature should the interior of the building reach during the unoccupied hours for the air conditioner to cool the building down to 75 degrees by 7 A.M. the following morning? If this were to be determined by guessing, a great deal of energy probably would be wasted allowing the cooling system to run unregulated during the evening hours.

A computerized building system can calculate the most energy efficient operation considering exterior temperatures and the direction and speed of the wind. Basically, the computer relays to the operating engineer or the controls directly how the system should be operated to obtain the required temperatures during the work day using the least amount of energy.

This concept first surfaced in the early 1960s when energy was cheap and computers were expensive, so it took many years to adopt. Even now, few buildings are making full use of available technology.

VI. CHAPTER SUMMARY

While preventative maintenance should be the main focus, breakdowns will occur which require repairs and/or replacements.

Economic factors as well as management requirements play a part in decisions about what maintenance, if any, shall be performed by employees or contract services. Some management firms have their own separate maintenance companies. These firms avoid a conflict of interest by fully informing owners about how they charge for the work. The property owners, in turn, must give informed permission to use these maintenance firms.

By developing work specifications, you can get truly competitive bids with bidders conducting their bidding on a level playing field.

Standardizing replacement hardware makes future repairs less costly.

Repairs should be prioritized so that minor jobs are not performed first while major problems are placed on a waiting list. Repairs should not be "first come first served."

As the property manager, you should develop a core group of responsible contractors who can be counted on to do a proper job. Price alone is not enough. Reliability and service are also of great importance.

In scheduling work as needed rather than performing work by the calendar, you might be able to free personnel for other tasks.

Maintenance records are important to track work and identify problems.

Maintenance personnel should wear identifying uniforms and name tags for tenants to recognize and build up a relationship with your personnel.

Staffing requirements will vary as to the particular property and management needs.

Specific maintenance tasks include:

1. Roofs. Repair or replacement may be necessary. Pitch and the load-bearing capabilities of the roof would determine the type of roof replacement.

2. Roof leaks can often be visually identified. If not, areas to check are around vents and chimneys, where the flat area meets the pitched area or where the roof meets a wall.

3. Plumbing. You may want to negotiate with a plumbing firm to contract on a per-call basis to include one-half hour of labor plus an hourly rate thereafter.

4. Furnace and Air Conditioning. An annual service contract as well as a per-call contract should be considered.

5. Paint. Limiting the colors makes touch-up jobs easy. Exterior paint jobs can be limited to only those sides that require paint or just the trim or part of the trim.

6. Carpeting. A quality pad is important to the life of the carpet. Try standardizing and contracting for quality carpet at a price per-square yard to include labor and material. This arrangement can apply to multiple properties.

7. Air Filters. You should be in charge of replacement to make certain the job has been done. Clean filters reduce wear on equipment and interior painting needs.

8. Pressure Washing. Sidewalks, patios, garage floors, driveways and parking areas and walls should be cleaned periodically.

9. Graffiti. Graffiti should be removed as soon as it appears. Pressure washing, painting or even sandblasting may be required for removal.

10. Exterminators. Exterminating jobs should be contracted for as to price per unit to ensure savings.

11. Pigeons. Pigeons create problems for office buildings and require frequent cleanups. Prohibiting the feeding of pigeons by tenants will help alleviate the problem.

12. Gulls, Ducks and Geese. They also create problems such as cleaning. Contact your state Department of Fish and Game for control possibilities.

13. Temporary Clean-Up Work. Consider using a temporary-help service for special jobs. The cost is usually less and the work is often done faster than if contracted for.

Improvements involve providing something new that was not there before. The owner must write off costs over the life of the improvements while repairs are expensed out during the year in which the repairs were made.

Economic decisions about improvements include the return on the investment in increased revenue, the effect on vacancy rate and future revenues.

Unpaid contractors, subcontractors, or material providers have a right to file a mechanic's lien after a preliminary notice. After filing a notice of completion the period for the mechanic to file a lien is set.

If a tenant authorizes work to be done, you will want a notice of nonresponsibility recorded and posted so that the property does not become subject to a lien.

Energy conservation is important to reduce costs and help preserve our environment. Heating and air conditioning engineers can recommend cost savings. Individual heating and cooling units give tenants an incentive to save energy.

Automatic damper controls reduce the loss of heat through the flue. Some electric companies give reduced rates if you agree to have your air conditioning units equipped with a shut-off unit to allow your electric provider to turn off your air conditioner for brief periods should a threatened overload occur.

Consider one of the new more energy-efficient water heaters when replacement is needed. Existing water heaters should be wrapped with an insulation blanket.

Outside lighting should be connected to timers or photo electric cells. Florescent lights are less costly to operate.

Fireplaces draw hot and cold air from the building when left open.

Solar heat may be cost effective for swimming pools. Solar lights can be used for lighting landscapes.

Water conservation is possible by using low flow adapters on faucets and showers, the use of low water requirement commodes, use of bricks in commode tanks, and checking sprinkler systems.

Venting dead air space reduces the heat build-up. Passive vents, air turbine or wind power vents, are available as well as the preferred fan-operated power vents.

Additional insulation can be installed in both ceilings and walls to conserve energy. Caulking and weatherstripping will also reduce energy needs. Double-glazed windows provide better insulation than single glazed windows.

Styrofoam insulation can be applied with mastic to basement walls and weather shields can be place around basement windows.

Radiance paint is purported to radiate heat back into a building and prevent heat from entering during hot summer months. Reflective paint on a roof can reduce heat absorption. Light color shingles also reduce heat absorption.

Dirty ducts impede air flow. Ducts should be cleaned periodically and wrapped with insulation if used for hot or cold air.

Computerized systems installed in a building determine how heating and cooling systems should be operated.

VII. CHAPTER QUIZ

1. Which of the following repairs should be given the highest priority?
   a. Dripping faucet
   b. An inoperable commode
   c. An electrical outlet that does not work
   d. A broken bath tile

2. A roof with a one-inch pitch every 12 inches needs new roofing. You would NOT use:
   a. a built-up roof.
   b. tile.
   c. rubber roofing.
   d. foam roofing.

3. The location of a roof leak is not evident. Areas to consider as to likely spots would be:
   a. around vents.
   b. around the chimney.
   c. where the roof meets a wall or parapet.
   d. all of the above.

4. To reduce summer air conditioning costs, the best color for roof shingles would be:
   a. white.
   b. black.
   c. brown.
   d. green.

5. Dirty air filters:
   a. reduce cooling and heating effectiveness.
   b. cause additional wear on equipment.
   c. both a and b.
   d. neither a nor b.

6. Pigeons can be completely eliminated as a problem by:
   a. using recordings of wounded birds.
   b. placing plastic owls on the property.
   c. placing plastic snakes on window ledges.
   d. none of the above.

7. The advantages in using temporary service workers rather than a contractor for unskilled labor jobs would be:
   a. speed in getting the job done.
   b. a likely lower cost.
   c. both a and b.
   d. neither a nor b.

8. From an owner's point of view, the difference between improvements and repairs would be:
   a. repairs are more costly.
   b. improvements must be written off over the life of the improvement.
   c. repairs can be shown as an expense in the year of the repair.
   d. both b and c.

9. An insulated blanket would likely be used to cover a(n):
   a. water heater.
   b. air filter.
   c. sprinkler system.
   d. solar collector.

10. The purpose of placing bricks in a commode tank would be to:
   a. soften the water.
   b. reduce the use of water.
   c. prevent the tank from cracking.
   d. increase the water pressure.

ANSWERS: 1. b; 2. b; 3. d; 4. a; 5. c; 6. d; 7. c; 8. d; 9. a; 10. b

DANGER
TRUCTION AREA
EP OUT

CONSTRUCTION SITE
SAFETY RULES

1. HARD HATS REQUIRED.
2. PROPER WORK SHOES REQUIRED.
3. NO SHORTS.
4. NO RADIOS.
5. NO GLASS BOTTLES.
6. NO ALCOHOL OR DRUGS ALLOWED.

Chapter 11
Records and Controls

KEY WORDS AND TERMS

1099
Ad Register
Annual Statement
Audits
Beneficiary Ledger
Broker Funds
Cash Ledger
Commingling
Comparative Operating Statement
Computer Management Software
Employee Files
Eviction Register
Good Funds
Inactive Files
Inspection Report
Insurance Register
Interpleader Action
Interest-Bearing Trust Account
Inventory File
Journal

Lease Files
Monthly Statement
Mortgage File
Move-Outs Owing
Occupancy Factor
Offset of Trust Funds
Operating Budget
Operational Costs and Expenses
Pass-Through Funds
Payroll Records
Percentage Lease Verification
Purchase Orders
Reconciliation of Trust Account
Rent Rolls
Telephone Records
Trust Account
Trust Fund Account
Utility Files
Vendor Files

CHAPTER 11 OUTLINE

I. Trust Fund Accounting

Property management involves the receipt of funds such as rents, security deposits, and money received for a particular service or disbursement. Document all revenue and expenses clearly for landlord's files and information.

*Money that is not the funds of the property manager, or is not yet the funds of the property manager, but are being held for some purpose or future disbursement, would be considered **TRUST FUNDS**.*

Funds received on behalf of a principal or others would be trust funds. *NONTRUST FUNDS would be broker/property manager-owned funds.*

Trust funds do not have to be cash. They could be a personal note, or a note secured by a trust deed or even a pink slip to a car given as a deposit (these would be trust assets). The property owner must be informed of the nature of any deposit not in the form of cash, check or money order.

A. FUNDS RECEIVED BY PROPERTY MANAGER

As a property manager who receives funds of others, you may properly do the following:

Trust Account. Funds can be placed in the your trust account. In most states, the deadline is the end of the third business day following the receipt of the funds.

Service Provider. You may pay the funds to a service provider such as a credit agency or for a repair bill if authorized to do so. (The checks received might be made out to the service provider.)

Be extremely cautious when disbursing trust funds.

Principal. If the principal is entitled to the funds, they can be given directly to the principal. Payment to the principal could create a problem if the deposit has to be returned to the person who made it because the principal fails to perform some condition or the funds were otherwise subject to some condition or required performance that fails to occur.

Chapter 11

B. CHECKS HELD NOT CASHED

VOICE OF EXPERIENCE:

Disclosure to all parties is a must. The owner must be informed if any deposit is not in the form of cash, check, or money order. He/she must also be notified if any tenant payments are held uncashed.

As a property manager, you may hold a lease deposit check and other deposits not cashed if the tenant or prospective tenant has instructed you not to cash the checks until something happens, such as the lessor agreeing to the lease. The property owner must be informed when tenant payments are held uncashed.

Upon satisfaction of any condition placed by the person depositing the funds, the funds must be placed in your trust account or must otherwise be disbursed.

C. FUNDS RECEIVED BY EMPLOYEES/AGENTS

No more than two people should be authorized to handle trust fund accounts.

Generally, funds received by your employees or agents must be either turned over to you, as the property manager, or deposited directly into your trust account if the person receiving the funds is authorized to do so.

D. THE TRUST ACCOUNT

In most states, the property manager's trust account must be a non interest-bearing demand account (checking account).

It should be in a financial institution insured by the Federal Deposit Insurance Corporation (FDIC).

Customarily, there is no interest earned on brokers' trust accounts.

The account must clearly indicate that it is a trust account held by the property manager as a trustee. Otherwise, your bankruptcy, death, or creditor judgements could tie up and possibly reach assets that were intended to be held in trust for others.

E. INTEREST-BEARING TRUST ACCOUNTS

Lessees may demand interest for their funds as part of the lease.

Interest-bearing trust accounts are not commonly maintained by property managers, but they are possible. As an example, an industrial lease for a long term, such as ten years, might have a $20,000 security deposit. If this were the case, the person depositing these funds might want the funds to be in an interest-bearing account as the interest over the lease period could be considerable.

The owner of the funds, who would be the lessee, could request the funds be placed in an interest-bearing account in a bank, savings bank, credit union, or industrial loan company providing the account is insured by the Federal Deposit Insurance Corporation.

As the property manager, in order to deposit funds in an interest-bearing account, the following criteria should be met for the account:

Name of Property Manager. The account must be in your name as trustee.

Insurance. All of the funds must be covered by insurance. (Deposits over the FDIC insurance limit might have to be placed in several accounts.)

Separation. The account must not only be separate from any of your funds, it should also be kept separate from trust funds held for others (this requires a separate trust fund for each such account). This relieves you, the property manager, of responsibility for determining interest allocations among a number of holders covering various time periods.

Disclosure. As the property manager, you must disclose to the person from whom the funds were received and the beneficiary of the funds:

1. the nature of the account;
2. how interest will be calculated and paid;
3. whether service charges will be paid to the depository and by whom, and
4. possible notice requirements or penalties for withdrawal.

Property Manager May Not Benefit. Interest earned on funds may not benefit you or any person licensed to you as the property manager (directly or indirectly).

F. DISBURSEMENTS FROM TRUST ACCOUNT

Withdrawals can generally be made from trust funds by you as the property manager, or by an employee (under a written contract) who has been specifically authorized in writing to make withdrawals.

As a property manager, an unlicensed employee of yours can also be authorized to make withdrawals. However, the unlicensed employee should be covered by a fidelity bond that is at least equal to the amount of the trust funds that the employee would have access to at any time.

Your state law will govern trust fund handling. California law is typical of state requirements. The California Code of Regulations 2834 covers trust fund withdrawals.

(a) Withdrawals may be made from a trust fund account of an individual broker only upon the signature of the broker or one or more of the following persons if specifically authorized in writing by the broker:

(1) A salesperson licensed to the broker.
(2) A person licensed as a broker who has entered into a written agreement pursuant to Section 2726 with the broker.
(3) An unlicensed employee of the broker with fidelity bond coverage at least equal to the maximum amount of the trust funds to which the employee has access at any time.

(b) Withdrawals may be made from the trust fund account of a corporate broker only upon the signature of:

(1) an officer through whom the corporation is licensed pursuant to Section 10158 or 10211 of the Code, or

(2) one of the persons enumerated in paragraph (1), (2), or (3) of subdivision (a) above, provided that specific authorization in writing is given by the officer through whom the corporation is licensed and that the officer is an authorized signatory of the trust fund account.

(c) An arrangement under which a person enumerated in paragraph (1), (2), or (3) of subdivision (a) above is authorized to make withdrawals from a trust fund account of a broker shall not relieve an individual broker, nor the broker-officer of a corporate broker licensee, from responsibility or liability as provided by law in handling trust funds in the broker's custody.

G. COMMINGLING TRUST FUNDS

COMMINGLING is the prohibited practice of mixing broker or general account funds with trust funds. Commingling could also be holding cash or checks uncashed without approval of the parties involved. Commingling is generally grounds for suspension or revocation of a real estate license.

Section 10176 of the California Business and Professions Code provides for revocation or suspension of a real estate license because of commingling.

leginfo.ca.gov/.html/bpc_table_of_contents.html
California Business and Professions Code

Grounds for Revocation or Suspension

10176. The commissioner may, upon his own motion, and shall, upon the verified complaint in writing of any person, investigate the actions of any person engaged in the business or acting in the capacity of a real estate licensee within this state, and he may temporarily suspend or permanently revoke a real estate license at any time where the licensee, while a real estate licensee, in performing or attempting to perform any of the acts within the scope of this chapter has been guilty of any of the following:

(e) Commingling with his own money or property the money or other property of others which is received and held by him.

Article 8 of the National Association of REALTORS® (NAR) Code of Ethics states:

"Realtors shall keep in a special account in an appropriate financial institution, separated from their own funds monies coming into their possession in trust for other persons, such as escrows, trust funds, client monies, and other like items."

realtor.org/mempolweb.nsf/pages/code
National Association of REALTORS® Code of Ethics

In California, it is considered commingling for a broker to fail to deposit designated trust funds into his or her trust account within three business days following receipt.

VOICE OF EXPERIENCE:

"Conversion" is the misappropriation and use of a client's funds. Spending (converting) funds that should be deposited in a trust account without your principal's authorization is a much more serious violation than commingling. The consequences may also be much more serious, including heavy criminal penalties.

H. PROPERTY MANAGER/BROKER FUNDS IN TRUST ACCOUNT

Property managers/brokers can keep a small amount of personal funds (according to state law) in the trust account.

The reason for allowing property managers to keep some of their own money in the account is to avoid any bank charges creating a shortage in the account. (Some property managers have the bank charges for their trust accounts charged against their general account.)

Depending on the laws in your state, you may also keep earned commissions in your trust account for a designated time period, such as 30 days.

I. RETURN OF TRUST FUNDS

Funds must be verified prior to disbursement.

If a lease or other transaction cannot be completed for reasons other than the default of the depositor, unexpended funds must be returned to the person making the deposit.

A shortage in the trust account could result if a deposit is returned before the deposit check has cleared and the deposit check fails to clear. This problem can be avoided by a

contract that clearly indicates that any check deposited must clear before any funds will be returned.

*Once a deposit has cleared a bank, it is considered **GOOD FUNDS***. As a property manager, you should not return a deposit or write a check to a service provider unless the check is written on good funds.

J. CONFLICTING CLAIMS ON TRUST FUNDS

Should both owner and tenant make a claim to funds held by you, the property manager, you should not turn the disputed funds over to either party.

If you turned over funds to one party without approval of the other party and a court later determined that the party receiving the funds was not entitled to them, you could be liable if the party receiving the funds was unwilling or unable to return those funds.

If the parties are unable to reach an agreement on disposition of trust funds, you could commence an ***INTERPLEADER ACTION***, *which is a legal proceeding where the stakeholder (property manager) deposits the funds with the court and asks the court to determine the rightful claimant.*

An "interpleader action" forces the parties to plead their case in court, which can be an expensive process for both parties.

Frequently, the legal expense is not justified by the dollars involved. As the property manager, you should recommend that the parties reach an agreement or compromise. Some contracts call for mandatory arbitration of disputes involving entitlement to trust funds.

K. OFFSET OF TRUST FUNDS

As a property manager, trust money held by you cannot be used to offset claims that you may have against the party depositing the funds or your principal.

As an example, suppose a prospective tenant placed a deposit with a lease application. Suppose the lease application was not accepted and the prospective tenant was entitled to the return of the deposit. Even though the prospective tenant may owe you money because of another transaction, you must return the funds in full and may not use such funds to offset the debt.

As a property manager with access to trust monies, you cannot take trust funds out of the account because the owner or tenant owes you a debt. The money remains trust money until the funds are disbursed.

L. TRUST FUND RECORDS

In your position as a property manager, you should keep a record of all trust funds received, including uncashed checks held. This record (including computer records) must set forth in chronological order the following information in columnar form:

Date. Date the trust funds are received.

Source. From whom trust funds were received.

Amount. Amount received.

Date Deposited. With respect to funds deposited in an account, date of said deposit.

Disbursement Data. With respect to trust funds previously deposited to an account, check number and date of related disbursement.

Pass-Through Funds. With respect to trust funds not deposited in an account, identify other depository and the date that the funds were forwarded. (If the funds pass through the broker's hands, even though the check or note is made out to another party, they are still considered to be trust funds.)

Daily Balance. Daily balance of said account. (Trust accounts should be balanced daily and reconciled with the bank account at least once a month.)

A separate record must be kept for each beneficiary or transaction that sets forth information sufficient to identify the transaction and the parties to the transaction, and also include the information required above.

While computer records may be kept rather than using forms, a backup disk is a safety factor that should be considered. There are a number of excellent software programs available for trust account record keeping.

Most states do not require that records be kept on particular forms, but we have included the following forms that have been prepared by the California Association of REALTORS®:

Figure 11-1. Trust Bank Account Record For All Trust Funds Deposited and Paid Out.

Figure 11-2. Trust Bank Account Record For Each Beneficiary.

Figure 11-3. Trust Funds Received and Released (Not Placed In Trust Bank Account).

M. RECONCILIATION OF TRUST ACCOUNT

The trust account should be reconciled at least once a month with the record of all trust funds received and disbursed (this applies to separate beneficiary records).

A record of the reconciliation should be maintained. This record must identify the:

Figure 11-1

**TRUST BANK ACCOUNT RECORD FOR ALL TRUST FUNDS
DEPOSITED AND WITHDRAWN**

(C.A.R. Form TAA, Revised 11/07)

Broker: _____

Address: _____

DATE	DEPOSIT (Received From)	OR	WITHDRAWAL (Paid To)	AMOUNT	BALANCE
					Forward from previous page $
	Name: _____ ☐ check ☐ cash ☐ _____ For: _____		Name: _____ Check # _____ For: _____	$	$
	Name: _____ ☐ check ☐ cash ☐ _____ For: _____		Name: _____ Check # _____ For: _____	$	$
	Name: _____ ☐ check ☐ cash ☐ _____ For: _____		Name: _____ Check # _____ For: _____	$	$
	Name: _____ ☐ check ☐ cash ☐ _____ For: _____		Name: _____ Check # _____ For: _____	$	$
	Name: _____ ☐ check ☐ cash ☐ _____ For: _____		Name: _____ Check # _____ For: _____	$	$
	Name: _____ ☐ check ☐ cash ☐ _____ For: _____		Name: _____ Check # _____ For: _____	$	$
	Name: _____ ☐ check ☐ cash ☐ _____ For: _____		Name: _____ Check # _____ For: _____	$	$
	Name: _____ ☐ check ☐ cash ☐ _____ For: _____		Name: _____ Check # _____ For: _____	$	$
	Name: _____ ☐ check ☐ cash ☐ _____ For: _____		Name: _____ Check # _____ For: _____	$	$
	Name: _____ ☐ check ☐ cash ☐ _____ For: _____		Name: _____ Check # _____ For: _____	$	$

TAA REVISED 11/07 (PAGE 1 OF 1)

Reviewed by _____ Date _____

EQUAL HOUSING OPPORTUNITY

TRUST BANK ACCOUNT RECORD FOR ALL TRUST FUNDS DEPOSITED AND WITHDRAWN (TAA PAGE 1 OF 1)

Agent: WALT HUBER	Phone:	Fax:	Prepared using zipForm® software
Broker: WALT HUBER REALTOR			

Figure 11-2

TRUST BANK ACCOUNT RECORD FOR EACH BENEFICIARY
(C.A.R. Form TAB, Revised 11/07)

Owner: _____

Address: _____

Remarks: _____

DATE	DEPOSIT (Received From)	OR	WITHDRAWAL (Paid To)	AMOUNT	BALANCE
	✕	✕	✕	✕	Forward from previous page $
	Name: _____ ☐ check ☐ cash ☐ ____ For: _____		Name: _____ Check # _____ For: _____	$	$
	Name: _____ ☐ check ☐ cash ☐ ____ For: _____		Name: _____ Check # _____ For: _____	$	$
	Name: _____ ☐ check ☐ cash ☐ ____ For: _____		Name: _____ Check # _____ For: _____	$	$
	Name: _____ ☐ check ☐ cash ☐ ____ For: _____		Name: _____ Check # _____ For: _____	$	$
	Name: _____ ☐ check ☐ cash ☐ ____ For: _____		Name: _____ Check # _____ For: _____	$	$
	Name: _____ ☐ check ☐ cash ☐ ____ For: _____		Name: _____ Check # _____ For: _____	$	$
	Name: _____ ☐ check ☐ cash ☐ ____ For: _____		Name: _____ Check # _____ For: _____	$	$
	Name: _____ ☐ check ☐ cash ☐ ____ For: _____		Name: _____ Check # _____ For: _____	$	$
	Name: _____ ☐ check ☐ cash ☐ ____ For: _____		Name: _____ Check # _____ For: _____	$	$
	Name: _____ ☐ check ☐ cash ☐ ____ For: _____		Name: _____ Check # _____ For: _____	$	$

TAB REVISED 11/07 (PAGE 1 OF 1)

Reviewed by _____ Date _____

EQUAL HOUSING OPPORTUNITY

TRUST BANK ACCOUNT RECORD FOR EACH BENEFICIARY (TAB PAGE 1 OF 1)

Agent: WALT HUBER	Phone:	Fax:	Prepared using zipForm® software
Broker: WALT HUBER REALTOR			

Figure 11-3

TRUST FUNDS RECEIVED AND RELEASED
(NOT PLACED IN TRUST BANK ACCOUNT)

CALIFORNIA ASSOCIATION OF REALTORS®

Broker: _____

Address: _____

Received From		Description	Value	Where Kept	Agent Initials	Instructions	Released To	
Name	Date						Name	Date
		☐ check ☐ cash ☐ note				☐ Hold until Acceptance + 3 Bus. Days		
		☐ check ☐ cash ☐ note				☐ Hold until Acceptance + 3 Bus. Days		
		☐ check ☐ cash ☐ note				☐ Hold until Acceptance + 3 Bus. Days		
		☐ check ☐ cash ☐ note				☐ Hold until Acceptance + 3 Bus. Days		
		☐ check ☐ cash ☐ note				☐ Hold until Acceptance + 3 Bus. Days		
		☐ check ☐ cash ☐ note				☐ Hold until Acceptance + 3 Bus. Days		
		☐ check ☐ cash ☐ note				☐ Hold until Acceptance + 3 Bus. Days		
		☐ check ☐ cash ☐ note				☐ Hold until Acceptance + 3 Bus. Days		
		☐ check ☐ cash ☐ note				☐ Hold until Acceptance + 3 Bus. Days		
		☐ check ☐ cash ☐ note				☐ Hold until Acceptance + 3 Bus. Days		
		☐ check ☐ cash ☐ note				☐ Hold until Acceptance + 3 Bus. Days		
		☐ check ☐ cash ☐ note				☐ Hold until Acceptance + 3 Bus. Days		
		☐ check ☐ cash ☐ note				☐ Hold until Acceptance + 3 Bus. Days		

Published and Distributed by:
REAL ESTATE BUSINESS SERVICES, INC.
a subsidiary of the California Association of REALTORS®
• 525 South Virgil Avenue, Los Angeles, California 90020

SM - OCT 99

REVISED 10/99

FORM TF-11

Agent: **WALT HUBER**
Broker: **WALT HUBER REALTOR**

Phone: _____ Fax: _____

Prepared using zipForm® software

OFFICE USE ONLY
Reviewed by Broker
or Designee _____
Date _____

EQUAL HOUSING OPPORTUNITY

1. **Identification of Account.** Bank account name and number;
2. **Date.** Date of the reconciliation;
3. **Beneficiaries.** Account number or name of the principals or beneficiaries or transactions, and
4. **Property Manager Liability.** The trust fund liability of the broker to each of the principals, beneficiaries or transactions.

N. RETENTION OF TRUST RECORDS

Files must be retained by broker for three years.

A real estate broker/property manager must maintain trust records (as well as other records relating to a transaction) for a statutory period, such as three years.

The retention period shall run from the date of closing of the transaction.

After notice, the records shall be made available for examination, inspection and copying by the Department of Real Estate, and be subject to audit without notice.

O. DRE AUDITS

Careless handling of trust funds may have dire consequences.

Your state Department of Real Estate views a shortage in a trust account and an unauthorized use of funds as very serious violations of the law. Because of the importance of safeguarding funds of others, there is a continuous program of examination of broker's records. Audits may result in disciplinary action if the trust fund is not in balance or if dangerous handling procedures are discovered. Criminal violations may be referred to the appropriate district attorney for possible criminal prosecution.

II. Owner Reports

A. MONTHLY STATEMENT

The monthly statement to an owner should show gross revenues and expenses paid. Expenses should be broken down by category so that an owner can see what has happened during the prior month. Figures for both income and expenses from a prior year for the same month can be included.

The check and monthly statement should be mailed so that they will be received by the owner on or about the same date each month. Some property managers beat their contractual obligation date for their monthly accounting.

VOICE OF EXPERIENCE:

If a check accompanying a monthly statement will appear to an owner to be surprisingly large or small, then the statement should include a notation explaining the inconsistency.

B. ANNUAL STATEMENT

The *ANNUAL STATEMENT is more than just a compilation of monthly statements for an owner's account to use in preparing taxes. It can also be a management tool to keep business, better owner/management relations and to use to upgrade the property.*

Some property managers like to meet with the owners to give them the annual statement. It provides an opportunity to strengthen owner/manager relations. It puts a face and adds a personality to letters and telephone calls. An owner who knows and likes you is less likely to get angry at you because of a single problem.

1. Multiple-Owner Properties

When an owner has multiple properties, there should be separate statements for each property, as well as a combined statement.

2. Comparative Operating Statement

Comparing actual data to the previous year is a good practice.

A comparative operating statement can show the past year and prior year figures. A benefit of such a statement is that it points out the problems and the strengths relating to the property and/or the economy. It is easy to understand and quickly explain where the differences are that relate to changes in the bottom line.

Expenses should be broken down into categories that can be clearly understood. If you receive a call from an owner asking what something means, it is an indication that the annual statement needs clarification.

3. Occupancy Factor

Some management firms include an occupancy factor in their annual statement. They will also indicate the occupancy rates for the prior year or prior years. It shows changes and helps to explain bottom line changes.

4. Average Rents

Some annual statements show average rent for the year to per unit or per square foot. The average rent is shown on prior years and the percentage change is noted.

5. Balance in Account

The annual statement should show the balance in the account as well as deposits held in trust, such as security deposits, with an explanation as to why fixed costs or variable costs have risen or decreased. An annual report might point out that while the occupancy rate declined 1.7 percent from the prior year, the area occupancy rate for similar property has declined by 2.4 percent. This is not "spin control"; it's a legitimate explanation of changes.

Everything but the "notes" on an annual report can be computer generated.

6. Addendums

As an addendum to the annual report, you should include an inspection report. The inspection report should be a detailed form with comments. Future significant expenses should be noted. When owners are informed of work required a year or more ahead of actual expenses, they accept the expenses more readily. The inspection report could indicate that a patched roof may require full replacement within the next three years.

Some property managers like to include estimated expenses and income for the coming year (operating budget). They will try to be realistic, which means not overly conservative or optimistic. They will also include a paragraph comparing how the annual statement related to the prior year estimates and reasons for deviation.

Some management firms like to provide an insurance summary showing the amount and type of insurance coverage for each property, as well as the name of the carrier.

The summary would footnote any changes made in insurance coverage and why.

The annual statement is an excellent communication tool if used properly.

The owner's 1099 statement should be included with the annual statement if applicable.

III. Management Records and Controls

A. LEASE FILES

Lease files will have the original lease signed by the tenant. Computer files should show lease termination dates, dates for extensions or exercise of options, as well as lease clauses or reference to a standard form if one were used. By use of a scanner, the entire lease can be available for computer viewing. The file should include a subfile of expiration dates.

B. PERCENTAGE LEASE VERIFICATION

Percentage leases need to be carefully monitored.

While percentage leases generally require that tenants use a totalizing cash register (a register that cannot be turned back), some tenants will find ways to avoid paying the required percentage on every sale. While larger retailers will seldom "play games," some smaller retailers will use every opportunity to avoid reporting sales.

Some lessors use the services of an investigative firm, like Wilmark, to run periodic checks on the honesty of their tenants. A "checker" employed by the firm will often arrive just at closing time, select a small item, and take it to the store owner. The checker will make itclear that he/she is in a hurry, pay with exact change including tax, and leave with the merchandise before the sale can be rung up. If the sale is not shown as one of the last sales of that day or the first of the following day, the owner has pocketed the money.

C. INSURANCE REGISTER

The *INSURANCE REGISTER should indicate the insurance coverage on every property managed, the name of the carrier and policy due dates.* The policy due dates should also be flagged on a computer tickler file to make certain that coverage does not lapse on a property. It is not an excuse to claim you were never billed when you have an uninsured loss.

Insurance coverage should be reviewed for every property managed upon taking over management duties and on an annual basis thereafter.

An insurance review can be done when the annual statement is prepared.

D. MORTGAGE FILE

The mortgage file shows mortgage payments to be made, to whom, the amounts, and due dates.

Not receiving a bill is no excuse for neglecting to make a payment.

E. RENT ROLLS

The rent rolls of all tenants, the rent they pay, as well as due dates can be broken down by individual properties.

The rolls should show when tenants paid rent, any checks that failed to clear, late charges assessed against the tenants, and any rental arrearage.

With computer programs, you can check on all tenants or tenants as to a particular property and can retrieve data on current rent status. The rent rolls would also show dates for scheduled rent increases.

F. EVICTION REGISTER

Some firms having a great many residential units track evictions using a separate register that shows when notices were sent and dates for unlawful detainer actions.

G. MOVE-OUTS WHO OWE

Keep track of undesirable tenants and your efforts to remedy the situation.

Some tenants will move out either owing rent or with property damage bond that is insufficient to cover damaged or missing property. A file should be kept on these persons and indicate your efforts to collect amounts due and accounts sent to collection services or attorneys.

VOICE OF EXPERIENCE:

Quick action should be taken to collect from "move-outs." While some of these accounts will be legally or practically uncollectible, others will be paid willingly but often over a protracted period of time.

Your initial collection effort should be letters and/or telephone calls. Collection agencies and attorneys may charge up to 50 percent of a claim, depending upon the amount. Sometimes it's better to get half of what you're owed than nothing. You have a duty to your owner to make a reasonable effort to collect all rents and damages due the owner.

VOICE OF EXPERIENCE:

When you can't locate a past renter who owes you money, consider using a "skip tracer." These persons and firms have broad computer-based access to locate the missing person. Once the person is located, you can use an attorney or collection agency to collect your past due account.

H. INVENTORY FILE

An inventory file should be maintained by property detailing equipment, furnishings, and appliances that are owned by the property owner and their condition.

I. VENDOR FILES

VENDOR FILES would include approved vendors to be used by resident managers. It would include vendor history.

J. UTILITY FILES

UTILITY FILES would show dates for utility payments and payments made.

K. PAYROLL RECORDS

Payroll records must be sufficient for preparation of annual W-2 forms for employees showing income and deductions.

Records must show federal and state tax withholding as well as employee and employer social security contributions. Separate records must be kept for your payments to the government.

Computer systems will compute and prepare checks for employees as well as for tax and social security payments.

Worker's compensation and unemployment compensation payments will also have to be scheduled and appropriate checks sent.

L. PURCHASE ORDERS FILES

Purchase order numbers should be assigned to purchases of material or services above a particular figure, such as $50. The purchase order should be tracked as to receipt of goods or completion of service. There are computer systems to aid in preparation of and tracking purchase orders.

M. INACTIVE FILES

Files should be maintained for a **minimum of three years** after management ceases.

IV. Your Own Records and Controls

A. OPERATION COSTS AND EXPENSES

Besides maintaining records for owners, you need records for your own management use. They can be monthly or just annual. They would show your firm's income and expenses by category.

By using a spread sheet format showing prior years, significant changes become readily apparent.

Besides just profit and loss, you should have records listing occupancy factors for all the properties you manage. You should also have records addressing the type of property and annual percentage changes in rents for the same properties from the prior year by type of property.

Records could include the number of units and/or square feet under management as well as figures from prior years. You can prepare a realistic budget from all this information.

Quarterly reports showing budgeted and actual figures can help you recognize areas that need to be addressed as well as changes in your operating budget.

B. MANAGEMENT OFFICE INSURANCE FILE

Besides keeping records of owner property insurance, you must make certain you keep records of your own property insurance covering office equipment, maintenance equipment, vehicles as well as liability coverage. Your insurance might also include bonding of employees.

Do not rely on others to make certain that you are covered. Use your computer to track coverage.

VOICE OF EXPERIENCE:

You should also make certain that any employee using his/her own vehicle for company-related business has adequate liability coverage. The employee can request coverage information be supplied to your firm by the employee's carrier.

C. AD REGISTER

Keeping track of what is being advertised is very important for a number of reasons.

1. **Owners.** You can show owners what you are doing to rent their properties.

Send your owners copies of all advertisements, including websites.

2. **Agents.** Agents will know what is being advertised so that they can be prepared to answer inquiries.

Keep copies of all ads at the front desk.

3. **Management Evaluation.** By evaluating ads and cost of ads for individual properties, you can evaluate the economic effectiveness of the ad, the advertising media and the management contract.

If the marketing you're using doesn't work, change it!

D. TELEPHONE AND WALK-IN RECORDS

Records of telephone calls and walk-ins for rentals should be maintained. When the caller is asking about a particular property, the person answering the telephone should find out if the party is calling from a rental sign or an ad. The same should apply to walk-ins.

Whatever works should be repeated.

Records should also be kept regarding rental showings that result from telephone calls. From these records a great deal can be learned.

Should there be a change in terms, previous callers should be contacted and informed.

1. **Ad Response.** The effectiveness can be gauged by knowing the number of calls resulting from an ad. As a property manager, you're likely to find that ads in a particular price range, area, or emphasizing particular features are more effective then others.

Check your competitors' comparable listings to use as potential switchs for your own listings. Also contact these agents to make them aware of your listings.

2. **Is the Ad on Target?** If an ad brings many calls but few showings, it indicates that the ad is not giving the reader a true impression of the property. The same would be true for a property that has been shown many times but has not been rented.

3. **Are the Employees Properly Trained?** If some employees are having a high percentage of telephone calls resulting in showings and have good sales while other employees have a very low percentage of calls resulting in showings, it would indicate that the less successful employee needs help with his or her telephone techniques, as well as closing training.

E. EMPLOYEE FILE

You should keep an employee file that includes employment applications and any pre-employment checks that were performed.

The file should include employee reviews. The file should also indicate employee wages and include copies of any employment contracts signed employees, as well as emergency contact information.

If a complaint has been received about an employee's work-related activities, the complaint should be included in the file and what investigation or disposition was made about the complaint.

Keep a paper trail of all complaints and problems.

An employee file could be important to you in case of a lawsuit for wrongful termination or for a claim that you failed to adequately check on an employee's background or failed in a duty of supervision.

F. AUDIT

If you do not personally handle bookkeeping tasks, you should either perform your own audit or hire someone from outside the firm to perform one. In addition to an annual audit, it would be money well spent to have an accountant spend at least one full day going over records, deposits and disbursements at least once per quarter.

VOICE OF EXPERIENCE:

It's not a matter of your trusting your employees, it's a matter of your agency duty to protect funds of others. You would be remiss in this obligation not to make certain that all funds are properly accounted for. It's a good business practice.

V. Computer Management Software

There are a number of firms that offer computer management software programs. Most of the programs are for MS Windows® compatible computers.

We have included information on just a few of the available programs. You will likely be able to evaluate programs at real estate trade conventions or by writing software firms. Most firms offer demonstration disks so that you can see what the program is capable of performing.

A. REALTY AUTOMATION, INC.

Realty Automation, Inc. offers residential and commercial software for:

1. Single-family and multi-family residentials,
2. Commercial office buildings,
3. Commercial strip centers and shopping malls,
4. Mini-storage or self-service storage facilities,
5. Condominium or owner associations, and
6. Marinas, warehouses, airports, etc.

fullhousesoftware.com

Realty Automation

Features of the program include:

1. Complete accounting (Cash or Accrual),
2. Complete tenant (or member) tracking,
3. Manual or automatic check-writing capabilities, and
4. Extensive report generating capabilities.

B. AMT DIRECT

The **AMTdirect Real Estate and Lease Administration Solution** reduces operational management costs, enhances profits, and generates cash flow by uncovering hidden value within complex portfolios of leased and owned properties.

AMTdirect is powerful, yet easy to use, and is considered one of the most complete Real Estate Administration applications on the market by leading retailers, corporations, and service providers.

AMTdirect provides both large and small companies with an economical lease administration solution that reduces the financial, legal and operational costs associated with managing complex portfolios of leased and owned properties.

 amtdirect.com
AMTdirect

C. PROMAS PROPERTY MANAGEMENT SOFTWARE

PROMAS Property Management Accounting Software is a family of products for professional property managers, association management companies and self-managed associations. Integrated accounting and property management reporting functions form the backbone of a feature-rich, affordable, easy-to-use product line. A fully functional demo is available from the Promas website.

 promas.com
Promas Property Management Software

D. RESORT MANAGEMENT SYSTEMS

Resort Management Systems software is designed to meet the special needs of firms handling resort rentals. The system helps you determine which units are available and their features for your reservations. It provides arrival and departure lists, owner statements, and commonly used reports including income projection.

resortmanagementsystem.com
Resort Management Systems

VI. CHAPTER SUMMARY

Funds of others or for some later disbursement that come into the control of the property manager are trust funds until disbursed. When trust money is received, it can be placed in a trust account, paid to a service provider if that was its purpose, or given to the principal if the principal is entitled to the funds.

The property manager's trust account should be a non-interest-bearing demand deposit (checking) account in an FDIC insured institution. The account must be clearly titled identifying it for trust purposes. Funds from multiple beneficiaries can be in the same account.

If the depositor of funds requests, funds received can be placed in an interest-bearing account with interest benefiting the owner of the funds. Interest-bearing accounts should not mix funds of more than one owner.

Funds can be withdrawn from the trust account by the broker/property manager, a licensed employee with written authorization, or an unlicensed bonded person.

A broker/property manager may not commingle personal funds with trust funds, but may keep a small amount of his or her own funds in the trust account.

If two or more persons claim an interest in trust funds, the broker should commence an interpleader action. Trust funds cannot be used to offset other claims owed to the broker. Records must be kept for trust funds showing the date money was received, from whom, the amount, the date deposited, and the disbursement data. A record must be kept of payments made directly to service providers or returned uncashed.

Trust accounts should be reconciled monthly.

Owners should receive a monthly statement as well as an annual operating statement. The statement might compare income, expenses, etc. by category with the prior year or years. Owners like to know changes in rents and occupancy factors.

The annual statement might include an inspection report, operating budget, insurance summary and the owner's 1099.

Additional records that will aid management, include:

1. Lease files
2. Insurance register
3. Mortgage file
4. Rent rolls
5. Eviction register
6. Move-outs owing funds
7. Inventory files

8. Vendor files
9. Utility files
10. Payroll records
11. Purchase order files
12. Inactive files

A property management firm would also want records of its operations for budgeting and to consider operational adjustments. Records would include:

1. Profit and loss statements
2. Management office insurance files
3. Ad registers
4. Telephone records
5. Employee files
6. Audit reports

Most record keeping can be handled utilizing readily available computer software programs that are available from a number of firms.

VII. CHAPTER QUIZ

1. A property manager may hold a check received as a rental deposit uncashed:
   a. if the manager does not think the prospective tenant's rent application will be approved.
   b. until the lease has been signed and the rent is actually due.
   c. if the prospective tenant requests it be held until lessor agrees to the tenancy.
   d. at his or her own discretion.

2. Which of the following constitutes commingling of trust funds?
   a. A property manager who leaves $1 of his/her own money in the trust account
   b. A trust account containing funds belonging to several different owners
   c. A trust account that is interest-bearing
   d. Trust money deposited in a broker's/property manager's personal account

3. A broker's/property manager's trust account was not designated as a trust account. Claims of third parties for the trust monies would result from:
   a. creditor judgments against the broker.
   b. bankruptcy of the broker.
   c. death of the broker.
   d. all of the above.

4. Information that an owner would find beneficial with an annual statement includes:

   a. occupancy rates for theprevious year or years.
   b. a comparison of expenses and income with prior years.
   c. both a and b.
   d. neither a nor b.

5. A skip tracer would be used to:

   a. audit trust funds.
   b. locate former tenants.
   c. reproduce lost documents.
   d. copy computer programs.

6. Payroll records would include:

   a. income.
   b. social security deductions.
   c. income tax deductions.
   d. all of the above.

7. Keeping telephone records allows a property manager to evaluate:

   a. responses to an ad.
   b. effectiveness of an ad.
   c. effectiveness of an agent.
   d. all of the above.

8. An employee file should include:

   a. employees' applications.
   b. employees' employment contracts.
   c. employees' evaluations.
   d. all of the above.

9. A property manager's audit of his or her firm's bookkeeping:

   a. is required by law.
   b. indicates a distrust of employees.
   c. is good business practice.
   d. is a waste of money.

10. Computer software is capable of:

    a. producing graphs of income and expenses.
    b. automatically calculating late fees.
    c. preparing and tracking work orders.
    d. all of the above.

ANSWERS: 1. c; 2. d; 3. d; 4. c; 5. b; 6. d; 7. d; 8. d; 9. c; 10. d

Chapter 12
Promotion and Advertising

KEY WORDS AND TERMS

Advance Fee Rental Agencies
Billboards
Bird Dogs
Blog
Bulletins
Business Cards
Car Signs
Chambers of Commerce
Classified Ads
Code Violations
Craigslist
Daily Newspapers
Display Ads
Evictions
Facebook
Fee Splitting
For Lease Sign
Foreign Language Papers
Internet
Junior Posters
LinkedIn

Logos
Movie Screen Ads
Name Tags
Newspaper Columns
Personal Promotion
Personnel Office
Press Releases
Public Transit Ads
Radio
Referral Fees
Referrals
Rental Magazines
Social Networking
Speculators
Standard Billboards
Talking Signs
Telephone Solicitation
Throwaway Papers
Twitter
Yellowpages.com
YouTube

CHAPTER 12 OUTLINE

I. Promoting Your Firm

When you promote the name and image of your firm to the general public or to specific groups, your greatest benefit is likely to be the effect of the promotion on owner attitudes or perception of your firm.

A positive image will increase your business. Be sure to include the Internet and "social networking" in your promotion plans.

Prospective tenants don't buy "name brands." They are not likely to rent because of your name recognition and your accomplishments. They rent because they desire benefits of a particular property.

Your firm name and image can be presented in a positive light in a number of ways.

A. MEETING OWNERS

You should attempt to meet people who can help you in your business. These would be owners of investment property as well as people who have business and/or social relationships with property owners. Uploading your business profile to social networking sites such as Facebook, LinkedIn, and YouTube increases your exposure.

1. Membership in Property Owner's Groups

By being an active member or leader in your local chapters of property owner's groups (See Chapter 1), you will get to meet owners of property. By making presentations to the group on areas of management and showing a common and knowledgeable interest, you can build up a rapport that can lead to significant management contracts.

2. Public Speaking

Most service organizations, such as Rotary Clubs, are constantly looking for speakers. If you develop a presentation on an area or areas of interest to most business people, the organizations will be happy to have you as a speaker. As an example, a subject you could speak on, "O.K.! We have a new tax law, but what does it mean?" With that example you could cover the changes in the law in general and tie in examples as they relate to your property management business.

Accountants are a good group to speak to because they can influence clients into seeking professional management.

3. Teaching

Teaching a class or seminar at a local community college will enhance your professional image. If you teach a real estate class, such as real estate practices, your students will likely be real estate agents who could refer business your way.

Students can become good referral ambassadors.

VOICE OF EXPERIENCE:

If you teach a class in property management, your class will likely consist of both real estate agents and property owners. You will have an opportunity to sell yourself to owners because you're the "expert."

4. Religion

Being active in a religious group may show others that you are a moral and ethical person and this can lead to business.

5. Organization Membership

Taking an active role in service organizations such as Rotary and Kiwanis and lodges such as the Masonic Order and Lions' Clubs, will give you a wide group of acquaintances who will likely view you in a positive light.

B. PRESS RELEASES

Press releases can sell your firm as a "can do" professional management firm. Press releases could herald accomplishments such as the following:

New Management. Being chosen to manage a significant property or development.

VOICE OF EXPERIENCE:

Announcements regarding new property management laws are always appreciated. Many potential clients will be impressed with your knowledge of the law and your fast actions in notifying the community.

Professional Achievements. The fact that the property manager or an employee received professional designations should be announced with a press release.

Major New Tenant. The fact that your firm has negotiated a lease with a major local or national tenant is newsworthy and reflects favorably on your firm.

Don't hesitate to discreetly blow your own horn.

Achievements of Individuals. The fact that a property manager has received an award from your firm will reflect well on that individual and your firm when dealing with third parties. As an example, the fact that an agent has leased 1,000,000 square feet of commercial space in one year would be a remarkable and newsworthy achievement.

It pays to advertise.

Project Leasing. Leasing a major project, such as a new shopping center, warehouse complex or industrial park, could lead to a number of press releases. Promoting events such as "Leasing Ahead of Schedule," "50% Leased in Only 50 Days," "100% Lease," "First Lease Finalized," etc. is a good business decision.

Promote your people and their achievements.

New Employee. If you hire a new property manager, a press release covering the new employee's prior work history and education and family data would be in order. It should also cover the duties of the new employee.

VOICE OF EXPERIENCE:

A new hire press release makes new hires feel good about themselves and it also informs those who know the new hires that they will be working in property management for your firm.

Promotions. When an employee receives a promotion or change in job title, this information could be used in an effective press release.

Change in Office Location. Opening an office for the first time, a change in office location, or opening another office can be the subject of a press release.

C. PERSONAL PROMOTION

Individual managers within your firm can help your firm and themselves with personal promotion:

Business Cards. A distinctive business card with the name of your firm and clear indication that your firm is in the property management business will help spread the name of your firm. The card should also have the agent's photograph, name, telephone/fax numbers, etc., to benefit the agent.

Name Tags. Name tags with your firm name and logo help identify the agents employed with your firm. The name tags should be readable from a distance of about six feet.

Car Signs. Car signs with the name of your firm and the agent's name are beneficial to the firm and the agent because of the exposure possible.

D. NEWSPAPER COLUMNS/INTERNET BLOGS

Writing a "Tenant and Landlord" column for a local newspaper, or as an online "blog" covering tenant and landlord rights and obligations, as well as interesting legal cases in the management area, will serve to enhance your professional status in the community.

If you're a significant advertiser in the newspaper and if you are willing to provide the column at no charge to the paper, your request will likely be accepted. It is important that the column bear your photograph and that it be well written. Consider using a professional writer to prepare the column.

If you start a blog, you should be prepared to spend considerable time devoted to updating your posts.

Your reputation as a "cutting edge" presence in the real estate/property management community may be outweighed by the time and effort necessary to maintain that status.

E. PROFESSIONAL JOURNALS

Writing articles for professional journals will help your reputation within the property management profession. It can lead to referral management or consulting work.

F. PROFESSIONAL ASSOCIATIONS

Active participation and leadership positions within professional associations of property managers will enhance the professional reputation of your firm.

Gaining professional designations within the association you are active in will increase your personal reputation as well as that of your firm.

G. MANAGEMENT SIGNS

Discreet signs or plaques placed on quality properties that are managed by your firm will help your image. Some firms place these plaques in the elevators where they are likely to be read, while others place them at the entryway to the building. The signs might also indicate that your firm should be contacted for leasing information or give the location of the management office.

H. LEASED SIGNS

While signs indicating property is for rent or lease are effective tenant promotional tools, the fact that it has been leased can help you promote your firm to owners of other properties.

A "Leased" banner over a "For Lease" sign is much the same as a "Sold" banner is over a "For Sale" sign. It indicates success, and people like to deal with winners.

I. LOGO IDENTIFICATION

Consistent design is important.

A **LOGO** *is a special or unique design applicable to your firm.* You want to have your logo on all of your signs, business cards, stationery and in your advertisements. With a well-developed logo, persons interested in investment property will recognize and relate your logo with your firm's name. There are commercial artists who specialize in logos.

> ### VOICE OF EXPERIENCE:
> *Your logo should be associated with a color so that you always see the logo with a particular color. This enhances logo identification.*

J. YELLOW PAGES

Yellow Page advertisements are well-worth their costs.

A yellow page ad under "Real Estate Property Management" will bring in inquiries about management and rentals. Many larger management firms use display ads in the yellow pages.

To the reader, a larger ad relates to a larger management firm, although this is not necessarily the case.

You should consider more than a bare minimum yellow page ad. Also, don't forget to upload information to Yellowpages.com®.

K. INSTITUTIONAL ADVERTISING

Institutional advertising sells your name rather than a product.

A yellow page ad is institutional advertising as would be an ad in a program book for a charitable event.

These ads merely note your presence in the marketplace and sell your firm based on what you do.

While most ads placed by a property management firm will be to lease property, some ads will be institutional in nature.

II. Sources for Obtaining Management

The basis of property management is to have property to manage. Without management contracts there can be no property manager.

Obtaining new contracts is a continuing necessity as contracts will be lost for many reasons. As an example, when a shopping center or large apartment complex is sold to a REIT, management will be lost since REITs manage their own property.

Searching for new contacts on a continuing basis is a must.

There are many sources to use to obtain property management as well as leads to management opportunities. Most property managers use a combination of sources or programs to obtain management. Some management firms have an ongoing promotional program to obtain management and follow carefully thought out plans.

We endorse planning. We feel that just as a property should have a management plan, so should the property manager have his or her plan to maintain and increase inventory to manage.

A. REFERRALS FROM OWNERS

As in all real estate transactions, referrals for property management are highly beneficial.

Owners who are your clients are an excellent source of business. If they are pleased with the work you do for them, they generally are willing to refer you to other owners they know. If an owner contacts you from a personal referral, you know that owner has been half sold by the referral source. You also know that it is unlikely that you are competing with other firms for the management.

Watch the news for potential property management opportunities.

There is much more to do than wait for referrals to come to you. By discussing your needs with owners, you can get information about other owners. You can make the initial contact. A good time to ask owners for help is at a face-to-face meeting, such as when you have gone over an annual statement or have brought an owner good news such as an advantageous lease. When an owner is pleased with your services, the owner is likely to be very willing to tell you about other owners who they feel could use your management skills.

B. REFERRAL FEES FOR MANAGEMENT

Generally, brokers can pay referral fees for property management to other brokers. This can provide a huge source of referrals since most real estate offices do not handle property management, but will handle the sale of properties that may need professional management.

By letting other brokers know about your organization and what you do, as well as the benefits to the office making the referral, can result in your services being half sold to referral clients before you've ever met them.

Some offices use open houses and holiday parties to invite real estate agents to their offices and to sell them on the benefits the firm offers to owners and to referring agents.

Some large companies have a property management department and do not allow their residential agents to do property management.

Brokers who have the greatest chance to provide you with management opportunities are brokers who specialize in investment property.

VOICE OF EXPERIENCE:

It might benefit you to recommend other property managers. This would be the case when a property manager is specializing in an area or type of property that your firm does not manage. Referrals in such cases are likely to be mutual.

C. BIRD DOGS

BIRD DOG is not a derogatory term. It refers to a person who points you toward opportunities. A mother who keeps her eye out for a future daughter-in-law for her son would be a bird dog.

In property management, bird dogs should look for management opportunities and tenants. The best bird dogs are relatives or friends who want you to be successful.

Bird dogs need reassurances that you appreciated their help even if it didn't lead to success. Sooner or later they will come across opportunities that can be of help to you. Remember them regularly with a call or a card.

D. NEIGHBORS

Owners of income property adjacent to property that you manage can often be convinced, by logic, that you should also manage their property.

The economics of scale start with resident managers. One resident manager or management office could be shared by adjacent similar properties. If there are maintenance staffs or contracts, the costs could likely be reduced because of the advantage of having side-by-side work sites. Advertising costs could also be shared. While both owners would have to agree, expanding management to a contiguous property or properties makes economic sense.

E. GETTING OWNERS TO BUY

When a rental property comes on the market for sale and it is located adjacent or close to a similar property you manage, you could have an opportunity to gain another management opportunity.

By providing your owner with purchase information and the benefits of owning an adjacent property, you can at times earn a sales commission, as well as obtain another property to manage—a win/win situation.

VOICE OF EXPERIENCE:

If your owner is not interested in purchasing because of the need to work with tenants, you should point out to the listing agent that you would like to show a prospective buyer the economics possible with joint management.

F. PROPERTY SALES

Sales of income property, as reported through local MLS services or press releases, can mean a new owner and often new management. New owners will often be very interested in a management proposal.

Don't be a "secret agent." Promote the benefits of using your services.

G. BANKS

Banks and other lending institutions have an inventory of properties from foreclosures. Some lenders have huge property inventories, while others have just the occasional properties. Sometimes the lenders only wish to protect the property from vandalism, while other times active management is required.

You should begin lender contacts with your present bank and find out about their needs and how they are handling them. You should also contact other lenders. Some management firms specialize in relatively short-term management of foreclosed properties.

In addition to foreclosures, banks often gain control of property through their trust departments. Since trust departments prefer to deal with securities rather than real estate, they will generally sell the real estate, but management is necessary until the properties can be disposed of.

While you want a lender's management business, the lender likely desires your business. Property management firms have large trust accounts containing rental and security deposits, as well as rents received, but not yet disbursed. Lenders like the idea of having a large account for which they need not pay any interest.

The size of your trust account will dictate the leverage you have in dealing with a lender.

H. VACANT PROPERTY

Vacant property or property having a high vacancy rate will likely have an unhappy owner and are often ripe for management. County records will make it fairly easy to determine ownership. If an owner resides outside of the area, your chances for obtaining management will increase dramatically.

Contact absentee owners. They usually need you.

One property manager, in obtaining management for vacant single tenant properties, asks for a management contract with the provision that no management fees shall be owed until the property has been leased. If not leased within a designated period of time (from three to six months), the owner can cancel the management contract without obligation. If the property has been vacant for a long period of time, such as over one year, the owner would view this approach as a no-lose situation.

Some property management contracts allow for cancellation with a 30-day notice to the other party.

I. PROBLEM PROPERTY

Sometimes it is relatively easy to obtain management of problem property, but you must determine if you want the management on a case-by-case basis.

1. Code Violations

Health, safety, and building code violations are a matter of public record. Code violations often indicate problems. The problems could relate to poor management and/or financial problems of the owner. An owner plagued with problems, especially if he or she lives outside the area, can be ripe for management.

2. Evictions

The records of unlawful detainer actions are indicative of problems. Sometimes they relate to poor tenant qualifying.

Where the tenant owes many months' rent, it is indicative of poor management.

Substandard housing might also result in renting to tenants who are more likely to default.

3. Tax Delinquent Properties

All taxes must be paid on time.

When an owner of income property does not pay his or her taxes when due, it indicates a financial problem. While the problem could stem from other reasons, it could be management related, which professional management could solve.

4. Poor Maintenance

If you see an income property that is poorly maintained with poor or nonexistent landscaping, broken screens, etc., the problem could be management related. You should contact the owner about your services.

VOICE OF EXPERIENCE:

Look for opportunities in your community. A property that is increasingly rundown may have a recent change in ownership, and the new owner does not know, or is over his/her head, in keeping up with maintenance duties.

J. NEWSPAPER ADS

Classified ads are not going to read "I need a property manager," but they can indicate the need for management, and you should contact the owner offering your services.

1. Rental Ads

Rental ads that seem to appear in the newspaper forever either indicates a great many vacancies or the inability to fill a vacancy, both of which indicate a need for management.

Rental ads offering significant concessions like free rent, or otherwise indicate a desperate owner, are clues to management needs. They too need your services.

2. Ads for Trade

When an owner wants to trade an income property, it usually means that the owner is not happy with his or her situation. Such an owner could be a likely management prospect if you can show the owner a different vision of the benefits of ownership with professional management. You may also use a 1031 exchange for a larger property.

3. For Sale By Owner

"For Sale By Owner" ads often contain clues revealing the need for professional management. "100% Occupancy" could mean that the owner is not realizing rental potential. "Raisable Rents" means that the owner realizes rents are too low but isn't doing anything about it. You should wonder why the owner is not asking for the market rate.

Words indicating desperation, such as "Submit All Offers" or "Must Sell," indicate a problem.

Property management should be an economical benefit to the owners.

A good approach to use for this situation, as well as some of the other situations noted, would be to offer to prepare an analysis of the property showing the income that can reasonably be obtained over expenses. Ask the owner, "If you could remove yourself from management problems and maximize your income, would you be interested in retaining ownership?"

K. REAL ESTATE INVESTORS

REAL ESTATE INVESTORS buy property primarily for income and/or value appreciation. They expect a relatively long holding period. Discussion with brokers in your area should likely reveal major players.

Investors are usually willing to talk to anyone. The fact that they are open to ideas is what has led them to success. Offering to evaluate a property they own, or are considering buying, and preparing a management plan for them will give you an opportunity to prove you are a professional. It is an offer hard to turn down.

A free property evaluation is a great door opener with excellent financial opportunities.

Many property management firms will start a management relationship with an investor on a single property. It is likely to be the investor's biggest headache. The firm's performance on one problem property can not only lead to handling all of the investor's property, but a close relationship that includes evaluation of purchase opportunities.

L. DEVELOPERS

Developers of investment properties may be developing for particular buyers or with the intention of selling. Many developers develop for their own property portfolios. They keep what they develop and consequently must either become involved in management or use a professional manager.

Building permits issued will help you in locating developers. Since proper property management really begins with the planning, it is never too early to contact a developer.

Developers are generally willing to schedule an appointment. You want to show the benefits you can offer to the developer. A similar approach would be used with an investor.

M. SPECULATORS

SPECULATORS differ from investors in that they buy, try to enhance value and sell. With the change in capital gains, speculators now want to hold properties for at least 18 months to take advantage of the 20-percent capital gain's rate.

Speculators are active players in the real estate market. Many property managers work closely with speculators and consult with them when considering property changes to enhance value and likely rents that are possible. In return, they expect and get the property management. They are often able to retain management when the property is sold to new owners.

Local brokers dealing in investment properties can give you the names of many speculators active in your market area.

N. FEDERAL NATIONAL MORTGAGE ASSOCIATION ("FANNIE MAE")

The Federal National Mortgage Association ("Fannie Mae") will designate brokers to handle the renovation of its properties. The services are short term and do not include leasing. If you are interested in handling this work, contact a Fannie Mae office near you.

O. WHEN THERE IS A MANAGER

You will contact some owners who appear to be in need of professional property management only to find that the owner has a management contract with another firm.

The property problems that you perceived might not be the result of management deficiencies, but rather owner limitations.

Do not criticize the property management firm handling the property.

Without knowledge of all the facts, you do not know if you could do a better job. We strongly recommend that you leave your name, or card, if a face-to-face meeting and end the conversation. If you have mentioned any reason why the owner needs management, we suggest, "I am quite sure that _____ has the situation under control." While stealing accounts might be okay for garbage haulers, it should not play a part in property management or any other type of transaction.

We regard property management as a profession and those engaged in it should act as professionals.

If an owner who has a property management firm contacts you, there is nothing wrong with showing the owner what you can do. However, do not denigrate the work or ability of the current property management.

P. CONSULTING CONTRACTS

Some owners want your services and are willing to pay for them, but they do not wish to give up property management.

As an example, some Real Estate Investment Trusts will hire consultants to evaluate a property for management or evaluate an ongoing management operation of a large property or complex.

Contacts will be initiated by the property owner based upon the reputation of the property manager being hired.

Beware of the owners who want your services, but have no intention of paying for them.

Some owners will take advantage of you by asking you to evaluate a property and prepare a management plan so that you can be considered for management, when they have no intention of hiring you.

VOICE OF EXPERIENCE:

If you have reason to believe that the owner does not intend to hire outside management, no matter how good a plan you prepare, you might consider contracting for this work. Ask the owner to agree to a fixed fee for this effort with the provision that it will be waived if you receive a management contract.

Q. LEASING

Many management companies will also take exclusive listings to lease nonresidential property.

Such agency agreements do not provide full management services. Nevertheless, these agreements are worthwhile because they offer an opportunity for you, as the property manager, and your firm to significantly increase earnings.

Many property management firms take these listings because working closely with an owner can result in an excellent owner-agent relationship. After an owner realizes what you can do for them, it is often just a short step to obtaining a management contract for the property that was leased and other properties that he or she owns.

Figure 12-1 is the CAR® **Commercial, Residential Income and Vacant Land Listing Agreement**.

III. Promoting Space

There are many ways of marketing space, some more effective than others and some more expensive.

PROMOTING SPACE refers to getting the message out to prospective tenants that you have space available for lease. In other words, it deals with "advertising."

If you are not successful in finding tenants, then you will have failed as a manager, because without tenants you are looking after an empty shell.

A. FEE SPLITTING

Just as you can cooperate with other brokers in obtaining property management you can cooperate with others by your willingness to split leasing fees with firms that have a tenant for your space.

This cooperation should go both ways. Prospective tenants with whom you are working can be rented space controlled by another management firm if space that you control does not meet the tenant's needs.

Just because you might compete vigorously to get management accounts does not mean that you shouldn't cooperate with others.

Cooperation is in the best interest of your owners and your refusal to do so could raise questions about ethics, and could be a breach of fiduciary duties.

B. ADVANCE FEE RENTAL AGENCIES

There are rental agencies that charge prospective renters a fee for a list of available rentals. People who pay these advance fees are usually very serious about renting.

If there are advance fee rental agencies active in your area, you should provide them with weekly updated lists of your available rentals. It is a no-cost method of spreading the word about your rentals.

Figure 12-1

CALIFORNIA
ASSOCIATION
OF REALTORS®

COMMERCIAL, RESIDENTIAL INCOME AND VACANT LAND LISTING AGREEMENT
(C.A.R. Form CLA, Revised 4/06)

1. **EXCLUSIVE AUTHORIZATION:** _____ ("Owner")
hereby employs and grants _____ ("Broker")
beginning (date) _____ and ending at 11:59 P.M. on (date) _____ ("Listing Period")
the exclusive and irrevocable right to ☐ SELL, ☐ LEASE, ☐ EXCHANGE, ☐ OPTION, or ☐ OTHER _____
the real property in the City of _____ *Marina del Rey* _____, County of _____,
California, described as: _____ *123 Sail Avenue* _____ ("Property").

2. **ITEMS EXCLUDED AND INCLUDED:** Unless otherwise specified in an agreement between Owner and transferee, all fixtures and fittings that are attached to the Property are included, and personal property items are excluded from the price.
ADDITIONAL ITEMS EXCLUDED: _____.
ADDITIONAL ITEMS INCLUDED: _____
Owner intends that the above items be excluded or included in listing the Property, but understands that: **(i)** the Agreement between Owner and transferee supersedes any intention expressed above and will ultimately determine which items are excluded and included in the transaction; and **(ii)** Broker is not responsible for and does not guarantee that the above exclusions and/or inclusions will be in the Agreement between Owner and transferee.

3. **LISTING PRICE AND TERMS:**
   A. The listing price shall be _____ Dollars ($ _____).
   B. Additional Terms: _____

4. **COMPENSATION TO BROKER:**
   Notice: The amount or rate of real estate commissions is not fixed by law. They are set by each Broker individually and may be negotiable between Owner and Broker (real estate commissions include all compensation and fees to Broker.)
   A. Owner agrees to pay to Broker as compensation for services irrespective of agency relationship(s): ☐ _____ percent of the listing price (or if an agreement is entered into, of the contract price), ☐ $ _____ , OR ☐ in accordance with Broker's attached schedule of compensation; as follows:
   (1) If during the Listing Period, or any extension, Broker, Owner, cooperating broker, or any other person, procures a buyer(s) who offers to acquire the Property on the above price and terms, or on any price and terms acceptable to Owner. (Broker shall be entitled to compensation whether any Escrow resulting from such offer closes or tenancy begins during or after the expiration of the Listing Period.)
   (2) If within _____ calendar days after the end of the Listing Period or any extension, Owner enters into a contract to sell, lease, exchange, option, convey or otherwise transfer the Property to anyone ("Prospective Transferee") or that person's related entity: **(i)** who physically entered and was shown the Property during the Listing Period or any extension by Broker or a cooperating broker; or **(ii)** for whom Broker or any cooperating broker submitted to Owner a signed, written offer to acquire, lease, exchange or obtain an option on the Property. Owner, however, shall have no obligation to Broker under this paragraph 4A(2) unless, not later than **3 calendar days** after the end of the Listing Period or any extension thereof, Broker has given Owner a written notice of the names of such Prospective Transferees.
   (3) If, without Broker's prior written consent, the Property is withdrawn from sale, lease, exchange, option or other, as specified in paragraph 1, or is sold, conveyed, leased, rented, exchanged, optioned or otherwise transferred or made unmarketable by a voluntary act of Owner during the Listing Period, or any extension thereof.
   B. If completion of the transaction is prevented by a party to the transaction other than Owner, then compensation due under paragraph 4A shall be payable only if and when Owner collects damages by suit, arbitration, settlement, or otherwise, and then in an amount equal to the lesser of one-half of the damages recovered or the above compensation, after first deducting title and escrow expenses and the expenses of collection, if any.
   C. In addition, Owner agrees to pay Broker: _____
   D. **(1)** Broker is authorized to cooperate and compensate brokers participating through the multiple listing service(s) ("MLS"): **(i)** by offering MLS brokers either: ☐ _____ percent of the purchase price, or ☐ $ _____ ; **OR (ii)** (if checked) ☐ as per Broker's policy.
   (2) Broker is authorized to cooperate and compensate brokers operating outside the MLS as per Broker's policy.
   E. Owner hereby irrevocably assigns to Broker the above compensation from Owner's funds and proceeds in escrow. Broker may submit this Listing Agreement, as instructions to compensate Broker pursuant to paragraph 4A, to any escrow regarding the Property involving Owner and a buyer, transferee or Prospective Transferee.
   F. **(1)** Owner represents that Owner has not previously entered into a listing agreement with another broker regarding the Property, unless specified as follows: _____
   (2) Owner warrants that Owner has no obligation to pay compensation to any other broker regarding the Property unless the Property is transferred to any of the following Prospective Transferees: _____
   (3) If the Property is transferred to anyone listed above during the time Owner is obligated to compensate another broker: **(i)** Broker is not entitled to compensation under this Listing Agreement; and **(ii)** Broker is not obligated to represent Owner in such transaction.

Owner acknowledges receipt of a copy of this page.
Owner's Initials (_____) (_____)
Reviewed by _____ Date _____
EQUAL HOUSING OPPORTUNITY

CLA REVISED 4/06 (PAGE 1 OF 4)
COMMERCIAL, RESIDENTIAL INCOME AND VACANT LAND LISTING AGREEMENT (CLA PAGE 1 OF 4)

Agent: WALT HUBER	Phone:	Fax:	Prepared using zipForm® software
Broker: WALT HUBER REALTOR			

Property Address: *123 Sail Avenue*
*Marina del Rey, CA 90292*_____ Date: _____

5. **OWNERSHIP, TITLE AND AUTHORITY:** Owner warrants that: **(i)** Owner is the owner of the Property; **(ii)** no other persons or entities have title to the Property, and **(iii)** Owner has the authority to both execute this Listing Agreement and transfer the Property. Exceptions to ownership, title and authority are as follows: _____

6. ____ **MULTIPLE LISTING SERVICE:** Information about this listing will (or ☐ will not) be provided to the MLS of Broker's selection. All terms of the transaction, including financing, if applicable, will be provided to the selected MLS for publication, dissemination and use by persons and entities on terms approved by the MLS. Owner authorizes Broker to comply with all applicable MLS rules. MLS rules allow MLS data to be made available by the MLS to additional Internet sites unless Broker gives the MLS instructions to the contrary. MLS rules generally provide that residential real property and vacant lot listings be submitted to the MLS within 48 hours or some other period of time after all necessary signatures have been obtained on the listing agreement. However, Broker will not have to submit this listing to the MLS or can prohibit this listing or certain information from or about it from appearing on a certain internet sites if, within that time, Broker submits to the MLS a form signed by Seller (C.A.R. Form SEL or the locally required form) instructing Broker to withhold the listing from the MLS. Information about this listing will be provided to the MLS of Broker's selection unless a form instructing Broker to withhold the listing from the MLS is attached to this listing Agreement.

7. **OWNER REPRESENTATIONS:** Owner represents that, unless otherwise specified in writing, Owner is unaware of: **(i)** any Notice of Default recorded against the Property; **(ii)** any delinquent amounts due under any loan secured by, or other obligation affecting, the Property; **(iii)** any bankruptcy, insolvency or similar proceeding affecting the Property; **(iv)** any litigation, arbitration, administrative action, government investigation, or other pending or threatened action that affects or may affect the Property or Owner's ability to transfer it; and **(v)** any current, pending or proposed special assessments affecting the Property. Owner shall promptly notify Broker in writing if Owner becomes aware of any of these items during the Listing Period or any extension thereof.

8. **BROKER'S AND OWNER'S DUTIES:** Broker agrees to exercise reasonable effort and due diligence to achieve the purposes of this Listing Agreement. Unless Owner gives Broker written instructions to the contrary, Broker is authorized to order reports and disclosures as appropriate or necessary, and advertise and market the Property in any method and medium, including the Internet, selected by Broker, and, to the extent permitted by these media, including MLS, control the dissemination of the information submitted to any medium. Owner agrees to consider offers presented by Broker, and to act in good faith toward accomplishing the transfer of the Property by, among other things, making the Property available for showing at reasonable times and referring to Broker all inquiries of any party interested in the Property. Owner agrees to provide Broker and transferee(s) all disclosures required by law. Owner further agrees to immediately disclose in writing any condition known to Owner that affects the Property, including but not limited to, any past or current generation, storage, release, threatened release, disposal, and presence and location of asbestos, PCB transformers, petroleum products, flammable explosives, underground storage tanks and other hazardous, toxic or contaminated substances or conditions on, or about the Property. Owner shall maintain public liability and property damage insurance on the Property during the Listing Period or any extension and waives all subrogation rights under any insurance against Broker, cooperating brokers or employees. Owner is responsible for determining what price to list and transfer the Property. **Owner further agrees to indemnify, defend and hold Broker harmless from all claims, disputes, litigation, judgments and attorney's fees arising from any incorrect information supplied by Owner, or from any material fact that Owner knows but fails to disclose.**
   ☐ **(If checked)** The attached property disclosure is part of this Listing Agreement and may be provided to Prospective Transferees.

9. **DEPOSIT:** Broker is authorized to accept and hold on Owner's behalf any deposit to be applied toward the contract price.

10. **AGENCY RELATIONSHIPS:**
   A. **Disclosure:** If the Property includes residential property with one to four dwelling units and this Listing Agreement is used to list the Property for sale, exchange or lease for a period of greater than one year, a "Disclosure Regarding Agency Relationships" form is required to be provided to Owner prior to entering into this Listing Agreement.
   B. **Owner Representation:** Broker shall represent Owner in any resulting transaction, except as specified in paragraph 4F.
   C. **Possible Dual Agency With Buyer:** Depending upon the circumstances, it may be necessary or appropriate for Broker to act as an agent for both Owner and buyer, exchange party, or one or more additional parties ("Buyer"). Broker shall, as soon as practicable, disclose to Owner any election to act as a dual agent representing both Owner and Buyer. If a Buyer is procured directly by Broker or an associate licensee in Broker's firm, Owner hereby consents to Broker acting as a dual agent for Owner and such Buyer. In the event of an exchange, Owner hereby consents to Broker collecting compensation from additional parties for services rendered, provided there is disclosure to all parties of such agency and compensation. Owner understands and agrees that: **(i)** Broker, without the prior written consent of Owner, will not disclose to Buyer that Owner is willing to transfer the Property at a price less than the listing price; **(ii)** Broker, without the prior written consent of Buyer, will not disclose to Owner that Buyer is willing to pay a price greater than the offered price; and **(iii)** except for (i) and (ii) above, a dual agent is obligated to disclose known facts materially affecting the value or desirability of the Property to both parties.
   D. **Other Owners:** Owner understands that Broker may have or obtain listings on other properties, and that potential buyers may consider, make offers on, or acquire through Broker, property the same as or similar to Owner's Property. Owner consents to Broker's representation of owners and buyers of other properties before, during, and after the end of this Listing Agreement.
   E. **Confirmation:** If the Property includes residential property with one to four dwelling units, Broker shall confirm the agency relationship described above, or as modified, in writing, prior to or concurrent with Owner's execution of an agreement to sell.

11. **SECURITY AND INSURANCE:** Broker is not responsible for loss of or damage to personal or real property or person, whether attributable to use of a keysafe/lockbox, a showing of the Property, or otherwise. Third parties, including but not limited to, appraisers, inspectors, brokers and prospective buyers, may have access to, and take videos and photographs of the interior of the Property. Owner agrees: **(i)** to take reasonable precautions to safeguard and protect valuables that might be accessible during showings of the Property; and **(ii)** to obtain insurance to protect against these risks. Broker does not maintain insurance to protect Owner.

Owner acknowledges receipt of a copy of this page.
Owner's Initials (_____)(_____)

Reviewed by _____ Date _____

CLA REVISED 4/06 (PAGE 2 OF 4)

COMMERCIAL, RESIDENTIAL INCOME AND VACANT LAND LISTING AGREEMENT (CLA PAGE 2 OF 4)
Untitled

Property Address: *123 Sail Avenue*
Marina del Rey, CA 90292 _____ Date: _____

12. KEYSAFE/LOCKBOX: A keysafe/lockbox is designed to hold a key to the Property to permit access to the Property by Broker, cooperating brokers, MLS participants, their authorized licensees and representatives, authorized inspectors and accompanying prospective buyers. Broker, cooperating brokers, MLS and Associations/Boards of REALTORS® are **not** insurers against injury, theft, loss, vandalism, or damage attributed to the use of a keysafe/lockbox. Owner does (or if checked ☐ does not) authorize Broker to install a keysafe/lockbox. If Owner does not occupy the Property, Owner shall be responsible for obtaining occupant(s)' written permission for use of a keysafe/lockbox. (C.A.R. Form KLA)

13. SIGN: Owner authorizes Broker to install a FOR SALE/SOLD/LEASE sign on the Property unless otherwise indicated in writing.

14. EQUAL HOUSING OPPORTUNITY: The Property is offered in compliance with federal, state, and local anti-discrimination laws.

15. ATTORNEY'S FEES: In any action, proceeding, or arbitration between Owner and Broker regarding the obligation to pay compensation under this Listing Agreement, the prevailing Owner or Broker shall be entitled to reasonable attorney's fees and costs, except as provided in paragraph 19A.

16. ADDITIONAL TERMS: _____
_____
_____
_____
_____
_____
_____
_____
_____
_____

17. MANAGEMENT APPROVAL: If an associate-licensee in Broker's office (salesperson or broker-associate) enters into this Listing Agreement on Broker's behalf, and Broker or Manager does not approve of its terms, Broker or Manager has the right to cancel this Listing Agreement, in writing, within 5 days after its execution.

18. SUCCESSORS AND ASSIGNS: This Listing Agreement shall be binding upon Owner and Owner's successors and assigns.

19. DISPUTE RESOLUTION:

A. MEDIATION: Owner and Broker agree to mediate any dispute or claim arising between them out of this Listing Agreement, or any resulting transaction, before resorting to arbitration or court action, subject to paragraph 19B(2) below. Paragraph 19B(2) below applies whether or not the Arbitration provision in initialed. Mediation fees, if any, shall be divided equally among the parties involved. If, for any dispute or claim to which this paragraph applies, any party commences an action without first attempting to resolve the matter through mediation, or refuses to mediate after a request has been made, then that party shall not be entitled to recover attorney's fees, even if they would otherwise be available to that party in any such action. THIS MEDIATION PROVISION APPLIES WHETHER OR NOT THE ARBITRATION PROVISION IS INITIALED.

B. ARBITRATION OF DISPUTES: (1) Owner and Broker agree that any dispute or claim in law or equity arising between them regarding the obligation to pay compensation under this Agreement, which is not settled through mediation, shall be decided by neutral, binding arbitration, including and subject to paragraph 19B(2) below. The arbitrator shall be a retired judge or justice, or an attorney with at least 5 years of residential real estate law experience, unless the parties mutually agree to a different arbitrator, who shall render an award in accordance with substantive California law. The parties shall have the right to discovery in accordance with Code of Civil Procedure §1283.05. In all other respects, the arbitration shall be conducted in accordance with Title 9 of Part III of the California Code of Civil Procedure. Judgment upon the award of the arbitrator(s) may be entered in any court having jurisdiction. Interpretation of this agreement to arbitrate shall be governed by the Federal Arbitration Act.

(2) EXCLUSIONS FROM MEDIATION AND ARBITRATION: The following matters are excluded from mediation and arbitration: (i) a judicial or non-judicial foreclosure or other action or proceeding to enforce a deed of trust, mortgage, or installment land sale contract as defined in Civil Code §2985; (ii) an unlawful detainer action; (iii) the filing or enforcement of a mechanic's lien; and (iv) any matter that is within the jurisdiction of a probate, small claims, or bankruptcy court. The filing of a court action to enable the recording of a notice of pending action, for order of attachment, receivership, injunction, or other provisional remedies, shall not constitute a waiver of the mediation and arbitration provisions.

"NOTICE: BY INITIALING IN THE SPACE BELOW YOU ARE AGREEING TO HAVE ANY DISPUTE ARISING OUT OF THE MATTERS INCLUDED IN THE 'ARBITRATION OF DISPUTES' PROVISION DECIDED BY NEUTRAL ARBITRATION AS PROVIDED BY CALIFORNIA LAW AND YOU ARE GIVING UP ANY RIGHTS YOU MIGHT POSSESS TO HAVE THE DISPUTE LITIGATED IN A COURT OR JURY TRIAL. BY INITIALING IN THE SPACE BELOW YOU ARE GIVING UP YOUR JUDICIAL RIGHTS TO DISCOVERY AND APPEAL, UNLESS THOSE RIGHTS ARE SPECIFICALLY INCLUDED IN THE 'ARBITRATION OF DISPUTES' PROVISION. IF YOU REFUSE TO SUBMIT TO ARBITRATION AFTER AGREEING TO THIS PROVISION, YOU MAY BE COMPELLED TO ARBITRATE UNDER THE AUTHORITY OF THE CALIFORNIA CODE OF CIVIL PROCEDURE. YOUR AGREEMENT TO THIS ARBITRATION PROVISION IS VOLUNTARY."

"WE HAVE READ AND UNDERSTAND THE FOREGOING AND AGREE TO SUBMIT DISPUTES ARISING OUT OF THE MATTERS INCLUDED IN THE 'ARBITRATION OF DISPUTES' PROVISION TO NEUTRAL ARBITRATION."

Owner's Initials _____ / _____   Broker's Initials _____ / _____

Owner acknowledges receipt of a copy of this page.
Owner's Initials (_____)(_____)
Reviewed by _____ Date _____

CLA REVISED 4/06 (PAGE 3 OF 4)

COMMERCIAL, RESIDENTIAL INCOME AND VACANT LAND LISTING AGREEMENT (CLA PAGE 3 OF 4)

Untitled

123 Sail Avenue
Property Address: <u>Marina del Rey, CA 90292</u>_____ Date: _____

20. ENTIRE CONTRACT: All prior discussions, negotiations, and agreements between the parties concerning the subject matter of this Listing Agreement are superseded by this Listing Agreement, which constitutes the entire contract and a complete and exclusive expression of their agreement, and may not be contradicted by evidence of any prior agreement or contemporaneous oral agreement. If any provision of this Agreement is held to be ineffective or invalid, the remaining provisions will nevertheless be given full force and effect. This Listing Agreement and any supplement, addendum, or modification, including any photocopy or facsimile, may be executed in counterparts.

By signing below, Owner acknowledges that Owner has read, understands, received a copy of and agrees to the terms of this Listing Agreement and any attached schedule of compensation.

Date _____ at _____

Owner _____

By _____ Title _____

Address _____ City _____ State _____ Zip _____

Telephone _____ Fax _____ E-mail _____

Date _____ at _____

Owner _____

By _____ Title _____

Address _____ City _____ State _____ Zip _____

Telephone _____ Fax _____ E-mail _____

Date _____ at _____

Owner _____

By _____ Title _____

Address _____ City _____ State _____ Zip _____

Telephone _____ Fax _____ E-mail _____

Date _____ at _____

Owner _____

By _____ Title _____

Address _____ City _____ State _____ Zip _____

Telephone _____ Fax _____ E-mail _____

Real Estate Broker (Firm) _____ DRE Lic. # _____

By (Agent) _____ DRE Lic. # _____ Date _____

Address _____ City _____ State _____ Zip _____

Telephone _____ Fax _____ E-mail _____

Published and Distributed by:
REAL ESTATE BUSINESS SERVICES, INC.
a subsidiary of the California Association of REALTORS®
525 South Virgil Avenue, Los Angeles, California 90020

Reviewed by _____ Date _____

CLA REVISED 4/06 (PAGE 4 OF 4)

COMMERCIAL, RESIDENTIAL INCOME AND VACANT LAND LISTING AGREEMENT (CLA PAGE 4 OF 4)

Untitled

C. USE OTHER TENANTS

An excellent way to fill vacancies is to inquire of other tenants if they have any friends (in the case of residential vacancies) or firms that they do business with and would like to have in the property.

In cases of residential rentals, a tenant who has close friends living in the property is less likely to move out than are other tenants.

Firms like to have other firms that they do business with close at hand to enhance communications. All firms benefit by this arrangement.

D. "FOR LEASE" SIGNS

Signs and banners proclaiming space or units available for rent or lease are the most cost effective advertising available.

In very desirable, high-trafficked areas, many managers are able to use property signs as their only source for tenants.

You can also obtain institutional benefits from signs that include your firm name and logo.

For maximum effectiveness, you want large letters and good contrast for your signs. The most effective contrasting colors are yellow and black.

Your sign may capitalize the first letter of each word, but the rest of the sign should be lower-case lettering. Avoid stylized fancy lettering as it is difficult to read. Also keep sign wordage to a minimum for quick comprehension.

If your property has something special like "Pets Allowed" or "Health Club," these features can be added using a strip sign attached to the "For Lease" sign.

E. TALKING SIGNS

Talking signs simply indicate that interested parties can get greater information by dialing their radio to a particular frequency. The signs do not talk, but low-frequency radio waves do.

These signs can be FM or AM. AM models have a slightly longer range, but are still under 300 feet. The transmitters are in the building and use continuous tapes broadcasting a message. Installation simply requires that they be plugged in. Machines are available for under $200 each through radio supply and real estate supply vendors.

The signs give a 24-hour message which could include the size of available rentals, when they can be shown, rental rates, property damage bonds, pet restrictions or allowances, special amenities included, parking information, etc. Talking signs can be a prerental

tool in that, after hearing the message, anyone who views a unit or space available has probably found what meets his/her needs.

Some property managers who use talking signs use a locally recognized voice for the message.

F. FLAGS, BALLOONS, AND THE OPEN HOUSE

When a unit with vacancies is on a well-travelled street, simply placing an "Open House" sign with a few balloons or flags outside will bring in traffic. This works best on Saturdays and Sundays from the hours of 11 A.M. to around 3 P.M.

G. THE INTERNET

Craigslist is rapidly replacing classified ads for advertising rental properties.

The Internet can be an effective and low-cost tool to rent all kinds of property. You can include photographs, as well as detailed rental information. An "800" number will increase the volume of contacts that you receive from your website.

Take advantage of "social networking" sites, such as Facebook, Twitter, and YouTube, to increase your "sphere of influence" as well as advertise your rental property.

H. PERSONNEL OFFICES

Large employers in your area will probably have new and transferred employees relocating to your area.

VOICE OF EXPERIENCE:

By talking with company personnel managers, you should be able to work out a mutually beneficial arrangement. Knowing the names of employees moving to the area gives you the opportunity to contact them and find out their needs prior to actually meeting with them.

I. CHAMBERS OF COMMERCE

Chambers of Commerce receive area inquiries in a constant stream. They will supply you with the names and addresses of persons and firms interested in or who are moving to the area.

You can mail out information on your rentals including an "800" number for them to call for further information. If you have one, you may also want to include your Internet address.

J. BILLBOARDS

Billboards can be effectively used to promote new, large rental developments where the owners wish to stabilize the property quickly. Billboards are expensive. They fall into different categories, including.

Bus Stop Displays. Bus stop displays are usually about 3 feet by 6 feet, and are limited by their size according to the message.

Junior Posters. Junior posters are also known as 8-sheet displays. They have a 5 foot x 11 foot viewing area.

Standard Billboards. Standard billboards are 12 feet x 25 feet in size.

Bulletins. These are the large highway billboards. They are 14 feet x 48 feet. A bulletin in a well-trafficked area could cost $3,000 to $5,000 per month, and this is without special effects.

K. PUBLIC TRANSIT ADS

Ads are sold on the inside and outside of buses. While the outside ads are traveling billboards, the inside ads are studied by many transit passengers simply because there is nothing else to do.

These ads can be effective for low-range and mid-range rentals that emphasize transit convenience and price.

L. CLASSIFIED ADS/CRAIGSLIST

People looking for rentals do check the local newspapers. However, classified ads are more effective for bringing inquires than for actually renting properties. As mentioned previously, **Craigslist** is rapidly replacing classified newspaper ads for advertising rental properties.

Whether in a newspaper or online, ads should indicate area, size (number of bedrooms), and monthly rent. If there are unusually positive features, like a garage or pets allowed, this should be emphasized.

The heading should be the strongest feature or a combination of features, such as:

West Hollywood - $900
Bring Your Dog
2BR - West L.A.

VOICE OF EXPERIENCE:

Newspaper classified ads are being replaced by the more immediate and cost-effective websites such as Craigslist and Yellowpages.com. You can also post a video of your available rental property on YouTube and see your ad go "viral" all over the world. Talk about increasing the circulation of an ad!

Newspapers offer lower rates for classified ads that run for longer periods of time. We feel this is a false economy. The greatest effect is when the ad first appears. People seeking rentals check the classifieds for new rentals. We believe that an ad should run for no more than three days. The ad should then be rewritten for a later insertion.

The best days to advertise are generally on the highest circulation days, which are normally weekends, since this is when many people search for rentals.

The best time to advertise is at the first of the month when 30-day notices are often given out. Even if nothing is available, you can advertise what will be available at the end of the month. Being able to avoid a break in rent production is good management.

M. DISPLAY ADS

DISPLAY ADS are block ads. They are costly and should be reserved for advertising a large number of properties to rent or for a large nonresidential property. They are good for initial leasing of new units.

If you use models in the display ad photographs, be careful that the photos do not raise the question of discrimination. As a rule of thumb, when you use models in your photographs, try for 20 percent to 25 percent minority representation.

N. SELECTION OF NEWSPAPERS

The media choices you make are important, as ads for particular properties will be more effective in particular papers.

1. Daily Newspapers

Chances are your daily newspaper is the newspaper with the greatest number of classified rental ads for the type of property and area in which you are advertising.

Your area may be served by a local daily newspaper such as the *Orange County Register* and an area daily such as the *Los Angeles Times*. Because of the huge circulation area for the *Los Angeles Times*, advertising rates are significantly higher. Since most persons renting come from within a 20-mile area, the *Orange County Register* would likely be more cost effective to advertise a rental in Orange County than the *Los Angeles Times*.

2. Weekly Throwaway Papers

Throwaway papers give you the opportunity to target a smaller area. An advantage of the throwaways is that many lower income households today do not subscribe to newspapers on a regular basis and these free papers are readily available.

The ads are usually mixed so that readers must search for what they are looking for. These throwaways are effective for rentals and should be utilized where applicable. You can use classified as well as display advertising at a relatively low cost.

3. Foreign Language Papers

Foreign language papers can target readers who are interested in what you have to lease.

As an example, in advertising a commercial location or residential unit in an area having a significant Korean presence, you might consider using a Korean language newspaper, in addition to other advertising.

When advertising, you must be careful to avoid illegal steering.

VOICE OF EXPERIENCE:

If you only advertise property in the Korean newspaper for renting property in the Korean neighborhood, you could be suspected of steering. Advertise property located in other areas in the same newspaper to avoid any hint of your discriminating in advertising.

4. Special Interest Papers

There are a wide variety of English language papers that target national origin groups, religious groups, as well as racial groups.

Gay-orientated publications can be productive for upscale area residential rentals and unusual rentals, such as lofts. Because many of the readers are in business for themselves, they are also a good media for advertising commercial space.

O. RENTAL MAGAZINES

When you have a number of residential units available and your property has good curb appeal, you should consider rental magazines which, like home sale magazines, are available free in newspaper racks in most areas of the country. Rental magazines are usually monthly pictorial magazines and are quite effective in reaching people relocating to the area.

P. MOVIE SCREEN ADS

Movie theaters advertise on screen before the feature films. An ad in a local theater featuring rentals in the area can be effective if the screen advertising indicates that brochures are available in the lobby that provide additional information. Otherwise, viewers will forget who the advertiser was for the rental that appeared interesting.

Q. RADIO

Radio stations can supply you with a great deal of information about the demographics of their listeners. The information includes age, education, income, etc.

With this information you can target rental audiences to the group or groups likely to be renters. As an example, a station having a great many educated, affluent young listeners would probably include many who were interested in one-bedroom units with pool and health club facilities in a desirable location.

Ad times are 15 seconds, 30 seconds or one minute. Your local radio station can help prepare your radio ads. Morning or afternoon "drive time" is usually the most expensive.

R. TELEVISION ADS

Television advertising is generally expensive, but many communities now have classified advertising cable channels that project your ads. Some of the channels allow you to include a voice override. These cable classifieds appear to be an effective way to promote residential rentals. We don't think that they will be effective advertising for commercial, office or industrial space.

S. TELEPHONE SOLICITATIONS

Many leasing agents who handle nonresidential property will analyze who can use the property and then start calling using the yellow pages of their local telephone book. It is tedious, but one or two successes per month can produce above-average income, depending upon the rent.

T. NEIGHBORHOOD WALK-AROUND

Some agents who have available vacant commercial, industrial or office space will walk the areas talking to other tenants about the available space. A side benefit of this procedure is that an agent discovers the needs of renters in the area for other properties that the agent may have available.

U. FURTHER AD HELP

If you want assistance in the actual composition of ad copy and greater insight into the use of advertising media, we suggest two books published by Real Estate Education Company. They are *The Big Book of Real Estate Ads* and *Power Real Estate Advertising*, by William and Bradley Pivar.

IV. CHAPTER SUMMARY

There are a number of ways to promote your firm and personal image.

Meeting people who can help you, which would include:

1. membership in property owner groups;
2. public speaking before groups such as Rotary Clubs;
3. teaching real estate related classes at your local community college;
4. being active in religious organizations, and
5. belonging to service organizations and/or lodges.

Don't be a "secret agent."

Press releases can positively portray you and/or your firm. Press releases could cover:

1. new management contracts;
2. professional achievements of you or employees;
3. a major new tenant for a property;
4. achievements of individual agents within the firm;
5. the leasing activity of a major new project;
6. a new property manager in your firm;
7. promotion of a property manager, and
8. a change in office location, new office or opening of a satellite office.

Personal promotion of an individual would include:

1. business cards,
2. name signs, and
3. car signs.

Writing a newspaper column or Internet blog will help your image with the general public.

Writing an article for a professional journal or active participation within a professional organization will enhance your image within the profession.

Management signs on quality properties will show the presence of your firm. Strip "Leased" signs over "For Lease" signs indicate the success of your firm.

Use of a logo on all your firm's signs and ads tends to increase the market presence of your firm in the minds of the public as well as within the profession.

Many people will view the size of a yellow page ad with the firm's importance within the marketplace.

Institutional ads for your firm do not rent a particular property.

There are many sources for obtaining management as well as leads to management opportunities.

Referrals from owners are a quality source because contacts will be half sold before you talk with them. By paying referral fees, you gain management opportunities from the contacts of other brokers.

Bird dogs are people who like you, and are concerned with your success. A bird dog will keep his or her eyes peeled for opportunities of management or leasing.

Owners of properties contiguous to properties you manage are a natural for management because of savings possible in managing contiguous properties. When property comes available for sale adjacent to a property you manage, you should point out to your owner the management economies possible if he or she would purchase the property.

New owners of income property should be contacted about management.

Lending institutions require management for their foreclosures and trust inventories of real estate.

A property that has been vacant for a long period of time or has a high vacancy factor will likely have an unhappy owner who could be ripe for management.

Problem properties are often those where obtaining management might be relatively easy, but you must decide if you want to manage them.

Problem properties include:

1. properties having outstanding code violations;
2. properties having a high number of evictions;
3. properties where the owners are delinquent in taxes, and
4. poorly managed property evidenced by the physical condition of the premises.

Newspaper advertising can hint at an owner's need for management. Advertising hints may include:

1. continuously running rental ads;
2. ads indicating an owner wants to trade income property for something else, and
3. an owner's For Sale ad that indicates the owner is extremely motivated to sell.

Real estate investors, developers and speculators are all excellent sources for management opportunities.

Fannie Mae is a source of contracts to manage and renovate (usually single-family homes) until they can be sold.

If an owner indicates he or she already has a property manager, don't pursue management unless instigated to do so by the owner. Never criticize your competition.

Consulting contracts involve advice without action. Leasing contracts involve leasing activity without management. However, many successful leases have led to management.

You market your vacant property by seeking tenants. There are many ways to locate persons and firms that can use your space. They include:

1. referrals from other brokers wishing to cooperate and share in the leasing commission;

2. providing advance fee rental agents with the information on residential vacancies;

3. canvassing tenants to see if their friends or firms they deal with would like to live or occupy space close to the tenants.

4. "For Lease" signs are the most cost effective way to find tenants;

5. talking signs give a radio message about the property;

6. weekend open houses for residential vacancies are effective on high-traffic streets;

7. the Internet; a low-cost method to spread information about your inventory of vacancies;

8. major area personnel offices that can give you information on new hires and job transfers;

9. Chambers of Commerce that can supply information about firms and persons interested in relocating in your area;

10. billboards that can be used for large leasing projects. They include:

    a. bus stop displays,
    b. junior posters,
    c. standard billboards, and
    d. bulletins.

11. public transit ads that can be outside the bus or inside placards;

12. using the classified columns as part of their marketing plan, as people do check classified ads;

13. display ads. These are block ads and are fairly costly;

14. rental magazines that cover residential projects;

15. a selection of newspapers, which include:

    a. daily newspapers;
    b. weekly throwaway papers;
    c. foreign language papers, and
    d. special interest papers.

16. movie screens that can be used for area residential rental ads;

17. radio ads that can be used for property likely to appeal to the demographics of a station's listeners;

18. television ads, which are expensive, but there are cable television stations that run a classified channel, which can be an effective residential rental medium;

19. telephone solicitations targeted at firms who can use particular nonresidential space can be very effective;

20. persons you may discover who are interested in nonresidential vacancy space by knocking on doors in the area.

V. CHAPTER QUIZ

1. You can personally promote yourself by all of the following, except:
    a. business cards.
    b. name tags.
    c. car signs.
    d. fee splitting.

2. A logo refers to a(n):
    a. geographical location.
    b. identifying design.
    c. operational plan.
    d. estimated operating budget.

3. Which of the following ads would be an institutional ad?
    a. An ad that simply gives the firm name and the words "Property Management"
    b. A letter to an owner requesting property management
    c. A classified "For Rent" ad for an apartment
    d. A "For Lease" sign on a commercial building

4. The term "bird dog" refers to a(n):
    a. illegal practice.
    b. problem property.
    c. teaser contract offer.
    d. person who watches for opportunities for you.

5. Indications of a problem property include:
    a. code violations.
    b. frequent evictions.
    c. poor maintenance.
    d. all of the above.

6. Speculators differ from investors in that speculators:
   a. buy with cash.
   b. expect to have a shorter holding period.
   c. buy more expensive property.
   d. only buy raw land.

7. When you discover that a prospect you have contacted for management already has a management firm, the professional approach would be to:
   a. ask when the contract expires.
   b. agree to cut the price.
   c. thank the owner and end the discussion.
   d. sign a contract that does not take effect until the other contract expires.

8. Which of the following contracts include partial management duties?
   a. An exclusive right to lease
   b. A management consulting contract
   c. An offer to purchase
   d. Both a and b

9. Advance fee rental agencies:
   a. charge a fee to prospective tenants.
   b. charge owners to advertise their properties.
   c. provide prospective tenants with lists of vacancies.
   d. both a and c.

10. The most cost effective method of advertising to fill a vacancy would be a:
   a. television ad.
   b. radio ad.
   c. "For Rent" sign.
   d. classified ad.

ANSWERS: 1. d; 2. b; 3. a; 4. d; 5. d; 6. b; 7. c; 8. d; 9. d; 10. c

Chapter 13
Fair Housing and Ethics

KEY WORDS AND TERMS

Americans With Disabilities Act
Blockbusting
Civil Rights Act of 1866
Civil Rights Act of 1964
Civil Rights Act of 1968
Civil Rights Act of 1870
Equal Credit Opportunity Act
Equal Housing Opportunity
Equal Housing Opportunity Poster
Executive Order 11603
Fair Housing

Fair Housing Amendment Act
Familial Status
Fourteenth Amendment
Jones v. Mayer
Mental Handicap
Physical Handicap
Readily Achievable
Redlining
Reverse Caregiver Law
Steering
Voluntary Affirmative Marketing Agreement

CHAPTER 13 OUTLINE

I. Fair Housing (Federal)

Fair housing does not mean "equal housing." You need to know the law to keep out of trouble and be sensitive to discrimination issues.

People are not equal in their energy and productivity regarding income and savings. Equal housing would not be fair because it could reward sloth rather than accomplishments. Fair housing refers to equal housing opportunity. The right of all persons to live where they wish to live, subject only to economics, without artificial barriers being placed before them.

There are a number of federal as well as state laws and court decisions that provide for fair housing. As a property manager, you must realize that fair housing is the law of our land and that discriminatory practices will not be tolerated by the courts, the public or your profession.

A. THE CIVIL RIGHTS ACT OF 1866

This act, passed shortly after the Civil War, actually predated the 14th Amendment to the Constitution. The act provides that "all citizens of the United States shall have the same right in every state and territory as is enjoyed by white citizens thereof to inherit, purchase, lease, sell, hold, and convey real and personal property."

The act had not been enforced by the courts until 1968 when, in the case of *Jones v. Mayer*, the U.S. Supreme Court held that the Civil Rights Act of 1866 could be enforced by a private citizen. Until that time, it had become a forgotten relic that courts had refused to enforce because of some very narrow interpretations.

What is important about the Civil Rights Act of 1866 is:

Application. It applies to race only.

Property. It applies to both real and personal property.

No Exceptions. Since there are no exceptions to this act, it serves to wipe out exceptions set forth in some later acts.

Violations. Violations of the act could result in a judgment for compensatory and even punitive damages. The court could also order an injunction to make a person cease from discriminatory activities. Continuance would place that party in contempt of court.

B. 14TH AMENDMENT

The **14TH AMENDMENT** *provides that no state can abridge the privileges of citizens or deprive them of property without due process.* It also provides for the equal protection of all persons under the law. It is a broad civil rights act that implicitly provides for fair housing.

C. CIVIL RIGHTS ACT OF 1870

This law was really just the reiteration of the 1866 law. It was passed since Congress was worried that courts might later claim that the 14th Amendment superceded the Civil Rights Act of 1866.

D. EXECUTIVE ORDER 11603

This 1962 order, issued by President John F. Kennedy, prohibited discrimination in housing where there was federal involvement, such as loan programs or federal grants.

E. CIVIL RIGHTS ACT OF 1964

This act simply made law what was set forth in the prior executive order. The application of this act was still very limited.

F. CIVIL RIGHTS ACT OF 1968

This is our basic Fair Housing Act.

The **CIVIL RIGHTS ACT OF 1968** *prohibits housing discrimination based upon race, color, national origin, and religion*. In 1974, coverage was extended to **sex** and the 1988 amendment extended coverage to **handicapped** as well as for **familial status**.

1. Exemptions

There are four exemptions to the Civil Rights Act of 1968. However, these are not exempt by the Civil Rights act of 1866:

1. Nonprofit housing owned or leased by religious groups may limit sale or lease to members of their group as long as membership in the religion is not discriminatory.
2. Private clubs can discriminate in the sale or lease of housing if they limit the sale or lease to members and it is for noncommercial purposes.
3. Owner occupants, who do not use agents, may discriminate for one-to-four residential units providing no discriminatory advertising is used.
4. Persons who own three or less single-family rental homes are exempt if they do not use an agent, do not use discriminatory advertising and are not in the rental business.

2. Prohibitions

1. Agents cannot discriminate against owners, buyers, lessors, or lessees.
2. It is illegal to claim a property is unavailable when it is actually available.
3. Directing prospective buyers or tenants towards or away from property based on race, color, etc., is illegal. This is known as **"steering."**

4. Refusal to loan within an area is known as **"redlining"** and is an illegal practice.

5. Inducing panic selling by representing that minority groups entering the area will lead to crime or reduced values is illegal. This is known as **"blockbusting."**

6. Discriminatory advertising is prohibited (this was covered in more detail in Chapter 12).

7. Different lease terms based upon race, color, etc., would be illegal. A lessor, seller or lender cannot hold a party to different qualifications because that party is a member of a protected group.

8. An owner or manager cannot take retaliatory action against a tenant because of a just complaint about property condition or violation of statute.

9. Agents may not discriminate by refusing access to multiple listing services.

From the National Fair Housing Advocate November 1996:

Orthodox Jews cannot break an electrical circuit on the Sabbath as it constitutes working on the Sabbath. A New York apartment complex installed electronic locks on the entryway. Orthodox Jews had to wait until another nonorthodox tenant opened the door in order to gain access. The plaintiffs asked the management company to go back to manual locks.

In reversing the decision of a trial court that the landlord had acted in a discriminatory manner, the court on appeal indicated that the fact that an act creates a burden on some individuals does not make the action discriminatory. It was obvious that electric locks were installed for the sole purpose of deterring crime. There was no allegation that the act had discriminatory intent. The court held that the inconvenience placed on some could not be deemed discriminatory (Seigel v. Blair Hall).

Note: This case points out that innocent acts can be deemed discriminatory by others and could require you to defend your actions.

Remember: Presumed discrimination may still need to be addressed.

From the National Fair Housing Advocate October 1996:

A discrimination case against a Florida mobile home park was settled for $81,250.

A Hispanic couple alleged that they were discouraged from applying to rent lot space at the park. They had reached an agreement to purchase a mobile home in the park and when the resident manager met the couple, they were told they would not like living in the park. They nevertheless applied for a lot and their application was rejected.

▼

The park did not require a minimum income level. They required only good credit and one financial reference. The park management, however, required the Hispanic couple to submit three credit references, three personal references and identify three bank accounts in their names. The couple met all of these additional requirements but were still rejected.

The park owners claimed that the reason the couple was rejected was that it was a seniors-only complex and the Hispanic couple were not over 55. However, the owner of the mobile home that they wished to buy was only 52 years of age at the time her application to rent was approved.

A young white, non-Hispanic tester was told of several available lots and no age restriction was mentioned. A young Hispanic tester was told that he would not be able to rent because he was too young.

After the court ordered the owners of the park to submit income and net worth information to support a punitive damage claim, the park settled. (*Pina v. Mutchnik* No. 94-6084 [S.D. Fla]).

Do not accept a property management contract where you can perceive discrimination of any kind.

From the National Fair Housing Advocate October 1996:

A white woman won a settlement from the owners of a rental house in Lincoln, Nebraska.

She applied for an apartment with her black boyfriend. Her daughter would also be living with them. The rental application was denied because the references were deemed inadequate, the boyfriends' income was not considered sufficient if anything happened to her and the landlord wanted no more than two persons in the unit.

The apartment in question was later rented and occupied by five people (a couple, their children and a grandchild). This cast doubt on the real reason why the rental application was refused.

From the National Fair Housing Advocate September 1997:

A Minnesota mother of three received a large awarded by a jury based on discrimination. She charged that her landlord discriminated based upon race, sex, and disability.

She was awarded $153,000 for racial discrimination, $105,000 for emotional distress, $60,000 in punitive damages and $18,000 for out-of-pocket expenses.

▼

The lawsuit alleged that the landlord treated African-American tenants differently than white tenants. She referred to African Americans as "You people" and let herself into apartments without notice or knocking. She also allegedly refused to schedule maintenance for African-American tenants.

It was also alleged one of the landlords chased the tenant's daughters with a stick and called a daughter a "crazy nigger." Witnesses claimed she had chased an African-American boy with a hammer after he rode his bike on her lawn and had called him a "nigger."

The plaintiff, who has a mental disability, claimed one of the landlords called her "crazy," "goofy," "cockeyed," and "idiot."

The husband of the landlord allegedly told the plaintiff that "girls could be short on the rent" and that he became sexually aggressive and intimidating.

There were numerous other complaints in this case. The award, when given, was the largest housing award to a single-family since the Fair Housing Act was passed in 1968.

Note: Discrimination applies to all aspects of dealing with tenants, not just refusal to rent and rental terms.

These landlords outdid themselves on many levels. A competent property manager could have saved the money and grief.

G. 1988 FAIR HOUSING AMENDMENT ACT

This act extended the coverage afforded by the 1968 act to handicapped as well as familial status.

1. Handicapped

HANDICAPPED includes both physical and mental handicaps. Physical handicaps affect a life function. Hearing, sight and mobility would be covered. While drug addiction is not considered a protected category under handicaps, alcoholism, AIDS, cancer, etc., are protected.

Important points for property managers are:

1. A lessor cannot refuse a handicapped tenant who has a seeing eye dog or other support animal even if the lessor otherwise has a no pets policy. Security deposits cannot be increased over what others are charged because of the seeing eye dog or support animal.

2. A tenant may modify his/her unit and common areas at the tenant's expense so that he/she can enjoy the premises as would a nonhandicapped tenant. No additional security deposit may be charged because of the modifications although

the tenant may have to agree to restore the premises at the end of the tenancy if a nonhandicapped tenant would not wish the modifications. The tenant need not restore modifications to common areas.

3. The owner must make reasonable accommodations to rules and policies to allow the handicapped tenant to enjoy his or her unit. This could include a designated parking space close to the unit.

4. A landlord need not rent to a handicapped tenant whose presence would pose a health or safety danger to other tenants. Example would be a highly contagious disease or mental disorder that results in violent behavior toward others.

From the National Fair Housing Advocate October 1996:

A HUD administrative law judge approved a $13,000 settlement based on a claim of racial and disability discrimination.

The resident manager of an apartment complex refused to allow an elderly black couple to move from a second story unit to a ground floor unit. The complex had no elevator and the couple complained of poor health and had difficulty using the stairs. The manager told the couple that no units were available.

After the couple wrote the management company about their requests to move to the first floor, the management company notified them that their lease would not be renewed and that they would have to vacate upon its termination.

A HUD investigation revealed that a ground floor unit was available at the time the couple made their requests and that white disabled tenants were transferred to the first floor without written request. HUD alleged that the property management firm was not able to explain why white tenants were transferred to other apartments regularly but the black couple was told that units were not available. The management company claimed that they did not intentionally discriminate.

You need to be careful that your resident manager is well versed on fair housing issues.

From the National Fair Housing Advocate November 1996:

A $60,000 settlement was reached in a lawsuit against a California Homeowner's Association. It was alleged that a condominium association refused to allow a woman in a wheelchair the right to make reasonable modifications to her rental unit to accommodate her physical disability.

▼

She wished to build a ramp for access to her unit. The association denied her the request to build a ramp. She paid rent to the owner of the unit for three months without being able to use it. She then installed a temporary ramp. She was ordered by the association to remove it since "ramps displace landscape."

In addition to the refusal to allow a ramp, the condominium association complex was not accessible to the handicapped in other ways. Some walkways were too narrow for wheelchairs and there were no ramps at the clubhouse, denying wheelchair access.

In addition to the monetary award, the settlement required the property be inspected for accessibility, establish procedures for dealing with accessibility requests and the members of the association were required to attend training in fair housing.

From the National Fair Housing Advocate November 1996:

The owners and managers of a Maryland apartment complex settled a disability discrimination lawsuit by agreeing to furnish the plaintiff with an apartment for life (lifetime value estimated at $340,000 plus pay $160,000 in compensatory damages).

The plaintiff, who is deaf, blind and has Usher's Syndrome wished to rent a unit. He made it clear that he was able to live independently and even offered to pay a full year's rent in advance. The agent refused the offer stating that the complex did not have facilities for the handicapped and recommended a nearby complex.

The federal lawsuit alleged intentional discrimination because of the plaintiff's disability and steering him to alternate housing (both fair housing violations).

Fair housing violations can be expensive in more than monetary penalties, i.e., lack of empathy!

From the National Fair Housing Advocate December 1997/January 1998:

A disabled person wished to purchase a unit modified for a handicapped person. He asked the association to make accommodations to the rules prohibiting a home business. Since he had been unable to work outside his home since the late 1980s, he wished to meet clients in his home.

The board of directors told him that two-thirds of the residents had to agree to grant the exception. There were two votes, both of which resulted in disapproval. The unit was not purchased by him. He purchased another unit elsewhere that required expensive modifications for his handicapped use.

The Fair Housing Council of Greater Washington filed a complaint resulting in a $180,000 settlement. It was noted that a disabled person's need to work at home should have been accommodated if it did not interfere with the quiet enjoyment of other owners.

There is no substitute for common sense and fair play.

From the National Fair Housing Advocate November 1996:

A San Jose woman settled a discrimination lawsuit for $126,000. She was confined to a wheelchair and her only access was using the apartment elevator. The elevator was frequently out of order forcing her husband to take her up and down the stairs if she wanted to leave the apartment.

The defendants were repeatedly notified of the condition of the elevator and their solution allegedly was to have her call a maintenance man to help her up and down the stairs.

Note: Apparently failure to properly maintain the premises can be discriminatory if it unreasonably denies handicapped access.

In some instances, lack of adequate maintenance may be viewed as discrimination.

From the National Fair Housing Advocate November 1996:

An appellate court in New York determined that a co-op must make reasonable alterations of common areas to accommodate handicapped residents.

The co-op had a policy that no co-op funds could be spent installing wheelchair ramps or other accommodations for handicapped residents.

The court ruled that the refusal violated federal law.

From the National Fair Housing Advocate November 1996:

Owners and managers of a California apartment complex agreed to a $100,000 settlement of a claim that they discriminated against a tenant with a mental disability.

The apartment manager told a tenant she could not keep her dog since they had a no-pet policy. The tenant's doctor wrote a letter to the owners and managers that the tenant needed the companion dog to help in controlling her mental disability. Attempts to mediate the problem failed and the tenant was served with an eviction notice. The tenant's suit resulted in the settlement.

Note: The 1988 amendment to the Fair Housing Act adds mental disability as well as physical disability to the protected group. The law allows support animals. The only defense the apartment complex could raise is that a "companion dog" is not a support animal. The landlord and manager decided to settle rather than risk an adverse court decision coupled with the cost of litigation.

This case indicates a manager should seek legal counsel before evicting a tenant with a pet if it is claimed that a pet serves a necessary purpose for a handicapped person.

A similar case reported in the February 1997 National Fair Housing Advocate involved a man who had several stress related disabilities. One of the few sources of relief was his cat. His mental health counselor wrote to the management that the cat was a necessary service animal. The complex began eviction proceedings. The HUD administrative law judge awarded the man $5,569 and a penalty to HUD of $5,000.

Always check with legal counsel prior to eviction when facing a problematic issue.

2. Familial Status

FAMILIAL STATUS relates to family. Important aspects of the amendment as it relates to familial status are:

1. A lessor cannot discriminate because there are children under the age of 18 living with the parent (parent, guardian or custodian).

2. A lessor cannot discriminate because a person is pregnant or in the process of gaining custody.

3. Exemptions that apply to familial status would be housing occupied by at least one person age 55 or older when at least 80 percent of the units have persons 55 or older (formerly this exemption required that the units have facilities that are special to the needs of older persons but this limitation has been removed).

Several states, such as California, have *REVERSE CAREGIVER LAWS, which allow persons who do not meet the age restrictions for senior housing to move in if they are providing*

needed care for someone who lives in the complex. The person need not have medical training.

Non-seniors claiming to be providing needed assistance to a person in a senior community could likely reside as a permanent guest, if state law or state court decisions allowed caregivers in senior housing.

Asking the marital status of prospective tenants could be dangerous if the tenants later claim that the refusal to rent to them was based on their marital status.

While state courts differ, the California Supreme Court has held that lessors may not refuse to rent to unmarried couples even though the lessors' religious beliefs were that they were aiding in sin if they allowed the couples to cohabit in the lessors' dwellings. The U.S. Supreme Court is likely to rule in this matter. Freedom of religion in this case is colliding with the basic rights of tenants.

From the National Fair Housing Advocate September 1997:

An Ohio landlord settled a familial status lawsuit by paying $100,000, agreeing to attend fair housing training along with his employees and to apologize to a family for not allowing them to move into a building he had designated adult only.

The landlord in this case had wrongfully designated some buildings for adults and some for families. At the time the family applied, the only vacancies were in adult buildings and the family was denied a rental in a family building.

Case Example

Smith v. Fair Employment and Housing Commission, 12 Cal.4th 700 (1996)

The California Fair Employment and Housing Act (FEHA) declared it unlawful for any housing accommodation to discriminate against any person on the basis, among other things, of marital status. The Fair Employment Housing Commission ruled a landlord violated the statute by refusing to rent an apartment to an unmarried couple. The Court of Appeal reversed on the grounds that the state may not apply FEHA to a landlord whose religious beliefs make it sinful to rent to an unmarried couple. ▼

The California Supreme Court reversed that decision. The Court stated: "The First Amendment does not support Smith's claim. Her religion may not permit her to rent to unmarried cohabitants, but "the right of free exercise does not relieve an individual of the obligation to comply with a valid and neutral law of general application on that ground that the law proscribes (or prescribes) conduct that his religion prescribes (or proscribes).' .... The statutory prohibition against discrimination because of marital status ... is a law both generally applicable and neutral towards religion."

Case Example

PFAFF v. U.S. Dept. of Housing and Urban Development, 88 F. 3d 739 (1996)

Owners told their rental agent that occupancy of a 1,200 square foot two bedroom home would be limited to four persons because of its small size and lack of a basement or backyard. A rental application had been received from a family of five. The rental applicants then filed a complaint with HUD based on discrimination as to family status. An administrative law judge awarded $4,212.61 in compensatory damages, $20,000 for emotional distress and $8,000 in civil penalties.

The U.S. Court of Appeals reversed the administrative law judge's decision. The Appellate Court pointed out that landlords do not have to prove a compelling business reason for limiting occupancy since HUD has not set occupancy guidelines. The court held that occupancy of four was not unreasonable to protect the property. Since HUD has in the past used a two-person per bedroom rule of thumb, four persons should be presumed to be reasonable.

Note: The Appellate Court was strongly critical of HUD for going after the property owner when they had no guidelines.

Tenants do not always win. Common sense prevails.

From the National Fair Housing Advocate October 1996:

The Fair Housing Council of Orange County settled a racial and family status lawsuit for $775,000 against Clark Biggers, the owner of four apartment complexes in Southern California.

FHC alleged that Biggers discriminated against minorities and families with children. Families complained that they were either charged higher rents or were denied apartments at Bigger's complexes.

The Los Angeles Times felt that the FHC got "the short end of the settlement because an attorney for the FHC received $645,000 of the $775,000 settlement."

Note: A settlement does not mean admittance of guilt. Defendants often find it is cheaper to settle than to fight, even when they dispute the merit of the allegations.

H. ADVERTISING

Discriminatory advertising is prohibited by the Civil Rights Act of 1968.

Advertising that a property is close to a minority area or with a minority connotation such as "only two blocks from Martin Luther King High School" could be discriminatory. Mentioning a preference such as "females preferred" in an ad would be discriminatory even though expressed as a preference not an absolute.

HUD discourages use of specific words in advertising that indicate discrimination. Words included are, black, white, colored, Catholic, Protestant, Jew, Chicano, restricted, etc.

Selective use of advertising media, such as advertising a property in a minority area in papers only aimed at that minority group, could be discriminatory (**steering**).

VOICE OF EXPERIENCE:

There has been a great deal of confusion about what can or cannot be advertised. Some "experts" claim that it is discriminatory to advertise a view as it might offend the blind. While this may seem confusing or even ridiculous to you personally, it's best not to take any chances. Always err on the side of caution.

On January 9, 1995, HUD supplied a memo to its staff as to guidelines for discrimination investigation. The memo covered several points:

1. **Race, color and national origin.** Terms such as "master bedroom," "rare find" or "desirable neighborhood" are allowable. There had been concern that "master" was masculine and sexually discriminatory as well as being a term common to slavery.

2. **Religion.** Statements such as "apartment complex with chapel" or "kosher meals available" does not show preference for persons who might use these facilities.

3. **Sex.** "Master bedroom," "mother-in-law suite" and "bachelor apartment" are permissible. Many state organizations had been advising members that these terms were discriminatory.

4. **Handicap.** Reference to "view," "walk-up," "walk-in closets," etc. do not violate the act nor does "jogging trails" or "walk to bus stop." It is also acceptable to advertise "nonsmoking" or "sober" as these are prohibited activities. You cannot advertise "no alcoholics" or "nonsmokers" as these refer to groups of people.

5. **Familial Status.** Advertisements using terms such as "2 BR," "cozy," "familyroom," "no bicycles allowed" and "quiet streets" are allowed, but limiting age or sex of children is not allowed.

Advertising for singles or even a preference for adults would be discriminating.

Despite the HUD memorandum, there are still many unanswered questions about what HUD will or will not allow. A complicating factor is that words have different meanings in different areas of the country, as well as among different ethnic groups. Several state organizations have come up with guidelines addrerssing "acceptable," "caution," and "not acceptable" language.

Figure 13-1 is a list prepared by the Oregon Newspaper Publishers Association.

I. ENFORCEMENT OF THE CIVIL RIGHTS ACT OF 1968 (As Amended)

Remedies include:

1. HUD initiation of complaints on its own authority.
2. Individuals can file complaints with HUD.
3. Individuals can commence legal action.
4. Remedies:

The court could award:

a. actual damages;
b. punitive damages;
c. court costs and attorney fees, and/or
d. the court could issue an injunction.

1. Equal Housing Opportunity Poster

Failure of a leasing agent to prominently post the Equal Housing Opportunity Poster (**Figure 13-2**) will shift the burden of proof of discriminatory practices from the person claiming discrimination to the agent. This can be an extremely difficult task.

From the National Fair Housing Advocate January 1997:

A 20-year-old man and his 19-year-old wife were not allowed to fill out a rental application because they were both under the age of 21 and the apartment complex had a 21 and over policy. The age to contract is 18. It was alleged that the age policy was discriminatory and illegal. The apartment complex settled the matter for $5,200.

Figure 13-1

Discriminatory and Nondiscriminatory Advertising Language

Not Acceptable

able-bodied	Caucasian	membership approval
adult living	Chicano	required
adult community	Chinese	mentally handicapped, no
adults only	impaired, no	mentally ill, no
African	Indian	Mexican-American
agile	integrated	Mormon Temple
alcoholics, no	Irish	responsible
Asian	Jewish	retarded, no
bachelor	landlord (description of)	shrine
bachelor pad	Latino	stable
blacks, no	married	white
blind, no	mature couple	white only
board approval required	mature individual	
Catholic	mature person(s)	

Caution

active	fisherman's retreat	one person
children, no	gays, no	Oriental
church(es), near	gender	physically fit
colored	gentlemen's farm	Polish
close to	golden-agers only	Puerto Rican
country club, near	grandma's house	quiet tenants
couple	handyman's dream	responsible
couples only	healthy only	retarded, no
crippled, no	Hispanic	season worker, no
deaf, no	lesbians, no	single person
desirable neighborhood	male roommate	singles only
domestic's quarters	mosque	smokers, no
drinkers, no	must comply with	SSI, no
employed, must be	nationality	stable
empty nestors	newlyweds	synagogue, near
ethnic references	nondrinkers	temple, near
exclusive	nonsmokers	tenant (description of)
executive	no play area	unemployed, no
female roommate	older person(s)	
female(s) only	one child	

Acceptable

apartment
bus, near
credit check required
den
drinking, no
drugs, no
drug users, no
Equal Housing Opportunity
family, great for
family room
fixer-up neighborhood
hobby farm
male(s) only
man (men) only
mature
mother-in-law
nanny's room
near
neighborhood
name
no student(s)
number of bedrooms

number of persons
number of sleeping areas
nursery
nursing home
play area
prestigious
privacy
private
private driveway
private entrance
private property
public transport, near
quality
restricted
retired
retirees
school district
school name
secluded
Section 8, no
secure
senior citizen(s)

senior discount
senior housing
senior(s)
sex or gender
single woman, man
smoking, no
square feet
sophisticated
students
townhouse
traditional style
tranquil setting
two people
verifiable income
view of
view with
walking distance of
within
woman (women)

From the National Fair Housing Advocate March 1997:

Glendale Federal and the management company they used had to pay $440,000 to settle a discrimination case based on race, national origin, and family status.

After foreclosure, Glendale Federal hired a management company that terminated the tenancies so that the building could be renovated. The building was in a white neighborhood close to the U.C. Santa Barbara campus.

It was alleged that evictions were not necessary as the work contemplated could be performed without dislocating the tenant. It was alleged that the evictions had a disparate impact on Hispanics and families with children. The allegations were that Glendale wished to replace the Hispanic tenants and families with children with college students without children.

Note: It used to be considered good management if the character of a building could be changed resulting in higher rents. Now, you must be concerned with who will be replaced and are they members of a protected group. The management company could have simply raised rents which would have provided vacancies.

Figure 13-2

U.S. Department of Housing and Urban Development

**EQUAL HOUSING
OPPORTUNITY**

We Do Business in Accordance With the Federal Fair Housing Law

(The Fair Housing Amendments Act of 1988)

> **It is Illegal to Discriminate Against Any Person Because of Race, Color, Religion, Sex, Handicap, Familial Status, or National Origin**

- ■ In the sale or rental of housing or residential lots

- ■ In advertising the sale or rental of housing

- ■ In the financing of housing

- ■ In the provision of real estate brokerage services

- ■ In the appraisal of housing

- ■ Blockbusting is also illegal

Anyone who feels he or she has been discriminated against may file a complaint of housing discrimination:
   1-800-669-9777 (Toll Free)
   1-800-927-9275 (TDD)

U.S. Department of Housing and
Urban Development
Assistant Secretary for Fair Housing and
Equal Opportunity
Washington, D.C. 20410

Previous editions are obsolete

form HUD-928.1A(8-93)

From the National Fair Housing Advocate November 1997:

A California landlord agreed to a $7,500 settlement of a federal lawsuit alleging discrimination based on family status.

The plaintiff inquired as to a rental. When the landlord found out about two young sons, the landlord indicated that he did not want to rent to a family with children because the property was on a steep hill. A tester then inquired about the rental and the owner again stated that children would not be appropriate because of the steep slope and the fact that there was a creek running through the backyard that presented a safety hazard. The tester told the owner she did not think her children would be in danger. Upon later contact with the owner, the owner told the tester the property had been rented to persons without children.

VOICE OF EXPERIENCE:

Rather than refusing to rent to tenants with children because of the potential safety hazard of a steep slope and a creek running through the backyard, the lessor could have taken precautions to minimize the risks by erecting a fence around the dangerous areas. Potential liability may also be minimized by having tenants sign a document acknowledging their awareness of the situation. Even better, the tenant and landlord might agree to split the cost of improving the property so as to lessen the risk of harm.

J. AMERICANS WITH DISABILITIES ACT

The ***AMERICANS WITH DISABILITES ACT*** *protects those with physical and mental disabilities. It requires owners, operators, lessees, and managers of commercial facilities to make their facilities accessible to the extent that is readily achievable.* The reasonableness of providing access would be based on the difficulty of achieving access and the expense involved considering the total property value and the financial ability of the person responsible.

The Americans with Disabilities Act makes it discriminatory to deny equal enjoyment of goods, services, facilities, and accommodations in an existing place of public accommodation (nonresidential).

This would include stores, offices and service providers.

To comply with the act, a leasing office might have to:

1. provide handicap parking close to an office;
2. ramp the curb or steps;
3. lower a front counter for wheelchair access;
4. move furniture to provide wheelchair access;
5. add a paper cup dispenser by a water fountain;
6. install grab bars in washrooms;

7. any other reasonably achievable action that will allow full use and enjoyment of facilities by the handicapped.

An owner can charge more for sale or lease of handicapped accessible facilities.

1. Enforcement

The Americans with Disabilities Act can be enforced by:

1. an action by a citizen;
2. an action by the U. S. Attorney.

2. Penalties

Penalties for violations are severe:

1. $50,000 for first discriminatory act;
2. $100,000 for each additional act;
3. Damages (compensatory);
4. Attorney fees.

K. EQUAL CREDIT OPPORTUNITY ACT

As a property manager, the importance of this act relates to qualifying prospective renters.

You may not ask applicants questions about their childbearing intentions.

Applicants cannot be refused because of race, color, religion, national origin, sex, marital status, age, or because the source of income is public assistance.

Case Example

Gilligan v. Jamco Development Corp., 108 F. 3d 246 (1997)

This case involved a family who contacted a property manager about a vacancy. They indicated that their source of income was Aid To Families With Dependent Children (AFDC). The property manager refused to allow them to inspect units or to apply for a rental because they were on AFDC. The property manager never inquired about the amount of income the plaintiffs received nor did the manager inform them of the rent. A fair housing tester then contacted the property manager. The tester told the property manager she received welfare income. The tester was informed that Verduga Gardens was not a "Welfare Building." This tester was immediately followed by a second tester who indicated that he was working. The second was shown an apartment.

▼

The U.S. Court of Appeals held that discrimination applied to the application process and that AFDC did not make the plaintiff ineligible. Refusal to accept a rental application was discriminatory.

All rental applicants must be treated equally!

Can a property manager refuse to rent to a person who can be expected to lose assistance in the future? Unless the law is changed, the answer appears to be "No."

II. Fair Housing (State)

The reason that states have fair housing laws is primarily because the state legislation preceded the federal laws. As an example, California passed the **Unruh Act** that prohibits any business from discriminatory practice. This was interpreted to include real estate agents and property owners.

The Unruh Act provides for actual damages plus $250 for each offense.

California later passed a comprehensive fair housing act (**California Fair Employment and Housing Act**). The only exceptions to this act were for owners renting a room in their own housing unit as well as nonprofit religious, charitable and fraternal organizations. These exceptions were not applicable to the Unruh Act or the 1866 federal act.

California's Fair Employment and Housing Act provides that an owner or manager could be required to rent another available unit to the person discriminated against and be subject to a $10,000 civil penalty.

Many discrimination cases are brought under state law rather than federal law because of generally lower costs for litigation.

Most states also provide that discriminatory actions of a real estate licensee shall be grounds for disciplinary action that could include revocation of license.

III. HUD/NAR® Fair Housing Partnership

The National Association of REALTORS® (NAR) entered a Fair Housing Partnership with the Department of Housing and Urban Development (HUD). The Partnership focuses on identifying and eradicating housing discrimination. Because those issues and the priorities differ from community to community, NAR and HUD did not develop a specific model for local partnerships. Local NAR associations and HUD field offices are encouraged to develop local partnerships based on the following principles of the national partnership:

1. Sharing responsibility for the achievement of fair housing, identifying fair housing issues and concerns;

2. Developing measurable strategies and actions to address identified issues and concerns;

3. Evaluating the process of actions taken, and

4. Determining future strategies and actions based on that evaluation.

Your own association of REALTORS® offers training and guidance. Attend these informational seminars regularly.

IV. Ethics

Ethics is simply doing what is right.

If a wrong was committed, ethics would dictate that the wrong be corrected.

The problem that arises is, "What is right?" Some persons analyze actions from their own viewpoint. We have grown beyond the "If it's right for General Motors, it's right for America" way of thinking. We have gone beyond absolute self interest as justification of actions. However, beyond is actually back in a historical perspective. We are coming to realize that ethics isn't that difficult to understand.

Ethics is the application of the oldest rule for distinguishing right from wrong—The Golden Rule (Do unto others as you would have them to do unto you).

If you wouldn't want to be treated in a particular manner, you cannot ethically justify treating others in that manner.

Placing the interests of a client first is not incompatible with ethics. It is in the best interests of owners to treat employees, contractors and tenants in a fair manner. Actually, if you were to take advantage of others it would be detrimental to you in the long run.

Good ethics is good business.

Ethics differs from the law. Ethics is what is right. The law sets minimum standards of behavior. The law, however, could be unethical, such as early laws mandating racial segregation.

The following management situations and suggestions will help you understand the ethical considerations of property management.

A. SITUATION 1

Your firm, which manages Crayton Towers, has just merged with a competing firm that manages the adjacent and identical Winston Towers. Both of these high-rise apartment buildings have a 10 percent vacancy factor. You intend to establish just one rental contract offered for both buildings. You feel that this would be more efficient and that costs could be reduced. The Winston Towers' contract calls for the reimbursement of advertising costs, an agent rental bonus, and a slightly higher management fee than the Crayton Towers' contract. The Crayton Towers' contract has no charge for rentals.

What, if any, are the ethical problems involved?

Analysis: With the difference in costs and commissions, you are bound to have problems as to perception of wrongdoing. At the very least, the owner of Winston Towers should know how you will be allocating advertising costs since one office will be handling all advertising calls and walk-ins. However, this in itself would not be enough. Because the Winston Towers' contract is more lucrative, the owner of Cranston Towers could feel that Winston Towers would be getting preference in rentals. Even if you did not intend to give preference, your onsite leasing agent would be influenced by the bonus offer for Winston Towers' rentals.

Avoid any perceived conflict of interest at all costs.

There are two ways you could be fair to both owners. One way would be to continue two separate management arrangements with separate leasing offices. The other way would be to combine the offices, but negotiate identical contracts so that it would not be in the best interest of the onsite manager or the leasing agent to prefer one building over the other when leasing.

B. SITUATION 2

You are the managing agent for a freestanding single-tenant office structure. The building is in a racially integrated middle-class neighborhood. The property has been vacant for over one year because of a high office vacancy factor in the area coupled with insufficient off-street parking. The out-of-state owner is desperate for a tenant because of high mortgage payments.

Another agent has procured a prospective tenant for the structure. It is the "Hitler Society of America," a new Anglo-Saxon hate organization. They have been endowed by a wealthy benefactor who has agreed to a ten-year lease with one year's rent in advance. The benefactor has also agreed to sign as a guarantor on the lease. The Hitler Society of America wishes to use the structure as a national headquarters that will handle its publications and training of cadre for the various state organizations that will be established.

While the group's activities are obnoxious, checking with the State Attorney General, the FBI and local law enforcement officials indicates that, as of now, the group has managed to remain inside the law.

What should you do?

Analysis: This situation can be ethically decided two ways. If you believe that the First Amendment rights of free speech are so important that they must be protected at all costs, then you could ethically lease the property. However, you should fully disclose to the owner the nature of the tenant's activity before leasing. You should also check with your insurance carrier to ascertain if the carrier will continue to insure the structure based on the tenant. To not do so could be negligence on your part. If, after full disclosure, the owner wishes the leasing to go forward, you can then ethically execute the lease.

On the other hand, if you feel that leasing to this tenant is the equivalent of yelling "Fire" in a crowded theater, then you believe that free speech should not be paramount in this situation. Because you are an agent, you have to tell the owner about the tenant and you can ethically recommend that the prospective tenant be rejected. If the owner wishes to rent anyway, you can ask to be relieved of management.

If you signed the lease and kept management, your actions would be unethical because you believed them to be dangerous to the community without any overriding principal such as free speech.

VOICE OF EXPERIENCE:

Ethical decisions are not always obvious. They are influenced by your own application of the golden rule. Your owner's agenda, personal beliefs, and/or prejudices should not influence your decisions if they force yo to discard your integrity. Your honor should not be for sale at any cost.

C. SITUATION 3

You are managing a spectacular 4,200 square-foot oceanfront home that was built for the view. It sits atop of a 300-foot cliff that drops vertically only 75 feet from the patio. There is no fence by the cliff as the owners did not want to obstruct their view.

You feel you will have no trouble renting the home even though the rent is $10,000 per month and, in fact, the first persons to view it placed a rental deposit. They are a family with three children ages two, four and six. You warn them of the dangers for small children because of the cliff. You also tell them about the small child who was killed falling off the cliff at the home next door. However, the parents love the view and indicate that they will make certain that their children do not get too close to the cliff. Checking their application reveals that the prospective tenants are well qualified.

Analysis: If you truly believe that the children are in danger, you should do all in your power to prevent the family from renting the property. You could ask the parents to sign a waiver of liability in the hopes that it would make them reconsider renting.

Sometimes there are no easy decisions.

The 1988 Amendment to the Civil Rights Act of 1968 prohibits you from refusing to rent to a family because of the age or presence of children. However, law is not the same as ethics. Ethics is the way things should be. Law, on the other hand, sets legal limits to behavior. You could ethically violate the law in refusing the tenants, but legally you would be liable and subject to legal sanctions.

D. SITUATION 4

A tenant in a building with many small children has been criminally charged with child molestation. He denies the charge and is out on bail. Other tenants have asked you to evict the tenant.

Analysis: The tenant has not violated lease provisions and should not be considered guilty until proven so. The tenant should only be given notice to leave if you now were aware of something prior to his rental that, had you known, you would have refused the rental. As an example, you discover that the tenant has a previous conviction for child molestation, then you could be acting in an ethical manner in giving the tenant notice to vacate.

VOICE OF EXPERIENCE:

If possible, you should establish screening criteria that includes written consent to conduct a thorough criminal history background check. All criteria for applicant screening, lease enforcement, or eviction must be applied consistently for every applicant and/or resident. You should also make your tenants aware of "Megan's Law," which is federal legislation requiring law enforcement officials to make information available regarding the presence of sex offenders.

V. CHAPTER SUMMARY

The Civil Rights Act of 1866 provided that every citizen shall have the same rights as white citizens to purchase and lease real as well as personal property. There were no exceptions to the act. The Civil Rights Act of 1870 simply reiterated the 1866 Act. The act was not enforced by the courts until 1968 when the Supreme Court held in *Jones v. Mayer* that the act could be enforced by a private citizen.

The 14th Amendment to the Constitution is a broad statement of civil rights that implies fair housing.

In 1962, President John F. Kennedy issued Executive Order 11603 that bans discrimination in housing with federal involvement. The Civil Rights Act of 1964 made this executive order into law.

The Civil Rights Act of 1968 is also known as our Fair Housing Law. It prohibits discrimination in housing based on race, color, national origin, and religion. It was amended to cover sex, handicapped, and familial status. The act provides that:

1. agents cannot discriminate;
2. it is illegal to claim a unit is unavailable when it is available;
3. it is illegal to steer prospective tenants based on race, etc.;
4. refusal to loan within a designated area is illegal redlining;
5. blockbusting, the inducement of panic selling, is illegal;
6. discriminatory advertising is illegal;
7. lease terms that differ based on race, etc., are illegal;
8. retaliatory action against a tenant exercising legal rights is an illegal practice;
9. agents may not discriminate by refusal of multiple listing access.

The 1988 Fair Housing Amendment Act protects persons with mental and physical handicaps as well as to familial status. An owner cannot refuse to rent because of a seeing eye dog or support animal. Tenants may modify units to provide handicap access. Lessors cannot discriminate because there are children under the age of 18 or because the lessee is pregnant. Qualified senior housing (55 or older) is exempt.

The Americans With Disabilities Act requires places of public accommodation to provide that handicap access is readily achievable.

Ethics is simply doing what is right. It differs from law, which sets a minimum standard. Ethics goes beyond the law to the way things should be. However, ethical action could be illegal and legal action could be unethical. The Golden Rule is the best test for determining if a course of action is ethical.

VI. CHAPTER QUIZ

1. The Civil Rights Act that applied only to race was the Civil Rights Act of:

    a. 1866.
    b. 1964.
    c. 1968.
    d. 1988.

2. Directing a prospective tenant away from a property because you did not feel that he/she would be comfortable there based on the race of the current residents would be:

    a. blockbusting.
    b. steering.
    c. redlining.
    d. legal.

3. Which of the following is NOT be a member of a protected group under the 1988 Fair Housing Amendment Act?

    a. A blind person
    b. A person with AIDS
    c. A drug addict
    d. An alcoholic

4. A tenant has a seeing eye dog. The lessor can:

   a. charge an increased rent because of the pet.
   b. increase the security deposit to cover possible damage by the dog.
   c. refuse to rent to the person if there is a no-pet policy that is uniformly enforced.
   d. do none of the above.

5. An exception to the prohibition against discrimination as to familial status would be:

   a. children under the age of 18.
   b. a prospective tenant who is pregnant.
   c. housing for the elderly.
   d. an unmarried mother.

6. Which of the following advertising language would be acceptable?

   a. "Mother-in-Law suite"
   b. "Walk-up"
   c. "Family room"
   d. All of the above

7. A property management office installed a wheelchair ramp. They also installed grab bars in their washrooms. They did this to comply with:

   a. the Unruh Act.
   b. Americans With Disabilities Act.
   c. Executive Order 11603.
   d. Fair Housing Amendment Act of 1988.

8. In qualifying a tenant, a property manager can refuse a tenant for all, except:

   a. poor credit history.
   b. problems with prior landlords.
   c. no verifiable source of income.
   d. income from public assistance programs.

9. A property management office failed to display an Equal Housing Opportunity poster. The result would be:

   a. revocation of the broker's license.
   b. a $1,000 fine only.
   c. a $10,000 fine only.
   d. shifting of the burden of proof if discrimination is claimed.

10. The best test to determine if an action is ethical would be to consider the:

   a. cost.
   b. legality.
   c. Golden Rule.
   d. benefits.

ANSWERS: 1. a; 2. b; 3. c; 4. d; 5. c; 6. d; 7. b; 8. d; 9. d; 10. c

BELLEVUE
REALTORS®
SALES ~ RENTALS
INVESTMENT
PROPERTIES
PARKING
c1859
STUDENT RENTALS

Chapter 14
Tenant and Owner Relations

KEY WORDS AND TERMS

Alternative Dispute Resolution (ADR)
Change In Terms
Confidentiality
Constructive Eviction
Eleven-Month Year
Eviction
Fair and Honest Dealing
Fiduciary Duty
Full Disclosure
Honesty
Leases in Spanish
Low-Balling
Loyalty
Mediation
Mitigation of Damages

Negotiation
Obedience
Physical Eviction
Quit or Cure
Quit or Pay Rent
Reasonable Care and Skill
Retaliatory Eviction
Seizure of Property
Surrender
Tenant Complaints
Tenant Repair Rights
Unlawful Detainer
Waiting List
Waste

Chapter 14

CHAPTER 14 OUTLINE

I. Tenant Relations

A. TENANT EDUCATION

As previously stated, tenants should fully understand the lease provisions as well as the property rules and regulations at the time the lease is signed. You can do this by going through the lease paragraph by paragraph. You can do the same with the occupancy rules and regulations. A great many of the tenant problems that occur can be prevented by carefully explaining what is expected of the tenants.

In California, and several other states, if a lease is negotiated in Spanish, then a Spanish translation must be provided to the tenant.

Spanish translations of commonly used residential leases are readily available. For other tenants who do not speak English, you should arrange to have someone present when the lease is signed who can explain the lease and occupancy rules. This is the time to avoid future problems.

You should not be the translator even if you speak the language.

State law generally requires that tenants in multifamily apartments be given the name and address of the person to whom notices and demands are to be sent and who is responsible for management of the property.

B. RENTING TO FRIENDS AND RELATIVES

Your relationship with tenants should be on a business basis.

While you should be friendly and fair, you do not want a situation to develop where there could be any perception or misunderstanding about your loyalties. Your fiduciary duties lie with your principal, the owner of the property that you manage.

People close to you make terrible tenants. They tend to feel they are special and expect special treatment and relaxed occupancy rules. When your aunt buys a poodle, do you give her notice? If Uncle Charley promised to have the rent to you on Thursday and didn't, do you give him a three-day notice?

In addition, if you gave the person any inducement to rent, such as free rent, it could appear to be a breach of your fiduciary duty of loyalty to the owner. At the very least, when renting to a relative or close friend, you should inform the owner prior to the rental and give the owner all rental details and explain how you qualified the tenant.

Full disclosure of all relationships must be made. When in doubt, disclose. Better yet, avoid renting to any close relatives or friends.

C. ROMANTIC ENTANGLEMENTS

Don't get involved with a tenant or rent to anyone with whom you are involved. Romantic entanglements can be costly, especially clandestine ones.

Enforce this prohibition with employees in your office. To start with, you could put yourself in a position of having divided loyalties. Should the relationship sour, you also have a good chance of losing a tenant.

A property manager related to us how he rented an apartment he managed to a girlfriend. When the girlfriend failed to pay the rent on time and he called her about it, she told him, "Do you think your wife would like to know about our relationship?" Although that ended the relationship, he ended up paying the rent for over two years.

D. TENANT COMPLAINTS

You should keep a record of every tenant complaint.

Using your computer, you can relate complaints by tenant, time period and type of problem. This ability can help you in a number of ways. It can indicate maintenance deficiencies, personnel problems, service contract problems and problems relating to the tenant.

It is not enough that you record the complaint. When the action was taken and by whom is also important. You don't want a tenant to have to make a second call asking why nothing was done. It indicates a disgruntled tenant.

VOICE OF EXPERIENCE:

If the tenant was not told what action would be taken about a complaint at the time it was received, the tenant should be notified as soon as possible thereafter about what action has or will be taken and by whom.

Tenants should never be led to believe that their complaint has fallen on deaf ears. Similarly, tenants should never be led to believe that you will do something when you will not. As an example, suppose a tenant complains that the automatic sprinkler system wakes him up and he wants the sprinklers set to run during the daytime rather than at night. Assume you run them at night because of better water pressure and to avoid interference with the gardeners and use of walkways by the tenants. If you are not going to make any correction based on this tenant's complaint, you should explain this to the tenant and give truthful reasons.

Some property managers take the easy way out and lie. They might say the water district requires them to run sprinklers at night. A lie such as this puts the blame on someone else and the property manager comes off as being on the side of the tenant. The problem with lies is they tend to be forgotten by the teller who will come up with a different story at a later date. Another problem is the person might carry it one more step and by calling the water department and discover the lie.

It is not enough to be technically honest with answers; you should be scrupulously honest when servicing tenant complaints and all other aspects of tenant relations.

E. LET THE TENANT GO

Some people do not have the temperament to live in close quarters with others in an apartment building. They may be constantly complaining to management about noise such as another tenant flushing a toilet in the middle of the night. They might also harangue other tenants about what they perceive as significant problems. You will encounter such tenants and you will swear that their purpose in life is to make you miserable. A "tenant from hell" could result in the loss of other tenants, so something has to be done.

Eviction may not be an option as the tenant's actions may needle others, but might not be sufficient cause for eviction. If you start an eviction action, this tenant might be able to successfully defeat your action by claiming retaliatory eviction and you could even end up paying damages.

A first step would be to talk to the tenant. From our experience, talking is often ineffective because of the selective listening of such a tenant. We have let such tenants out of their leases, and in one case, we actually paid the moving costs to arrive at our solution.

F. DEATH OF A TENANT

The death of a wage earner in the case of a residential tenant, or the death of a business owner in the case of a commercial rental, could result in future rent collection difficulties.

One property manager always sends flowers and a kind note in such a case. About 10 days after the funeral, she makes an appointment to see the spouse or survivor and lets the party know that she is willing to help. For residential property, she offers to release the tenant from the lease and help find a less expensive rental if rent will be a problem. For commercial property, she offers to suggest business brokers if a business will have to be sold.

This property manager is careful to convey a helpful image. She is able to quickly discover if there will be a problem and, if so, to begin work to solve it. In some cases, she has shown tenants who to contact for public assistance. In other cases, she has recommended attorneys where she felt the survivor might have a worker's compensation or liability claim. If you are not comfortable with the above approach, don't use it.

VOICE OF EXPERIENCE:

It's important to be tactful when dealing with those impacted by a death. A little sensitivity goes a long way in easing the awkwardness of the situation. You should be as flexible as possible without compromising your owner's right to collect rent. It's a difficult job—but that's why the owner hired you!

G. WAITING LIST

You must be meticulous in following the order of the waiting list of your prospective tenants when taking applications for units and qualifying prospective tenants.

Not following the proper order of the list could result in charges of discrimination. However, this does not mean that you must accept the tenants at the top of the list. If they do not qualify because of income or credit history or if they are unable or unwilling to take the unit when it becomes vacant, you can go down the list to another party.

If an apartment consistently has a waiting list and the rents are not limited by rent control, it should be clear that the demand has exceeded the supply and rent increases would be in the best interest of the owner.

You should increase rents when it's obvious that the demand is higher than the supply.

H. TENANT'S RIGHT TO REPAIR

Many states allow a residential tenant to make repairs and deduct the costs from the rent in cases where the repairs are necessary for habitability and the lessor has failed, after reasonable notice, to make the repairs.

California Civil Code Section 1942 allows the tenant to make such repairs and deduct the cost of the repairs from the rent, providing that the cost of the repairs does not exceed one month's rent. The tenant may exercise this right no more than two times in any 12-month period. As to period of time for a notice, 30 days is presumed to be a reasonable period of time, but the period could be shorter based on the problem. A tenant who needed plumbing repairs on an inoperable toilet in a single-bath apartment would not have to wait 30 days.

A court might even consider failure to repair within 24 hours after notice is served to be a reasonable period.

As an alternative to making a repair, the tenant could, after the lessor's failure to correct the problem within a reasonable time, treat the failure as the landlord's constructive eviction and vacate the premises as well as be discharged from further rent payments and other conditions of the lease.

If a lessor attempts to evict or raise the rent on a tenant who has properly made repairs and deducted the cost from the rent, the tenant would have the defense of retaliatory eviction for the following 180 days.

I. TENANT PAINTING

Uniform paint color is an economical way to go.

Many landlords who deal directly with tenants supply the paint and allow tenants to paint their units. In some cases, the landlords give tenants rent credit for the work.

From experience, we don't believe this is a good practice. Besides poor workmanship, paint on woodwork and carpeting, plus work that may only get half finished, we no longer had control over the colors and quality of paint used. By limiting interiors to one or two colors, we can often have a maintenance person touch up a paint job with a roller in from 30 minutes to one hour per unit. In areas where there is not a great deal of airborne dirt, this is the norm rather than the exception.

Even where we have supplied tenants with paint, they have painted over varnished woodwork and kitchen cabinetry and even changed the colors by adding tints. Therefore, we ceased allowing tenants to paint units in properties we have managed.

In small units, such as fourplexes, where we did not have resident managers, we allowed a tenant to have a rent concession by taking care of the lawn, walkways, entryways and hallways. We have also hired retired tenants with maintenance skills to handle maintenance work within a complex. If you do so, make certain that your contract spells out that they are independent contractors rather than employees.

J. WASTE

WASTE is an abuse of property that impairs the value of the property. Waste could be an alteration of the premises, removal of a structure, removl of trees, etc. Waste results in substantial or permanent damage to the property that impairs value. A landlord is justified in terminating a lease for waste, and may also be entitled to damages.

K. EXTENDED TENANT ABSENCE

As the property manager, you should tell tenants that if they will be absent for a long period of time to notify you of the absence. Also request in writing that you have the right

Case Example

Freeze v. Brinsin, 4 C.A. 4th Supp 1 (1991)

Plaintiff brought action against a tenant for unlawful detainer alleging that the tenant had committed waste on the premises. The landlord claimed there was damage to a wall and floor caused by excrement of the tenant's dog. The trial court found for the plaintiff, but the Superior Court Appellate Department reversed the decision.

The court held that to declare waste there must be clear evidence of acts that seriously affect the market value of the property. The burden is on the landlord to show that the value was permanently or substantially impaired. While the landlord had shown damage to the premises, there wasn't any evidence to show the value of the premises was substantially or permanently diminished.

to enter their unit for inspection purposes and to place any mail, papers, and deliveries in the unit. You must impress upon tenants that they are responsible for any damage caused by failure to maintain utilities when absent. This is particularly important for property in northern or mountain areas where a freeze could destroy plumbing, as well as result in water damage.

If possible, ask tenants who will be gone for an extended period where they can be contacted or who to contact in an emergency.

L. CHANGE IN TERMS/END OF TENANCY

For a month-to-month tenancy, the lessor can change the rent or other terms of the tenancy. However, a notice (usually 30 days) is required to do so.

Similarly, to end a periodic tenancy, either tenant or landlord can generally give the other party a notice for the length of the rent paying period (but no more than 30 days—60 days for lessor starting in 2007) that the tenancy is to end.

VOICE OF EXPERIENCE:

When you raise the rent, it is good practice to justify the raise. As an example, painting hallways or doing landscaping work just prior to a rent increase will be accepted better than a raise without any improvement of the property or apparent increase in owner costs.

M. NEVER HAVE SURPRISE CHARGES

Some mobile home parks surprise tenants with a group of hidden charges, such as a charge to check the sewer hookups or to connect to the park's cable television system. Some charges are in the nickel and dime category while others are substantial.

All charges should be fully and clearly revealed before a tenant is obligated to the rental. Even a justified change will be resented if it comes as a surprise.

N. FAILURE TO TAKE POSSESSION

If a tenant fails to take possession after signing a lease, the tenant is liable under the lease even if he/she never moved in, and you have a right and duty to hold the tenant to his/her agreement. Sometimes tenants think that they can just forfeit what they paid if they find something they like better.

Your duty to your principal is to enforce the lease.

O. SURRENDER OF LEASE

A *SURRENDER OF A LEASE is the lessee giving the premises back to the lessor and the lessor accepting possession with the understanding that the lease is ended.* A surrender ends all lease obligations of the lessee at the time of surrender.

A tenant who vacates the premises prior to the end of the lease is likely to claim that he or she has surrendered the premises, However, the lessor would likely want to consider it an abandonment of the premises with the lessee remaining liable for future lease payments.

While there can generally be a verbal surrender of leases for one year or less, written leases for more than one year should not be surrendered orally.

You should always get a written surrender agreement from your tenant.

P. THE FIRST EXCUSE

If a tenant calls you to explain that he or she will be late with the rent, ask the tenant when the rent will be paid. Arrive at an agreement as to date of payment and inform the tenant that, if the rent is not paid by the agreed date, a three-day notice shall be given, followed by eviction if the tenant fails to pay or vacate.

If the rent is not paid by the date set, do not take a second promise. Go ahead with eviction proceedings. If the tenant brings in the money, never waive the late charge. Waiver of late charges condones being late.

Never allow the tenant to fall behind a full month's rent. If it happens, the majority of the time the rent never becomes current.

VOICE OF EXPERIENCE:

Don't waive late charges. This is a business, not a charity. You're first duty is to your owner. The expression, "give 'em an inch they'll take a mile" is true as far as property management is concerned, too!

Don't except second excuses. You may end up losing another month's rent!

Q. THE ELEVEN-MONTH YEAR

Owners may turn over property for management with tenants who are over a year in rent arrearage. This rent arrearage isn't necessarily because of a tenant's inability to pay; it is often because of the gullibility of the landlord.

A tenant may pay June rent on June 10. The tenant may pay rent for July on July 19. For August, the rent may be paid on August 26. The tenant may pay rent for September on October 3. You soon realize then that the tenant has become one month behind in rent in just a few months. Landlords are unwilling to evict such a tenant because the tenant pays rent, although a little slow. The owner will suddenly realize how far the tenant is in arrearage. Now the landlord believes that if he or she is just patient with the tenant, who appears to be trying, he or she will get caught up on the rent. It is not going to happen.

In management, you have a duty to the owner.

You cannot allow a tenant to get away with less than 12 monthly payments per year. Remember that fairness is a two-way street. While you want to be fair with tenants, they must also be fair with you and the landlord.

R. EVICTION

A tenant may be evicted for failure to pay rent or for the breach of a significant lease provision. The first step would be a notice (generally a three-day notice). The notice could be.

1. Quit or Pay Rent

The tenant can cure such action by paying the rent.

VOICE OF EXPERIENCE:

A lessor need not evict a tenant who is delinquent in rent. The lessor, as an alternative, could sue for rent as it becomes due. This alternative would only be feasible where the tenant has financial resources that make a judgment collectable.

2. Quit or Cure

Such a notice would require the tenant to cure the default. As an example, if the notice was based on the tenant having a pet in violation of the law, removing the pet from the premises would cure the default.

3. Quit

If the default is one that cannot be cured, the three-day notice to quit is appropriate. As an example, assume a tenant lied about the size of his or her family in order to rent a one-bedroom apartment. If there are six people rather than the two claimed, a three-day notice to quit is appropriate. (Three-day notices are included in Chapter 5.)

The three-day notice would be followed by an unlawful detainer action. After being served with this action, the tenant has a statutory period (five days in California) to file an answer. The tenant could claim a defense such as retaliatory eviction, the premises were uninhabitable or a denial of the charges. The tenant could also claim a procedural error in that the tenant had not been served with a three-day notice or that the notice was defective. Another possible defense would be a claim that eviction was based upon the race, religion, national origin, sex, etc. of the tenant so it would be a civil rights violation.

Never put yourself in a position where a tenant may claim discrimination.

If a lessor indicates in an unlawful detainer action, based on nonpayment of rent, that the amount due is greater than the amount the court determines is actually due, then the unlawful detainer action would be faulty and would likely fail.

A partial payment accepted after the three-day notice will also invalidate the unlawful detainer action.

If the tenant answers the unlawful detainer action, the tenant has his or her day in court and the court will decide if a judgement should be entered in favor of the landlord. The court will grant the landlord a judgement if the tenant fails to answer the unlawful detainer action.

If the tenant fails to vacate the premises, the landlord can obtain a **WRIT OF POSSESSION,** *authorizing the sheriff or marshal to physically remove the tenant and his or her possessions from the premises.* In most cases, the tenant will peacefully vacate, although damage to the premises is an all too common occurrence.

You should change the locks after the unit is vacated.

Case Example

City of South San Francisco Housing Authority v. Guillory, 41 C.A. 4th Supp 13 (1996)

A lease contained a "zero tolerance" drug clause. Drugs were found in the closet of the son of the tenant. The family was evicted.

The Superior Court affirmed the Municipal Court's decision that the housing authority had good cause for eviction. Parents can be held for the illegal conduct of their children.

Case Example

Lamanna v. Vagnor, 17 C.A. 4th Supp 4 (1993)

A tenant was served a three-day notice for rent delinquency on a Wednesday. On the following Tuesday, the day after Memorial Day, the landlord filed an unlawful detainer action.

The Appellate Court held that the unlawful detainer action was invalid because the tenant was not given a three-day notice, as required by California law, to quit or pay rent and retain possession.

In California, the time for a three-day notice is computed by excluding the day of service and including the last day. Therefore, the three days commenced on Thursday and Friday would have been the second day. Since business days only are counted and Monday was a holiday, the third day was Tuesday. The tenant had all of Tuesday to cure the rent arrearage. The unlawful detainer should not have been filed until Wednesday.

Note: Be certain that you count days properly in accordance with state law or your unlawful detainer will fail. You would then have to again give a new three-day notice followed by an unlawful detainer action.

You only count business days and not the 1st day the notice is served.

S. RENT AFTER NOTICE

After you have commenced an eviction with a three-day notice and/or unlawful detainer action, should you accept any rent, your notice will be canceled. Any further eviction will mean you must start over. Consider this when a partial rent payment is offered.

You may not want to accept partial rent as it will cancel your notice.

T. MENACING CONDUCT BY A LANDLORD IS PROHIBITED

A civil penalty of up to $2,000 may be imposed for each act of the landlord that is "made for the purpose of influencing the tenant to vacate a dwelling" by using force, threats, or menacing conduct that "would create an apprehension of harm" in a reasonable person. Oral or written warning notices given in good faith and explanations of the rental agreement do not constitute improper activities.

Also, the landlord may not recover possession of the premises in any action, increase the rent, or decrease services within 180 days of the tenant making a complaint to an agency, if the tenant is not in default on the payment of rent.

U. CONSTRUCTIVE EVICTION

A landlord's actions can negatively affect the use and enjoyment of premises to the extent that a tenant could get out of a lease under the doctrine of **CONSTRUCTIVE EVICTION**.

If a landlord fails to provide utilities as agreed or cuts off the tenant's utilities, these actions would allow a tenant to rescind the lease. Failing to correct a vermin or sanitation problem could also be grounds for a tenant's ending a lease. Failure to take action against another tenant's activities that materially affected the use and enjoyment of the property by others would also be grounds for a tenant to end a lease.

The tenant must declare constructive eviction within a reasonable period after the landlord's actions (or failure to act). If the tenant stays in possession, the tenant must pay rent. The tenant cannot use the landlord's action as an excuse not to live up to his or her rental obligations.

Case Example

Lee v. Placer Title, 28 C.A. 4th 503 (1994)

Placer Title moved out of its space in a shopping center prior to the expiration of its lease. In a suit for rent due, Placer claimed constructive eviction since the landlord failed to stop an adjoining dry cleaners from allowing toxic fumes to enter Placer's premises.

Court of Appeals affirmed the decision for the landlord since the lease provided that in "no event shall tenant have the right to terminate this lease as a result of landlord's default and tenant remedies shall be limited to damages and/or an injunction." Placer had breached the lease, giving up any rights to claim constructive eviction.

Note: This case applied to a commercial rental. Such a clause cannot be expected to be upheld for a residential rental.

▼

***Dinieu v. Groff Studios Corp.*, 690 N.Y.S.2d 220 (A.D.1Dept. 1999)**

A constructive eviction occurs when a tenant, though not physically barred from the area in question, is unable to use the area for the purpose intended. Where eviction is constructive, breach of the covenant of quiet enjoyment does not require a physical ouster. Rather, a showing of abandonment of the premises under pressure is sufficient.

V. RETALIATORY EVICTION

RETALIATORY EVICTION is eviction because the tenant exercised legal rights that have upset the landlord. Retaliatory eviction can result in not only losing at an attempt to evict, but also possible punitive damages.

You must avoid any appearances that an eviction is retaliatory. Treat all tenants similarly.

As an example, if you evict a tenant who has made frequent complaints to the health department or rent control board, but based your eviction on the fact that the tenant had a dog that was not permitted under the lease, it could be considered retaliatory if you had taken no action against other tenants with dogs who had not made similar complaints. In other words, selective enforcement of lease provisions or rules and regulations could be considered "payback" and determined by the court to be retaliatory.

W. PHYSICAL EVICTION

Years ago, landlords often took the physical evictions of tenants into their own hands. Some commonly used methods included removing front doors or turning off utilities. Other owners used physical threats or actually carted tenants' possessions out to the sidewalk. These illegal actions are no longer tolerated.

Don't do it! Resorting to inappropriate eviction methods may subject you to costly lawsuits. Damages for cutting off utilities, for example, are often set by state statute.

X. SEIZURE OF PROPERTY

In most states, a landlord has no lien on personal property of a tenant. The landlord can evict or sue for rent. If the landlord seizes property of the tenant because the tenant owes money to the landlord, the landlord could be exposing himself or herself to substantial damages (both compensatory and punitive) because of wrongful seizure.

Y. PAY THEM TO LEAVE

While it may go against your personal feelings, often the best way to get a tenant to leave is to offer them cash, providing they vacate by a particular date and the unit is left in a presentable condition.

As a property manager, what really counts is the bottom line.

A couple hundred dollars paid to a tenant to leave will reduce the probability of the unit being trashed by an evicted tenant. Ripped out plumbing fixtures, holes in the walls, and piles of trash are not the norm, but this does not have to happen too many times to realize that a few dollars paid can be well spent.

If a tenant has posted a property damage bond, your agreement could be that you will return the property damage bond and not apply it to rent due, which you would otherwise be entitled to do.

You might also have to agree to forget past-due rent. Because you're probably dealing with judgment-proof tenants, collection is unlikely anyway, so you won't be giving much.

An advantage to a tenant, in agreeing to leave, is that his/her credit report will not show an eviction.

Before you pay to have a tenant leave or give up any rights to past due rents, explain the situation to the owner and get the owner's written approval for your action. After the fact, an owner's attorney could make such action appear improper.

Z. MITIGATION OF DAMAGES

When a tenant breaches a lease by moving out before the lease period has expired or he or she has been evicted, the landlord has a duty to **MITIGATE DAMAGES**, *meaning the landlord must use reasonable steps to re-rent the premises.*

In trying to re-rent the premises, if a landlord asked for a higher rent than the defaulting tenant paid, the defaulting tenant would probably be excused as to any subsequent rent because the landlord was not reasonable in his or her attempt to mitigate damages. In the same respect, insisting on different lease terms, such as a longer lease, could also serve to relieve the former tenant of obligations under the lease.

If, in trying to re-rent the premises, the landlord refused a prospective tenant, the landlord could have relieved the prior tenant from the obligation unless the refusal can be shown to be reasonable.

If economic conditions require the landlord to rent at a lower figure, the former tenant's obligation would be for the period of vacancy plus the difference in the rent he or she had agreed to pay and the rent actually received.

A landlord can sue a former tenant for rent as it becomes due, but cannot sue for the entire amount owed on the lease because the actual damages have yet to be determined.

Zanker Dev. Co. v. Cogito Sys., Inc., 215 C.A. 3rd 1377 (1989)

This case involved a landlord who expended $1 million preparing a property for a tenant. As part of the seven-year lease, the landlord gave the tenant nine month's free rent. After the free rent period expired, the tenant never made rent payments on time. The landlord was nearly forced into bankruptcy. The landlord finally evicted the tenant and sought damages for the remainder of the lease. The trial court awarded the landlord $3.6 million in damages.

On appeal, the tenant claimed that the landlord failed to properly mitigate damages since the tenant wanted to renegotiate the lease with different terms. The Court of Appeals upheld the trial court and stated that the landlord had taken reasonable measures to re-let the premises to allow recovery. The court pointed out that a landlord should not have to renegotiate a lease with a tenant who had repudiated the original lease after the tenancy was terminated by an unlawful detainer.

Note: This case indicates that a landlord can refuse a lease with a tenant who has not met prior lease obligations without forfeiting rights for failure to mitigate damages. The landlord can be reasonable as to re-renting.

Quill v. R.A. Investment Corp., 707 N.E.2d 35, Ohio.App.2Dist. (1997)

Reviewing the lease agreement afresh, we find that this provision defines and limits the remedies of the lessors in the event of a breach by the lessee. Ohio courts recognize that such cure provisions are lawful and may be enforced.

II. Alternatives to Litigation

Today, litigation is only one of the ways used to resolve different types of controversies. Not only are contractual rights being decided outside of the courts, but also certain types of property rights.

A. ALTERNATIVE DISPUTE RESOLUTION (ADR)

Before they'll hear a case, California court judges routinely require litigants to go to negotiation, mediation, or arbitration, sometimes more than once. This saves judges time and taxpayers money.

Conflict between people is increasingly being resolved through the use of **Alternative Dispute Resolution (ADR)**. People and businesses dissatisfied with the time and expense of litigation are looking for alternatives to resolve their disputes. **Negotiation, mediation, and arbitration** are three types of ADR that are being utilized to avoid litigation when controversies surrounding contracts and property rights arise. Administrative hearings are used by the Department of Real Estate to avoid the use of courts when deciding issues surrounding real estate licensees.

ADR is a catchall term used to describe out-of-court methods to resolve disputes, including negotiation, arbitration, and mediation, among other methods.

In fact, California has indicated its support of ADR in the real estate industry by amending the **California Arbitration Act** (Code of Civil Procedure Sections 1298-1298.8) to **specifically address arbitration clauses in real estate contracts**.

Additionally, the Legislature has found that approaching dispute resolution from an adversarial position "can be unnecessarily costly, time-consuming, and complex when achieved through formal court proceedings." It therefore strongly encourages the parties to resolve their disputes outside of the judicial process. There are definite potential advantages to alternative dispute resolution when compared to litigation. Not all the advantages will be present in every situation. Among these advantages are:

1. **Speedier.** With the crowded court calendars, it may be years before the dispute is actually heard by the court.

2. **Less expensive.** Taking less time reduces the expense of resolving the dispute. Normally there is **LIMITED DISCOVERY**, *which is the process of determining what evidence exists prior to trial.*

3. **Use of an expert as the decision maker.** In most of the ADR processes, the parties are able to select the decision maker by agreement. This gives them the opportunity to have an expert knowledgeable in the field make a decision.

4. **Proceedings are confidential.** Most of the ADR processes are private affairs and closed to the public. Negotiations and decisions are confidential and not available for public inspection unless the parties approve.

5. **Decisions are final and not appealable.** Decisions reached through most of the ADR processes are final and binding upon the parties. This finality reduces the expense and time. However, there are very limited grounds for appeal that will be discussed later.

6. **Less formal.** ADR uses the parties themselves to determine how the process will run. The formalities of judicial procedures are not a normal aspect of many ADR processes.

B. NONADJUDICATIVE AND ADJUDICATIVE ALTERNATIVES

Alternatives to the judicial process may be classified into two categories: nonadjudicative and adjudicative. In the *NONADJUDICATIVE alternatives, the parties are encouraged to voluntarily enter into agreements that settle the controversy.* Many times the parties will use a neutral third party to assist in reaching an agreement among themselves. The *ADJUDICATIVE alternatives of dispute resolution mirror the judicial process in that a third party decides the controversy, much as a judge does in court.* The adjudicative processes may

be concerned with settling controversies among private parties or between regulatory agencies and individuals.

1. Negotiation

Although arbitration receives much of the focus in the ADR literature, negotiation continues to serve as the primary method by which conflicts are resolved. *NEGOTIATION is a voluntary process where parties attempt to settle their conflicts in a peaceful manner.*

To successfully negotiate, it is necessary to move beyond positions on issues and negotiate about the person's interests or needs. Looking past positions on issues can be hard for many people, yet, it is helpful to focus on underlying interests or needs if agreement is to be reached. By asking yourself "why" a person is taking a certain position, you can often determine what his or her true interests or needs are and then be better prepared to offer solutions that will lead to an agreement.

Negotiations may be either distributive or integrative. *DISTRIBUTIVE NEGOTIATION (win-lose or competitive) is where the goals of the parties are interdependent but not compatible.* It occurs when one person wins and the other person loses. *INTEGRATIVE NEGOTIATION (problem-solving) occurs when both parties win. The negotiators seek to achieve mutual gains and they focus on the needs and interests of both parties.* This means the negotiators look past their individual positions ("their" solution to the dispute) and identify "why" those solutions are being sought by each party.

2. Mediation (A Neutral Third Party)

In *MEDIATION, a neutral third party assists the parties in voluntarily negotiating a settlement to their dispute by helping them recognize their interests involved, developing choices, and analyzing the alternatives.* The goal is to overcome the problems and negotiate a mutually satisfying agreement.

Because mediation is voluntary, the parties must agree to the use of mediation in attempting to resolve the dispute. A **mediation clause** may be included in the contract the parties are executing. If there is an existing dispute but no contractually agreed-to clause to mediate the dispute, the parties may stipulate to mediating the dispute.

The most obvious advantage to mediation is that parties maintain an active role, even if they have an attorney. Because a neutral party assists to identify, develop, and explore viable settlement alternatives, mediation is likely to produce a settlement faster than litigation. Mediation may be preferred to arbitration for a number of reasons, such as:

1. parties retain greater control of proceeding;
2. parties know soon if the matter and issues may be resolved, and differences narrowed, and
3. the process is quicker and less expensive if it is resolved.

3. Arbitration (Commerical Leases)

In *ARBITRATION, the parties agree to submit the dispute (often through a contractual arbitration clause) to a neutral third party for a final, binding decision, unless agreed otherwise.* Arbitration awards can rarely be appealed.

Many contracts contain compulsory arbitration provisions. As a result, the parties forego enforcing their rights in court.

The scope of the arbitration provision is very important. For example, most state laws provide for a quick and inexpensive procedure to evict a non-paying tenant. Accordingly, a property manager would not want the scope of the arbitration clause, if any, to include eviction matters.

The arbitration clause may include the:

1. state in which the arbitration is to take place if it is not the state in which the property is located;
2. state law governing the contract;
3. amounts for the "prevailing parties" that may be awarded for attorney fees and arbitration expenses;
4. selection of the private arbitration firm, such as the American Arbitration Association, which has its own rules, and
5. choice of the number of arbitrators, which may significantly affect the expense of the arbitration proceeding.

Decisions about the arbitration provision affect the extent of the costs of the arbitration. Arbitration costs may be far higher than costs of the litigation process, because the parties are paying the costs of the arbitrators, which may range from $300 an hour and up, particularly if there is more than one arbitrator.

The arbitration procedure is flexible, confidential, and results in a decision. Parties may choose the rules to a certain extent. Typically, the rules of the private arbitration firm govern. The length of the arbitration hearing and the timing of the decision may be agreed to by the parties.

The arbitrators (one or more) are selected by the parties and are usually experts in particular areas of the law.

The binding arbitration decision is usually entered as a court order.

Arbitrations can be set for hearing in a short period of time by agreement of the parties. Attorney's fees and costs may be reduced depending on the scope of prehearing motions and discovery that has been agreed upon by the parties. If the arbitration clause includes many prehearing motions and extensive discovery, the costs of attorney fees that would be incurred in litigation may not be reduced at all.

Generally, the arbitrator makes a final resolution to the dispute.

III. Owner Relations

A. COMMUNICATION

As previously stated, there should be one contact person in a management office for an owner. This should be the person who directly supervises any onsite personnel and has the responsibility for management decisions involving the owner's property.

The communication lines must be kept open in that negative and positive information must be conveyed to the owner as soon as practical. As an example, if you discover that a major commercial tenant has just gone into Chapter 11 bankruptcy, let the owner know. Be prepared to explain what Chapter 11 is and its ramifications as to rent owed and future rent.

If the owner lives out of the area, an office "800" number will encourage owner communication.

Owner questions, letters and calls must be promptly acknowledged and questions answered fully and honestly.

At least one annual face-to-face encounter with the owner is desirable. A good time for this would be during delivery of the annual statement. You could then go over operations of the past year and future management plans.

B. FIDUCIARY DUTIES

In dealings with an owner, you must keep in mind that he or she is your principal and that you have fiduciary duties toward the owner. These duties include the following.

1. Loyalty

You must be loyal to your principal. Loyalty to an owner means being faithful to the owner's interests. If a lease expired, and you persuaded the tenant to move into another property you managed because you felt your management contract on the property the tenant occupied would not be renewed, then you would have breached your fiduciary duty of loyalty and could be held civilly liable for damages.

2. Confidentiality

Information received from the owner must be regarded as confidential unless it is clear that it is to be provided to prospective tenants. Assume that an owner told you that he wanted $1,500 per month for a property but, that if he had to, he could accept less because his payments were only $1,000 per month. If you revealed this information to a prospective tenant who offered to lease the premises for $1,000 per month, you would have breached the duty of confidentiality.

Confidentiality is the reason that you should not gossip about an owner, even within your office. The problem is that it is hard enough for one person to keep information private.

Once two people have been told something, it is on the verge of becoming public knowledge.

3. Fair and Honest Dealings

Ask yourself if you would consider your action fair if you were a third party. If you would not, the action would not be fair.

If you tell an unsophisticated owner that the management and leasing fees you charge are "customary" when in fact they are quite a bit higher than customarily charged for the type of property and services, you are not only treating the owner unfairly but your action is also dishonest.

4. Full Disclosure

Failing to inform an owner of any information you had (other than confidential) of a type that an owner could reasonably be expected to want to know would be a violation of your disclosure duty.

As an example, assume a major franchise has negotiated a lease with another agent for $1.80 per square foot. Assume the franchise is interested in a second location and is interested in leasing a property that you manage. While you're asking $1.60 per square foot, the franchise offers to lease the space for $1.40. The information about the other lease would be the kind of information the owner would want to know. The decision to hold firm at $1.60 would be reinforced by his/her awareness that the firm could pay that much. Failure to tell the owner would be a breach of your duty of full disclosure.

5. Reasonable Care and Skill

You have a duty to use the reasonable care and skill that an owner would expect and that a property manager should possess.

Telling an owner to sign a lease prepared by the tenant without reading it or having it checked by an attorney would not be the exercise of reasonable care and skill. A court would probably determine you to be negligent.

6. Obedience

The duty of obedience means that you must follow the lawful instructions of your principal. That does not mean that you should not disagree or make your opinions known. Failure to inform an owner that you feel that an owner's proposed action is a mistake could be a breach of your duty of due care.

C. UNDERESTIMATING COSTS AND OVERESTIMATING INCOME

While optimism has its place, realism is what an owner wants when dealing with what the owner holds dear: his or her pocketbook.

LOW-BALLING is a term that has its origin in used car sales. It is an estimate of what a car can be purchased for that is less than what the dealer will actually take. The purchaser is induced to begin the bargaining process with an offer and then later induced to raise it.

"Low-balling" has no place in property management.

If an estimate is given to an owner or tenant as to what modifications or repairs will cost, it should be based on experience or bids. You should never quote a figure to tease a person to act. In dealing with property owners, it would also be a breach of fiduciary duty.

Never surprise landlords. It's a recipe for disaster.

Did you ever take your car to a garage and sign an original estimate only to later receive a call or calls that it was going to cost considerably more than originally estimated. How did you feel?

On the other hand, if costs are less than estimated, your feelings towards the person who gave you the estimate would probably be positive. You are more likely to recommend to others the person who beat the estimate rather than the person who exceeded the estimate.

This lesson can be applied to property management:

1. Don't low-ball bids or be overly optimistic in estimating property returns, rental periods or expenses.
2. Be realistic. Prepare owners for your best estimate but give them some idea as to what could happen. A worst case scenario can make for a happy owner when it doesn't happen.

VOICE OF EXPERIENCE:

Keep track of reliable independent contractors. Let them know when you have recommended them for work with others. They may show their gratitude by putting your jobs at the top of their priority list and even cut their prices.

D. RELATIONSHIPS WITH OWNERS

While there can be a conflict of interest when you, as a property manager, have a close relationship with a tenant, this conflict would not exist in a relationship with an owner. The agent and the owner are on the same team and their interests should be the same. Many business relationships develop into close friendships.

Our personal preference is that relationships with both owners and tenants be kept on a friendly but business level.

Arm-length transactions are best. You should be fair to both parties.

Romantic relationships, however, should be discouraged because breakups often result in resentment or anger. This would mean one or both parties would want to limit future contact with the other. A breakup of a romantic relationship could likely result in a management contract not being renewed.

E. HOMEOWNER ASSOCIATION MANAGEMENT

Homeowner associations are often political hotbeds with groups that want to usurp the present association management.

As a property manager, you should avoid appearing too closely allied with either group. This would include social contacts. You want to be considered as a service provider who will do whatever the board of directors wants, but will, nevertheless, make recommendations that you feel are fair and in the best interests of the owners.

F. VIOLATING THE LAW

Never aid in illegal and untruthful dealings.

As a property manager, you may be asked to violate the law or to aid the property owner in violating the law. Generally, it is tax laws that are involved. Usually, the owner does not say, "Help me avoid paying taxes"; it is usually more subtle. It could be, "Please pay this billing," for services or material not supplied or supplied to the owner's personal residence. The check would possibly be made out to an illegitimate firm name or even a foreign firm. This particular tax scam takes the operating profits and turns them into a deductible expense.

VOICE OF EXPERIENCE:

Be neutral and listen to everyone with an opinion. Always bring a notebook to jot down ideas being presented at a tenant meeting. Dismissing someone's idea without careful consideration is insulting.

You must avoid gossip with or about any owner, and treat every owner with patience and courtesy even if you feel a complaint is frivolous or even mean spirited.

A variation of the above was a case where a property manager was asked to put the son of the owner on the property's payroll. The owner simply wanted to make the support of his son a tax-deductible expense. There would have been nothing wrong if the son had actually contributed services to the property, but in this case, it was simply a scam.

Owners have asked property managers for operating statements that don't reflect the true operations. These could be for lenders, as owners could intend to defraud the lender by obtaining a loan based on false figures.

VOICE OF EXPERIENCE:

If an owner asks you to prepare any false document or report, or to pay any bills where the recipient is not entitled to the monies as a property expense, don't do it.

You do not want to be a part of any unlawful activity or help to carry out any owner's secret agenda that would tend to deceive. Besides possible criminal and/or civil liability, it would be unethical behavior that would reflect upon your professionalism.

Accounting irregularities could also lead to suspension or revocation of your real estate license.

G. SUING A PRINCIPAL

While you represent an owner and have fiduciary duties toward that owner, you should realize that you have rights under the management contract and that it is not a breach of your fiduciary duty to enforce those rights.

As an example, assume that you have a management contract on a large freestanding property and are seeking a tenant. Assume also that you have interested Home Depot® in the property and are in the process of negotiating a lease that will provide you with significant leasing fees over the proposed 20-year term. Assume the owner, in an apparent effort to avoid paying the leasing fees, cancels the management contract and negotiates directly with Home Depot, signing a 20-year lease. Good business practice would dictate that you make demands for your commission, and if not forthcoming, seek to collect by legal means.

VOICE OF EXPERIENCE:

While suing an owner should be avoided, if a dispute can be resolved by agreement, it does not mean you should not vigorously defend your rights when there is an attempt to deprive you of them.

IV. CHAPTER SUMMARY

A great many tenant problems can be avoided by properly explaining to the tenant, at the time the lease is signed, what the tenant's obligations are under the lease as well as any property rules and regulations for the tenants.

Renting to friends or relatives could create significant problems, as they are likely to expect special treatment, and your relationship could likely affect your actions if the friend or relative breaches a lease clause or occupancy rule. There could also be an appearance of a possible conflict of interest. Romantic involvement with a tenant not only provides the appearance of a conflict of interest, it could also result in loss of a tenant, as well as other complications.

A record should be kept of all tenant complaints and the action taken. The tenant should be informed as to what, if anything, will be done. You should be entirely truthful with the tenant.

There may be problem tenants who have constant frivolous complaints or who bother other tenants. You should consider letting such a tenant out of his or her lease.

After the death of a tenant, by asking if you can help, you can ascertain any problems and possibly avoid problems relating to the tenancy.

The order of a waiting list should be followed without exception to avoid any chance of discrimination claims.

It is not a good policy to allow tenants to paint their own units because of workmanship problems.

A lessor has the right to terminate a lease if the tenant commits waste.

You should ask tenants to notify you when the tenant will be absent for a protracted period of time. You should also request the right to enter the unit for inspection purposes and to deposit mail and deliveries.

A notice is required to change the terms of tenancy on a month-to-month lease. It is a good policy to provide something extra prior to a rent increase. Tenants should not be surprised with expenses not revealed at the time of leasing. Failure to take possession after the lease has been signed would not relieve the tenant from the lease obligations.

A surrender of the premises that is accepted by the lessor would relieve the tenant of all further lease obligations. In accepting the premises from a vacating tenant when the lease has not expired, the lessor should make it clear that this is not a surrender and the lessor will hold the lessee liable for remaining lease obligations. As a matter of policy, allow only one excuse for late payment and then serve a three-day notice. Never allow a tenant to get more than one month behind in rent without commencing eviction action.

The eviction process begins with a three-day notice to quit or pay rent, quit or cure (when other than rent) or quit (when a cure is not possible). The three-day notice is followed by an unlawful detainer action. The tenant has five days to answer or a judgment will be entered for the lessor. Defenses of eviction include retaliatory eviction, uninhabitable premises, a denial of the charges, procedural error, discriminatory eviction, incorrect amount due stated or a payment made after the three-day notice was served.

If the tenant fails to answer or the court finds for the lessor, a judgment would be entered for the lessor. The lessor could get a Writ of Possession and the sheriff could remove the tenant and possessions from the property.

A landlord's actions in interfering with a tenant's rights could be viewed by the tenant as constructive eviction, which would allow the tenant to vacate without any further lease obligations.

Retaliatory eviction is not allowed. Examples would be evicting a tenant for exercising a legal right to complain or organizing a tenant's group.

A lessor cannot physically evict a tenant. To cut off utilities would likely subject a lessor to penalties. A lessor generally has no right to a tenant's property because of failure to pay rent.

Sometimes it can be advantageous to pay a tenant to vacate rather than to evict. It saves time, money, and the premises are likely to be left in better condition.

The lessor has a duty to keep the tenant's damages as low as possible. If the tenant has vacated prior to the expiration of the lease, the lessor has a duty to attempt to re-rent the premises.

Lease conflicts are increasingly being resolved through the use of Alternative Dispute Resolution (ADR) procedures such as mediation or binding arbitration. Renters and landlords frustrated with the time and expense of court litigation are looking for economical alternatives to resolve their disputes.

Owner relations are based on open and full communication. As the property manager, you also have a fiduciary duty toward the owner, which includes:

1. Loyalty
2. Confidentiality
3. Fair and honest dealings
4. Full disclosure
5. Reasonable care and skill
6. Obedience

You will have an unhappy owner if you tend to underestimate costs and are overly optimistic in revenue projections. You should be realistic in your estimates.

While a business relationship is best, personal relationships with owners do not create conflicts of interest. Romantic relationships, however, can create numerous problems leading to loss of management.

In dealing with homeowner associations, you must avoid owner politics and be fair and friendly to everyone. You should never get involved with owner deceit, fraud, or other activities that could be perceived as being illegal, even when asked to do so by the owner.

While, as the manager, you represent the owner, you should make certain that the owner meets his or her responsibilities to you. You can properly bring legal action to enforce these rights.

V. CHAPTER QUIZ

1. Which of the following is true about a lease "surrender" when one year is remaining on the lease?
   a. The tenant is liable for one month's rent.
   b. The tenant is not liable for the remaining rent.
   c. The landlord must mitigate damages.
   d. The tenant is immediately liable for total rent to the end of the lease.

2. As a property manager, it is NOT good business practice to lease to:
   a. close relatives.
   b. close friends.
   c. a person with whom you are romantically involved.
   d. any of the above.

3. In handling a tenant waiting list, you should give preference to:
   a. friends.
   b. women.
   c. families with children.
   d. time and date of application.

4. Fiduciary duty of a property manager to a property owner includes:
   a. loyalty.
   b. confidentiality.
   c. full disclosure.
   d. all of the above.

5. Tenant "waste" refers to:
   a. inefficient management.
   b. a high tenant turnover.
   c. tenant abuse of the property.
   d. the failure to conserve energy.

6. A tenant signed a one-year lease and failed to take possession. The maximum tenant obligation would be:

    a. one month's rent.
    b. 30 day's rent.
    c. rent for one year.
    d. none of the above.

7. The first notice to evict a tenant who has not paid rent would be a(n):

    a. Quit or Pay Rent notice.
    b. Unlawful Detainer Action.
    c. Writ of Possession.
    d. Notice of Nonresponsibility.

8. If correct, which of the following would be a defense against an unlawful detainer action?

    a. A claim of retaliatory eviction
    b. Partial rent payment after the three-day notice
    c. A claim that the residential premises was uninhabitable
    d. All of the above

9. Which of the following is an example of constructive eviction?

    a. Failure of the landlord to provide for contracted utilities
    b. Failure to take action against a tenant who is interfering with another tenant's use of the premises
    c. Failure to correct a sanitation problem, which is the landlord's responsibility
    d. Any of the above

10. Which of the following would be an act to mitigate damages after a tenant vacated the premises?

    a. Changing the use and asking for a higher rent
    b. Bringing legal action as each month's rent is due
    c. Waiting until the lease expires before placing the property on the rental market
    d. None of the above

ANSWERS: 1. b; 2. d; 3. d; 4. d; 5. c; 6. c; 7. a; 8. d; 9. d; 10. d

Chapter 15
Management Operations

KEY WORDS AND TERMS

Bonuses
Colorblind Management
Completed Staff Work
Dress Code
Economics of Scale
Employee Contract
Employee Evaluation
Employee File
Employment Application
Employment Interview
Employment Tests
Firing
Health Insurance
Hiring
Immigration Reform and Control Act
Interpersonal Relations

Job Description
Key Money
Leasing Fees
Management Fees
No-Tolerance Drug Policy
Opening a Management Office
Organizational Chart
Policy Manual
Profit Sharing
Staffing
Tenant Gifts
Tenant Exit Interview
Termination Fee
Theft
Training
Vacation Days

CHAPTER 15 OUTLINE

I. The Management Office

A. ORGANIZATIONAL CHART

The organizational chart of a property management office can vary significantly. In a small office with only a few properties, the chart might look like the following:

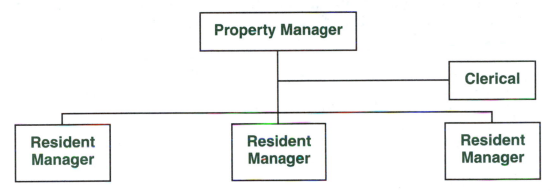

The organizational chart of a much larger operation might look like the following:

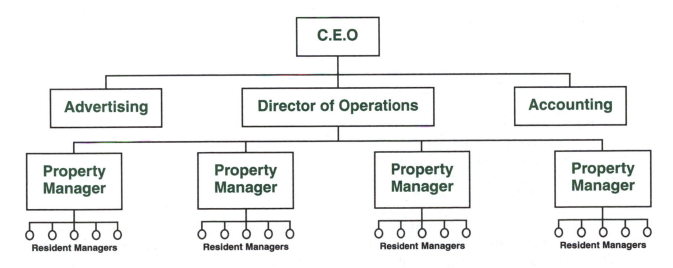

> ***VOICE OF EXPERIENCE:***
>
> *For purposes of this chapter, assume that you are the property manager in charge of a property management firm. As such, it would be your responsibility to supervise one or more resident managers. A resident manager (also called an onsite manager) might have under his/her supervision a director of maintenance and maintenance staff.*

Some property management firms have management property in a number of states. A wide geographical service area is possible because of the availability of fax machines, computer modems, cellular telephones, teleconferencing, etc. What formerly took days to resolve can now be done in minutes with better communication and flow of documents.

Most of these multi-state operations deal with large properties, allowing a strong onsite team. Nevertheless, regular visits are generally conducted by a management team to evaluate records, leasing activity and leases, maintenance, security, improvement planning, etc. By use of a team approach, it is possible to provide a wide area of expertise.

While multi-state management requires licensing in each state, we will see more of this in the future. We know of one firm operating in several states that specializes in managing condominium associations. Large REITs operate nationwide.

Widespread management operations might alter the organizational chart. A number of REITs have regional offices that appear to be working well.

B. STAFFING

There is no standard staffing plan for a property management office. Staffing must be based upon the specific needs of an office. This would be based on a number of factors such as:

1. number of separate properties managed;
2. number of individual tenants;
3. physical proximity of units;
4. type of units;
5. types of leases;
6. number and type of onsite employees;
7. duties of onsite employees;
8. advertising budget, and
9. contracted management duties.

There is also no standard staffing plan for an onsite office. During initial lease-up operations, there would be more rental agents than there would be after the property stabilizes. Factors affecting staffing of the onsite office include many of those for the property management office.

The number of maintenance employees is based on:

1. age, construction, and quality of the building;
2. number of units and/or total square footage;
3. the amount and type of landscaping;
4. special features such as waterfalls, playgrounds, pools, etc., and
5. the amount and type of work covered by contract labor.

C. POLICY MANUAL

As the property manager in a supervisory poition, you should supply all employees, including resident managers, with a policy manual. The *POLICY MANUAL should include the employee's job description as well as how tasks should be carried out, and the treatment regarding emergencies.* This can also be included in each independent contractor agreement.

1. Dealings with Owners

The policy manual should point out that the resident manager should not have any direct dealings with the owner unless directed to do so by you (the property manager), or unless contacted by the owner.

If the resident manager is contacted by the owner, he/she should answer any questions fully and honestly. The resident manager should then contact you, the property manager, about the owner's contact and convey any concerns of the owner.

The person who is directly responsible for a property should be the primary contact person with the owner because that person knows the property status better than anyone else. This person might be the onsite manager for a very large project. However, generally it's the person who is responsible for the property and directly supervises the onsite manager. If an owner has multiple properties, the same person should be responsible for all of them. However, this might require different levels of expertise where an industrial park and an office building are involved.

2. Dress Code

Your employees reflect the image of your firm. The employee manual should cover appearances, which could specify:

1. clean clothes;
2. for males, a shaved appearance;
3. hair that is short, tied or under a cap, and
4. cleanliness and avoidance of too much cologne.

The dress code in some projects include shirt, tie, and jacket for men, and dresses for women. The type of property and area where located should dictate the dress code.

Basically, the dress code should reflect the way you would expect a professional in the business to dress.

3. Interpersonal Relations

Some policy manuals forbid property managers from dating tenants or other employees they supervise. This type of policy makes sense because the end of a relationship could lead to loss of a tenant or an employee.

4. Theft

You should expect and receive complete honesty from your staff.

You can expect some theft and you will probably even condone some pilferage. As an example, there are probably very few parents who haven't given their school-age children pencils, pens, or other supplies that were paid for by the parents' employers. Actually, this kind of theft will probably be viewed more as an employee benefit than a crime. It is when theft gets out of hand that something must be done. Selling supplies, stealing cash, taking items of considerable value or stealing from tenants cannot be condoned.

The policy manual or employee manual should state that such action will result in discharge of the persons involved.

5. Completed Staff Work

All employees should be imbued with the principle of completed staff work.

Completed staff work is:

1. **Define the Problem**. What exactly is the problem.
2. **What Are Possible Solutions?** There could be a number of ways that a particular problem could be solved. Feedback at office meetings is good.
3. **What Do You Recommend?** The person presenting the problem should be expected to also provide the solution.
4. **Why is Your Recommendation Best?** The person who presents a problem should be able to defend the recommended course of action over other possible solutions.

Employees who understand "completed staff work" become part of the solution rather than part of the problem.

Neither the property manager, the owner, nor the tenant wants to know about problems; they want to know about solutions.

6. Tenant Gifts to Managers

All tenants are to be treated equally well.

Some property management firms have a policy that resident managers are not to accept gratuities or gifts from tenants, while in some apartment complexes the resident managers regard gifts and gratuities as an entitlement of the job.

A problem with allowing resident managers to accept gifts or gratuities is that those tenants who give greater amounts expect priority treatment regarding complaints.

The resident manager who accepts significant gifts or gratuities has priorities dictated by both his or her supervisor and a tenant who expects something in return. This conflict can result in resources of time and money being expended that may fail to meet the best interests of the owner.

7. Key Money

When a vacancy arises in a rent controlled area, there is no problem filling that vacancy. There is such a demand that prospective tenants are often willing to pay extra to get a rental.

Some resident managers have been receiving **KEY MONEY** *to give tenancy, which is simply a payment to the manager to give them occupancy.* One problem with allowing a resident manager to accept key money is that key money is illegal in many rent controlled areas because it amounts to rent.

Some resident managers have stocked units with a few pieces of old furniture and required prospective tenants to buy the furniture for thousands of dollars. This is really key money in a different form.

You cannot allow your resident manager to accept key money.

You could be viewed as a conspirator in an illegal act. You must demand absolute honesty of your resident managers and cannot allow a "secret profit."

D. MANAGEMENT COSTS

The larger a management complex, the greater the possibilities of operational efficiency.

For instance, the management costs per unit for a 1,200-unit residential development are likely to be significantly less than the management costs to operate a 100-unit development (management costs not directly reimbursed by the property owner). Therefore, lower management fees are possible on a per-unit or gross-rent basis when dealing with larger developments.

It also holds true that the more property a property firm manages, the lower the central office overhead costs are per unit. This is because many of the costs are fixed and not directly related to the number of units managed. *Even for variable costs, greater efficiency is possible as the numbers increase. This is often referred to as ECONOMICS OF SCALE.*

E. MANAGEMENT FEES

1. For Management

Most management fees are based on a percentage of the gross income.

The percentage might vary in a range from around three percent to 10 percent, depending upon the type of property, scheduled gross rents, services provided and the leasing fee schedule. As an example, a lower leasing fee might be coupled with a higher percentage of the gross.

VOICE OF EXPERIENCE:

Never agree to a percentage of the net; there might not be any net income because of expenses beyond the control of the property manager, such as a high debt service.

For a single-tenant building, you would want a minimum fee coupled with a percentage of the gross. The reason for the minimum fee is that a vacant property is likely to require as much or greater management effort than one that is occupied. The property must be protected and maintenance is still required. A percentage fee without a minimum would mean a "zero" management fee for considerable expenditure of management resources.

For some properties, you might negotiate a fee per unit rather than a percentage of the gross. A bachelor apartment building consisting of 140 units would likely take the same or greater management effort than would be required to manage 140, two-bedroom units with a gross rental that might be 150 percent to 200 percent greater than the rents from the bachelor units. A price per unit or a higher percentage would be a fairer approach for the bachelor units.

2. Leasing Fees

"Management fees" and "leasing fees" are related.

As a manager, if you charged a higher than normal management fee, the leasing fee might be reduced or eliminated. If the management fee were quite low, the leasing fee would probably be higher.

If an owner reimbursed you for advertising costs, the leasing fee would likely be significantly lower than if the advertising costs were your responsibility. Leasing fees may be one or two month's rent (based on the length of the lease and the type of property), but leasing fees are more likely to be a percentage of the entire lease. The percentage might be flat for the entire lease or it may be structured so that a higher percentage is charged in the first year with lower charges for subsequent years.

A management contract that doesn't provide for leasing fees is a disservice to an owner.

VOICE OF EXPERIENCE:

Leasing fees are for renting. Property management is an ongoing fee for conducting property management activities and is usually a percentage of gross monthly receipts.

Because there is a leasing fee, many property managers and their agents cooperate with each other in directing prospective tenants to each other's properties when management would otherwise be unable to meet the tenant's needs. Without a leasing fee, any fee to a cooperating broker would have to come from the pocket of the property manager. Cooperation is particularly important in nonresidential leasing.

3. Lease Renewals and Options

As the property manager, you might renew the lease when the lease expires. The leasing commission for the renewal might be the same or less than the original leasing commission, but only when it contains a renewal option.

When a lease contains a renewal option and the tenant exercises the option, the management agreement would likely provide that the commission structure for the original lease would continue.

4. Termination Fee

Some owners want the right to terminate the management contract. If there were no termination fee, an owner could take advantage of a property manager who had expended a great deal of effort to solve property problems by simply terminating the agreement. The California property management agreement allows each party to terminate the contract, without penalty, with a 30-day notice.

A termination fee is really called "liquidated damages"; it is a penalty agreed to in advance by the manager and owner.

With an agreed termination fee, you (the property manager) do not have to prove the amount of damages for an owner's renunciation of the contract.

II. Employees

A. STATUS OF THE RESIDENT MANAGER

Your resident manager is treated by law as an employee.

The resident manager would either be employed by the owner (in most cases) or you, the property manager. Therefore, the employee would be eligible for worker's compensation and unemployment insurance. The resident manager is also protected against wrongful discharge as is any employee.

Resident managers are subject to minimum wage laws. There have been cases where resident managers won lawsuits entitling them to back pay for minimum wages and payments for far more than 40 hours a week. Thus, you should consider an employment contract that clearly specifies that your resident manager is not to work more than 40 hours per week without specified authorization for the additional hours, except in emergency situations.

If you provide your resident manager with an apartment and the resident manager is required to reside in the unit, then the value of the apartment would not be shown as part of the employee's gross salary for determining withholding tax or social security contributions. However, should the resident manager not be required to reside on the premises, then the apartment that is furnished would be part of the wages. Some property management companies collect rent on the apartment managers' units, which tends to separate the rental units from the employment contracts.

If you discharge a resident manager who is not paying rent, the former resident manager generally need not be given notice because he/she would not be considered a tenant. An unlawful detainer action would be proper. However, if you give the former manager a 30-day notice, he/she could be considered to be on a month-to-month tenancy and might be able to raise the defense of retaliatory eviction.

Once you give a 30-day notice, you may have created a tenancy.

While large nonresidential properties will often have a management office on the premises, smaller properties, as well as some small residential properties such as single-family homes and duplexes, are unlikely to have resident managers.

VOICE OF EXPERIENCE:

Where there are no resident managers, the rentals would be handled out of the management office. In order to show a prospective tenant properties at various locations, lock boxes would likely be used.

Case Example

Brewer v. Patel, 20 C.A. 4th 1017 (1993)

A motel manager was required to remain on the premises 24 hours a day. The manager could remain in his apartment during the hours the office was not open. The manager filed a claim for overtime wages.

The Superior Court ruled that the manager was not entitled to wages during those hours when he was not required to work. The Court of Appeals affirmed the trial court holding that only those hours carrying out employee duties need be compensated.

Note: This decision would apparently apply to resident managers who were required to reside on the premises. However, your contract should specify the hours to be worked and specify authorization requirements as to overtime so that you are protected against a manager who claims to have worked excessive hours.

Case Example

Chan v. Antepenko, 203 C.A. 3rd 21 (1988)

This case held that a discharged property manager is not a tenant at sufferance but is a licensee. The agreement between the landlord and the property manager only gave the property manager a license, not a tenancy. While the case covered whether or not the discharged manager was protected by San Francisco's rent control ordinance, the reasoning of the court would indicate that a notice is not required to terminate occupancy since no tenancy existed.

The proper action would be one for ejection since the former property manager is no longer legally in possession of the premises.

In order to preserve a licensee relationship, no notice is required to eject the resident manager, as there is no tenancy.

B. QUALITIES OF A GOOD RESIDENT MANAGER

As a property manager, it's your responsibility to hire a resident manager who possesses all the qualities your owners and tenants have a right to expect.

There are a number of qualities that make a good resident manager. These qualities include:

People Oriented. The resident manager should like dealing with people and care for their interests. The interpersonal skill of presenting a problem and getting others to help in its solution is important. A resident manager, you must be able to correct behavior without antagonizing and be able to refuse a request without resulting animosity.

Reliable. The resident manager cannot be a procrastinator. When the resident manager states that something will be done, then he or she must be the type of person who will make sure that something will be done. The resident manager should be the kind of person others can rely on (a self-starter).

Organized. A good resident manager must organize his or her time and that of others who the resident manager supervises to accomplish the required tasks in order of reasonable priority. The time and resources must be allocated to best meet the needs of the tenants and owners.

Salesmanship. The resident manager must be able to efficiently close a rental by asking for a deposit.

Good Character. The resident manager must be of good character to be bonded. The resident manager can't have any vices that would reflect negatively on the owner or property management firm.

Trade Skills. An important asset is the ability to actually do a job or to understand what is needed so that the manager can adequately prepare purchase orders and/or supervise the work.

Positive Attitude. This is extremely important in a resident manager. Tenants and owners don't want negativism; they want, instead, to know what can be done and how and when.

C. RESIDENT MANAGER JOB DESCRIPTION

Your resident manager's job description should outline the responsibilities of the position. They might include many of the following tasks:

1. Showing units to prospective tenants.
2. Taking rental applications and deposits.
3. Faxing or sending applications to credit reporting company and/or the property management office.
4. Making calls to verify employment and checking prior rental history.
5. Contacting prospective tenant as to the acceptance or rejection of his or her application.
6. Going over the lease with the tenant and having the tenant sign it.
7. Collecting balance of rent and security deposit.
8. Reviewing property rules and regulations with tenant and having tenant sign and date a copy.

9. Receiving tenant complaints and answering the tenant's questions.
10. Supervising maintenance.
11. Supervising service contracts.
12. Preparing work orders.
13. Tracking work in progress.
14. Conducting move-in and exit inspections.
15. Inventory preparation of furnished units.
16. Serving three-day, 30-day and unlawful detainer notices.
17. Maintaining records.
18. Mediating tenant disagreements.
19. Advising property management office to report problems.

In some cases, the resident manager might also have maintenance and repair duties.

VOICE OF EXPERIENCE:

The duties of the resident manager vary greatly. What is important is that he/she fully understands these duties. This onsite manager should not establish rental rates or modify standard leases or contracts without your approval as the property manager.

D. MANAGERIAL PROBLEMS

Be sure to reprimand in private and praise in public.

When a property has operational problems, it could be related to problems concerning the manager, the communication process or to extraneous factors.

If work is not completed, you want to find out why.

1. Did the employee know what was expected of him or her?
2. Did the employee know how to get the job done?
3. Was there an extenuating circumstance beyond the employee's control? It could be the unavailability of a part or problems of a contractor.
4. Was the problem the result of the employee's action? By giving priority to jobs using resources that could have been allocated elsewhere, it could have resulted in another job not being accomplished.

You must try to avoid using 20/20 hindsight to criticize. If you did not cover how a situation should have been handled, you must be willing to share the blame. It shows your support of the employees.

Employees should feel that management supports them when a discretionary decision later turned out to be wrong.

Consider asking the employee how you both can avoid similar problems in the future. You want positive suggestions with open communications. Yelling at employees only creates a me-against-you attitude when you really want a team feeling.

When employees realize that you value their opinions, then they will help you devise the solution to problems and ways to prevent others.

VOICE OF EXPERIENCE:

Even if you don't totally accept an employee's suggestion, you should try to incorporate it into part of the solution. You can then explain how you used the employee's idea. This serves to reinforce the employee's self image.

The tendency of many firms is to overlook problems in more productive employees. Don't do it. Other employees will resent the difference in treatment and the problem will probably only get worse rather than better. Correct all problems as they occur.

When there is a problem, unless it is a group problem, be private in your discussion with the employee. If an employee feels you were critical of him or her in front of others, then that employee's self-esteem will suffer. You could also place the employee in a position where he or she will act defensively or even offensively and verbally retaliate and later regret the incident. An employee does not have to take abuse, but must maintain his/her professionalism.

If a resident manager engaged in a shouting match with a tenant, you could explain to the manager, "If you have any problem in the future, tell the tenant to call me." However, if you wanted to handle the incident through the resident manager, then you could suggest, "Count to ten first, be calm and tell it the way it is! If the tenant abuses you verbally, walk away."

If an employee appears to have personal problems, or what you suspect is an alcohol problem, ask the employee what's wrong. Ask also if you can help. Let the employee know that you will be supportive. Should he or she resist admitting to what you are reasonably sure is the problem, suggest AA or a similar self-help group. If the employee indicates that the problem is not that bad, you know you're on target. Let the employee know that you want his/her employment to continue, but that the employee must want to solve the problem. Suggest that they think about it and come and see you the next day.

Sometimes good employees begin to slack off. Let them know that you noticed, and ask how you can be of any help.

If an employee is continuously late and unreliable, then point this out to the employee. Again, ask if you can help. If the employee claims it was only once or twice, be prepared to show the employee that it has been more than a few times. End the discussion of the problem on an upbeat tone. Let the employee know that you regard him or her as a valuable asset.

III. Employee Hiring

A. APPLICATION

In hiring any employee, you should have the employee complete a job application. Most companies have general employment application forms. As a matter of policy, you should not hire anyone until an application has been received.

Things of particular interest to you would be:

1. Long gaps in employment.
2. Short periods for the last few jobs.
3. Employers listed who are no longer in business and so can't be checked.
4. Last job or jobs at a significantly lower wage and/or level of responsibility than prior jobs.

The employment application should include the authorization to check references given and to investigate an applicant's work history. Also check on personal traits, which could include a credit check. Constant late payments and collection accounts could indicate a reliability problem as well as other problems.

VOICE OF EXPERIENCE:

In verifying prior employment and employment dates, ask why the employee left and if the employers would hire the former employee again and the reason why or why not.

Many applications for employment include a statement above the applicant's signature that states that the application is truthful and that the applicant understands that any false representation made shall be considered sufficient grounds for termination of employment.

Don't require a photograph of the applicant with the application. It could be viewed as an attempt to weed out minority applicants without an interview.

You want to go over all employee policies when hiring. You should have an employee handbook that sets forth policies.

You should have a no-tolerance drug policy where the possession or use of drugs during duty hours or on managed property shall result in dismissal and that reporting for work under the influence of drugs and/or alcohol shall be grounds for dismissal.

B. TESTS

You should avoid giving prospective employees written tests.

While they were popular in past years, a number of cases have held that written tests for job applicants were discriminatory when the employer could not show that the knowledge tested was really necessary for performance of the job. The reasoning is that minorities who may have less education and take a test that does not relate directly to the job would therefore be discriminated against.

However, you can test typing, shorthand, and computer aptitude, as these are measurable skills that could be directly job related.

C. EMPLOYEE INTERVIEW

The interviewing process can weed out possible problem employees, but it is not infallible. While an interviewer might lack training in psychology, asking the proper questions can reveal positive and negative features in a prospective employee. Chances are you don't want employees who always have excuses or someone to blame. Some people feel that the whole world is out of step with them rather than vice versa.

VOICE OF EXPERIENCE:

You don't need a gossip who will tell tenants about other tenants. If all of a prospective employee's prior supervisors were "idiots," watch out. If an employee is personally defensive over any questioning, view that attitude as a red flag!

If a prospective employee expresses unsolicited strong views as to religion, politics, or antipathy towards any group of people, watch out! That person could be disruptive to other employees and tenants.

Keep in mind that the interviewee might have his or her guard up. Your questions should be friendly and nonintimidating so that the person will relax and open up to you. Some of the questions you could ask that might reveal the nature of the prospective employee would be:

1. Tell me about your last supervisor. (If you are told about the supervisor being a drunk, drug user or womanizer, the chances are that the interviewee is a gossip.)

Criticism of a previous employer can be a red flag.

2. What could (your last employer) have done to make you stay?
3. Who was your best boss? Why?
4. Who was your worst boss? Why?
5. What is there about this job that interests you?
6. What is your strongest asset?
7. What is your major weakness?
8. How long do you expect to work for us?
9. What aspects of this job interest you the most?

10. What aspects of this job least interest you?
11. What previous job did you like best? Why?
12. How would previous co-workers describe you?
13. How would previous employers describe you?
14. Can you get a recommendation from a previous employer?
15. Do you have a current driver's license?
16. If you could do something to improve yourself, what would it be?
17. How many traffic citations have you received in the last three years? For what?

You can also use the interview process to present hypothetical situations relating to interpersonal relationships that relate to the job. The answers could be very revealing.

You might want to include an employee who the new hire would be working with or who has a similar position at another property as a co-interviewer. Allowing other employees to have a voice in hiring will help your employee relations. They realize that you regard their views and the job as being important. In addition, other employees are often valuable in discovering the strengths and weaknesses in prospective employees.

While you will get some half-truths, the interview will give you quite a bit of information about the job applicant. Coupling the interview with the employment application and checking prior employers, you will have a far better chance of hiring a person with whom you will be satisfied than you would hiring at random. You will be fooled; you just don't want it to be too often.

D. TEMPORARY WORKERS

Some firms will use temporary workers to fill positions when their contracts with the temporary worker firm allows them to convert to employee status.

By taking this approach, a firm can observe the actual performance of the person. They can also ask for other workers or can hire the worker supplied. It allows for a relatively inexpensive trial period without obligations.

E. COLORBLIND MANAGEMENT

We realize that we should not discriminate in leasing or in hiring, yet we see results that do not indicate a colorblind approach in promotions. While there are a number of minority-owned property management firms, the upper echelon of corporate property management and REITs indicate that few people of color reach the vice presidential or director status.

The authors selected 20 annual reports of Real Estate Investment Trusts (REITs) at random. Most of the annual reports displayed photographs of the officers as well as the directors. From the photographs, it did not appear that any of the officers or directors were African American. Furthermore, women were completely absent at the Director's level and represented only 12 percent of corporate officers. There wasn't one case where a woman was listed as the President of a REIT.

Photographs in the annual reports did indicate a great many African Americans and women in the onsite leasing and maintenance categories.

Although these figures may have recently changed, the authors view this as a significant problem which the profession will have to address. It is not enough that we "talk the talk." We must "walk the walk."

F. ILLEGAL ALIENS

To be protected against any claim that you violated the Immigration Reform and Control Act of 1986 by hiring an illegal alien, you should require employees to complete Immigration and Naturalization Form I-9 shown as **Figure 15-1**.

Don't assume from a person's accent or appearance that they are not a citizen of the United States.

Do not refuse to hire a person because of these reasons since it could amount to a civil rights violation on your part. Simply give all employees the Form I-9 and have them complete it and return it to you. You are not required or expected to investigate the facts, but you should complete part two of Form I-9 and retain it for three years from the end of employment.

IV. Working With Employees

A. EMPLOYEE FILE

You should keep a file for every employee. This file should include:

1. employee application,
2. information on employee and pre-employment check,
3. employee's employment contract,
4. copies of all employee evaluations,
5. payroll records,
6. complaints received and any action taken or praise about employee's work, and
7. Form I-9.

The file should not contain hearsay evidence. The information in the file should be as factual as possible.

B. EMPLOYEE EVALUATION

All employees should be evaluated.

Evaluation serves to point out areas of concern to help in the employee's development. By pointing out strengths and good performance, it also helps to reinforce the employee's self-image.

Figure 15-1

OMB No. 1615-0047; Expires 08/31/12

Department of Homeland Security
U.S. Citizenship and Immigration Services

Form I-9, Employment Eligibility Verification

Read instructions carefully before completing this form. The instructions must be available during completion of this form.

ANTI-DISCRIMINATION NOTICE: It is illegal to discriminate against work-authorized individuals. Employers CANNOT specify which document(s) they will accept from an employee. The refusal to hire an individual because the documents have a future expiration date may also constitute illegal discrimination.

Section 1. Employee Information and Verification *(To be completed and signed by employee at the time employment begins.)*

Print Name: Last	First	Middle Initial	Maiden Name

Address *(Street Name and Number)*	Apt. #	Date of Birth *(month/day/year)*

City	State	Zip Code	Social Security #

I am aware that federal law provides for imprisonment and/or fines for false statements or use of false documents in connection with the completion of this form.

I attest, under penalty of perjury, that I am (check one of the following):

☐ A citizen of the United States
☐ A noncitizen national of the United States (see instructions)
☐ A lawful permanent resident (Alien #) _____
☐ An alien authorized to work (Alien # or Admission #) _____
until (expiration date, if applicable - *month/day/year*)

Employee's Signature	Date *(month/day/year)*

Preparer and/or Translator Certification *(To be completed and signed if Section 1 is prepared by a person other than the employee.)* I attest, under penalty of perjury, that I have assisted in the completion of this form and that to the best of my knowledge the information is true and correct.

Preparer's/Translator's Signature	Print Name

Address *(Street Name and Number, City, State, Zip Code)*	Date *(month/day/year)*

Section 2. Employer Review and Verification *(To be completed and signed by employer. Examine one document from List A OR examine one document from List B and one from List C, as listed on the reverse of this form, and record the title, number, and expiration date, if any, of the document(s).)*

	List A	OR	List B	AND	List C
Document title:					
Issuing authority:					
Document #:					
Expiration Date *(if any)*:					
Document #:					
Expiration Date *(if any)*:					

CERTIFICATION: I attest, under penalty of perjury, that I have examined the document(s) presented by the above-named employee, that the above-listed document(s) appear to be genuine and to relate to the employee named, that the employee began employment on *(month/day/year)* _____ and that to the best of my knowledge the employee is authorized to work in the United States. (State employment agencies may omit the date the employee began employment.)

Signature of Employer or Authorized Representative	Print Name	Title

Business or Organization Name and Address *(Street Name and Number, City, State, Zip Code)*	Date *(month/day/year)*

Section 3. Updating and Reverification *(To be completed and signed by employer.)*

A. New Name *(if applicable)*	B. Date of Rehire *(month/day/year) (if applicable)*

C. If employee's previous grant of work authorization has expired, provide the information below for the document that establishes current employment authorization.

Document Title:	Document #:	Expiration Date *(if any)*:

I attest, under penalty of perjury, that to the best of my knowledge, this employee is authorized to work in the United States, and if the employee presented document(s), the document(s) I have examined appear to be genuine and to relate to the individual.

Signature of Employer or Authorized Representative	Date *(month/day/year)*

Form I-9 (Rev. 08/07/09) Y Page 4

1. 30-Day Evaluation

The initial evaluation period of 30 days allows the employee time to learn the job and be exposed to problems.

You want employees to tell you about what they like and/or dislike about the job and get their own evaluations before you give any input. It pays to be a better listener than talker.

2. Subsequent Evaluations

A subsequent evaluation might be at the 90-day or 6-month period. After that, evaluations should be at least on an annual basis and be regularly scheduled as a priority item.

You must convey the attitude that you care about the employee and you want the employee to be both productive and happy.

The time to give any salary raise or bonus would be at the close of an evaluation session.

The employee should be given a copy of a written evaluation at the time of the evaluation meeting. The employee should sign and date the management copy showing the receipt of his or her evaluation.

3. Tenant Exit Interview

A tenant exit interview can help you in that it can show areas where improvement is needed on the property and/or the property management.

An exit interview can be a short telephone call. A sample script of such a call would be:

[Mrs. Jones] this is [Alice Smith] from [Morgan Management]. I wonder if you could take just a little time to answer a few questions. By knowing why tenants give notice to leave, we feel we can better serve tenant needs in the future.

1. Why did you decide to leave [Glenview Terrace]?
2. Where will you be moving to?
3. Why did you choose…?
4. During the [two years] you have lived here at [Glenview Terrace], how would you rate the cooperation of [the resident manager]? Why?
5. What did you like about living at [Glenview Terrace]?
6. What, if any, were problems that you saw with the property?

Thank you very much for your time. Your cooperation is appreciated.

C. EMPLOYEE RELATIONS

You want your employees to feel that they have a common goal and are members of a team where every person is important.

You should always address an employee with respect. Never use derision, sarcasm, or talk "down" to someone.

Never gossip with employees about other employees or owners.

If any decision has been made that will affect an employee's work hours or working conditions, you should tell the employee as soon as possible and the reason for the decision.

Occasionally, accounts are lost despite excellent management results. Try to relocate the resident manager to another property. When you take care of your own, your people will have greater respect for you.

An incentive for resident property managers to excel can be promotion to larger units offering higher earnings and/or better living conditions.

Many management firms always remember birthdays and anniversaries of employees with a gift. As an example, it might be a certificate for dinner for two at one of the area's better restaurants. Whatever it is, you want your employees to know you care about them.

Besides treating employees with respect on the job, many firms have social events to bring employees from different properties together. Social events might include an annual picnic, a holiday party, or tickets to a circus for employees and families.

VOICE OF EXPERIENCE:

You must be careful if supplying alcoholic beverages. A drunk and loud employee can undo everything you are trying to do. In addition, an accident involving an intoxicated employee could subject you to liability because he or she was drunk at a company-sponsored event where you supplied the liquor. Soft drinks and good food is a better idea.

One property manager, who operates in a college community, annually hosts a tailgate party, complete with grilled hot dogs and hamburgers prior to a football game. He provides every employee and family members with tickets to the game.

Another manager we know invites two resident managers and their spouses to a dinner at his home. This way, every resident manager is invited at least once every 18 months.

The reason that he uses his home rather than a restaurant is because he feels it helps create a more personal relationship. The managers who ordinarily would seldom meet each other are encouraged to talk about amusing problems, etc. He reports that these dinners have led to managers developing a personal relationship with one another and calling each other to discuss ideas and problems.

D. EMPLOYEE RETENTION

Owners of property management offices tend to lose qualified employees to other firms who offer higher salaries, higher commissions or a particularly desirable property situation.

There are ways a management firm can keep most of their core employees without getting involved in a bidding war. They can offer:

Health Insurance. The insurance can vary from full coverage to the firm paying just half the premium on a high-deductible policy.

The better the coverage offered, the more difficult it becomes for an employee to leave.

Vacation Days. By offering paid vacation days that increase as the length of employment increases, it serves as a disincentive to leave.

Retirement Program. Some firms have a retirement program where the company will match the employees' contribution to the plan up to a specified dollar amount or where the employer doesn't require the employee to contribute matching funds. The retention kicker is that the employer's contribution to the plan does not vest with the employee until he or she has been with the firm a stated period, such as three to five years. If the employee leaves before the pension funds have vested, the employee could be walking away from thousands of dollars.

Profit Sharing. A profit-sharing program can mean a bonus of several thousand dollars each year for an employee.

An employee gets used to this end-of-the-year bonus, so it becomes difficult to accept another position where such a bonus is not given.

Management Fees. Many management offices give management responsibility plus a percentage of the management fees to the person who brings in the management contract. As a person builds up his or her portfolio of contracts, his or her monthly check increases. Many managers get several thousand dollars every month from the management contracts in addition to their leasing commissions. If a person has $40,000 a year coming in for management contracts and is averaging $50,000 per year in leasing fees, it is difficult to walk away from the job.

Contract Rights. Most offices provide employees with a contract that spells out their rights and commissions.

One firm that we know of gives retiring management employees 40 percent of the management fee that they would receive for handling properties that they signed up for as long as the firm retains management. The other 60 percent is given to the manager who is assigned the management responsibility for the property. In addition, this particular firm encourages retirees who remain in the area to attend staff meetings and social functions and to sign up new management accounts so that their income flow increases rather than decreases.

Seeing affluent retirees attending staff meetings and social functions makes managers realize that this is more than a job, it is a career with a firm that cares.

Bonuses. In property management, you should try to arrive at a reasonable annual operating budget for repairs and maintenance. Rewarding resident managers who are able to maintain the property, but come well below budget estimates can be good business. One property manager told us that he has given annual bonuses of over $4,000 to resident managers with the concurrence of the property owner. He gives the managers a percentage of the savings for costs below the budget. According to the property manager, the reason for the savings realized is that his resident managers are more aware of what the maintenance personnel can do and they have cut down the number of purchase orders for outside contractors.

E. TRAINING

Employee training can involve new employees as well as all employees in various categories.

One large management firm schedules several full-day sessions for resident managers each year. The sessions cover cost-saving methods, computer programs to aid the resident manager and other topics of interest. A benefit of bringing the managers together is that they get to know each other and build a professional rapport. Resident managers tend to contact other resident managers to brainstorm ideas and solutions to problems.

O.K.- NOTICE HOW WILCOX RUNS AFTER THE PROSPECT... TACKLES HIM... AND DRAGS HIM BACK INTO THE REAL ESTATE OFFICE

New resident managers should work several days with another resident manager for initial indoctrination. There should also be formal training that would include:

Job Description. By discussing the job description with the resident manager and asking and answering questions, you will ascertain the manager's understanding about what is expected. You should also go over the job descriptions of any maintenance personnel who will be supervised by the resident property manager.

Service Contracts. As the property manager, you and the resident manager should review all service contracts, purchase order procedures and preferred contractors.

Office Policy Manual. Discussing and asking questions will insure that the employee fully understands office policy.

Property Rules and Regulations. Discussing with and questioning the resident manager about the tenant rules and regulations concerning specified properties will insure that the new resident fully understands what is required.

Telling. The first step in learning any procedure is to tell the person how to do it. For instance, you could tell the resident manager how to fill out a rental application.

Show and tell—a great way to teach and learn.

Demonstration. The learning process is enhanced by watching the application being filled out by another.

Doing It! This is the most important step of training. The resident manager at this stage would actually fill out the application.

Paper Backup. The process of telling, demonstration and performance should be backed up by a policy manual or other written material that clearly shows how the task should be performed.

Proper training of new hires and explaining what is expected is well worth the few days needed for training.

During the first few weeks, as the property manager, you should make numerous visits to the resident manager to ascertain how the resident manager has been doing his or her job. Suggestions for improvements should be given as required.

Professional Organizations. As indicated in Chapter 1, many professional organizations offer educational opportunities for professional advancement.

VOICE OF EXPERIENCE:

You should encourage resident property managers to take applicable courses. Many management offices pay for these courses. It is good employee relations and makes for better employees.

F. FIRING AN EMPLOYEE

You should document the reasons with written statements of others, if applicable, before you fire an employee. Be factual, not subjective. After the fact, former employees could claim the reasons for firing were because of race, sex, etc., or because of retaliation against a whistle blower. You can't stop the claims, but you can have a file to support your actions.

When defending your actions, state the facts, and nothing but the facts.

It is unfortunate, but unsubstantiated claims could place you in a situation where you are forced to let an employee go even if you don't really believe the claims. A property manager we know fired a resident manager because a tenant claimed that her child said that the manager "talked dirty" to her. While the manager denied the charges, the property manager felt he had no alternative but to fire the resident manager. If the manager was not fired and later assaulted a child, the property manager could haved faced a lawsuit seeking significant damages.

From the National Fair Housing Advocate: April 1997

It cost a building owner $200,000 plus an agreement to terminate the building superintendent to settle a sexual harassment suit in Washington, D.C.

According to the lawsuit, which was brought by a preschool teacher, the supervisor grabbed her in an elevator and later pinned her against a table rubbing himself against her. She reported the facts to the management company. After the management company failed to reprimand or fire the building superintendent, she began legal action.

Note: This case points out the necessity of taking sexual harassment charges very seriously.

It is unfortunate, but in most of these cases, the charges are denied and the property manager does not know who is telling the truth.

Firing an employee should be done on a face-to-face basis if at all possible.

The firing might be based on other than employee performance or employee problems. In this type of situation, the employee should be told and offered a letter of recommendation.

If you fire an employee because of job performance, interpersonal problems or unacceptable behavior, you don't want to go into a litany of transgressions. You don't want to argue fault or even the truth of allegations made against an employee if the employee is aware of such allegations.

You should have the employee's check available to pay them. In some instances, you might want to give severance pay.

At the time of the firing, the employee must surrender all keys to property or vehicles and any other company property.

If the firing is for cause, you can dispute the employee's entitlement to unemployment insurance. However, you may not wish to do so, depending upon the circumstances.

V. Opening a Management Office

Property management requires analysis and planning. Going into the property management business also requires analysis and planning. The following should be done before you consider opening a management office:

A. YOUR COMPETITION

Property Type. What type of property do property managers in the area manage? Do they specialize in particular types of property?

Fees. What are the fee ranges for property management and leasing in the area?

Success (Financial). Do the property managers in the area appear to be doing well economically?

Meeting Needs. What owner needs are there that local property management firms have not or only partially fulfilled? Can you do the job as good or better?

B. YOURSELF

Owner Contacts. What owner contacts do you currently have that could aid you in obtaining property management?

Broker Contacts. Do you have broker contacts who will help you obtain property management?

Type of Property. What type or types of property are you most capable of managing?

Personal Attributes. What important personal attributes do you have to be successful in property management?

Experience. What experience do you have in regards to:

1. property management in general,
2. specified areas of property management,
3. computer use for property management accounting and recordkeeping,
4. supervisory experience in maintenance and management personnel and
5. are you willing to obtain experience or training to augment what you have?

Financial Resources. What financial resources can you bring to property management including personal and borrowed funds?

Financial Risk. Are you willing to risk your financial resources for your success?

C. YOUR PLAN

You must plan a business. However, your plan should not be cast in concrete. Changing circumstances should allow flexibility. Your plan should include:

Type of Management Activity. Are you going to specialize in an area or areas of management or take a general management approach?

Office.

1. Location for the office.
2. Equipment, supplies, telephone service, utilities, signage, furniture, computers, programs, etc., required to open the office.

Staffing. Initial staffing that will be required to open the office. Do you have experienced people willing to join you?

Insurance. Will you have adequate insurance coverage when you open your office?

Initial Management. Will you have any management contracts when you open your office?

Contractors and Service Providers. Have you assembled a group of contractors and service providers who you feel will meet owner needs?

Financial.

1. Estimated costs to open the office. (Historically, most brokers underestimate costs by about 50 percent.)
2. Estimate your monthly fixed operational costs. Be certain to include any monies you require for personal living expenses.
3. How much must you generate in monthly fees to reach your break-even point?
4. Plot your planned revenue growth month-by-month until you reach your break-even point. Your financial reserves must allow you to comfortably reach this point.

Goal Setting. Your goals should be set forth in writing. They should be divided into short-term goals (1 to 12 months), intermediate-term goals (1 to 5 years) and long-term goals (over five years).

Your short-term goals would include weekly and monthly goals as to contacts to make and things that you will be doing to obtain management contracts and service the contracts you have.

Intermediate-term and long-term goals might be based on measurable number of units or dollar volume. Your short-term goals should be constantly revised as they are accomplished. The short-term goals should lead to the intermediate-term goals that are milestones on the way to your career goal.

Just setting a direction to your career will not guarantee success. However, success is more likely when planned than managing by crisis, where the first telephone call of the day determines the direction of your efforts.

VI. CHAPTER SUMMARY

The organizational chart for a property management firm will vary based on the number of properties managed, the number of employees, and even geographical distribution of management properties.

Staffing of a management office will be based on the number of properties managed, number of tenants, types of properties, types of leases, onsite employees supervised, duties of onsite managers, advertising budget, and management duties contracted for.

The policy manual should cover the employees' job descriptions and how tasks are to be carried out. Other areas to be addressed are dealing with owners, dress codes, interpersonal relations with subordinates and tenants, theft by employees, the necessity of never having a supervisor handle a problem without providing a supportive solution, and the prohibition of accepting gifts from tenants or key money.

Management costs of larger properties go down per unit, which, in turn, allows for lower management fees. Management fees include a percentage of the gross and leasing fees. The fees are interrelated because a lower management fee could be offset by a higher leasing fee. Lower leasing fees are probable when owners pay the advertising costs. Besides fees for initial leasing, fees are customarily charged for lease renewal and the exercise of options to extend leases.

The resident manager is an employee, and is subject to minimum wage laws. If the resident manager must reside on the premises, then the apartment provided is not considered part of the wages. In such a case, the resident manager is not regarded as a tenant, so a notice to vacate is not required for an unlawful detainer action.

The resident manager's duties vary by owner requirements and the property being managed. It is important to discover the "Why?" when evaluating problems with managers.

All new hires should complete an employment application. You should be interested in gaps in employment, short periods with employers, employers listed who are no longer in business and, therefore, cannot be checked, and acceptance of jobs having a lower wage or lower level of responsibility.

The employment interviewing process can tell you positive and negative things about a potential employee. You want to search for the true person by asking revealing questions.

By hiring temporary workers who then could become permanent employees, you really have a trial employee.

You must strive to hire without any element of discrimination.

By having new hires fill out a residency form, you can be protected against liability for hiring an illegal alien.

The employee files should include employment application and pre-employment checks, employee contracts, employee evaluations, pertinent correspondence, payroll records, complaints, and commendations.

Employees should be evaluated to assist the employee's development and point out areas of strength and areas that require more attention. Tenant exit interviews can reveal positive and negative areas of management, the problems and strengths of individual managers and the property.

You want employees to feel that they are worthwhile. They should be treated with respect and kept informed. Remembering birthdays, and anniversaries, and social events can be used to reinforce employee morale.

Employee retention can be aided by health insurance, vacation days, a retirement program, profit sharing, sharing in fees and the use of bonuses.

Training of new hires should include:

1. job description,
2. understanding of service contracts,
3. understanding the office policy manual, and
4. understanding property rules and regulations.

The training process should involve telling, showing and the employee performing the task. Additional training is available through professional organizations.

Before you fire an employee, document your reasons. Don't get into an argument. Pay the employee any amount owed at the time of firing and get any keys or property belonging to your firm.

Before starting a property management business, you should analyze your competition and yourself as to:

1. owner contacts,
2. broker contacts for referrals,
3. the type of property you wish to manage,
4. your experience,
5. available financial resources, and
6. if you are willing to risk your resources.

For success, property managers should have a plan as to where they will locate, the type of management activity that they will engage in, preliminary staffing requirements, what management contracts that they will have to start with, what service providers and contractors will be used, an estimate of start-up costs, an estimate of fixed monthly costs, and what it will take to reach a break-even point.

Success should be planned and one element of planning is goal setting. Setting measurable goals of short-term, intermediate-term and long-term duration that leads to what you are after is a plan for success.

VII. CHAPTER QUIZ

1. As used in this chapter, "key money" refers to:
    a. a form of security deposit.
    b. a lease deposit.
    c. a payment to be given occupancy.
    d. none of the above.

2. Management costs per unit managed:
    a. increase as the number of units increase.
    b. decrease as the number of units increase.
    c. decrease as the number of units decrease.
    d. are not related to the number of units.

3. As to management and leasing fees, which of the following is a true statement?
    a. Larger complexes would probably have a lower percentage of the gross as management fees.
    b. Below-normal management fees could be compensated for with higher leasing fees.
    c. When the owner pays for advertising costs, leasing fees will probably be lower.
    d. All of the above.

4. A resident manager lives in the complex she manages but does not pay any rent. Which of the following is true?
    a. If he/she is not required to live there, the value of the apartment counts as wages.
    b. If he/she is required to live there, the apartment value does not count as wages.
    c. Both a and b.
    d. Neither a nor b.

5. A property manager would probably be worried about hiring an individual if the application showed:
    a. a history of work going to more and more responsible positions.
    b. the employee had not worked for one employer more than two months.
    c. no period of unemployment greater than three weeks.
    d. any of the above.

6. A prospective employee looks foreign and speaks with an accent. You should:
    a. assume that he or she is an illegal alien.
    b. offer below-minimum wages.
    c. have the person complete a government form to show citizenship or alien status.
    d. refuse to interview or hire the person.

7. The main purpose of an employee evaluation is to:
    a. justify firing the employee.
    b. help the person to be a better employee.
    c. comply with the law.
    d. both a and c.

8. Ways to discourage employees from accepting a position with another broker would be to offer:
    a. health insurance coverage.
    b. a retirement program.
    c. profit sharing program.
    d. all of the above.

9. By contributing to an employee's retirement program where your contribution will not vest for five years, you:
    a. need not part with any money.
    b. make it difficult for the employee to leave before five years.
    c. encourage job-hopping.
    d. avoid minimum wage restrictions.

10. Before you go into your own property management business, you should consider:
    a. your financial resources.
    b. the cost to open an office.
    c. your contacts who will help you gain management business.
    d. all of the above.

ANSWERS: 1. c; 2. b; 3. d; 4. c; 5. b; 6. c; 7. b; 8. d; 9. b; 10. d

A-B

Accredited Management Organization (AMO): A professional designation available to a management firm that meets IREM specifications.

Accredited Resident Manager (ARM): A professional designation of the Institute of Real Estate Management (IREM).

Accredited Marketing Director: A professional designation of the International Council of Shopping Centers.

Accredited Shopping Center Manager (ASM): A professional designation of the International Council of Shopping Centers.

Agent: A person who acts for another such as a property manager.

American Industrial Real Estate Association: An organization that provides educational material including lease forms.

Americans With Disabilities Act: An act prohibiting discrimination, as well as allowing and requiring modifications for handicapped.

Anchor Tenant: The major tenant(s) who act(s) as an attraction in a shopping center.

Appreciation: An increase in value.

Arbitration: Nonjudicial process of a dispute resolution before a party agreed to by the parties (arbitrator).

Assignment of Lease: Transfer of all lease interests by the lessee. Assignee becomes the tenant of lessor.

Association Management Specialist (AMS): A professional designation of the Community Associations Institute.

Attornment: A tenant agrees to be the tenant of a prior lienholder who forecloses.

Automatic Renewal: A clause that the lease renews itself unless notice of termination is given.

Binder: Authorized insurance coverage prior to the issuance of a policy of insurance.

Boiler Insurance: Insurance that covers losses from a boiler explosion.

Budget: A financial plan for operation.

Building Owners and Managers Association International (BOMA): A major property management organization.

Built-Up Roof: A layered roof of hot tar and roofing paper.

C-D

CAL OSHA: California Occupational Safety and Health Act

Capital Gains: Gains on the sale of a capital asset (real estate) that are subject to a preferred tax rate.

Cash Flow: Cash left over from all cash receipts after cash expenses (net spendable).

Certified Leasing Specialist (CLS): A designation of the International Council of Shopping Centers.

Certified Manager of Community Associations (CMCA): A professional designation of the Community Associations Institute.

Certified Property Manager (CPM): The highest professional designation of the Institute of Real Estate Management (IREM).

Certified Shopping Center Manager (CSM): A professional designation of the International Council of Shopping Centers.

Civil Rights Act of 1866: The first federal civil rights act. The act applies to racial discrimination.

Civil Rights Act of 1968: This is our Federal Fair Housing Act.

Class A Building: The best quality of office building.

Class B Building: An older quality office building.

Class C Building: Older office building of lesser desirability in a less than prime area.

Class D Building: The least desirable category of office buildings.

Clothing Optional: Developments catering to nudists.

Co-Insurance: An insurer requirement that the insured carry a set percentage of replacement value (usually 80 percent) to be fully covered up to policy limits.

Commingling: Mixing broker funds with funds of others.

Common Interest Development (CID): Includes condominiums, stock cooperatives, community apartment projects, and planned developments.

Community Associations Institute (CAI): An association of persons having an interest in common ownership developments.

Community Shopping Center: A shopping center where the anchor tenant would be a department store.

Condominium: An ownership in common of common areas with each unit owner owning his or her own air space.

Consumer Price Index (CPI): A government index often used for rent increases in a lease subject to rent adjustments.

Constructive Eviction: An action by the lessor that can be treated by the tenant as an eviction to end lease obligations.

Contract of Adhesion: A take-it-or-leave-it contract or lease offered by one who has great bargaining power.

Covenant to Remain in Business: Tenant on a lease agrees that he or she will not terminate the business during the term of the lease.

Depreciation: A noncash expense taken for tax purposes to shelter income from taxation.

Development Fees: Fees charged for new developments to cover infrastructure costs.

DRAM Shop Liability: Liability of a property owner for injuries resulting from an intoxicated customer of a tavern.

E-K

Earthquake Insurance: A high deductible policy covering earthquake damage.

Elevator Insurance: A liability coverage policy for losses due to elevator malfunctions.

Eminent Domain: The taking of property by a public entity.

Equal Credit Opportunity Act: Prohibits lessor discrimination as to source of income (public assistance).

Errors and Omission Insurance: Protects a property manager as to liability for mistakes.

Escalation Clause: A clause in a lease calling for rent increases.

Estate for Years: A lease having a definite termination date.

Estoppel Certificate: Certificate by lessee (or lessor) setting forth all rights under a lease.

Excess Parking: Parking space that exceeds normal needs.

Facilities Management Administrator (FMA): A professional designation of BOMA.

Factory Outlet Centers: Shopping centers where the tenants are manufacturers or off-price merchandisers.

Fair Employment and Housing Act (FEHA): California's fair housing act.

Familial Status: Family status as to married, children and age.

Fidelity Bond: A bond that protects against employee theft.

Fiduciary Duty: Duties owed by a property manager to an owner client.

Fixtures: Items that were personal property that have become real property.

Flood Insurance: Insurance coverage for flood damage.

Footloose Industry: A business that can locate anywhere.

Garden Office Buildings: Single-story office structure.

Gentlemen Farms: Farms where appearance is more important than profit.

Good Funds: Cash, cashiers checks, or other checks that have cleared the maker's bank.

Gross Lease (Flat Lease): A level payment lease. The owner pays taxes, insurance, etc.

Gross Multiplier: The relationship between gross income and the sale price determined by dividing the sale price by the gross income.

Ground Lease: Lease of the land. Tenant builds improvements.

Guarantor: A party who guarantees a lease by agreeing to be liable.

Hazardous Substances: Substances declared hazardous by governmental agencies.

Hold Harmless Clause: A clause whereby the lessee agrees that they will not hold an owner liable for personal or property losses.

Holdover Clause: Clause in a lease that increases rent should a tenant hold over after the end of the lease.

Homeowner Association: The managing association of a common interest development.

Homeowner Policy: A fire, liability policy that covers a wide range of perils.

HVAC: Heating, ventilating, and air conditioning.

Improvements: Improving a property by providing something the property did not have before.

Independent Contractor: A contractor hired for results who is not directly supervised by his or her principal.

Independent Living Facilities: Elderly housing where tenants live independently of one another.

Industrial Parks: Industrial subdivisions.

Inland Marine Insurance: Insurance for property in transit or storage, as well as for specific items of personal property.

International Council of Shopping Centers (ICSC): An organization of Shopping Center operators.

International Real Estate Institute: An international association that includes property managers.

Institute of Real Estate Management (IREM): The property management association of the National Association of Realtors®.

Joint and Several Liability: Parties agree to be both jointly and separately liable under a contract.

Key Man Insurance: Life insurance on the life of a key employee payable to the employer.

L-Q

Labor-Oriented Business: Manufacturer located close to labor supply.

Late Charges: A charge for a late rent payment.

Lead-Based Paint: Oil-based paint containing lead.

Lead-Based Paint Disclosure: Federally mandated disclosure required for residential property built prior to 1978.

Lease: The occupancy and possession contract between an owner and a tenant.

Letter of Intent: While not a lease, it is an agreement to negotiate for a lease.

Liability Insurance: Insurance that covers injuries to third parties and their property.

Libel: Written false statement that injures another.

Life-Care Facilities: Facilities where the management agrees to provide the degree of housing or care required for life (from independent living units to nursing facilities).

Low-Rise Buildings: Buildings of two to three stories.

Maintenance: The care and repair of property.

Management Contract: The agency agreement between the owner and the property manager.

Management Plan: An operation plan for property management of a property.

Manufactured Home: A home that is transported on its own chassis.

Market-Oriented Business: A manufacturer located close to market for its goods.

Master Lease: The lease of the entire premises to a tenant who will sublease all or part.

MAXI Award: An award given by the International Council of Shopping Centers.

Mechanic's Lien: A lien by a contractor, subcontractor or material provider who has not been paid for the job.

Medical-Pay Insurance: An insurance policy that covers medical expenses of persons injured on a property without regard to liability.

Mid-Rise Buildings: Buildings of four to eight stories.

Mini-Mall: Small centers with a convenience or fast food store as the anchor tenant.

Mini-Storage: Small warehouse rental units.

Mitigation of Damages: A duty of a lessor to keep damages as low as possible by trying to rerent property vacated prior to the end of a lease.

Motion Sensor: A sensor that turns on lights or an alarm if the sensor detects motion.

Negative Cash Flow: A loss operation where cash expenditures exceed cash receipts.

Negotiation: The process of give and take where lease terms are arrived at.

Neighborhood Shopping Center: A shopping center where the anchor tenant is a major food store.

Net Lease: A lease where the tenant pays a set rent plus taxes, insurance and maintenance.

Nondisturbance Clause: Prior mortgage holder agrees not to terminate tenancy if the mortgage is foreclosed.

Notice of Nonresponsibility: Notice posted by lessor that lessor will not be obligated for work authorized by tenant.

Occupational Safety and Health Act (OSHA): Federal act that sets safety standards and provide for reporting of injuries and illnesses of employees.

Option to Purchase: A right given to purchase property at an agreed price.

Option to Renew: A right given a tenant to renew a lease.

Overimprovement: An improvement that is not economically justified.

Partnership Insurance: Term life insurance on all partners payable to the surviving partners in order to buy out the deceased partner's interests in the business.

Percentage Lease: A lease where the rent is set at a percentage of gross income.

Periodic Tenancy: A tenancy from period-to-period that renews itself unless notice is given to terminate.

Pitch (Roof): The vertical drop per horizontal foot.

Proactive Guard Patrol: A patrol whose job is to prevent crime.

Professional Community Associations Manager (PCAM): The highest professional designation of the Community Associations Institute.

Pro-Forma Statement: An estimated operating statement.

Property Management Association (PMA): A professional management organization.

Proximate Cause: An action must be the cause of the injury to make the perpetrator liable.

Psychic Income: The benefit of pride of ownership.

Qualifying Tenants: The process of determining if a tenant has the income, credit and character to be a good tenant.

Quiet Enjoyment: Lessor agrees not to interfere with the tenant's use of premises or permit others to do so.

R-S

R-Factor: Resistance factor used to measure effectiveness of insulation.

Radius Clause: The tenant agrees not to open a competing location within a stated distance.

Reactive Guard Patrol: A patrol that responds to alarms in order to catch a criminal.

Real Estate Investment Trust (REIT): A publicly traded ownership that avoid double taxation of corporations.

Real Property Administrator (RPA): A professional designation of BOMA.

Recapture Clause: Clause in a percentage lease providing that the lessor can terminate the lease if a stated volume of sales is not reached.

Recreational Vehicle Park: Park where spaces are rented to mobile units.

Recording: Process of filing a document with the country recorder so constructive notices may be given of an interest.

Regional Shopping Center: A major shopping center anchored by several department stores.

Registered Property Manager (RPM): A designation of the International Real Estate Institute.

Rent: Compensation for possession.

Rent Control: Political limitations on rents and/or rent increases.

Rent Incentives: Free or reduced rent given to a tenant to induce the tenant to sign a lease.

Rental Interruption Insurance: Insurance covering rent loss due to a casualty loss.

Research and Development Buildings: Office and laboratory structures that might conduct prototype manufacturing.

Resident Manager: Manager who lives in the managed property.

Residential Property: Property where people live.

Restoration: Return of premises to an original condition.

Retaliatory Eviction: Unlawful eviction for making proper complaints to public authorities or for organizing a tenant organization.

Right of First Refusal: The right to buy or lease at terms offered by another by agreeing to meet those terms. It is a preemptive right.

Security Deposit: A deposit that insures the lessor against tenant damage or default.

Self Insured: A party bearing the risk without insurance company protection.

Semi-Independent Living: Elderly housing where services are provided, but tenants have their own apartments.

Sick Buildings: Buildings associated with tenant illnesses from fumes or bacteria.

Single Room Occupancy (SRO): Motel and hotel facilities converted to permanent housing.

Slander: Verbal false statement that injures another.

Smart Building: A building equipped with electronic and communications equipment for tenant use.

Square Footage: Measurement of floor space to compute rents.

Stabilization: The process of renting a new or vacant property to the point where vacancy factor is reduced to a reasonable level.

Standard Policy (fire insurance): A policy covering loss by fire, lightning and removal of property because of those perils.

Statute of Frauds: The requirement that certain agreements must be in writing to be enforceable.

Steering: The illegal process of directing prospective tenants based on race, sex, marital status, etc.

Stigmatized Property: Property with an undesirable reputation.

Storage Yards: Outside storage areas.

Strip Center: A line of shops catering to vehicular traffic.

Sublease: A lease by the lessee. The sublessee is the tenant of the original lessee.

Subordination: An agreement to be secondary to another agreement.

Subsidized Housing: Below-market rent housing subsidized by government ownership or low-interest financing.

Supply-Oriented Business: A manufacturer located close to supply of material used.

Surrender: Turning over the premises that terminates the lease obligations.

Systems Maintenance Technician (SMT): A professional BOMA designation.

T-Z

Theme Buildings: Buildings where all tenants have similar businesses.

Thirty-Day Notice: Notice given on a periodic tenancy to terminate or change tenancy terms.

Three-Day Notice: A notice given prior to an unlawful detainer action to quit or pay rent, quit or cure or quit.

Time is of the Essence: An agreement that dates set are material and are not approximate.

Time Share: A divided-unit ownership where each owner is entitled to occupancy of a unit during a specified time period.

Trade Fixtures: Fixtures installed for a business or trade. They remain personal property.

Trophy Building: A pride of ownership structure.

Trust Account: Account holding funds of others prior to disbursement.

Unlawful Detainer: The legal eviction notice.

Unruh Act: California act that prohibits a business from discriminating.

Urban Land Institute (ULI): A research and publishing organization with emphasis on development.

Urban Pedestrian Mall: A foot traffic only open mall.

Utility-Oriented: Manufacturer that wants to be located where utility costs are low.

Vacancy Factor: The percentage of vacancies.

Waiver of Subrogation: An insurer giving up rights to make a claim for a covered loss against the property manager.

Waste: Tenant causing damage to property.

Worker's Compensation Insurance: Required coverage covering employee job related injuries.

Zero-Based Budgeting: Budgeting based on the idea that every expense must be justified.

Index

Index

Textbooks From Educational Textbook Company

etctextbooks.com or etcbooks.com

Sometimes our textbooks are hard to find!

If your bookstore does not carry our textbooks, please send us a check or money order and we'll mail them to you with our 30-day money back guarantee.

Other Great Books from Educational Textbook Company:

California Real Estate Principles, 12th ed., by Huber. . . . . $100.00 ____
California Real Estate Practice, 6th ed., by Huber & Lyons. . . . . $100.00 ____
How To Pass The Real Estate Exam (850 Exam Questions), by Huber. . . . . $100.00 ____
California Real Estate Law, 7th ed., by Huber & Tyler. . . . . $100.00 ____
Real Estate Finance, 7th ed., second printing, by Huber & Messick. . . . . $100.00 ____
Real Estate Finance: Appraiser's Edition, 6th ed., by Huber & Messick. . . . . $100.00 ____
Real Estate Economics, 4th ed., by Huber, Messick, & Pivar. . . . . $100.00 ____
Real Estate Appraisal – Principles and Procedures, 3rd ed., by Huber, Messick, & Pivar. . $100.00 ____
Residential Real Estate Appraisal, by Huber & Messick. . . . . $100.00 ____
Mortgage Loan Brokering, 4th ed., by Huber, Pivar, Zozula. . . . . $100.00 ____
Property Management, 5th ed., by Huber, Lyons, & Pivar. . . . . $100.00 ____
Escrow I: An Introduction, 3rd ed., by Huber & Newton. . . . . $100.00 ____
Real Estate Computer Applications, by Grogan & Huber. . . . . $100.00 ____
Homeowner's Association Management, by Huber & Tyler. . . . . $100.00 ____
California Business Law, 2nd ed., by Huber, McGrath, & Tyler. $100.00 ____
Hubie's Power Prep 700 CD – 700 Questions, by Huber. . . . . $100.00 ____

Subtotal _____
Add shipping and handling @ $10.00 per book _____
Add California sales tax @ 9.75% _____
TOTAL _____

Allow 2-3 weeks for delivery

Name: _____
Address: _____
City, State, Zip: _____
Phone: _____

Check or money order: Educational Textbook Company, P.O. Box 3597, Covina, CA 91722